新 时 代 高 等 院 校 法 学 专

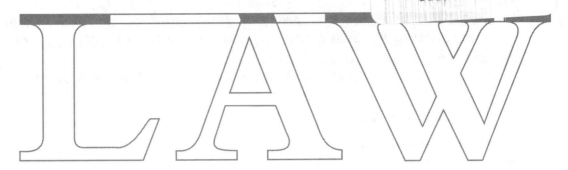

U0607126

国际经济法案例选编（双语）

◎主　编　曾文革　陈咏梅　◎副主编　张　路　胡　斌

重庆大学出版社

内容提要

本书编写遵循国际经济法教学特点，紧密结合曾文革教授主编的《国际经济法（双语）》教材内容，分别就国际货物买卖法、国际技术贸易法、国际贸易管理法、国际投资法、国际金融法、国际税法、国际经贸争端解决等章节内容编写了相关案例。

本书主要供法律专业本科生、研究生，以及国际经贸法律从业人员及水平相当的学习者使用。

图书在版编目（CIP）数据

国际经济法案例选编：汉、英／曾文革，陈咏梅主
编. -- 重庆：重庆大学出版社，2021.1
新时代高等院校法学专业系列教材
ISBN 978-7-5689-2434-4

Ⅰ.①国… Ⅱ.①曾… ②陈… Ⅲ.①国际经济法—
案例—高等学校—教材—汉、英 Ⅳ.①D996

中国版本图书馆CIP数据核字（2020）第189349号

国际经济法案例选编（双语）
GUOJI JINGJIFA ANLI XUANBIAN（SHUANGYU）

主 编：曾文革 陈咏梅
副主编：张 路 胡 斌
策划编辑：贾 曼 唐笑水
责任编辑：陈 力 王廷兴 版式设计：贾 曼
责任校对：万清菊 责任印制：张 策
 ＊
重庆大学出版社出版发行
出版人：饶帮华
社址：重庆市沙坪坝区大学城西路21号
邮编：401331
电话：（023）88617190 88617185（中小学）
传真：（023）88617186 88617166
网址：http://www.cqup.com.cn
邮箱：fxk@cqup.com.cn（营销中心）
全国新华书店经销
重庆升光电力印务有限公司印刷
 ＊
开本：787mm×1092mm 1/16 印张：26 字数：743千
2021年1月第1版 2021年1月第1次印刷
印数：1—2 000
ISBN 978-7-5689-2434-4 定价：78.00元

| 编委会 |

总 主 编

黄锡生

副总主编

王本存

编委

（按姓氏拼音排序）

陈 晴　陈咏梅　黄锡生

苗文龙　史玉成　宋宗宇

王本存　徐信贵　杨春平

杨疏影　张 舫　赵 谦

曾文革

| 总 序 |

在中华民族复兴关键时刻，中国特色社会主义进入新时代之时，在宪法不断完善、民法典颁布，全面依法治国向纵深发展之时，法学教育日新月异，要更好满足人民群众需求之时，重庆大学启动了"新时代高等院校法学专业系列教材"建设，严格遵循《普通高等学校教材管理办法》，紧跟新时代需求，紧跟党和国家重大战略、学生成长发展的关键需求，侧重一个"新"字，策划出版该系列教材。

内容新。充分反映时代新发展，积极响应党和国家新要求，紧跟法律体系新进展，紧盯经济社会、科学技术的变迁，与时俱进更新教材内容。守正创新，在新视角和新要求下重述和深化对经典法学知识的理解和表述，及时更新法学知识体系；语言活泼，凝练，短小精悍；久久为功，推陈出新，不断发展。

形式新。形式多样，既包括讲义、辅导用书，也包括案例用书、习题作业等各类教学用书；既支持跨学校、跨专业团队的编写，也支持教师个人富有个性的独立写作；教辅的编写与慕课、翻转课堂等新型教学形式深度结合；拓展材料、案例、法条"互联网化"，探索运用"互联网+"等技术手段，构建更新内容的新机制和新方法。

目标新。在详细调研"互联网新生代"新学情的基础上，将关键知识传授与学生学习的客观需求、主观动机紧密结合，尊重新生代学生的认知学习规律，抓住学生学习的"痛点""关键点"，"以学生为中心"，精准发力，使这套系列教材成为学生们喜爱的图书。

希望这套教材能够成为符合国家要求、教师教学的好帮手，学生学习的倍增器，为中国法学教育注入一股清新有活力的"新动能"。

新时代高等院校法学专业系列教材编委会
2019 年 10 月

| 前言 |

为践行法律与英语、理论与实务之结合，提升实际教学效果，重庆大学法学院法学专业核心课程"国际经济法"采用双语教学模式。于2011年和2012年被建设为重庆市本科双语示范课程和研究生教育优质课程（双语）。重庆大学法学院法学双语教学工作由此得到了稳步扎实的推进。双语课程建设的目的是培养能够熟练运用英语并精通国际经济法相关理论和制度的高端法律专业人才，让学生能够通过对本课程的学习，提升法律英语综合能力、促进赴国外进行学术交流或参加相关国际法律实务领域的工作。课程建设的关键和核心是教材，双语课程尤其如此。为满足"国际经济法"双语示范课程和优质课程建设的需要，2012年，重庆大学法学院组织了国际法学科教师编写《国际经济法》双语教材并在对外经贸大学出版社出版。该教材得到学界同行和学生欢迎，反响良好。为进一步推进国际经济法教学工作，重庆大学法学院国际法学科于2020年在此基础上进一步编写了《国际经济法案例选编（双语）》，以此作为"国际经济法"双语教材的配套教学材料于2021年1月出版。

本书参照"国际经济法"双语教材内容编排，分章节编选了相关案例。选取的案例均为本专业典型案例，虽然囿于篇幅限制，无法面面俱到，但选取的案例基本涵盖了各章节的核心知识点。基于国际经济法这一学科综合性的特点，本书选取的案例极具多样性。从内容上而言，案例涵盖国际货物、技术、服务贸易，国际金融、国际运输、国际投资、国际税法、国际经贸争端解决等诸多方面。从形式上而言，选取的案例裁判文书风格各异，既有法院裁判，也有仲裁庭裁定；既有相关国家的国内裁判文书，也有国际争端解决机构的裁判文书。

本书基于信息化时代特点对编排内容、体例、电子化查阅做的新尝试。在裁判文书的选择和案件分析、思考题和延伸资料阅读、信息化手段查阅等方面具有较为鲜明的特色。在选择相关裁判文书方面本书尽量保留了案例裁判文书的原始风貌，以便让读者尽可能地接触到第一手资料和信息。在保留裁判文书全文的同时，为方便读者快速了解案例背景和相关裁判内容，本书除了在每一章首部就整章内容进行概括性介绍的同时，还分别在每个案例前面以中文形式简要介绍了案件背景和裁判结果，并就案件核心争议进行了法律分析。当然，此处的法律分析仅系一家之言，读者也可从案例英文摘录中获取更多信息并得出自己的结论。在相关资料支持和深度学习方面，在每个案例的结尾还附有启发性思考题供读者参考，同时附有相关核心法律术语、延伸阅读材料和与案例相关的法律法规和条约供读者查阅。为方便读者，这些相关配套资料全部以信息化手段进行了处理，通过扫描书中二维码，读者可以通过便携式移动电子设备进行查阅。

本书可以作为高等院校法学类、财经类专业本科生和研究生国际经济法双语课程的配套案例教材，也可以作为 MBA、EMBA 等双语教学用书；同时，也是各类国际经济法与法律培训和国际经济法专业实务工作者的理想读物和参考资料。

本书由重庆大学曾文革教授、西南政法大学陈咏梅教授担任主编，重庆大学张路教授、胡斌副教授担任副主编。主编和副主编负责本书的总体策划、大纲制订、编写组织和统稿定稿，各位撰写者及其分工如下：第一章，唐仙丽（重庆大学法学院副教授）；第二章，师怡（西北政法大学副教授）；第三章，曾文革（重庆大学法学院教授）；第四章，陈咏梅（西南政法大学国际法学院教授）；第五章，吴雪燕（重庆大学法学院副教授）；第六章，张路（重庆大学法学院教授）；第七章，张宁宁（西南大学法学院讲师）；第八章，胡斌（重庆大学法学院副教授）。

本书编写得到重庆大学法学院的出版资助和西南政法大学、西北政法大学、西南大学等合作单位的大力支持，重庆大学出版社在书籍内容策划、内容编排、信息化手段等方面也付出了大量努力，在此一并致谢！

由于编者水平有限，不足甚至错漏之处在所难免，真诚欢迎各位读者批评指正。本书主编的电子邮箱：zengwenge@126.com。

编　者

2020 年 12 月

于重庆大学法学院

各章二维码扫描配套数据资料简介

为帮助读者进一步拓展阅读，本书每个项目都附有相应二维码供读者扫描查阅，包括法律术语、思考题答题要点、延伸阅读，以及与正文内容紧密相关的国际条约与法律法规，字数约合计20万字。

Ⅰ 国际货物买卖法二维码拓展阅读材料主要包括本章主要贸易和法律术语、思考题答题要点、八篇延伸阅读英文论文材料，以及正文涉及的《联合国国际货物销售合同公约》主要条款。

Ⅱ 国际货物运输法二维码拓展阅读材料主要包括本章主要法律术语、思考题答题要点、Wea Farms,Lima Peru vs.American Airlines,Inc.,31 Avi.18,739(S.D.Fla.2007)、Delta Airlines,Inc.vs.Chimet,S.p.A.,33 Avi.17,330(E.D.Pa.2008)、Vigilant Insurance Co.vs.World Courier,Inc.,32 Avi.16,436(S.D.N.Y.2008)等案例材料和一篇延伸阅读英文论文，以及正文涉及的1978年《汉堡规则》主要条款。

Ⅲ 国际技术贸易法二维码拓展阅读材料主要包括本章主要法律术语、思考题答题要点，Mark D. Janis, Patent Law in the Age of the Invisible Supreme Court, 2001 U. ILL. L. REV.387, 387 (2001)等案例和两篇延伸阅读英文论文，以及正文涉及的TRIPS协定、《中国人民共和国刑法》主要条款。

Ⅳ 国际贸易管理与世界贸易组织法二维码拓展阅读材料主要包括本章主要法律术语、思考题答题要点，并分别在案例一和案例二下安排了各四篇延伸阅读英文论文，以及正文涉及的《补贴与反补贴协定》《中国加入世界贸易组织工作组报告》《中国入世议定书》《1994年关税与贸易协定》和《关于实施1994年关税与贸易总协定第6条的协定》主要条款。

Ⅴ 国际投资法二维码拓展阅读材料主要包括本章主要法律术语、思考题答题要点、四篇延伸阅读论文，以及正文涉及的《华盛顿公约》《乌克兰—立陶宛双边投资条约》主要条款。

Ⅵ 国际货币金融法二维码拓展阅读材料主要包括本章主要法律术语、思考题答题要点、两本外文专著节选，以及正文涉及的TPP主要条款。

Ⅶ 国际税法二维码拓展阅读材料主要包括本章主要法律术语、思考题答题要点、四篇延伸阅读英文论文，以及正文涉及的《英美双边税收协定》主要条款。

Ⅷ 国际经济贸易争端解决二维码拓展阅读材料主要包括本章主要法律术语、思考题答题要点。针对国际投资、国际商事贸易和WTO贸易争端三个领域分别提供了六篇延伸阅读英文论文，以及三个案例分别涉及的《联合国国际货物销售合同公约》《华盛顿公约》《中韩双边投资协定》《1994年关税与贸易总协定》《WTO争端解决程序谅解》主要条款。

目　录
CONTENTS

I

国际货物买卖法

【内容摘要】

本章分为两节，精选两个 CISG 案例。第一个案例是奥地利液化气购销合同案（Austria-LPG Sales Contract, 10 Ob 518/95），主要争议焦点是本案中双方是否订立了有效的天然气销售合同，即双方是否作出了适格的要约和有效的承诺。第二个案例是加利福尼亚州灯杆销售案（California-light Poles Business Sales No. 07-161-JBT)，主要争议焦点在于卖方没有及时做出不符的通知却已将灯杆使用在其项目建设中是否依然享有救济权利。

Case1 Austria-LPG Sales Contract（GZ 10 Ob 518/95）

【案情说明】

一、案件事实

1990 年 9 月 26 日，居住在德国的买方和居住在奥地利的卖方就天然气的销售进行初步商业洽谈。在谈判过程中，卖方出具了一份手册，该手册中包含卖方的商业标准条件（含卖方仅接受以书面形式签订合同的条件），但无法确定买方是否收到该手册以及是否同意将该手册纳入双方将来签订的合同中。1990 年 10 月 8 日，双方进行了进一步的会谈，卖方在此次会谈中提出了一份框架协议草案（含卖方仅接受以书面形式签订合同的条件；该草案并未采用国际贸易术语，无法根据《国际贸易术语解释通则》执行），但买方认为该草案过于片面，并未进一步研究。其后，双方通过电话和传真进行了磋商。

1990 年 12 月 18 日，买方提出购买 700~800 吨天然气，卖方于 1990 年 12 月 19 日（上午 10 时 17 分）以传真回应买方，内容如下：

"丁烷和丙烷可以立即交货，FOB：ARA，价格为 18 美元 / 公吨。购买数量最好超过 1 000 吨。（ARA 的缩写是指阿姆斯特丹—鹿特丹—安特卫普的较大区域）"

同日上午，卖方向买方发送了另外一份传真，内容为：

"根据我们的酌处权，目前我们最多可以接受 376 美元的平均价格。"

同日下午，买方向卖方发送一份传真，内容为：

"我们很高兴确认第一个关于天然气的合同。根据你方报盘，我方已购买如下：

产品：丙烷，经双方同意，丁烷最多 2%，烯烃最多 5%；数量：700~800 吨；价格：最高 376 美元离岸价，鹿特丹炼油厂，出口比利时；交付：1990 年 12 月交付。

由于我们打算在 1990 年 12 月 20 日开始接收货物，请向我方提供交货详情。

付款方式：我们建议在收到单据后 10 天内以电传方式付款。另外，我们今年正在处理大约 1 000 吨的船货。

等待你方关于 1991 年 1 月 2 日装船的通知。更多细节将在下午讨论。"

同日，卖方向买方发送一份传真，内容如下：

"……我们得在接下来的两个小时内确认货物在美国的确切装运地点以及装船时间，尽管我们还有付款问题仍需进一步商谈。"

"付款不得迟于接管货物后三天。由于几乎在所有方面都建立了这种新的业务关系，因此我们必须要求银行对订单进行确认。"

"装船日期确定为 1991 年 1 月 2 日。请告知我方，你方银行什么时候能予以确认，然后我们会立即向您提供我们的账户信息。同时，我们希望从美国方面得到更多信息。"

之后，双方继续通过电话进行谈判沟通，最终商定货物数量为 3 000 吨，付款方式为收到货物并开出信用证后三天内付款。但不能确定卖方是否同意买方所指定的以比利时为最终目的地。

在与卖方洽谈的过程中，买方与"G-T Holland"公司联系，讨论上述货物的转售问题。最初，"G-T Holland"公司同意从买方处买入 700~800 吨的天然气。但由于买方与卖方于 1990 年 12 月 19 日最终达成的销售货物数量为 3 000 吨，因此买方请求"G-T Holland"公司将上述天然气全部购入。最终，"G-T Holland"公司同意以 381 美元 / 吨的价格向买方购买 3 000 吨天然气。

此后，买方曾催促卖方向其告知确切装货地点，但卖方并未回应。1991 年 1 月 3 日，买方通知卖方，由于没有必要的单据，银行当天无法办理信用证。卖方于 1991 年 1 月 7 日向买方发出传真，表明由于没有供应商的授权，无法将天然气出口到荷兰、比利时或卢森堡，因此卖方无法向买方交付天然气。

二、裁判结果

买方向奥地利萨尔茨堡地方法院提起诉讼，要求卖方赔偿损失。萨尔茨堡地方法院于 1995 年 1 月 23 日作出判决，认为原告买方与被告卖方于 1990 年 12 月 19 日的洽谈符合《联合国国际货物销售合同公约》（CISG）中对合同订立的规定，因此双方之间的天然气买卖协议已经于 1990 年 12 月 19 日达成，双方应当按照约定履行义务。但由于卖方未取得供应商的授权，无法将货物出口到比利时，构成违约，因此被告卖方应当赔偿原告买方损害赔偿金 16.8 万先令以及因无法按期向"G-T Holland"公司交付天然气而产生的额外费用（144 131 美元加上 1% 的利息）。卖方对判决结果不满，向林茨法院提起上诉，林茨法院于 1995 年 5 月 23 日驳回了卖方的上诉。其后，卖方继续向奥地利最高法院提起上诉，奥地利最高法院于 1996 年 2 月 6 日判决驳回被告的上诉，并确认了萨尔茨堡初审法院的判决。

【法律分析】

本案的关键问题是明晰原告与被告之间是否存在有效的货物销售合同，主要法律问题如下：1. 本案是否适用 CISG？ 2. 本案所涉合同是否仅能以书面形式签订？ 3. 若本案合同形式不受约束，那么本案原、被告是否订立了有效的货物销售合同？

焦点一：本案是否适用 CISG。CISG 作为以国际条约形式出现的统一实体法，本来可以不经冲突规范援用而直接适用于缔约国及其自然人和法人，但由于本案纠纷发生于

CISG 在德国生效前（前德意志民主共和国 1981 年 8 月 13 日签署，1989 年 2 月 23 日批准了该公约，公约于 1990 年 3 月 1 日生效），故本案不能以"不经援用冲突规范而直接适用于缔约国及其自然人和法人"为依据直接适用公约。但根据 CISG 第 1 条第 1 款之规定"本公约适用于营业地在不同国家的当事人之间所订立的货物销售合同：……（b）如果国际私法规则导致适用某一缔约国的法律"，即如果冲突规范援用某一国际条约缔约国的法律为准据法，该缔约国参加的这一国际条约可视同该国国内法并可被作为准据法予以适用。本案中，原告买方主营地位于德国，被告卖方主营地位于奥地利，双方营业地位于不同国家，且双方于 1990 年 12 月 19 日进行磋商时，CISG 已在被告卖方所在地奥地利生效，故本案仍可根据国际私法规则适用 CISG。

焦点二：本案所涉合同是否仅能以书面形式签订。本案中，双方争论的根本问题是双方是否签订了一份关于以 3 000 吨天然气为标的的货物销售合同。卖方对此持否定态度，认为双方此前的业务洽谈（卖方出具的商业标准条件、框架协议草案以及双方的传真来往），已经表明了卖方仅以书面形式签订合同，由于双方并未以书面形式签订合同，因此合同尚未成立。但卖方的主张事实上并无法律依据。首先，根据 CISG 第 11 条及第 14 条之规定，合同由两份相应的意向声明订立，即一方的要约和另一方的承诺，且销售合同不必以书面形式订立，也不受任何其他形式要求的约束，即公约本身对合同的形式没有强制性规定。其次，关于卖方主张其曾在商业标准条件、框架协议草案中明确表明其仅以书面形式签订合同的问题，根据 CISG 第 8 条第 3 款之规定，在确定一方当事人的意旨或一个通情达理的人应有的理解时，应适当地考虑到与事实有关的一切情况，包括谈判情形、当事人之间确立的任何习惯做法、惯例和当事人其后的任何行为。结合本案，第一，关于商业标准条件是否应当作为双方合同成立基础的问题。CISG 并未对将商业标准条件纳入合同作出具体规定，但可根据合同成立规则来进行调整和解释，即在受要约人知道或者应当知道该条件，并在接受该条件时，该一般销售条件可被纳入合同。本案中，由于不能确定买方是否了解卖方的一般销售条件，因此卖方曾向买方提供的商业标准条件无法作为合同签订的基础。第二，关于框架协议草案能否成为双方合同成立基础的问题，只有在买方了解该框架协议草案且打算使其成为双方所有合同的基础时，该框架协议草案才能够成为双方合同的基础。本案中，由于买方认为该框架协议草案过于片面，双方并未进行进一步探讨，故买方实质上拒绝以上述框架协议草案作为双方此后合同的基础。第三，双方之间的传真往来也无法证明卖方曾明确向买方表示仅能以书面形式订立合同。第四，根据 CISG 第 9 条第 2 款之规定，"除非另有协议，双方当事人应视为已默示地同意对他们的合同或合同的订立适用双方当事人已知道或理应知道的惯例，而这种惯例，在国际贸易上，已为有关特定贸易所涉同类合同的当事人所广泛知道并为他们所经常遵守"，即如果双方在订立合同时提及行业惯例，则该行业惯例对双方当事人产生拘束力。但本案中，卖方从未提及行业惯例，且石油工业中亦无仅能以书面形式签订合同的惯例。因此，本案所涉合同并非仅能以书面形式签订，双方未能以书面形式签订合同不能成为合同成立的阻碍。

焦点三：若本案合同形式不受约束，那么本案原、被告是否订立了有效的货物销售合同。根据 CISG 的规定，判断双方是否订立有效合同的关键是判断双方是否作出了适格的要约和有效的承诺。本案中，双方的谈判沟通可分为两个阶段，传真联络阶段和电话磋商阶段。第一阶段中，卖方曾向买方发出要约，买方以传真方式回复卖方。这一阶段的关键问题为买方于 1990 年 12 月 19 日（下午 2 时 16 分）给卖方的回复中提到的"在收到单据后 10 天内以电传方式付款"是否构成买方接受卖方要约的实质性偏差。根据 CISG 第 19 条之规定"有关货物价格、付款、货物质量和数量、交货地点和时间、一方当事人对另一方当事人的赔偿责任范围或解决争端等的添加或不同条件，均视为在实质上变更发价的条件"，买方的此份传真属于还价，这就要求双方必须达成新的一致意见。因此，在该阶段中，双方并未就货物销售合同达成一致意见。第二阶段中，双方通过电话磋商货物买卖的相关事宜，最终商定销售数量为 3 000 吨天然气，支付方式为买方于收到货物三天后付款。结合在焦点二中的论述，CISG 本身对合同的形式没有强制性规定，故双方以口头形式达成的合同是有效的。

综上所述，双方实际上已经于 1990 年 12 月 19 日缔结了销售合同，双方存在合法有效的合同。卖方未按照约定向买方交货构成违约，因此应当承担违约责任。

【英文案例裁决摘录】

下文的摘录是奥地利最高法院判决中论述合同成立与否的部分。

I. THE FACTS

On 26 September 1990 the manager of the plaintiff [buyer][1], Juergen S, and the managing partner of the defendant [seller], Harald D., engaged in a preliminary business conversation. In the course of that conversation Harald D. purposes a blue brochure [page 153] with the title "H. Cooperationsgesellschaft GmbH. & Co. KG" [firm of the sellers]. It cannot be established whether the [buyer] has ever received this brochure containing a supplement with the AGB (general conditions of sale of the [sellers]), whether thereafter the [buyer] ever agreed to include these general conditions of sale into future contracts, or that the [buyer] specifically agreed to include these terms into the contract during the contract negotiations on 19 December 1990.

On 8 October 1990, a further conversation between the parties took place in Stuttgart. In the course of this conversation, the draft of a framework agreement serving as the basis for

---

1 All translations should be verified by cross-checking against the original text. For purposes of this translation, the German Defendants-Appellants are referred to as [sellers], the Austrian Plaintiff-Respondent as [buyer]. Monetary amounts in Austrian schillings are indicated as [sA].

business contacts with Saudi Arabia was generally agreed upon. This framework agreement was not to be applied to the so-called routine contracts, which are usually carried out under Incoterms. Subsequently, on 17 October 1990, the [sellers] sent to the [buyer] a draft of the framework agreement, which the [buyer], however, regarded as too one-sided and therefore did not pursue any further. The framework agreement was not suitable for routine contracts because these involve finding buyers for specific products on short notice, and are therefore primarily agreed upon and executed by phone. As the business relationship between the parties was new, they agreed to secure every contract with a letter of credit.

Following several offers by fax, which were not accepted by the [sellers], on 18 December 1990, the [buyer] made an offer to purchase approximately 700 to 800 tons of natural gas. In response to this offer, the [sellers], sent a fax to the [buyer] on 19 December 1990 (10:17 a.m.), which read:

"Butane and propane can be delivered immediately FOB: ARA, with a price of US $18/mt. However, preferably, we should … a larger quantity than the 1,000/mt. mentioned by you … This deal is ready to be concluded in all its details. As we have larger quantities at our disposition due to term contracts, since today, we are making every effort to find a customer." [The abbreviation ARA refers to the greater area of Amsterdam-Rotterdam-Antwerp.]

Another fax of the [sellers] dated 19 December 1990 (11:46 a.m.) said:

"In accordance with our discretionary powers, we can currently accept an average price of US $376 at the maximum."

Then, the [buyer] sent a fax to the [sellers] on 19 December 1990 (2:16 p.m.):

"We are pleased to confirm the first contract regarding liquid gas. According to your offer, we have bought as follows:

Product: propane, upon mutual agreement a maximum of 2% butane and a maximum of 5% olefin.

Quantity: approximately 700~800 tons.

Price: up to US $376 FOB, refinery Rotterdam for export to Belgium.

Delivery: December 1990.

As we intend to begin to take the merchandise over on 20 December 1990, please provide us with the details of delivery.

Payment: We suggest ten days after date of delivery upon invoice by telex. In addition, we are working on the delivery of a shipload of approximately 1,000 tons this year.

"We are a Payment: We suggest ten days after date of delivery upon invoice by telex. In addition, we are working on the delivery of a shipload of approximately 1,000 tons this year.

Waiting your immediate notification regarding the ship to be loaded on 2 January 1991.

Further details will be discussed in the course of the afternoon."

Belgium was mentioned as the final destination for export in order to inform the refinery of the country for which the customs documents should be prepared. The last written communication on 19 December 1990 was the fax of the [sellers] to the [buyer] (3:19 p.m.), which read as follows:

"… I still have to confirm the exact place of loading in the US within the next two hours. This also applies to the time of loading, despite the fact that we still have the problem of payment."

"Payment should not be made later than three days after takeover of the goods. Due to this new business relationship in almost all regards, we have to ask for a bank confirmation of the order. This would be the easiest way."

"And the date of 2 January 1991 could also be already confirmed. Please let us know, at what time your bank will be able to confirm. Then we will immediately provide you with our account information. Meanwhile, we will hopefully have further information from the US. Unfortunately, this does not go faster."

Beside this ample communication by fax, the parties equally communicated by phone on 19 December 1990, whereby the negotiations were conducted by Juergen S. and Harald D. Following the fax of the [buyer] of 2:16 p.m., another telephone conversation took place, in the course of which in contrast to the initial proposal of the [buyer] the parties agreed upon a deadline of payment of three days after takeover of the goods and a letter of credit of the [buyer] to secure this contract of sale. It could not be established whether the [sellers] still had reservations regarding the final destination of Belgium.

During the negotiations with the [sellers], the [buyer] made contacts with the company of "G-T Holland" to discuss the resale of the merchandise ordered from the [sellers]. As the [buyer] opportunity to sell took a more concrete shape, the [buyer] agreed upon the takeover of the first 700 to 800 tons with the [sellers]. When Harald D. urged the [buyer] [page 155] to purchase a larger quantity, the [buyer] made every effort to sell a larger quantity, in which [buyer] finally succeeded on that very afternoon. When a corresponding offer of [buyer's customer] G-T was made, the [buyer] finally agreed upon a quantity of approximately 3,000 tons instead of the 700-800 tons initially envisaged. The [buyer] and G-T agreed upon a resale price of US $381 per ton.

II. PROCEDURE

On 23 May 1995, the Oberlandesgericht Linz, acting as a Court of Appeals (GZ 1 R 64/95-34), rejected the defendants appeal and affirmed the decision by the Court of First

Instance, the Landesgericht Salzburg, of 13 January 1995, GZ 9 Cg 398/93t-28.

The Oberster Gerichtshof [Supreme Court of Austria], composed of the President of this Senate of the Supreme Court, Dr. Kropfitsch, as chairman and Dr. Bauer, Dr. Ehmayr, Dr. Steinbauer und Dr. Danzl as accompanying judges, sitting over the case of plaintiff Friedrich S. OHG, represented by Dr. Utho Hosp, attorney in Salzburg, versus the defendant parties H. GmbH and Z. GmbH & Co Betriebs KG, both represented by Dr. Michael Wonisch and Dr. Hansjrg Reiner, attorneys in Salzburg, over 168,000 sA [Austrian shillings] and a declaratory judgment, has come to the following decision:

The appeal is denied.

The defendant parties [sellers] are ordered to reimburse the plaintiff [buyer] for the costs of the proceedings in this final instance set at sA 22,671 (including sA 3,778.50 of turnover tax) within fourteen days.

III. ANALYSIS

1. JURISDICTION

Therefore, the decision of the Court of Appeals is upheld and the appeal is dismissed.

2. MERITS

The District Court (ErstG or Court of First Instance) granted the [buyer] claim with the exception of a part of the claim for interest.

The reasoning for this decision was as follows:

The business relationship between the parties to this lawsuit is governed by the CISG. According to the CISG, the parties reached an agreement upon the amount, quality and price of the natural gas to be sold by the [sellers]. The terms of payment (i.e., by letter of credit) and the deadlines for payment were agreed upon contractually on the evening of 19 December 1990. Only the nomination of a place of loading by the [sellers] was still left open. This means that a valid contract without conditions was in existence.

The Court of First Instance found that the terms of the framework agreement never constituted the basis for the specific deal. The general conditions of sale of the [sellers] were not agreed upon. According to Article 53 CISG, the [buyer] was under a contractual obligation to make sure the letter of credit would be granted. A clause to open a letter of credit serves to secure the obligations of both parties to a contract; especially the buyer wants to make sure that payment is only made when the contractual obligations of the [sellers] (i.e., delivery of the mutually agreed upon amount and quality at the mutually agreed upon time) have been fulfilled. This means that the buyer has an overwhelming interest in determining the details of the letter of credit and of the documents to be presented already upon conclusion of the contract. In the case of an FOB clause, the [sellers] has to deliver the goods onboard a ship named by the [buyer] at a mutually agreed upon harbor according to the customs of the harbor, and at a mutually agreed upon time or within a mutually agreed upon time framework.

Furthermore, the [sellers] has to inform the [buyer] immediately that the goods have been delivered to the ship. This means that the [sellers] has to bear the costs and risk of the goods until the time when the goods actually cross the railing of the ship in the mutually agreed upon harbor of shipment. In order to completely secure the contractual rights of the [buyer] by letter of credit, the nomination of the harbor of loading by the [sellers] is of utmost importance to the [buyer]. The fact that a letter of credit can be opened without naming the exact place of loading, is not a decisive factor here, because the [buyer] explicitly asked the [sellers] to name the place of loading to completely secure the [buyer] order. The [sellers] had assured the [buyer] they would inform the [buyer] of the place of loading within two hours, which, however, did not happen. Therefore, the non-issuance of a letter of credit was due to an omission of the [sellers]. If the [sellers] had ever considered the issuance of a general letter of credit as a fulfillment of their contractual obligations, they should have informed the [buyer] about this. Failing to act or merely waiting for the remittance of any kind of letter of credit by the [buyer] is contrary to the legal principle of bona fide [good faith]. Furthermore, one has to note, that in the end not the non-issuance of the letter of credit by the [buyer], but the determination of the final place of export by the [supplier] of the [sellers] led to the failure of the contract. Therefore, the reason for the non-fulfillment of the delivery of the goods can be found in the sphere of the [sellers], i.e., their inability to get clearance from their [supplier] to export the goods to the Benelux countries.

The Court of First Instance concluded that according to Art. 74 CISG, the [sellers] are obligated to indemnify the [buyer] for the loss of profit in the amount of $5 m/t. The [buyer] proved its special interest to be granted a declaratory judgment by showing the existence of a business relationship and a contractual obligation towards G-T. The motion for declaratory judgment was justified following the [sellers] rejection of any of [buyer] claims, especially with regard to the running of the limitation period and the doubtful outcome of the suit for damages in Rotterdam.

The Court of Appeals rejected the [sellers'] appeal, basing its decision on the lower courts factual findings on the grounds that they were the result of a flawless procedure.

The Court of Appeal's reasoning was as follows:

The contract of sale at issue is governed by the UN Sales Convention according to Art. 1(1)(b) CISG. According to the CISG, as under Austrian law, a contract is formed by two corresponding declarations of intent. Art. 11 CISG does not provide for any form requirements for the conclusion of a contract. In this case, the framework agreement does not apply, because it had not been concluded. The CISG does not put up specific requirements for the inclusion of general conditions of sale in a contract. The necessary rules are to be developed employing Art. 8 CISG. Consequently, general conditions of sale of one party can be a part of the offer due to the contract negotiations between the parties or the practices developed between them. In all other cases, a reference to general conditions of sale which are not attached to the offer, has to be so explicit that a reasonably prudent person from the perspective of the recipient is able to understand it.

The contract at issue was the first one in the newly developed business relationship between the parties. Therefore, practices between the parties could not have been developed yet. The lower court did not find that the general conditions of sale of the [sellers] were part of the contract negotiations. The [sellers] did not explicitly note that they would only be willing to enter into the contract if their general conditions of sale were included. Therefore, the inclusion of the [sellers] general conditions of sale into the contract was not agreed upon. Consequently, the written form stipulated therein did not apply to the confirmation of the acceptance of an order and does not have an effect on the validity of the sales contract. Furthermore, the estoppel exception of Art. 29(2), sentence two, CISG would apply here, if the parties agreed orally on the conclusion of a sales contract without one of the parties informing the other party about the requirement of a written form for the conclusion of said contract. As a result, the parties agreed partly orally and partly in writing upon a contract of sale for approximately 3,000 tons of liquid gas on 19 December 1990. In addition, agreement was reached about the terms of payment, i.e., a deadline for payment of three days after acceptance of the goods by the [buyer] and the securing of the sale by a letter of credit were agreed upon in detail. The [buyer] did not open the letter of credit and the [sellers] did not deliver the goods of sale, i.e., the liquid gas.

The Court of Appeals held that it was irrelevant whether the non-opening of the letter of credit by the [buyer] represented a breach of contract, which would have given the [sellers] the right to declare the contract avoided under Art. 64(1) CISG. The performance of the contract failed, not because the [buyer] did not open the letter of credit, but because the [sellers] were not able to get approval from their [supplier] to export the liquid gas to Belgium. If it is already certain that the [seller] is unable to fulfill his obligation to deliver the purchased goods, then the [buyer] is entitled to suspend its duty to open a letter of credit (Art. 71 CISG). Furthermore, the [sellers] never explicitly declared to the [buyer] the avoidance of the contract according to Art. 26 CISG. Instead, the [sellers] always claimed that a contract of sale was never concluded in the first place. The [sellers] did not fulfill their obligation to deliver the purchased goods, and as a consequence the [buyer] can demand damages according to Arts. 45(1)(b), 74-77 CISG. According to Art. 74 CISG, damages for breach of contract by one party consist of a sum equal to the loss, including loss of profit, suffered by the other party as a consequence of the breach. According to the findings of the lower court, the loss to the [buyer] amounts to 168,000 Austrian Schillings. Consequently, the [buyer] has already suffered damages resulting from the breach of contract. Additionally, it is a fact that the [buyer] has been sued by its business partner, G-T, for damages in the Circuit Court of Rotterdam with the consequence that the [buyer] could suffer additional damages resulting from the [sellers] breach of contract. There are no reasons to assume collusive conduct between the [buyer] and G-T, as claimed by the [sellers].

The Court of Appeals authorized this appeal on points of law (revision).

The [sellers] appeal the decision of the Court of Appeals to this Court on grounds of a faulty procedure and incorrect legal assessment of [buyers] claim. They request the Supreme Court to overturn the appealed decision as well as the decision of the Court of First Instance and to reject the claim. In the alternative, they request a setting-aside of the above-mentioned judgments.

The [buyer] requests dismissal of this appeal.

The appeal is dismissed.

A reason to decide in favor of the [sellers] on procedural grounds does not exist. According to the [sellers], the appellate procedure was faulty because further factual findings were necessary to adequately make a decision. Therefore, the [sellers] claim the existence of secondary mistakes of findings, which, however, cannot be advanced by an appeal under 503 No. 2 ZPO [Austrian Code of Civil Procedure], but can only be claimed in connection with an appeal on material grounds (SSV-NF 3/29; EFSlg 55.115; JBl 1982, 311; EFSlg 34.500, ua).

Before the Court of Appeals, the [sellers] claimed that the Court of First Instance had made procedural mistakes by failing to take evidence in several ways (testimony of the parties, the reading of the motions of the foreign suit between the [buyer] and G-T, the questioning of an informed witness belonging to G-T). As the Court of Appeals rejected the [sellers] submissions, the alleged mistakes of the Court of First Instance cannot be examined by the Supreme Court as a mistake of the appellate proceeding itself (for consistent case law of the Supreme Court; see JUS 1989 Z/265; EvBl 1989/165=NRsp 1989/159 = WBl1989, 317; SSV-NF 3/18, 7174, ua).

Insofar as the [sellers] claim as a ground for appeal that the lower courts found that the [buyer] had suffered a loss of profit of $5 / mt of propane gas, they attack the factual findings, which is not allowed before this Court. The lower courts found that the parties agreed upon a price of $376/mt and that the [buyer] sold the natural gas to G-T at a price of $381/mt. The Supreme Court does not decide on the facts, but on the law only. The Supreme Court is not entitled to examine whether the lower courts in their taking of evidence established the facts of the case correctly.

Both parties in this case assume correctly that the question whether a contract of sale was concluded on 19 December 1990 between the [buyer] residing in Germany and the [sellers] with their residence in Austria, as well as the decision about the obligations resulting from such a contract and the consequences arising from the breach of such a contract, are governed by the UN Convention on Contracts for the International Sale of Goods (CISG); the parties have their places of business in different countries. Though the contract of sale was concluded one day before the CISG entered into force in Germany (on 1 January 1991, BGBl. 1990/303), Art. 1(1)(b) CISG provides for the application of this Convention if the rules of private international law lead to the application of the law of one of the Contracting States to the Convention (Vorschaltloesung cf. Karollus, CISG, 30). According to Art. 36 IPRG [Austrian Code of Private International Law], synallagmatic contracts, whereby one party at least predominantly owes money to the other party, and for which a choice of the applicable law has not been made by the parties, are governed by the law of the country in which the other party has its usual residence. Consequently, Austrian law applies to the business relationship between the parties, because the [sellers] place of business is in Austria. As the CISG was already in force in Austria (since 1 January 1989, BGBl 1988/96) at the time the contract at issue was concluded, the contract is governed by this Convention (cf. RIW 1991, 952).

According to Art. 14 CISG, a contract is concluded by two corresponding declarations of intent, that is, the offer of one party and the acceptance of the other party, and the contract of sale does not have to be in writing nor is it subject to any other form requirements (Art. 11 CISG). The offer, which must be sufficiently definite in that it indicates the goods, the quantity and the price (the latter two must be at least determinable), is interpreted according to the offerors intent where the offeree could not have been unaware of such intent (Herber/ Czerwenka, Internationales Kaufrecht, Art. 14 n. 10). According to Art. 8(3) CISG, when interpreting the offer, the negotiations of the parties, the practices which the parties have established between themselves, and the subsequent conduct of the parties have to be taken into consideration.

The CISG does not contain specific requirements for the incorporation of standard business conditions, such as the [sellers] general conditions of sale, into a contract. Therefore, the necessary requirements for such an inclusion are to be developed from Art. 14 et seq. CISG, which contain the exclusive requirements for the conclusion of a contract (cf. Piltz, Internationales Kaufrecht, Art. 5 n. 75). Consequently, the general conditions of sale have to be part of the offer according to the offerors intent, where the offeree could not have been unaware of that intent, in order to become a part of the contract (Art. 8(1) and (2) CISG). This inclusion into the offer can also be done implicitly or can be inferred from the negotiations between the parties or a practice which has developed between them.

The fundamental question at issue is whether the parties concluded a contract of sale regarding 3,000 mt propane gas, which the lower courts decided in the affirmative. In denial of the existence of a contract of sale, the [sellers] argue that it can be inferred from the general conditions of sale, the draft of the framework agreement, and the correspondence between the parties that the [sellers] generally only conclude contracts in writing and only when the payment is guaranteed by letter of credit or some other means of securing payment; in addition, in the preliminary correspondence, the [buyer] explicitly referred to the "usual conditions" and "delivery on a contractual basis". The [sellers] admit that no prior contract has been concluded between the parties and that this, therefore, would constitute their first contract if a contract was ever concluded, which is still denied by the [sellers] with the consequence that practices in the meaning of Art. 9 CISG could not have been developed between the parties. The [sellers] claim, however, that prior business conversations between the parties (the general conditions of sale, the prior correspondence and the draft of the framework agreement) show the [sellers] usual approach when concluding contracts, i.e., their principle of concluding contracts in writing only. According to the [sellers], this prior conduct can qualify as practices in the sense of Art. 9 CISG, which means that a contract has not been agreed upon, because the written form requirement was not observed.

The argument of the [sellers] is without merit:

It is generally possible that intentions of one party, which are expressed in preliminary business conversations only and which are not expressly agreed upon by the parties, can become practices in the sense of Art. 9 CISG already at the beginning of a business relationship and thereby become part of the first contract between the parties. This, however, requires at least (Art. 8, especially paragraph (1) of Art. 8 CISG) that the business partner realizes from these circumstances that the other party is only willing to enter into a contract under certain conditions or in a certain form. In the present case, it cannot be determined whether the [sellers] general conditions of sale were given to the [buyer], whether agreement was reached about their application, or whether the [buyer] got to know them at all. The lower courts could not determine that the [buyer] general contract manager had ever received the brochure containing the general conditions of sale; and the findings of the lower courts do not support the conclusion that the [buyer] was informed of the contents of the general conditions of sale in the aftermath (i.e., following the first informational conversations). As it cannot be determined that the [buyer] had knowledge of the general conditions of sale of the [sellers], the Court cannot draw the conclusion that they formed the basis of the contractual agreement between the parties in the meaning of Art. 9 CISG.

The parties also discussed the draft of a framework agreement. The intended framework agreement, which in the end was not concluded, because the parties could not agreed upon it, was supposed to form the basis for so-called tender contracts. According to the findings of the lower courts, these are principally different from routine contracts, such as the contract in question. Routine contracts involve the finding of customers for specific products on short notice; they are mainly negotiated and executed by phone. It cannot be assumed that the [buyer] knew or had reason to know that the [sellers] intended to make those conditions the basis for the conclusion of routine contracts, which were discussed, and finally rejected, in the framework of negotiations for the conclusion of a framework agreement for tender contracts. Only if the [buyer] had been aware of both of these conditions and the [sellers] intent to make them a basis for all of their contracts, these conditions could have been part of the contractual agreements pursuant to Art. 9 CISG without special agreement.

The correspondence of the parties does not support the [sellers] point of view either. The mere allusion to "usual conditions" or to "on a contractual basis" does not mean that the [buyer] was referring to the [sellers] general conditions of sale or to general contractual conditions, which were discussed in connection with the completely different framework agreement, which ultimately was not agreed upon and which did not even cover the kind of contract at issue here.

As the [sellers] general conditions of sale did not become part of the contract, their content is of no relevance here and no determinations regarding their content had to be made by the courts. It was equally unnecessary to determine the content of the parties correspondence (as the [sellers] demanded), because even if the [sellers] claims regarding those facts could be substantiated, this would not lead to a different result.

As a specific form for the conclusion of a contract was not agreed upon during the negotiations of 19 December 1990 and the facts do not establish that it was self-evident for the parties (Art. 9(1) CISG) that contracts could only be agreed upon in writing as a condition for the conclusion of a contract, the observance of the form requirement, i.e., the written form, was not a condition for the formation of a valid contract (Art. 11 CISG). When deciding this question, oral declarations of the parties have to be equally taken into consideration.

Therefore, the Court of Appeals correctly decided that neither the contractual negotiations nor the practices having developed between the parties could have made the general conditions of sale of the [sellers] part of their offer. It is true that the usual requirements for the formation of a contract can be modified by industry usages (Karollus, UN-K, 52), if the parties refer to such usages upon conclusion of the contract (Art. 9(2) CISG); however, a custom in the oil industry to conclude contracts of sale in writing only was neither found nor claimed by the [sellers] in this case.

The [sellers] argue in their appeal in this regard that the existing written documents (telefaxes) are insufficient to assume the existence of an agreement of the parties. The [sellers], however, neglect essential factors, if they argue only based on the contents of the telefaxes that the declarations of the parties are not sufficient to assume the existence of an agreement. Indeed, it is certain that several telephone conversations were made between the parties on 19 December 1990, the contents of which need to be considered when answering the essential question whether a contract was concluded. Accordingly, on 19 December 1990 the parties agreed partially orally and partially in writing upon the delivery of 700 to 800 tons of liquid gas at a price of $376 per mt. The mere approximate determination of the quantity was customary in the natural gas industry; the quality or other characteristics of the natural gas have never been disputed by the parties not even at the trial level.

The terms of payment, i.e., a deadline of three days after acceptance of the goods and secured payment by letter of credit, were also agreed upon in detail. Therefore, it is irrelevant whether the proposal of the [buyer], which was mentioned in the telefax of 19 December 1990, to pay ten days after delivery of the goods and after telex invoice, constituted a material deviation of the [buyer] acceptance from the [sellers] offer (in that case, the response of the [buyer] would have to be regarded as a counter-offer according to Art. 19(1) CISG, which would require a new consensus of the parties) or just a proposal of the offeree mentioned for future business between the parties, which does not fall under Art. 19(1) CISG (cf. von Caemmerer/Schlechtriem, Kommentar zum [page 164] einheitlichen UN-K, Art. 19 n. 7). In fact, in a telephone conversation, the parties reached agreement about a deadline of three days.

The fact that the parties in this case did not pursue the quantity originally agreed upon, but instead agreed upon the delivery of 3,000 tons of liquid gas, is valid with regard to Art. 29(1) CISG (providing for a subsequent modification of the contract by agreement of the parties), and does not prevent the conclusion of a contract regarding the quantity, which was finally agreed upon. Furthermore, the [sellers] are precluded by the factual findings of the lower courts from challenging the agreement of the parties about the quantity of 3,000 mt propane gas. The lower courts decided that the increase of the quantity to be delivered (which was incidentally desired by the [sellers]) was agreed upon by phone on the afternoon of 19 December 1990. According to the factual findings, an agreement was also reached about the opening of a letter of credit.

The deal between the parties, therefore, was concluded on the evening of 19 December 1990. In the aftermath, however, neither did the [buyer] open the letter of credit nor did the [sellers] deliver the sold goods, i.e., the liquid gas.

According to Art. 54 CISG, the [buyer] has the obligation to pay the purchase price and to comply with such formalities as may be required under the contract or any laws and regulations to enable payment to be made. If, as in this case, the opening of a letter of credit was agreed upon, the [buyer] is obligated to make sure it is opened on time. This can only be assumed as being done when the [sellers] has acquired the claim against the bank. Therefore, the agreement about a letter of credit requires the [buyer] to perform before the [sellers] does. It is only after the letter of credit is opened that the [buyer] acquires the claim against the [sellers] to perform as agreed upon (Avancini/Iro/Koziol, Bankvertragsrecht II, n. 4/26). According to the unanimous opinion of scholars (cf. Karollus, 171; von Caemmerer/Schlechtriem, Art. 54 n. 3), the opening of a letter of credit is part of the obligation to pay the purchase price with the consequence that the non-performance in this regard triggers the legal remedies of breach of contract (Art. 61 et seq. CISG) and not just the remedies of an anticipatory breach (Arts. 71 to 73 CISG, cf. von Caemmerer/Schlechtriem, Art. 54 n.7).

However, the letter of credit was not issued because the [sellers] did not inform the [buyer] of the place of loading despite their obligation to do so and their express confirmation in this regard (last telefax of 19 December 1990). Though Juergen S., even when on Christmas vacation, urged the [sellers] to release this information, the [sellers] did not even inform him of the place of loading at the beginning of January. As a consequence, the notice of the [buyer] in the telefax of 2 January 1990 can only mean that [buyer] obviously thought that the release of this information would happen on that very day, but that [buyer] could not take any measures anymore on that very day due to the little time left. The fact that the [buyer] did not fulfill its obligation the advance performance by means of opening a letter of credit until the beginning of January, is the [sellers] fault, who did not name the place of loading despite their corresponding obligation, even though they had reason to know that the [buyer] would only issue the letter of credit after being informed of the place of loading. It is irrelevant whether the opening of a letter of credit would have been possible even without information about the place of loading, because the parties expressly agreed upon the naming of the place of loading by the [sellers]. Due to this agreement, the [sellers] had the primary duty to name the place of loading.

Only after this act on the part of the [sellers], did the [buyer] have the obligation to issue the letter of credit. The non-issuance of the letter of credit, therefore, was caused by an omission of the [sellers], and following Art. 80 CISG the latter cannot rely on the [buyer] failure to open the letter of credit.

Furthermore, the non-issuance of the letter of credit was not the cause for non-fulfillment of the contract. In accordance with the holdings of the lower courts, this Court finds that the [sellers] are responsible for the non-fulfillment of the contract, because they did not obtain clearance of their supplier for export of the liquid gas into Belgium. According to Art. 30 CISG, the [sellers] is obligated to deliver the goods in accordance with the terms of the contract. The argument of the [sellers] in their appeal to the effect that the prohibition of export into Belgium and the resulting consequences are part of the sphere of the [buyer], because the latter did not make the possibility of export into Belgium a condition of the contract, is without merit. Upon conclusion of a contract of sale, the buyer can generally assume in the absence of special circumstances (embargo, legal restrictions, general restrictions known to the industry) that the further use the goods is unlimited and is not subject to further restrictions. It is not the duty of the [buyer] to obtain an assurance that further delivery restrictions do not exist. To the contrary, it is the obligation of the [sellers] to mention such restrictions of delivery, which limit the normally unrestricted use of the goods. If the [sellers] omits to mention such restrictions, the [buyer] can justifiably assume that such restrictions do not exist. According to Art. 41 CISG, the [sellers] has to deliver goods, which are not subject to the rights of third parties, unless the [buyer] has previously agreed to accept such goods in fulfillment of the contract. If the supplier of the [sellers] has restricted the export of the goods, then the goods are burdened with such a restriction. This consequently means that the delivery of goods, which are subject to such a restriction, constitutes non-fulfillment of the contract in the absence of the [buyer] consent.

As the [sellers] did not fulfill this obligation, the [buyer] has the right to full indemnification of its damages (Karollus, 211). This means that the aggrieved party always has to be placed in the position that he or she would have been in if the other party had fulfilled the contractual obligation breached by him (Karollus, 215). The other party does not have to be at fault or have to act illegally to be held liable in this respect (Karollus, 206). In its Arts. 75 and 76, the CISG contains specific provisions about the calculation of damages only for the case of avoidance of a contract following a breach. The breach of a contractual obligation never leads to the automatic avoidance of the contract by law even if, as is the case here, one party is substantially deprived of what she is entitled to expect under the contract (Art. 25 CISG; cf. Karollus,151; von Caemmerer/Schlechtriem, Art. 49 and 28). The avoidance of a contract is made by unilateral declaration of the party faithful to the contract to the other party (cf.

Karollus,151); it does not require a specific form and generally, with the exception of the cases of Art. 49(2) CISG, is not subject to a specific deadline (cf. Karollus,146).

In this case, the controversy about whether the declaration to avoid the contract in the sense of Art. 49(1) CISG has to be explicit (cf. Karollus, 151) or whether conclusive conduct is sufficient (cf. von Caemmerer/Schlechtriem, Art. 49 and 29), is irrelevant. For even if a conclusive declaration to avoid a contract is regarded as sufficient, the intention of the [buyer] not to adhere to the contract anymore has to be obvious beyond any doubt (cf. LG Frankfurt aM, RIW 1991, 952/953). In this respect, the requirements for the clarity of the declaration have to be set at a high level (cf. von Caemmerer/Schlechtriem, Art. 26 and 10). The factual findings of the lower courts do not suggest that the contract of sale in this case has been explicitly avoided by the [buyer], which, besides, has never been argued by the [buyer] itself. Furthermore, a declaration to avoid the contract cannot be concluded beyond any doubt from the fact that the [buyer] provided the [sellers] with a list of the losses of [buyer] customer. Consequently, the [buyer] damages in the present case have to be calculated in a way that is based on the existence and performance of the contract according to Art. 74 CISG. This may include the damages resulting from the delay of the delivery of the goods or from defects of the product, including loss of profit as consequential damages (cf. von Caemmerer/Schlechtriem, Art. 74 and 5). However, if the [buyer] loses profits, which [buyer] could have realized by reselling the goods had the [sellers] not breached his obligations, the [sellers] is only liable for this loss of profit if he had to reckon with the [buyer] resale. In the case of the sale of commercial goods to a merchant, this can always be assumed without any further indications (cf. von Caemmerer/Schlechtriem, Art. 74 and 41). In addition, the [sellers] themselves admit that they knew that the [buyer] would sell the goods.

However, insofar as the damages for breach of contract, including the loss of profit, could have been mitigated by measures reasonable in the circumstances, compensation cannot be demanded (cf. von Caemmerer/Schlechtriem, Art. 77 and 3 ; Karollus, 225). A possible measure to reduce damages is reasonable, if it could have been expected as bona fides [good faith] conduct from a reasonable person in the position of the claimant under the same circumstances (cf. von Caemmerer/Schlechtriem, Art. 77 and 9). Apparently, the [sellers] refer to this provision when they claim a breach of the duty to mitigate damages. However, this argument has to be rejected because the [sellers] have not advanced any detailed facts to support it. The claim of the breach of the duty to mitigate damages is an exception leading to the loss of the claim for damages. It requires the [sellers] to put forward detailed facts and the supporting evidence showing why the [buyer] has breached its duty to mitigate damages, the possibilities of alternative conduct and which part of the damages would have been prevented by this alternative conduct. The [sellers] did not bring forward any of these submissions. They solely claimed the breach of the duty to mitigate damages in a general manner in the course of the suit, and it was not until the appellate level that they raised the argument that the [buyer] was obligated to conclude substitute contracts at an appropriate time and in an appropriate time framework according to Art. 75 CISG. Beside the fact that new arguments cannot be raised on the appellate level, these arguments themselves contain only the legal language of Art. 77 CISG without even trying to advance specific facts such as the ones mentioned above.

In addition, the arguments raised by the [sellers] against a declaratory judgment are without merit. Upon the sale of commercial goods to a merchant, the [sellers] has reason to believe that the [buyer] will be held liable by her customers if the [sellers] delivers non-conforming goods or does not fulfill his duty to deliver at all (cf. von Caemmerer/Schlechtriem, Art. 74 and 42). Therefore, the [buyer] has a legal interest in the award of a declaratory judgment regarding the [sellers] liability for all future damages resulting from the breach of contract, in particular because the possibility exists that the breach may cause even further damages (EFSlg 55.030). Besides, in this case it is certain that the [buyer] has already been held liable by its customer, which is the subject of a lawsuit in Rotterdam. When the [sellers] claim collusive conduct of the [buyer] and G-T to the detriment of the [sellers], these are mere presumptions without any substance whatsoever.

【思考题】

1. 根据《联合国国际货物销售公约》，一个合格的要约需满足哪些条件？买方于 1990 年 12 月 18 日向卖方提出购买 700~800 吨的天然气是否属于要约？

2. 根据《联合国国际货物销售公约》，一个有效的承诺需满足哪些条件？买方于 1990 年 12 月 19 日向卖方发送的传真是否构成有效的承诺？

3. 一方对要约作出附加条件的答复能否构成承诺？

4. 何种情况下，商业标准条件能够被纳入合同？

5. 口头的国际货物买卖合同是否有效？

Case1 · 拓展阅读

Case2 California – Light Poles Business Sales（No. 07–161–JBT）

【案情说明】

一、案件事实

原告 Sky Cast Inc.（以下简称"天空公司"）是一家外国公司，其主要营业地在加拿大安大略省圭尔夫，对被告 Global Direct Distribution, LLC（以下简称"全球公司"）提起诉讼，该有限责任公司的主要营业地在美国肯塔基州列克星敦。天空公司指控全球公司亏欠混凝土灯杆款项 83 203.78 美元，并就全球公司管理层员工 David J. Dixon（"Dixon"）和 Raymond A. Sjogren（"Sjogren"）的欺诈陈述提出诉讼。天空公司根据签订生效的合同，要求全球公司赔偿因违约行为而带来的判决前利息、判决后利息以及相关律师费用。作为回应，全球公司反诉天空公司违反合同，没有按照全球公司同意的方式交付混凝土电线杆，以及天空公司未能及时履行合同给全球公司造成损失。全球公司寻求未指明的补偿性损害赔偿、判决后利息、成本和律师费。

天空公司作为一家混凝土电线杆的制造商，在这起诉讼发生的过去三年里，向全球公司销售混凝土电线杆和其他相关产品，用于美国东南部的建筑项目。2006 年 4 月之前的一段时间里，天空公司与全球公司就电线杆买卖形成一种模式或程序。一般来说，全球公司的代表会联系天空公司的销售团队讨论计划全球公司的投标项目，在交换了工作规范和成本等信息后，全球公司将对该项目进行投标，如果投标成功，全球公司会向天空公司发送采购订单，然后天空公司根据订单制造并运送相关产品至项目现场。2006 年 4 月，天空公司和全球公司刚刚在佛罗里达州完成了一个项目——提供安装在停车场的灯杆，该停车场位于土地开发项目的新目标商店，这个订单的总金额是 115 658.30 美元。2006 年 4 月 20 日，根据合作实况和习惯，天空公司开发了三种不同类型、不同数量的电线杆，供全球公司土地开发项目的新目标商店使用，并且由天空公司将它们运送到佛罗里达州圣露西港的项目现场，并要求在两周内装运一卡车的电线杆（即 20 个电线杆）。

2006 年 5 月 4 日，天空公司向佛罗里达州圣露西港运送了两批 25 根电线杆（总共50 根电线杆）。另外在执行本合同过程中，天空公司遇到了生产问题，无法每两周用卡车将一车电线杆运至项目现场。但是天空公司最终还是提供了全球公司四个采购订单（2006 年 2 月 16 日、2006 年 4 月 20 日、2006 年 7 月 19 日和 2006 年 10 月 13 日的采购订单）中要求的产品和服务，全球公司接受了天空公司提供的产品和服务。此后，天空公司向全球公司发送了这些产品和服务的发票，但全球公司没有全额支付这些发票款项并欠天空公司 83 203.78 美元的本金。

二、裁判结果

（一）天空公司部分简易判决

天空公司认为它提供的货物虽然有问题，但全球公司接受并用于了项目的建设，因此全球公司必须按合同规定的价格支付已接受的任何货物。而对于全球公司的反诉认为灯杆的迟延装运给全球公司带来了经济损失其应该得到救济，天空公司认为全球公司并没有在合理的期限内通知己方，根据《美国统一商法典》（UCC）第 2 条的规定，全球公司接收了货物取得了对货物的实际占有，且接收货物的法律后果就是：（1）买方必须就所接收的货物付款；（2）丧失拒绝接受的权利；（3）开始计算卖方的违约时效[1]。

全球公司认为合同争议是在不同国家的当事人之间进行的，应由 CISG 而不是通过 UCC 所规范。

法院认为 CISG 管辖的是主要营业地点在不同国家的缔约方之间的货物销售合同，在这个案例中，全球公司的主要业务所在地美国和天空公司的所在地加拿大都是 CISG 的签署国，而且双方没有明确排除公约的适用，因此双方的合同争议适用 CISG。在责任方面，全球公司接收了有问题的货物并用于项目的建设，却没有足额支付其应付的款项构成违约，天空公司享有违约索赔的权利。天空公司违约索赔唯一剩余的问题是是否有权获得损害赔偿金。

（二）全球公司部分简易判决

全球公司认为根据 CISG 第 39 条的规定，假设灯杆因装运延误而不合格，全球公司有两年时间即从灯杆交货之日起至施工项目期间向天空公司发出货物不合格的通知。由天空公司提供的发票可以推出两年的诉讼时效最早也要到 2008 年 8 月 14 日才能到期。其次，全球公司认为其有权就其所提供的电子邮件证明天空公司向其传达的有关灯杆交付的虚假信息而造成的经济损失进行赔偿。

作为回应，天空公司认为全球公司声称的疏忽性误述部分的判决请求应该被驳回。理由是全球公司未能提供任何证据证明天空公司存在疏忽性虚假陈述以及证明它依赖于任何此类虚假陈述。其次，全球并没有提供其损失的具体证据，它所提交的有关其损失的证据只是推测性的。

法院认为全球公司对疏忽性误述的主张应受到州法律的控制，其次根据其提供的电子邮件并不支持全球公司就其疏忽性误述的索赔要求作出简易判决。

（三）全球公司对于天空公司向其传达灯杆交付的虚假信息造成的经济损失赔偿的简易判决

全球公司提供了三份电子邮件作为证据证明天空公司传达灯杆交付的虚假信息使其遭受损失，分析这三份电子邮件内容可以看出争议点是灯杆的使用目的是用于土地项目还是城市花园项目。然而从记录来看，在 2006 年 5 月 4 日天空公司发出的 50 根

---

1 王慧 . 国际货物买卖合同中买方"拒受权"辨析 [J]. 北大法律评论，2009，10（02）：398-425.

灯杆与土地项目无关，因此不能证明天空公司传达虚假信息。且本案中全球公司对于天空公司的疏忽性误述是一种完全不同于违约索赔的侵权索赔，不适用 CISG 中的侵权索赔。由此可以看出双方对于事实以及适用法律条款都存在争议，因此被告提出简易判决不被允许。

（四）天空公司诉全球公司管理层人员 Dixon 和 Sjogren 的欺诈陈述的简易判决

要在肯塔基州建立欺诈索赔，索赔人必须以明确和令人信服的证据证明以下六个要素：（a）实质陈述，（b）虚假陈述，（c）已知为虚假陈述或不顾后果的陈述，（d）作出有关陈述的诱因，（e）作出有关陈述及（f）造成损害。而天空公司没有提出任何证据来证实最后三个要件，即这些欺诈声明（ⅰ）的目的是引导天空公司签订合同，（ⅱ）实际上推动了天空公司签订合同，以及（ⅲ）对天空公司造成伤害。因此本案中天空公司诉全球公司管理成员 Dixon 和 Sjogren 的欺诈陈述并不存在实质事实争议点，可以进行简易判决。

【法律分析】

天空公司诉全球公司损害赔偿一案一共涉及四个法律问题，分别是简易判决的适用标准；CISG 适用范围；CISG 中第 39 条不符通知的合理期限；CISG 中损害赔偿范围。由于第一个法律问题简易判决的适用范围和国际货物买卖关联不大，因此在这里不详细分析，本文将着重对后面三个问题进行探讨。

一、CISG 的适用范围

CISG 第 1 条详细规定了公约的适用范围：（1）本公约适用于营业地在不同国家的当事人之间所订立的货物销售合同：（a）如果这些国家是缔约国；或（b）如果国际私法规则导致适用某一缔约国的法律。在本案中天空公司和全球公司的主营业地属于不同的国家且美国和加拿大都是 CISG 的缔约国，此外，两公司间的货物买卖合同是关于混凝土灯杆的交易，根据 CISG 第 2 条的规定：本公约不适用于以下的销售：（a）购供私人、家人或家庭使用的货物的销售，除非卖方在订立合同前任何时候或订立合同时不知道而且没有理由知道这些货物是购供任何这种使用；（b）经由拍卖的销售；（c）根据法律执行令状或其他令状的销售；（d）公债、股票、投资证券、流通票据或货币的销售；（e）船舶、船只、气垫船或飞机的销售；（f）电力的销售。本案中两公司的货物交易不属于公约不适用的情形。更为重要的一点是天空公司和全球公司并没有明确表示不接受公约的调整，CISG 第 6 条规定：双方当事人可以不适用本公约。但是双方当事人应明确做出表示。因此本案中天空公司根据 UCC 的相关规定做出的诉求并不能得到支持，而应该适用 CISG。

题的货物后没有拒绝而直接使用在项目建设中其定由……为全球公司失去救济的权利是根据 UCC 第 1 条的规定，一旦买方有合理机会检验货物，而没有提出有效的拒受，就视为接受货物，即使真的有瑕疵，此时想要再拒绝接受，就必须使用撤销接受的条件。但是根据 CISG 第 39 条的规定：（1）买方发现货物不符规格后，在合理的时间内，或者应当发现货物不符规格后，不通知卖方，指明不符规格的性质，就失去了货物不符规格的申诉权利。（2）在任何情况下，如果买方在货物实际移交给买方之日起两年内不提出通知，他将丧失因货物不符规格而提起诉讼的权利，除非这个期限是不符合合同担保的。在上一个问题中已分析得出本案应适用 CISG 而不是 UCC，因此似乎全球公司通知天空公司货物不符合规定是及时的。

但是我们不难看出，CISG 中第 39 条至第 44 条有关不符通知合理期限的规定是不明确的，大陆法系、英美法系、伊斯兰法系在实践中也有不同的做法。大陆法系中，德系国家主要按照"尊贵月"规则来解释不符通知的合理期限，而非德系国家则主要根据具体案情来界定合理期限。英美法系则适用灵活的解释规则来规范不符通知的合理期限；而伊斯兰法系似乎与 CISG 相违背，没有要求买方具体说明不符点。其中最具影响力的是德系国家"尊贵月"规则，其主要观点为不符通知的期限为一个月最适宜，但一个月的期限针对耐用性的商品[1]，其他商品不符通知的期限需要具体分析。"尊贵月"规则被众多国家所接受，对 CISG 中第 39 条规定的"合理的期限"的适用提供了一定程度的实践证明。但是我们也看到了"尊贵月"规则不是万能的，它因受制于一个月的期限而具有局限性，因此灵活的解释规则大量适用成为英美法系的潮流。灵活的解释规则似乎更受青睐，具体案件具体分析具体适用，不受制于具体期限。但正是由于其不受限制，"合理期限"才显得"不合理"，合理期限具有不确定性、随意性与难以判断性。但这似乎与 CISG 中规定的"合理的期限"立法意图相吻合，CISG 的规定越来越朝着客观、科学的方向发展，这既是各方妥协所致，也是追求内部统一的结果。CISG 中的第 7 条的规定：（1）在解释本公约时，应考虑到本公约的国际性质和促进其适用的统一以及在国际贸易上遵守诚信的需要。（2）凡本公约未明确解决的属于本公约范围的问题，应按照本公约所依据的一般原则来解决，在没有一般原则的情况下，则应按照国际私法规定适用的法律来解决。第 7 条作为原则性条文规定具有统领性，它规定了在公约没有规定的情况下适用条约时应遵守的原则，因此在适用第 39 条的规定时不是不受限制，而是在诚信的基础上进行解释。

---

1 殷涛 .CISG 第三十九条中不符通知的合理期限之探讨 [J]. 四川职业技术学院学报，2018，28（06）：12-19.

三、CISG 中损害赔偿范围及标准之分析

根据 CISG 第 74 条规定："一方当事人违反合同应负的损害赔偿额，应与另一方当事人因他违反合同而遭受的包括利润在内的损失额相等。这种损害赔偿不得超过违反合同一方在订立合同时，依照他当时已知道或理应知道的事实和情况，对违反合同预料到或理应预料到的可能损失。"我们可以看出国际货物买卖合同中受害方所受到的损害赔偿的具体范围包括实际损失以及利益损失。实际损失包括合同一方因违约行为造成的财产直接减少、灭失以及为避免损失而采取补救措施所支付的费用。利益损失相比之下较难以计算，其范围的界定也模糊，总的来说是指订立合同时当事人预期会获得利益的损失。

由于第 74 条并没有具体说明损害赔偿的计算标准和方法，因此，获利机会、汇率、律师费以及商誉损失等损失是否应计算在内？在实践中，各国有不同的做法。实践中并不是所有国家对以上几种损失都支持为受害方应获得的损失赔偿。但是笔者认为如果受害方能提供确切的证据证明其受到了利益损失，那么以上所涉及的几种损失都可以获得支持。然而又不得不承认，损害赔偿的证明标准以及证明的确切程度各国在实践中也有所不同，大陆法系国家的证明标准通常较英美法系严格；其次，在证明损害标准时法官的自由裁量权也占据一定因素，至于法院的自由裁量权，各国又有不同的规定，或限制或宽松。对于损害金额的确定，法官在现有证据的基础上公平、合理地进行"自由裁量"。再者，CISG 没有规定损害赔偿的具体数额，是全额赔偿还是最高额赔偿，并没有做出明确规定。最后，对于非物质性利益的损害赔偿例如在当事人名誉受到损害时，应如何得到救济以及获得怎样的救济，CISG 并没有涉及。

在 CISG 具有广泛适用性以及影响力的今天，我们仍不能否认 CISG 中损害赔偿范围及标准规定的适用仍存在不确定性和争议，为了促进国际贸易社会交往的公平、稳定和发展，推动损害赔偿范围及标准规定之完善具有现实意义。

【英文案例裁决摘录】

下文摘录的是案例判决书原文。

I. INTRODUCTION

Plaintiff Sky Cast Inc. ("Sky Cast"), a foreign corporation with its principal place of business in Guelph, Ontario, Canada, brings this action against defendants Global Direct Distribution, LLC ("Global"), a limited liability company with its principal place of business in Lexington, Kentucky; David J. Dixon ("Dixon"), a managing member of Global; and Raymond A. Sjogren ("Sjogren"), a managing member of Global, for breach of contract, alleging that Global is indebted to it in the principal amount of $83,203.78 for concrete light poles that Sky Cast made and delivered to Global's customer in Florida in 2006. Sky Cast also asserts claims against the defendants for unjust enrichment and fraud.

Sky Cast seeks judgment in the amount it is owed under its contract with Global, prejudgment interest, post judgment interest, and its costs and attorney's fees.

In response, Global has counterclaimed, alleging that Sky Cast breached their contract by failing to deliver the concrete light poles in question as Sky Cast had agreed to do and that Global sustained damages by Sky Cast's failure to perform the contract in a timely manner. Global also asserts claims for negligent misrepresentation and fraud and concealment. Global seeks unspecified compensatory damages, post judgment interest, its costs and attorney's fees.

This matter is presently before the court on (1) plaintiff's motion for partial summary judgment on its breach of contract claim and on the defendant's counterclaim for breach of contract, (2) defendant's motion for partial summary judgment on its claim for negligent misrepresentation, and (3) the motion of the individual defendants Sjogren and Dixon for summary judgment on all claims asserted against them individually. Plaintiff's motion for partial summary judgment on its breach of contract claim and on the defendant's counterclaim for breach of contract and defendants' motion for partial summary judgment on their claim for negligent misrepresentation have been fully briefed and are ripe for review. Plaintiff has filed no response to the motion of the individual defendants for summary judgment on all claims, and the time for responding thereto has expired; therefore, this motion is also ripe for review.

II. FACTUAL BACKGROUND

For approximately three years prior to the events giving rise to this lawsuit, Sky Cast, a manufacturer of concrete light poles, sold concrete light poles and related products to Global for use in various construction projects in the south eastern United States. Global supplied concrete light poles to Tradition, one of Global's customers in Florida, for use in its construction/development projects.

During the period of time prior to April of 2006, a pattern or a course of dealing had developed between Sky Cast and Global in relation to Global's purchase of light poles from Sky Cast. Generally, representatives from Global would contact members of Sky Cast's sales team and talk with them about upcoming projects on which Global planned to bid. After exchanging information including job specifications and costs, Global would submit a bid on the project. If Global were awarded the project, then Global would send a purchase order to Sky Cast. Sky Cast would then produce the items ordered and ship them to the project site pursuant to its agreement with Global. In April 2006, Sky Cast and Global had just completed a project in Florida, and the parties then engaged in preliminary discussions concerning a new job in the Landings development in Florida. Global had been awarded a contract by Tradition to supply the light poles for installation in the parking lot at a new Target store location in the Landings development.

Subsequently, after all of the details concerning the specifications had been provided to Sky Cast, on April 20, 2006, pursuant to the practice and custom that had developed between Global and Sky Cast, Global sent a Purchase Order to Sky Cast for various quantities of three different types of light poles for the Target store in the Landings development, which Sky Cast was to ship to the project site in Port St. Lucie, Florida. The total amount of this Purchase Order was $115,658.30. The purchase order also requested Sky Cast to provide wind-load certifications and requested that one truck load of light poles (viz., 20 light poles) be shipped within two weeks.

By e-mail dated April 25, 2006, Sky Cast advised Global that it could have two loads leaving on Monday afternoon (presumably May 1, 2006) to arrive mid-week of that week. Apparently, on May 4, 2006, Sky Cast shipped two (2) separate loads of 25 light poles (for a total of 50 light poles) to Town Park in Port St. Lucie, Florida, consistent with Romi Pop's e-mail dated April 25, 2006. However, as explained in greater detail below, it is unclear whether this shipment of light poles was for the Landings project or whether it was for a different project.

Additionally, during the course of performing this contract, Sky Cast encountered problems with production and was unable to ship a truck load of poles to the Landings project site every two weeks, consistent with the customary practice previously followed by Sky Cast and Global on this type of construction project. Nevertheless, Sky Cast ultimately supplied the products and/or services requested by Global in the four Purchase Orders at issue (Purchase Orders dated February 16, 2006, April 20, 2006, July 19, 2006, and October 13, 2006), and Global accepted the products and/or services provided.

Thereafter, Sky Cast sent invoices to Global for these products and/or services. The invoices specify a payment term of 30 days. Sky Cast asserts that Global has failed to pay these invoices in full and is indebted to it in the principal amount of $83,203.78.

III. THE MOTIONS FOR SUMMARY JUDGMENT

A. Standard for Summary Judgment

In Menuskin v. Williams, 145 F.3d 755 (6th Cir.1998), the Sixth Circuit reiterated the standard to be employed when considering a motion for summary judgment, as follows:

"… Summary judgment is appropriate 'if the pleadings, depositions, answers to interrogatories, and admissions on file, together with the affidavits, if any, show that there is no genuine issue as to any material fact and that the moving party is entitled to a judgment as a matter of law.' In applying this standard, we view the evidence so that all justifiable inferences are drawn in favor of the non-moving party…"

With this standard in mind, the court will proceed to Sky Cast's motion for partial summary judgment on its breach of contract claim and on Global's counterclaim for breach of contract.

B. Sky Cast's motion for partial summary judgment

In support of its motion for summary judgment on its breach of contract claim and on Global's counterclaim for breach of contract, Sky Cast contends that the contract at issue is governed by Article 2 of the Uniform Commercial Code, codified in Kentucky as Chapter 355 of the Kentucky Revised Statutes (KRS). More particularly, Sky Cast submits that since it supplied the goods in question and that since Global accepted these goods, this contract is controlled by KRS 355.2-606 and KRS 355.2-607. KRS 355.2-607, provides that "[a] buyer must pay at the contract rate for any goods accepted," and KRS 355.2-606(1)(b) specifies that "[a]cceptance of goods occurs when the buyer … fails to make an effective rejection."Based on these undisputed facts and the applicable law, Sky Cast asserts that it is clear that Global is in breach of contract and that it is entitled to summary judgment on its breach of contract claim because (1) Sky Cast supplied the light poles specified in the Purchase Orders (albeit untimely), and (2) Global accepted the light poles, made no efforts to reject the light poles, and used these light poles in the construction project.

With this claim resolved, Sky Cast notes that the only other contract issue remaining is whether it was in breach by the delays in shipment of the light poles and, if so, whether Global is entitled to a set-off against the contract price for damages resulting from any breach by Sky Cast. Sky Cast points out that pursuant to KRS 355.2-607(3)(a), "where tender has been accepted the buyer must within a reasonable time after he discovers … any breach notify the seller of breach or be barred from any remedy."Based on this provision, Sky Cast argues that if Global desired to deduct any damages for Sky Cast's breach of contract from the contract price, it was required to do the following: (1) notify Sky Cast of its breach within a reasonable time after discovering the breach, and (2) notify Sky Cast of its intent to deduct damages resulting from the breach. Sky Cast contends that since Global did not follow the foregoing procedure, it is now barred from any remedy. Sky Cast states that prior to the filing of this action, Global never notified it that Global considered Sky Cast to be in breach of contract and that it intended to offset its alleged damages against the contract price. For these reasons, Sky Cast also contends that Global has waived its claim for damages under KRS 355.2-607 and that it is entitled to summary judgment on Global's counterclaim for breach of contract.

In opposing Sky Cast's motion for summary judgment on its breach of contract claim against Global and on Global's counterclaim for breach of contract, Global submits that since the contract in dispute is between parties in different nations, it is governed by the United Nations Convention on Contracts for the International Sale of Goods ("CISG") rather than by Article 2 of the Uniform Commercial Code, as urged by Sky Cast. Therefore, Sky Cast is not entitled to summary judgment on its breach of contract claim against Global or on Global's counterclaim for breach of contract.

Discussion/Analysis

Since Sky Cast is a foreign corporation with its principal place of business in Guelph, Ontario, Canada, and since Global is a company with its principal place of business in Lexington, Kentucky, U.S.A., it appears that the contract in dispute is contract is controlled by the CISG, which governs a contract for the sale of goods between parties whose principal places of business are in different nations if those nations are signatories to the treaty. In this case, both the United States of America, where Global's principal place of business is located, and Canada, where Sky Cast is located, are signatories to the CISG. Although the parties to a contract normally controlled by the CISG may exclude the applicability of the CISG to their contract, any such exclusion must be explicit. See PetroEcuador, 332 F.3d at 337. In this case, there is no indication that the parties elected not to have the CISG apply to their contract.

The CISG preempts state law contract claims. Since this contract concerns the sale of goods between parties in different countries (Canada and the United States of America), since these two countries are signatories to the CISG, and since there is no indication that the parties opted out of the CISG, the court concludes that the CISG governs this contract and that it preempts the applicability of Article 2 of the UCC to this transaction for the sale of goods that ordinarily would be controlled by Article 2 of the UCC. However, even though the CISG, rather than Article 2 of the UCC, controls this contract, the court also concludes that that fact does not operate to defeat Sky Cast's motion for summary judgment on its breach of contract claim, and the court further concludes that based on the undisputed facts of this case, at least as to liability, Sky Cast is entitled to summary judgment on its breach of contract claim. This conclusion is based on the fact that Sky Cast supplied the goods that were purchased by Global in the various Purchase Orders, that Global accepted these goods and made no efforts to reject these goods, that these goods were used in the construction project, and that Global failed to pay Sky Cast in full for the total amount of the invoices Sky Cast sent to Global concerning these goods.

Therefore, liability on Sky Cast's breach of contract claim against Global is no longer an issue. The only remaining aspect of Sky Cast's claim for breach of contract is the amount of damages to which Sky Cast is entitled.

Global's counterclaim for breach of contract

Sky Cast also contends that it is entitled to summary judgment on Global's counterclaim for breach of contract because Global is barred from deducting from the balance owed on the contract price for any damages it may have sustained by reason of Sky Cast's delay in shipping the light poles to the construction project. In support of this argument, Sky Cast relies on Article 2 of the UCC and asserts that since Global did not follow the foregoing procedure, set out in detail above, Global has waived any claim it might have had under Article 2 of the UCC for damages and is now barred from any remedy. Therefore, it is entitled to summary judgment on Global's counterclaim for breach of contract.

Sky Cast's motion for summary judgment on Global's counterclaim for breach of contract is premised on Article 2 of the UCC, which is not applicable to this contract. As previously stated, the CISG governs this contract. Article 39 of the CISG contains the following provision concerning lack of conformity of the goods:

Article 39

"(1) The buyer loses the right to rely on a lack of conformity of the goods if he does not give notice to the seller specifying the nature of the lack of conformity within a reasonable time after he has discovered it or ought to have discovered it."

"(2) In any event, the buyer loses the right to rely on a lack of conformity of the goods if he does not give notice thereof at the latest within a period of two years from the date on which the goods were actually handed over to the buyer, unless this time-limit is inconsistent with a contractual period of guarantee."

See CISG, Article 39.

Although Global has not asserted as a defense that the goods were non-conforming, per se, Global impliedly asserts that the goods were non-conforming because they were not shipped within the time-frame customarily followed by the parties on contracts for similar construction projects, and that it sustained damages by the delay in shipments. Thus, Article 39 of the CISG is applicable by analogy. Assuming the light poles were non-conforming because of the delay in shipments, under Article 39, it appears that Global had two years from the date of delivery of the light poles to the construction project within which to give Sky Cast notice that the goods were non-conforming.

In this case, the exact dates of Sky Cast's shipments of the light poles to the construction project are not clear from the record as it presently stands. However, all light poles were shipped to the construction project in the summer and early fall of 2006, and Sky Cast sent Global invoices to Global for these shipments, presumably at the time the light poles were shipped or shortly thereafter. Of the twelve (12) invoices attached to Sky Cast's complaint, two are dated August 14, 2006, three are dated August 31, 2006, three are dated September 14, 2006, and four are dated October 4, 2006. Thus, under Article 39 of the CISG, Global had a two years thereafter in which to notify Sky Cast that the light poles were non-conforming goods. Therefore, Global's two-year statute of limitations would not expire, at the earliest, until August 14, 2008. Global's counterclaim herein was filed on July 26, 2007. Consequently, the court concludes that under Article 39 of the CISG, Global's notice to Sky Cast that its goods were non-conforming was timely.

Nevertheless, even though Global's notice to Sky Cast that there was a problem with its goods, in the sense that Global considered the late delivery of the goods to have violated the terms of their contract, was timely, such notice does not mean that Global will or should prevail on its counterclaim for breach of contract. Article 74 of the CISG provides, in part, that a party can recover for damages for breach of contract "equal to the loss, including loss of profit, suffered by the other party as a consequence of the breach." Global claims that it was damaged by Sky Cast's late shipments of the light poles in that (1) in order to appease its customer, Tradition, it had to pay the storage charges of certain materials that had to be placed in storage awaiting the delivery of the light poles, and (2) it has also incurred a loss of profits in that its volume of business with Tradition has declined as the result of this situation. As to proof of its damages, Global advises that its out-of-pocket expenses for the storage charges were $13,156.02 and that it lost profits in the amount of $146,885.76. However, at this juncture, Global has come forward with no concrete proof of its loss of profits.

Consequently, for all of the foregoing reasons, the court concludes that neither Sky Cast nor Global is entitled to summary judgment on Global's counterclaim for breach of contract.

C. Global's motion for partial summary judgment

In support of its motion for summary judgment on its counterclaim for negligent misrepresentation, Global relies on 552 of the Restatement (Second) of Torts, which was adopted in Kentucky in 2004 in Presnell Construction Managers, Inc. v. EH Construction, LLC, 134 S.W.3d 575 (Ky.2004). Global contends that under 552 of the Restatement (Second) of Torts, it is entitled to recover for pecuniary loss resulting from the false information on which it relied that was conveyed to it by Sky Cast concerning the deliveries of the light poles. Global also points out that while the CISG preempts Article 2 of the UCC in respect to the breach of contract claim, it does not preempt state law tort claims. Additionally, Global notes that Article

74 of the CISG provides for the award of lost profits.

In response, Sky Cast contends that Global's motion for partial summary judgment on its claim for negligent misrepresentation should be denied because Global has failed to produce any evidence of a negligent misrepresentation by Sky Cast and/or any evidence that it relied on any such misrepresentation. Sky Cast also asserts that Global has provided no concrete evidence as to its damages and that the evidence it has submitted concerning its loss is speculative. For all of these reasons, Sky Cast submits that there are genuine issues of material fact concerning Global's claim for negligent misrepresentations and that Global's motion for partial summary judgment on this claim must be denied.

Discussion/Analysis

In Presnell Construction Managers, Inc. v. EH Construction, LLC, supra, the Restatement (Second) of Torts 552, was adopted as the law in Kentucky. 552 concerns the tort of negligent misrepresentation and provides, as follows: "One who, in the course of his business … supplies false information for the guidance of others in their business transactions, is subject to liability for pecuniary loss caused to them by their justifiable reliance upon the information, if he fails to exercise reasonable care or competence in obtaining or communicating the information. In adopting 552, the Kentucky Supreme Court held that [w]e agree that privity is not necessary to maintain a tort action, and, by adopting 552, we agree that the tort of negligent representation defines an independent duty for which recovery in tort for economic loss is available." Id.

Thus, negligent misrepresentation is a tort claim completely different from a claim for breach of contract. Being a tort claim, the court concludes that it is not controlled by the CISG, which only concerns the sales of good between merchants in different countries, and that since this action is a diversity action, Global's claim for negligent misrepresentation is controlled by state law.

Global's claim for negligent misrepresentation is based on the premise that Sky Cast provided it with false information concerning the delivery of the light poles. In support of this claim, Global relies on the following three e-mails from Romi Pop at Sky Cast to Global: (1) an email dated April 25, 2006 to Ray Sjogren, (2) an e-mail dated June 7, 2006 to Ray Sjogren, and (3) an e-mail dated June 8, 2006 to Dave Dixon. These three e-mails are examined in greater detail, as follows:

1. The e-mail dated April 25, 2006 to Ray Sjogren

In responding to an e-mail from Ray Sjogren to Ron and Romi dated April 25, 2006, inquiring about the 50 poles shipping for Town Park, Romi Pop stated:

"Hi Ray,

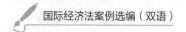

If it's OK, we can have two loads leaving on Monday afternoon, for mid-week arrival. Would that work?

Please let me know.

Thanks,

Ron"

Exhibit 4 to Sky Cast's response to Global's motion for summary judgment reflects that on May 4, 2006, in Shipping Order Nos. 30277 and 30278, Sky Cast shipped 50 light poles (two loads of 25 poles each) to Town Park. Thus, this e-mail does not appear to contain false information. Based on a review of this e-mail and Exhibit 4 to Sky Cast's response to Global's motion for summary judgment, it appears that Sky Cast shipped 50 light poles to Town Park in Port St. Lucie, Florida, on May 4, 2006, consistent with Romi Pop's e-mail dated April 25, 2006.

However, the inquiry does not end here. Ray Sjogren's e-mail to Ron Wagen and Romi Pop at Sky Cast dated April 25, 2006, inquiring about the shipment of 50 light poles concerns the shipping of light poles for Town Park. Exhibit 4 to Sky Cast's response to Global's motion for summary judgment reflects that on May 4, 2006, 50 light poles were shipped to Town Park at the following address: 11209 S.W. Springtree Terrace, Port St. Lucie, FL 34987. This Delivery Notice (Exhibit 4) identifies this project as Project No. 06-19, which appears to be the Town Park project, which also appears to be a project different from the Landings project, which is identified by Sky Cast in its invoices to Global as Project No. 06-74 with the following shipping address: 10521 SW Village Center Drive, Port St. Lucie, FL 34987.

Thus, it is unclear whether Ray Sjogren's e-mail to Ron Wagen and Romi Pop at Sky Cast dated April 25, 2006, inquiring about the shipment of 50 light poles and Romi Pop's response thereto on April 25, 2006, concerned the light poles that were to be shipped to the Landings project. If Project No. 06-19 and Project No. 06-74 concern the same project and/or if the Town Park project and the Landings project are one and the same, then it is clear that Romi Pop's e-mail to Ray Sjogren dated April 25, 2006, concerned the light poles that were to be shipped to the Landings project, that those light poles were in fact shipped as Sky Cast represented they would be, and that these light poles were shipped to Port St. Lucie, Florida, on May 4, 2006.

However, it further appears from the record that the 50 light poles Sky Cast shipped on May 4, 2006, did not concern the Landings project, as evidenced by an e-mail from Dave Dixon to Romi Pop at Sky Cast dated June 6, 2006, which states, as follows:

"Romi,

Can you give me an update on delivery for the 1st release on the Landing job? We need those poles ASAP. I am still waiting for the prints on the balance of the poles to advise you on the GFI and hand hold placement. Please send good news!"

Additionally, on June 7, 2006, Ray Sjogren sent an e-mail to Romi Pop and Ron Ragwen at Sky Cast, stating:

"We really need a truck load of poles immediately for the Tradition Landing Job. Can you advise on where you are on that order?"

On June 7, 2006, Romi Pop responded with the following e-mail:

"Gents, the first full load of poles will be ready to ship on week of June 19/06.

Regards,

Romi"

Consequently, it appears that while Sky Cast shipped 50 poles to Port St. Lucie, Florida on May 4, 2006, the record is not entirely clear whether this shipment of light poles concerned the Landings project. Therefore, this e-mail does not support Global's motion for summary judgment on its negligent misrepresentation claim.

2. The e-mail dated June 7, 2006 to Ray Sjogren

To reiterate, on June 7, 2006, Ray Sjogren sent Romi and Ron at Sky Cast an e-mail advising that Global really needed a truck load of poles immediately for the Tradition Landing Job and requested a status report on where Sky Cast was on that order. In response to this e-mail, Romi Pop stated:

"Gents, the first full load of poles will be ready to ship on week of June 19/06.

Regards,

Romi"

3. The e-mail dated June 8, 2006 to Dave Dixon

In response to Romi Pop's e-mail dated June 7, 2006, on June 8, 2006, Dave Dixon at Global sent Romi Pop an e-mail at Sky Cast, which stated in part, as follows:

"… Please tell me you have the 1st truck load going out this week. This order is 8 weeks old and we are getting much heat on this. Please get with Ron if you are having a problem with production. He said at time of order that we could get 1st truck out very QUICKLY. Please advise us today as we need to respond to our customer NOW."

In response to this e-mail, on June 8, 2006, Romi stated:

"Gentlemen, please be assured that we have our full resources working on this order. The best that we can do is shipping at the end of next week, and we will have approximately 17 poles at that time.

Thank you for your patience and understanding,

Romi"

It is clear from the foregoing e-mails that they concerned the Landings project. Summarizing these e-mails, on June 7, 2006, Global advised Sky Cast that they "really need a truck load of poles immediately for the Tradition Landing Job," and requested a status report on those poles. Sky Cast responded that it had encountered some production problems, but that it expected to be able to have a full load of poles ready to ship on the week of June 19, 2006. The record reflects that on June 19, 2006, Sky Cast shipped a load of fourteen (14) poles and that on July 7, 2006, Global received another shipment containing twenty-one (21) poles.

Consequently, the court concludes that these two e-mails in question, viz., the e-mail dated June 7, 2006 to Ray Sjogren, and the e-mail dated June 8, 2006 to Dave Dixon, do not contain any false information. Therefore, these two e-mails do not support Global's motion for summary judgment on its claim for negligent misrepresentation.

For these reasons, the court also concludes that Global is not entitled to summary judgment on its counterclaim for negligent misrepresentation.

D. The motion for summary judgment filed Sjogren and Dixon on Sky Cast's fraud claim

Defendants Sjogren and Dixon have moved for summary judgment on plaintiff 's claim for fraud asserted against them individually concerning representations they made to state officials in Florida in order to effectuate the dissolution in Florida of Global Direct's predecessor, Global Direct Distribution, LLC, a limited liability company in Florida. Sky Cast has filed no response to the motion of defendants Sjogren and Dixon for summary judgment, and the time for responding thereto has expired. Thus, this matter is ripe for review.

Discussion/Analysis

Defendant Global is presently a limited liability in Kentucky, with its principal place of business in Lexington, Kentucky. However, Global is successor in interest to Global Direct Distribution, LLC, in Palm City, Florida, which was dissolved in Florida on or about November 28, 2006. In the Articles of Dissolution for a Limited Liability Company filed with Florida officials, Global's managing members, Sjogren and Dixon, stated that the Global entity in Florida was being dissolved because the "company has relocated to Kentucky and has no physical location in Florida," that dissolution was approved on November 21, 2006, that all debts, obligations and liabilities of the limited liability had been paid or discharged, and that there were no suits pending against Global in any court. Subsequently, defendant Global became a Kentucky limited liability company on or about December 4, 2006.

Sky Cast asserts that in effectuating the dissolution of Global Direct Distribution, LLC, in Palm City, Florida, defendants Sjogren and Dixon fraudulently represented to Florida officials in November of 2006, that all of Global's debts, obligations and liabilities had been paid or discharged, when in fact Global was indebted to Sky Cast at that time in the principal amount of $83,203.78 stemming from the light poles Sky Cast shipped to the Landings project, which Global accepted and which were used in the Landings project.

To establish a fraud claim in Kentucky, a claimant must prove, by clear and convincing evidence, the following six elements: (a) a material representation, (b) which is false, (c) and which is known to be false or made recklessly, (d) made with inducement to be acted thereon, (e) which is acted thereon, and (f) causes injury.

Assuming the truthfulness of Sky Cast's claim that defendants Sjogren and Dixon made fraudulent statements to state officials in Florida in order to effectuate the dissolution of Global Direct Distribution, LLC, in Florida, which would establish the first three of the six elements required to state a viable fraud claim in Kentucky, Sky Cast has not come forward with any evidence to establish the last three elements required to establish a fraud claim, viz., that these fraudulent statements (i) were made to induce action thereon by Sky Cast, (ii) were, in fact, acted thereon by Sky Cast, and (iii) caused injury to Sky Cast. This conclusion is based on the chronology of events occurring between Sky Cast and Global, set out below:

1.The agreements between Sky Cast and Global that comprise the contract in question occurred in April of 2006, prior to the allegedly fraudulent statements made in November of 2006.

2.Sky Cast's invoices to Global dated October 4, 2006, are the last documentation regarding Sky Cast's claim; these invoices predate the dissolution of Global Direct Distribution, LLC, in Florida, which was not dissolved until November 28, 2006, nearly two months after the date of the Sky Cast's last invoice to Global.

Any fraudulent statements that were made to Florida officials were made to induce action thereon not by Sky Cast, but by Florida officials by approving the dissolution of Global Direct Distribution, LLC, the Florida entity. Assuming that these statements were fraudulent and that Florida officials acted thereon by allowing Global Direct Distribution, LLC, to be dissolved in Florida, Sky Cast has not established that it was induced to act by these fraudulent statements and/or that it was injured by these fraudulent statements. It is clear that the dissolution of Global Direct Distribution, LLC, in Florida, in November 2006, had no bearing on any agreement made between Sky Cast and Global at any time prior thereto. In short, Sky Cast simply cannot claim to have relied to its detriment on an event that had not occurred when its claim for breach of contract arose.

Thus, Sky Cast has not established that it relied to its detriment on the November 28, 2006, dissolution filing or that it suffered any damage as a result of any statement contained in the dissolution filing. Based on the foregoing, the court concludes that there is no genuine issue of material fact and defendants Sjogren and Dixon are entitled to judgment as a matter of law.

【思考题】

1. 根据 CISG，不适用于该公约的销售类型有哪些？
2. 根据 CISG，当事人可以采取的主要救济措施有哪些？
3. 根据 CISG，在条文没有具体规定时，解释该公约应遵循的原则有哪些？
4. 根据 CISG，买方的义务有哪些？本案中全球公司是否违背其义务？

Case2·拓展阅读

II

国际货物运输法

【内容摘要】

　　本章分为两节，精选两个国际货物运输法案例。第一个案例是美国航空货物运输承运人责任案（Eli Lilly and Co.v. Air Express International USA），主要涉及航空货物运输公司在 1999 年《蒙特利尔公约》下的赔偿责任问题和责任限制问题。第二个案例是英国海洋货物运输承运人责任案（East West Corporation *v* DKBS 1912），主要涉及海洋货物运输公约《汉堡规则》中提单项下的交货义务。

Case1 Eli Lilly and Co.vs. Air Express International USA,Inc.,33 Avi.17,530 （S.D.Fla.2009）

【案情说明】

一、案件事实

被告美国国际航空快递公司（DHL）是一家物流供应链的供应商。原告 Eli Lilly 公司与被告 DHL 签订了一项《长期服务协议》，根据该协议，被告同意提供与原告国际货运相关的物流服务。被告安排了第三方汉莎航空货运公司将货物从欧洲运往美国。运送的货物是对温度敏感的胰岛素产品，这些产品从法国空运到印第安纳州，途中存储于低于冰点的温度下。尽管低于冰点的温度是由于汉莎航空货运公司的人为失误造成的，但被告作为缔约承运人应对货物的任何损坏承担赔偿责任。

为了弥补因胰岛素失效对公司造成的损失，原告及其保险公司起诉被告违反了《长期服务协议》和两份关于运送胰岛素产品的航空运单，致其产品受损。美国佛罗里达州南区地方法院仅认为被告违反了航空运单，因此，就被告违反航空运单的责任问题作出简易判决，并驳回了原告关于被告违反《长期服务协议》的主张。此外，法院认为，根据《长期服务协议》中的一项条款，被告放弃了《统一国际航空运输某些规则的公约》（《蒙特利尔公约》）的责任限制。

被告不服，提起上诉。被告认为，在责任承担问题上，法院做出了有利于原告的简易判决。被告主张，他有权根据《蒙特利尔公约》承担有限责任，但地方法院却认为被告已经约定取消《蒙特利尔公约》的限制。被告还辩称，原告无权获得简易判决，因为他们未能证明货物在运输过程中受损，而且提供的某些证据不具有证明力。

二、裁判结果

在责任承担问题上，上诉法院支持了美国佛罗里达州南区地方法院的简易判决，支持了原告所提出的赔偿请求。在承运人责任限制问题上，被告主张应根据《蒙特利尔公约》，但地方法院认为被告已经约定取消《蒙特利尔公约》的限制。上诉法院认为地方法院的该项判决错误，因此，推翻了被告责任限制不受《蒙特利尔公约》约束而应受《长期服务协议》条款约束的裁决。法院最终判决，根据《蒙特利尔公约》第 22 条，应对被告的赔偿责任进行限制，即被告赔偿责任的上限是每公斤货物 17 特别提款权。

【法律分析】

本案主要涉及两个争议点：航空货物运输公司（即被告）的赔偿责任问题和责任限制问题。

第一，航空货运公司的赔偿责任问题。由于原告提出了两项无可争辩的证据：一是胰岛素被承运人存放于零度以下的环境中；二是在上述情况下，无论是否遭受实际损坏，胰岛素都无法销售。因此，法院作出的关于产品在运输过程中受到损坏的简易判决是正确的，被告应当对胰岛素损害造成的损失承担赔偿责任。

第二，责任限制问题。《蒙特利尔公约》限制国际航空运输承运人对货物损坏的赔偿责任，本案所涉合同涉及对这些限制的放弃。初审法院认定，根据《长期服务协议》中的一项条款，被告放弃了《蒙特利尔公约》的责任限制，公司承担的责任应受《长期服务协议》中的责任条款规制。上诉法院认为，初审法院的此种认定是错误的。如果承运人有意在一份与航空运单分开的文件中约定放弃《蒙特利尔公约》的责任限制，就应当将《长期服务协议》中的责任条款纳入航空运单，以免除公约的责任限制，但他们没有采取这样的做法。航空运单中没有提到《长期服务协议》对责任限制的修改。因此，上诉法院不认为此种放弃是有效的，故撤销初审法院以下判决内容：《长期服务协议》对责任限制的约定优于《蒙特利尔公约》关于责任限制的规定。

【英文案例裁决摘录】

Procedural Posture

Plaintiffs, a company and its insurers, sued defendant corporation for breach of a long-term service agreement and for breach of two air waybill contracts for carriage of damaged insulin products. The United States District Court for the Southern District of Florida dismissed the claim for breach of the service agreement and granted summary judgment on the issue of liability for breach of the air waybill contracts. The corporation appealed.

Overview

The corporation challenged: summary judgment in favor of plaintiffs on liability issue; the ruling that the corporation's liability was governed by the liability provision in the long-term service agreement; and the denial of its motion for sanctions for spoliation of evidence. Assuming that a carrier could stipulate to waive the limits of the Convention for the Unification of Certain Rules for International Carriage in a document separate from the air waybill, the parties did not intend for the liability provision in the long-term service agreement to be such a stipulation. There was no mention of the service agreement in the air waybill contracts and had the parties agreed to incorporate the service agreement's liability provision so as to waive the Convention's limits, they could have noted their intent to do so. As plaintiffs presented undisputed evidence that the insulin was subjected to sub-freezing temperatures and undisputed evidence that the insulin was unsaleable regardless of whether actual damage occurred, summary judgment on whether the products were damaged in transit was correct. As the corporation suffered no prejudice, denial its spoliation claim was not in error.

Outcome

The appellate court affirmed the grant of summary judgment to plaintiffs on the issue of liability and the denial of the corporation's motion for spoliation sanctions, but reversed the ruling that the corporation stipulated that the air waybill contracts were subject to limits of liability greater than those provided for in the Montreal Convention.

The Convention for the Unification of Certain Rules for International Carriage ("Montreal Convention") limits international air carrier liability for damage to cargo. This case involves a purported contractual waiver of those limits.

Defendant Air Express International USA, Inc. (DHL) is a provider of supply chain logistics. Plaintiff Eli Lilly and Company and DHL entered into a long-term service agreement under which DHL agreed to provide logistics services related to the international shipment of Eli Lilly pharmaceuticals. Among other things, DHL arranged for third-party air cargo carriers to transport pharmaceuticals from Europe to the United States. This case arises out of the spoliation of temperature-sensitive insulin products, which were shipped by air from France to Indiana and were exposed to sub-freezing temperatures en route. Pursuant to its service agreement with Eli Lilly, DHL arranged for Lufthansa Cargo AG to transport the insulin. Although the exposure to sub-freezing temperatures was the result of human error attributable to Lufthansa, DHL is liable as a contracting carrier for any damage to the cargo.

Seeking to recover for damage to the insulin products, Eli Lilly and its insurers sued DHL for breach of the long-term service agreement and for breach of two air waybill contracts for carriage of the damaged products. The district court dismissed the claim for breach of the service agreement because it was preempted by the Montreal Convention. In the same order, the court granted Plaintiffs summary judgment on the issue of liability for breach of the air waybill contracts. And, the court held that, under a provision in the long-term service agreement, DHL waived the liability limitations of the Montreal Convention. DHL appeals; its primary contention is that its liability should be limited pursuant to the Montreal Convention. DHL also argues that Plaintiffs are not entitled to summary judgment because they failed to show that the cargo was damaged in transit and because certain evidence offered to prove its damage is inadmissible. DHL further argues that the court abused its discretion in denying its motion for sanctions for spoliation of evidence. After review, we affirm the grant of summary judgment to Plaintiffs on the issue of liability and the denial of DHL's motion for spoliation sanctions. But we reverse the ruling that DHL stipulated that the air waybill contracts are subject to limits of liability greater than those provided for in the Montreal Convention.

I. BACKGROUND

A. The Montreal Convention

We consider in this case certain provisions of the Montreal Convention, a treaty which sets forth uniform rules for international air carriage. We begin with a brief overview of the Convention and its relevant provisions.

International air carrier liability for damage to cargo and injury to passengers has been governed by a set of uniform rules since 1933, when the Warsaw Convention, adopted by delegates of thirty-three nations in 1929, took effect. The Warsaw Convention created a liability scheme which served as the sole means to remedy injuries suffered in the course of international air transportation of persons, baggage, or goods. See King v. Am. Airlines, Inc., 284 F.3d 352, 356-57 (2d Cir. 2002) (summarizing provisions of the Convention for the Unification of Certain Rules Relating to International Transportation by Air, Oct. 12, 1929, 49 Stat. 3000, T.S. No. 876 (1934), reprinted in 49 U.S.C. § 40105 note (1997) (hereinafter "Warsaw Convention")). To shield air carriers from catastrophic liability, the Convention set limits on damages, and it restricted the types of claims that could be brought against carriers. To protect passengers and shippers, it required carriers to issue air waybills detailing the conditions of carriage, and it created a presumption of liability against carriers for injuries to passengers or damage to cargo. Over the years, subsequent international agreements changed its liability scheme, but several features of the Warsaw Convention—caps on damages for injuries suffered in international air transportation, a presumption of liability against carriers, and a requirement that carriers issue air waybills—remain in effect in some form today.

In 1999, fifty-two nations including the United States signed the Montreal Convention, a treaty to replace the Warsaw Convention. Convention for the Unification of Certain Rules for International Carriage by Air, ICAO Doc. 9740, reprinted in Treaty Doc. No. 106-45, 1999 WL 33292734 (2000). The United States Senate ratified the Montreal Convention in September 2003, and it entered into force on November 4, 2003, after at least thirty nations did the same.

The Montreal Convention provisions related to carrier liability for damage to baggage and cargo are relevant to this case. Article 22(3) of the Convention limits potential liability to seventeen "Special Drawing Rights" ("SDRs") per kilogram of cargo shipped. An SDR is an artificial currency, published daily by the International Monetary Fund, which fluctuates based on the global currency market. Sompo Japan Ins., Inc. v. Nippon Cargo Airlines Co., 522 F.3d 776, 779 n.3 (7th Cir. 2008). These limits may be increased in one of two ways. First, Article 22(3) provides that damages may exceed 17 SDRs per kilogram if "the consignor has made, at the time when the package was handed over to the carrier, a special declaration of interest in delivery at destination and has paid a supplementary sum if the case so requires." This provision did not represent a change in the law; it is nearly identical to Article 22(2) of the original Warsaw Convention. Second, Article 25 of the Montreal Convention, entitled "Stipulation on Limits," states "[a] carrier may stipulate that the contract of carriage shall be subject to higher limits of liability than those provided for in this Convention or to no limits of liability whatsoever." Article 25 is new; there is no parallel provision in the Warsaw Convention or its subsequent amendments. So, the Warsaw Convention as amended expressly provided that limits on liability for damage to cargo could be increased if a shipper declared a value for the cargo and paid a supplementary sum if the case so required; it is unclear whether this was the sole means to increase a carrier's potential liability. After November 2003, when the Montreal Convention entered into force, limits on carrier liability could be increased either by the shipper declaring a value for the cargo or by the carrier stipulating that the contract of carriage, i.e. the air waybill, shall be subject to higher limits of liability. See St. Paul Ins. Co. v. Venezuelan Int'l Airways, Inc., 807 F.2d 1543, 1547 n.6 (11th Cir. 1987) (noting that one of the functions of an air waybill is to serve as the contract of carriage of goods).

B. Factual Background

Eli Lilly is one of the world's largest pharmaceutical companies. It has manufacturing plants in thirteen countries, conducts clinical research in more than fifty countries, and markets products in 143 countries. Eli Lilly regularly ships products around the world, and due to its complex supply chain, it engages providers of international logistic services who assist Eli Lilly in coordinating shipping, warehousing, and distribution of its products. DHL is the world's largest provider of logistics services. Among other things, it provides international freight forwarding services; it arranges, through various third-party carriers, air and ocean freight services, ground transportation, and warehousing.

DHL and Eli Lilly entered into a long-term service agreement covering a period of five-years beginning on January 1, 2003, eleven months before the Montreal Convention entered into force. The agreement states that DHL will provide Eli Lilly the following services related to the transport of pharmaceuticals to and from Europe and the United States: airfreight, ocean freight, multimodal service, customs clearance and brokerage services, land transportation, warehousing and distribution, project management, and customer service support. It further states that DHL "is to utilize high quality airfreight service providers or if requested, to use a carrier selected by Lilly." Article Five of the agreement is entitled "Indemnification." The first paragraph provides that DHL agrees to indemnify Eli Lilly against third-party claims arising from breach of the service agreement. The second paragraph contains a limitation of liability stating, in part, that damages that either party is required to pay for whatever reason shall be limited to two times the amount of the total fees payable to DHL under the service agreement. It also states that neither party shall be liable for loss of profits arising out of obligations under the agreement.

Eli Lilly France, S.A., an Eli Lilly affiliate, manufactures pharmaceuticals at a plant in Fegersheim, France. Eli Lilly France regularly ships pharmaceuticals between Fegersheim and the United States. Lufthansa is Eli Lilly's preferred carrier for these shipments, and Eli Lilly purchased a shipping service from Lufthansa called "Cool/td." Through this service, Lufthansa ships products in insulated containers designed to keep cargo cool during transit. The containers do not protect cargo from freezing temperatures, but Eli Lilly France places temperature recording devices in the containers to monitor the air temperature to which the container and cargo are exposed during transit. Under the Cool/td service, Lufthansa provides trucking from the Fegersheim plant to the airport of departure, airport storage of the containers, loading of the containers onto airplanes, air transport to Chicago O'Hare airport, and trucking service from O'Hare to an Eli Lilly facility in Indiana.

Eli Lilly regularly directed DHL, pursuant to the long-term service agreement, to arrange for Lufthansa to ship containers of pharmaceuticals by air from Fegersheim to the United States. In December 2004, Eli Lilly France requested that DHL arrange a shipment from Fegersheim to Indiana of eight containers of cold-sensitive insulin and growth hormone utilizing the Cool/td service. The eight containers were divided into two shipments, and DHL arranged for the shipments to depart from Munich, Germany. DHL then issued two "house air waybills," which are contracts of carriage between Eli Lilly and DHL. It also issued two "master air waybills," which are contracts of carriage between DHL and Lufthansa. All waybills contained a box labeled "Declared Value for Carriage." Eli Lilly's practice with respect to the shipments handled by DHL and Lufthansa was never to declare any value for the shipments. Consistent with this practice, the boxes were marked "NVD," or no value declared. The waybills also instructed the carrier to refrigerate the cargo at eight degrees Celsius and to avoid freezing.

The shipments were transported from the Fegersheim plant to the Munich airport in heated trucks hired by Lufthansa. Due to admitted human error by Lufthansa personnel, the containers were left outside in sub-freezing temperatures before they were loaded on to airplanes for shipment to the United States. When the shipments arrived in Indiana, temperature recording devices inside the insulated containers showed that the contents of seven of the eight containers had been subjected to sub-freezing temperatures.

A few days after the shipments arrived in Indiana, Eli Lilly France gave notices of claim to DHL for damage to the cargo, and DHL gave notices of claim to Lufthansa. A DHL agent then sent an e-mail to Eli Lilly's insurance company representatives requesting that the damaged insulin products not be destroyed. Eli Lilly permitted DHL representatives to examine the insulin products, but did not allow them to be removed from the Eli Lilly facility. Eli Lilly asserts that it destroyed the insulin products shipped in the containers in which temperature recording devices registered below freezing temperatures, but that it salvaged some of the growth hormone. It claims that destroying the insulin was necessary because determining whether it remained viable after being exposed to sub-freezing temperatures would have required that the insulin be subjected to destructive testing. Eli Lilly has not produced records documenting the destruction of the insulin products, and DHL contests whether they were actually destroyed.

Eli Lilly made a claim to its insurer, Elgo Insurance Company, in the amount of $ 10,251,432.50, which represented the "transfer price" of the insulin products. The transfer price is the price at which an Eli Lilly affiliate in the supply chain that is in possession of a product at a certain point in time sells the product to another Eli Lilly affiliate or a third-party. It encompasses all of the costs incurred throughout the Eli Lilly supply chain and all of the profit that is earned in each step of the supply chain by an Eli Lilly affiliate up to that point in time. The insurer and reinsurers ultimately paid Eli Lilly $ 9,000,000 to satisfy the claim.

II. PROCEDURAL HISTORY

Eli Lilly, individually and for the use and benefit of its insurer Elgo Insurance Company Limited, individually and for the use and benefit of Certain London Market Reinsurance Underwriters, filed this action against DHL and Lufthansa in the United States District Court for the Southern District of Florida. The complaint asserts a claim against DHL for breach of the long-term service agreement. It also asserts claims for breach of the air waybill contracts against Lufthansa and DHL. Defendants answered the complaint, and DHL filed a cross-claim against Lufthansa for breach of contract and indemnification or contribution.

All parties moved for summary judgment and moved to strike certain affidavits. Defendants also sought sanctions for spoliation of evidence. The district court issued an omnibus order in which it (1) dismissed the claim for breach of the service agreement because it is preempted by the Montreal Convention, Eli Lilly & Co. v. Air Express Int'l USA, Inc., 602 F. Supp. 2d, 1260, 1268-69 (S.D. Fla. 2009); (2) held that DHL, as a contracting carrier, and Lufthansa, as an actual carrier, are liable under the Montreal Convention for breach of the air waybills; (3) held that Lufthansa's liability for the damaged cargo is capped at seventeen SDRs per kilogram pursuant to Article 22(3) of the Montreal Convention; (4) held that DHL's liability is not limited by the Montreal Convention and is instead governed by the terms of the liability provision contained in the long-term service agreement; (5) held that damages are to be calculated based on the transfer price of the damaged cargo; (6) held that Eli Lilly did not commit spoliation of evidence; and (7) denied all motions to strike. Thereafter, Plaintiffs settled all claims against Lufthansa and all parties stipulated to Lufthansa's dismissal from the case. (R.5-258.) In addition, Plaintiffs and DHL stipulated, without waiving DHL's rights to contest certain rulings contained in the omnibus order, that judgment may be entered against DHL and in favor of Plaintiffs for the sum of $ 10,216,958.12. (R.5-259.) The court then entered a final judgment in favor of Plaintiffs against DHL and dismissed all claims against Lufthansa with prejudice. DHL appeals, challenging: (1) the grant of summary judgment in favor of Plaintiffs on the issue of liability and the denial of its motion for summary judgment on that issue; (2) the ruling that DHL's liability is governed by the liability provision in the long-term service agreement; and (3) the denial of its motion for sanctions for spoliation of evidence.

III. ISSUES ON APPEAL AND CONTENTIONS OF THE PARTIES

The main issue on appeal is whether DHL's liability should be limited to seventeen SDRs per kilogram of the damaged cargo pursuant to Article 22(3) of the Montreal Convention, or whether the long-term service agreement between DHL and Eli Lilly constitutes a stipulation to waive those limits. DHL argues: (1) because the court dismissed Plaintiffs' claim for breach of the service agreement as preempted by the Montreal Convention, it erred in applying the terms of that agreement to Plaintiffs' remaining claims for breach of the air waybill contracts; (2) the court improperly incorporated the terms of the service agreement into the separate air waybill contracts because the air waybill contracts were marked "no value declared"; (3) DHL did not breach the service agreement, and the liability limitation contained therein applies only if Eli Lilly sought indemnity from third-party claims arising from breach of the agreement; and (4) the liability limitation in the service agreement is ambiguous, and the court erred in interpreting that provision in favor of the drafter, Eli Lilly. Plaintiffs counter that: (1) the service agreement provides that all air waybill contracts between the parties would be subject to limits of liability in excess of 17 SDRs per kilogram; (2) the Montreal Convention permits parties to enter into an agreement collateral to the air waybill contracts waiving the Convention's limits; (3) there was no reason for Eli Lilly to declare a value on the air waybills because under the service agreement the parties opted out of the Montreal Convention liability regime; (4) the liability provision applied not only to indemnity claims but to all claims arising from the agreement; and (5) it was not ambiguous.

DHL also contends that in concluding that the pharmaceuticals were damaged, the court erred in considering an affidavit of Rene Scheer, an Eli Lilly logistics manager. It argues that the contents of the affidavit were not based on Scheer's personal knowledge, that they were hearsay, that attached documents were not authenticated, and that the documents were translated from French to English by Scheer himself, who is not a certified translator. Plaintiffs counter that the district court did not rely on the challenged portions of the affidavit, that the contents of the affidavit were drawn from Scheer's personal knowledge gained from his job duties as a logistics manager, that the translations comport with the Federal Rules of Evidence, and that the attached documents fall under the business records exception to the hearsay rule.

DHL further contends that summary judgment was inappropriately granted on the issue of whether the pharmaceuticals were damaged in transit. It points out that Plaintiffs did not present proof that the pharmaceuticals were in fact destroyed, and it claims that Eli Lilly refused to produce the pharmaceuticals for testing and inspection by DHL. Plaintiffs counter that they presented evidence that the insulin products were subjected to sub-freezing temperatures during transit, and this exposure rendered them worthless whether or not actual damage occurred.

Finally, DHL contends that the court abused its discretion in holding that Eli Lilly did not commit spoliation of evidence by refusing to permit testing and inspection of the pharmaceuticals. Plaintiffs counter that a party moving for sanctions for spoliation of evidence must prove prejudice. And, federal regulations mandate destruction of pharmaceutical products subjected to sub-freezing temperatures whether or not they are in fact damaged. Given that the pharmaceuticals were worthless regardless of their condition, Plaintiffs argue that DHL did not suffer prejudice from not having the opportunity to inspect the pharmaceuticals before they were destroyed.

IV. STANDARD OF REVIEW

We consider *de novo* a grant or denial of summary judgment, applying the same legal standards as the district court. Baker v. Birmingham Bd. of Educ., 531 F.3d 1336, 1337 (11th Cir. 2008).

A district court's evidentiary rulings are reviewed for abuse of discretion. General Elec. Co. v. Joiner, 522 U.S. 136, 141, 118 S. Ct. 512, 517, 139 L. Ed. 2d 508 (1997).

A district court's decision regarding spoliation sanctions is reviewed for abuse of discretion. Harris v. Chapman, 97 F.3d 499, 506 (11th Cir. 1996).

V. DISCUSSION

A. The Montreal Convention limits DHL's liability to 17 SDRs per kilogram of the damaged pharmaceuticals.

The Montreal Convention limits on liability may be waived under Article 22(3) if the shipper declares a value for the cargo or under Article 25 if the carrier stipulates that the contract of carriage shall be subject to higher limits of liability. It is undisputed that Eli Lilly did not declare a value for the cargo. At issue is whether a provision in the long-term service agreement constitutes a stipulation to waive the Montreal Convention limits.

The district court dismissed Plaintiffs' claim for breach of the long-term service agreement because it was preempted by the Montreal Convention, and this ruling is not contested on appeal. Plaintiffs' remaining claims allege breach of the air waybill contracts. The court noted that "[t]he parties did not stipulate in any of the air waybills that the shipments in question would be subject to higher limits of liability than those provided for in the Montreal Convention." Eli Lilly, 602 F. Supp. 2d at 1276. Nevertheless, it held that DHL stipulated to waive the Convention's limits through the liability provision in the long-term service agreement. The court explained that "the Liability Limitation clearly and unambiguously establishes that DHL's liability is limited to two times the total fees payable to DHL for the duration of the Service Agreement." The air waybills and the service agreement are separate contracts, and they were not executed contemporaneously. Therefore, in concluding that a provision in the service agreement serves as a stipulation to subject the waybills to increased limits on liability, the court implicitly held that the service agreement is incorporated into the air waybill contracts.

In addressing whether the liability provision of the service agreement constitutes a stipulation to waive the Montreal Convention limits, we first interpret the terms of the service agreement and the air waybill contracts; we must discern the meaning of the liability provision and discern whether the parties intended to incorporate that provision into the air waybill contracts. We generally apply state law to such questions of contract interpretation, and the parties assume that Florida law controls. If we conclude that the parties did intend for the liability provision to serve as such a stipulation, we would have to consider whether that stipulation is effective. We would examine Article 25 of the Montreal Convention to determine what a carrier must do to effectively stipulate that a contract of carriage shall be subject to limits of liability in excess of seventeen SDRs per kilogram. Because this involves interpretation of an international treaty, it is a question of federal law. (See Maugnie v. Compagnie Nationale Air France, 549 F.2d 1256, 1258 (9th Cir. 1977) ("The scope of the

Warsaw Convention is a matter of federal law and federal treaty interpretation, and must be determined from an examination of the 'four corners of the treaty.'")

Before turning to whether the parties intended to incorporate the liability provision of the service agreement into the air waybill contracts, we pause to note that it is an open question whether Article 25 of the Montreal Convention permits parties to agree to waive the Convention's limits in a document separate from the air waybills. DHL contends that a stipulation under Article 25 is valid only if contained in the contract of carriage, i.e. the air waybill, itself. We are aware of no authority supporting this position. And, Article 25 does not state that the stipulation must be "in" the contract of carriage. Further, Article 27 provides that "[n]othing contained in this Convention shall prevent the carrier … from waiving any defences available under the Convention, or from laying down conditions which do not conflict with the provisions of this Convention." So, it appears from the language of the Montreal Convention that a stipulation to increase a carrier's potential liability may be valid even if it is not set forth in the waybill itself. Nevertheless, we need not decide this issue. We assume that a carrier may stipulate to waive the Convention's limits in a document separate from the air waybill. But, we conclude that the parties did not intend for the liability provision in Article 5 of the long-term service agreement to be such a stipulation.

The first paragraph of Article 5 is a third-party indemnity provision. It reads:

Article 5: Indemnification

Except for claims for personal injury or property damage which are caused by the failure of Lilly to observe any of the terms and conditions of this agreement and those claims for personal injury or property damage which arise from the gross negligence or willful misconduct of Lilly, Supplier hereby agrees to indemnify and hold Lilly harmless against and from any and all claims arising from any breach or default in the performance of any obligation on Supplier's part to be performed under the terms of the agreement, or arising from any act, neglect, fault, or omission of Supplier or of its agents, employees, visitors, invitees, or licensee and from and against all costs, attorney's fees, expenses, and liabilities incurred in or about any such claims or any action against customer by reason of such claim. Supplier, upon notice of Lilly, shall defend same at Supplier's expense.

This provision appears to require DHL to indemnify Eli Lilly from third-party claims that arise from DHL's breach of the service agreement. The second paragraph of Article 5 is entitled "Liability Limitations." It reads:

Except for a party's obligations of this Agreement, any damages that either party is required to pay for any reason whatsoever and regardless of the form of action, in the aggregate, shall be limited to two times the amount of the total fees payable to Supplier hereunder. Neither Supplier nor Lilly shall be liable for any special, punitive or consequential damages, or loss of profits arising out of or in connection with their respective obligations under this Agreement. Notwithstanding the foregoing, if any claim against Supplier is a claim covered by any insurance policy maintained by Supplier, any recovery of proceeds under such policy shall be paid to Lilly to the extent Lilly's damages exceed the foregoing limitation of liability.

This provision appears to cap either party's potential liability to two times the amount of the total fees payable to DHL under the agreement. Because the liability provision is contained in a section of the agreement addressing indemnification, the parties dispute whether it applies only where Eli Lilly seeks indemnification from third party claims arising from DHL's breach of the service agreement, or whether it applies to any and all claims arising from the service agreement. We need not resolve this dispute. Whatever the scope of the liability provision, we have no reason to conclude that the parties intended for it to apply to the separate air waybill contracts so as to subject those contracts to limits of liability in excess of those imposed by law.

The service agreement took effect January 1, 2003, eleven months before the Montreal Convention entered into force. The governing law in January 2003 (the Warsaw Convention as amended by subsequent international agreements) did not include a provision parallel to Article 25 of the Montreal Convention—one providing that a carrier may stipulate that a contract of carriage would be subject to increased limits on liability. Had the parties intended for the service agreement to constitute a stipulation to waive limits on liability, this would not have been expressly permitted by the Warsaw Convention, and may have been invalid. This suggests that the parties did not intend such a result. In addition, the service agreement makes no mention of the Montreal Convention, the Warsaw Convention, the concept of declared value, or limits of liability imposed by law. Nor does it contemplate that the service agreement would modify any subsequently executed air waybill contracts. In sum, there is no indication that the parties intended to opt out of the Montreal Convention liability regime through Article 5 of the service agreement.

The air waybill contracts at issue were executed after the Montreal Convention took effect. The parties knew of the limits on air carrier liability and the ways to contract around those limits—declaring a value for the cargo or stipulating to waive the limits. The waybills show that the parties declined to do so. They note that potential liability is limited to seventeen SDRs per kilogram of cargo and state, "[t]he shipper's attention is drawn to the notice concerning carrier's limitation of liability. Shipper may increase such limitation of liability by declaring a higher value for carriage and paying a supplemental charge if required." (R.1-1 Ex's A-D.) Furthermore, the air waybill contracts indicate no intent to incorporate the service agreement's liability provision. "Where a written contract refers to and sufficiently describes another document, that other document or so much of it as is referred to, may be regarded as part of the contract and therefore is properly considered in its interpretation." See e.g. Hurwitz v. C.G.J. Corp., 168 So. 2d 84, 86 (Fla. 3d DCA 1964) (internal quotation and citation omitted). There is no mention of the service agreement in the air waybill contracts. Had the parties agreed to incorporate the service agreement's liability provision so as to waive the Convention's limits, they could have noted their intent to do so. But they did not.

The conduct of and course of dealings between the parties supports our conclusion. Eli Lilly purchased insurance to fully cover the value of the cargo in the event of its damage or loss in transit (R.5-218 at 89). This suggests that Eli Lilly declined to opt out of the Montreal Convention liability regime. See Groupe Chegaray/V. De Chalus v. P&O Containers, 251 F.3d 1359, 1363 (11th Cir. 2001) (noting that shippers, instead of paying increased freight by declaring the value of what is shipped, generally buy insurance from cargo insurers). And, in 2002, before the service agreement took effect, DHL arranged for air cargo transport of a number of shipments of Eli Lilly pharmaceuticals. Eli Lilly, 602 F. Supp. 2d at 1265 ("Since at least 2002, Lilly France instructed DHL to arrange bookings with Lufthansa for six to eight containers to be shipped per week"). Eli Lilly declined to declare a value for these shipments. (R.5-218 at 68) (acknowledging that Eli Lilly never declared a value for cargo). After the service agreement became effective, DHL arranged for additional shipments, including the two that gave rise to this case. Eli Lilly declined to declare a value for these shipments as well. This suggests that the parties did not intend for the long-term service agreement to have any effect on DHL's potential liability under the air waybills; it shows that, before and after the agreement commenced, they intended for all air waybill contracts to be subject to limits of liability imposed by the Warsaw or Montreal Conventions.

The long-term service agreement makes no mention of the Montreal Convention, its predecessor the Warsaw Convention, or to limits on air carrier liability imposed by law. Nor does the face of the air waybill contracts show that the parties intended to incorporate the terms of the service agreement into those contracts. And, the conduct and course of dealings between the parties does not suggest otherwise. For these reasons, we conclude that the parties did not intend for the liability provision of the long-term service agreement to subject the air waybill contracts to increased limits of liability. We need not reach the question whether that provision constitutes an effective stipulation under Article 25 of the Montreal Convention. Our conclusion is drawn solely from our interpretation of the contracts, not by considering whether Article 25 of the Convention would have permitted the purported stipulation.

B. The district court did not abuse its discretion in considering certain affidavits and deposition testimony.

DHL argues that the court erred in considering an affidavit of Rene Scheer, logistics manager of Eli Lilly France, in determining whether the cargo was delivered to DHL and Lufthansa in good condition According to DHL, the affidavit is not based on Scheer's personal knowledge, is hearsay, attached documents were not authenticated, and those documents were not translated from French to English by a certified translator. These arguments are without merit. The court "only relied on that portion of Scheer's affidavit that sets forth and attaches the business records relating to the shipments in question: i.e., packing lists for the subject cargo generated by Lilly France, protocols of manufacture, analysis, and release; certificates of analysis; and checklists for the containers." Eli Lilly, 602 F. Supp. 2d at 1280. We find no error in the district court's analysis in its omnibus order concluding that Scheer is qualified to testify concerning the documents at issue, that those documents fall within the business records exception to the hearsay rule, Fed. R. Evid. 803(6), and that Scheer's translations of the documents from French to English could be considered. (Id. at 1280-81.)

C. Summary judgment was appropriately granted on the issue of whether the cargo was damaged in transit, and Plaintiffs did not commit spoliation of evidence.

DHL argues that because Plaintiffs failed to produce documents showing that the pharmaceuticals had been destroyed, they failed to present evidence sufficient to show that they were damaged in transit. DHL further argues that because Plaintiffs denied DHL an opportunity to inspect and test the pharmaceuticals, they committed spoliation of evidence warranting an adverse inference on this issue. But, Plaintiffs produced records showing that the insulin was subjected to sub-freezing temperatures and evidence showing that the devices which measured the temperatures were tested and certified for accuracy before and after use. Further, federal regulations provide that pharmaceuticals subjected to sub-freezing temperatures must be tested for safety and purity prior to being salvaged. 21 C.F.R. § 211.208. And, Plaintiffs presented uncontradicted expert testimony that any testing of insulin subjected to sub-freezing temperatures would result in destruction of the insulin. Because Plaintiffs presented undisputed evidence that the insulin was subjected to sub-freezing temperatures and undisputed evidence that the insulin is unsaleable regardless whether actual damage occurred, Plaintiffs are entitled to summary judgment on the issue of whether the insulin products were damaged in transit.

As to DHL's spoliation claim, a party moving for sanctions must establish, among other things, that the destroyed evidence was relevant to a claim or defense such that the destruction of that evidence resulted in prejudice. See Flury v. Daimler Chrysler Corp., 427 F.3d 939, 943 (11th Cir. 2005) (explaining that spoliation analysis hinges upon the significance of the evidence and the prejudice suffered as a result of its destruction). The destruction of the insulin products did not affect DHL's ability to make a claim or defense; the exposure to sub-freezing temperatures rendered the products worthless regardless of the results of any tests that DHL may have conducted. Because DHL suffered no prejudice, the district court did not abuse its discretion in denying its claim for spoliation of evidence.

VI. CONCLUSION

For the reasons stated in this opinion, we affirm the grant of summary judgment in favor of Plaintiffs on the issue of liability, affirm the denial of DHL's motion for summary judgment, and affirm the denial of DHL's motion for sanctions for spoliation of evidence. We reverse the ruling that DHL's liability shall be governed by the terms of the long-term service agreement and therefore vacate the final judgment entered by the district court. We remand to the district court for proceedings not inconsistent with this opinion and with instructions that DHL's liability shall be capped at 17 SDRs per kilogram of the damaged cargo pursuant to Article 22 of the Montreal Convention.

【思考题】

1. 什么是承运人赔偿责任限制？《蒙特利尔公约》对航空承运人责任限制是如何规定的？

2. 航空货物运输合同的当事人能否通过约定取消《蒙特利尔公约》中的责任限制？本案中的此种约定是否有效？

3. 在何种情况下，航空运输承运人赔偿责任需要高于航空运输公约规定的责任限额？

4. 缔约承运人与实际承运人的责任承担如何划分？这种划分在本案中是如何体现的？

Case1·拓展阅读

Case2　East West Corporation vs DKBS 1912 and Anothers（Utaniko Ltd. vs P&O Nedloyd BV）

【案情说明】

一、案件事实

原告在中国香港从事向世界各地出口中国制造的商品的业务。长期以来，他们一直向总部位于智利圣地亚哥的金皇冠公司销售产品。1998 年，他们同意以货到付款的方式出售更多的货物。原告在中国香港用集装箱装运货物，然后用班轮运往智利。第一次由 Maersk 于 1998 年 9 月 22 日到 1998 年 10 月 19 日运输，第二次由 P&O 于 1999 年 2 月 5 日装运。

原告与银行做出有关安排，将货运单据汇寄给智利的银行，委托银行付款交单。九批货物被告都已经按时签发班轮运输项下的提单并交给原告。每份提单中，原告都是托运人，收货人是金皇冠公司。所有提单都是以智利银行为指示人的指示提单，只有一份由 Maersk 签发的提单例外，这份是以智利银行为收货人的记名提单。这些银行将作为原告的银行的代理行，接受金皇冠公司的付款赎单。提单经原告背书，并由原告的银行寄给其在智利的代理银行，从而取得货款。

Maersk 运输的货物在 1998 年 10 月底到 11 月初，运抵智利的圣安东尼奥；P&O 运输的货物在 1999 年 3 月 10 日经由特许的航道运送至圣安东尼奥。P&O 签发的提单规定货物运送至瓦尔帕莱索。依据智利的海关法，在未提前缴纳海关税时，货物必须存放在指定的仓库中内：由 Maersk 运输的货物，由其代理人存放在圣安东尼奥海港运营的海关仓库之中；由 P&O 负责运送的货物由船上的代理商，先行存放在集装箱堆场，然后再转移到圣安东尼奥市的特许海关仓库。

海关将已经缴纳关税的货物，在未出示正本提单时，交给金皇冠公司的海关代理，再由其移交给金皇冠公司。由 Maersk 运输的七个集装箱的货物，四个于 1998 年 11 月放行，剩下两个于 1999 年 1 月 19 日放行，还有一个提货日期不详。由 P&O 运输的货物于 1999 年 3 月 15 日放行。

尽管金皇冠向原告支付了一些款项，但没有对 P&O 运输的两个集装箱和 Maersk 运输的七个集装箱中的货物付款。原告要求银行返还提单后，未经银行背书的提单被返还。

每份提单中都记载着一项条款，表明该合同适用英国法律并由英国管辖。原告在英国提起诉讼，理由是 Maersk 和 P&O 无单放货。原告向 Maersk 索赔 134 807.40 美元，对 P&O 索赔 95 147.20 美元。

承运人做出如下抗辩：

ⅰ）原告无权提起诉讼。

ⅱ）根据智利法律，承运人必须将货物运送至海关指定的仓库中。一旦他们把货物送到指定的海关仓库，而不必出示提货单，他们就履行了自己的义务，运输合同也就终止了。此外，《联合国海上货物运输公约》（《汉堡规则》）在智利生效，根据《汉堡规则》第4条，Maersk和P&O在此种情况下免责，而无须对无单放货承担责任。

ⅲ）即使他们对智利法律的理解不正确，他们也可以根据提单上的免责条款免除责任。

ⅳ）Maersk和P&O在无单放货问题上不存在过失。

二、裁判结果

法院认为，认可承运人没有义务将货物交给海关；承运人虽不需将货物交付给海关，但是要将货物置于海关指定的仓库之中并接受海关仓库运营人员的管辖。双方约定，在未出示提单时不对货物放行。如果承运人的义务是将货物交给其他当局的海关、港口保管，则这种移交，应构成根据提单向商户交付货物。

【法律分析】

本案涉及1992年《海上货物运输法》关于提单项下的交货义务和智利国内法，包括在智利生效的《汉堡规则》（尤其是第4条）的规定。

智利于1988年将《汉堡规则》纳入其《商法典》中。《汉堡规则》第1条第7款规定："提单，是指用以证明海上运输合同和货物由承运人接收或装船，以及承运人保证据以交付货物的单证。单证中关于货物应按记名人的指示交付、或者按指示交付、或者向提单持有人交付的规定，构成此种保证。"

《智利商法典》第977条指出："提单是用以证明海上货物运输合同成立，证明承运人接管或装载货物并且按照委托人的指示交付货物或者将货物交付给提单持有人的单证。"

《汉堡规则》第4条题为"责任期间"，规定：

"1.承运人对本[公约]项下货物的责任包括承运人在装货港、运输期间和卸货港负责货物的期间。《智利商法典》第982条也作了同样的规定：'承运人对货物的责任包括其保管期间、在岸上或实际运输期间。'"

《汉堡规则》第4条第2款规定：

"就本条第1款而言，在下述期间，承运人应被视为已经掌管货物：

（a）自承运人从下述各方接管货物时起：（ⅰ）托运人或代其行事的人；或者（ⅱ）根据装货港适用的法律或规章，须将货物交其装运的当局或其他第三方。

（b）直至他按下列方式交付货物之时为止：（ⅰ）将货物交付收货人；或者；（ⅱ）如果收货人不向承运人提货，则依照合同或在卸货港适用的法律或特定商业习惯，将货物置于收货人支配之下；或者（ⅲ）根据卸货港适用的法律或规章，将货物交付所需交付的当局或其他第三方。"

专家们对《智利商法典》条款（第983条）中西班牙文的准确译文存在争议，特别是西班牙文"货物必须移交"是否应改为"可以移交"。因为该案文与《汉堡规则》的案文在所有实质性方面完全相同；所以可以参考《汉堡规则》的措辞，理解为"必须移交"。

《汉堡规则》第5条（《智利商法典》第984条）题为"责任基础"，其表述为：

"1. 第4条所规定的货物在承运人掌管期间所发生的货物灭失、损坏以及迟延交付所造成的损失，承运人应当承担赔偿责任，除非承运人证明其受雇人或代理人采取了一切合理要求的措施以避免事故的发生或后果。

……

3. 如果货物没有按照第4条的要求在连续60天内交付，有权对货物损失提出索赔的人可以认为货物已经丢失……"

基于上述理由，法院认为，认可承运人没有义务将货物交给海关；承运人虽不需将货物交付给海关，但是要将货物置于海关指定的仓库之中并接受海关仓库运营人员的管辖。承运人不可以依赖第4.2（b）（ⅲ）条［《智利商法典》第983（c）条］的规定。但是双方可以约定，不出示提单就不能放货。

【英文案例裁决摘录】

R Waller for the Claimants

M Davey for the Defendants

Goods shipped by the Claimants in Hong Kong in containers were carried to Chile on the Defendants' liner services; they were cleared through customs and delivered to a person not entitled to the goods without presentation of the bills of lading. To such a claim, a shipowner would normally have no defence, but the circumstances in this case are said by the Defendants to provide them with a defence on several cumulative and alternative grounds. The issues give rise to points on the Carriage of Goods by Sea Act 1992, the delivery obligations under bills of lading and the law of Chile, including an issue on the scope of art 4 of the Hamburg Rules which are in force in Chile.

Facts

The Claimants are related companies and carry on in Hong Kong a business of exporting goods manufactured in China to other countries in the world. For some time they had been selling goods to Gold Crown, a company based in Santiago, Chile. In 1998 they agreed to sell further consignments to them on terms of cash against delivery. The Claimants shipped goods at Hong Kong in containers on liner services for delivery in Chile. Those that were carried by the Defendants in the first action (Maersk) were shipped between 22 September 1998 and 19 October 1998 and those carried by the Defendants in the second action (P&O) were shipped on 5 February 1999.

The Claimants had made arrangements with their bankers for the shipping documents to be remitted to banks in Chile so that the documents would only be released on payment. Liner bills of lading were duly issued for each of the nine shipments and delivered to the Claimants. The Claimants were named as the shippers in each bill of lading and the notify party was Gold Crown. The goods were consigned to the order of named Chilean Banks in all the Bills of Lading, save one of the Maersk bills where the goods were simply consigned to a named Chilean bank and not to its order; these banks were to act as the correspondents of the Claimant's bankers to obtain payment from Gold Crown in return for the bills of lading.

The bills of lading were endorsed by the Claimants and sent by the Claimants' bankers to their correspondent bankers in Chile for them to obtain payment. There were some transfers between the banks in Chile to which it will be necessary to refer.

The containers carried by Maersk arrived at San Antonio, Chile between the end of October and November 1998; those carried by P&O (on a chartered vessel) arrived at San Antonio and were discharged from the vessel on 10 March 1999. The bills of lading issued by P&O provided for them to be shipped to Valparaiso, but no point arose on this for various reasons which it is not necessary to set out. In accordance with the Customs laws of Chile, as duty had not been paid in advance, the containers had to be placed on arrival in a licensed Customs warehouse: The goods carried by Maersk were placed by their agents AJ Broom in a Customs warehouse operated by Seaport SA at San Antonio; those carried by P&O were placed by the ship's agents, Agencias Universales SA, first in a container yard and then moved to a licensed customs warehouse operated by Empressa Porturia de Chile de San Antonio at San Antonio. It will be necessary to examine in more detail the detailed provisions of these laws and the arrangements for the operation of licensed warehouses and Customs clearance.

Customs duty was paid on the goods and the goods in the containers were released to the Customs agent of Gold Crown without presentation of the original bills of lading and handed over to Gold Crown. Four of the seven containers carried by Maersk were released in November 1998, two after 19 January 1999 and one at an unknown date. Those carried by P&O were released on 15 March 1999.

Although Gold Crown made some payments to the Claimants, they did not pay for the goods in two of the containers carried by P&O and seven of the containers carried by Maersk. The banks were requested to return the bills of lading to the Claimants which they did without endorsing them back.

Each of the bills of Lading contained a clause subjecting the contract to English law and jurisdiction. The Claimants commenced proceedings in this court against P&O and Maersk on the basis that they had delivered the cargo without presentation of the bills of lading. They claimed $134,807.40 against Maersk and $95,147.20 against P&O.

In the ordinary case, a carrier would have no defence to such a claim properly made by a person entitled to bring a claim under the bill of lading. However, Maersk and P&O have raised a number of defences:

i) The Claimants had no title to sue.

ii) Under the law of Chile carriers were required to deliver the goods to the licensed Customs warehouse. Once they had delivered the goods to licensed Customs warehouse which they had to do without presentation of the bills of lading, they had discharged their obligations and the contract of carriage came to an end. Furthermore the Hamburg Rules were in force in Chile; under art 4 of the Hamburg Rules, Maersk and P&O were discharged from responsibility in such circumstances. As they had acted in accordance with the law of Chile, they were not liable for delivery without presentation of the bills of lading.

iii) If they were not correct in their contentions as to the law of Chile, the express terms of the bills of lading exempted them from liabilty.

iv) They were not negligent in delivering the goods without production of the bills of lading.

At an earlier stage, Maersk and P&O both contended that the Claimants had not properly mitigated their loss, but at the conclusion of the evidence that allegation was quite properly abandoned.

It is convenient to consider the issues that arise under four main headings — (1) title to sue, (2) the delivery obligation, (3) the exceptions in the bill of lading and (4) the claim in negligence. I was greatly assisted by the very thorough and detailed research and submissions made by counsel for the parties.

Issue 1: Do the Claimants have title to sue?

The Claimants contended that they had title to sue on a number of different bases:

i) They had retained their rights of suit as shippers and these had not transferred to the Chilean banks even though the banks were named as consignees and the banks had obtained physical possession of the bills of lading.

ii) If the rights of suit had been transferred to the Chilean banks, the Claimants had title to sue as undisclosed principals of the Chilean banks named as consignees.

iii) If they had lost their rights of suit and did not have them as undisclosed principals of the Chilean banks, the rights of suits had been transferred back to them.

iv) They had, in any event, title to sue in bailment.

v) They had the right to sue in negligence for the loss of their proprietary interest.

Before considering each of these contentions, it is necessary to set out my further findings of fact.

Further findings of fact

It was quite clear on the evidence that the capacity in which the Claimants' own bankers in Hong Kong acted was to put in place arrangements for payment to be made by Gold Crown to the correspondent bank before the bills of lading were transferred to Gold Crown. The correspondent banks in Chile which were named as the consignees were appointed only for the purpose of collecting the price from the buyers as the agents (or subagents) of the Claimants. The goods remained in the ownership of the Claimants and neither their bankers in Hong Kong nor the correspondent bankers in Chile obtained any security or other interest in them. As between the banks in Chile and the Claimants, the banks had no right to take delivery from the carrier.

That was all clear both from the documents and from the evidence of Mr Deepak Balani, a director and principal in the Claimants, which I accept; he was an honest and clear witness. His evidence was that the Claimants had named the banks as consignees as that was their practice. Their own bankers wanted this done so that the payments were routed through their correspondent banks in Chile.

I am also satisfied on his evidence and from the documents that the Claimants retained full control over the documents, as the banks at all times held them to the order and direction of the Claimants. The clearest proof of this was the transfers of the documents between banks in Chile to which I briefly referred at para 5. For example, one of the Maersk bills for goods which the Claimants intended to sell to Gold Crown was issued with the Banco Credito e Inversiones as consignee; the Claimants decided to sell the goods to another buyer and recalled the bills from that bank. The Claimants then asked Maersk to issue new bills naming Banco de Chile as consignee and the new buyer as the notify party. Maersk issued a new bill. All of this was done on the instructions of the Claimants; it was a clear illustration of the fact that they exercised control over the bills, even though the banks were the named consignees and the bills were in the possession of the banks. At the time the goods were delivered to Gold Crown, five of the seven Maersk bills were in the hands of a bank other than the bank named in the bill of lading as the consignee.

(i) Did the Claimants lose their rights of suit?

The position was agreed to be the same for all the bills of lading, save for the Maersk bill of lading no 4 where the goods were consigned simply to a bank in Chile and not to its order. It is therefore convenient to consider first all the bills of lading except no 4.

It is clear that the Chilean banks were named as the consignees in the bills of lading, the bills of lading were endorsed by the Claimants to them and they obtained physical possession of the bills of lading. Maersk and P&O contended that on these facts and by reason of the provisions of Carriage of Goods by Sea Act 1992 (the 1992 Act), the Chilean banks became the persons entitled to sue and the Claimants lost their rights of suit.

Under s 2(1) of the 1992 Act, the lawful holder of a bill of lading, by virtue of becoming the lawful holder of the bill of lading, has transferred to him and vested in him all rights of suit under the contract of carriage. A holder of a bill of lading includes, under s 5(2)(a) of the 1992 Act: "a person with possession of the bill, who by virtue of being identified in the bill, is the consignee of the goods to which the bill relates" Section 2(5) provides for the extinguishment of the shippers' rights: "Where rights are transferred by the operation of subsection (1) above in relation to any document, the transfer for which the subsection provides shall extinguish any entitlement to those rights which derives — (a) where that document is a bill of lading, from a person's having been an original party to the contract of carriage."

The submission of Maersk and P&O was that on an ordinary reading of the 1992 Act, the Chilean banks to which the bills of lading were originally endorsed and transferred became the lawful holder of those bills of lading as they obtained possession of the bills in which they were the named consignees. These banks therefore obtained the rights of suit and those of the Claimants as the shippers were extinguished.

The Claimants' submission was more complex: Section 2(1) and s 5(2)(a) of the 1992 Act [as defined in para 18] should not be read in the way suggested by Maersk and P&O. These provisions were only intended to apply where the person who became the lawful holder was not only in physical possession of the bill and the named consignee, but was also in fact in control of the goods and the bills and entitled to take delivery of the goods. Where the person was not entitled to take delivery of the goods, such a person was not in truth the consignee. It was not enough that he was named on the face of the bill as consignee; the true position had to be ascertained. If the person named as consignee did not have authority to take delivery, then he should not be treated as a "consignee" of the bill for the purposes of s 5(2)(a) and hence was not a holder. Section 2(1) and s 5(2)(a) did not apply where the shipper still retained constructive possession of the bills and the physical possession was held by a person acting in a ministerial capacity. In this case, control remained in the Claimants and the banks never treated their physical possession of the bills as giving them a right to possess the goods. The Claimants as shippers had retained constructive possession of the bills, as they had complete control over them.

Although the Claimants' submission was complex, there is, in my view, a short answer, as the issue depends upon the construction of the 1992 Act. It is clear, in my judgment, that the Chilean banks to whom the bills of lading were sent initially were the consignees identified in the bills of lading within the ordinary meaning of those words in the 1992 Act. I cannot see that it is possible to give the word "consignee" any other construction. When they received the bills, they held possession of them. They therefore fulfilled the definition set out in s 5(2) (a) and became the lawful holders. In my view, it is not appropriate to go behind the facts as they would appear from the face of the bill of lading. As the Law Commission pointed out in their joint Report with the Scottish Law Commission which led to the passing of the 1992 Act, "Rights of Suit in respect of Carriage of Goods by Sea", under the law as it then stood a carrier was bound to make delivery against presentation of the bill of lading without enquiry as to the way in which he had acquired the property in the goods; the object of the change was to simplify the law. The construction advanced by the Claimants would return a substantial degree of complexity. For example if the Claimants were correct, there would need to be an enquiry into the question as to whether the consignee named on the face of the bill of lading had, as between the shipper and the person named as consignee, an entitlement to delivery. It would in another guise re-open the enquiry into the contractual arrangements that the reform brought about by the 1992 Act sought to remove. It will be necessary to consider whether the Chilean banks held them as agents and other issues raised by the Claimants, but as regards this first question, the answer is in my view clear.

Maersk bill of lading No 4 was, it seems, originally issued as a bill of lading where the goods were consigned to the order of the Banco de Credito e Inversiones. The Claimants wanted it amended to the order of the Banco de Chile; a new bill of lading was issued with the consignee named as the Banco de Chile, but the words "or order" omitted, in error. Maersk decided to make no claim to rectify this bill of lading.

The Claimants contended that in these circumstances the bill of lading was therefore a "straight" or "non-negotiable" bill — whatever is the appropriate terminology in English law: see Carver on Bills of Lading at para 1-007; that therefore the Claimants' rights had not been extinguished by the provisions of the 1992 Act. The position under such a bill of lading is summarised in Carver on Bills of Lading at para 6-007. The bill is not a document of title at common law, the transfer does not operate as a transfer of constructive possession; the carrier is bound to deliver to the consignee without presentation of the bill.

The effect of s 2(5) of the 1992 Act in such circumstances is not to extinguish the rights of the Claimants as the original party to this bill of lading, as Maersk accepted would follow if they did not seek to rectify this bill of lading. The Claimants are therefore entitled to maintain their claim in respect of this bill as the shippers.

(ii) Were the Claimants the undisclosed principals of the banks named as consignees and therefore had title to sue in that capacity?

The first alternative case of the Claimants was that, if the rights of suit were transferred to the Chilean banks as consignees, they were transferred to those banks in their capacity as agents for the Claimants who were their undisclosed principals. They submitted that at all times the Chilean banks were doing no more than acting as agents for the Claimants; had the Chilean banks been asked whether rights should vest in the banks or in the Claimants, they would have said that they should vest in the Claimants. Thus the necessary intention that the banks should act as agents could easily be inferred. They relied on this argument only in relation to the banks named as consignees and where transferring possession to those banks had the effect of extinguishing the rights of the Claimants as shippers under the original contract. They did not seek to contend that the banks to which the bills were subsequently transferred at the Claimants' direction were such agents for the purposes of this argument.

The Claimants contended that in so far as the effect of the 1992 Act was to create rights in contract between the carrier and the holder of the bill, there was no reason why the undisclosed principal could not sue under such a contract just as in any other contract. Similarly, there was no reason why in so far as the rights of suit were transferred, they could not be transferred to the banks as agents for the Claimants as undisclosed principals.

They contended that the same policy considerations that enabled the principal of a consignee or a consignor to sue under an air waybill under the provisions of the Warsaw and Guadalajara Conventions should apply; they relied particularly on the judgment of Mance LJ in Western Digital v BA [2000] 2 Lloyd's Rep 142 at paras 43, 44 and 81.

It is suggested in Carver on Bills of Lading at para 5-017, that where a bearer bill of lading is delivered to an agent, then it may be the case that the principal can be the holder for the purposes of the Act; it seems to me that this must be so, for in such a case the real question which arises is who is in possession as the actual holder. For example, if a bearer bill (or a bill endorsed in blank) is received by an employee of a company, the answer to the question is simple. The employee is not in possession; he can be described as having custody. His employer is in possession and is the holder. It does not seem to me that there can be any material distinction between such a person and any other agent. The agent holds custody of the bill for his principal and it is the principal who has possession and is the holder for the purposes of the 1992 Act; P&O and Maersk did not seek to contend to the contrary.

Where, however, under s 5(2)(a) of the 1992 Act, the person who becomes the holder is the named consignee, is that right personal to him as the person upon whom the 1992 Act confers the right? It is clear that there is scope for the operation of the doctrine of undisclosed principals in relation to rights of suit under bills of lading at common law: see for example the speech of Lord Blackburn in Sewell v Burdick (1884) 10 App Cas 74 at 90-1. It is also the case that the policy considerations referred to in the cases on air waybills may also be applicable in certain circumstances. For example in Gatewhite v Iberia Airlines [1990] 1 QB 326, [1989] 1 Lloyd's Rep 160, Gatehouse J referred to the curious position that could arise if the right of suit depended on the willingness of the consignee to sue, as in such cases he might have little incentive being a customs agent or forwarding agent or bank; the same point was made by the Hong Kong Court of Appeal in Regaalite International Limited v Air Cargo Consolidation Service (UK) Ltd [1966] 3 HKLR 453 and by Pritchard J in Tasman Pulp & Paper Co v Brambles [1981] 2 NZLR 225.

However the scheme of the Conventions governing carriage by air is very different; serious practical problems would, as the judgment of Mance LJ in Western Digital demonstrates, arise if the rights of suit in carriage by air were confined to the actual consignee or the consignor and their principals were excluded. The Conventions contain no definition of consignor or consignee; often in air transport, the consignee named in the air way bill is purely nominal. However both the scheme of the 1992 Act and the practice as to the naming of the shipper and the consignee are very different. The 1992 Act provides a detailed scheme for the transfer of the bill of lading and clear definitions as to the parties involved. There can be no difficulty in identifying the holder in the case of a consignee who becomes the lawful holder under s 5(2)(a); he is the person who by virtue of being identified in the bill is the consignee. The legal regime relating to airway bills is very different. I can see no reason for overriding what are in my view clear statutory definitions.

(iii) Were the rights of suit transferred back to the Claimants?

Although the bills of lading were delivered back to the Claimants, they were never endorsed by the banks to them. Was endorsement necessary? The issue turned substantially upon the meaning of the definitions of holder in s 5(2)(b) and (c) of the 1992 Act.

The simple contention advanced by Maersk and P&O was that by reason of s 5(2)(b) of the 1992 Act, the rights of suit could only be transferred back by endorsement. This sets out the second definition of a holder as: "a person with possession of the bill as a result of the completion, by delivery of the bill, of any indorsement of the bill, or in the case of a bearer bill, of any other transfer of the bill." There had been no endorsement back; therefore, as the Claimants accepted, they could not establish title to sue on this basis. Maersk and P&O stressed that the simple step of endorsement back could have been taken and there was no need to attempt to complicate the simple scheme of the 1992 Act.

The Claimants contended that endorsement was unnecessary because by the time of the return of the bills of lading to the Claimants, the goods had been delivered and the bills of lading therefore no longer gave a right to possess as against the carrier. If the goods had not been delivered, then the bills would have been endorsed back to the Claimants to enable them to take delivery of them. The Claimants were therefore holders of the bills under s 5(2)(c) of the 1992 Act and rights of suit vested in them; s 5(2)(c) sets out the third definition of a holder as:

"a person with possession of the bill as a result of any transaction by virtue of which he would have become a holder falling within paragraph (a) or (b) above had not the transaction been effected at a time when possession of the bill no longer gave a right (as against the carrier) to possession of the goods to which the bill relates." They contended that once the cargo had been discharged, the bill of lading no longer gave a right to possession, only to a claim for damages; they relied on a series of decisions to which I refer at para 35 and following. As holders they were entitled to bring a claim under s 2(2):

"Where, when a person becomes the lawful holder of a bill of lading, possession of the bill no longer gives a right (as against the carrier) to possession of the goods to which the bill relates, that person shall not have any rights transferred to him by virtue of subsection (1) above unless he becomes the holder of the bill — (a) by virtue of a transaction effected in pursuance of any contractual or other arrangements made before the time when the right to possession ceased to attach to the bill … "

The first question which arises is whether there was a right to possess as against the carrier after the goods had been wrongly delivered to Gold Crown. There are a number of cases prior to the 1992 Act where the courts considered the circumstances in which a bill of lading is discharged or spent. In Barclays Bank v Commissioners of Customs and Excise [1963] 1 Lloyd's Rep 81, Diplock LJ summarised the general rule at p 89: "The contract for the carriage of goods by sea is a combined contract of bailment and transportation … Such a contract is not discharged by performance until the shipowner has actually surrendered possession (that is divested himself of all powers to control any physical dealing in the goods) to the person entitled under the terms of the contract to obtain possession of them."

The specific issue, however, is whether the contract of carriage is discharged if the goods are delivered to a person other than the person entitled under the bill of lading. In Glynn Mills v The East & West India Dock Co (1882) 7 App Cas 600, Willes J said in the Court of Common pleas:

"I think the bill of lading remains in force at least so long as complete delivery of possession of the goods has not been made to some person having a right to claim under it. I believe that will be found not only to be the law but also to be in accordance with the convenience and practice of carriers and merchants."

In the House of Lords, Lord Hatherly LC agreeing with this went on to state:

"When they have arrived at the dock, until they are delivered to some person who has the right to hold them, the bill of lading remains the only symbol that can be dealt with by way of assignment, or mortgage or otherwise … Until that time bills of lading are effective representations of the ownership of the goods, and their force does not become extinguished until possession, or what is equivalent in law to possession, has been taken on the part of the person having the right to demand it."

In London Joint Stock Bank v British Amsterdam Maritime Agency (1910) 16 Com Cas 102, Channell J observed that the question as to whether the bill of Lading was discharged depended upon whether the person who took delivery was entitled to delivery.

Although Diplock LJ left the question open in Barclays Bank v Customs and Excise, in The Delfini [1988] 2 Lloyd's Rep 599, the correctness of the observations of Channell J was accepted by the parties. In that case, it was contended that a bill of lading for 24,540 mt of oil remained in force because 275.79 mt had been short delivered; the bill of lading would only be discharged upon delivery of the full cargo. Phillips J rejected that argument; after analysing the cases to which I have referred, he added at p 608: "So long as the contract is not discharged, the bill of lading in my view, remains a document of title by endorsement and delivery of which the rights of property in the goods can be transferred … The discharge of the contract referred to by Diplock J occurs, in my view, when the primary obligations of the contract of carriage come to an end, notwithstanding that the carrier may have incurred secondary obligations as a consequence of the breach of those primary obligations. In this case, once the Delfini had arrived at [the discharge port], discharged the vast majority of the cargo loaded … and sailed away, the contract of carriage was discharged by performance. Thereafter any remedy against the Defendants lay in a claim for damages for breach." In the Court of Appeal [1990] 1 Lloyd's Rep 252, the court did not find it necessary to deal with the issue as to whether the bills of lading were discharged.

In the Future Express [1992] 2 Lloyd's Rep 79, the cargo was delivered against an indemnity to a person who did not have a right to delivery under the bill of lading; one of the many issues that arose was whether the bill of lading was spent. Judge Diamond QC held, following the passage from the judgment of Willes J, that the bill of lading had not become spent, as the goods had not been delivered to a person who had a right to demand delivery or was entitled to them. He went on to observe that it was a difficult question as to whether the bill of lading was spent as a document of title, if the cargo was delivered against an indemnity to a person authorised to receive delivery; he said:

"To hold that a bill of lading becomes spent when goods are delivered against an indemnity would greatly detract from the value of bills of lading as documents of title to goods, would diminish their value to bankers and other persons who have to rely upon them for security and would facilitate fraud."

He held that it was not necessary to decide the question, in view of the fact that the bill was not in any event spent as delivery had not been made to the person entitled. In the Court of Appeal [1993] 2 Lloyd's Rep 542, the decision was affirmed on grounds which made it unnecessary for the Court of Appeal to decide the issue on whether the bill of lading was spent.

As Gold Crown had no right to take delivery, it is my view that the bills of lading were not spent when the goods were delivered to them. It is clear on the basis of the long accepted dictum of Willes J that a bill of lading remains in force even if the goods are misdelivered to a person not entitled to them. The reason is clear. At or after the time of misdelivery to a person not entitled, the bill of lading may be being negotiated between banks on the basis that it is still a valid document of title. In short haul bulk trades, it is not uncommon that the cargo arrives at the port of destination whilst the documents are still being negotiated (see for example the practice in the European oil trade described by Staughton J in The Sagona [1984] 1 Lloyd's Rep 194 at 200). Until the goods are delivered to the person actually entitled, the bill of lading must remain the document of title to the goods. Although there may be a debate as to whether a bill is or is not spent when the goods are delivered against an indemnity to a person entitled to them (cf Carver on Bills of Lading at para 6-009), there can be no doubt that they are not spent when the goods are delivered to a person not entitled.

But even if the bill of lading is not in these circumstances spent and thus remains the document of title to the goods, can it be said that there is still a right to possess as against the carrier within the meaning of the 1992 Act, when the carrier no longer has the goods? The Claimants contended that there was no right to possess, as there could not be a right to posses that which the carrier did not have; there only existed a secondary right to damages. I do not agree. It seems to me clear from the 1992 Act that the reference to the right to possess is a reference to one of the primary rights emanating from the bill of lading's function as a document of title. Even if it were not clear from the wording of the 1992 Act, the explanatory notes to s 2(2) and s 5(2) make it clear that the references are to circumstances where the bill of lading has ceased to be a transferable document of title; the note also refers to paras 2.43-2.44 of the Law Commissions Report which also makes this clear.

I therefore conclude that the s 2(2) was not applicable, as the bills of lading still gave a right to possession of the goods as against the carrier. If, contrary to that view, I had concluded that s 2(2) was applicable, then I would have been satisfied that there were arrangements in force from the outset of the transaction under which the Chilean banks would return the documents to the Claimants in the event that they were not taken up by Gold Crown. This seems to me to have been implicit in the way in which the Chilean banks were retained in this case to collect payment from Gold Crown.

(iv) Did the Claimants have rights of suit in bailment?

The Claimants contended that rights of suit in bailment subsisted, even if they had no rights of suit under the bill of lading contract because of the provisions of the 1992 Act. As bailors they were entitled to sue Maersk and P&O in conversion.

The principal question to which the submission gave rise was whether the Claimants retained an immediate right as against Maersk and P&O as carriers to possess the goods. It was common ground that the Claimants could only claim in bailment, if they were at all times entitled to immediate possession of the goods.

Maersk and P&O contended that as the Chilean banks became the lawful holders of the bills under the provisions of the 1992 Act, they became the parties entitled to immediate possession. The Claimants could not therefore be entitled to immediate possession.

The Claimants' answer to this short contention was as follows: A bailment arose on shipment between the Claimants as shippers and the carriers (Maersk and P&O). At common law the transfer of a bill of lading to another did not transfer constructive possession unless that was the intention of the parties; they relied on the judgment of Lloyd LJ in the Future Express in the Court of Appeal [1993] 2 Lloyd's Rep 542 at p 547. There had been no such intention, as the Claimants intended to retain control over the goods. There was also no attornment as there was no intention to transfer title to the goods; the Claimants relied on the judgment of Judge Diamond QC in The Federal Express [1992] 2 Lloyd's Rep 79 at 95 and a passage in the speech of Lord Brandon of Oakbrook in The Aliakmon[1986] AC 785, [1986] 2 Lloyd's Rep 1 at 10 of the latter report. The 1992 Act did not affect that position; the Act only transferred rights in contract and not in bailment. Furthermore the only rights of suit transferred in contract were "rights of suit" and not primary rights such as the right to possess. As between the Chilean Banks and the Claimants, it was the Claimants as the owners of the goods and the persons entitled to them who were entitled to immediate possession of the goods; Maersk and P&O would have been bound to deliver to the Claimants as the true owners, if the Claimants had sought delivery. The Chilean banks had at most a contractual right to possession under the bills of lading. A mere contractual right to possession was not sufficient to found a right to sue in conversion: Jarvis v Williams[1955] 1 All ER 108, [1955] 1 WLR 71; International Factors v Rodriguez[1979] QB 351, [1979] 1 All ER 17 at 357 of the former report. If, contrary to their submissions, the Chilean banks had a right to immediate possession, they had a right to do so only as agents of the Claimants. It is necessary to examine each stage of this argument, beginning with the position at common law.

At common law, the right to possession under the bailment created on the issue of the bill of lading was, by mercantile custom, capable of transfer by endorsement of the bill of lading; the indorsement and delivery of the bill of lading were capable of transferring the endorser's right to possession of the goods to the endorsee. What effect that had on rights of property depended on the intention of the parties. A special or general property in goods was only passed if that was the intention; as Lord Bramwell said in Sewell v Burdick(1884) 10 App Cas 74 at 105: "the property does not pass by the indorsement, but by the contract in pursuance of which the indorsement is made." For example, if the bill was endorsed to an agent to enable him to sell the goods, no property would pass to the agent: see Scrutton (20th edition): Article 104(3) and the old cases of Waring v Cox (1808) 1 Camp 369 and Patten v Thompson (1816) 5 M&S 350 (which explains this partly on the grounds that no consideration or value was given for the transfer). The position was summarised by Lloyd LJ in The Future Express in accepting the correctness of counsel's submission that: "… just as the transfer of the bill of lading only operates to transfer the general property in the goods if that is the intention of the parties, so it only operates to transfer the special property when the transferor so intends."

Contractual rights were not transferred by mercantile custom and so the transferee of the bill of lading could not sue under the contract of carriage contained in the bill of lading; the purpose of the Bills of Lading Act 1855 was to remedy this in situations where the common law had been unable to provide a remedy – see the analysis of Lord Hobhouse of Woodborough in The Berge Sisar[2001] UKHL 17, [2001] 2 All ER 193, [2001] 2 WLR 1118 at paras 18 to 21. Under the law prior to the 1855 Act, the rights and obligations in contract could become separated from the right of the endorsee to the possession, and to demand delivery, of the goods: (see para 19 of his speech). The 1855 Act, however, only transferred the rights under the contract contained in the bill of lading when the property in the goods passed upon or by reason of the consignment or endorsement; this gave rise to difficulties where the property did not pass in such circumstances.

The intention and effect of the 1992 Act was to sever the link between the transfer of rights under the contract of carriage and the passing of property which the Law Commission considered had caused the difficulties. The effect of the 1992 Act was, however, only on the contract of carriage. This was made clear by Lord Hobhouse of Woodborough in The Berge Sisar. After referring to the Report of the Law Commission, he stated at p1134:

"But it must be observed that all these statements in the report, like the terminology used in the Act are expressed in terms which refer explicitly to 'the contract of carriage' and not to the right of the holder of the endorsed bill of lading to possession of the goods as against the bailee. It is thus categorising the delivery up of the goods in this context as the performance of a contractual obligation and not a bailment obligation. This is not objectionable since where there is a contract of carriage, the contract certainly includes a contractual obligation to deliver the goods… .the bailment is a contractual bailment. The relationship of the original parties to the contract of carriage is a contractually mutual relationship, each having contractual rights against the other. The important point which is demonstrated by this part of the report, and carried through into the Act is that the contractual rights, not the proprietary rights (be they special or general), that are to be relevant. The relevant consideration is the mutuality of the contractual relationship transferred to the endorsee and the reciprocal contractual rights and obligations that arise from that relationship."

Thus rights are acquired under the 1992 Act irrespective of the contractual provisions as to the passing of property between the shipper and the person who becomes the holder.

The rights transferred to the lawful holder under the 1992 Act are the "rights of suit"; this phrase was taken from the 1855 Act. Although "rights of suit" have been described as rights of "suing upon the contract" [as in The Freedom (1871) LR 3 PC 594 at 599], the phrase was not used to distinguish "rights of suit" from "rights under the contract". It is clear, in my view, that the phrase refers not merely to the right to sue, but the rights under the contract. These include the contractual right as against the carrier to demand delivery against presentation of the bill of lading and hence the right to possess. Not only is the language of the 1992 Act clear, but it is also clear from the Law Commission Report and in particular paras 2.34 and 3.13-3.21 that it was intended that "rights of suit" include the right to demand delivery. It would make no sense to the scheme of the 1992 Act if the contractual right to demand delivery from the carrier was excluded from the rights transferred.

The 1992 Act does not in terms affect rights in bailment: see the Report of the Law Commission and the speech of Lord Hobhouse to which I have referred. But the question arises as to whether there are rights in bailment to immediate possession independent of the contract contained in the bill of lading. Rights in bailment subsist in many cases independent of a contract, as the obligations between bailor and bailee arise out of the bailment and are not dependent on there being a contract. I accept that the analysis of Professor Palmer in Bailment can apply in such cases and the duties of the bailor can be seen as arising out of the voluntary assumption of possession of another's goods.

However, the rights as between bailor and bailee are often governed by a contract; where there is a contract, the contract may modify or define the obligations in bailment. In the present case, the right to possess the goods entrusted to the carrier was governed by the contract contained in the bill of lading; it was not independent of it. As between the carriers (P&O and Maersk) and the Claimants as shippers, there was no agreement as to the terms of the bailment other than the terms set out in the bill of lading. Under the terms of the contract contained in the bill of lading, the goods were to be delivered against presentation of the bill of lading (as I subsequently discuss at paras 120 to 129 where I accept the submissions of the Claimants on that issue). There was no separate agreement with the Claimants as shippers that the rights of the consignees or holders of the bill of lading should be other than those set out in the bill of lading. When these contractual rights were transferred by s 2(1) of the 1992 Act to the Chilean Banks, the Claimants lost their contractual right to immediate possession under s 2(5) of the Act for the reasons set out. As between themselves and the carriers (Maersk and P&O) their rights in bailment and their rights under the contract were the same; there were no separate rights. It was only as between the Claimants and the Chilean banks that the rights were different, but the position under the arrangements between the Chilean banks and the Claimants did not affect the contractual rights under the bills of lading between the carriers and the Chilean banks.

The lawful holder of a bill of lading clearly cannot acquire under the 1992 Act rights which the transferor did not have (see the discussion of Finlay v The Liverpool and Great Western Steamship Co (1870) 23 LT 251 at para 5-027 of Carver on Bills of Lading and at p 578 of "The Bill of Lading as a Document of Title" at Ch 22 of Palmer & McKendrick: Interests in Goods). Therefore as between the carrier and the lawful holder of the bill of lading, the right of the lawful holder to immediate possession of the goods can be defeated where the transferor to him did not have the right to transfer the bill. However, if the shipper was the true owner of the goods and had the right to immediate possession under the bill of lading, then by operation of the 1992 Act that contractual right to immediate possession is transferred, even if the shipper remained as between the shipper and the transferee the party entitled to delivery. The rights under the bill of lading operate independently of the arrangements under the banking relationships.

The right so transferred is not a "mere contractual" right to possession of the goods of the kind discussed in Jarvis v Williams and International Factors v Rodriguez. The contractual rights that are transferred by transfer of the bill of lading include the obligation to delivery under the bailment. Though the rights under the contract and possessory rights can be separated, they are not separated in these circumstances for the reasons I have given.

Thus I have reached the view that there were no separate rights in bailment that were retained by the Claimants. But the question remains as to whether the Chilean banks acquired the rights as agents for the Claimants? It seems clear that if an agent has a right to possession for an undisclosed principal that right can in many circumstances be exercised by the principal: see the judgment of Hope JA in Maynegrain Pty Ltd v Compafina Bank [1982] 2 NSWLR 141. However in this case the rights so obtained were obtained by the Chilean banks as consignees under the 1992 Act and for the reasons given in para 31, they could not have been acquired by them in their capacity as agents.

Conclusion on title to sue

I have therefore come to the view that the Claimants can maintain a claim on one of the grounds they have advanced on all the bills of lading and also a claim under Maersk bill No 4 on a further ground.

Issue 2: The obligation to deliver

The bills of lading were governed by an express choice of English law. Under art 10 of the Rome Convention, English law therefore applied to the performance of the contract, though by art 10(2) "in relation to the manner of performance and the steps to be taken in the event of defective performance, regard is to be had to the law of the country where performance is to take place."

The Claimants contended that the obligation to deliver was governed entirely by English law and that Maersk and P&O were in breach by delivering without presentation of the bill of lading. Maersk and P&O denied that they were in breach as a matter of English law, but also contended that under the law of Chile which was material to the performance of that obligation they were plainly not in breach. Three questions therefore arose:

i) Was the law of Chile relevant to the delivery obligation?

ii) If it was, what were its provisions and were the carriers discharged from responsibility under that law?

iii) What were the consequences under the terms of the bills of lading which were governed by English law ?

The effect of art 10 of the Rome Convention is to maintain a distinction between the substance of the obligation which is governed by the proper law (in this case English law) and the mode (or manner and method) of performance which is governed by the law of the place of performance – Chile. Before considering this distinction, it is necessary first to set out my findings in relation to the law of Chile.The provisions of the law of Chile relating to delivery: the Customs laws [65] Maersk and P&O accepted that there was no provision in the Commercial Code of Chile that expressly relieved a carrier of any obligation to deliver goods otherwise than against presentation of an original bill of lading. However, they contended that it was the inevitable result of Chilean customs law and procedure that they were obliged to deliver the goods without presentation to them of an original bill of lading. They submitted that under the Customs law of Chile a carrier was obliged to deliver goods on which duty had not been paid to the Customs Authority; the carrier lost all control over the goods and the Customs determined who had the right to take delivery of the cargo.

Furthermore under the Hamburg Rules this constituted good delivery under the bill of lading.

The general provisions of the Customs laws and the areas of dispute.

The general provisions of the Customs laws and procedures were not in dispute and must briefly be described. The provisions of Chilean Customs law are primarily contained in the Customs Ordinance; the version before the court was one promulgated in 1998 which came into force on 17 January 1999; it was common ground that there was no material distinction with the version which was in force in 1998 when some of the goods arrived in Chile.

The procedure for dealing with goods imported into Chile depended upon whether goods had been cleared through Customs in advance (retiro directo) or not (retiro indirecto). The goods shipped by the Claimants had not been cleared through Customs in advance and therefore it is necessary only to consider the law and procedure applicable to such goods (retiro indirecto).

The normal procedure was a two stage one. First the cargo manifest had to be submitted and "presented" to Customs by the carrier (arts 35 and 37 of the Customs Ordinance). Second, the carrier was also obliged to deliver the goods to a warehouse subject to the jurisdiction of the Customs – the Customs primary zone (arts 16, 34, 44 and 46). Warehouse facilities were operated by the state corporation, Empressa Porturia de Chile (Emporchi) or private companies licensed by Customs to operate Customs warehouses. Until December 1997, Emporchi operated the ports in Chile as a single state corporation. It was then divided into ten separate companies including Empressa Porturia de Chile de San Antonio (Emporchi de San Antonio). Article 9 of the law which effected this change (Law 19542 of 19 December 1997) permitted the new entities to enter into contracts with others which were to be governed by private law. Customs warehouses were either within the limits of the port or could be outside them; wherever they were, they were within the jurisdiction of the Customs and within the Customs primary zone; their operation was governed by the Customs Ordinance (in particular arts 44, 45, 56, 57 and 60).

Regulations provided that cargo had to be delivered to the warehouse within 24 hours of unloading (art 2.3 of the Customs Compendium and art 9 of Presidential Decree 298 of 24 March 1999).

In this particular case the warehousing of the goods, as summarised in para 6 was: The goods carried by Maersk were placed in a warehouse operated by Seaport SA, a private operator licensed by Customs; on 19 January 1999 (before 2 out of the 7 consignments carried were released to Gold Crown), Maersk entered into a service agreement with Seaport; this provided by cl 6 for Seaport to take custody of cargo until the consignee withdrew the cargo. Under App 1 to this agreement entitled "Reception and Storage of Import Cargo", Seaport agreed to:

"deliver the cargo to the consignee or its representative after the consignee has completed all Customs clearing procedures involved." The goods carried by P&O were placed by the ship's agents, Agencias Universales SA, in a warehouse operated by Emporchi de San Antonio.

Upon receipt of the goods, the operator of the warehouse issued a "Documento Portuario Unico" (DPU) which operated for the carrier or his agent as a receipt of the goods received into the warehouse; it recorded matters such as the time and date of receipt and the condition of the goods.

The goods then had to remain "under jurisdiction [control] in the authorised premises" or "in the Customs depots" until they were withdrawn (arts 45 and 56 of the Customs Ordinance). Goods in practice remained in the warehouses until Customs clearance was obtained and the warehouse provider was paid for its services. This was done by the consignee's Customs agent.

A Customs agent (who acted for the consignee) was licensed by the National Director for Customs; regulations govern what he could do. The usual practice was for the consignee to endorse the bill of lading to the customs agent (see art 222); this constituted his authority. The Customs agent also had a duty to verify to the Customs that his principal was entitled to the goods. The Customs agent was a ministro de fe – an "attesting witness" or "attesting judge"; thus he could certify photocopies of documents used in Customs procedures. Other duties were imposed on him such as keeping the documents for 5 years (art 77).

The normal practice was for the Customs agent to present to the warehouse operator the appropriate documentation – a Customs Destination Document legalised by the Customs, normally a Import Declaration. The Compendium of Customs Regulations provided that the Import Declaration was to be drawn up on the basis of various documents, including the original bill of lading (art 5.1). The Import Declaration duly legalised by the Customs and the payment voucher in respect of Customs duty were presented to the warehouse operator prior to release of the goods.

There were some differences in procedure in the case of containers. Because of the increase in container traffic, administrative functions relating to Customs were transferred to persons known as "Container Operators" in 1995 under Regulation made under Customs Resolution No 2808 of 12 April 1995. It was very common for the agent of the carrier to act as a Container Operator. Container Operators were authorised to issue a form called a TATC (Title for the Temporary Admission of Containers). The form enabled the container, once the form was legalised by Customs and had been presented to the warehouse operator, to leave the Customs primary zone on a temporary basis. Strictly the TATC applied only to the container.

In this particular case, Maersk's agent, AJ Broom, were also licensed Container Operators and by an agreement with Maersk made in 1994 were remunerated for issuing TATC forms. In the case of P&O, its contract for the period 1 January 1997 to 31 December 1999 with its agents in Chile, Sudamericanan Agencias Aereas Y Maritimas SA (SAAM) provided that SAAM, as a licensed Container Operator, should provide a service in respect of container discharge and should issue TATC forms; SAAM was to be responsible for "whole containers TATC processes which include all diligences related with matter according to Customs Services rules." SAAM issued the TATC form for the goods carried by P&O on 15 March 1999. Neither Container Operator asked for an original bill of lading before allowing the goods to be taken by Gold Crown's agent.

The main dispute between the experts related to the questions as to (a) whether receipt into the Customs warehouse constituted delivery by the carrier to Customs and the end of the carrier's responsibility, (b) whether the warehouse had to accept the statement of the Customs agent that a copy bill of lading was sufficient and (c) whether the carrier could ask the warehouse to demand an original bill of lading or ensure that under the TATC procedure the Container Operator asked for presentation of an original bill of lading.

It was, in summary, the evidence of Mr Sahurie: The carrier was not obliged to deliver the cargo to Customs; the duty to "present" was the duty to place the goods under the jurisdiction of the customs authorities so that they could collect the duty. Goods were not received by the Customs into their possession; they merely came within their jurisdiction. It was possible for the carrier to enter into contracts with warehouses on terms which enabled the carrier to insist on the presentation of original bills of lading. Even if there was no such contract, nothing prevented the carrier instructing the warehouse to withhold delivery of the goods unless an original bill of lading was presented. There was nothing that prevented the warehouse checking the authority of the Customs agent to withdraw the goods. In the case of containers, it was a matter for the carrier's agent as Container Operator to refuse to issue the TATC without presentation of the original bill of lading; in his experience the refusal to issue the TATC was used to ensure freight was collected. Although technically the TATC might only apply to the container itself, the goods within the container and the container were an indivisible unit for the purposes of withdrawing the goods from the primary zone. Whilst it was rare in Chile for the Customs agent to be asked for the original bill of lading (as the warehouse normally relied on the Customs Destination Document), any interested party could require presentation of the bill of lading.

Mr Tomasello's evidence, in summary, was that: there was nothing that obliged a carrier to deliver at all if he did not want to and wished to keep the cargo aboard the vessel, though he might be in breach of his contract of carriage. If the carrier did discharge the cargo, he had to "present" the cargo directly to the Customs at the warehouse without presentation of a bill of lading; once he had done that his responsibility was at an end and he had lost control over and possession of the cargo. His action in presenting was a delivery to the Customs; he relied particularly on art 16 of the Customs Ordinance. Thereafter it was the responsibility of Customs to determine who had the right to collect the cargo. It was accepted by Maersk and P&O that the warehouse operator was not acting as agent of the consignee and delivery to the warehouse was not delivery to the consignee. I did not understand Mr Tomasello's evidence to be to the contrary. The carrier had no dealings with the Customs agent of the consignee, as it was the responsibility of the Customs agent to obtain delivery from the warehouse operator. He relied heavily on a decision of the Court of Appeal of Valparaiso dated 7 December 1972 in which the court stated:

"In Chile, there is no direct or immediate relationship between [the ocean carrier] and the consignee of the cargo, but there is an intermediary who receives the goods and keeps them on deposit until corresponding customs formalities and requirements are fulfilled. This intermediary is Emporchi to whom the law has entrusted the reception of the goods that are in the possession of the [ocean carrier] who deposits them in their warehouses … until the entire customs procedure of revision and cataloguing of the goods, determination of their origin and their import, … is fulfilled. [Emporchi] are a corporate body of public law which has been created precisely for the purpose of receiving the goods in possession [of the ocean carrier] and subsequently delivering them to the consignee."

Although since that decision Emporchi had been broken into 10 separate companies and private warehouses also operated, all of these new companies fulfilled precisely the same functions as Emporchi had done. In 1981 the rule that required the Customs agent to obtain the approval of the vessel's agents for the cargo to be withdrawn from the warehouse had been abolished.

When the original bill of lading was not available to the Customs agent when he completed the Customs declaration, a copy could take its place if that was authorised by the carrier and the copy annotated to the effect that it replaced the original for all legal purposes. The Customs agent was then obliged to keep the copy until the original bill of lading was provided. It was the responsibility of the Customs Service to verify the entitlement of the consignee to the cargo, but they relied heavily on the status of the customs agent as an "attesting judge" or "attesting witness". Once the Import Declaration was legalised by the Customs, the Customs warehouse operator was not entitled to question the right of the Customs agent to collect the goods on behalf of the consignee. The warehouse operator had no right to demand to see the original bill of lading. The entitlement of the Customs agent to obtain the cargo could only be challenged by the Customs.

It was not permissible for the operator of a Customs warehouse to enter into a contract incompatible with its status in performing its public duty; in particular, a contractual obligation could not entitle the warehouse operator to question the authority of the Customs agent to withdraw the goods. The TATC was issued by the Container Operator in his capacity as Container Operator and not as agent for the carrier. As such he was performing a public function and could not demand sight of an original bill of lading as a condition of issuing a TATC.

(a) The effect of delivery to the Customs warehouse

The first question to consider is the effect under Chilean Customs law of the requirement that the goods be delivered to the Customs warehouse. I have come to the clear view that, under the law of Chile, delivery by a carrier to the Customs warehouse was not a delivery to Customs and was not a delivery of the goods in the sense that this relinquished the carrier's control over them.

In considering the effect and meaning of the Customs Ordinance, it is necessary as a matter of the law of Chile to consider the purpose of that Ordinance as set out in art 1.2. That Article provided that the role of the Customs was to watch over and supervise the passage of merchandise through the coastlines and frontiers of Chile for purposes of collecting Customs duty and for producing statistics.

In my view Mr Sahurie was right in the distinction he drew under the Ordinance construed in the light of art 1.2 between on the one hand delivery to the Customs of Chile and on the other hand delivery to a Customs warehouse licensed by Customs and operated either by Emporchi or by a private operator. In my view he was correct in his opinion that goods never came into the physical possession of the Customs; they only came under its jurisdiction. The goods were to be physically delivered to and received by the Customs warehouse operator; the Customs warehouse operator then became responsible for them if they were damaged or lost. Two key articles were arts 16 and 17:

国际经济法案例选编（双语）

"Article 16 The goods which must enter or leave through the ports of other authorised places, shall be delivered to Customs at the point of its primary zone indicated by its administrator or Head, at the request of the consignee without further formality. This article has to be understood as covering the two stage process that customs clearance involves – first the presentation of the manifest and the subsequent delivery to the Customs warehouse operator. The same is the case in Article 46 which uses similar words. Article 17 While within the primary zone of jurisdiction and without prejudice to the attributions of the competent authorities, all vehicles, their vehicles, their passengers and their cargoes, shall be submitted to the authority of the respective Customs, but the latter shall only respond [have responsibility for damage to] for the goods after having been checked and finally received by them."

I accept the evidence of Mr Sahurie that art 17 means that the goods come under the power or jurisdiction of the Customs; but, as the Customs never take possession of the goods, they did not become responsible for the goods. It was the warehouse operator that was responsible. Mr Sahurie's evidence (which I accept) was that many years ago the Customs authorities actually received the goods themselves; the system had then changed to a mixed system. From the 1980s or 1990s, the goods were received by Customs warehouses; in so doing the Customs warehouses were not carrying out a delegated function of the state of Chile. The system had changed. It was entities such as Emporchi against whom claims were made, as they were in physical possession of the goods. There is a clear distinction drawn between the warehouses being within and subject to the jurisdiction of Customs and the warehouses being treated as if they were part of the Customs. In performing their functions, the warehouse operators were not carrying out any delegated function of the state save in relation to obligations owed to Customs such as the collection of taxes.

I also accept the evidence of Mr Sahurie that the decision of the Valparaiso Court of Appeal of 7 September 1972 (to which I referred in summarising the evidence of Mr Tomasello at para 81) was not determinative of the position in Chile in 1998/9. Mr Sahurie accepted in oral evidence that this decision represented the law of Chile at the time it was given; Emporchi then was the state monopoly which arranged the warehousing of all imports into Chile. However, the position had changed in many respects, including the incorporation of the Hamburg Rules, Chile's adherence to the UN Convention on the sale of goods and changes in Emporchi and to practice. The position was very different to what had been the case in 1972. Emporchi has been broken into 10 companies and there were also the private warehouse operators. Carriers were in a position to enter into contracts with them in relation to delivery to the consignee, as I discuss below at para 98.

There are two further factors which support this view. First, in the event of misdelivery, if the carrier's responsibility had terminated on delivery to the Customs, the only claim would be that of an unsecured claim against the Customs agent. That can hardly have been intended. In view of the provisions of art 97, it seems unlikely that a claim against the Customs would be successful. Mr Tomasello initially stated that a claim could not be made against the Customs agent because he was part of the state, but later suggested that he could be sued and the bond the Customs agent provided would amount to security. I accept that there might be a claim against the Customs agent, but the bond would not respond under the terms of art 230. Second, as bills of lading continue to play an essential role in the financing of international trade by sea, I have no doubt that a Chilean Court would prefer a construction of the Customs Ordinance which protected the security of banks; that could only be achieved, given the changes that had occurred, by holding that delivery to the Customs warehouse did not mean that the responsibility of the carrier was at an end.

(b) The effect of the demand of the Customs agent

The second question is whether the operator of the Customs warehouse had to accept the entitlement of the Customs agent to obtain the delivery of the goods and could not require the presentation of an original bill of lading.

Mr Tomasello relied on arts 56 and 104 of the Customs Ordinance. However, all that art 56 provided was that the goods had to remain in the Customs warehouse until they were withdrawn for import or export or to be sent to another Customs destination; it did not deal with the question as to the terms upon which goods were to be withdrawn. Article 104 provided: "The declaration duly processed and the payment voucher as may be the case shall entitle the interested party to withdraw goods from the Customs depot."

This meant no more than, as far as Customs were concerned that, when Customs duty was paid, goods could be withdrawn from the Customs warehouse and from the jurisdiction of Customs. It obliged the warehouse operator, so far as Customs were concerned, to release the goods to an interested party which presented the appropriate documentation to show the goods had been cleared through Customs. It had no other consequence. I accept the evidence of Mr Sahurie to this effect; he was correct in my view in stating that although normally a warehouse operator would accept the legalised Import Declaration as sufficient, trusting that the Customs agent had done his work properly, and not ask to see the original bill of lading, he was entitled to ask for it to satisfy himself that the goods were, after Customs clearance, being delivered to the person entitled under the bill of lading.

Nor does art 220 assist Maersk and P&O This Article provides, in part:

"The Customs agent is a professional assistant or auxiliary to the Customs public function and his license enables him before Customs to render services to third parties as a representative when obtaining clearance of the goods. These Customs agent shall have the capacity as Ministros de fe in so far that Customs may consider as a true fact that the data requested in the declarations contained in the relevant dispatch documents, including the liquidation of Customs duties are in accordance with the antecedents which legally must serve as a basis. The above is without prejudice to the checking which may be undertaken by Customs public officials in any moment in order to verify that the statement/certificate is correct. …"

There was a dispute as to the correct translation of Ministros de fe; Mr Sahurie considered that it meant qualified attesting witness, Mr Tomasello that it meant "attesting judge". It may not matter which was correct; it is clear that the function was one of certifying the fact that a copy was a true copy or that a fact stated was true. I accept Mr Sahurie's evidence that the certification of a document by the customs agent in his capacity of "Ministero de Fe" only entitled him to certify as true copies, the documents he had in his file.

The creation of and terms of the mandate of the Customs agent was governed by art 222; its opening phrase was: "The act by means of which the owner, consignor or consignee entrusts the clearance of his goods to a Customs agent who accepts this job is a mandate ruled by the provisions of this Ordinance … and, alternatively by the provisions of the Civil Code."

Reading these Articles together and taking account of art 1.2, it is clear that the mandate of the Customs agent under the Ordinance was for the purpose of clearing the goods through Customs; Mr Tomasello accepted that the passage from art 220 which I have quoted referred to "clearance" and not "delivery". The Customs agent's function under that Ordinance (in attesting that the copies were true and the truth of which could not then be challenged) was a function in that capacity. For Customs purposes he authenticated copies and for that purpose and third parties were not entitled to question for Customs purposes what he stated, but that did not mean that they were authenticated for other purposes. It did not mean that they had to be accepted for other purposes. I accept the evidence of Mr Sahurie to that effect. Furthermore Mr Tomasello accepted that although Customs had to accept the truth of what was stated in the declaration, there was only a presumption to that effect in respect of others. Maersk and P&O relied upon a letter written by the Inspection sub-Directorate of the National Customs Office to a judge of the Criminal Court in Valparaiso about the events in this case; the letter concluded that the Customs agent had been guilty of a serious breach of the Customs Ordinance and of the trust placed in him. Part of the letter stated:

"At the time when the goods are withdrawn from deposit premises, presentation of the relevant bill of lading is not required. The Customs agent signing the Customs delivery statements must have prepared it in accordance with … the original bill of lading … It is necessary to notify you that the Service only inspects delivery statements selectively…"

This letter did not detract at all from Mr Sahurie's evidence; it was looking at the issue from the perspective of Customs and did not deal with the distinction drawn by Mr Sahurie.

It was common ground that the Customs agent had to retain all three original bills of lading; he could not surrender one to the carrier for the carrier to keep. However I accept the evidence of Mr Sahurie that this did not mean that the original bill of lading did not have to be produced and shown before the goods were released.

Nor do I consider that legal report 009 of 26 February 1986 assists. In that report the Head of the Customs Legal Department advised that the Customs had no right to retain goods until security was provided for contributions in general average; their powers were restricted to the collection of duties as set out in art 1 of the Customs Ordinance; they were not entitled to use their powers for other purposes by intervening in a private dispute. This was simply, as Mr Sahurie stated, a report concerned with the powers of Customs and had no bearing on the entitlement to demand presentation of an original bill of lading. Furthermore, I accept the evidence of Mr Sahurie that the law of Chile has changed. At the time of the report, a carrier had to go to court to obtain an order entitling him to retain the goods; by express provision under art 1114 of the Code of Commerce, the carrier has since 1988 been entitled to retain the goods until general average is paid or secured.

Under the law of Chile, I accept the evidence of Mr Sahurie that there was nothing that precludes the warehouse operator from requesting sight of an original bill of lading before the goods were released. Indeed the evidence of Mr Parra, P&O's cargo claims representative for Latin America based in Santiago Chile, was to the effect that, although the carrier's agents acted on the basis of the Customs agent's statements, they could ask for the original bill of lading; the Customs agent would in effect be bound to produce it as otherwise he would be denounced to Customs who would then check his file to see if it contained the original.

There is one further matter. After the conclusion of the evidence and the hearing, I allowed the parties further time to make and respond in writing to submissions of law, given the number of legal issues that had arisen and the wish of the court and the parties not to prolong the oral hearing. During the course of those responses, P&O sought to adduce further evidence; although initially they sought to put several further documents before the court, they confined their final application to a letter dated 5 October 2001 from Emporchi Valparaiso to P&O. The last paragraph of the letter stated: "The withdrawal of goods from the warehouse limits is authorised by our Company in its capacity as a Warehouse only upon presentation of the legalised entry declaration (DI) and upon payment of duties (where appropriate). Consequently, it is not for us under any circumstances to require the original bill of lading as a requirement for delivery of the cargo, as this is not a function of this Company, given that this is a power only given to the National Customs Directorate."

I am prepared to admit this document as evidence from Emporchi Valparaiso, but its weight must be affected by the fact that it was not available to be put to Mr Sahurie at trial, that it was produced after a meeting between P&O and Emporchi, Valparaiso in circumstances which are not clear and that it deals essentially with a legal issue. The letter did not address the distinction which Mr Sahurie drew between the duties of a warehouse operator in respect of Customs and other duties that he could assume under contract with the shipowner. Although the letter stated that Emporchi Valparaiso could not require the original bill of lading in "any circumstances", it addressed only their relationship with Customs in the letter and not their ability to assume by contract the kind of duty about which Mr Sahurie gave evidence. I therefore found it of little assistance. (c) Could the owner contract with the warehouse operator on terms requiring him to release only on presentation of the original bill of lading and use the TATC procedure for the same purpose?

It was common ground that a carrier could enter into a contract with a Customs warehouse operator or container operator provided that it was not inconsistent with their public duties. This had been so for the new Emporchi companies since the 1997 law to which I referred at para 71.

Article 1 of Resolution No 05274 of 13 November 1987 promulgated by the Customs stated that goods within the confines of Customs areas managed by private enterprises had to be carried out in accordance with the rules promulgated. However, there was nothing express in the Rules or elsewhere that prevented the warehouse operator asking for an original bill of lading.

I have set out above my acceptance of the evidence of Mr Sahurie that under the law of Chile goods were not delivered to Customs; that there was nothing in the status of the Customs agent that obliged a Customs warehouse operator to accept his entitlement to demand the goods without presentation of an original bill of lading. I have also considered art 104 at para 88; that Article imposed a public duty on the warehouse operator. However, I accept the clear distinction drawn by Mr Sahurie between the public duties of a warehouse operator and other duties; the public duties were those that related to the discharge of his Customs function. Although the warehouse operator could not be given instructions that contradicted the public duty under art 104 entitling the Customs agent to withdraw the goods once the Customs requirements were complied with, that only applied to the duties of the warehouse operator as regards Customs. It did not affect obligations that arose under the contract of carriage and instructions could be given as regards obligations under the contract of carriage not inconsistent with that public duty. It is clear therefore that there was nothing in the law of Chile which made it inconsistent with the public duties of a Customs warehouse operator for that operator to be required by private contract between him and the carrier to demand presentation of an original bill of lading before delivering the goods after they had been cleared through Customs; I accept the evidence of Mr Sahurie there was nothing to prevent, and in particular nothing in art 104 to prevent, a carrier asking for the presentation of an original bill of lading as envisaged by art 977 of the Chilean Commercial Code, referred to at para 112 below.

In 1981 the rule that required the Customs agent to obtain the approval of the vessel's agents for the cargo to be withdrawn from the warehouse was abrogated. That, however, pertained before the changes to status of Emporchi; at that time, there was no need for the Customs agent to obtain approval as the carrier was protected by the then status of Emporchi. The change in 1981 had no bearing on this issue as the position had changed and it did not affect the contractual position between the warehouse operator and the carrier.

I am satisfied on the basis of Mr Sahurie's evidence that, although cargo imported into Chile subject to the retiro indirecto system had to be delivered into Customs warehouses, the carrier could choose the Customs warehouse to which the goods were to be delivered and contract with that warehouse operator on terms that delivery of the goods should only be delivered against presentation of a bill of lading. Furthermore a prudent carrier should do so to fulfil his obligation under the bill of lading only to deliver to the holder of the bill of lading. Mr Sahurie accepted that in 1998 and 1999 some carriers did not enter into contracts with warehouse operators on terms that required warehouse operators only to deliver against presentation of an original bill of lading, though some did. Those who had not done this, acted as they did because of the historical position of Emporchi; they wanted to avoid a grey area and the cost of assuring goods were delivered correctly. The position had changed and many carriers were instructing their agents and the warehouse operators to ensure that the person withdrawing the goods had the original bill of lading.

As I have mentioned at para 77, the procedure for containers differed; the carrier's agent would commonly act as a Container Operator under a special licence from Customs and issue the TATC form; this was the case for both Maersk and P&O Mr Sahurie was correct in my view in saying that when the carrier's agent issued TATC forms he was acting as a Container Operator; in that capacity he was performing an obligation under private law and not a public law function. He was performing a function of facilitating paperwork and his responsibility to Customs was for any Customs duty that was not paid if the container was not re-exported. I reject the evidence of Mr Tomasello to the contrary; there is nothing to support his evidence that the function in issuing the form was a public one. Mr Sahurie was correct in saying this was essentially a paper work function.

It was clear that a Container Operator could demand to see an original bill of lading before the TATC was issued. On 29 December 1987, the head of the legal department of the Customs issued report no 74 which stated that it was in order for the container operator to demand the original bill of lading before issuing the TATC; if the original was not available, then a non negotiable copy certified by the bank which was the consignee could be used. The report observed:

"… the general rule when clearing goods from customs is that the consignment be established in the original B/L or an equivalent document which complies, amongst others, with the function of entitling the consignee in respect of the goods, being generally transferable by a simple endorsement all of which justify this requirement in full." This report was confirmed by the National Director of Customs by resolution 284 of 1987. The arguments and conclusion of this report also support the evidence of Mr Sahurie in relation to the right of the warehouse operator to demand an original bill of lading.

I do not accept Mr Tomasello's evidence to the contrary; in his expert report, Mr Tomasello made a number of criticisms of report no 74, but I do not accept them. For example, I have already set out my conclusion as to why a statement of a Customs agent can be questioned; nor is there a duty to issue a TATC, only a right to do so. Furthermore, it is in my view of no significance that the ruling is not mentioned in the regulations made under Resolution 2808 of 12 April 1995; these regulations deal with matters that concern the Customs, not the obligations of the carrier to the consignee.

Mr Parra accepted that a container operator could demand to see an original bill of lading before the TATC was issued and said that container operators often asked to see such documents to ensure that the container was delivered to the person entitled. Although Mr Parra said subsequently in his evidence that there was no obligation on a Customs agent to comply with the request other than by producing a copy certified by the Customs agent himself, he was unaware of report No 74 and wrong about the ability of carriers to enter into contracts with Emporchi and Seaport. Furthermore, as I have set out at para 95, it was also Mr Parra's evidence that if the original was not produced, the Customs agent could be reported to Customs. I therefore do not accept him as an altogether reliable witness and reject the subsequent qualification that he gave to his earlier evidence that a Container Operator could and did demand sight of an original bill of lading. The practice of AJ Broom, according to the written evidence of Mr Malinarich, their operations manager, was not to ask for the original bill of lading before issuing the TATC, though in his written evidence he accepted that it had become the practice of some, though by no means all, container operators to demand sight of a bill of lading or a copy before issuing the TATC. He also stated that it was only the Customs who could ask to see the original bill of lading and it was impossible to ask to see the TATC. He was not cross examined and his evidence is inconsistent with the practice of other operators and with report no 74. I therefore attach little weight to it.

Conclusion on the Customs law

I am satisfied that: – An ocean carrier carrying goods to Chile was not obliged, as a matter of the Customs law of Chile to deliver goods to the physical possession of Customs, but only to a Customs warehouse licensed by Customs and subject to the jurisdiction of Customs. Customs did not deliver the goods. – Ocean carriers were not precluded from entering into contracts requiring the Customs warehouse operator to deliver against presentation of an original bill of lading. – Neither the carrier nor the Customs warehouse keeper nor the Container Operator had to accept the entitlement of the Customs' agent to possession of the goods without presentation of an original bill of lading.

I am therefore satisfied that Maersk and P&O were able to enter into contracts with both Customs warehouse operators and with Container Operators on terms that required them to deliver or issue a TATC only against presentation of a bill of lading. They had undertaken in the contract contained in the bill of lading that delivery should be against presentation of an original bill of lading and they should have ensured that they could discharge that obligation by an appropriate contract with Customs warehouse operators and Container Operators.

Was there a custom or usage of the ports in Chile that cargo could be delivered without presentation of a bill of lading?

It was also contended by Maersk and P&O that there was a custom at the ports in Chile to the effect that carriers delivered goods to a Customs warehouse without presentation of an original bill of lading and the warehouse then delivered without presentation. They relied on the evidence of Mr Parra and Mr Marlinarich.

I do not consider that their evidence established any such custom. I have referred at para 106 to some of their evidence and the weight of their evidence. In my view there was clearly no custom of the ports of Chile that cargoes could be delivered to Customs warehouses in discharge of the carrier's delivery obligations or could be delivered without presentation of a bill of lading. I have already referred to the evidence of Mr Sahurie, the ability of carriers to enter into agreements with Customs warehouse operators and Container Operators, the changes that have taken place in Chile and the practice of agents and container operators. I am therefore quite satisfied that there was no such custom or usage for which Maersk and P&O contended. It is not necessary therefore to consider the further submissions of the Claimants that any such custom would have been unreasonable.

The Hamburg Rules

Chile incorporated the Hamburg Rules into its Code of Commerce in 1988. Article 1.7 of the Hamburg Rules provides:

"The bill of lading is a document which evidences a contract of carriage by sea and the taking over or loading of the goods by the carrier, and by which the carrier undertakes to deliver the goods against surrender of the document. A provision in the document that the goods are to be delivered to the order of a named person, or to order, or to bearer, constitutes such an undertaking."

It was common ground that this was the basis of art 977 of the Chilean Code of Commerce: "The bill of lading is a document which establishes the existence of a contract of maritime transport and verifies that the carrier has taken charge of or has loaded the goods and has undertaken to deliver them against the presentation of that document to a determined person to his order or to the bearer."

Article 4 of the Hamburg Rules is entitled "period of responsibility"; it provides: "1. The responsibility of the carrier for the goods under this [Convention] covers the period during which the carrier is in charge of the goods at the port of loading, during the carriage and at the port of discharge." The equivalent provision of the Chilean Code of Commerce is art 982 which provides: "The liability of the carrier for the cargo comprises the period during which it is under his custody, be this ashore or during its actual transport."

Article 4 of the Hamburg Rules continues:

"2. For the purposes of para 1 of the Article, the carrier is deemed to be in charge of the goods.

…

(b) until the time he has delivered the goods:

(i) by handing over the goods to the consignee; or

…

(iii) by handing over the goods to an authority or other third party to whom, pursuant to the contract of carriage or with the law or with the usage of the particular trade applicable at the port of discharge, the goods must be handed over".

There was some dispute between the experts over the precise translation of the Spanish text in the equivalent Article of the Chilean Commercial Code (art 983) and in particular as to whether the Spanish text "the goods must be handed over" should read "may be handed over". The text is identical to the text of the Hamburg Rules in all material respects; I therefore consider it correct to use the official language version of the Article contained in the Hamburg

Rules, even though Mr Sahurie considered that the translation "may be handed over" was the preferred translation.

Article 5 of the Hamburg Rules (art 984 of the Chilean Code of Commerce) is entitled "basis of liability"; it provides that:

"1. The carrier is liable for loss resulting from loss of or damage to the goods, as well as from delay in delivery, if the occurrence took place while the goods were in his charge as defined in art 4, unless the carrier proves that he his servants or agents took all measures that could reasonably be required to avoid the occurrence or its consequences.

......

3. The person entitled to make a claim for the loss of the goods may treat the goods as lost if they have not been delivered as required by art 4 within 60 consecutive days …"

P&O and Maersk contended (supported by the evidence of Mr Tomasello) that under the Hamburg Rules, if the carrier was obliged to deliver to the Customs, that constituted due delivery under the contract. The Claimants (supported by Mr Sahurie) contended that art 4 did not stipulate what constituted good delivery, only when the responsibility for loss or damage ended, though Mr Sahurie accepted that, if the carrier was obliged to deliver to Customs, then art 4.2(b) (iii) (art 983(c) of the Chilean Code) would be satisfied for the purposes of establishing the period of custody.

For the reasons I have given I am satisfied that a carrier was not obliged to hand over the goods to Customs; he did not deliver them to Customs, but placed them with a Customs warehouse operator subject to the jurisdiction of Customs. He could enter into a contract with that operator that the goods should not be released without presentation of the bill of lading. Thus in my view the carrier could not rely on art 4.2(c) (art 983 (c) of the Chilean Code of Commerce).

If, however, I had concluded that the carrier was obliged to make a delivery to Customs, then I would have found it difficult to accept the distinction that the Claimants sought to make between the end of the carrier's period of responsibility and custody for the purposes of a claim for loss or damage of the goods and the carrier's continuing responsibility to deliver only against presentation of a bill of lading. The purpose of art 4.2 (b) (iii) was in my view accurately stated in a report of the UNCTAD secretariat entitled "The economic and commercial implications of the entry into force of the Hamburg Rules" (December 1987) at p 36:

"These provisions concern port authorities and other third parties to whom the goods must be handed over before shipment or after discharge in accordance with the laws or regulations of the loading or discharge ports. National laws or regulations frequently grant monopolies to State-owned or private warehouses or docks for handling and storage of goods, particularly in connection with Customs procedures. The policy of these provisions is that if the carrier is not free to chose such a facility, he should not be liable for damage to the goods caused by the facility. Article 4.2(b) (iii) states that he is not in charge of the goods in those circumstances."

Although it is not necessary for me to express a concluded view on this issue, it is difficult to see what proper distinction can be made on the basis of the policy of the Hamburg Rules between damage to the goods by a warehouse the carrier is forced to use to and misdelivery of the goods by the warehouse. The loss has occurred when the goods are not in the carrier's custody as a result of the action of a person which the carrier was not free to chose.

There is one further issue. If contrary to the clear view I have formed, the delivery to the Customs warehouse was delivery to the Customs, then the Claimants accepted that on the terms of the P&O bills of Lading that constituted due delivery under the contracts. This was because cl 20 (6) provided: "If the carrier is obliged to hand over the goods into the custody of a Customs, port of other authority, such hand over shall constitute due delivery to the Merchant under the bill of lading."

The obligation under English law to deliver under the bills of lading

It has been made clear in decisions of the highest authority that a carrier must under the usual terms of a bill of lading deliver the goods only against presentation of an original bill of lading; the case most commonly cited is Sze Hai Tong Bank v Rambler Cycle Co[1959] AC 576, [1959] 3 All ER 182. In The Houda [1994] 2 Lloyd's Rep 541, Leggatt LJ expressed the position in this way:

"Under a bill of lading contract a shipowner is obliged to deliver goods upon production of the original bill of lading. Delivery without production of the bill of lading constitutes a breach of contract even when made to the person entitled to possession…"

There is no need to rehearse the importance to international commerce of this obligation under a bill of lading.

Furthermore the contract of carriage generally continues and the bill of lading remains effective, as set out in paras 35 to 38 above, until the goods are delivered to the person entitled under the bill of lading.

The bills of lading contained express terms which Maersk and P&O contended modified that usual obligation. Maersk relied on the following provisions of their bills of lading: "The face of the bill of lading … for delivery unto the Consignee mentioned herein or to his or their assigns, where the Carrier's responsibilities shall in all cases and in all circumstances finally cease… In witness whereof the number of original bills of lading stated on this side, one of which being accomplished, the other(s) to be void.

Clause 17: METHODS AND ROUTES OF TRANSPORTATION

1. The carrier may at any time

(e): comply with any orders or recommendations given by any government or authority or …

2. Anything done or not done in accordance with this provision is deemed to be within the contractual carriage and shall not be a deviation" P&O relied on the following provisions of their bills of lading (and cl 20(6) in respect of which I have set out the concession of the Claimants at para 119): "The face of the bill of lading … If the Carrier so requires, before he arranges delivery of the goods one Original bill of lading, duly endorsed, must be surrendered by the Merchant to the Carrier at the Port of Discharge or at some other location acceptable to the carrier." The bills of lading also contained provisions identical to cl 17 of the Maersk bills.

First it was contended that under the terms of the P&O bills of lading, the presentation of an original was only the carrier's prerogative rather than his obligation, in view of the words "if he so requires". I do not accept that contention. Clear language would be needed to discharge the carrier from his obligation to deliver in accordance with the bill of lading; this clause does not contain any such language.

Second, it was contended that cl 17.1(e) in the Maersk bill and the identical clause in the P&O bill entitled the carrier to comply with any government order; on the findings I have made in relation to the law of Chile, there was no such order.

In my view therefore there was no relevant qualification to the usual delivery obligation by reason of the clauses in the bill of lading.

Maersk and P&O next contended that there was an implied term of the bill of lading that entitled them to deliver without presentation of a bill of lading in circumstances where there was a reasonable explanation of its absence. They relied on a short passage in the judgment of Clarke J in The Sormovskiy 3068 [1994] 2 Lloyd's Rep 266. Goods were delivered at Vyborg by the Defendant carrier without seeking presentation of the bills of lading. The carrier contended that he was not liable because he had delivered the goods in accordance with the practice and custom of the port of Vyborg and he had delivered to the plaintiff's agents. Clarke J held that the although the carrier was generally obliged to deliver only against presentation of an original bill of lading, there were circumstances where the carrier was entitled to deliver other than against presentation. After a review of the authorities, Clarke J concluded that there were two such circumstances – where there was a reasonable explanation for the non availability of the bill of lading and where the law or custom of the port required such delivery.

It is convenient to deal subsequently with the position relating to the law and custom of the port of delivery. As regards a reasonable explanation for the absence of the bill of lading, Clarke J said at 274:

"In trades where it is difficult or impossible for bills of lading to arrive in the discharge port on time, the problem is met by including a contractual term requiring the master to deliver against a letter of indemnity or a bank guarantee. That is common place and indeed there was a provision to that effect here. The simple rule to which I referred does require some exceptions because the bill of lading might have been lost or stolen. In order to cater for that problem it is no doubt necessary to imply a term that the master must deliver cargo without production of an original bill of lading in circumstances where it is proved to his reasonable satisfaction both that the person seeking delivery of the goods is entitled to possession and what has become of the bills of lading. The precise nature of the exceptions will no doubt require further consideration on the future."

In Motis Exports v Dkbs 1912 [1999] 1 Lloyd's Rep 837, [1999] 1 All ER (Comm) 571, Rix J took a contrary view. He had to consider as a preliminary issue the liability of Maersk line for the loss of goods after discharge where forged bills of lading were used to obtain delivery orders for the goods at the port of discharge. One of the arguments made was that there was an exception to the rule that a shipowner must deliver against presentation of a bill of lading where the carrier was deceived without fault into parting with the goods; the carrier relied upon the passage in the judgment of Clarke J in The Sormovskiy 3068 which I have set out in para 126. After referring to the Houda and noting that The Sormovskiy 3068 did not appear to have been cited to the Court of Appeal in that case, Rix J expressed the view that the exception which the carrier sought to derive from the The Sormovskiy 3068 did not exist; the remedy in circumstances where the original bill of lading could not be produced was to persuade the carrier to accept an indemnity or go to Court. In the Court of Appeal, the argument on this point was not pursued by the carrier [2000] 1 Lloyd's Rep 211 at 213, para 7.

I agree with the views of Rix J Furthermore if the carrier is not protected by a reasonable belief in the genuineness of the bill presented (as was held in Motis Exports), it is difficult to see how he can be protected in the circumstances suggested by Clarke J: see Carver on Bills of Lading, para 6-005. Moreover the exception suggested by Clarke J was by way of implied term. But, in my view, no such implied term could ever be said to be necessary; on the contrary the right of the carrier to deliver where he had a reasonable explanation as to the absence of the bill and reasonable evidence of the entitlement of the person seeking delivery to delivery would undermine the security of the bill of lading. The position of the consignee and the shipowner can and should in the circumstances envisaged by Clarke J be protected by an indemnity or an application to court as is made clear in the judgments in the Court of Appeal in The Houda. There are occasions, for example in the short haul trades, where the bills usually do not reach the port of discharge until after the ship has discharged; the documents have usually pointed to the consignee being entitled to delivery. However, in my experience, in such circumstances, although there rarely is a problem, there have been occasions where insolvency has supervened in the contractual chain and banks have exercised their rights under the bills of lading. It is for that reason it has been the practice of P&I clubs to insist an indemnity always be provided where a bill of lading is not available even in the most plausible of circumstances and have generally excluded insurance cover for a carrier who delivers in such circumstances without obtaining an indemnity or court order.

Even if, contrary to my view there was such an exception, I do not consider it would avail the carriers in the present case. They received no explanation of the whereabouts of the original bills of lading and a copy of a bill of lading produced by Gold Crown's Customs agent was not reasonable evidence of entitlement to possession. No one questioned whether the Customs agent had the original. The obligation under the bills of lading and the law and custom at the port of discharge in Chile.

Thus as a matter of English law, I am satisfied that the obligation in bailment and contract upon P&O and Maersk was only to deliver against presentation of an original bill of lading. However, these carriers relied on the distinction under art 10 of the Rome Convention between the substance of that obligation and the manner and mode of its performance to which I referred at para 64.

To the extent that the law of Chile contained provisions specifying the manner in which cargo in Chile had to be delivered, then in my view it must be correct to have regard to the law of Chile under art 10. Thus, for example, under the law of Chile, as set out in para 75, the original bills of lading had to be retained by the Customs agent. They could only therefore be presented to the carrier and had to be returned (marked if necessary to show delivery had been made); to that extent the obligations under the bill of lading are modified by the law of Chile.

A similar result to that to which I referred in para 131 is reached on the basis of another part of the decision in The Sormovskiy 3068 relating to the law and custom at the port of discharge. Clarke J said at 275: "If it were a requirement of the law of the place of performance that the cargo must be delivered to the [the Commercial Sea Port at Vyborg] as agent of the plaintiffs without presentation of an original bill of lading the Defendants would in my judgment have performed their obligations under the contract of carriage. Any other conclusion would mean that the contract could not lawfully be performed, which could not have been intended by the parties. Equally if there was a custom … However, custom in this context means custom in its strict sense… It would not however, in my judgment, be good performance of the Defendants' obligations under the contract if it were mere practice…"

I agree with the views of Clarke J; they seem to me to accord entirely with the authorities to which he refers and with the broader principle of art 10 of the Rome Convention.

I accept that the obligation under the bills of lading in English law contemplated the bill being surrendered to the carrier and kept by him, but either under the principle in The Sormovskiy 3068 or under art 10, I consider that the modification in the manner of the discharge of that obligation set out in para 131 is permissible and is in no way inconsistent with the basic obligation under these bills of lading in English law to deliver against presentation of the bill of lading.

If under the law of Chile I had concluded that Maersk and P&O were under an obligation to deliver the cargo to a Customs warehouse without presentation of a bill of lading and that discharged their delivery obligations, that would have given rise to more difficult questions as to the scope of the principle in The Sormovskiy 3068 and of art 10. It was contended by the Claimants that the exception in The Sormovskiy 3068 did not apply because the basis of such an exception was the intention of the parties and such an exception could not be implied because of the terms of the bills of lading. Article 10 did not assist Maersk and P&O as the substance of the obligation was the obligation to deliver against presentation of the bill of lading. Furthermore the Claimants did not know of the law of Chile and therefore Maersk and P&O could not rely on the provisions of that law; there was no supervening illegality. Maersk and P&O contended that the exception in The Sormovskiy 3068 was of wide application and consistent with cases such as Petrocochino v Bott(1874) LR 9CP 355 and The Asiatic Prince 108 Fed Rep 287 (1901, CA, 2 Cir). It was consistent with the principle, set out for example by Staughton J in Libyan Arab Bank v Bankers Trust[1989] QB 728 that performance was excused if the act required was necessarily unlawful in the place of performance and therefore performance was discharged by illegality. In view of the conclusion to which I have come on the law of Chile, it is not necessary for me to lengthen this judgment by a consideration of these conflicting arguments.

Issue 3: The exceptions in the bill of lading

Although the terms of the Maersk and P&O bills of lading were similar (as is to be expected as each company operates a liner service) and both bills could be used either as port to port bill or combined transport bill, it is necessary to consider them separately.

The terms of the Maersk bills

Maersk relied first on cl 5:

CARRIER'S RESPONSIBILITY

The carrier undertakes responsibility from the place of receipt if named herein or from the port of loading to the port of discharge or the place of delivery if named herein.

3. Carriage to and from Countries other than the USA

b. Where the carriage called for commences at the port of loading and finishes at the port of discharge, the Carrier shall have no liability whatsoever for any loss or damage to the goods while in its actual or constructive possession before loading or after discharge over the ship's rail, or if applicable over the ship's ramp, however caused.

The Claimants first submitted that the clause did not in any event apply as the carriage was not port to port. On the face of the bill of lading, the spaces for port of loading and for place of receipt were each filled in as "Hong Kong" and the spaces for port of discharge and place of delivery were also filled in. The spaces for place of receipt and place of delivery were marked "Only applicable when the document used as a combined transport bill". It would seem therefore that this was not carriage that finished within the terms of cl 5.3.b at the port of discharge; it finished only at the place of delivery. But it is not necessary to consider this at length, as I am satisfied that in any event that the clause is inapplicable on the basis of the Claimants' second submission relying on Motis Exports v Dkbs 1912.

In Motis Exports v Dkbs. 1912, Rix J and the Court of Appeal held that cl 5.3.b did not cover misdelivery without presentation of a bill of lading. Stuart Smith LJ said at para 20: "Clause 5(3)(b) is not apt on its natural meaning to cover delivery by the carrier or his agent, albeit the delivery was obtained by fraud." "The natural subject matter of clause 5(3)(b) is consists in loss or damage caused to the goods while in the carrier's custody, but not deliberate delivery up of the goods, whether without any bill of lading or against a forged and therefore nul document believed to be a bill of lading."

Maersk argued that the facts of the present case were different; Maersk had not handed over the goods to the wrong person, but the wrong person had obtained the goods without the consent of the carrier as in the case of theft. In the case of theft, it was accepted in Motis Exports that the clause would apply (see also The Ines [1995] 2 Lloyd's Rep 144). In my view this was not a case of theft; it was a simple case of misdelivery without presentation of a bill of lading and to persons, Gold Crown, who were not in any event entitled. Maersk were under an obligation to deliver to the person who presented a bill of lading; this they did not do.

Maersk next relied on the Hague-Visby Rules. It was accepted by the Claimants that the Hague-Visby Rules applied by reason of cl 5.3.a. Maersk contended that the Hague-Visby Rules exceptions in art IV r 2 (g) and (q) provided them with a defence. Assuming that these exceptions applied to misdelivery (though the Claimants contended that they only applied to physical loss and damage), they do not assist Maersk. There was no restraint of princes (on the law of Chile as I have found it to be) and the loss did not occur without their fault or privity (for the reasons given in paras 148 to 149 in relation to negligence). Maersk did not seek to rely on the package limitation as it was greater than the amount claimed.

The terms of the P&O bills

P&O relied on cl 5 of their bills:

……

5. CARRIER'S RESPONSIBILITY

The carrier shall be under no liability whatsoever for loss or damage to the Goods, howsoever occurring, if such loss or damage arises prior to loading onto or subsequent to discharge from the vessel. Nothwithstanding the above, in case and to the extent that any applicable law provides for any additional period of responsibility, the carrier shall be entitled to every … limitation and liberty in the Hague Rules, notwithstanding that the loss or damage did not occur at sea.

It was the Claimant's case that cl 5 did not apply as the carriage under the bills of lading was not port to port. Under the terms of the definition clause, a bill of lading was port to port if it was not combined transport; a bill was a combined transport bill if the "place of receipt" and/or "the place of delivery" were so indicated on the face of the bill in the relevant spaces. On face of the bills the space for "place of receipt" was filled in "Hong Kong Cy", and the "place of delivery" filled in "Valparaiso". The space for the port of loading was filled in as "Hong Kong" and the space for the port of discharge "Valparaiso". The spaces for "place of delivery" and "place of discharge" were marked "applicable only when this document is used as a combined transport bill of lading". The Claimants therefore contended that, as the spaces had been filled in, cl 5 did not apply. P&O contended that even though the spaces had been filled in, this did not make the carriage combined transport as it was necessary for the place of receipt and the place of delivery to be different to the places loading and discharge. I do not accept P&O's argument. There may be many reasons why the combined transport provisions were chosen even if the places were the same; as the provision in cl 6 dealing with combined transport makes clear (and as is emphasised in P&O's guide) this makes the carrier liable throughout the carriage; the combined transport provisions also extends the period of responsibility beyond discharge from the vessel to storage at the place of delivery until collection. Thus there are sensible reasons why the parties might have filled the spaces in; they did so in this case and in my view, these bills of lading were not port to port. P&O also contended that even if the carriage was combined transport, cl 5(b) applied by reason of cl 6(3) (b); I cannot accept that argument, on the terms of the clause, given the way the face of the bill of lading was completed.

But even if cl 5(b) applied, I do not consider it would assist P&O The clause is in most respects similar to cl 5.3.b in the Maersk bill; the difference between the phraseology is in my view immaterial. However, the P&O bill contains cl 7(5)(b) which provides:

7. SUNDRY LIABILITY PROVISIONS

(5) Scope of application

P&O relied on the Hague-Visby and Hague Rules exceptions. For the reasons given in respect of Maersk, I do not consider they assist P&O They also relied on cl 7(2) which applied a limit of £100 sterling per package or unit if the Hague Rules were applicable other than by national law. There are a number of reasons why this does not assist P&O; the clause applying the Hague Rules only applied to port to port bills and in any event the applicable limit would be the Hague-Visby limits which do not assist P&O.

Conclusion

I therefore hold that the Claimants succeed in their claims for $134,807.40 against Maersk and for $95,147.20 against P&O Judgment for the Claimants.

【思考题】

1. 什么是无单放货?

2. 根据《汉堡规则》，承运人在何种情况下无权享有责任限制?

3.《汉堡规则》对于过失索赔的规定有哪些?

Case2·拓展阅读

III

国际技术贸易法

【内容摘要】

　　本章分为两节，精选两个案例。第一个案例 "Genentech, Inc.vs. MedImmune, Inc." 主要关注点为国际技术转让合同履行过程中有关确认不侵权之诉的程序要求。传统知识产权法的重心放在对知识产权权利人专有权的保护上，但在这一过程中也随之出现了知识产权人权利滥用的现象，确认不侵权之诉即为应对后一现象而产生，其允许被指控侵权人在满足特定条件下向法院请求确认自身是否侵权，从而避免自身陷入长期的权利不确定状态。第二个案例选取美国诉中国某些影响知识产权保护和执行措施案（China-Measures Affecting the Protection and Enforcement of Intellectual Property Rights, DS362），主要争议点为中国海关对于侵权产品的处置，中国刑法对于知识产权侵权的处罚门槛规定是否符合 WTO/TRIPS 相关规定。

Case1　Genentech, Inc.vs. MedImmune, Inc. ［549 US 118（2007）］

【案情说明】

一、案件事实

　　Genentech, Inc. 和 MedImmune, Inc. 是全球两大生物医药巨头。作为生物医药领域的先驱，Genentech 主要关注上游的基因信息研发。而 MedImmune 主要针对各种疾病进行具体的医药研发。1997 年双方就 Genentech 的两套技术签订了许可协议。其中一份协议涉及的技术属于已经获得专利的技术；但另一份协议涉及一项尚在专利申请审批过程中的技术。MedImmune 在协议中承诺支付 Genentech 专利许可费，以此获准制造、使用、销售通过上述技术制造的产品，双方同时约定，前者若要提前终止许可协议应提前 6 个月通知后者。当专利最终被授予后，Genentech 向 MedImmune 发函，声称该新的专利涵盖了 MedImmune 生产的 Synagis（药物），该药物主要用来避免婴幼儿呼吸道疾病，其销售占 MedImmune 销售总额的 80%。Genentech 的上述做法让 MedImmune 处于一个极为困窘的立场，对它而言，除非另外与 Genentech 达成一项支付更多特许费的协议，否则可能面临 Genentech 终止原有许可协议及其侵权指控。最终，MedImmune 一方面按照 Genentech 的要求支付了更高的许可费；另一方面向美国加州地方法院提起了确认判决，请求法院判定当事方的权利和法律关系。

二、裁判结果

　　美国加州地方法院驳回了原告主张，认为其对本案缺乏对物管辖。案件上诉至美国联邦巡回法院之后，巡回法院肯定了地方法院判决。最终，在美国联邦最高法院发出提审令后，案件由联邦巡回法院转呈到了美国联邦最高法院。最高法院推翻了下级法院对本案的判决，肯定专利被许可人在不终止许可协议或不违反许可协议情况下，仍可针对被许可专利提出专利无效之诉。换言之，专利被许可人可以在专利许可协议有效存续期间就被许可专利提出无效之诉。

【法律分析】

　　确认之诉也常常被称为宣示判决或确认不侵权之诉。其主要存在于知识产权保护法领域。在知识产权法领域，传统层面关注的只是知识产权权利人专有权的保护，但随着知识产权保护法律制度的发展，权利人滥用权利的现象也频频出现。例如现实中，可能某个知识产权人会发出警告，认为他人存在侵犯本人知识产权的行为，但前者可能并不会马上起诉。此时被控侵权人就面临着不确定性：为应对起诉，后者理应进行相应的准备；但如果准备好了而对方又不起诉了呢？但如果不准备的话，又存在被对方突袭起诉的风险。而且当对方指控自身侵权而没有及时提起诉讼的情况下，后者的商誉也会因此受到影响，一些准备与此发展商业往来的客户也会因为担心其交易货物涉及知识产权纠纷而停留在观望阶段或放弃交易。面对这种情况，英美法系国家率先提出了所谓的确认不侵权之诉。即在满足一定条件下，被控侵权方可以向法院提出确认不侵权之诉，以解除自身的不确定状态。美国为此专门制定了成文法《宣示判决法案》。

本案中，MedImmune 同样面临这种不确定状态，其或者维持现状，但这样做的后果将是 Genentech 终止原有许可协议并诉其侵权，MedImmune 将面临三倍损害赔偿、律师费和其他商业损失；或者通过确认不侵权之诉来排除这种不确定性。但按照美国此前判例法的要求，采取后一行动的前提是 MedImmune 先有违约行为，换言之，MedImmune 首先要拒绝签订新的许可协议，在此前提下方有可能提起确认不侵权之诉，但这样做存在败诉并最终承担侵权责任的风险。基于这种考虑，MedImmune 最终采取了第三条路径，即一方面同意向 Genentech 支付许可费；另一方面向法院提起无效之诉。美国联邦最高法院最终认可了它的这种做法。

在本案之前，美国地方法院和巡回法院在解释《宣示判决法案》第 3 条时，将宣示判决之诉提起前提条件解释为需要经历一个所谓的"合理诉讼担忧（Reasonable Apprehension of Suit, RAS）"测试。根据巡回法院确定的这一标准，原告只有在满足以下标准的前提下方可提起专利确认之诉：（1）专利权人明确的威胁或其他行动使得提起确认之诉的原告对自身将面临侵权之诉存在合理担忧。（2）原告是否实施侵权或有侵权意图的行动。但最高法院的解释显然已经推翻了下级法院的判决。美国联邦最高法院认为，专利被许可人即便未违反合同，在依据许可协议支付了专利许可费之后，仍得提出确认不侵权之诉。换言之，上述两个要件中，原告违约不再是提起确认不侵权之诉的必要条件。

【英文案例裁决摘录】

JUSTICE SCALIA delivered the opinion of the Court.

We must decide whether Article Ⅲ's limitation of federal courts' jurisdiction to "Cases" and "Controversies," reflected in the "actual controversy" requirement of the Declaratory Judgment Act, 28 U. S. C. §2201(a), requires a patent licensee to terminate or be in breach of its license agreement before it can seek a declaratory judgment that the underlying patent is invalid, unenforceable, or not infringed.

Because the declaratory-judgment claims in this case were disposed of at the motion-to-dismiss stage, we take the following facts from the allegations in petitioner's amended complaint and the unopposed declarations that petitioner submitted in response to the motion to dismiss. Petitioner MedImmune, Inc., manufactures Synagis, a drug used to prevent respiratory tract disease in infants and young children. In 1997, petitioner entered into a patent license agreement with respondent Genentech, Inc. (which acted on behalf of itself as patent assignee and on behalf of the coassignee, respondent City of Hope). The license covered an existing patent relating to the production of "chimeric antibodies" and a then-pending patent application relating to "the coexpression of immunoglobulin chains in recombinant host cells. Petitioner agreed to pay royalties on sales of "Licensed Products," and respondents granted petitioner the right to make, use, and sell them. The agreement defined "Licensed Products" as a specified antibody, "the manufacture, use or sale of which … would, if not licensed under th[e] Agreement, infringe one or more claims of either or both of [the covered patents,] which have neither expired nor been held invalid by a court or other body of competent jurisdiction from which no appeal has been or may be taken. App. 399. The license agreement gave petitioner the right to terminate upon six months' written notice."

In December 2001, the "coexpression" application covered by the 1997 license agreement matured into the Cabilly II" patent. Soon thereafter, respondent Genentech delivered petitioner a letter expressing its belief that Synagis was covered by the Cabilly II patent and its expectation that petitioner would pay royalties beginning March 1, 2002. Petitioner did not think royalties were owing, believing that the Cabilly II patent was invalid and unenforceable,1 and that its claims were in any event not infringed by Synagis. Nevertheless, petitioner considered the letter to be a clear threat to enforce the Cabilly II patent, terminate the 1997 license agreement, and sue for patent infringement if petitioner did not make royalty payments as demanded. If respondents were to prevail in a patent infringement action, petitioner could be ordered to pay treble damages and attorney's fees, and could be enjoined from selling Synagis, a product that has accounted for more than 80 percent of its revenue from sales since 1999. Unwilling to risk such serious consequences, petitioner paid the demanded royalties "under protest and with reservation of all of [its] rights." Id., at 426. This declaratory-judgment action followed.

Petitioner sought the declaratory relief discussed in detail in Part II below. Petitioner also requested damages and an injunction with respect to other federal and state claims not relevant here. The District Court granted respondents' motion to dismiss the declaratory-judgment claims for lack of subject-matter jurisdiction, relying on the decision of the United States Court of Appeals for the Federal Circuit in Gen-Probe Inc. v. Vysis, Inc., 359 F. 3d 1376 (2004). Gen-Probe had held that a patent licensee in good standing cannot establish an Article

III case or controversy with regard to validity, enforceability, or scope of the patent because the license agreement "obliterate[s] any reasonable apprehension" that the licensee will be sued for infringement. Id., at 1381. The Federal Circuit affirmed the District Court, also relying on Gen-Probe. 427 F. 3d 958 (2005). We granted certiorari. 546 U. S. 1169 (2006).

At the outset, we address a disagreement concerning the nature of the dispute at issue here—whether it involves only a freestanding claim of patent invalidity or rather a claim that, both because of patent invalidity and because of noninfringement, no royalties are owing under the license agreement. That probably makes no difference to the ultimate issue of subject-matter jurisdiction, but it is well to be clear about the nature of the case before us.

Respondents contend that petitioner "is not seeking an interpretation of its present contractual obligations. Brief for Respondent Genentech 37; see also Brief for Respondent City of Hope 48-49. They claim this for two reasons: (1) because there is no dispute that Synagis infringes the Cabilly II patent, thereby making royalties payable; and (2) because while there is a dispute over patent validity, the contract calls for royalties on an infringing product whether or not the underlying patent is valid. See Brief for Respondent Genentech 7, 37. The first point simply does not comport with the allegations of petitioner's amended complaint. The very first count requested a DECLARATORY JUDGMENT ON CONTRACTUAL RIGHTS AND OBLIGATIONS," and "stated that petitioner disputes its obligation to make payments under the 1997 License Agreement because [petitioner's] sale of its Synagis® product does not infringe any valid claim of the [Cabilly II] Patent." App. 136. These contentions were repeated throughout the complaint. Id., at 104, 105, 108, 147.3 And the phrase "does not infringe any valid claim" (emphasis added) cannot be thought to be no more than a challenge to the patent's validity, since elsewhere the amended complaint states with unmistakable clarity that the patent is ... not infringed by [petitioner's] Synagis product and that [petitioner] owes no payments under license agreements with [respondents]. Id., at 104.

As to the second point, petitioner assuredly did contend that it had no obligation under the license to pay royalties on an invalid patent. Id., at 104, 136, 147. Nor is that contention frivolous. True, the license requires petitioner to pay royalties until a patent claim has been held invalid by a competent body, and the Cabilly II patent has not. But the license at issue in Lear, Inc. v. Adkins, 395 U. S. 653, 673 (1969), similarly provided that "royalties are to be paid until such time as the 'patent ... is held invalid, and we rejected the argument that a repudiating licensee must comply with its contract and pay royalties until its claim is vindicated in court. We express no opinion on whether a non-repudiating licensee is similarly relieved of its contract obligation during a successful challenge to a patent's validity—that is, on the applicability of licensee *estoppel* under these circumstances. Cf. Studiengesellschaft Kohle, M.

B. H. v. Shell Oil Co., 112 F. 3d 1561, 1568 (CA Fed. 1997)" ("[A] licensee … cannot invoke the protection of the Lear doctrine until it (i) actually ceases payment of royalties, and (ii) provides notice to the licensor that the reason for ceasing payment of royalties is because it has deemed the relevant claims to be invalid"). All we need determine is whether petitioner has alleged a contractual dispute. It has done so.

Respondents further argue that petitioner waived its contract claim by failing to argue it below. Brief for Respondent Genentech 10-11; Tr. of Oral Arg. 30-31. The record reveals, however, that petitioner raised the contract point before the Federal Circuit. See Brief for Plantiff- Appellant MedImmune, Inc. in Nos. 04-1300, 04-1384 (CA Fed.), p. 38 ("Here, MedImmune is seeking to define its rights and obligations under its contract with Genentech precisely the type of action the Declaratory Judgment Act contemplates"). That petitioner limited its contract argument to a few pages of its appellate brief does not suggest a waiver; it merely reflects counsel's sound assessment that the argument would be futile. The Federal Circuit's Gen-Probe precedent precluded jurisdiction over petitioner's contract claims, and the panel below had no authority to overrule Gen-Probe. Having determined that petitioner has raised and preserved a contract claim, we turn to the jurisdictional question. The Declaratory Judgment Act provides that, "[i]n a case of actual controversy within its jurisdiction … any court of the United States … may declare the rights and other legal relations of any interested party seeking such declaration, whether or not further relief is or could be sought. 28 U. S. C. §2201(a). There was a time when this Court harbored doubts about the compatibility of declaratory judgment actions with Article III's case-or-controversy requirement. See Willing v. Chicago Auditorium Assn., 277 U. S. 274, 289 (1928); Liberty Warehouse Co. v. Grannis, 273 U. S. 70 (1927); see also Gordon v. United States, 117 U. S. Appx. 697, 702 (1864) (the last opinion of Taney, C. J., published posthumously) ("The award of execution is … an essential part of every judgment passed by a court exercising judicial power"). We dispelled those doubts, however, in Nashville, C. & St. L. R. Co. v. Wallace, 288 U. S. 249 (1933), holding (in a case involving a declaratory judgment rendered in state court) that an appropriate action for declaratory relief can be a case or controversy under Article III. The federal Declaratory Judgment Act was signed into law the following year, and we upheld its constitutionality in Aetna Life Ins. Co. v. Haworth, 300 U. S. 227 (1937). Our opinion explained that the phrase case of actual controversy in the Act refers to the type of Cases and Controversies that are justiciable under Article III. Id., at 240.

Aetna and the cases following it do not draw the brightest of lines between those declaratory-judgment actions that satisfy the case-or-controversy requirement and those that do not. Our decisions have required that the dispute be definite and concrete, touching the legal relations of parties having adverse legal interests"; and that it be "real and substantial" and "admi[t] of specific relief through a decree of a conclusive character, as distinguished from an opinion advising what the law would be upon a hypothetical state of facts.Id., at 240-241." In Maryland Casualty Co. v. Pacific Coal & Oil Co., 312 U. S. 270, 273 (1941), we summarized as follows: "Basically, the question in each case is whether the facts alleged, under all the circumstances, show that there is a substantial controversy, between parties having adverse legal interests, of sufficient immediacy and reality to warrant the issuance of a declaratory judgment."

There is no dispute that these standards would have been satisfied if petitioner had taken the final step of refusing to make royalty payments under the 1997 license agreement. Respondents claim a right to royalties under the licensing agreement. Petitioner asserts that no royalties are owing because the Cabilly II patent is invalid and not infringed; and alleges (without contradiction) a threat by respondents to enjoin sales if royalties are not forthcoming. The factual and legal dimensions of the dispute are well defined and, but for petitioner's continuing to make royalty payments, nothing about the dispute would render it unfit for judicial resolution. Assuming (without deciding) that respondents here could not claim an anticipatory breach and repudiate the license, the continuation of royalty payments makes what would otherwise be an imminent threat at least remote, if not nonexistent. As long as those payments are made, there is no risk that respondents will seek to enjoin petitioner's sales. Petitioner's own acts, in other words, eliminate the imminent threat of harm. The question before us is whether this causes the dispute no longer to be a case or controversy within the meaning of Article III.

Our analysis must begin with the recognition that, where threatened action by government is concerned, we do not require a plaintiff to expose himself to liability before bringing suit to challenge the basis for the threat—for example, the constitutionality of a law threatened to be enforced. The plaintiff's own action (or inaction) in failing to violate the law eliminates the imminent threat of prosecution, but nonetheless does not eliminate Article III jurisdiction. For example, in Terrace v. Thompson, 263 U. S. 197 (1923), the State threatened the plaintiff with forfeiture of his farm, fines, and penalties if he entered into a lease with an alien in violation of the State's anti-alien land law. Given this genuine threat of enforcement, we did not require, as a prerequisite to testing the validity of the law in a suit for injunction, that the plaintiff bet the farm, so to speak, by taking the violative action. Id., at 216. See also, e.g., Village of Euclid v. Ambler Realty Co., 272 U. S. 365 (1926); Ex parte Young, 209 U. S. 123 (1908). Likewise, in Steffel v. Thompson, 415 U. S. 452 (1974), we did not require the plaintiff to proceed to distribute handbills and risk actual prosecution before he could seek a declaratory judgment regarding the constitutionality of a state statute prohibiting such distribution. Id., at 458 460. As then-Justice Rehnquist put it in his concurrence, the declaratory judgment procedure is an alternative to pursuit of the arguably illegal activity. Id., at 480. In each of these cases, the plaintiff had eliminated the imminent threat of harm by simply not doing what he claimed the right to do (enter into a lease, or distribute handbills at the shopping center). That did not preclude subject matter jurisdiction because the threat-eliminating behavior was effectively coerced. See Terrace, supra, at 215-216; Steffel, supra, at 459. The dilemma posed by that coercion—putting the challenger to the choice between abandoning his rights or risking prosecution—is "a dilemma that it was the very purpose of the Declaratory Judgment Act to ameliorate." Abbott Laboratories v. Gardner, 387 U. S. 136, 152 (1967).

Supreme Court jurisprudence is more rare regarding application of the Declaratory Judgment Act to situations in which the plaintiff's self-avoidance of imminent injury is coerced by threatened enforcement action of a private party rather than the government. Lower federal courts, however (and state courts interpreting declaratory judgment Acts requiring "actual controversy"), have long accepted jurisdiction in such cases. See, e.g., Keener Oil & Gas Co. v. Consolidated Gas Utilities Corp., 190 F. 2d 985, 989 (CA10 1951); American Machine & Metals, Inc. v. De Bothezat Impeller Co., 166 F. 2d 535 (CA2 1948); Hess v. Country Club Park, 213 Cal. 613, 614, 2 P. 2d 782, 783 (1931) (in bank); Washington-Detroit Theater Co. v. Moore, 249 Mich. 673, 675, 229 N. W. 618, 618-619 (1930); see also Advisory Committee's Note on Fed. Rule Civ. Proc. 57.

The only Supreme Court decision in point is, fortuitously, close on its facts to the case before us. Altvater v. Freeman, 319 U. S. 359 (1943), held that a licensee's failure to cease its payment of royalties did not render non justiciable a dispute over the validity of the patent. In that litigation, several patentees had sued their licensees to enforce territorial restrictions in the license. The licensees filed a counterclaim for declaratory judgment that the underlying patents were invalid, in the meantime paying under protest "royalties required by an injunction the patentees had obtained in an earlier case. The patentees argued that so long as [licensees] continue to pay royalties, there is only an academic, not a real controversy, between the parties." Id., at 364. We rejected that argument and held that the declaratory-judgment claim presented a justiciable case or controversy: "The fact that royalties were being paid did not make this a difference or dispute of a hypothetical or abstract character."

(quoting Aetna, 300 U. S., at 240). The royalties were being paid under protest and under the compulsion of an injunction decree, and [u]nless the injunction decree were modified, the only other course [of action] was to defy it, and to risk not only actual but treble damages in infringement suits."319 U. S., at 365. We concluded that the requirements of [a] case or controversy are met where payment of a claim is demanded as of right and where payment is made, but where the involuntary or coercive nature of the exaction preserves the right to recover the sums paid or to challenge the legality of the claim." Ibid.

The Federal Circuit's Gen-Probe decision distinguished Altvater on the ground that it involved the compulsion of an injunction. But Altvater cannot be so readily dismissed. Never mind that the injunction had been privately obtained and was ultimately within the control of the patentees, who could permit its modification. More fundamentally, and contrary to the Federal Circuit's conclusion, Altvater did not say that the coercion dispositive of the case was governmental, but suggested just the opposite. The opinion acknowledged that the licensees had the option of stopping payments in defiance of the injunction, but explained that the consequence of doing so would be to risk "actual [and] treble damages in infringement suits" by the patentees. 319 U. S., at 365. It significantly did not mention the threat of prosecution for contempt, or any other sort of governmental sanction. Moreover, it cited approvingly a treatise which said that an "actual or threatened serious injury to business or employment" by a private party can be as coercive as other forms of coercion supporting restitution actions at common law; and that "[t]o imperil a man's livelihood, his business enterprises, or his solvency, [was] ordinarily quite as coercive" as, for example, "detaining his property." F. Woodward, The Law of Quasi Contracts §218 (1913), cited in Altvater, supra, at 365.

Jurisdiction over the present case is not contradicted by Willing v. Chicago Auditorium Association, 277 U. S. 274. There a ground lessee wanted to demolish an antiquated auditorium and replace it with a modern commercial building. The lessee believed it had the right to do this without the lessors' consent, but was unwilling to drop the wrecking ball first and test its belief later. Because there was no declaratory judgment act at the time under federal or applicable state law, the lessee filed an action to remove a cloud on its lease. This Court held that an Article III case or controversy had not arisen because "[n]o defendant ha[d] wronged the plaintiff or ha[d] threatened to do so. Id., at 288, 290." It was true that one of the colessors had disagreed with the lessee's interpretation of the lease, but that happened in an "informal, friendly, private conversation, id., at 286, a year before the lawsuit was filed; and the lessee never even bothered to approach the other colessors. The Court went on to remark that "[w]hat the plaintiff seeks is simply a declaratory judgment, and [t]o grant that relief is beyond the power conferred upon the federal judiciary." Id., at 289. Had Willing been decided after the enactment (and our upholding) of the Declaratory Judgment Act, and had the legal disagreement between the parties been as lively as this one, we are confident a different result would have obtained. The rule that a plaintiff must destroy a large building, bet the farm, or (as here) risk treble damages and the loss of 80 percent of its business, before seeking a declaration of its actively contested legal rights finds no support in Article III.

Respondents assert that the parties in effect settled this dispute when they entered into the 1997 license agreement. When a licensee enters such an agreement, they contend, it essentially purchases an insurance policy, immunizing it from suits for infringement so long as it continues to pay royalties and does not challenge the covered patents. Permitting it to challenge the validity of the patent without terminating or breaking the agreement alters the deal, allowing the licensee to continue enjoying its immunity while bringing a suit, the elimination of which was part of the patentee's *quid pro quo*. Of course even if it were valid, this argument would have no force with regard to petitioner's claim that the agreement does not call for royalties because their product does not infringe the patent. But even as to the patent invalidity claim, the point seems to us mistaken. To begin with, it is not clear where the prohibition against challenging the validity of the patents is to be found. It can hardly be implied from the mere promise to pay royalties on patents which have neither expired nor been held invalid by a court or other body of competent jurisdiction from which no appeal has been or may be taken, App. 399. Promising to pay royalties on patents that have not been held invalid does not amount to a promise not to seek a holding of their invalidity.

Respondents appeal to the common-law rule that a party to a contract cannot at one and the same time challenge its validity and continue to reap its benefits, citing Commodity Credit Corp. v. Rosenberg Bros. & Co., 243 F. 2d 504, 512 (CA9 1957), and Kingman & Co. v. Stoddard, 85 F. 740, 745 (CA7 1898). Lear, they contend, did not suspend that rule for patent licensing agreements, since the plaintiff in that case had already repudiated the contract. Even if Lear's repudiation of the doctrine of licensee estoppel was so limited (a point on which, as we have said earlier, we do not opine), it is hard to see how the common-law rule has any application here. Petitioner is not repudiating or impugning the contract while continuing to reap its benefits. Rather, it is asserting that the contract, properly interpreted, does not prevent it from challenging the patents, and does not require the payment of royalties because the patents do not cover its products and are invalid. Of course even if respondents were correct that the licensing agreement or the common-law rule precludes this suit, the consequence would be that respondents win this case on the merits—not that the very genuine contract dispute disappears, so that Article III jurisdiction is somehow defeated. In short, Article III jurisdiction has nothing to do with this insurance-policy contention.

Lastly, respondents urge us to affirm the dismissal of the declaratory-judgment claims on discretionary grounds. The Declaratory Judgment Act provides that a court "may declare the rights and other legal relations of any interested party, 28 U. S. C. §2201(a) (emphasis added), not that it must do so. This text has long been understood "to confer on federal courts unique and substantial discretion in deciding whether to declare the rights of litigants." Wilton v. Seven Falls Co., 515 U. S. 277, 286 (1995); see also Cardinal Chemical Co. v. Morton Int'l, Inc., 508 U. S. 83, 95, n. 17 (1993); Brillhart v. Excess Ins. Co. of America, 316 U. S. 491, 494-496 (1942). We have found it "more consistent with the statute, however, to vest district courts with discretion in the first instance, because facts bearing on the usefulness of the declaratory judgment remedy, and the fitness of the case for resolution, are peculiarly within their grasp." Wilton, supra, at 289. The District Court here gave no consideration to discretionary dismissal, since, despite its "serious misgivings" about the Federal Circuit's rule, it considered itself bound to dismiss by Gen-Probe. App. to Pet. for Cert. 31a. Discretionary dismissal was irrelevant to the Federal Circuit for the same reason. Respondents have raised the issue for the first time before this Court, exchanging competing accusations of inequitable conduct with petitioner. See, e.g., Brief for Respondent Genentech 42-44; Reply Brief for Petitioner 17, and n. 15. Under these circumstances, it would be imprudent for us to decide whether the District Court should, or must, decline to issue the requested declaratory relief. We leave the equitable, prudential, and policy arguments in favor of such a discretionary dismissal for the lower courts' consideration on remand. Similarly available for consideration on remand are any merits based arguments for denial of declaratory relief.

We hold that petitioner was not required, insofar as Article III is concerned, to break or terminate its 1997 license agreement before seeking a declaratory judgment in federal court that the underlying patent is invalid, unenforceable, or not infringed. The Court of Appeals erred in affirming the dismissal of this action for lack of subject-matter jurisdiction. The judgment of the Court of Appeals is reversed, and the cause is remanded for proceedings consistent with this opinion.

It is so ordered.

【思考题】

1. 按照美国联邦最高法院判决，在什么情况下，被控侵权人可以提起确认不侵权之诉？

2. 美国联邦最高法院的上述判例对于美国专利保护会造成何种影响？

Case1·拓展阅读

| Case2 China-Measures Affecting the Protection and Enforcement of Intellectual Property Rights（DS362） |

【案情说明】

一、案件事实

美国对中国知识产权保护一直以来予以高度关注。2007 年 4 月 10 日，美国分别就"中国知识产权保护和实施有关措施"和"中国影响部分出版物和视听娱乐产品贸易权和分销服务措施"向 WTO 提出磋商请求。2007 年 4 月 20 日，中方致函美方同意就相关事项展开磋商，但磋商未果。美国遂于 2007 年 8 月 13 日请求 WTO 成立专家组，9 月 25 日，专家组正式成立，12 月 13 日，WTO 总干事任命艾德里安·麦凯（Adrino Macey）担任专家组主席，斯瓦坎特·提瓦里(Sivakante Tiwari)、马力诺·波奇奥(Marino Porzio) 为专家组成员。与此同时，阿根廷、澳大利亚、加拿大等 12 个其他 WTO 成员作为第三方加入了专家组程序。美方要求中国就知识产权侵权刑事处罚门槛、知识产权侵权产品的海关处置措施以及对未在中国出版或发行作品版权及相关权利的保护和执行等方面措施加以调整，以符合 WTO 相关协定的要求。

具体而言，美方认为中方《中华人民共和国刑法》第 213 条、214 条、215 条、217 条、218 条和 220 条，2004 年《最高人民法院、最高人民检察院关于办理侵犯知识产权刑事案件具体应用法律若干问题的解释》（《2004 年解释》）和 2007 年《最高人民法院、最高人民检察院关于办理侵犯知识产权案刑事案件具体应用法律若干问题的解释》（《2007 年解释》）中对恶意商标侵权或商业规模的盗版行为给予刑事处罚时所设定的相应"门槛"标准的规定违反了中国在 TRIPS 协定第 41.4 条和 61 条下的义务。

中国刑法第 213 条、214 条、215 条就有关商标侵权的刑事处罚进行了规定。按照这三条刑法条文，只有在"情节严重""销售金额数额较大"时方可入罪。刑法第 217 条就"著作权侵权"、第 218 条就"销售侵权复制品"两类侵权行为入罪进行了规定。类似的，这两条规定也分别设立"违法所得数额较大或有其他严重情节"这样一个入罪门槛标准。刑法本身并未对"严重""特别严重""较大""巨大"等进行量化解释，但《2004 年解释》和《2007 年解释》分别对"非法经营数额""数额相对较大""违法所得数额""情节严重""其他严重情节"等进行了解释。美方认为，这种门槛规定违反了 TRIPS 协定第 41.1 条和第 61 条的规定。其中第 41.1 条规定，"各成员方应保证其国内法中包括关于本部分规定的实施程序，以便对任何侵犯本协定所涵盖知识产权的行动采取有效行动，包括防止侵权的迅速救济措施和制止进一步侵权的救济措施。这些程序的实施应避免对合法贸易造成障碍并为防止这些程序被滥用提供保障"。

除此以外，美方还指控中方依据《中华人民共和国知识产权海关保护规定》及其实施细则，以及 2007 年 4 月 2 日颁布的海关总署第 16 号公告及其修正案对海关在没收知识产权侵权产品后的处置办法违反了 TRIPS 协定的要求。美方认为，按照现行中国海关立法，中国海关未获得授权以便按照 TRIPS 第 46 条的规定，对侵权产品予以销毁或处置。中国此举也有违其在 TRIPS 协定第 59 条下的义务。美国第三个诉求称《中华人民共和国著作权法》拒绝对未在中国出版或发行作品版权和相关权利予以保护和执行违反了 TRIPS 协定下的义务。美方特别指出《著作权法》第 4 条与 TRIPS 协定第 9.1 条、第 14 条、第 61 条第 1、2 句，以及第 41.1 条规定不符。

二、裁判结果

专家组报告裁定如下：第一，中国著作权法第 4 条不符合中国在 1971 年《伯尔尼公约》第 5 条（1）款下承担的义务，也违反了 TRIPS 协定第 9.1 条和 41.1 条。第二，就中国海关执法措施的合规性而言，专家组认为中国有关海关措施违反了 TRIPS 协定第 59 条所纳入的 TRIPS 协定第 46 条所设立的原则。即相关海关措施必须是为有效制止侵权。第三，由于美国无法证明中国对于知识产权侵权的刑事处罚门槛违反 TRIPS 协定第 61 条（1）的规定，因此，专家组驳回了美国上述请求。同时，基于司法经济的理由，专家组未进一步就中国知识产权侵权刑事处罚门槛是否违反 TRIPS 第 41 条（1）的规定予以分析。

【法律分析】

本案主要涉及以下几个方面的问题：

（一）中国《著作权法》是否违反 TRIPS 协定第 9.1 条和第 41.1 条

关于这一诉求，核心争议点在于中国《著作权法》第 4 条的第 1 句话的规定是否剥夺了依法被禁止出版和传播作品作者依据《伯尔尼公约》所享有的其他权利。回答这一问题，首先需要肯定的是，首先，《伯尔尼公约》允许缔约方禁止某些作品的出版和传播，这是肯定的。其次，《伯尔尼公约》同时并非否定这些作品作者的著作权。在此前提基础之上，专家组需要解答的问题是，中国《著作权法》第 4 条第 1 句是否否定了此类作者的著作权。专家组分析后认为，该句"不受本法保护"实际上等同于剥夺了此类作者的著作权，因此裁定中国该规定违反了 WTO 成员的相关条约义务。

（二）中国海关措施是否违反 TRIPS 规定

对于该诉求，专家组从三个方面进行了分析：第一，TRIPS 第 46 条创设的原则究竟为何？第二，中国海关处理知识产权侵权货物的方式是否符合 TRIPS 协定第 46 条相关原则的要求；第三，中国海关将知识产权侵权产品予以拍卖的做法是否违反了 TRIPS

的要求。对于第一个问题，第46条的共同目标是"有效制止侵权"。专家组分析认为，不合格或危险产品的捐赠的确可能导致对权利人名誉的损害，但本案中，美国并非提出此类证据加以证明。对第二个问题，专家组分析认为，中国《海关条例》第27条的规定均为选择性规定，拍卖只是其中一种方式。美国主张认为拍卖排除了销毁这一方式，但因为无法证明而不予支持。对于第三个问题，专家组认为，中方仅仅去除侵权产品商标即允许进入商业渠道的做法不足以有效制止侵权，因此裁定中方这一做法违反 TRIPS 协定第59条纳入的第46条第4句的原则要求。

（三）中国对知识产权刑事处罚门槛是否过高

美方认为，对于某些"具有商业规模"的故意假冒商标和盗版案件，按照中国当前刑事法律的相关规定无法入刑处罚。因此，本案的核心争议实际上也就是确定何谓"具有商业规模"的侵权。也因此，专家组首先澄清了商业规模的通常含义。按照专家组的分析，商业规模的假冒或盗版应根据特定市场来判定，即根据特定市场中特定产品的数量或范围来决定某种蓄意假冒或盗版是否达到了商业规模。在此基础上，专家组接着分析了中国刑事法是否规定了过高的刑事门槛。专家组认为，美方未能提供相关产品和市场的数据或其他因素用以证明到底什么样的水平构成在中国市场的具有商业规模的蓄意假冒或盗版。因此，对此专家组并未予以支持。

【英文案例裁决摘录】

I. Thresholds for criminal procedures and penalties

The Panel notes that this claim challenges China's criminal measures "as such". The parties disagree on certain aspects of the measures at issue. The Panel is therefore obliged, in accordance with its mandate, to make an objective assessment of the meaning of the relevant provisions of those measures. The Panel recalls its observations at paragraph 7.28 above and confirms that it examines these measures solely for the purpose of determining their conformity with China's obligations under the TRIPS Agreement.[1]

Normative effect of the Judicial Interpretations

Under the 1982 Constitution of the People's Republic of China, the National People's Congress is the highest organ of State power and its permanent body is its Standing Committee. The National People's Congress and its Standing Committee exercise the legislative power of the State. The National People's Congress enacts and amends basic laws, such as the Criminal

---

1 Panel Report, para. 7.416.

Law, whilst its Standing Committee enacts and amends other statutes.[1]

In 1981, the Standing Committee of the National People's Congress adopted a Resolution on Improving the Work of Interpreting the Law, in which it decided as follows:

"Questions involving the specific application of laws and decrees in court trials shall be interpreted by the Supreme People's Court. Questions involving the specific application of laws and decrees in procuratorial work shall be interpreted by the Supreme People's Procuratorate."[2]

In 1997, the Supreme People's Court formulated Certain Provisions on Judicial Interpretation Work. In March 2007, it replaced these with new Provisions on Judicial Interpretation Work, which may be translated as follows:

"Judicial interpretations issued by the Supreme People's Court shall have legal effect."[3]

In 1996 the Supreme People's Procuratorate formulated Provisional Provisions on Judicial Interpretation Work. In May 2006, it replaced these with Provisions on Judicial Interpretation Work, which may be translated as follows:

"Judicial interpretations made by the Supreme People's Procuratorate have legal effect. People's procuratorates may use provisions of judicial interpretation in legal documents such as bills of indictment or protest."[4]

The Provisions of the Supreme People's Court on Judicial Interpretation Work and the Provisions of the Supreme People's Procuratorate on Judicial Interpretation Work both provide for the joint formulation of judicial interpretations by the Supreme People's Court and the Supreme People's Procuratorate when an issue involves both judicial and prosecutorial work.[5]

The United States submits that, in light of the above, the Judicial Interpretations at issue in

---

1 1982 Constitution of the People's Republic of China, Articles 62 and 67, explained in China's WTO Trade Policy Review, Report by the Secretariat, WT/TPR/S/161, Chapter II(2), referenced in United States' first written submission, para. 22, set out in Exhibit US-16 (quoiting Panel Report, para. 7.417).

2 1981 Resolution of the Standing Committee of the National People's Congress on Improving the Work of Interpreting the Law, paragraph 2, in Exhibit US-13(quoiting Panel Report, para. 7.418).

3 Provisions of the Supreme People's Court on Judicial Interpretation Work, Article 5, 法发 [2007] No. 12 in Exhibit US-14(quoiting Panel Report, para. 7.419).

4 Provisions of the Supreme People's Procuratorate on Judicial Interpretation Work, Article 5, 高检发研字 [2006] No. 4 in Exhibit US-15(quoiting Panel Report, para. 7.420).

5 Provisions of the Supreme People's Court on Judicial Interpretation Work (referred to in note 394 above), Article 7, and Provisions of the Supreme People's Procuratorate on Judicial Interpretation Work (referred to in note 395 above), Article 21(quoiting Panel Report, para. 7.421).

this dispute are binding and have the force of law.[1]

China submits that the Judicial Interpretations are issued "in order to ensure a uniform understanding and application of the law".[2] China does not disagree with the United States 'description of the legal basis and binding nature of the Judicial Interpretations at issue as set out in the United States' first written submission.[3] China confirms that if an illegal act does not meet one of the pertinent thresholds set out in the Judicial Interpretations at issue, prosecution of that act is legally impossible.[4]

In light of the above, the Panel finds that the Judicial Interpretations of the Articles of the Criminal Law at issue are binding and have the force of law.[5]

Thresholds under the Criminal Law in general

The Panel observes that Part One of the Criminal Law sets out general provisions. Within Part One, Chapter II, Section 1 provides for "Crimes and Criminal Responsibility". Article 13 defines a crime and may be translated in fine as follows:

"However, if the circumstances are obviously minor and the harm done is not serious, the act shall not be considered a crime."[6]

The Panel notes China's acknowledgement that a total of 11 crimes out of 117 crimes set out in these relevant Parts and this relevant Section of the Criminal Law are not subject to any specific threshold.[7] Therefore, whilst China may for internal policy reasons frequently use thresholds to define the point at which many classes of illegal act are considered serious enough to be criminalized, China's legal structure is capable of criminalizing certain acts without recourse to thresholds.[8]

Thresholds for conviction or aggravation

The Panel notes that some thresholds in the Criminal Law set minimum requirements for conviction ("conviction thresholds") whilst others set minimum requirements for higher penalties ("aggravation thresholds"). Most of the Articles at issue in this dispute include both. The conviction thresholds comprise "serious circumstances" in Articles 213 and 215, "relatively large amount of sales" in Article 214, "relatively large amount of illegal gains" or

---

1 United States' first written submission, para. 24(quoiting Panel Report, para. 7.422).

2 China's first written submission, para. 22(quoiting Panel Report, para. 7.423).

3 China's response to Question No. 10, referencing paras 20-24 of that submission(quoiting Panel Report, para. 7.423).

4 China's response to Question No. 55(quoiting Panel Report, para. 7.423).

5 Panel Report, para. 7.424.

6 Exhibit CHN-1(quoiting Panel Report, para. 7.427).

7 China's response to Question No. 57(quoiting Panel Report, para. 7.429).

8 Panel Report, para. 7.429.

"other serious circumstances" in Article 217 and "huge amount of sales 'in Article 218. The aggravation thresholds comprise' especially serious circumstances" in Articles 213, 215 and 217 and "huge amount of sales" in Article 214.[1]

The United States only challenges the conviction thresholds as these render prosecution impossible in the absence of certain criteria. Therefore, the Panel does not consider the aggravation thresholds further.[2]

General provisions on inchoate crimes

The Panel observes that Part One, Chapter II, Section 2 of the Criminal Law sets out three inchoate crimes of preparation for a crime, criminal attempt and discontinuation of a crime.[3]

The Panel notes that each of these Articles contains provisions that appear to be of general application and that relate explicitly to "a crime" (犯罪). The Articles to which China refers contain no express limitation to certain specific provisions of the Criminal Law. They form part of Chapter II on "Crimes" found in Part One on "General Provisions", which also sets out the aim, basic principles and scope of application of the Criminal Law in Chapter I, provisions on punishments in Chapter III and the concrete application of punishments in Chapter IV. On their face, there is no reason to suppose that Articles 22 and 23 do not apply to the crimes of infringing intellectual property rights in Articles 213, 214, 215, 217 and 218 of the Criminal Law. This reading is confirmed by examples of judicial decisions submitted by China that show courts applying Articles 22 and 23 of the Criminal Law in cases of crimes of infringing intellectual property rights.[4]

The Panel also notes that China has referred to the offences of preparation for a crime and attempted crime to show that packaging and product components can be taken into account in determining the availability of criminal procedures to enforce the substantive crimes of infringing intellectual property rights. However, the Panel notes that China has not alleged that the offences of preparation and attempt render activities falling below the thresholds in Articles 213 to 220 generally subject to criminal prosecution.[5]

General provisions on joint crimes

The Panel observes that Part One, Chapter II, Section 3 of the Criminal Law provides for "Joint crimes". It sets out five provisions. Article 25 may be translated, relevantly, as follows:

---

1 Panel Report, para. 7.430.

2 Panel Report, para. 7.431.

3 The parties have not referred to Article 24 on discontinuation of a crime(quoiting Panel Report, para. 7.434).

4 The United States refers to these judicial decisions and appears to acknowledge that the Articles were applied in these cases: see United States' response to Question No. 8(quoiting Panel Report, para. 7.436).

5 Panel Report, para. 7.437.

"A joint crime refers to an intentional crime committed by two or more persons jointly. ..."[1]

The Panel observes that Articles 26 and 27 are limited to "joint crimes" which are defined by Article 25 as "intentional crimes". On their face, there is no reason to suppose that Articles 25, 26 and 27 do not apply to the crimes of infringing intellectual property rights in Articles 213, 214, 215, 217 and 218 of the Criminal Law. Several judicial decisions submitted by China show one or more of these Articles being cited in relation to Article 213.[2] The decisions show that the relevant factors were aggregated among several offenders in order to reach a criminal threshold.[3]

China submitted that it may apply criminal procedures and penalties, on the basis of joint crimes and criminal group membership, to infringers that would not otherwise reach the criminal thresholds of the substantive criminal laws.[4] However, in response to a question, China confirmed that the numerical thresholds under Articles 213, 214, 215, 217 and 218 of the Criminal Law apply to joint crimes under Articles 25, 26 and 27 of the Criminal Law.[5]

Therefore, the Panel considers that the concept of joint crimes is relevant to the capacity of the Criminal Law to take into account an element of organization among different offenders. However, it does not alter the lack of criminal procedures and penalties for acts of infringement falling below the thresholds in Articles 213 to 220.[6]

The Panel observes that, as regards the trademark offences, two of the thresholds under Article 213 of the Criminal Law, as interpreted by Article 1 of Judicial Interpretation No. 19 [2004], are set in terms of "illegal business operation volume" and "illegal gains" (i.e. amount of profits obtained[7]). Article 214 of the Criminal Law applies to the act of selling, and the corresponding threshold in Article 2 of Judicial Interpretation No. 19 [2004] is set in terms of "amount of sales". These all imply a purpose of obtaining financial gain or making profits. Article 215 of the Criminal Law does not expressly refer to a profit-making purpose.[8]

As regards the copyright offences, both Articles 217 and 218 of the Criminal Law expressly refer to acts carried out for "the purpose of making profits". This language is

---

1 Exhibit CHN-1(quoiting Panel Report, para. 7.441).

2 Exhibits CHN-4, CHN-6, CHN-9, CHN-12, CHN-13 and CHN-16(quoiting Panel Report, para. 7.444).

3 Panel Report, para. 7.444.

4 China's rebuttal submission, para. 46(quoiting Panel Report, para. 7.445).

5 China's response to Question No. 56(quoiting Panel Report, para. 7.445).

6 Panel Report, para. 7.446.

7 See paragraph 7.402 above(quoiting Panel Report, para. 7.448).

8 Panel Report, para. 7.448.

reiterated in the corresponding interpretations in Articles 5 and 6 of Judicial Interpretation No. 19 [2004] and Article 1 of Judicial Interpretation No. 6 [2007].[1]

Therefore, Articles 213, 214, 217 and 218 of the Criminal Law take account of at least one qualitative factor in conjunction with the numerical thresholds. In this dispute, the United States does not challenge this aspect of the measure.[2]

Alternative thresholds

The Panel observes that Articles 213 and 215 of the Criminal Law each contain a single threshold. However, these are interpreted by Articles 1 and 3 of Judicial Interpretation No. 19 [2004] in terms of a series of distinct circumstances. It is clear from the text of Articles 1 and 3 that each of these circumstances applies in the alternative as Articles 1 and 3 each provide that the conviction threshold under the relevant Article of the Criminal Law shall be deemed satisfied in "any of the following circumstances".[3]

The Panel observes that Article 217 of the Criminal Law contains two conviction thresholds namely, "the amount of illegal gains" and "other serious circumstances". The text of Article 217 makes it clear that these are alternatives to each other by the use of the word "or". Both of these thresholds are interpreted by Article 5 of Judicial Interpretation No. 19 [2004]: the former in terms of a numerical amount and the latter in terms of a series of distinct circumstances. It is clear from the text of Article 5 that each of these circumstances applies in the alternative as Article 5 provides that the conviction threshold of "other serious circumstances" under Article 217 of the Criminal Law shall be deemed satisfied in "any of the following circumstances". Satisfaction of any one of those circumstances, or "the amount of illegal gains" threshold, shall be deemed to satisfy the relevant conviction threshold.[4]

This means, for example, that the use of a counterfeit trademark where the illegal business operation volume is, say, ¥40,000 (i.e. below the threshold of ¥50,000 applicable under Article 213 of the Criminal Law) is not exempt from criminal prosecution unless the amount of illegal gains, the number of registered trademarks involved in the offence, and other circumstances all fail to fulfil the other applicable thresholds. However, where an act of infringement falls below all the applicable thresholds, criminal prosecution and penalties are not available.[5]

It is not disputed that the crimes of selling under Articles 214 and 218 of the Criminal Law each contain only one conviction threshold. Therefore, those thresholds do not apply as

---

1 Panel Report, para. 7.449.

2 See paragraphs 7.659 and 7.660 below(quoiting Panel Report, para. 7.450).

3 Panel Report, para. 7.453.

4 Panel Report, para. 7.454.

5 Panel Report, para. 7.455.

alternatives.[1]

Cumulative calculation over time

The Panel observes that Part One, Chapter IV, Section 8 of the Criminal Law sets out limitation periods for the prosecution of crimes. Article 87 provides for limitation periods calculated according to the maximum punishment for the relevant crime, of which the shortest period is five years. Article 89 of the Criminal Law provides that the limitation period for a criminal act of a continual or continuous nature shall be counted from the date the criminal act is terminated.[2]

The Panel also notes that article 12(2) of Judicial Interpretation No.19 [2004][3] already show that the thresholds may take into account multiple acts of infringement, and not simply the income, profits, sales or number of copies in a single transaction or at a single point in time. This point is confirmed by examples of judicial decisions submitted by China showing that, when calculating whether thresholds had been met, courts have taken into account infringements during periods of up to five years.[4] An administrative penalty for a particular act of infringement excludes that act from the cumulative calculation of the "illegal business operation volume", "the amount of illegal gains", or "the amount of sales" thresholds and, hence, from criminal procedures and penalties.[5]

Calculation of illegal business operation volume—goods

The Panel observes that three conviction thresholds under Articles 213, 215 and 217 of the Criminal Law are set in terms of "illegal business operation volume". The definition of "illegal business operation volume" in Article 12(1) of Judicial Interpretation No. 19 [2004][6] refers to infringing products "manufactured, stored, transported or sold"during the course of commission of the act of infringing intellectual property rights. On its face, this does not restrict the calculation of these thresholds to the value of goods seized in a single place at the same point in time. This interpretation is confirmed by examples of judicial decisions submitted by China showing that courts have taken into account the value of goods already sold[7] , as well as of

---

1 Panel Report, para. 7.456.

2 Exhibit CHN-1(quoiting Panel Report, para. 7.459).

3 Panel Report, para. 7.460.

4 Exhibits CHN-4, CHN-13 and CHN-14(quoiting Panel Report, para. 7.461).

5 Panel Report, para. 7.461.

6 Set out at paragraph 7.401 above(quoiting Panel Report, para. 7.464).

7 Exhibits CHN-4, CHN-5 and CHN-6(quoiting Panel Report, para. 7.464).

goods seized at different locations[1] when calculating the illegal business operation volume.[2]

Calculation of illegal business operation volume—price

The Panel observes that three conviction thresholds under Articles 213, 215 and 217 of the Criminal Law are set in terms of "illegal business operation volume", which can be calculated by alternative methods. Ultimately, the parties agree that, in accordance with the definition of "illegal business operation volume" in Article 12(1) of Judicial Interpretation No. 19 [2004][3], the primary method of calculation of those thresholds is based on the actual price at which infringing goods were sold or labelled or, if unsold, the average actual sales price of the infringing products as verified. It is only where there is no labelled price or the actual sales price is unable to be verified that the illegal business operation volume is calculated according to the "middle" market price of the infringed products. In other words, the threshold primarily relates to the value of the counterfeit trademark or copyright infringing goods but may, as a last resort, relate to the value of the genuine products.[4]

It is not disputed that the value of the counterfeit trademark goods or copyright infringing goods will be less than the value of the corresponding genuine goods. This has the effect of making the illegal business operation threshold harder to satisfy in those cases where the price of the genuine goods is not used. The number of cases that will fall below the thresholds is therefore greater than if the price of the infringed goods is used in all cases.[5]

Number of goods and prices

The Panel observes that, in accordance with the definition of "illegal business operation volume" in Article 12(1) of Judicial Interpretation No. 19 [2004][6], these thresholds are calculated in terms of the price of goods. Naturally, the number of goods required to meet the threshold is inversely proportional to the value of those goods. Therefore, the threshold is flexible enough to capture a small number of high-value goods or a large number of low-value goods. However, where the number of goods multiplied by the value of the goods is less than the threshold and not captured by any alternative applicable threshold, no criminal procedures and penalties will apply.[7]

---

1 Exhibit CHN-7(quoiting Panel Report, para. 7.464).

2 Panel Report, para. 7.464.

3 Set out at paragraph 7.401 above(quoiting Panel Report, para. 7.467).

4 Panel Report, para. 7.467.

5 Panel Report, para. 7.468.

6 Set out at paragraph 7.401 above(quoiting Panel Report, para. 7.470).

7 Panel Report, para. 7.470.

Residual thresholds

The Panel observes that, on the face of the measures at issue, one of the thresholds applicable to three crimes infringing intellectual property rights is a residual category of "other serious circumstances". In the case of Articles 213 and 215 of the Criminal Law, this threshold only appears in the text of Judicial Interpretation No. 19 [2004]. In the case of Article 217 of the Criminal Law, this threshold actually appears in the text of the Article itself, but is later defined in terms of two specific thresholds plus an identically worded residual category of "other serious circumstances". This bears out China's explanation that this threshold is a legislative device that allows for the future development of laws. However, it is not alleged that any other thresholds have yet been devised beyond those set out in this Report.[1]

Moreover, it is not alleged that the courts or prosecutors would treat all infringing acts that fall below the numerical thresholds as criminal acts by virtue of this residual threshold. China confirms that if an illegal act does not meet one of the pertinent thresholds set out in the Judicial Interpretations at issue, prosecution of that act is legally impossible.[2] China also confirms that these residual thresholds apply to other acts that are "comparable and equivalent" to the defined thresholds. Therefore, these residual thresholds do not significantly alter the legal position but rather help define the class of trademark- and copyright-infringing acts that are not treated as criminal.[3]

Administrative enforcement

The Panel notes that administrative sanctions, including fines, are available for intellectual property infringement falling below the criminal thresholds in China. Therefore, the thresholds do not create a "safe harbor". However, neither party to the dispute[4] argues that administrative enforcement may fulfil the obligations on criminal procedures and remedies set out in Article 61 of the TRIPS Agreement. Therefore, the Panel does not consider this issue further.[5]

Conclusion regarding construction of the measures at issue

For the above reasons, the Panel concludes that, whilst the structure of the thresholds and the method of calculation of some of them can take account of various circumstances, acts of trademark and copyright infringement falling below all the applicable thresholds are not subject to criminal procedures and penalties. The Panel will now consider whether any of those acts of

---

1 Panel Report, para. 7.474.

2 See paragraphs 7.423 and 7.455 above(quoiting Panel Report, para. 7.475).

3 Panel Report, para. 7.475.

4 Contrast Brazil's third party written submission, paras 39-42(quoiting Panel Report, para. 7.478).

5 Panel Report, para. 7.478.

infringement constitute "willful trademark counterfeiting or copyright piracy on a commercial scale" within the meaning of Article 61 of the TRIPS Agreement.[1]

Claim under the first sentence of Article 61 of the TRIPS Agreement

The Panel decides that the United States' claim relates to cases of wilful trademark counterfeiting and copyright piracy in respect of which China does not provide for criminal procedures and penalties to be applied but which the United States claims are "on a commercial scale".[2] The claim is based on two alleged "fundamental problems" referred to in this Report as the two limbs of this claim. The first limb concerns the level and method of calculation of the thresholds. By specifying certain levels, the thresholds allegedly eliminate whole classes of counterfeiting and piracy from risk of criminal prosecution and conviction.[3] The second limb concerns the limited set of numerical tests in the thresholds. By focusing solely on these tests, the thresholds allegedly require law enforcement officials to disregard other indicia of counterfeiting and piracy.[4]

The Panel notes that the first limb of the claim addresses the numbers specified in the numerical tests, and the way in which some of them are calculated, in order to show that the thresholds are too high. These are quantitative issues. The second limb addresses certain factors that the numerical tests do not take into account. These are qualitative issues. Neither limb is a broad claim that numerical thresholds cannot capture all cases "on a commercial scale". In response to the Panel's requests for clarification of the claim after both the first and the second substantive meetings, the United States clarified that it did not object to the use of numerical thresholds *per se*.[5]

Accordingly, the Panel is not asked to consider whether numerical thresholds, as a matter of principle, can implement an obligation in terms of cases "on a commercial scale".[6]

Therefore, in its assessment of this claim, the Panel will proceed as follows:

(a) with respect to the first limb of the claim, the Panel will assess whether the levels in

---

1 Panel Report, para. 7.479.

2 United States' first written submission, paras 116 and 143(quoiting Panel Report, para. 7.494).

3 United States' first written submission, para. 112; rebuttal submission, para. 74(quoiting Panel Report, para. 7.494).

4 United States' first oral statement, para. 36; first oral statement (closing statement), para. 16(quoiting Panel Report, para. 7.494).

5 United States' responses to Questions Nos. 25 and 54. It seems pertinent to note that during the negotiations of the terms of China's accession to the WTO, some members of the Working Party took a similar position. In particular, they expressed concerns that the monetary thresholds were very high and seldom met. They considered that those thresholds should be lowered: see the Working Party Report, para. 304. China subsequently reduced certain thresholds with the adoption of Judicial Interpretation No. 19 [2004]: see United States' first written submission, para. 27(quoiting Panel Report, para. 7.495).

6 Panel Report, para. 7.495.

China's thresholds are too high to capture all cases on a commercial scale; and

(b) with respect to the second limb of the claim, the Panel will assess whether the other factors raised by the United States can be taken into account by China's thresholds to capture all cases on a commercial scale and, if not, whether this is a TRIPS requirement.[1]

Procedural issues

The Panel notes that this claim is brought under Article 61 of the TRIPS Agreement, which concerns criminal procedures and penalties.[2] Article 64.1 of that Agreement provides that: "The provisions of Articles XXII and XXIII of GATT 1994 as elaborated and applied by the Dispute Settlement Understanding shall apply to consultations and the settlement of disputes under this Agreement except as otherwise specifically provided herein."[3]

The application of the rules and procedures of the DSU to the settlement of disputes under the TRIPS Agreement is confirmed by Article 1.1 of the DSU, in conjunction with Appendix 1 of the DSU which lists the TRIPS Agreement as a "covered agreement". In accordance with Article 3.2 of the DSU, the Panel applies "the customary rules of interpretation of public international law" to its task of interpreting the TRIPS Agreement in this dispute. The general rule of interpretation, expressed in Article 31 of the Vienna Convention, and the rules on supplementary means of interpretation in Article 32 of the Vienna Convention, have attained the status of rules of customary or general international law.[4] The Panel will apply the general rule of interpretation and, to the extent warranted, supplementary means of interpretation. The Panel is mindful that Article 3.2 of the DSU also provides that "recommendations and rulings of the DSB cannot add to or diminish the rights and obligations provided in the covered agreements".[5]

The Panel acknowledges the sensitive nature of criminal matters and attendant concerns regarding sovereignty. These concerns may be expected to find reflection in the text and scope of treaty obligations regarding such matters as negotiated by States and other Members.[6] Section 5 of Part III of the TRIPS Agreement, dedicated to criminal procedures and remedies, is considerably briefer and less detailed than the other Sections on enforcement in Part III.

---

1 Panel Report, para. 7.496.

2 Despite use of the word "remedies" in the second and third sentences, it seems clear that criminal sanctions are "penalties" (quoiting Panel Report, para. 7.499).

3 Panel Report, para. 7.499.

4 Appellate Body Reports in US – Gasoline, at p. 17; and Japan – Alcoholic Beverages II, at p. 10(quoiting Panel Report, para. 7.500).

5 Panel Report, para. 7.500.

6 Articles 3, 4 and 41, in particular paragraph 4, of the TRIPS Agreement inter alia also apply to criminal enforcement procedures(quoiting Panel Report, para. 7.501).

Brief as it is, the text of Section 5 also contains significant limitations and flexibilities. The customary rules of treaty interpretation oblige the treaty interpreter to take these limitations and flexibilities into account in interpreting the relevant provision.[1]

Nature of the obligation

This claim is brought under the first sentence of Article 61 of the TRIPS Agreement.[2] The first sentence of this Article uses the word "shall", indicating that it is mandatory. This stands in contrast to the fourth sentence, which addresses the same issue with respect to other cases of infringement of intellectual property rights but uses the word "may", indicating that it is permissive. Unlike the third sentence, the first sentence contains no language such as "in appropriate cases" which might expressly introduce some margin of discretion. The terms of the first sentence of Article 61, read in context, impose an obligation.[3] This interpretation is confirmed by Article 41 of the TRIPS Agreement on "General Obligations", which is the first provision of Part III of the TRIPS Agreement and forms part of the context of Article 61.[4]

In the Panel's view, the general obligation in Article 41.1 confirms that Article 61 contains obligations, as one of the specific provisions on enforcement procedures in Part III.[5]

China submits that the first sentence of Article 61 cannot set forth a specific obligation because it provides for enforcement against certain types of infringement but neither the TRIPS Agreement nor the Berne Convention (1971) define what constitutes substantive infringement. Rather, they defer to national discretion to define the rights being infringed.[6]

The Panel agrees with China that the first sentence of Article 61 contains a number of terms that are not defined by the Agreement and that this can affect the proper interpretation of the provision. However, even though the first sentence does not use the term "infringement", it is important to note that Part II of the TRIPS Agreement, including the provisions of the Paris Convention (1967) incorporated by Article 2.1, and the provisions of the Berne Convention (1971) incorporated by Article 9.1, provide for minimum standards concerning the availability, scope and use of intellectual property rights that apply irrespective of national treatment. These provisions define the rights conferred by intellectual property and the circumstances in which those rights are infringed. Part III of the TRIPS Agreement provides for the enforcement of those rights, to varying degrees. Therefore, the Agreement contains substantive obligations that

1 Panel Report, para. 7.501.

2 Panel Report, para. 7.502.

3 Panel Report, para. 7.503.

4 Panel Report, para. 7.504.

5 Panel Report, para. 7.505.

6 China's first written submission, paras 80-82(quoiting Panel Report, para. 7.506).

are not simply matters of national discretion.[1]

China submits that Article 61 of the TRIPS Agreement is less specific than the Anti-Dumping Agreement and the Agreement on Subsidies and Countervailing Measures and lacks the clarity required to demonstrate a specific, concrete obligation. China also argues that the TRIPS Agreement lacks a provision such as Article 18.4 of the Anti-Dumping Agreement requiring Members to take steps to ensure the conformity of their laws with its provisions.[2]

The Panel agrees that the TRIPS Agreement differs from trade remedy agreements. However, the Panel will apply the usual rules of treaty interpretation to the terms used in the TRIPS Agreement and make its assessment on that basis in accordance with Article 11 of the DSU. The Panel draws China's attention to Article XVI:4 of the WTO Agreement which provides as follows:

"Each Member shall ensure the conformity of its laws, regulations and administrative procedures with its obligations as provided in the annexed Agreements."[3]

The "annexed Agreements" include the TRIPS Agreement. Therefore, Members are obliged to ensure conformity of their respective laws with their respective obligations as provided in the TRIPS Agreement.[4]

China submits that the third sentence of Article 1.1 of the TRIPS Agreement sets forth the overall context for interpreting the specificity of the standards in the TRIPS Agreement. It describes Article 1.1 as a specific "caveat" that establishes boundaries on obligations, specifically in the realm of enforcement.[5]

The Panel observes that Article 1.1 of the TRIPS Agreement[6] that, The first sentence of Article 1.1 sets out the basic obligation that Members "shall give effect" to the provisions of this Agreement. This means that the provisions of the Agreement are obligations where stated, and the first sentence of Article 61 so states. The second sentence of Article 1.1 clarifies that the provisions of the Agreement are minimum standards only, in that it gives Members the freedom to implement a higher standard, subject to a condition. The third sentence of Article 1.1 does not grant Members freedom to implement a lower standard, but rather grants freedom to determine the appropriate method of implementation of the provisions to which they are required to give effect under the first sentence. The Panel agrees that differences among

---

1 Panel Report, para. 7.507.

2 China's first written submission, paras 83-87(quoiting Panel Report, para. 7.508).

3 Panel Report, para. 7.509.

4 Panel Report, para. 7.510.

5 China's first written submission, paras 89-97(quoiting Panel Report, para. 7.511).

6 Panel Report, para. 7.512.

Members' respective legal systems and practices tend to be more important in the area of enforcement. However, a coherent reading of the three sentences of Article 1.1 does not permit differences in domestic legal systems and practices to justify any derogation from the basic obligation to give effect to the provisions on enforcement.[1]

Therefore, the standard of compliance with Article 61 is the minimum internationally agreed standard set out in that Article. The minimum standard in Article 61 does not defer to China's domestic practice on the definition of criminal liability and sanctions for other wrongful acts in areas not subject to international obligations under the TRIPS Agreement, unless it so states. For example, the second sentence refers to "crimes of a corresponding gravity" which might refer to domestic practice in other areas. However, the first sentence of Article 61 does not make any such reference.[2]

For the above reasons, the Panel confirms its view at paragraphs 7.503 to 7.505 above that the first sentence of Article 61 of the TRIPS Agreement imposes an obligation. The Panel will now turn to the terms used in that provision, read in context and in light of the object and purpose of the Agreement, to determine the scope and content of that obligation.[3]

Scope of the obligation

The terms of the obligation in the first sentence of Article 61 of the TRIPS Agreement are that Members shall "provide for criminal procedures and penalties to be applied". That obligation applies to "wilful trademark counterfeiting or copyright piracy on a commercial scale". Within that scope, there are no exceptions. The obligation applies to all acts of wilful trademark counterfeiting or copyright piracy on a commercial scale.[4]

The Panel recalls its conclusion at paragraph 7.479 above that, in China, acts of trademark and copyright infringement falling below the applicable thresholds are not subject to criminal procedures and penalties. The issue that arises is whether any of those acts of infringement constitute "wilful trademark counterfeiting or copyright piracy on a commercial scale" within the meaning of the first sentence of Article 61. This requires the Panel to consider the interpretation of that phrase.[5]

The Panel notes that the first sentence of Article 61 contains no fewer than four limitations on the obligation that it sets forth. These define the scope of the relevant obligation and are not exceptions. The first limitation is that the obligation applies to trademarks and copyright rather

---

1 Panel Report, para. 7.513.

2 Panel Report, para. 7.514.

3 Panel Report, para. 7.515.

4 Panel Report, para. 7.516.

5 Panel Report, para. 7.517.

than to all intellectual property rights covered by the TRIPS Agreement. The fourth sentence of Article 61 gives Members the option to criminalize other infringements of intellectual property rights, in particular where they are committed wilfully and on a commercial scale. Despite the potential gravity of such infringements, Article 61 creates no obligation to criminalize them. This can be contrasted with Sections 2 and 3 of Part III of the TRIPS Agreement, regarding civil and administrative procedures and remedies, which apply to any act of infringement of intellectual property rights covered by the Agreement. It can also be contrasted with Section 4 of Part III which attaches conditions to the option to apply its procedures to other infringements of intellectual property rights.[1]

The second limitation in the first sentence of Article 61, which is related to the first, is that it applies to counterfeiting and piracy rather than to all infringements of trademarks and copyright. This can also be contrasted with Sections 2 and 3 of Part III of the TRIPS Agreement. This limitation, like the first, indicates an intention to reduce the scope of the obligation. Indeed, the records of the negotiation of the TRIPS Agreement confirm that the term "infringements of trademarks and copyright" on a commercial scale was considered in the draft provision on criminal procedures but ultimately rejected.[2]

The terms "trademark counterfeiting" and "copyright piracy" are not defined in the TRIPS Agreement. They are distinct from the concepts of "trademark infringement" and "copyright infringement". They are similar to the terms "counterfeit trademark goods" and "pirated copyright goods" which are defined for the purposes of the TRIPS Agreement[3] in footnote 14.

The terms used in the first sentence of Article 61 denote classes of acts or activity whilst the terms used in footnote 14 denote classes of goods only. This reflects the fact that Article 61 provides for criminal enforcement against infringing acts whilst Section 4 of Part III (in which the terms defined in footnote 14 are used) provides for enforcement at the border against infringing goods. The definitions in footnote 14 also refer to the law of the country of "importation" whilst Article 61 relates to the law of the Member to which the obligation applies – generally speaking, the law of the Member where the infringing act occurs. Subject to these observations, the Panel considers that the definitions in footnote 14 are relevant in

1 See paragraph 7.223 above(quoiting Panel Report, para. 7.518).

2 The Panel has recourse to this supplementary means of interpretation in accordance with Article 32 of the Vienna Convention in order to confirm the meaning resulting from the application of the general rule of interpretation in Article 31. See, for example, the Chairman's draft text of 23 July 1990 (document MTN.GNG/NG11/W/76)(quoiting Panel Report, para. 7.519).

3 The terms "counterfeit trademark goods" and "pirated copyright goods" are used not only in Section 4 of Part III but also in Article 69 of the TRIPS Agreement. The identical term "counterfeit trademark goods" is also used in Article 46(quoiting Panel Report, para. 7.520).

understanding the terms used in Article 61.[1]

The United States does not claim that Articles 213, 214, 215, 217 and 218 of the Criminal Law fail to cover the full extent of the terms "trademark counterfeiting" and "copyright piracy" as used in Article 61 of the TRIPS Agreement.[2] China does not contest that each of the thresholds established by the Criminal Law, in particular Articles 213, 214, 215, 217 and 218, applies to acts of "trademark counterfeiting" and "copyright piracy". Therefore, it is unnecessary for the Panel to interpret those terms in greater detail at this stage.[3]

The third limitation in the first sentence of Article 61 is indicated by the word "wilful" that precedes the words "trademark counterfeiting or copyright piracy". This word functions as a qualifier indicating that trademark counterfeiting or copyright piracy is not subject to the obligation in the first sentence of Article 61 unless it is "wilful". This word, focussing on the infringer's intent, reflects the criminal nature of the enforcement procedures at issue. It is absent from Section 4 of Part III, even though that Section is similarly limited, as a minimum, to counterfeit trademark goods and pirated copyright goods. The penalties for criminal acts, such as imprisonment, fines and forfeiture of property, are relatively grave, as reflected in the second sentence of Article 61. There is no obligation to make such penalties available with respect to acts of infringement committed without the requisite intent.[4]

The fourth limitation in the first sentence of Article 61 is indicated by the phrase "on a commercial scale" that follows the words "trademark counterfeiting or copyright piracy". This phrase, like the word "wilful", appears to qualify both "trademark counterfeiting" and "copyright piracy". The limitation to cases on a commercial scale, like the limitation to cases of wilfulness, stands in contrast to all other specific obligations on enforcement in Part III of the TRIPS Agreement.[5]

The principal interpretative point in dispute is the meaning of the phrase "on a commercial scale". This phrase functions in context as a qualifier, indicating that wilful trademark counterfeiting or copyright piracy is included in the scope of the obligation provided that it also satisfies the condition of being "on a commercial scale". Accordingly, certain acts of wilful trademark counterfeiting or copyright piracy are excluded from the scope of the first sentence of Article 61.[6]

---

1 Panel Report, para. 7.521.

2 United States' first written submission, paras 101 and 106(quoiting Panel Report, para. 7.522).

3 Panel Report, para. 7.522.

4 Panel Report, para. 7.523.

5 Section 4 contains a de minimis exception, discussed at paragraph 7.553 below(quoting Panel Report, para. 7.524).

6 Panel Report, para. 7.525.

Despite the fact that trademark counterfeiting and copyright piracy infringe the rights of right holders, and despite the fact that they can be grave, the two qualifications of wilfulness and "on a commercial scale" indicate that Article 61 does not require Members to provide for criminal procedures and penalties to be applied to such counterfeiting and piracy per se unless they satisfy certain additional criteria. This is highlighted by the fourth sentence of Article 61, which allows Members to provide for criminal procedures and penalties to be applied in other cases of infringement, "in particular" where they are committed wilfully and on a commercial scale. This indicates that the negotiators considered cases of wilful infringement on a commercial scale to represent a subset of cases of infringement, comprising the graver cases. This is useful context for interpreting the first sentence of Article 61, even though it does not refer to "infringement" in general, because the first sentence refers to both "counterfeiting" and "piracy" and wilfulness and commercial scale, evidently to limit the cases of infringement in different ways. Therefore, the text of Article 61 indicates that it must not be assumed that the nature of counterfeiting and piracy per se is such that Members are obliged to provide for the application of criminal procedures and penalties.[1]

This is consistent with the nature of the obligation, being a minimum standard, as expressly confirmed by the use of the words "at least" in the first sentence of Article 61 and, more generally, by the second sentence of Article 1.1, quoted at paragraph 7.512 above. Members may, and many do, criminalize other acts of trademark counterfeiting, other acts of copyright piracy, other acts of infringement of trademarks and copyright, and acts of infringement of other intellectual property rights such as patents, but there is no obligation to do so under the TRIPS Agreement.[2]

Part III of the TRIPS Agreement distinguishes between the treatment of wilful trademark counterfeiting and copyright piracy on a commercial scale, on the one hand, and all other infringements of intellectual property rights, on the other hand, in that only the former are subject to an obligation regarding criminal procedures and penalties. This indicates the shared view of the negotiators that the former are the most blatant and egregious acts of infringement. This view must inform the interpretation of Article 61.[3]

The Panel recalls its findings at paragraph 7.241 above as to the circumstances of conclusion of the TRIPS Agreement with respect to enforcement procedures. Whilst some of the pre-existing international intellectual property agreements or conventions contain provisions on the characteristics of enforcement mechanisms, it is striking that none of them

---

1 Panel Report, para. 7.526.

2 Panel Report, para. 7.527.

3 Panel Report, para. 7.528.

create any specific minimum standard for criminal enforcement procedures.[1] Among the international intellectual property agreements with wide membership, Article 61 of the TRIPS Agreement is, in this sense, unique.[2]

This reflects, in part, the fact that intellectual property rights are private rights, as recognized in the fourth recital of the Preamble to the TRIPS Agreement. In contrast, criminal procedures are designed to punish acts that transgress societal values. This is reflected in the use of the word "penalties" in Article 61.[3]

Bearing in mind these aspects of the context of the first sentence of Article 61, and the object and purpose of the TRIPS Agreement, the Panel now turns to the ordinary meaning of the words "on a commercial scale".[4]

"on a commercial scale"

The parties adopt different approaches to the task of interpreting the phrase "on a commercial scale". The Panel will examine each of these approaches in turn, beginning with that of the complainant.[5]

The ordinary meaning of the word "scale" is uncontroversial. It may be defined as "relative magnitude or extent; degree, proportion. Freq. in on a grand, lavish, small, etc. scale".[6] The ordinary meaning of the word includes both the concept of quantity, in terms of magnitude or extent, as well as the concept of relativity. Both concepts are combined in the notions of degree and proportion. Therefore, a particular "scale" compares certain things or actions in terms of their size. Some things or actions will be of the relevant size and others will not.[7]

The relevant size is indicated by the word "commercial". The ordinary meaning of "commercial" may be defined in various ways. The following two definitions have been raised in the course of these proceedings:

"1. Engaged in commerce; of, pertaining to, or bearing on commerce.

2. (…)

3. Interested in financial return rather than artistry; likely to make a profit; regarded as a

---

1 The Convention for the Protection of Producers of Phonograms against Unauthorized Duplication of their Phonograms, Article 3, expressly

provides that each Contracting State may implement the Convention by means of penal sanctions(quoiting Panel Report, para. 7.529).

2 Panel Report, para. 7.529.

3 Panel Report, para. 7.530.

4 Panel Report, para. 7.531.

5 Panel Report, para. 7.532.

6 New Shorter Oxford English Dictionary (1993). Mexico notes a definition in Spanish that refers to degree, but that is not apposite in context:

see Mexico's third party oral statement, fn. 8(quoiting Panel Report, para. 7.533).

7 Panel Report, para. 7.533.

mere matter of business."[1]

The Panel considers the first definition to be apposite. It includes the term "commerce" which may, in turn, be defined as "buying and selling; the exchange of merchandise or services, esp. on a large scale".[2] Reading this definition into the definition of "commercial" indicates that "commercial" means, basically, engaged in buying and selling, or pertaining to, or bearing on, buying and selling.[3] A combination of that expanded definition of "commercial" and the definition of "scale" would render a meaning in terms of a relative magnitude or extent (of those) engaged in buying and selling, or a relative magnitude or extent pertaining to, or bearing on, buying and selling. This draws a link to the commercial marketplace.[4]

The United States also submits that the word "commercial" scale draws a link to the commercial marketplace. However, it refers to elements of the first and third meanings in definition 3., but dismisses the relevance of the second meaning, "likely to make a profit", because it is different from the other two.[5]

The Panel notes that the third definition, which includes the qualifiers "rather than artistry" and "mere", refers to usages such as a "commercial artist", "commercial film" or "commercial writing" in the sense of those who are more interested in financial return than the artistic merit of a work, works that are of such a nature that they are likely to make a profit and works that are regarded as a mere matter of business rather than as expressions of other values. This definition is not apposite in the first sentence of Article 61.[6]

Therefore, the Panel considers that the first definition set out at paragraph 7.534 above is appropriate. However, the combination of that definition of "commercial" with the definition of "scale" presents a problem in that scale is a quantitative concept whilst commercial is qualitative, in the sense that it refers to the nature of certain acts. Some acts are in fact commercial, whilst others are not. Any act of selling can be described as commercial in this primary sense, irrespective of its size or value. If "commercial" is simply read as a qualitative term, referring to all acts pertaining to, or bearing on commerce, this would read the word "scale" out of the text. Acts on a commercial scale would simply be commercial acts. The

1 New Shorter Oxford English Dictionary (1993)(quoiting Panel Report, para. 7.534).

2 New Shorter Oxford English Dictionary (1993)(quoiting Panel Report, para. 7.535).

3 The Panel also observes that the definition of "commerce" itself expressly includes a notion of "scale", but this appears to refer to commerce in a general sense, such as "trade and commerce", which does not appear apposite within the word "commercial"(quoiting Panel Report, para. 7.535).

4 Panel Report, para. 7.535.

5 See United States' first written submission, paras 109, 110 and 123(quoiting Panel Report, para. 7.536).

6 Panel Report, para. 7.537.

phrase "on a commercial scale" would simply mean "commercial". Such an interpretation fails to give meaning to all the terms used in the treaty and is inconsistent with the rule of effective treaty interpretation.[1]

There are no other uses of the word "scale" in the TRIPS Agreement, besides the first and fourth sentences of Article 61. However, the wider context shows that the TRIPS Agreement frequently uses the word "commercial" with many other nouns, although nowhere else with "scale". The other uses of the word "commercial" include "commercial rental"[2], "commercial purposes"[3], "commercial exploitation"[4], "commercial terms"[5], "public non-commercial use"[6], "first commercial exploitation"[7], "honest commercial practices"[8], "commercial value"[9], "unfair commercial use"[10], "non-commercial nature"[11] and "legitimate commercial interests".[12]

The provisions of the Paris Convention (1967) incorporated by Article 2.1 of the TRIPS Agreement include uses of the word "commercial" in the phrase "industrial or commercial establishment" (in the singular or plural)[13] and in the phrases "industrial or commercial matters" and "industrial or commercial activities".[14] The provisions of the Berne Convention (1971) incorporated by Article 9.1 of the TRIPS Agreement include the phrase "any commercial purpose".[15] The provisions of the IPIC Treaty incorporated by Article 35 of the TRIPS Agreement include the phrase "commercially exploited" and "exploits ordinarily

---

1 See, for example, Appellate Body Reports in US – Gasoline, at p. 23; Japan – Alcoholic Beverages II, at p. 12(quoiting Panel Report, para. 7.538).

2 Articles 11 and 14.4 of the TRIPS Agreement(quoiting Panel Report, para. 7.539).

3 Articles 26.1 and 36 of the TRIPS Agreement(quoiting Panel Report, para. 7.539).

4 Article 27.2 of the TRIPS Agreement(quoiting Panel Report, para. 7.539).

5 Article 31(b) of the TRIPS Agreement(quoiting Panel Report, para. 7.539).

6 Article 31(b) and (c) of the TRIPS Agreement(quoiting Panel Report, para. 7.539).

7 Article 38.1 and 38.2 of the TRIPS Agreement(quoiting Panel Report, para. 7.539).

8 Article 39.2 of the TRIPS Agreement(quoiting Panel Report, para. 7.539).

9 Article 39.2(b) of the TRIPS Agreement(quoiting Panel Report, para. 7.539).

10 Article 39.3 of the TRIPS Agreement(quoiting Panel Report, para. 7.539).

11 Article 60 of the TRIPS Agreement(quoiting Panel Report, para. 7.539).

12 Article 63.4 of the TRIPS Agreement(quoiting Panel Report, para. 7.539).

13 Articles 3, 5C(3), 6quinquiesA(2) and 7bis(1)) of the Paris Convention (1967). This phrase also appears in footnote 1 to the TRIPS Agreement(quoiting Panel Report, para. 7.540).

14 Article 10bis of the Paris Convention (1967)(quoiting Panel Report, para. 7.540).

15 Articles II(9)(a)(iv) and IV(4)(c)(iii) of the Appendix to the Berne Convention (1971)(quoiting Panel Report, para. 7.540).

commercially".[1]

The context shows that the negotiators chose to qualify certain activities, such as rental, exploitation and use, as "commercial". They also chose to qualify various nouns, such as "terms", "value", "nature" and "interests", as "commercial" or "non-commercial". In a similar way, they could have agreed that the obligation in the first sentence of Article 61 would apply to cases of wilful and "commercial" trademark counterfeiting or copyright piracy. This would have included all commercial activity. Indeed, the records of the negotiation of the TRIPS Agreement show that this formulation was in fact suggested (by the United States) at an early stage.[2]

The context shows that the negotiators used the term "commercial purposes" in two provisions on the scope of protection of certain categories of intellectual property rights, and that the Appendix to the Berne Convention (1971) already did use that term in the singular in provisions on possible limitations to particular rights. However, the negotiators did not agree that the obligation in the first sentence of Article 61 would apply to cases of wilful trademark counterfeiting or copyright piracy "for commercial purposes". This would have included all activity for financial gain or profit.[3]

Instead, the negotiators agreed in Article 61 to use the distinct phrase "on a commercial scale". This indicates that the word "scale" was a deliberate choice and must be given due interpretative weight. "Scale" denotes a relative size, and reflects the intention of the negotiators that the limitation on the obligation in the first sentence of the Article depended on the size of acts of counterfeiting and piracy. Therefore, whilst "commercial" is a qualitative term, it would be an error to read it solely in those terms. In context it must indicate a quantity.[4]

A review of the uses of the word "commercial" throughout the TRIPS Agreement indicates that it links various activities, not simply selling, to the marketplace. It also shows that "commercial" activities cannot be presumed to be on a larger scale than others, such as "public non-commercial" activities, even though they would generally be larger than, say, "personal" or "domestic" use. The distinguishing characteristic of a commercial activity is that it is carried

---

1 Article 7(1) and (2), of the IPIC Treaty(quoiting Panel Report, para. 7.540).

2 The United States suggested in October 1988 a provision applying to trademark counterfeiting and copyright infringement that were "wilful and commercial" (see document MTN.GNG/NG11/W/14/Rev.1). This suggestion was not taken up. A later US proposal, like certain other proposals, used the phrase "on a commercial scale" (see document MTN.GNG/NG11/W/70)(quoiting Panel Report, para. 7.541).

3 Panel Report, para. 7.542.

4 The Panel is not required, for the purposes of this claim, to express a view as to whether "commercial" also indicates certain qualitative factors, such as a profit-seeking purpose(quoiting Panel Report, para. 7.543).

out for profit.[1] The review of the uses of the word "commercial" also shows that, unlike all the others, Article 61 uses the word "commercial" to qualify a notion of size.[2]

In the Panel's view, the combination of the primary definition of "commercial" and the definition of "scale" can be reconciled with the context of Article 61 if it is assessed not solely according to the nature of an activity but also in terms of relative size, as a market benchmark. As there is no other qualifier besides "commercial", that benchmark must be whatever "commercial" typically or usually connotes. In quantitative terms, the benchmark would be the magnitude or extent at which engagement in commerce, or activities pertaining to or bearing on commerce, are typically or usually carried on, in other words, the magnitude or extent of typical or usual commercial activity. Given that the phrase uses the indefinite article "a", it refers to more than one magnitude or extent of typical or usual commercial activity. The magnitude or extent will vary in the different "cases" of counterfeiting and piracy to which the obligation applies. In the Panel's view, this reflects the fact that what is typical or usual varies according to the type of commerce concerned.[3]

Turning to the arguments of the parties and various third parties on this point, they have attempted to give due meaning to both the terms "commerce" and "scale" in different ways. Initially, the United States submitted as follows:

"those who engage in commercial activities in order to make a 'financial return' in the marketplace ... are, by definition, therefore operating on a commercial scale"[4]

Similarly, Canada submitted that "commercial scale" refers to activities undertaken with a view to profiting.[5] The European Communities submitted that the terms "commercial" and "scale" denote activities that pertain to a business or to "the generation of profits".[6]

The Panel considers these interpretations unsatisfactory, as they seem to equate "commercial scale" with "commercial purpose" or merely "commercial", which are not the term used in Article 61.[7]

The United States then clarified that it does not read the word "scale" out of the term

---

1 At the same time, some activities — such as experimentation — may be conducted in the course of business or in connection with a business without a specific profit-making purpose(quoiting Panel Report, para. 7.544).

2 Panel Report, para. 7.544.

3 Panel Report, para. 7.545.

4 United States' first written submission, para. 110. This submission also interpreted "scale": see paragraph 7.659 below(quoiting Panel Report, para. 7.546).

5 Canada's third party written submission, para. 5(quoiting Panel Report, para. 7.547).

6 European Communities' third party oral statement, paras 4 and 14(quoiting Panel Report, para. 7.547).

7 Panel Report, para. 7.548.

"commercial scale" and added a qualifier or two to its initial position, submitting that: "an infringer seriously engaged in pursuing financial gain in the marketplace is necessarily acting on a 'scale' that is 'commercial' and therefore falls within the ordinary meaning of the term." (emphasis added and removed)[1]; and

"'commercial scale' certainly extends to those who are genuinely engaged in commercial activities in order to make a financial return."[2]

In response to a request for clarification from the Panel, the United States explained: "The United States has employed the words 'seriously' or 'genuinely' to underscore that the IPR infringer must be actually engaged in pursuing financial gain through non-trivial commercial activities in the marketplace, as opposed to, for example, a one-off entry into the marketplace of a limited nature. Whether an infringer is 'seriously' or 'genuinely' engaged in commercial activities would depend on the facts and circumstances of the activity. (…)"[3]

The Panel understands that this refined approach interprets "commercial scale" as basically everything that is "commercial" with the exception of some trivial or de minimis activities. It is not clear how "seriously" and "genuinely" indicate "non-trivial" activities – if anything, "seriously" indicates something more important. However, there is no need to consider its meaning further as the word "seriously" is not used in the terms of the treaty, nor is it implied by the terms that are used.[4]

Whilst the United States' refined approach has the merit of ensuring that its interpretation of "commercial scale" does not capture an identical class of acts as the term "commercial purpose", the difference seems minimal. This refined approach does not read the word "scale" out of the text but nevertheless it reads the word down to such an extent that it lacks the significance that the negotiators evidently intended. The negotiators chose the word "scale", which refers to size, rather than other words that they actually used elsewhere in the Agreement that do not exclude activities on the basis of size. They also used the word "scale" in the fourth sentence of Article 61, together with the term "in particular", which would be virtually redundant if the sentence simply meant that Members could provide for criminal procedures and penalties to be applied "in particular" to more than trivial or de minimis cases. The context throughout Part III shows that the limitations in Section 5 reflect an effort to address only the more blatant and egregious infringements.[5]

---

1 United States' rebuttal submission, para. 17(quoiting Panel Report, para. 7.549).

2 United States' closing oral statement at the second substantive meeting, para. 15(quoiting Panel Report, para. 7.549).

3 United States' response to Question No. 63(quoiting Panel Report, para. 7.550).

4 Panel Report, para. 7.551.

5 Panel Report, para. 7.552.

As to the view that "on a commercial scale" is basically a de minimis provision, the Panel need look no further than the preceding provision, Article 60, to see how the negotiators addressed that issue. Article 60 forms part of Section 4 on special requirements related to border measures and serves an analogous purpose to the phrase "on a commercial scale" in Article 61 in that both define the lower end of infringement at which a particular type of enforcement procedure must be available. However, the terms of each are quite different: Article 60 defines de minimis infringement in terms of volume ("small quantities"), nature ("of a non-commercial nature") and circumstances ("in travellers' personal luggage or sent in small consignments"). Had the negotiators wanted to exclude only de minimis infringement from the minimum standard of Article 61, they had a model in Article 60, or they could have used words such as "except for minor or personal use". However, they did not.[1] Instead, Article 61 refers to size ("scale") qualified only by the word "commercial". This indicates that the negotiators intended something different from de minimis. Article 60 also indicates that the negotiators did not equate small with non-commercial, confirming that a "commercial" scale is not necessarily small-scale nor large-scale.[2]

The Panel considers that these interpretations, whilst they may reflect sound domestic policy considerations, lack a clear basis in the rules of treaty interpretation which the Panel is obliged to apply. All of these interpretations are valid explanations as to why such infringement should be unlawful but they do not explain why it must be a crime. The answer to that question must be found in the terms of the treaty as finally agreed.[3]

In this connection it seems pertinent to recall that the negotiators chose a term that was different from the commercial purpose or financial return standards used in the national legislation of a number of the participants.[4]

Turning now to the respondent's approach to the interpretation of "on a commercial scale", China submits that these words should be interpreted as a single term.[5] The United States proposes that each of the terms in the two-word term be interpreted and does not submit that there are other ordinary uses of the phrase that would be relevant.[6]

The Panel observes that the general rule of treaty interpretation in Article 31 of the

---

1 Indeed, the United States expressed a similar view in order to explain why a reference to "exceptional cases" in Article 46 of the TRIPS

Agreement is not a de minimis test (see paragraph 7.387 above)(quoiting Panel Report, para. 7.553).

2 Panel Report, para. 7.553.

3 Panel Report, para. 7.555.

4 Panel Report, para. 7.556.

5 China's first written submission, paras 69-71(quoiting Panel Report, para. 7.557).

6 United States' response to Question No. 68(quoiting Panel Report, para. 7.557).

Vienna Convention refers in paragraph 1 to the ordinary meaning of the terms of the treaty, read in context. Where the terms are a single term, or ordinarily used together, then the treaty interpreter should refer to the ordinary meaning of that single term, or of each term in the particular context of each other. This is a distinct exercise from that in paragraph 4 of Article 31 of the Vienna Convention which requires a "special meaning" to be given to a term if it is established that the parties so intended. No party to this dispute considers that a "special meaning" should be given to the phrase "on a commercial scale", and nor does the Panel.[1]

The Panel recalls that the dictionary definition of "scale" (quoted at paragraph 7.533 above) includes the entry "Freq. in on a grand, lavish, small, etc. scale". These examples show that the phrase "on a ... scale" is frequently used. Therefore, the use of the words "on a commercial scale" as a phrase appears to be relevant to their ordinary meaning.[2]

The circumstances surrounding the inclusion of the phrase "on a commercial scale" show that the phrase has been used and, in some cases, defined in the intellectual property legislation of various countries for periods stretching back almost a century. Specifically, the patent laws of these countries refer to the working of inventions, or failure to work inventions, "on a commercial scale".[3] The term is used in relation to the exploitation of protected subject matter, as in Article 61, but the purpose of these non-working provisions, and the considerations relevant to their operation, are distinct from those of criminal procedures and penalties as addressed in Article 61 of the TRIPS Agreement. There is insufficient indication that the meaning ascribed to the term "on a commercial scale" in such legislation was that intended by the negotiators of the TRIPS Agreement when they used the term in the first and fourth sentences of Article 61. However, this circumstance shows the phrase in use in an intellectual property context long before the negotiation of the TRIPS Agreement.[4]

The term "on a commercial scale" was also used in the specific context of trademark counterfeiting and copyright piracy in the WIPO Committee of Experts on Measures Against Counterfeiting and Piracy in 1988 contemporaneously with the earlier part of the negotiations of the TRIPS Agreement. Draft Model Provisions for National Laws set out in a Memorandum

---

1 Panel Report, para. 7.558.

2 Panel Report, para. 7.560.

3 See, for example, the Australian Patent Act 1990, s. 135(1) (mentioned in response to Third Party Question No. 9); Indian Patents Act 1970, ss. 83-84; South African Patent Act 1978, s. 56; United Kingdom Patent Act 1977-1988, s. 50; Zimbabwean Patents Act 1971, s. 31, in Exhibit CHN-198, and the patent laws of other Commonwealth countries. Earlier, the United Kingdom Patents and Design Act 1919, s. 27, had referred to working a patent "on a commercial scale"(quoiting Panel Report, para. 7.561).

4 Panel Report, para. 7.561.

by the International Bureau of WIPO for that Committee included, in Article A(1), (2) and (3), three draft Model Provisions on manufacturing as an act of counterfeiting, manufacturing as an act of piracy and additional acts of counterfeiting and piracy, respectively. Each of those draft Model Provisions contained a proviso that such goods were manufactured, or the act was committed, "on a commercial scale". An explanatory observation accompanied the term "commercial scale" as a phrase.[1]

The evidence on the record includes many other uses of the words "commercial scale" and "on a commercial scale" in a variety of contexts. Accordingly, the Panel considers that the words "commercial" and "scale" provide important context for the ordinary meaning of each other when used together in the phrase "on a commercial scale" as in the first sentence of Article 61 of the TRIPS Agreement.[2]

China submits that the phrase "on a commercial scale" refers to "a significant magnitude of infringement activity".[3] China refers to four isolated uses of the phrase "commercial scale" spread out over a period of forty years: one at the 1947-1948 Havana Conference, one in a 1985 GATT Council meeting, and two in US national legislation on alternative energy development. From these uses, China posits an interpretation suggestive of industrial scale activity.[4]

The Panel considers that this interpretation is predetermined by the context of the uses that China has selected, which refer to commercial scale activities at an industrial level. This is inapposite in the context of Article 61 of the TRIPS Agreement which applies to acts of infringement of individual rights, including those subsisting in individual products. This interpretation simply replaces the term "commercial", that is used in the text, with "significant", that is not used in the text, effectively reading out the term "commercial".[5]

China also argues that the explanatory observation that accompanied the draft Model Provisions is an example of ordinary usage of the term "commercial scale".[6]

The Panel notes that the explanatory observation did not purport to be a definition but was prepared by the International Bureau of WIPO for the specific purpose of accompanying a

---

1 That explanatory observation read as follows: "'Commercial scale' is a notion which will have to be applied taking into consideration the circumstances accompanying the manufacture. The quantity of the goods manufactured, the way in which they were, are or are intended to be used and the will to make profit are among the factors that the courts will have to take into consideration." See WIPO document C&P/CE/2 of 18, 19 February 1988, para. 17, set out in Exhibit CHN-43(quoiting Panel Report, para. 7.562).

2 Panel Report, para. 7.563.

3 China's first written submission, para. 64(quoiting Panel Report, para. 7.564).

4 Exhibits CHN-44, CHN-45, CHN-46 and CHN-47(quoiting Panel Report, para. 7.564).

5 Panel Report, para. 7.565.

6 China's first written submission, para. 72; rebuttal submission, para. 76(quoiting Panel Report, para. 7.566).

provision on manufacturing in the draft Model Provisions. The Report of the WIPO Committee of Experts on Measures against Counterfeiting and Piracy of April 1988 shows that the concept of "commercial scale" proved controversial.[1] Accordingly, it is not an example of ordinary usage. In any event, the draft Model Provisions of the Committee of Experts themselves were never agreed.[2] Therefore, it would not be appropriate to select an explanatory observation that accompanied them and elevate it to the status of the proper interpretation of a treaty text that was negotiated in another forum and that was finally agreed.[3]

Turning to other evidence on the record, two third parties contrasted "commercial scale" production with "pilot scale" production or "small scale test" production.[4] The Panel finds these contrasting terms relevant because they indicate a quantity, and because production can be an act of counterfeiting or piracy.[5]

In response to questions from the Panel, China, but not the United States, provided other examples of ordinary uses of the phrase "commercial scale", including in company press releases, filings with the US Securities and Exchange Commission and patent applications. The United States argues that these examples are functions of individuals' "own lexicography" and are not used in the same fashion or manner.[6] The United States also notes that patent applications are unrelated to the first sentence of Article 61 of the TRIPS Agreement.[7]

The Panel considers that each of the uses on the record, being in the English language, reflects the understanding of the authors as to the ordinary meaning of those words and phrases in that language. That is the reason why a language allows its speakers to render themselves mutually intelligible. These are the very meanings that dictionaries catalogue. Naturally, words and phrases in the same language may have more than one meaning, "common or rare, universal or specialized".[8] It is incumbent on the Panel to assess these usages in context to discern which is relevant to the question of interpretation at hand, just as the Panel has done when confronted with multiple definitions of the words "commercial" and "scale" in the same

---

1 See Report adopted by the WIPO Committee of Experts on Measures Against Counterfeiting and Piracy, WIPO document C&P/CE/4 of 28 April 1988, reproduced in Exhibit CHN-72, at paras 71-81 and 94(quoiting Panel Report, para. 7.567).

2 The April 1988 session of the Committee of Experts could not complete its work and it was envisaged that a revised text would be prepared: see Report in note 543 above, at para. 177(quoiting Panel Report, para. 7.567).

3 Panel Report, para. 7.567.

4 Australia's and Mexico's respective responses to Third Party Question No. 4(quoiting Panel Report, para. 7.567).

5 Panel Report, para. 7.568.

6 United States' response to Question No. 69; comments on China's response to Question No. 68(quoiting Panel Report, para. 7.569).

7 Panel Report, para. 7.569.

8 Appellate Body Report in US — Gambling, para. 164(quoiting Panel Report, para. 7.569).

dictionary. The Panel also notes that Article 61 of the TRIPS Agreement specifically relates the concept of infringement "on a commercial scale" to other intellectual property rights, which include patents, in the fourth sentence of that Article.[1]

Turning to the ordinary meaning of the term "on a commercial scale", the evidence includes examples of uses of that precise term and also the words "commercial scale" followed by a noun. It is not suggested that this changes the meaning. The nouns include "manufacturing", "production", "facility", "processes", "reactor", "composition" and "cultivation", and the term also follows "manufacture" and "employ".[2] This confirms that the phrase can be used in different contexts as a single term.[3]

Some of these nouns, notably manufacturing and production, refer to acts that could constitute trademark counterfeiting and copyright piracy, and are therefore particularly apposite to the interpretation of the first sentence of Article 61 of the TRIPS Agreement. However, counterfeiting and piracy include other acts besides manufacturing and production. There are no uses on the record of the phrase with the word "sales" or "selling".[4]

Simple searches of online patent databases of the Patent Cooperation Treaty, the United States Patent and Trademark Office and the European Patent Office, reveal many patent applications that use the phrase "commercial scale". China has provided abstracts of some applications that define the phrase "commercial scale" in precise, quantitative terms of volume, weight or speed. [5]These definitions vary greatly and relate to different factors, according to the invention claimed in the application. From this evidence, China concludes that:

"In the context of patent applications, the phrase 'commercial scale' refers to a certain level of magnitude. This magnitude is not necessarily objectively high, but it is relatively high in the context of the operation involved."[6]

The United States finds this statement "telling" and recalls its view that:

"[B]ased on its ordinary meaning, what qualifies as 'commercial scale' piracy or

---

1 Panel Report, para. 7.570.

2 Press releases of Novovax and Dupont, and US Securities and Exchange Commission filings of Amylin Pharmaceuticals, Inc., Biocryst Pharmaceuticals, Inc., Cambridge Display Technology, Inc. and Verenium Corporation in Exhibit CHN-196; and China's original evidence in Exhibits CHN-44, CHN-45, CHN-46 and CHN-47(quoiting Panel Report, para. 7.571).

3 Panel Report, para. 7.571.

4 Panel Report, para. 7.572.

5 International applications published under the PCT: WO 00/61722; WO 2004/054949 A1; WO 2006/110534 A2; WO2008/020357 A2; United States patent no. 6,525,205 B2; United States patent application no. 2007/0202578 A1; in Exhibit CHN-197(quoiting Panel Report, para. 7.573).

6 China's response to Question No. 69(quoiting Panel Report, para. 7.573).

counterfeiting will vary among product and market, and therefore, what is 'commercial scale' can be determined using factors relevant to a particular situation."[1]

The Panel observes a certain degree of convergence between the parties' views, as compared to their initial positions, when addressing these ordinary uses of the phrase "commercial scale". The Panel considers that the contexts in which the term "on a commercial scale" or "commercial scale" is used, given their variety, indicate that each of the words "commercial" and "scale" provides important context for the interpretation of the other when used together. Their combined meaning varies greatly according to the context around them and the lack of precision in the term is apparent.[2] However, it is clear that none of these uses refer to activities that are simply commercial. Rather, they are evidently intended to distinguish certain activities (or premises) from others that pertain to or have a bearing on commerce but which do not meet a market benchmark in terms of what is typical. The precise benchmark in each case depends on the product and the market to which the phrase relates.[3]

Conformity of the measures at issue with respect to the level of the thresholds

The Panel recalls its view at paragraph 7.545 above and, in light of the evidence considered above, finds that a "commercial scale" is the magnitude or extent of typical or usual commercial activity. Therefore, counterfeiting or piracy "on a commercial scale" refers to counterfeiting or piracy carried on at the magnitude or extent of typical or usual commercial activity with respect to a given product in a given market. The magnitude or extent of typical or usual commercial activity with respect to a given product in a given market forms a benchmark by which to assess the obligation in the first sentence of Article 61. It follows that what constitutes a commercial scale for counterfeiting or piracy of a particular product in a particular market will depend on the magnitude or extent that is typical or usual with respect to such a product in such a market, which may be small or large. The magnitude or extent of typical or usual commercial activity relates, in the longer term, to profitability.[4]

The Panel observes that what is typical or usual in commerce is a flexible concept. The immediate context in the second sentence of Article 61, which is closely related to the first, refers to the similarly flexible concepts of "deterrent" and "corresponding gravity". Neither these terms nor "commercial scale" are precise but all depend on circumstances, which vary

---

1 United States' comment on China's response to Question No. 69, citing its response to Question No. 16 and second oral statement (closing statement), paras 10-11(quoiting Panel Report, para. 7.574).

2 The lack of precision is highlighted by the addition of specific definitions in the patent applications(quoiting Panel Report, para. 7.576).

3 Panel Report, para. 7.576.

4 This finding is without prejudice to the qualitative aspect of "commercial scale" considered with respect to the second limb of this claim(quoiting Panel Report, para. 7.577).

according to the differing forms of commerce and of counterfeiting and piracy to which these obligations apply.[1]

The Panel finds that the United States has not made a prima facie case with respect to the first limb of its claim under the first sentence of Article 61 of the TRIPS Agreement. [2]The Panel concludes that the United States has not established that the criminal thresholds are inconsistent with China's obligations under the first sentence of Article 61 of the TRIPS Agreement.[3]

Claim under the second sentence of Article 61 of the TRIPS Agreement

The Panel observes that the United States has made this claim contingent upon the outcome of its claims under the first sentence of Article 61 of the TRIPS Agreement. Additional findings regarding this claim under the second sentence of Article 61 would not contribute further to a positive solution to this dispute. Therefore, it is unnecessary for the Panel to rule on this claim.[4]

Claim under Article 41.1 of the TRIPS Agreement

The Panel observes that this claim is consequent upon the outcome of the claims regarding the criminal measures under Article 61 of the TRIPS Agreement. Additional findings regarding this claim under Article 41.1 of the TRIPS Agreement would not contribute further to a positive solution to this dispute. Therefore, it is unnecessary for the Panel to rule on this claim.[5]

The Panel concludes that the United States has not established that the criminal thresholds are inconsistent with China's obligations under the first sentence of Article 61 of the TRIPS Agreement. [6]The Panel exercises judicial economy with respect to the claims under Article 41.1 of the TRIPS Agreement and under the second sentence of Article 61 of the TRIPS Agreement (with respect to the criminal thresholds).[7]

II. Disposal of goods confiscated by customs authorities that infringe intellectual property rights

The Panel notes that this claim challenges the Customs measures "as such". The parties disagree on the proper interpretation of the measures at issue. The Panel is therefore obliged, in accordance with its mandate, to make an objective assessment of the meaning of the relevant

---

1 Panel Report, para. 7.578.

2 Panel Report, para. 7.632.

3 Panel Report, para. 7.669.

4 Panel Report, para. 7.675.

5 Panel Report, para. 7.680.

6 Panel Report, para. 7.681.

7 Panel Report, para. 7.682.

provisions of those measures. The Panel recalls its observations at paragraph 7.28 above and confirms that it examines the Customs measures solely for the purpose of determining their conformity with China's obligations under the TRIPS Agreement.[1]

Border measures

This claim is made under Article 59 of the TRIPS Agreement, which provides as follows: "Without prejudice to other rights of action open to the right holder and subject to the right of the defendant to seek review by a judicial authority, competent authorities shall have the authority to order the destruction or disposal of infringing goods in accordance with the principles set out in Article 46. In regard to counterfeit trademark goods, the authorities shall not allow the re-exportation of the infringing goods in an unaltered state or subject them to a different customs procedure, other than in exceptional circumstances."[2]

This Article contains a number of key terms, such as "the right holder", "the defendant", "competent authorities" and "infringing goods" which are not defined in the Article itself but can only be understood by reading the whole Article in context.[3]

Article 59 is found in Section 4 of Part III of the TRIPS Agreement on Special Requirements Related to Border Measures. Section 4 sets out procedures for the suspension at the border by the customs authorities of the release into free circulation of goods. Article 59 sets out the step in these procedures that applies after goods have been found to be infringing. As such, Article 59 forms part of a set of procedures and its key terms must be understood in that context.[4]

This reading is confirmed by the opening provision of Section 4. The first sentence of Article 51 provides as follows:

"Members shall, in conformity with the provisions set out below, adopt procedures to enable a right holder, who has valid grounds for suspecting that the importation of counterfeit trademark or pirated copyright goods may take place, to lodge an application in writing with competent authorities, administrative or judicial, for the suspension by the customs authorities of the release into free circulation of such goods."[5]

This sentence refers to "procedures to enable a right holder ... to lodge an application ... for the suspension by the customs authorities of the release into free circulation" of certain goods. These procedures must conform with "the provisions set out below". The "provisions

---

1 Panel Report, para. 7.212.

2 Panel Report, para. 7.213.

3 Panel Report, para. 7.214.

4 Panel Report, para. 7.215.

5 Panel Report, para. 7.216.

set out below" are the provisions of Section 4, which include Article 59.[1]

The description of the procedure as one for an "application" for "suspension" does not appear to exclude related aspects of the procedure in the provisions set out below, such as the provisions on ex officio action in Article 58 or the remedies as a result of application and/or suspension set out in Article 59. Rather, the procedures in Section 4 form a set that must be read together. This is reflected in the second sentence of Article 51 (with respect to other goods, set out below) that refers to "such an application" (i.e. an application such as that referred to in the first sentence) being subject to "the requirements of this Section". This tends to confirm that the "provisions set out below" Article 51 include the whole of Section 4.[2]

The need to read provisions in the context of the relevant Section is a feature of Sections 2, 3 and 4 of Part III of the TRIPS Agreement. Whilst some provisions refer expressly to prior provisions, such as Articles 52, 54 and 56, many others do not, such as Articles 53.1, 55, 57 and 59, but rather rely on context for clarity. This confirms that the provisions of Section 4 must be read as a coherent set of procedures and not in isolation.[3]

Therefore, the Panel will refer to other provisions of Section 4, in particular to Article 51, in its interpretation of certain terms used in Article 59.[4]

"infringing goods"

The first sentence of Article 59 applies to "infringing goods". The ordinary meaning of these words is not limited to goods that infringe any specific rights. However, read in context, there are certain limitations. The first sentence of Article 51 provides for the relevant procedures to apply, as a minimum, to "the importation" of "counterfeit trademark or pirated copyright goods". [5]

Article 51 expressly allows Members to provide for procedures at the border for other infringing goods as well. The second and third sentences of Article 51 provide as follows:

"Members may enable such an application to be made in respect of goods which involve other infringements of intellectual property rights, provided that the requirements of this Section are met. Members may also provide for corresponding procedures concerning the suspension by the customs authorities of the release of infringing goods destined for

---

1 Panel Report, para. 7.217.

2 Panel Report, para. 7.218.

3 Panel Report, para. 7.219.

4 Panel Report, para. 7.220.

5 Panel Report, para. 7.221.

exportation from their territories."[1]

Both these sentences use the word "may", indicating that they are optional provisions. The second sentence provides for an optional extension to "other infringements of intellectual property rights". This is a reference both to goods that infringe trademarks and copyright without constituting counterfeit trademark goods or pirated copyright goods, as well as to goods that infringe other categories of intellectual property rights, such as patents. The second sentence includes an express condition that applies where Members provide border measures for other infringements of intellectual property rights, namely "provided that the requirements of this Section are met". [2]The requirements of that "Section" include those found in Article 59. Therefore, to the extent that a Member provides for such an application to be made in respect of goods involving other infringements of intellectual property rights, such as patents, the obligation in Article 59 applies.

The third sentence of Article 51 provides for an optional extension to "infringing goods destined for exportation" from a Member's territory. The terms of the third sentence do not attach any express condition to this option. An option with respect to "corresponding procedures" is not, on its face, an obligation that procedures shall correspond. The omission of any express condition in the third sentence stands in contrast to the proviso in the second sentence, which also serves the purpose of providing for an optional extension of the border measures. Whilst it would not have been appropriate to include an identical condition to that found in the second sentence, as the requirements of Section 4 refer to importation, the third sentence could nevertheless have included an express condition that the procedures with respect to infringing goods destined for exportation shall correspond to those set out in the Section, or shall comply with the principles thereof.[3] However, it does not. Read in context, this omission is not ambiguous. Therefore, the Panel finds that there is no obligation to apply the requirements of Article 59 to goods destined for exportation.[4]

---

1 Panel Report, para. 7.222.

2 There are some express differences between the procedures applicable to different goods: Article 53.2 of the TRIPS Agreement only applies to goods involving industrial designs, patents, layout-designs or undisclosed information; the second sentence of Article 59 only applies to counterfeit trademark goods(quoiting Panel Report, para. 7.223).

3 For example, Articles 49 and 50.8 of the TRIPS Agreement provide for optional procedures, subject to a contingent obligation that they "shall conform to principles equivalent in substance to those set forth" in the relevant Sections. In contrast, footnote 13 to the TRIPS Agreement sets out an option but contains no contingent obligation. However, footnote 13 limits the scope of the obligation in the first sentence of Article 51 rather than providing for an optional extension(quoiting Panel Report, para. 7.224).

4 The text of Article 59 itself provides a confirmation of this point. The second sentence refers to the "re-exportation" of the infringing goods not "exportation", which implies that the counterfeit trademark goods are only presented for importation(quoiting Panel Report, para. 7.224).

Turning to the measures at issue, the Panel notes that the Customs IPR Regulations, in Article 2, provide that "Customs protection of intellectual property rights in these Regulations means the protection provided by the Customs for the exclusive rights to use a trademark, copyrights and their related rights, and patent rights (hereinafter referred to as intellectual property rights) ..." (emphasis added). The same is true of the Implementing Measures and Public Notice No. 16/2007, that both implement the Customs IPR Regulations.[1]

It is apparent that the intellectual property right infringements covered by the Customs measures include not only counterfeit trademark goods and pirated copyright goods, but certain other infringements of intellectual property rights, namely other trademark-infringing goods, other copyright-infringing goods, and patent-infringing goods. For the reasons set out in paragraph 7.223 above, the Panel finds that Article 59 applies to the Customs measures as those measures apply to all these infringements of intellectual property rights.[2]

The Panel notes that the Customs IPR Regulations, in Article 2, also provide that "Customs protection of intellectual property rights in these Regulations means the protection provided by the Customs ... related to imports or exports ..." (emphasis added). The same is true of the Implementing Measures and Public Notice No. 16/2007, that both implement the Customs IPR Regulations.[3]

In this respect, China's border measures provide a level of protection higher than the minimum standard required by Section 4 of Part III of the TRIPS Agreement. The practical effect of this is that, according to uncontested statistics prepared by China Customs, 99.85 per cent by value of infringing goods disposed of or destroyed under the measures at issue in the years 2005 to 2007 were destined for exportation.[4]

The United States' claim refers to "infringing goods"[5] and specifically notes that the

---

1 See paragraphs 7.194 and 7.195 above(quoiting Panel Report, para. 7.225).

2 This finding only applies with regard to imports, in accordance with paragraph 7.231 below(quoiting Panel Report, para. 7.226).

3 These measures implement the Customs IPR Regulations. Further, in the Implementing Measures, Article 4 refers to the intellectual property rights of imports and exports, ChapterIII on "Detention upon application" begins with Article 14 that refers to goods to be imported or exported imminently, Chapter IV on "Investigation by authority" begins with Article 20 that refers to discovery of any imports or exports by Customs and is followed by Chapter V on disposal of goods and expenses which begins with Article 30 that refers to infringing goods that Customs has confiscated. Public Notice No. 16/2007 was notified to regulate the auction of goods in accordance with Article 27 of the Customs IPR Regulations that applies to both imports and exports(quoiting Panel Report, para. 7.227).

4 See "Statistics on Disposition of Infringing Goods by China Customs In Years 2005 through 2007 prepared by China Customs" in Exhibits CHN-166 and CHN-167(quoiting Panel Report, para. 7.228).

5 United States' first written submission, para. 171, 2nd sentence, refers to imports "in particular"(quoiting Panel Report, para. 7.229).

measures at issue apply to imports and exports.[1] However, in response to a question from the Panel concerning its claim and the relevance of Article 51, the United States advised that it "takes no position" with regard to whether the first sentence of Article 59 also governs border authorities' actions with respect to goods destined for exportation.[2]

In light of the United States' response, and given the complainant's responsibility to assert and prove its claim, China submits that its measures are not subject to this claim with respect to goods destined for exportation.[3]

The Panel notes that the United States has not withdrawn its claim with respect to any aspect of the Customs measures. For the reasons set out in paragraph 7.224 above, the Panel concludes that Article 59 of the TRIPS Agreement is not applicable to the Customs measures insofar as those measures apply to goods destined for exportation.[4]

The Panel will continue to assess the claim insofar as it concerns goods destined for importation. Imports represented 0.15 per cent by value of the goods disposed of or destroyed under the measures at issue in the years 2005 to 2007. During that period, all confiscated infringing imports were either donated to the Red Cross Society of China (0.12%) or destroyed (0.02%).[5] The volume of infringing imports that was sold to the right holder, or auctioned, was zero.[6]

Nevertheless, the Customs measures on their face apply in the same way to both exports and imports. China confirms that its evidence, including of specific shipments of exports, is indicative of how the Customs measures operate with respect to both exports and imports. [7]The statistics comprising both exports and imports are a much larger, and therefore more reliable, sample. Therefore, the Panel considers that it may refer to evidence as it relates to both exports and imports in its assessment of this claim as it relates only to imports.[8]

"shall have the authority"

The obligation in the first sentence of Article 59 is that competent authorities "shall have the authority" to order certain types of remedies with respect to infringing goods. It is

---

1 United States' first written submission, para. 58, fn. 45; para. 179, fn. 117(quoiting Panel Report, para. 7.229).

2 United States' response to Question No. 28(quoiting Panel Report, para. 7.229).

3 China's second oral statement, paras 46-47(quoiting Panel Report, para. 7.230).

4 Panel Report, para. 7.231.

5 These figures do not total 0.15% due to rounding. See Customs Statistics in note 219 above(quoiting Panel Report, para. 7.232).

6 Panel Report, para. 7.232.

7 See provisions of the Customs IPR Regulations and Implementing Measures cited at para. 7.227 above, and China's confirmation of this point in its response to Question No. 30(quoiting Panel Report, para. 7.233).

8 Panel Report, para. 7.233.

clear from the context within Section 4 that the obligations in Article 59 apply where customs authorities have suspended the release into free circulation of goods suspected of infringing intellectual property rights. The fact that Article 59 applies to "infringing goods" indicates that the obligations in this Article are triggered when competent authorities find that the goods subject to the suspension are infringing. The fact that Article 59 addresses the authority to order remedies implies that the obligations continue until the time that a remedy has been ordered. The text of the Article does not indicate any other limitation on the temporal scope of the obligations. Therefore, the obligation that competent authorities "shall have the authority" to make certain orders applies from the time that competent authorities find that goods subject to suspension at the border are infringing, right up until the time that a remedy is ordered.[1]

The United States confirms that it does not claim that the obligation that competent authorities "shall have the authority" to order certain remedies requires Members to make those orders. Rather, the United States claims that "[t]he pertinent issue is what decisions China Customs is permitted by law to make in particular circumstances".[2]

The Panel notes that the word "authority" can be defined as "power or right to enforce obedience; moral or legal supremacy; right to command or give a final decision."[3] The obligation is to "have" authority not an obligation to "exercise" authority. [4]The phrase "shall have the authority" is used throughout the enforcement obligations in Sections 2, 3 and 4 of Part III of the TRIPS Agreement, specifically, in Articles 43.1, 44.1, 45.1, 45.2, 46, 48.1, 50.1, 50.2, 50.3, 50.7, 53.1, 56 and 57.[5] It can be contrasted with terminology used in the minimum standards of protection in Part II of the TRIPS Agreement, such as "Members shall provide" protection, or that certain material "shall be" protected. The obligation in Article 46 that certain authorities "shall have the authority" to make certain orders reflects inter alia that orders with respect to specific infringements are left to enforcement authorities' discretion.[6]

This is confirmed by the context. Article 41.1 of the TRIPS Agreement, quoted at paragraph 7.170 above, obliges Members to ensure that enforcement procedures as specified in Part III are "available" under their law so as to "permit" effective action against infringement,

---

1 Panel Report, para. 7.234.

2 United States' first oral statement, para. 55; rebuttal submission, para. 131(quoiting Panel Report, para. 7.235).

3 New Shorter Oxford English Dictionary (1993)(quoiting Panel Report, para. 7.236).

4 This is without prejudice to other obligations regarding enforcement(quoiting Panel Report, para. 7.236).

5 The phrasing in Article 57 is slightly different. The phrase "shall have the authority" is also used in Articles 31(g), (k) and 34.1 in Part II of the TRIPS Agreement(quoiting Panel Report, para. 7.236).

6 Certain obligations guide the exercise of that discretion, for example, the principle of proportionality and the need to take into account the interests of third parties under the third sentence of Article 46(quoiting Panel Report, para. 7.236).

which addresses the potential for action.[1]

Given the potential importance of this interpretation to the operation of much of Part III of the TRIPS Agreement, the Panel notes that it is further confirmed by the records of the negotiation of the Agreement.[2] Previous drafts of the TRIPS Agreement had provided that the authorities shall "provide for" certain remedies, but this phrasing was changed to read shall "have the authority", as were a number of other draft provisions.[3] Therefore, the obligation that competent authorities "shall have the authority" to make certain orders is not an obligation that competent authorities shall exercise that authority in a particular way, unless otherwise specified.

Moreover, the obligation to have the authority to order certain types of remedies is not an obligation to have the authority to order those remedies only. Both parties to the dispute, and certain third parties, expressly recognize that the obligation that competent authorities "shall have the authority" to order certain types of remedies leaves Members free to provide that competent authorities may have authority to order other remedies not required to be within their authority by Article 59 of the TRIPS Agreement.[4]

The Panel agrees. The terms of Article 59 do not indicate that the authority to order the specified types of remedies must be exclusive. This interpretation is confirmed by Article 46, which forms part of the context of Article 59, as Article 59 incorporates the principles of Article 46, and both Articles are phrased as obligations that authorities "shall have the authority" to order certain types of remedies. The first sentence of Article 46 provides, basically, that authorities shall have the authority to order that goods be disposed of outside the channels of commerce or destroyed. At the same time, the fourth sentence of Article 46 relates to release into the channels of commerce which does not correspond to either of the remedies required by the first sentence. This is an express recognition that the remedies set out in the first sentence of Article 46 are not exhaustive. The same position applies under Article 59.[5]

Given the potential importance of this interpretation to the operation of Part III of the

---

1 Panel Report, para. 7.237.

2 The Panel has recourse to this supplementary means of interpretation in accordance with Article 32 of the Vienna Convention on the Law of Treaties ("Vienna Convention") in order to confirm the meaning resulting from the application of the general rule of interpretation in Article 31(quoiting Panel Report, para. 7.238).

3 See, for example, the Composite Draft Text of 12 July 1990, MTN.GNG/NG11/W/76(quoiting Panel Report, para. 7.238).

4 United States' rebuttal submission, para. 163; response to Question No. 37; China's first written submission, para. 213; response to Question No. 37; Brazil third party written submission, para. 51; European Communities' third party written submission, para. 18(quoiting Panel Report, para. 7.239).

5 Panel Report, para. 7.240.

TRIPS Agreement, the Panel notes that it is confirmed by the circumstances of conclusion of the Agreement.[1] One of the most important such circumstances was the fact that the pre-existing international intellectual property agreements contained comparatively few minimum standards on enforcement procedures beyond national treatment and certain optional provisions.[2]One of the major reasons for the conclusion of the TRIPS Agreement was the desire to set out a minimum set of procedures and remedies that judicial, border and other competent authorities must have available to them.[3]

At the same time, the negotiators appear to have considered it unnecessary to state in either Article 46 or Article 59 that the authorities could not release goods that had been found infringing into the channels of commerce. This may have been due inter alia to the fact that such an action itself could constitute infringement or otherwise expose the authorities to liability. Such an action would not constitute infringement if the circumstances of disposal were non-commercial or if the state of the goods was altered so that the goods no longer infringed. The negotiators addressed both these issues: in the first sentence of Article 46, by providing for disposal outside the channels of commerce (and destruction) and, in the fourth sentence, in regard to counterfeit trademark goods, by setting a minimum degree of alteration of the state of goods before release into the channels of commerce.[4]

The European Communities submitted that all authority to order remedies, including those not required by Article 59, is subject to an overarching requirement that it be "in such a manner as to avoid any harm caused to the right holder".[5] China addressed the degree to which auction, even though it does not satisfy the requirement that disposal be outside the channels

1 The Panel has recourse to this supplementary means of interpretation in accordance with Article 32 of the Vienna Convention in order to confirm the interpretation resulting from application of the general rule of interpretation in Article 31. The Panel recalls the view of the Appellate Body in its report on EC – Computer Equipment (at para. 86), quoted in its report on EC – Chicken Cuts (at para. 284), referring to Sinclair, I., The Vienna Convention on the Law of Treaties, 2nd ed., (Manchester University Press, 1984) (at p. 141), that recourse to the circumstances of conclusion of a treaty "permits, in appropriate cases, the examination of the historical background against which the treaty was negotiated" (quoiting Panel Report, para. 7.241).

2 The Panel Report in US – Section 211 Appropriations Act noted that:"The inclusion of this Part on enforcement in the TRIPS Agreement was one of the major accomplishments of the Uruguay Round negotiations as it expanded the scope of enforcement (…) of intellectual property rights. Prior to the TRIPS Agreement, provisions related to enforcement were limited to general obligations to provide legal remedies and seizure of infringing goods." (at para. 8.97)(quoiting Panel Report, para. 7.241).

3 Panel Report, para. 7.241.

4 Panel Report, para. 7.242.

5 European Communities' response to Third Party Question No. 16(quoiting Panel Report, para. 7.243).

of commerce, might still avoid any harm caused to the right holder.[1] The United States also addressed this issue.[2]

In the Panel's view, an interpretation that applies the phrase "in such a manner as to avoid any harm caused to the right holder" to all authority to order remedies is based on a selective reading of Article 46. The requirement that authority to order a remedy be "in such a manner as to avoid any harm caused to the right holder" is linked in the text of Article 46 to one remedy only, namely disposal outside the channels of commerce. [3] This does not exclude the possibility that other actions, notably release into the channels of commerce, may be subject to requirements, provided that those requirements are set out in the terms of Article 46 or Article 59.[4]

The parties disagree as to the circumstances in which competent authorities may be considered to have "authority" in accordance with Article 59, in particular, the extent to which the availability of authority may be subject to conditions. China submits examples of other Members' legislation that, in its view, subject customs' authority to conditions.[5]

The Panel observes that the reference to alternatives in Article 59 of the TRIPS Agreement implies a particular type of condition. Article 59 requires authority to order "destruction or disposal" (emphasis added). It is not disputed that where competent authorities have authority in any given situation within the scope of Article 59 to order either destruction or disposal (in accordance with applicable principles), this is sufficient to implement the obligation in the first sentence of Article 59.[6] Therefore, a condition that precludes the authority to order one remedy (e.g. destruction) could be consistent with Article 59 as long as competent authorities still had the authority to order the other remedy (in this example, disposal).[7]

The Panel also observes that a common feature of Sections 2, 3 and 4 of Part III of the TRIPS Agreement is that the initiation of procedures under these Sections is generally the

---

1 China's first written submission, para. 214(quoiting Panel Report, para. 7.243).

2 United States' first written submission, para. 189; rebuttal submission, para. 161; response to Question No. 83(quoiting Panel Report, para. 7.243).

3 The European Communities appeared to acknowledge this initially in its third party written submission at para. 17(quoiting Panel Report, para. 7.244).

4 Panel Report, para. 7.244.

5 China's first written submission, paras 198-200, referring to Exhibits CHN-102, CHN-106 to CHN-112(quoiting Panel Report, para. 7.245).

6 United States' response to Question No. 41; China in fact submits that the minimum standard permits reasonable conditions and sequencing or structuring authority "in a conditional and circumstantial manner": see its first written submission, paras 196 and 202(quoiting Panel Report, para. 7.246).

7 Panel Report, para. 7.246.

responsibility of private right holders. This is reflected in the first sentence of Article 42 and the first sentence of Article 51, the reference to an "applicant" in Article 50.3 and 50.5, the reference to "request[s]" in Articles 46 and 48.1, and the option (not obligation) to make ex officio action available under Article 58. Viewed in context, the phrase "shall have the authority" does not require Members to take any action in the absence of an application or request. Therefore, a condition that authority shall only be available upon application or request seems to be assumed in much of Sections 2, 3 and 4 of Part III. This is consistent with the nature of intellectual property rights as private rights, as recognized in the fourth recital of the preamble of the TRIPS Agreement. Acquisition procedures for substantive rights and civil enforcement procedures generally have to be initiated by the right holder and not ex officio.[1]

The above observations do not imply that other types of conditions that do not find such a reflection in the text may not be attached to the required authority. However, the Panel does not consider it necessary, for the purposes of its examination of this claim, to consider what other conditions, if any, may be attached to "authority" consistently with Article 59. Therefore, other than the two conditions mentioned above, the Panel will accept arguendo that the availability of the "authority" required by Article 59 may not be subject to conditions in any given situation within the temporal scope of that Article, as described above.[2]

The "authority" required by Article 59 concerns two types of remedies, namely "destruction or disposal". The meaning of "destruction" is not controversial. As for "disposal", the Panel notes that the English text of Article 59 does not qualify this word so that it could, in accordance with its ordinary meaning, refer both to disposal outside the channels of commerce as well as to release into the channels of commerce. [3]However, read in context, the word "disposal" could be a reference to an order that goods be "disposed of" outside the channels of commerce as set out in Article 46. This ambiguity is resolved by reference to the French and Spanish texts, which are equally authentic.[4] The French text of Article 59 refers to authority to order "la mise hors circuit" which is a reference to the authority to order that infringing goods be "écartées des circuits commerciaux" in Article 46. The Spanish text of Article 59 refers to

---

1 Panel Report, para. 7.247.

2 Panel Report, para. 7.248.

3 The ordinary meaning of "disposal" can be defined as "the action of disposing of or getting rid of; the action of settling or dealing with". "Dispose" in turn can be defined as "get rid of; deal conclusively with, settle": see the New Shorter Oxford English Dictionary (1993). This would include release to an importer or third parties, whether or not in exchange for payment(quoiting Panel Report, para. 7.249).

4 See the final clause of the WTO Agreement. According to Article 33(3) of the Vienna Convention,the terms of the Agreement are presumed to have the same meaning in each authentic text(quoiting Panel Report, para. 7.249).

authority to order "eliminación" which, read in its context as an alternative to "destrucción", is evidently a reference to the authority to order that infringing goods be "apartadas de los circuitos comerciales" in Article 46. Accordingly, the correct interpretation of the term "disposal" in the first sentence of Article 59 is disposal "outside the channels of commerce".[1]

The Panel will refer to "destruction" and "disposal" collectively as "disposition methods" for ease of reference. It is not disputed that China's Customs measures provide the authority to order destruction of infringing goods in accordance with the principles set out in Article 46. However, the United States takes issue with what it considers the "highly limited circumstances" in which the Customs measures permit destruction.[2] China does not deny that its authority to order destruction is, in principle, subject to certain limitations but argues that China Customs has considerable discretion to decide whether such limitations apply. The statistics show that, in practice, over half of infringing goods seized by Customs in terms of value are in fact destroyed.[3]

The Panel recalls its finding at paragraph 7.246 above that China is permitted to limit the authority to order destruction of infringing goods provided that its competent authorities have the authority in such situations to order disposal of infringing goods in accordance with the principles set out in Article 46. The limitations on Customs' authority to order destruction of infringing goods are relevant to the claim only to the extent that they show that Customs has authority to order neither destruction of infringing goods nor disposal in accordance with those principles.[4]

It is in this context that the United States claims that the measures establish a mandatory sequence of steps, as the authorities will not have either of the required forms of authority in a given situation if the measures at issue compel them to order another disposition method that is not required by Article 59.[5]This raises the so-called "mandatory/discretionary distinction" that has been discussed in a number of GATT and WTO Panel Reports relating to trade in goods.[6]Whilst authority to order a disposition method not required by Article 59 does not, in itself, lead to WTO inconsistent action, to the extent that such authority mandates a disposition method in any given circumstance it may preclude authority that is required by Article 59. The preclusion of such authority may be WTO-inconsistent. For that reason, the Panel will examine

---

1 Panel Report, para. 7.249.

2 United States' second oral statement, para. 59; response to Question No. 81(quoiting Panel Report, para. 7.250).

3 China's rebuttal submission, para. 154. See the statistics at paragraph 7.349 below(quoting Panel Report, para. 7.250).

4 Panel Report, para. 7.251.

5 United States' rebuttal submission, para. 161; responses to Questions Nos. 39, 41, 80 and 83(quoiting Panel Report, para. 7.252).

6 See further paragraph 7.358 below(quoiting Panel Report, para. 7.252).

whether certain aspects of the Customs measures are mandatory.[1]

The Panel also notes that authority to order a disposition method within the scope of Article 59 will often be discretionary, as the obligation that Members' competent authorities "shall have the authority" to make particular orders applies to what those authorities are permitted to order by domestic law. Accordingly, the obligation in Article 59 is applicable to both mandatory and discretionary measures and, in principle, both mandatory and discretionary measures "as such" can be examined for conformity with that obligation.[2]

The Customs measures at issue provide for three disposal options besides destruction. These are donation to social welfare bodies; sale to the right holder; and auction. The United States claims that none of these disposal options is in accordance with the principles set out in Article 46 and that all preclude authority to order destruction.[3]China responds that the first two of these disposal options constitute authority to order disposal in accordance with the principles set out in Article 46, and that the United States has not established that China Customs lacks authority to order destruction. Therefore, the Panel will proceed as follows:

(a) First, the Panel will determine what are "the principles set out in Article 46";

(b) Second, the Panel will assess China Customs' authority to order donation to social welfare bodies and, if necessary, sale to the right holder, in order to determine whether they constitute authority to order disposal in accordance with the principles set out in the first sentence of Article 46; and

(c) Third, the Panel will assess China Customs' authority to order auction of infringing goods (plus either of the first two disposal options that is found to be disposal not in accordance with the principles set out in the first sentence of Article 46) to determine whether such authority mandates a particular disposition method and thereby precludes authority to order destruction.[4]

---

1 Panel Report, para. 7.252.

2 The Panel notes that its approach is consistent with the view of the Appellate Body in US – Corrosion-Resistant Steel Sunset Review (at para. 93) that "as with any such analytical tool, the import of the 'mandatory/discretionary distinction' may vary from case to case". The Panel also notes that the possibility of obligations which would render illegal even discretionary legislation was specifically envisaged in the Panel Report in US – Section 301 Trade Act (at para. 7.53) as follows:

"The question is then whether, on the correct interpretation of the specific WTO obligation at issue, only mandatory or also discretionary national laws are prohibited. We do not accept the legal logic that there has to be one fast and hard rule covering all domestic legislation. After all, is it so implausible that the framers of the WTO Agreement, in their wisdom, would have crafted some obligations which would render illegal even discretionary legislation and crafted other obligations prohibiting only mandatory legislation?"(quoiting Panel Report, para. 7.253).

3 United States' first written submission, paras 184, 189 and 191(quoiting Panel Report, para. 7.254).

4 Panel Report, para. 7.254.

"The principles set out in Article 46"

The first sentence of Article 59 provides that competent authorities shall have the authority to order the destruction or disposal of infringing goods "in accordance with the principles set out in Article 46". The phrase referencing the principles set out in Article 46 attaches to "the authority to order the destruction or disposal of infringing goods". This directs the treaty interpreter to those principles in Article 46 that attach to such authority.[1]

The Panel makes the following observations. First, Article 59 refers to "authority". Second, Article 59 incorporates principles that attach to authority to order "destruction or disposal". Third, Article 59 relates to the authority to order destruction or disposal of "infringing goods" but not principles applicable to the disposition of materials and implements.[2]

The first sentence of Article 46 refers to "authority" to order that "infringing goods" be "disposed of ... or ... destroyed". Therefore, it seems pertinent to Article 59.[3]

The second sentence of Article 46 refers to disposal of materials and implements and is therefore inapposite. Indeed, materials and implements used to create infringing goods would not normally be suspended at the border with the infringing goods, unlike during enforcement actions within a Member's territory.[4]

The third sentence of Article 46 refers to "such requests" although the previous sentences do not refer expressly to any requests. The content of the third sentence clearly relates to materials and implements as addressed in the second sentence but it could equally relate to infringing goods as addressed in the first sentence. The text is ambiguous on this point. This ambiguity can be resolved by reference to the records of the negotiation of the TRIPS Agreement.[5]

The TRIPS Agreement was negotiated during the Uruguay Round in the Negotiating Group on Trade-Related Aspects of Intellectual Property Rights, including Trade in Counterfeit Goods. The Chairman's draft text of the Agreement of 23 July 1990 included a draft article

---

1 Panel Report, para. 7.255.

2 Panel Report, para. 7.256.

3 Panel Report, para. 7.258.

4 Panel Report, para. 7.259.

5 The Panel has recourse to a supplementary means of interpretation in accordance with Article 32 of the Vienna Convention in order to determine the meaning when the interpretation according to the general rule of interpretation in Article 31 leaves the meaning ambiguous(quoiting Panel Report, para. 7.260).

corresponding to what is Article 46 in the text as finally agreed.[1] In that draft article, the principle of proportionality and the interests of third parties were related to a request of the right holder under the previous sentence. That request could be for remedies with respect to infringing goods as well as materials and implements. In a later draft[2], the first sentence of the provision on remedies was divided into two separate sentences, one with respect to infringing goods and the other with respect to materials and implements. Both sentences included the phrase "upon request from the right holder". In the same draft, the phrase "[i]n considering such a request" was revised to read "[i]n considering such requests" (in the plural). This is the version of the third sentence that was retained in the so-called "Brussels Draft"[3] and the final text of Article 46 of the TRIPS Agreement.[4]

Auction and authority to order the destruction of infringing goods

The Panel will now consider Customs' authority to order that infringing goods be auctioned. Auction is the third disposal method set out in the measures at issue. Auction is not a form of destruction, and it is undisputed that auction is not a form of disposal outside the channels of commerce. Accordingly, this disposal method is clearly not required by Article 59.[5] However, the Panel recalls its finding at paragraph 7.240 above that the remedies specified in Article 59 are not exhaustive. Therefore, the fact that authority to order auction of infringing goods is not required is not in itself inconsistent with Article 59.[6]

The Panel finds that the United States has not established that the authority to order auction of infringing goods under the Customs measures precludes authority to order destruction of

---

1 That draft article read as follows:

"10. Other Remedies 10A Where an intellectual property right has been found to be infringed, the court shall have the authority to order, upon request of the right holder, that the infringing goods, as well as materials and implements the predominant use of which has been in the creation of the infringing goods, be, without compensation of any sort, destroyed or disposed of outside the channels of commerce in such a manner as to minimise any harm caused to the right holder. In considering such a request, the need for proportionality between the seriousness of the infringement and the remedies ordered as well as the interests of third parties shall be taken into account. [In regard to counterfeit goods] [Other than in exceptional cases], the simple removal of the trade mark [or geographical indication] unlawfully affixed shall not be ordered." (emphasis added) See Part IV of document MTN.GNG/NG11/W/76(quoiting Panel Report, para. 7.261).

2 Chairman's revised draft text of 13 November 1990, document no. 2814(quoiting Panel Report, para. 7.261).

3 See draft Article 49 in document MTN.TNC/W/35/Rev.1 dated 3 December 1990 entitled "Draft Final Act Embodying the Results of the Uruguay Round of Multilateral Trade Negotiations – Revision"(quoiting Panel Report, para. 7.261).

4 Panel Report, para. 7.261.

5 See paragraph 7.244 above(quoiting Panel Report, para. 7.327).

6 Panel Report, para. 7.327.

infringing goods in accordance with the principles set out in the first sentence of Article 46.[1]

III. Denial of copyright and related rights protection and enforcement to works that have not been authorized for publication or distribution within China

The Panel notes that this claim challenges China's Copyright Law, in particular Article 4(1), not as it has been applied in any particular instance but "as such". The parties have disagreed on the proper interpretation of that measure since shortly after the first substantive meeting. Therefore, the Panel is obliged, in accordance with its mandate, to make an objective assessment of the meaning of the relevant provisions of that measure. In this context, the Panel is mindful that, objectively, a Member is normally well-placed to explain the meaning of its own law.[2] However, in the context of a dispute, to the extent that either party advances a particular interpretation of a provision of the measure at issue, it bears the burden of proof that its interpretation is correct.[3] The Panel emphasizes that it examines the measure solely for the purpose of determining its conformity with China's obligations under the TRIPS Agreement.[4]

The United States claims that Article 4(1) of the Copyright Law on its face denies immediate, automatic protection to certain works of creative authorship.[5]

China responds that this claim is based on the "mistaken view" that copyright protection in China is contingent upon successful completion of content review.[6] In the course of addressing the issue of when copyright vests under Chinese law, China acknowledged that Article 4(1) of the Copyright Law denies protection to certain works due to their content.[7]

The United States stated at the first substantive meeting that, in view of that acknowledgement, China appeared simply to concede that Article 4 of the Copyright Law was inconsistent with China's obligations under the TRIPS Agreement.[8] Canada and the European

---

1 Panel Report, para. 7.354.

2 China stresses that part of this claim involves "an arcane area of Chinese law, with little practical application, and with respect to which there is little or no practical experience on which to base legal judgments": see China's response to Question No. 52(quoiting Panel Report, para. 7.28).

3 See the Panel Reports in EC – Trademarks and Geographical Indications (US), at para. 7.55, and EC – Trademarks and Geographical Indications (Australia), at para. 7.106(quoiting Panel Report, para. 7.28).

4 See Appellate Body Report in India – Patents (US), paras 65-68(quoiting Panel Report, para. 7.28).

5 United States' first written submission, para. 196(quoiting Panel Report, para. 7.29).

6 China's first written submission, para. 8(quoiting Panel Report, para. 7.30).

7 China's first written submission, paras 229 and 243(quoiting Panel Report, para. 7.30).

8 United States' first oral statement, para. 79(quoiting Panel Report, para. 7.31).

Communities, as third parties, took the same view.[1] Argentina considered that the text of Article 4 was straightforward.[2]

After that meeting, China clarified the terms of its earlier acknowledgement. It clarified that Article 4(1) denies "copyright protection" in the sense of enforcement but does not disturb "copyright".[3]

The United States dismissed China's clarification as an "artificial distinction".[4] The Panel begins its assessment by observing that Chapter I of the Copyright Law comprises eight articles. Article 1 sets out the purpose of the law, which includes the purpose of protecting the copyright of authors in their literary, artistic and scientific works and the rights and interests related to copyright.[5]

The Berne Convention (1971) is defined as an "international copyright treaty" for the purposes of the Provisions on the Implementation of International Copyright Treaties.[6] Article 3 sets out a non-exhaustive list of "works" for the purposes of this Law, including works of literature, art, natural sciences, social sciences, engineering and technology which are created in the form of any of a series of enumerated works.[7] Article 4 provides inter alia that certain "works" shall not be protected by this Law.[8] Article 5 sets out subject matter to which this Law does not apply.[9] Article 6 provides that certain works will be dealt with in other measures.[10]

The Panel finds that the Copyright Law is sufficiently clear, on its face, to show that Article 4(1) denies the protection of Article 10 to certain works, including those of WTO

---

1 Canada's third party written submission, para. 22; European Communities' third party written submission, para. 22, third party oral statement, para. 21(quoiting Panel Report, para. 7.31).

2 Argentina's third party written submission, para. 82(quoiting Panel Report, para. 7.31).

3 China's response to Question No. 44; rebuttal submission, paras 280-281(quoiting Panel Report, para. 7.32).

4 United States' second oral statement (closing statement), para. 25(quoiting Panel Report, para. 7.33).

5 Panel Report, para. 7.34.

6 Provisions on the Implementation of International Copyright Treaties, promulgated by decree of the State Council in 1992 and effective from 1992, Article 3, reproduced in Exhibit CHN-117. These Provisions, which predate the TRIPS Agreement, do not refer to the TRIPS Agreement in the definition of "international copyright treaties", although other legal provisions might. The United States has not challenged this aspect of the measure(quoiting Panel Report, para. 7.36).

7 Panel Report, para. 7.37.

8 Panel Report, para. 7.38.

9 Panel Report, para. 7.39.

10 The remaining provisions of Chapter I concern the departments responsible for administration (Article 7); and collective copyright administration (Article 8)(quoiting Panel Report, para. 7.40).

Member nationals, as the United States claims. [1] The Panel finds that the Supreme People's Court letter confirms that Article 4(1) of the Copyright Law denies copyright protection and clarifies that Article 4(1) applies where the publication and/or dissemination of a work is prohibited due to its content. [2]

The Panel notes that China equates the "protection" of the Copyright Law referred to in Article 4(1) with enforcement rights. However, China does not show any suitable basis in the text of Article 4(1) that would limit its effect to a subset of the protection under the Copyright Law. China contrasts the "protection" of the Copyright Law referred to in Article 4(1) with the "enjoyment" of copyright in accordance with Article 2 of the Copyright Law. However, the concepts referred to in Articles 2(2) and 4(1), on their face, are identical. China points out that Article 4(1) does not state that certain works "shall not enjoy copyright". [3] That is true, but the protection of the Law is copyright. [4]

【思考题】

1.TRIPS 协定第 46 条创设的原则是什么，将知识产权侵权货物捐赠社会公益是否违反该原则？

2. 按照专家组的观点，TRIPS 协定第 61 条中的"具有商业规模"应如何确定？

Case2·拓展阅读

---

1 Panel Report, para. 7.50.

2 Panel Report, para. 7.52.

3 China's response to Question No. 88(quoiting Panel Report, para. 7.63).

4 Panel Report, para. 7.63.

IV
国际贸易管理与世界贸易组织法

【内容摘要】

本章精选两个 WTO 案例。第一个案例是中国原材料案（China-Raw Materials，DS394、395、398），主要争议焦点在中国是否可以援引 GATT1994 第 20 条为其实施的出口限制措施进行抗辩。GATT1994 第 20 条规定了一般例外，允许各成员为保护人类健康或公共道德等目的采取违反 GATT1994 规则或其所作相关承诺的措施。第二个案例是美国反倾销反补贴案（US - Anti-Dumping and Countervailing Duties，DS379），主要争议焦点是美国对来自中国的产品实施"双重救济"措施是否违反 WTO 成员的相关条约义务，涉及对来自非市场经济国家的同一产品同时征收反倾销税和反补贴税是否适当的问题。

Case1   China-Raw Materials （DS394、395、398）

【案情说明】

一、案件事实

2009 年 6 月 23 日和 8 月 21 日，美国、欧共体以及墨西哥分别要求根据《关于解决争端的规则和程序的谅解》第 1 条、第 4 条以及 GATT1994 第 22 条，与中国就其对各种形式的铝土矿、焦炭、萤石、镁、锰、碳化硅、金属硅、黄磷和锌采取的出口限制措施进行磋商。[1]2009 年 11 月 4 日，美国、欧共体以及墨西哥要求争端解决组织根据《关于解决争端的规则和程序的谅解》第 6 条成立专家组。[2]2010 年 3 月 29 日，专家组成立，并于 2011 年 7 月 5 日分发专家组报告。此后，中国、美国、欧共体和墨西哥分别就专家组报告中的法律以及法律解释问题提起上诉。[3]2011 年 6 月 5 日，上诉机构作出裁决报告。

这场争端起于中国对某些原材料出口实行的四种出口限制。受出口限制的原材料有各种形式的铝土矿、焦炭、萤石、镁、锰、碳化硅、金属硅、黄磷和锌。中国是这些原材料的主要生产国，这些原材料主要用于生产日常用品和科技用品。在专家组成立之前，美国、墨西哥和欧共体(以下简称"申诉方")质疑中国对原材料实施的以下四种出口限制：（一）出口税；（二）出口配额；（三）出口许可要求；（四）最低出口价格要求。[4]申诉方还质疑中国出口配额、出口许可证和最低出口价格分配和管理中的某些方面，以及某些未公布的出口措施。[5]申诉方称，这些出口限制不符合中国根据《中国入世议定书》和《中国入世工作组报告》所作的承诺，也不符合 GATT1994 第 8 条第 1 款（a）项、第 8 条第 4 款、第 10 条第 1 款、第 10 条第 3 款（a）项和第 11 条第 1 款的规定。[6]申诉方主张，中国的出口限制措施造成了国际市场上相关原材料的稀缺，并导致全球市场原材料价格上涨。此外，中国通过充足的供应和更低更稳定

---

1 Panel Report,para.1.1.

2 Panel Report,para.1.2.

3 中国于 2011 年 8 月 31 日提起上诉，美国、欧共体和墨西哥于 2011 年 9 月 6 日提起上诉。

4 Panel Reports,para.2.1.

5 Panel Report,para.2.1.

6 Appellate Report, para.2.

的原材料价格为中国国内产业提供了显著优势。

针对申诉方的主张，中国的主要辩护依据是 GATT1994 第 20 条（b）款和（g）款。在中国看来，基于保护可耗尽的自然资源以及减少污染和保护人类健康，对某些形式的焦炭、萤石、镁、锰和锌征收出口关税是合理的。对于出口配额，中国主张根据 GATT1994 第 11 条第 2（1）款，对一种被称为"耐火及铝土矿"的铝土矿采取的出口配额是合理的。

二、裁判结果

（一）专家组报告

专家组讨论了申诉人所称中国实施的四种出口限制，以及某些出口措施的管理和适用问题。1. 关于出口税，专家组首先审议了中国对某些形式的铝土矿、焦炭、萤石、镁、锰、金属硅、黄磷和锌征收的出口关税是否符合《中国入世议定书》第 11.3 段。第 11.3 段要求取消适用于出口的所有税费，除非《中国入世议定书》附件 6 特别规定或根据 GATT1994 年第 8 条适用。专家组发现，除了黄磷之外，附件 6 中没有包括其他任何有争议的原材料，因此这些材料不能免除取消出口税的要求。[1] 对此，中国辩称根据 GATT1994 第 20 条（b）款和（g）款，对某些形式的焦炭、萤石、镁、锰和锌征收出口税是合理的[2]，因为这些原材料是可耗尽的自然资源，征收出口税是基于减少污染和保护人类健康的目的。然而，专家组认为中国不能援引 GATT1994 第 20 条的例外来证明被认为不符合《中国入世议定书》第 11.3 段措施的合理性，因为这些例外仅适用于违反 GATT1994 的情形而非《中国入世议定书》，除非 GATT1994 被特别地纳入议定书的条款或文本中。而《中国入世议定书》第 11.3 段不包含任何允许援引 GATT1994 年第 20 条来证明中国采取的与第 11.3 段不符的出口关税措施的合理性的语言或提法。[3] 除此之外，专家组认为，即使假设中国根据《中国入世议定书》第 11.3 段可以援引第 20 条（b）款和（g）款下例外，中国也没有满足这些条款的要求。[4] 2. 关于出口配额，专家组认为，中国对某些形式的铝土矿、焦炭、萤石、碳化硅和锌实行的配额不符合 GATT1994 第 11 条第 1 款的规定。除此之外，出口配额没有"暂时适用"，以便"防止或缓解"GATT1994 第 11 条第 2（a）款所指的耐火级铝土矿的"严重短缺"。[5] 3. 关于出口许可证制度，该制度本身并不违背中国根据 GATT1994 第 11

---

1 Panel Report, sections Ⅶ.B.1-Ⅷ.B.4.

2 中国没有试图根据第 20 条证明对铝土矿、其他形式的锰或金属硅征收出口税是合理的。

3 Panel Reports, section Ⅷ.B.5.

4 Panel Reports, sections Ⅷ.D.2-Ⅷ.D.4.

5 Panel Report, section Ⅷ.D.1.

条第 1 款承担的义务。[1] 然而，专家组认为，中国出口许可证当局有权向申请此类许可证的企业要求未在界定内的"其他"文件或材料造成了不确定性，构成了第 11 条第 1 款所禁止的出口限制。[2] 此外，专家组认为，中国要求以协调的最低出口价格出口某些形式的铝土矿、焦炭、萤石、镁、碳化硅、黄磷和锌，也构成第 11 条第 1 款规定的禁止出口限制。4. 对于中国出口配额管理和分配的某些方面，专家组认为，中国对某些出口配额分配规定的出口业绩和最低注册资本要求不符合中国根据《中国入世议定书》和《中国入世工作组报告》承担的"贸易权"义务。[3]

（二）上诉机构报告

上诉机构基本维持了专家组的裁决，只对专家组报告中的以下两点做出更改。第一，申诉方未能在据称违反的涵盖协定条款里包含的广泛义务与其所质疑的 37 项措施中找到足够清晰的联系，因此申诉方的专家组请求第三节不符合 DSU 第 6 条第 2 款的要求；第二，上诉机构认为专家组在解释 GATT1994 第 20 条（g）款中的"与……一同实施"有误，上诉机构认为，第 20 条（g）款的文本中没有任何内容表明贸易限制除了"与国内生产或消费限制一同实施"之外，还必须旨在确保国内限制的有效性。[4]

【法律分析】

在本案争议中，最主要的争议焦点是中国是否可以援引 GATT1994 第 20 条来证明其实施的出口管制措施具备合法性。该出口关税被认为不符合中国在《入世议定书》第 11.3 款下承诺的义务。下面我们结合该案的专家组报告和上诉机构报告，对该争议点进行法律分析。

专家组解释《中国入世议定书》第 11.3 段时指出，第 11.3 段"不包括对 GATT1994 第 20 条或 GATT1994 条款一般性的明确提及"。[5] 特别是第 11.3 段仅包含"具体的例外：附件 6 所涵盖的例外和 GATT1994 第 8 条所涵盖的例外"。[6] 对专家组来说，第 11.3 段中的措辞，加上"省略对世贸组织协定或 GATT1994 的一般性提及"，表明世贸组织成员不打算将第 20 条规定的抗辩纳入议定书第 11.3 段。[7] 专家组还认为，《中国入世工作组报告》的规定并不支持中国可以援引 GATT1994 第 20 条来为违反《中国入世议定书》

---

1 Panel Report, para. 7.938.

2 Panel Report, para. 7.948.

3 Panel Reports, paras. 7.657-7.670.

4 Appellate Report, para. 362(e).

5 Panel Report, para. 7.124.

6 Panel Report, para. 7.126.

7 Panel Report, para. 7.129.

第 11.3 段的行为进行辩护。

中国声称专家组的分析存在错误，并要求上诉机构推翻专家组的裁决。认为中国其可以利用 GATT1994 第 20 条来证明争议措施的正当性。并且认为，世贸组织成员有"固有权利"来规范贸易，"包括利用出口关税来促进非贸易利益"。[1]

基于此，本案上诉机构分别从《中国入世议定书》第 11.3 段，《中国入世议定书》第 11.1 段、11.2 段，《中国入世工作组报告》第 170 段以及中国规范贸易的权利四个方面进行分析。

（一）《中国入世议定书》第 11.3 段

《中国入世议定书》第 11.3 段要求中国取消特定产品出口的全部税费，具体名录附件 6 有明确规定或按照 GATT1994 第 8 条规定适用除外。其中附件 6 列出了 84 种产品以及每种产品的最高出口税率，同时附件 6 注释指出，在例外情况下可提高目前适用的税率；GATT1994 第 8 条规定了世贸组织成员对进出口的规费和手续。上诉机构认为，《中国入世议定书》附件 6 的注释没有允许中国对未列入附件 6 的产品征收出口税，或者在没有"例外情况"发生的情况下，提高附件 6 所列 84 种产品的适用出口关税。[2] 除此之外，虽然 GATT1994 第 8 条涵盖了"世贸组织成员对进出口征收的任何性质的所有规费和费用"，但它明确排除了出口关税，由于出口关税不在第 8 条的范围内，因此本案中的中国措施不存在与该条相符或一致的问题。上诉机构认为，可以援引 GATT1994 第 20 条来证明违反第 8 条规定的规费和费用是合理的，但这并不意味着可以援引第 20 条来证明第 8 条未规定的出口关税是合理的。[3]

（二）《中国入世议定书》第 11.1 段、11.2 段

审查了《中国入世议定书》第 11.3 段的文本后，上诉机构审查了此条款的上下文。《中国入世议定书》第 11.1 段规定："中国应确保国家或地方当局适用或管理的海关规费或收费符合 GATT1994"。第 11.2 段进一步规定："中国应确保由国家或地方当局实施或管理的国内税费，包括增值税，符合 GATT1994。"上诉机构指出，第 11.1 段一般指"海关规费和费用"，第 11.2 段指"国内税收和费用"，而第 11.3 段指取消"适用于出口的税收和费用"。虽然第 11.1 段和第 11.2 段均提及 GATT1994，但是第 11.3 段未提及 GATT1994，并且这些条款所涵盖的义务主题和性质不同，因此中国不得援引 GATT1994 第 20 条作为其违反根据第 11.3 段取消出口关税的承诺的理由。[4]

（三）《中国入世工作组报告》第 170 段

鉴于《中国入世工作组报告》第 170 段所属小节的标题与《中国入世议定书》第

---

1 China's appellant's submission, para.208.

2 Appellate Report, para.287.

3 Appellate Report, para.290.

4 Appellate Report, para.293.

11 节的标题相同。两者都题为"对进出口征收的税费"。中国认为，这表明《中国入世议定书》第 11.3 段和《中国入世工作组报告》第 170 段适用的措施范围"有很大重叠"，它们对"税收"和"出口收费"规定了"累积义务"。[1]《中国入世工作组报告》第 170 段赋予中国适用与 WTO 不一致的出口"税收"和"收费"的灵活性，该灵活性应同样适用于《中国入世议定书》第 11.3 段。[2]（that "any flexibilities that Paragraph 170 affords to China to adopt otherwise WTO-inconsistent export 'taxes' and 'charges' must extend equally to Paragraph 11.3".）针对中国的主张，上诉机构认为，《中国入世工作组报告》第 170 段对解释《中国入世议定书》第 11.3 段的相关性有限，《中国入世工作组报告》第 170 段没有充分说明中国取消出口关税的承诺。相反，《中国入世工作组报告》第 155 段和第 156 段规定了中国对消除出口关税的承诺，尤其是第 155 段，其与《中国入世议定书》第 11.3 段的规定非常类似。[3]如同《中国入世议定书》第 11.3 段那样，《中国入世工作组报告》第 155 段和 156 段都没有提及 GATT1994 第 20 条，因此，中国不能援引 GATT 第 20 条来证明其采取的出口关税措施的合法性。

（四）中国规制贸易的权利

中国主张，每个国家都有权以促进保护环境和公共健康的方式规范贸易，并引用中美出版物和视听产品案的上诉机构报告，认为这是一种"固有权利"，而不是"WTO 协定等国际条约赋予的权利"。[4]除此之外，中国认为，专家组对《中国入世议定书》第 11.3 段的解释"将固有权利转化为既得权利"，并"扭曲了中国加入 WTO 时确立的权利和义务的平衡"。[5]针对此争议，上诉机构以《中国入世议定书》第 5.1 段的措辞为依据，并将其与第 11.3 段相比较，认为《中国入世议定书》第 11.3 段未涵盖第 5.1 段所表述的"在不损害中国以符合 WTO 协定的方式管理贸易的权利的情况下"等措辞，因此，中国不能以此来证明出口关税措施的合法性。

最终，上诉机构维持了专家组的结论，认为根据对《中国入世议定书》第 11.3 段的恰当解释，没有能够为中国提供适用 GATT1994 第 20 条例外条款的依据。[6]因此，中国不能依据 GATT1994 第 20 条来证明其出口关税措施的合理性。

1 China's appellant's submission, para.233. (original emphasis)

2 China's appellant's submission, para.246.

3 Appellate Report, para.299.

4 China's appellant's submission, para. 275 (quoting Appellate Body Report, *China-Publications and Audiovisual Products*, para. 222).

5 China's appellant's submission, para.274, subheading IV.C.5.d.

6 Appellate Report, para.307.

【英文案例裁决摘录】

下文的摘录是上诉机构报告中关于 GATT 第 20 条的适用部分。

VI. Applicability of Article XX

270. In this section, we address China's claim that Article XX of the GATT 1994 is available as a defence to China in relation to export duties found to be inconsistent with China's obligations under Paragraph 11.3 of China's Accession Protocol.

A. The Panel's Findings

271. The Panel began its interpretation of Paragraph 11.3 of China's Accession Protocol by observing that Paragraph 11.3 "does not include any express reference to Article XX of the GATT 1994, or to provisions of the GATT 1994 more generally".[1] In so doing, the Panel drew a contrast between the text of Paragraph 11.3 and the language contained in Paragraph 5.1 of China's Accession Protocol—"without prejudice to China's right to regulate trade in a manner consistent with the WTO Agreement"—which the Appellate Body examined in *China-Publications and Audiovisual Products*.[2] In particular, the Panel noted that Paragraph 11.3 contains only a "specific set of exceptions: those covered by Annex 6 and those covered by GATT Article VIII".[3] For the Panel, the language in Paragraph 11.3, together with the "omission of general references to the WTO Agreement or to the GATT 1994"[4], suggest that WTO Members did not intend to incorporate the defences available under Article XX into Paragraph 11.3.[5] The Panel also found no support in the provisions of China's Accession Working Party Report for the proposition that China could invoke Article XX of the GATT 1994 to justify violations of Paragraph 11.3 of China's Accession Protocol.

272. Regarding the context provided by the provisions of the other WTO agreements, the Panel noted that there are no general exceptions in the *WTO Agreement*, and that each of the covered agreements provides its own "set of exceptions or flexibilities" applicable to the

---

1 Panel Report, para. 7.124.

2 Paragraph 5.1 of China's Accession Protocol provides:

Without prejudice to China's right to regulate trade in a manner consistent with the WTO Agreement, China shall progressively liberalize the availability and scope of the right to trade, so that, within three years after accession, all enterprises in China shall have the right to trade in all goods throughout the customs territory of China, except for those goods listed in Annex 2A which continue to be subject to state trading in accordance with this Protocol.

3 Panel Report, para. 7.126.

4 Panel Report, para. 7.129.

5 Panel Report, paras. 7.126-7.129.

specific commitments in each agreement.[1]   Referring to Article XX of the GATT 1994, the Panel considered that the reference to "this Agreement" *a priori* suggests that the exceptions therein relate only to the GATT 1994.[2]   Noting that, in several instances, provisions of Article XX have been incorporated into other WTO agreements by cross-reference, the Panel observed that, since no such language is found in Paragraph 11.3 of China's Accession Protocol, Article XX could not be intended to apply to Paragraph 11.3.   Furthermore, whereas the Panel agreed that WTO Members have an "inherent right" to regulate trade, the Panel considered that China had exercised this right in negotiating and ratifying the *WTO Agreement*, including the terms of its accession to the WTO.[3]   On this basis, the Panel concluded that the defences of Article XX of the GATT 1994 are not available to justify violations of the obligations contained in Paragraph 11.3 of China's Accession Protocol.[4]

B. Arguments on Appeal

273. China alleges various errors in the Panel's analysis and requests the Appellate Body to reverse the Panel's finding that China may not seek to justify export duties pursuant to Article XX of the GATT 1994 that were found to be inconsistent with its commitment to eliminate export duties under Paragraph 11.3 of its Accession Protocol.[5]   China further requests us to find that Article XX is available to China to justify such measures.

274. China contends, in particular, that the Panel erred in determining that there is "no textual basis" in China's Accession Protocol for it to invoke Article XX in defence of a claim under Paragraph 11.3.[6]   In China's view, the Panel's finding that Paragraph 11.3 excludes recourse to Article XX of the GATT 1994 was based on the Panel's erroneous assumption that the absence of language expressly granting the right to regulate trade in a manner consistent with Article XX means that China and other Members intended to deprive China of that right.   Moreover, China argues that WTO Members have an "inherent right" to regulate trade, "including using export duties to promote non-trade interests".[7]

275. Although China takes issue with the Panel's finding that Article XX is not available to China to justify measures that would otherwise be inconsistent with its commitment to eliminate export duties under Paragraph 11.3 of its Accession Protocol, it does not request the

---

1 Panel Report, para. 7.150.

2 Panel Report, para. 7.153.

3 Panel Report, para. 7.156.

4 Panel Report, para. 7.158.

5 China's appellant's submission, para. 168 (referring to Panel Reports, paras. 7.158, 7.159, 8.2(b)-(c), 8.9(b)-(c), and 8.16(b)-(c)).

6 China's appellant's submission, para. 190.

7 China's appellant's submission, para. 208.

Appellate Body to reverse the Panel's finding that China failed to demonstrate that the export duties at issue in this dispute are justified under Article XX of the GATT 1994.

276. The United States, the European Union, and Mexico support the Panel's finding that Article XX of the GATT 1994 cannot be invoked to justify export duties that are inconsistent with Paragraph 11.3 of China's Accession Protocol. The United States and Mexico recall that, in *China-Publications and Audiovisual Products*, the Appellate Body interpreted the language of Paragraph 5.1 of China's Accession Protocol as including a reference to Article XX. They note, however, that the language of Paragraph 11.3 is "in sharp contrast" to that of Paragraph 5.1, as it is "specific and circumscribed", "sets forth particular commitments", and two exceptions to those commitments. According to the European Union, while WTO Members can "incorporate" Article XX of the GATT 1994 into another WTO agreement if they so "wish", the legal basis for "applying" that provision to another agreement would be the "very text of the incorporation", and not Article XX itself, as Article XX is limited by its "express terms" to the GATT 1994.[1] The European Union also asserts that the Panel was correct in finding that China had exercised its inherent and sovereign right to regulate trade by negotiating the terms of its accession to the WTO such that this inherent right to regulate trade, without more, does not permit recourse to Article XX.

277. Canada, Colombia, Japan, Korea, and Turkey generally agree with the complainants that Article XX of the GATT 1994 cannot be invoked in order to justify a violation of China's export duty commitments contained in Paragraph 11.3 of China's Accession Protocol.[2]

C. Availability of Article XX to Justify Export Duties that Are Found to Be Inconsistent with Paragraph 11.3 of China's Accession Protocol

278. Paragraph 1.2 of China's Accession Protocol provides that the Protocol "shall be an integral part" of the *WTO Agreement*. As such, the customary rules of interpretation of public international law, as codified in Articles 31 and 32 of the *Vienna Convention on the Law of Treaties*[3](the "*Vienna Convention*"), are, pursuant to Article 3.2 of the DSU, applicable

---

1 European Union's appellee's submission, para. 54.

2 See Canada's third participant's submission, paras. 14-24; Colombia's third participant's submission, paras. 11 and 12; and Japan's third participant's submission, paras. 26-30, 34-37, and 39-42. For its part, Korea considers that the "gravity" and importance of an Article XX defence suggests that "[m]ore explicit wording" should have been used to express the "relinquishment" of such an "important right". Nonetheless, in Korea's view, the difference in "tone and nuance" between Paragraph 11.3 and Paragraphs 11.1 and 11.2 of China's Accession Protocol, as well as the context of the other provisions of Section 11, support the Panel's ultimate conclusion in the present disputes and should be upheld by the Appellate Body. (Korea's third participant's submission, paras. 32 and 33)

3 Done at Vienna, 23 May 1969, 1155 UNTS 331; 8 International Legal Materials 679.

in this dispute in clarifying the meaning of Paragraph 11.3 of the Protocol.[1] Article 31(1) of the *Vienna Convention* provides that a "treaty shall be interpreted in good faith in accordance with the ordinary meaning to be given to the terms of the treaty in their context and in the light of its object and purpose." Therefore, we will begin our analysis with the text of Paragraph 11.3.

Paragraph 11.3 of China's Accession Protocol

279. Paragraph 11.3 of China's Accession Protocol provides that:

China shall eliminate all taxes and charges applied to exports unless specifically provided for in Annex 6 of this Protocol or applied in conformity with the provisions of Article VIII of the GATT 1994.

280. By its terms, Paragraph 11.3 of China's Accession Protocol requires China to "eliminate all taxes and charges applied to exports" unless one of the following conditions is satisfied: (i) such taxes and charges are "specifically provided for in Annex 6 of [China's Accession] Protocol"; or (ii) such taxes and charges are "applied in conformity with the provisions of Article VIII of the GATT 1994".

281. As noted, Paragraph 11.3 of China's Accession Protocol refers explicitly to "Annex 6 of this Protocol". Annex 6 of China's Accession Protocol is entitled "Products Subject to Export Duty". It sets out a table listing 84 different products (each identified by an eight-digit Harmonized System ("HS") number and product description), and a maximum export duty rate for each product.[2]Following the table, Annex 6 includes the following text (the "Note to Annex 6"):

China confirmed that the tariff levels in this Annex are maximum levels which will not be exceeded. China confirmed furthermore that it would not increase the presently applied rates, except under exceptional circumstances. If such circumstances occurred, China would consult with affected members prior to increasing applied tariffs with a view to finding a mutually acceptable solution.

282. Except for yellow phosphorus, none of the raw materials at issue in this dispute is listed in Annex 6 of China's Accession Protocol.[3] China argues that the use of the

---

1 See Appellate Body Report, *US – Gasoline*, p. 17, DSR 1996:I, 3, at 16; and Appellate Body Report, *Japan – Alcoholic Beverages II* , p. 10, DSR 1996:I, 97, at 104.

2 Panel Report, para. 7.66.

3 The Panel found that, on 21 December 2009, yellow phosphorous was subject to an export duty of 20 per cent, which did not exceed the maximum rate listed in Annex 6 of China's Accession Protocol. The Panel found, therefore, that the provision of the *2009 Tariff Implementation Program* applicable to yellow phosphorus that was in force at the time of the Panel's establishment was not inconsistent with China's WTO obligations. (See Panel Reports, para. 7.71) This finding by the Panel has not been challenged on appeal.

term "exceptional circumstances" in the Note to Annex 6 indicates "a substantive overlap between the scope of the exceptions set forth, respectively, in Annex 6 and Article XX of the GATT 1994".[1] In China's view, "by allowing China to adopt otherwise WTO-inconsistent export duties in 'exceptional circumstances', China and other WTO Members have demonstrated a shared intent that China is permitted to have recourse—whether directly or indirectly—to the 'exceptional circumstances' set forth in Article XX to justify such duties."[2] China suggests that such "exceptional circumstances" can be invoked both to exceed the maximum rates specified in Annex 6 for the 84 products listed in the Annex, and to impose export duties on non-listed products.

283. In response, the United States and Mexico assert that the first sentence of the Note "makes clear" that China committed not to impose export duties on the 84 products listed in Annex 6 above the maximum rates set out therein.[3] In their view, the second and third sentences of the Note also impose a further obligation upon China that, in the event that the applied rate for any of the 84 products listed in Annex 6 is less than the maximum rate, China can raise the applied rate only in "exceptional circumstances", and only after consulting with the affected Members. In the light of this additional obligation, the United States and Mexico consider that the Note to Annex 6 does not provide "any basis" for China to impose export duties on the 84 listed products above the maximum rates specified in Annex 6, or "to impose any export duties at all with respect to the products not listed in Annex 6".[4]

284. Paragraph 11.3 requires China to eliminate taxes and charges applied to exports unless such taxes and charges are "specifically provided for in Annex 6" of China's Accession Protocol. Annex 6 in turn "specifically provides for" maximum export duty levels on 84 listed products. The Note to Annex 6 clarifies that the maximum rates set out in Annex 6 "will not be exceeded" and that China will "not increase the presently applied rates, except under exceptional circumstances". The Note therefore indicates that China may increase the "presently applied rates" on the 84 products listed in Annex 6 to levels that remain within the maximum levels listed in the Annex. We find it difficult to see how this language could be read as indicating that China can have recourse to the provisions of Article XX of the GATT 1994 in order to justify imposition of export duties on products that are *not* listed in Annex 6 or the imposition of export duties on listed products in excess of the maximum levels set forth in Annex 6.

---

1 China's appellant's submission, para. 216.

2 China's appellant's submission, para. 220.

3 Joint appellees' submission of the United States and Mexico, para. 113.

4 Joint appellees' submission of the United States and Mexico, para. 113; see also Canada's third participant's submission, paras. 14 and 15.

285. We further note that the third sentence of the Note to Annex 6 refers to the "exceptional circumstances" described in the second sentence of that provision, stating that, "[i]f such circumstances occurred, China would consult with affected members prior to increasing applied tariffs with a view to finding a mutually acceptable solution." This language further supports our view that the "exceptional circumstances" referred to in the Note to Annex 6 are ones that, if shown to exist, would allow China to increase applied tariffs up to the maximum tariff levels set out in Annex 6 for the products listed. We therefore see nothing in the Note to Annex 6 suggesting that China could invoke Article XX of the GATT 1994 to justify the imposition of export duties that China had committed to eliminate under Paragraph 11.3 of China's Accession Protocol.[1]

286. China recalls that, before the Panel, the European Union claimed that China violated its obligations under Annex 6 by failing to consult with affected Members prior to the imposition of export duties on particular forms of bauxite, coke, fluorspar, magnesium, manganese, silicon metal, and zinc, none of which are among the 84 products listed in Annex 6.[2] Noting the Panel's finding that China has acted inconsistently with its obligations under Annex 6 because it failed to consult with other affected WTO Members prior to imposing export duties on the raw materials at issue[3], China argues that, because none of the products subject to the European Union's claim is included in the Annex 6 schedule, the European Union's claim and the Panel's finding necessarily mean that "the exception in Annex 6 permits China to impose export duties on all products, provided that there are 'exceptional circumstances', and that China consults with the affected Members."[4]

287. In our view, the use of the word "furthermore" in the second sentence of the Note to Annex 6 suggests that the obligations contained in the second and third sentences of the Note, including the consultation obligation, are "in addition" to China's obligation under the first sentence not to exceed the maximum tariff levels provided for in Annex 6. We see nothing in the Note to Annex 6 that would allow China to: (i) impose export duties on products not listed in Annex 6; or (ii) increase the applied export duties on the 84 products listed in Annex 6, in

---

1 Furthermore, as the European Union notes, the Note to Annex 6 resembles to some extent the situation envisaged in Article XXVIII of the GATT 1994 and Article XXI of the GATS (Modification of Schedules), which deal with changes in tariff bindings and changes in the Services Schedules of Specific Commitments. However in these situations, WTO Members are required to "compensate" by offering increased market access in other areas on different tariff lines or service sectors. (European Union's appellee's submission, para. 68)

2 China's appellant's submission, para. 213.

3 China's appellant's submission, para. 214 (referring to Panel Reports, para. 7.104).

4 China's appellant's submission, para. 215.

a situation where "exceptional circumstances" have not "occurred". We therefore disagree with the Panel to the extent it found that China's failure to consult with other WTO affected Members prior to the imposition of export duties on raw materials not listed in Annex 6 is inconsistent with its obligations under Annex 6.[1] The imposition of these export duties is inconsistent with Paragraph 11.3 of China's Accession Protocol, and because the raw materials at issue are not listed in Annex 6, the consultation requirements contained in the Note to Annex 6 are not applicable.

288. We turn next to examine the relevance of the reference to Article VIII of the GATT 1994 in Paragraph 11.3 of China's Accession Protocol. Article VIII provides, in relevant part, as follows:

All fees and charges of whatever character (other than import and export duties and other than taxes within the purview of Article III) imposed by contracting parties on or in connection with importation or exportation shall be limited in amount to the approximate cost of services rendered and shall not represent an indirect protection to domestic products or a taxation of imports or exports for fiscal purposes.

289. China asserts that the reference to Article VIII in Paragraph 11.3 confirms the availability of Article XX of the GATT 1994. China reasons that Paragraph 11.3 of its Accession Protocol "requires" that export taxes and charges be "applied in conformity with the provisions of Article VIII of the GATT 1994".[2] According to China, "[i]f they are not, the measure violates both Paragraph 11.3 and Article VIII."[3] China argues that, "[i]n the event that a measure violates Article VIII of the GATT 1994, it may, of course, be justified under Article XX of the GATT 1994".[4] It follows that "China is not deprived of its right to justify a measure that violates Article VIII through recourse to Article XX simply because a complainant chooses to bring a claim under Paragraph 11.3" of China's Accession Protocol.[5] In China's view, the fact that Article VIII applies to certain export charges and fees covered by Paragraph 11.3, and not to export duties, does not render the reference to Article VIII "irrelevant", as the reference shows that the obligations under Paragraph 11.3 are "not absolute and unqualified", and that China did not agree to abandon its right to resort to Article XX.[6]

290. Although Article VIII covers "[a]ll fees and charges of whatever character imposed

---

1 See Panel Reports, para. 7.104. We note that this finding by the Panel has not been appealed.

2 China's appellant's submission, para. 224.

3 China's appellant's submission, para. 224.

4 China's appellant's submission, para. 224.

5 China's appellant's submission, para. 225.

6 China's appellant's submission, para. 226.

by [WTO Members] on or in connection with importation or exportation", it expressly excludes export duties, which are at issue here. In our view, as export duties are outside the scope of Article VIII, the question of conformity or consistency with this Article does not arise. Consequently, the fact that Article XX may be invoked to justify those fees and charges regulated under Article VIII does not mean that it can also be invoked to justify export duties, which are not regulated under Article VIII.

291. As noted by the Panel, "the language in Paragraph 11.3 expressly refers to Article VIII, but leaves out reference to other provisions of the GATT 1994, such as Article XX."[1] Moreover, there is no language in Paragraph 11.3 similar to that found in Paragraph 5.1 of China's Accession Protocol—"[w]ithout prejudice to China's right to regulate trade in a manner consistent with the WTO Agreement"—which was interpreted by the Appellate Body in *China-Publications and Audiovisual Products*. In our view, this suggests that China may not have recourse to Article XX to justify a breach of its commitment to eliminate export duties under Paragraph 11.3 of China's Accession Protocol.

292. Having examined the text of Paragraph 11.3, we turn to examine the context of that provision.

2. Paragraphs 11.1 and 11.2 of China's Accession Protocol

293. Paragraph 11.1 of China's Accession Protocol provides that "China shall ensure that customs fees or charges applied or administered by national or sub-national authorities, shall be in conformity with the GATT 1994". Paragraph 11.2 further stipulates that "China shall ensure that internal taxes and charges, including value-added taxes, applied or administered by national or sub-national authorities shall be in conformity with the GATT 1994." Both of these provisions contain the obligation to ensure that certain fees, taxes or charges are "in conformity with the GATT 1994". This is not the case for Paragraph 11.3. We also note that Paragraph 11.1 refers to "customs fees and or charges" in general and Paragraph 11.2 refers in turn to "internal taxes and charges", while Paragraph 11.3 refers specifically to the elimination of "taxes and charges applied to exports". Given the references to the GATT 1994 in Paragraphs 11.1 and 11.2, and the differences in the subject matter and nature of the obligations covered by these provisions, we consider that the absence of a reference to the GATT 1994 in Paragraph 11.3 further supports our interpretation that China may not have recourse to Article XX to justify a breach of its commitment to eliminate export duties under Paragraph 11.3. Moreover, as China's obligation to eliminate export duties arises exclusively from China's Accession Protocol, and not from the GATT 1994, we consider it reasonable to assume that, had there

---

1 Panel Reports, para. 7.129.

been a common intention to provide access to Article XX of the GATT 1994 in this respect, language to that effect would have been included in Paragraph 11.3 or elsewhere in China's Accession Protocol.

3. China's Arguments concerning Paragraph 170

294. China relies on the wording of Paragraph 170 of China's Accession Working Party Report to support its position that China assumed a "qualified" obligation to eliminate export duties, and is entitled to have recourse to the provisions of Article XX of the GATT 1994 to justify export duties that would otherwise be inconsistent with Paragraph 11.3 of China's Accession Protocol.

295. Paragraph 170 of China's Accession Working Party Report is referenced in Paragraph 342 of China's Accession Working Party Report and is therefore, by virtue of Paragraph 1.2 of China's Accession Protocol, incorporated into the Protocol. Paragraph 170 falls under subsection D of China's Accession Working Party Report, which is entitled "Internal Policies Affecting Foreign Trade in Goods"; subsection D(1) is entitled "Taxes and Charges Levied on Imports and Exports". Paragraph 170 provides in relevant part:

The representative of China confirmed that upon accession, China would ensure that its laws and regulations relating to all fees, charges or taxes levied on imports and exports would be in full conformity with its WTO obligations, including Articles I, III:2 and 4, and XI:1 of the GATT 1994[.]

296. China points to the identical language in the title of the subsection under which Paragraph 170 falls, and that of Section 11 of China's Accession Protocol. Both are entitled "Taxes and Charges Levied on Imports and Exports". China argues that this demonstrates a "*very considerable* overlap" in the scope of measures to which Paragraph 11.3 and Paragraph 170 apply, and that they impose "cumulative obligations" with respect to "*taxes*" and "*charges on exports*".[1] China argues, in essence, that Paragraph 170 of China's Accession Working Party Report and Paragraph 11.3 of China's Accession Protocol both apply to export duties, and that "any flexibilities that Paragraph 170 affords to China to adopt otherwise WTO-inconsistent export 'taxes' and 'charges' must extend equally to Paragraph 11.3".[2]

297. The United States and Mexico consider China's arguments to be "without merit".[3] They submit that Paragraph 169 of China's Accession Working Party Report shows that some Members were concerned about China's internal policies, especially those of sub-national

---

1 China's appellant's submission, para. 233. (original emphasis)

2 China's appellant's submission, para. 246.

3 Joint appellees' submission of the United States and Mexico, para. 128.

governments imposing discriminatory taxes and other charges that would affect trade in goods, and that China responded to this concern in Paragraph 170 by confirming that its laws relating to all fees, charges, or taxes levied on imports and exports would be in full conformity with its WTO obligations. The United States and Mexico argue that it is "untenable to believe"[1] that Paragraph 170 reflects the negotiators' intent to apply Article XX of the GATT 1994 to Paragraph 11.3 of China's Accession Protocol, which sets forth a "new commitment with respect to export duties and the exceptions applicable to that commitment".[2] They further point out that it is Paragraph 155 of China's Accession Working Party Report that reflects concerns with respect to export duties, and which refers to the same specific exceptions as Paragraph 11.3 of China's Accession Protocol.[3]

298. We note that China's Accession Working Party Report sets out many of the concerns raised and obligations undertaken by China during its accession process. The various paragraphs contained in China's Accession Working Party Report are organized according to subject matter, such that the section on "Policies Affecting Trade in Goods" is divided into subsections dealing with "Trading Rights", "Import Regulation", "Export Regulations", and "Internal Policies Affecting Trade in Goods". Paragraph 170 of China's Accession Working Party Report falls under subsection D, entitled "Internal Policies Affecting Foreign Trade in Goods". This subsection contains only two paragraphs. Paragraph 169 indicates that some members of China's Accession Working Party expressed concern about the application of the [value-added tax ("VAT")] and additional charges levied by sub-national governments on imports" and considered "[n]on-discriminatory application of the VAT and other *internal* taxes"[4] to be "essential". The language in the title to subsection D and in Paragraph 169 suggests to us that Paragraph 170 is concerned with "internal policies" affecting "all fees, charges or taxes levied on imports and exports" and sets out China's commitment in response to the concern expressed by WTO Members at the time of China's accession regarding "the application of VAT and additional charges levied by sub-national governments on imports".

299. As we see it, Paragraph 170 of China's Accession Working Party Report is of limited relevance in interpreting Paragraph 11.3 of China's Accession Protocol. In particular, Paragraph 170 does not shed much light on China's commitment to eliminate export duties.

---

1 Joint appellees' submission of the United States and Mexico, para. 130.

2 Joint appellees' submission of the United States and Mexico, para. 132.

3 Joint appellees' submission of the United States and Mexico, para. 134 (referring to Panel Reports, para. 7.145).

4 Emphasis added.

Instead, it is Paragraphs 155 and 156 of China's Accession Working Party Report[1], found in the section entitled "Export Regulations", that deal with China's commitments with respect to the elimination of export duties. The language of Paragraph 155 is very similar to that found in Paragraph 11.3 of China's Accession Protocol, and provides that taxes and charges applied exclusively to exports "should be eliminated unless applied in conformity with GATT Article VIII or listed in Annex 6 to the Draft Protocol". Paragraph 156, in turn, provides: "China noted that the majority of products were free of export duty, although 84 items … were subject to export duties". As in the case of Paragraph 11.3, Paragraphs 155 and 156 make no reference to the availability of an Article XX defence for the commitments contained therein. This further supports our interpretation that China does not have recourse to Article XX of the GATT 1994 to justify export duties found to be inconsistent with China's obligations under Paragraph 11.3 of China's Accession Protocol.

4. China's Right to Regulate Trade

300. China argues that, "like any other state", it enjoys the right to regulate trade in a manner that promotes conservation and public health.[2] Referring to the Appellate Body report in *China-Publications and Audiovisual Products*, China points out that such a right to regulate trade is an "inherent right", and "not a 'right bestowed by international treaties such as the *WTO Agreement*'".[3] According to China, by acceding to the WTO, Members agree to exercise their inherent right in conformity with disciplines set out in the covered agreements, either by complying with affirmative obligations, or by complying with "the obligations attaching to an exception, such as those included in Article XX" of the GATT 1994.[4] China further emphasizes that China's Accession Protocol and Accession Working Party Report contain no language showing that China "abandon[ed]" its inherent right to regulate trade. Instead, China submits that its accession commitments "indicate" that it retains this right.[5] In China's view, the Panel's interpretation of Paragraph 11.3 "turns *inherent* rights into *acquired* rights"[6] and "distorts the balance of rights and obligations" established when China acceded

---

1 Paragraphs 155 and 156 are not referenced in Paragraph 342 of China's Accession Working Party Report. Nonetheless, we agree with the Panel that they are of interpretative relevance in that they articulate the concerns of WTO Members at the time with respect to China's use of export duties.

2 China's appellant's submission, para. 275.

3 China's appellant's submission, para. 275 (quoting Appellate Body Report, *China-Publications and Audiovisual Products*, para. 222).

4 China's appellant's submission, para. 278.

5 China's appellant's submission, para. 286.

6 China's appellant's submission, para. 291. (original emphasis)

to the WTO.[1]

301. The United States and Mexico begin by highlighting that, contrary to China's claims, the Panel "nowhere suggested" that WTO Members abandoned their right to regulate trade in entering the WTO.[2] They assert that the Appellate Body report in *China-Publications and Audiovisual Products* recognized that, because WTO Members have an inherent right to regulate trade, it was necessary in the context of the WTO agreements to agree on rules that constrain that right.[3] The United States and Mexico also rely upon the Appellate Body report in *Japan-Alcoholic Beverages II* to argue that China's obligation to eliminate export duties contained in Paragraph 11.3 of China's Accession Protocol is a "commitment" that conditions the exercise of China's sovereignty in exchange for the benefits it derives as a Member of the WTO.[4] Referring to China's contention that it is entitled to invoke Article XX exceptions for violations of Paragraph 11.3 of China's Accession Protocol in the absence of "specific treaty language", the United States and Mexico assert that this would render the introductory clause in Paragraph 5.1, and the references to the GATT 1994 in Paragraphs 11.1 and 11.2 of China's Accession Protocol, "superfluous".[5] The United States and Mexico emphasize that the Appellate Body's finding in *China-Publications and Audiovisual Products* that Article XX is available for violations of Paragraph 5.1 of China's Accession Protocol was "grounded" in the language of Paragraph 5.1 and is not a right to regulate trade in the "abstract".[6] The United States and Mexico note that the language in Paragraph 11.3 is in "contrast" to the language in the accession documents of other WTO Members with respect to their obligations on export duties.[7] They further assert that China's right to promote non-trade interests is not "at risk" in this dispute, and that there are a number of ways in which China may pursue such interests.[8] Specifically, they argue that Paragraph 11.3 does not prevent

---

1 China's appellant's submission, para. 274, subheading IV.C.5.d.

2 Joint appellees' submission of the United States and Mexico, para. 140.

3 Joint appellees' submission of the United States and Mexico, para. 142 (referring to Appellate Body Report, *China-Publications and Audiovisual Products*, para. 222).

4 Joint appellees' submission of the United States and Mexico, paras. 143 and 144 (referring to Appellate Body Report, *Japan – Alcoholic Beverages II*, p. 15, DSR 1996:I, 97, at 108).

5 Joint appellees' submission of the United States and Mexico, para. 145.

6 Joint appellees' submission of the United States and Mexico, para. 145 (referring to Appellate Body Report, *China-Publications and Audiovisual Products*, paras. 219-228).

7 Joint appellees' submission of the United States and Mexico, para. 145 (referring to Report of the Working Party on the Accession of Ukraine, WT/ACC/UKR/152, paras. 240 and 512).

8 Joint appellees' submission of the United States and Mexico, para. 149.

China from adopting measures other than export duties to promote legitimate public health or conservation objectives, and suggest that China has a number of "tools at its disposal" to pursue these ends.[1]

302. The European Union argues that China exercised its inherent right to regulate trade when it completed the accession process and became a Member of the WTO. According to the European Union, the provisions of the covered agreements and China's Accession Protocol in fact "delineate" China's exercise of its inherent and sovereign right to regulate trade.[2] The European Union also highlights the Panel's finding that there is no contradiction between China's inherent right to regulate trade and the commitments undertaken by China in its Accession Protocol.[3] The European Union further argues that China's obligation under Paragraph 11.3 of the Accession Protocol should not be viewed in isolation, because it is "only a small part" of the rights and obligations that China "entered into and acquired" through its WTO accession.[4]

303. We note, as did the Panel, that WTO Members have, on occasion, "incorporated, by cross-reference, the provisions of Article XX of the GATT 1994 into other covered agreements".[5] For example, Article 3 of the *Agreement on Trade-Related Investment Measures* (the "*TRIMs Agreement*")explicitly incorporates the right to invoke the justifications of Article XX of the GATT 1994, stating that "[a]ll exceptions under GATT 1994 shall apply, as appropriate, to the provisions of this Agreement". In the present case, we attach significance to the fact that Paragraph 11.3 of China's Accession Protocol expressly refers to Article VIII of the GATT 1994, but does not contain any reference to other provisions of the GATT 1994, including Article XX.

304. In *China-Publications and Audiovisual Products*, in the context of assessing a claim brought under Paragraph 5.1 of China's Accession Protocol, the Appellate Body found that China could invoke Article XX(a) of the GATT 1994 to justify provisions found to be inconsistent with China's trading rights commitments under its Accession Protocol and Accession Working Party Report. In reaching this finding, the Appellate Body relied on the language contained in the introductory clause of Paragraph 5.1,which states "[w]ithout prejudice

1 Joint appellees' submission of the United States and Mexico, para. 150.

2 European Union's appellee's submission, para. 109.

3 European Union's appellee's submission, para. 110 (quoting Panel Reports, para. 7.157).

4 European Union's appellee's submission, para. 114.

5 Panel Reports, para. 7.153.

to China's right to regulate trade in a manner consistent with the *WTO Agreement*".[1] As noted by the Panel, such language is not found in Paragraph 11.3 of China's Accession Protocol. We therefore do not agree with China to the extent that it suggests that the Appellate Body's findings in *China-Publications and Audiovisual Products* indicate that China may have recourse to Article XX of the GATT 1994 to justify export duties that are inconsistent with Paragraph 11.3.

305. China refers to language contained in the preambles of the *WTO Agreement*, the GATT 1994, and the *Agreement on the Application of Sanitary and Phytosanitary Measures* (the "*SPS Agreement*"), *Agreement on Technical Barriers to Trade* (the "*TBT Agreement*"), the *Agreement on Import Licensing Procedures* (the "*Import Licensing Agreement*"), the GATS, and the *Agreement on Trade-Related Aspects of Intellectual Property Rights* (the "*TRIPS Agreement*") to argue that the Panel distorted the balance of rights and obligations established in China's Accession Protocol by assuming that China had "abandon[ed]" its right to impose export duties "to promote fundamental non-trade-related interests, such as conservation and public health."[2]

306. The preamble of the *WTO Agreement* lists various objectives, including "raising standards of living", "seeking both to protect and preserve the environment" and "expanding the production of and trade in goods and services, while allowing for the optimal use of the world's resources in accordance with the objective of sustainable development." The preamble concludes with the resolution "to develop an integrated, more viable and durable multilateral trading system". Based on this language, we understand the *WTO Agreement, as a whole*, to reflect the balance struck by WTO Members between trade and non-trade-related concerns. However, none of the objectives listed above, nor the balance struck between them, provides specific guidance on the question of whether Article XX of the GATT 1994 is applicable to Paragraph 11.3 of China's Accession Protocol. In the light of China's explicit commitment contained in Paragraph 11.3 to eliminate export duties and the lack of any textual reference to Article XX of the GATT 1994 in that provision, we see no basis to find

---

1 The Appellate Body referred to the question before it as being to assess whether "the introductory clause of paragraph 5.1 allows China to assert a defence under Article XX(a)". (Appellate Body Report, *China-Publications and Audiovisual Products*, para. 215) The Appellate Body characterized China's obligation under Paragraph 5.1 as "a commitment in respect of traders, in the form of a commitment to grant to all enterprises in China the right to import and export goods." (*Ibid.*, para. 226) The Appellate Body added, however, that this commitment is qualified by the introductory clause of Paragraph 5.1. On the basis of the introductory clause to Paragraph 5.1, the Appellate Body found that China's right to regulate trade "may not be impaired by China's obligation to grant the right to trade, provided that China regulates trade 'in a manner consistent with the *WTO Agreement*'". (*Ibid.*, para. 221)

2 China's appellant's submission, para. 290; see also para. 274.

that Article XX of the GATT 1994 is applicable to export duties found to be inconsistent with Paragraph 11.3.

5. Conclusion

307. In our analysis above, we have, in accordance with Article 3.2 of the DSU, applied the customary rules of interpretation of public international law as codified in the *Vienna Convention* in a holistic manner to ascertain whether China may have recourse to the provisions of Article XX of the GATT 1994 to justify export duties that are found to be inconsistent with Paragraph 11.3 of China's Accession Protocol. As we have found, a proper interpretation of Paragraph 11.3 of China's Accession Protocol does not make available to China the exceptions under Article XX of the GATT 1994. Consequently, we *find* that the Panel did not err, in paragraph 7.159 of the Panel Reports, in finding that "there is no basis in China's Accession Protocol to allow the application of Article XX of the GATT 1994 to China's obligations in Paragraph 11.3 of the Accession Protocol." We therefore *uphold* the Panel's conclusion, in paragraphs 8.2(b), 8.9(b), and 8.16(b) of the Panel Reports, that China may not seek to justify the application of export duties to certain forms of fluorspar pursuant to Article XX(g) of the GATT 1994 and the Panel's conclusion, in paragraphs 8.2(c), 8.9(c), and 8.16(c) of the Panel Reports, that China may not seek to justify the application of export duties to certain forms of magnesium, manganese and zinc pursuant to Article XX(b) of the GATT 1994.

【思考题】

1. GATT1994 例外是否适用于所有 WTO 协定？

2. "出口规费"与"出口关税"的区别是什么？

3. 中国援引《中国入世工作组》报告第 170 段抗辩的依据是什么？

Case1 · 拓展阅读

Case2   US — Anti-Dumping and Countervailing Duties（DS379）

【案情说明】

一、案件事实

2008 年 9 月 19 日，中国根据 DSU 第 4 条、GATT1994 第 23 条第 1 款、《补贴与反补贴措施协定》第 30 条以及《反倾销协定》第 17 条要求与美国进行磋商。磋商涉及美国对从中国进口的四种产品（圆形焊接碳质钢管、充气越野轮胎、薄壁矩形管、层压编织袋）征收的最终反倾销和反补贴税。2008 年 11 月 14 日，中国与美国进行磋商，但磋商未能解决双方争议。[1] 2008 年 12 月 9 日，中国要求根据 DSU 第 4 条第 7 款、第 6 条、GATT1994 第 23 条第 2 款、《补贴与反补贴措施协定》第 30 条以及《反倾销协定》第 17 条成立专家组。2009 年 1 月 20 日，专家组成立，并于 2010 年 10 月 22 日散发专家组报告。中国认为专家组适用的某些法律和法律解释有误，于 2010 年 10 月通知 DSB 上诉。2011 年 3 月 11 日，上诉机构将裁决报告散发各 WTO 成员。

二、裁判结果

（一）专家组报告

在报告中，专家组处理了中国就美国商务部关于财政资助、利益、专项性、双重救济以及调查程序问题提出的诉求。1. 关于财政资助，中国质疑美国商务部将某些向被调查的生产者给予支持（supplying inputs）的国有企业和提供贷款的国有商业银行定义为"公共机构"的决定，专家组驳回了中国的这一诉求，认为中国未能证实美国的行为与其承担的义务不一致。[2] 2. 关于利益（benefit）决定，中国质疑美国在调查中拒绝将中国国内私人价格（private price）作为决定政府提供支持和土地使用权存在的决定，专家组仍然驳回了中国的诉求。[3] 3. 关于专项性，中国反对美国商务部将国有商业银行向越野轮胎行业提供的贷款在法律上具有专项性的调查结果，专家组驳回了中国的诉求；对于中国反对美国商务部认为政府向被调查生产商提供土地使用权的行为具有区域专项性的诉求，专家组予以支持。[4] 4. 关于双重救济问题，专家组认为中国未能证明双重救济与

---

1 Panel Report, para.1.1.

2 See Panel Report, para. 17.1(a).

3 See panel Report, para. 17.1(c).

4 See Panel Report, para. 17.1(b).

《补贴与反补贴措施协定》的不一致性。[1] 5. 关于程序问题，中国认为美国商务部未能为中国政府以及被调查生产商提供至少 30 天的时间以回应关于新补贴指控的问题，专家组驳回了中国的诉求。6. 除此之外，中国质疑美国商务部利用"现有事实"确定被调查生产商在两项有争议的调查中从国有企业的贸易公司购买热轧钢材的数量，在这一点上，专家组支持了中国的诉求。[2]

（二）上诉机构报告

在专家组报告基础之上，上诉机构进行了进一步的分析，推翻了专家组关于"公共机构"和"双重救济"的裁决。1. 对于"公共机构"问题，上诉机构推翻了专家组报告第 8.94 段认为《补贴与反补贴措施协定》第 1 条第 1 款（a）（1）项规定的"公共机构"是指"所有由政府控制的实体"的裁决，[3] 并认为"公共机构"是指拥有、行使或被赋予政府权力的实体；同时推翻了专家组报告第 17.1（a）（1）段的裁决。2. 关于"双重救济"问题，上诉机构推翻了专家组报告中认为《补贴与反补贴措施协定》第 19 条第 3 款未处理双重救济的裁决，推翻了专家组关于中国未能证实基于非市场经济计算方法征收反倾销税的同时，对同一产品征收反补贴税的行为与《补贴与反补贴措施协定》第 19 条第 3 款不符的裁决。上诉机构裁决认为，上述双重救济措施不符合《补贴与反补贴措施协定》第 19 条第 3 款的规定，并与《补贴与反补贴措施》协定第 10 条和第 32.1 条也不相符合。[4]

【法律分析】

在双方争议中，本案最主要的争议焦点是美国对来自中国的同一产品在基于非市场经济计算方法征收反倾销税的同时征收反补贴税，从而导致的"双重救济"措施是否合法。"双重救济"，也称为"双重计算"，并不仅仅指对同一产品同时征收反倾销税和反补贴税的事实，还指对同一产品同时征收反倾销税和反补贴税从而导致至少在某种程度上双重抵消了同一补贴的情况。在专家组审理阶段，专家组支持了美国的主张，并裁决中国未能证明美国的行为不符合《补贴与反补贴措施协定》第 10 条、第 19 条第 3 款和第 32 条第 1 款和 GATT1994 第 6 条第 3 款的规定。[5] 中国对这一裁决提起上诉，要求上诉机构裁决专家组在解释和适用《补贴与反补贴措施协定》第 10 条、第 19 条第 3 款、

---

1 See Panel Report, para. 17.1(e).

2 See panel Report, para. 17.1(f).

3 Appellate Report, para. 611(a)(i).

4 Appellate Report, para. 611(d)(ii).

5 See Panel Report, paras. 17.1(e)(ii).

第 19 条第 4 款和第 32 条第 1 款以及 GATT1994 第 6 条第 3 款方面存在错误；推翻专家组对美国"双重救济"措施的裁定；以及裁决美国违反其在《补贴与反补贴措施协定》以及 GATT1994 下的义务。[1]因此本案的法律分析主要集中于对"双重救济"这一法律问题的分析。

（一）《补贴与反补贴措施协定》第 19 条第 3 款

对于《补贴与反补贴措施协定》第 19 条第 3 款，专家组认为，1. 只要征收的金额未超过"认定存在"的补贴金额，反补贴税的征收即是在"适当的金额"范围内；[2] 2. 征收基于非市场经济方法计算的反倾销税对同时征收反补贴税的金额"是否合当"没有影响；[3]3. 根据起草者的意图，《补贴与反补贴措施协定》第 19 条第 3 款未处理双重救济问题。[4]在解释这一条款时，上诉机构将重点放在分析"在每一案件的情况下以适当金额征收"这一条文要求上，认为以"适当的金额"征收意味着根据具体情况对金额进行一定的调整，不应过于僵化或拘泥于形式。[5]上诉机构继续分析《补贴与反补贴措施协定》第 19 条第 4 款，第 19 条第 4 款规定了反补贴税的数量上限，要求该上限不得超过补贴金额。因此，上诉机构认为，如果任何不超过补贴金额的反补贴税是第 19 条第 3 款意义上的"适当"金额，那么第 19 条第 3 款的要求将变得多余，因为第 19 条第 4 款已经规定征收的关税不得超过被认定存在的补贴金额。[6]也就是说，专家组对"适当"的解释不符合 GATT1994 第 19 条第 3 款应当内涵（即不是多余）的条约解释方法。上诉机构继续分析了《补贴与反补贴措施协定》第 19 条第 2 款，认为反补贴税的实际金额应与需要消除的损害联系起来。接着上诉机构分析了《补贴与反补贴措施协定》第五部分第 10 条，该条规定反补贴税的征收必须符合 GATT1994 第 6 条和《补贴与反补贴措施协定》的规定；对补贴的影响"只能有一种形式的救济"；以及"反补贴税"是为"抵消"补贴而征收的特别税。[7]上诉机构继而分析了 GATT1994 第 6 条第 5 款，第 6 条第 5 款规定"在任何缔约方领土的产品进口至任何其他缔约方领土时，不得同时征收反倾销税和反补贴税以补偿倾销或出口补贴所造成的相同情况。"也就是说，针对同一情形，如倾销或出口补贴，GATT1994 第 6 条第 5 款禁止同时采取反倾销和反补贴双重救济。专家组认为，该条意在将禁止

---

1 See Appellate Report, para. 540.

2 Panel Report, para. 14.128.

3 ibid.

4 Panel Report, para. 14.129.

5 Appellate Report,para.553.

6 Appellate Report,para.555.

7 Appellate Report,para.560.

范围限制在涉及出口补贴的情况下，WTO 成员并没有打算在《补贴与反补贴措施协定》第 19 条第 3 款或第 19 条第 4 款中禁止对国内补贴施加双重救济措施，因为这两条表面上均对双重救济措施问题保持沉默。[1] 上诉机构不同意专家组的观点，认为专家组的解释拘泥于条款的字面意思，同时认为，在以国内市场价格作为正常价值时，国内补贴对倾销幅度的确没有影响，但在对非市场经济国家采用特殊方法（替代国价格）计算正常价值时，在国内补贴的情况下，对同一产品同时适用反倾销税和反补贴税就可能导致"双重救济"。[2] 即在使用非市场经济方法计算倾销幅度的情况下，"双重救济"是"可能"发生的。上诉机构认为，在针对某一产品的反补贴税时，将已经抵消了同一补贴的反倾销税考虑进去才是适当的。[3] 基于以上分析，上诉机构认为专家组对《补贴与反补贴措施协定》第 19 条第 3 款的解释有误，推翻了专家组针对该款解释的裁决。

（二）《补贴与反补贴措施协定》第 19 条第 4 条以及 GATT1994 第 6 条第 3 款

对于《补贴与反补贴措施协定》第 19 条第 4 条以及 GATT1994 第 6 条第 3 款，专家组认为，第 19 条第 4 款规定了与认定存在的补贴金额相对应的可征收关税的最高限额，在反倾销调查中使用非市场经济计算方法并没有消除补贴的效果。[4] 并认为《补贴与反补贴措施协定》第 19 条第 4 款未处理"双重救济"问题。上诉机构认为，《反倾销协定》和《补贴与反补贴措施协定》的条款应以连贯一致的方式一起解释，以避免任何可能规避这两项协定条款中规定的反倾销和反补贴税相关规则和上限的行为。[5] 基于已经认定双重救济措施不符合《补贴与反补贴措施协定》第 19 条第 3 款的规定，上诉机构不需要继续分析和处理中国关于解释和适用《补贴与反补贴措施协定》第 19 条第 4 款和 GATT1994 第 6 条第 3 款的上诉，并认定专家组对这些条款的解释没有实际意义和法律效力。[6]

【英文案例裁决摘录】

下文摘录的是上诉机构报告中关于"双重救济"的部分。

---

1 Panel Report, para.14.118.

2 Appellate Report,para.569.

3 Appellate Report,para.574.

4 Panel Report, para. 14.113.

5 Appellate Report,para.589.

6 Appellate Report,para.560.

VII. Articles 10, 19.3, 19.4, and 32.1 of the *SCM Agreement* and Article VI:3 of the GATT 1994: "Double Remedies"

A. *Introduction*

538. Before the Panel, China made both "as such"[1] and "as applied"[2] claims in connection with the alleged imposition by the United States of "double remedies" resulting from the application, in each of the four sets of investigations at issue, of anti-dumping duties calculated under the United States' NME methodology simultaneously with countervailing duties on the same products.

539. With respect to one of China's "as applied" claims[3], the Panel found that:

China did not establish that the United States acted inconsistently with its obligations under Articles 10, 19.3, 19.4, and 32.1 of the SCM Agreement or under Article VI:3 of GATT 1994 by reason of the USDOC's use of its NME methodology in the four anti-dumping investigations at issue and the imposition of anti-dumping duties on that basis concurrently with the imposition of countervailing duties on the same products in the four countervailing duty investigations at issue.[4]

540. China appeals this finding and requests us to: (i) find that the Panel erred in its

---

1 China claimed that the United States' failure to provide sufficient legal authority for the USDOC to avoid the imposition of double remedies when it imposes anti-dumping duties determined pursuant to its NME methodology simultaneously with the imposition of countervailing duties on the same products was inconsistent with Articles 10, 19.3, 19.4, and 32.1 of the *SCM Agreement* and Articles I:1 and VI of the GATT 1994 (Panel Report, paras. 14.11 and 14.12). The Panel found that the measure to which these claims related and, thus, the claims fell outside its terms of reference. (*Ibid.*, paras. 14.11, 14.12, 14.42, and 17.1(e)(i))

2 Panel Report, para. 14.44. China claimed that in each of the four sets of anti-dumping and countervailing determinations at issue: (i) the USDOC's use of its NME methodology to determine normal value in anti-dumping determinations, concurrently with the imposition of countervailing duties on the same products, was inconsistent with Articles 10, 19.3, 19.4, and 32.1 of the *SCM Agreement* and Article VI:3 of the GATT 1994 (*Ibid.*, para. 14.8); (ii) the USDOC's failure to extend to imports from China the same unconditional entitlement to the avoidance of double remedies that the USDOC extends to like products originating in other Members was inconsistent with Article I:1 of the GATT 1994 (*Ibid.*, para. 14.9); and (iii) the United States had acted inconsistently with Articles 12.1 and 12.8 of the *SCM Agreement*, due to the USDOC's failure to provide interested parties notice of the information that the USDOC required to evaluate the existence of double remedies, and failure to inform China and interested parties of the essential facts under consideration that would "form the basis" for the USDOC's determinations in respect of the issue of "double remedy" (*Ibid*, para. 14.10).

3 With respect to the other "as applied" claims raised by China, the Panel found that China had not established that the United States had acted inconsistently with its obligations under Articles 12.1 and 12.8 of the *SCM Agreement* or under Article I:1 of the GATT 1994 (Panel Report, para. 17.1(e)(iii) and (iv)).

4 Panel Report, para. 17.1(e)(ii).

interpretation and application of Articles 10, 19.3, 19.4, and 32.1 of the *SCM Agreement* and Article VI:3 of the GATT 1994; (ii) reverse the Panel's finding that China did not establish that the United States had acted inconsistently with its obligations under these provisions by imposing anti-dumping duties calculated under its NME methodology concurrently with the imposition of countervailing duties on the same products, without taking steps to avoid offsetting the same subsidies twice; and (iii) complete the analysis and conclude that the USDOC acted inconsistently with the obligations of the United States under Articles 10, 19.3, 19.4, and 32.1 of the *SCM Agreement* and Article VI:3 of the GATT 1994, in all of the investigations at issue, by failing to take steps to avoid offsetting the same subsidies twice.

541. Before turning to the specific issues on appeal, we consider it useful to outline the concept of "double remedies" at issue in this dispute. In essence, "double remedies" may arise when both countervailing duties and anti-dumping duties are imposed on the same imported products. The term "double remedies" does not, however, refer simply to the fact that both an anti-dumping and a countervailing duty are imposed on the same product. Rather, as explained below, "double remedies", also referred to as "double counting", refers to circumstances in which the simultaneous application of anti-dumping and countervailing duties on the same imported products results, at least to some extent, in the offsetting of the same subsidization twice. "Double remedies" are "likely" to occur in cases where an NME methodology is used to calculate the margin of dumping.[1]

542. A more detailed explanation of how and why double remedies may occur is set out in paragraphs 14.67 through 14.75 of the Panel Report. We recap the main points here. When investigating authorities calculate a dumping margin in an anti-dumping investigation involving a product from an NME, they compare the export price to a normal value that is calculated based on surrogate costs or prices from a third country.[2] Because prices and costs in the NME are considered unreliable, prices, or, more commonly, costs of production, in a market economy are used as the basis for calculating normal value.[3] In the dumping margin calculation, investigating authorities compare the product's constructed normal value (not

---

1 The Panel had "no difficulty" accepting:

... the general proposition that the use of an NME methodology likely provides some form of remedy against subsidisation, and therefore, that the simultaneous imposition of anti-dumping duties calculated under an NME methodology and of countervailing duties likely results in any subsidy granted in respect of the good at issue being offset more than once. (Panel Report, para. 14.67)

2 Panel Report, para. 14.68.

3 Panel Report, para. 14.68. The use of surrogate, market economy values presumptively puts the producer in the position of having unsubsidized costs of production. (*Ibid.*, footnote 965 to para. 14.69)

reflecting the amount of any subsidy received by the producer) with the product's actual export price (which, when subsidies have been received by the producer, is presumably lower than it would otherwise have been). The resulting dumping margin is thus based on an asymmetric comparison and is generally higher than would otherwise be the case.[1]

543. As the Panel explained, the dumping margin calculated under an NME methodology "reflects not only price discrimination by the investigated producer between the domestic and export markets ('dumping')", but also "economic distortions that affect the producer's costs of production", including specific subsidies to the investigated producer of the relevant product in respect of that product.[2] An anti-dumping duty calculated based on an NME methodology may, therefore, "remedy" or "offset" a domestic subsidy, to the extent that such subsidy has contributed to a lowering of the export price.[3] Put differently, the subsidization is "counted" within the overall dumping margin. When a countervailing duty is levied against the same imports, the same domestic subsidy is also "counted" in the calculation of the rate of subsidization and, therefore, the resulting countervailing duty offsets the same subsidy a second time. Accordingly, the concurrent imposition of an anti-dumping duty calculated based on an NME methodology, and a countervailing duty may result in a subsidy being offset more than once, that is, in a double remedy. Double remedies may also arise in the context of domestic subsidies granted within market economies when anti-dumping and countervailing duties are concurrently imposed on the same products and an unsubsidized, constructed, or third country normal value is used in the anti-dumping investigation.[4]

544. The Panel understood the United States to have accepted the principle that double remedies may result from the concurrent imposition, on the same product, of countervailing duties and anti-dumping duties calculated using an NME methodology.[5] The United States nevertheless argued that the existence of a double remedy depends on whether the subsidy leads to a reduction in the export price in any given instance, and contended that it cannot be

---

1 The asymmetry is due to the comparison of *an actual, subsidized* export price to a *constructed, unsubsidized* normal value, rather than to an actual, subsidized normal value. (Panel Report, paras. 14.69 and 14.72)

2 Panel Report, para. 14.69.

3 Panel Report, para. 14.70. The potential for double remedies is even greater in the context of export subsidies, which benefit only exported goods and therefore presumably lower the export price. (*Ibid.*, footnote 972 to para. 14.72)

4 However, double remedies are unlikely to result in the context of domestic subsidies granted within market economies if normal value is based on domestic sales. In such cases, both the normal value and the export price will be lowered as a result of the domestic subsidy, so that the dumping margin should not be affected. (See Panel Report, footnote 972 to paragraph 14.72)

5 Panel Report, para. 14.71.

presumed that domestic subsidies lower export prices pro rata,or one-for-one.[1] The Panel was of the view that it would "be a rare case in which a subsidy … has *no effect at all* on either the producer's costs of production or … export prices."[2] In any event, the Panel considered that the answer to the question of "whether a *complete* double remedy *necessarily* results from *all instances* of concurrent imposition of anti-dumping duties calculated under an NME methodology and of countervailing duties" would not "invalidate the general proposition that at least *some* double remedy will *likely* arise from the concurrent imposition of countervailing duties and anti-dumping duties calculated under an NME methodology."[3]

B. Interpretation of Articles 19.3 and 19.4 of the SCM Agreement and Article VI:3 of the GATT 1994

545. On appeal, China contends that the Panel erred in its interpretation of the relevant provisions of the *SCM Agreement* and the GATT 1994, and in reasoning that, because these provisions do not *expressly* prohibit a Member from offsetting the same domestic subsidies through the imposition of two different duties, it was the intention of the drafters to *authorize* such actions. China emphasizes that an importing Member is under an affirmative legal obligation to ensure that it does not impose countervailing duties to offset a subsidy that is simultaneously offset through the manner in which it calculates anti-dumping duties in respect of the same imported product. In China's view, such obligation arises from: (i) Article 19.3 of the *SCM Agreement*, which requires investigating authorities to impose countervailing duties in the "appropriate" amounts; (ii) Article 19.4 of the *SCM Agreement* and Article VI:3 of the GATT 1994, which prohibit Members from levying countervailing duties in excess of the amount of the subsidy found to exist; (iii) Article 10 of the *SCM Agreement*, which requires Members to "take all necessary steps to ensure that the imposition of a countervailing duty … is in accordance with the provisions of Article VI of [the] GATT 1994 and the terms of [the SCM] Agreement"; and (iv) Article 32.1 of the *SCM Agreement*, which prohibits Members from taking "specific action against a subsidy of another Member … except in accordance with the provisions of [the] GATT 1994, as interpreted by [the SCM] Agreement".

---

1 Panel Report, footnote 968 to para. 14.71, and para. 14.73. The United States observed that, while certain domestic production subsidies will result in increased production and a reduction in export prices, other more general subsidies may be used for other purposes (payments of dividends, severance payments, research and development), thus not resulting in any increase in production. (Panel Report, para. 14.71 and footnote 968 thereto; United States' responses to Panel Questions 72 and 73 after the first Panel meeting) A similar point is made by the European Union in its third participant's submission, at paragraph 56.

2 Panel Report, para. 14.74. (original emphasis)

3 Panel Report, para. 14.75. (original emphasis) See also para. 14.67.

546. In addressing China's appeal of the Panel's "as applied" finding on double remedies in the four investigations at issue, we turn to the provisions of the *SCM Agreement* relied upon by China, beginning with Article 19.3.

Article 19.3 of the *SCM Agreement*

547. In its analysis of Article 19.3 of the *SCM Agreement*, the Panel found that: (i) countervailing duties are collected "in the appropriate amounts" insofar as the amount collected does not exceed the amount of subsidy "found to exist"[1]; (ii) "the imposition of anti-dumping duties calculated under an NME methodology has no impact on whether the amount of the concurrent countervailing duty collected is 'appropriate' or not"[2]; and (iii) "it was not the intention of the drafters [of] the SCM Agreement to address the question of double remedies in Article 19.3".[3] Accordingly, the Panel found that: … China has failed to establish that the USDOC's use of its NME methodology in the anti-dumping determinations at issue in this dispute, concurrently with its determination of subsidization and the imposition of countervailing duties on the same products in the four countervailing duty determinations at issue, was inconsistent with Article 19.3 of the SCM Agreement.[4]

548. China claims that these findings, and the Panel's interpretation of Article 19.3 of the *SCM Agreement*, were in error. China relies on the reasoning of the panel in *EC – Salmon (Norway)*, which interpreted the corresponding provision set forth in Article 9.2 of the *Anti-Dumping Agreement*, and found that the "appropriate" amount of an anti-dumping duty "is the amount of duty that is 'proper' or 'fitting' in the context of an anti-dumping investigation".[5] China submits that under Article 19.3 of the *SCM Agreement* "any determination of the 'appropriate amount' of a countervailing duty must take into account the extent to which the investigating authority offsets the same subsidies through the manner in which it calculates anti-dumping duties in respect of the same imported products."[6]

549. The United States considers that the Panel correctly found under Article 19.3 of the *SCM Agreement* that countervailing duties are collected in the "appropriate" amounts where the amount of countervailing duties collected does not exceed the amount of subsidy found to exist.[7]

---

1 Panel Report, para. 14.128.

2 ibid.

3 Panel Report, para. 14.129.

4 Panel Report, para. 14.130.

5 China's appellant's submission, para. 550 (quoting Panel Report, *EC-Salmon (Norway)*, para. 7.704).

6 China's appellant's submission, para. 554.

7 United States' appellee's submission, para. 382.

550. Thus, the main interpretative question before us concerns the meaning of the phrase "in the appropriate amounts in each case" in Article 19.3 of the *SCM Agreement* and whether, as China contends, it would *not* be appropriate, within the meaning of that provision, to levy countervailing duties that result in, or are likely to result in, the imposition of double remedies.

551. Article 19.3 of the *SCM Agreement* reads:

When a countervailing duty is imposed in respect of any product, such countervailing duty shall be levied, *in the appropriate amounts in each case*, on a non-discriminatory basis on imports of such product from all sources found to be subsidized and causing injury, except as to imports from those sources which have renounced any subsidies in question or from which undertakings under the terms of this Agreement have been accepted. Any exporter whose exports are subject to a definitive countervailing duty but who was not actually investigated for reasons other than a refusal to cooperate, shall be entitled to an expedited review in order that the investigating authorities promptly establish an individual countervailing duty rate for that exporter. (emphasis added)

552. The first sentence of Article 19.3 of the *SCM Agreement* contains two elements: first, a requirement that countervailing duties be levied in the appropriate amounts in each case, and, second, a requirement that these duties be levied on a non-discriminatory basis on imports of such product from all sources found to be subsidized and causing injury, except for imports from sources that have renounced the relevant subsidies or from which undertakings have been accepted. Beginning with the term "appropriate amounts", we note that relevant dictionary definitions of the term "appropriate" include "proper", "fitting" and "specially suitable (*for, to*)".[1] These definitions suggest that what is "appropriate" is not an autonomous or absolute standard, but rather something that must be assessed by reference or in relation to something else. They suggest some core norm—"proper", "fitting", "suitable"—and at the same time adaptation to particular circumstances. Within Article 19.3, the circumstance-specific quality of "the appropriate amounts" is further reinforced by the immediate context provided by the words "in each case". We also note that the term "amount" is defined as something quantitative, a number, "a quantity or sum viewed as the total reached".[2]

553. We consider that the two requirements in the first sentence of Article 19.3 inform each other. Thus, it would not be appropriate for an importing Member to levy countervailing duties on imports from sources that have renounced relevant subsidies, or on imports from sources whose price undertakings have been accepted. Similarly, because the requirement

1 *Shorter Oxford English Dictionary*, 6th edn, A. Stevenson (ed.) (Oxford University Press, 2007), Vol. 1, p. 106.

2 ibid.

that the duty be levied in "appropriate amounts" implies a certain tailoring of the amounts according to circumstances, this suggests that the requirement that the duty be imposed on a non-discriminatory basis on imports from all subsidized sources should not be read in an overly formalistic or rigid manner. The second sentence of Article 19.3 provides a specific example of circumstances in which it is permissible not to differentiate amongst individual exporters, as well as of when and how differentiated treatment in the establishment of a countervailing duty rate is required.

554. We continue our consideration of the meaning of the term "appropriate amounts" in its context, by turning to other paragraphs of Article 19 of the *SCM Agreement*.[1] We observe, in this regard, that in interpreting "appropriate amounts" in Article 19.3, the Panel appears to have ascribed great significance to Article 19.4 of the *SCM Agreement*, which provides that "[n]o countervailing duty shall be levied on any imported product in excess of the amount of the subsidy found to exist, calculated in terms of subsidization per unit of the subsidized and exported product." Article 19.4 thus places a quantitative ceiling on the amount of a countervailing duty, which may not exceed the amount of the subsidization.

555. The Panel's finding that countervailing duties are collected "in the appropriate amounts insofar as the amount collected does not exceed the amount of subsidy found to exist"[2] points to Article 19.4 as the key determinant of what is an "appropriate" amount, for purposes of Article 19.3. We share the Panel's view that Article 19.4 provides context relevant to the interpretation of Article 19.3. Yet, we are not persuaded, as the Panel seems to have been, that Article 19.4, alone, defines when the amount of duty is "appropriate". Indeed, if any amount of countervailing duty that does not exceed the amount of the subsidy is an "appropriate" amount within the meaning of Article 19.3, then the requirement in Article 19.3 would be rendered redundant, as Article 19.4 already prescribes that duties not be levied in excess of the amount of the subsidy found to exist.

556. Thus, while we agree that Article 19.4 informs Article 19.3, we do not see any indication that Article 19.4 exhausts the universe according to which "appropriateness" is to be gauged. Article 19.4 makes clear that the amount that could be "appropriate" cannot be *more than* the amount of the subsidy. However, Article 19.4 neither requires that the amount of countervailing duties *equal* the full amount of the subsidy found to exist, nor

---

1 The Panel reviewed what it considered to be relevant contextual elements for its interpretation of Article 19.4 of the *SCM Agreement*. However, the Panel also recalled these contextual elements in its interpretation of Article 19.3 and noted that "[t]he same considerations likewise suggest that it was not the intention of the drafters [of] the SCM Agreement to address the question of double remedies in Article 19.3 of the SCM Agreement". (Panel Report, para. 14.129)

2 Panel Report, para. 14.128.

bears upon the question of whether there may be circumstances in which the "appropriate amount" of a countervailing duty will be an amount *less than* the full amount of the subsidy found to exist.[1]

557. It is, rather, Article 19.2 of the *SCM Agreement* that appears more relevant to this question.　While expressly leaving to the importing Member's investigating authorities the decision as to whether the amount of the countervailing duty to be imposed shall be the full amount of the subsidy or less, Article 19.2 nevertheless states that it is "desirable" that "the duty should be less than the total amount of the subsidy if such lesser duty would be adequate to remove the injury".[2]　Article 19.2 thus encourages such authorities to link the actual amount of the countervailing duty to the injury to be removed.

558. Moreover, once a causal link between the subsidized imports and injury has been demonstrated, the imposition and levying of countervailing duties are not hermetically isolated from any consideration related to injury.　In addition to Article 19.2, a link between the amount of the countervailing duty and the injury that the subsidized imports are found to be causing is reflected in Article 19.3 itself, which provides that a "countervailing duty shall be levied, in the appropriate amounts in each case … on imports of such product … found to be subsidized and *causing injury*" (emphasis added).　Other provisions of the *SCM Agreement* also link the countervailing duty to the injury that the subsidized imports are found to be causing.　Article 19.1 allows for the imposition of countervailing duties when subsidized imports "are causing injury".[3]　The use of the present tense in this provision suggests that injury is a continuing prerequisite for the imposition and levying of countervailing duties.　This is confirmed by

---

1 We would like to emphasize that, in this context, we are considering Article 19.4 as context relevant to our interpretation of Article 19.3. In doing so, we are not addressing China's claim that the Panel erred in finding that a double remedy does not result in an amount of countervailing duty in excess of the subsidy found to exist, within the meaning of Article 19.4.

2 Article 19.2 of the *SCM Agreement* reads:

The decision whether or not to impose a countervailing duty in cases where all requirements for the imposition have been fulfilled, and the decision whether the amount of the countervailing duty to be imposed shall be the full amount of the subsidy or less, are decisions to be made by the authorities of the importing Member. It is desirable that the imposition should be permissive in the territory of all Members, that the duty should be less than the total amount of the subsidy if such lesser duty would be adequate to remove the injury to the domestic industry, and that procedures should be established which would allow the authorities concerned to take due account of representations made by domestic interested parties whose interests might be adversely affected by the imposition of a countervailing duty. (footnote omitted)

3 Article 19.1 of the *SCM Agreement* reads:

If, after reasonable efforts have been made to complete consultations, a Member makes a final determination of the existence and amount of the subsidy and that, through the effects of the subsidy, the subsidized imports are causing injury, it may impose a countervailing duty in accordance with the provisions of this Article unless the subsidy or subsidies are withdrawn.

Article 21.1 that states that "[a] countervailing duty shall remain in force only as long as and to the extent necessary to counteract subsidization which is causing injury."

559. Continuing with our examination of the context provided by other provisions of the *SCM Agreement*, we turn to Article 10, the first provision in Part V of the *SCM Agreement*, which provides:

Application of Article VI of GATT 1994[*]

Members shall take all necessary steps to ensure that the imposition of a countervailing duty[**]on any product of the territory of any Member imported into the territory of another Member is in accordance with the provisions of Article VI of GATT 1994 and the terms of this Agreement. Countervailing duties may only be imposed pursuant to investigations initiated[***] and conducted in accordance with the provisions of this Agreement and the Agreement on Agriculture.

The provisions of Part II or III may be invoked in parallel with the provisions of Part V; however, with regard to the effects of a particular subsidy in the domestic market of the importing Member, only one form of relief (either a countervailing duty, if the requirements of Part V are met, or a countermeasure under Articles 4 or 7) shall be available. …

The term "countervailing duty" shall be understood to mean a special duty levied for the purpose of offsetting any subsidy bestowed directly or indirectly upon the manufacture, production or export of any merchandise, as provided for in paragraph 3 of Article VI of GATT 1994.

The term "initiated" as used hereinafter means procedural action by which a Member formally commences an investigation as provided in Article 11.

560. We believe that there are three main features of Article 10 of the *SCM Agreement* that are relevant to the interpretative task before us. First, Article 10 establishes that Part V of the *SCM Agreement* relates to the application of Article VI of the GATT 1994, and that countervailing duties must conform to the dictates of that provision as well as to the *SCM Agreement*. Second, by providing that "only one form of relief shall be available" for the effects of a subsidy, footnote 35 makes clear that, at least within the four corners of the *SCM Agreement*, there can be no "double remedies" against the same subsidization. Third, footnote 36 to Article 10 defines a "countervailing duty" as a special duty levied for the purpose of "offsetting" a subsidy.

561. The link between the GATT 1994 and the *SCM Agreement* also figures prominently in Article 32.1 of the *SCM Agreement*, which states:

No specific action against a subsidy of another Member can be taken except in accordance with the provisions of GATT 1994, as interpreted by this Agreement.[*]

This paragraph is not intended to preclude action under other relevant provisions of GATT 1994, where appropriate.

562. Article 32.1 reaffirms the right of Members to take action under other relevant provisions of the GATT 1994, and at the same time recognizes that not all such action will be "appropriate".

563. In our view, therefore, Articles 10, 19.1, 19.2, 19.4, 21.1, and 32.1 all provide context relevant to the interpretation of Article 19.3. These provisions identify two situations in which the importing Member is prohibited from imposing two remedial measures as a response to the same subsidization. Importing Members are required to choose between accepting price undertakings *or* imposing countervailing duties, and between taking countermeasures under Parts II and III of the *SCM Agreement or* imposing countervailing measures under Part V of that Agreement. These provisions also confirm the close link between the GATT 1994, in particular its Article VI, and Part V of the *SCM Agreement*, and suggest that, among the purposes of countervailing duties are: to offset or counteract injurious subsidization, and to remove the injury to the domestic industry. Moreover, they indicate that the appropriateness of the amount of countervailing duties is not unrelated to the injury that is being caused. We note, in this connection, that the *Anti-Dumping Agreement* contains provisions that parallel Articles 10, 19.2, 19.3, 19.4, 21.1 and 32.1 in the context of anti-dumping duties, a subject to which we return below.[1]

564. Before doing so, we turn to Article VI of the GATT 1994, which also provides context relevant to Article 19.3 of the *SCM Agreement*. Article VI, entitled *"Anti-dumping and Countervailing Duties"*, is the genesis of both the *SCM Agreement* and the *Anti-Dumping Agreement*. Paragraphs 1 and 2 deal exclusively with anti-dumping duties, paragraph 3 deals exclusively with countervailing duties, and the remaining four paragraphs each deals with both anti-dumping and countervailing duties. Article VI:2 authorizes Members to levy anti-dumping duties "[i]n order to offset or prevent dumping", and Article VI:3 specifies that a countervailing duty is levied "for the purpose of offsetting any bounty or subsidy".

565. Article VI:5 is the provision most pertinent to our inquiry. It provides:No product of the territory of any contracting party imported into the territory of any other contracting party shall be subject to both anti-dumping and countervailing duties to compensate for the same situation of dumping or export subsidization.

566. The Panel relied on this provision as contextual support for its findings that Articles

---

19.3 and 19.4 of the *SCM Agreement* do not address the issue of double remedies. The Panel considered that "these terms are self-explanatory in their intention to limit the scope of the prohibition in Article VI:5 to situations involving *export subsidies*".[1] The Panel considered that, because the explicit prohibition in Article VI:5 is limited to potential double remedies in respect of *export* subsidies, Members could not have intended to prohibit the imposition of double remedies in respect of *domestic* subsidies in Articles 19.3 or 19.4 of the *SCM Agreement*, which are, on their face, silent on the issue of double remedies.[2]

567. We have concerns about the Panel's rather mechanistic, *a contrario* reasoning in this connection. While it is true that omissions have meaning[3], "omissions in different contexts may have different meanings, and omission, in and of itself, is not necessarily dispositive".[4] In this instance, we do not agree with the Panel that the "explicit terms in which the drafters addressed the issue" of double remedies in Article VI:5 make it "all the more unlikely that they sought to prohibit the imposition of double remedies in respect of other types of subsidies".[5] We note, rather, that Article VI:5 prohibits the concurrent application of anti-dumping and countervailing duties to compensate for the *same situation* of dumping or export subsidization. In our view, the term "same situation" is central to an understanding of the rationale underpinning the prohibition contained in Article VI:5, which in turn sheds light on the reason why, in the case of domestic subsidies, an express prohibition is absent.

568. We recall that, in principle, an export subsidy will result in a pro rata reduction in the export price of a product, but will not affect the price of domestic sales of that product.[6] That is, the subsidy will lead to increased price discrimination and a higher margin of dumping. In such circumstances, the situation of subsidization and the situation of dumping are the "same situation", and the application of concurrent duties would amount to the application of "double remedies" to compensate for, or offset, that situation. By comparison, domestic subsidies will, in principle, affect the prices at which a producer sells its goods in the domestic market and in export markets in the same way and to the same extent. Since any lowering of prices attributable to the subsidy will be reflected on both sides of the dumping margin calculation, the overall dumping margin will not be affected by the subsidization. In such circumstances, the concurrent application of duties would not compensate for the same situation, because no part of the dumping margin would be attributable to the subsidization. Only the countervailing duty

---

1 Panel Report, para. 14.117. (original emphasis)

2 Panel Report, para. 14.118. See also para. 14.129.

3 Appellate Body Report, *Japan – Alcoholic Beverages II*, p. 18, DSR 1996:I, 97, at 111.

4 Appellate Body Report, *Canada – Autos*, para. 138.

5 Panel Report, para. 14.118.

6 See *supra*, footnote 518 of this Report; and Panel Report, paras. 14.70, 14.72 and footnote 972 thereto, and 14.74.

would offset such subsidization.

569. To the extent that these assumptions hold true, then the presence, in Article VI, of an express prohibition on the concurrent application of duties to counteract the "same situation" of dumping or *export* subsidization, along with the absence of an express prohibition in connection with situations of *domestic* subsidization appears logical—at least when normal value is calculated on the basis of domestic sales prices. We note, in this regard, that Article VI:1(a) of the GATT 1994, like Article 2.1 of the *Anti-Dumping Agreement*, provides that the usual method for calculating normal value will be based on the comparable price for the like product in the exporter's domestic market. Thus, in anti-dumping investigations, normal value will typically be based on domestic sales prices and any domestic subsidy will have no impact on the calculation of the dumping margin. Nonetheless, Article VI:1(b), like Article 2.2 of the *Anti-Dumping Agreement*, sets out exceptional methods for the calculation of normal value, which are *not* based on actual prices in the exporter's domestic market. The second *Ad* Note to Article VI:1, which provides the legal basis for the use of surrogate values for NMEs in anti-dumping investigations[1], also authorizes recourse to exceptional methods for the calculation of normal value in investigations of imports from NMEs.[2] In case of domestic subsidization, it is only in these exceptional situations that there is any possibility that the concurrent application of anti-dumping and countervailing duties on the same product could lead to "double remedies".

570. In our view, the references to Article VI of the GATT 1994 in Articles 10 and 32.1 of the *SCM Agreement*, Article VI itself, and the many parallels between the obligations that apply to Members imposing anti-dumping duties and those imposing countervailing duties, suggest that any interpretation of "the appropriate amounts" of countervailing duties within the meaning of Article 19.3 of the *SCM Agreement* must not be based on a refusal to take account of the context offered both by Article VI of the GATT 1994 and by the provisions of the *Anti-Dumping Agreement*. While we agree with the Panel that Articles 19.3 and 19.4 of the *SCM Agreement* are concerned with countervailing duties and not with anti-dumping duties, we are not persuaded that it necessarily follows that these provisions are, as the Panel noted, "oblivious

---

1 *Ad* Note to Article VI:1 of the GATT 1994 reads:

It is recognized that, in the case of imports from a country which has a complete or substantially complete monopoly of its trade and where all domestic prices are fixed by the State, special difficulties may exist in determining price comparability for the purposes of paragraph 1, and in such cases importing Members may find it necessary to take into account the possibility that a strict comparison with domestic prices in such a country may not always be appropriate.

2 We observe that, while Article VI:5 was included in the original text of the GATT in 1947, the second *Ad* Note to paragraph 1 of Article VI was added subsequently, following the 1954-1955 Review Session. L/334, adopted 3 March 1955, p. 2, para. 6, and Annex I, Section I.B, p. 10; 3S/222, 223, para. 6.

to any potential concurrent imposition of anti-dumping duties".[1] Such an interpretative approach is difficult to reconcile with the notion that the provisions in the WTO covered agreements should be interpreted in a coherent and consistent manner, giving meaning to all applicable provisions harmoniously.[2] Members have entered into cumulative obligations under the covered agreements and should thus be mindful of their actions under one agreement when taking action under another. We are reinforced in this view by the fact that, although the disciplines that apply to a Member's use of anti-dumping duties and its use of countervailing duties are legally distinct, the remedies that result are, from the perspective of producers and exporters, indistinguishable.[3] Both remedial actions increase the amount of duty that must be paid at the border.

571. It follows that a proper understanding of the "appropriate amounts" of countervailing duties in Article 19.3 of the *SCM Agreement* cannot be achieved without due regard to relevant provisions of the *Anti-Dumping Agreement* and recognition of the way in which the two legal regimes that these agreements set out, and the remedies which they authorize Members to impose, operate. To us, the requirement that any amounts be "appropriate" means, at a minimum, that investigating authorities may not, in fixing the appropriate amount of countervailing duties, simply ignore that anti-dumping duties have been imposed to offset the same subsidization. Each agreement sets out strict conditions that must be satisfied before the authorized remedy may be applied. The purpose of each authorized remedy may be distinct, but the form and effect of both remedies are the same. Both the *Anti-Dumping Agreement*

---

1 Panel Report, paras. 14.112 and 14.129.

2 Appellate Body Report, *US – Upland Cotton*, paras. 549 and 550. We recall that in *Argentina – Footwear (EC)* and *US – Upland Cotton*, the Appellate Body affirmed that the Multilateral Agreements on Trade in Goods, contained in Annex 1A of the *WTO Agreement*, are "integral parts" of the same treaty, the *WTO Agreement*, and that their provisions, which are binding on all Members, are all provisions of one treaty, the *WTO Agreement*. The Appellate Body thus considered that a treaty interpreter must read all applicable provisions of a treaty in a way that gives meaning to all of them, harmoniously. (Appellate Body Report, *US – Upland Cotton*, para. 549 (quoting Appellate Body Report, *Argentina – Footwear (EC)*, para. 81 and footnote 72 thereto (referring, in turn, to Appellate Body Report, *Korea – Dairy*, para. 81; Appellate Body Report, *US – Gasoline*, p. 23, DSR 1996:I, 3, at 21; Appellate Body Report, *Japan – Alcoholic Beverages II*, p. 12, DSR 1996:I, 97, at 106; and Appellate Body Report, *India – Patents (US)*, para. 45))) In *US – Upland Cotton*, the Appellate Body agreed with the panel that "Article 3.1(b) of the *SCM Agreement* can be read together with the *Agreement on Agriculture* provisions relating to domestic support in a coherent and consistent manner which gives full and effective meaning to all of their terms". (Appellate Body Report, *US – Upland Cotton*, para. 549 (quoting Panel Report, *US – Upland Cotton*, para. 7.1071))

3 Moreover, it may well be the case that the injury that the duties seek to counteract is the same injury to the same industry. In this respect, we observe that, for each parallel anti-dumping and countervailing duty investigation at issue in this dispute, the USITC conducted a single injury determination in respect of imports of the relevant products. (United States' responses to questioning at the oral hearing)

and the *SCM Agreement* contain provisions requiring that the amounts of anti-dumping and countervailing duties be "appropriate in each case", as reflected in Articles 9.2 and 19.3 respectively. Both agreements also set ceilings on the maximum amount of duties that can be imposed to remedy dumping and subsidization, respectively. Article 19.4 of the *SCM Agreement* establishes that countervailing duties shall not exceed the amount of the subsidy found to exist and Article 9.3 of the *Anti-Dumping Agreement* establishes that anti-dumping duties shall not exceed the margin of dumping.

572. Only if these provisions are read in wilful isolation from each other can it be maintained that the respective rules on the imposition and levying of duties are complied with when double remedies are imposed. In contrast, reading the two agreements together suggests that the imposition of double remedies would circumvent the standard of appropriateness that the two agreements separately establish for their respective remedies. In other words, considering that each agreement sets forth a standard of appropriateness of the amount and establishes a ceiling for the respective duties, it should not be possible to circumvent the rules in each agreement by taking measures under both agreements to counteract the same subsidization. It is counterintuitive to suggest that, while each agreement sets forth rules on the amounts of anti-dumping duties and countervailing duties that can be levied, there is no obstacle to the levying of a total amount of anti-dumping and countervailing duties which, if added together, would not be appropriate and would exceed the combined amounts of dumping and subsidization found.

573. We consider, next, the object and purpose of the *SCM Agreement*, and whether this sheds light on the meaning of Article 19.3.[1] We recall that, in *US-Carbon Steel*, the Appellate Body explained that "Part V of the Agreement is aimed at striking a balance between the right to impose countervailing duties to offset subsidization that is causing injury, and the obligations that Members must respect in order to do so."[2] Similarly, in *US-Softwood Lumber IV*, the Appellate Body stated that "the object and purpose of the *SCM Agreement*, … is to strengthen and improve GATT disciplines relating to the use of both subsidies and countervailing measures, while, recognizing at the same time, the right of Members to impose such measures under certain conditions".[3] The object and purpose of the *SCM Agreement*, as identified by the Appellate Body in these disputes, sets important limitations to Members' right to impose countervailing duties. Members' right to impose countervailing duties to offset subsidies is not unfettered, but subject to compliance with the obligations set forth in the *SCM Agreement*. Such duties must be for the

---

1 See also *supra*, para. 301 of this Report.

2 Appellate Body Report, *US – Carbon Steel*, para. 74.

3 Appellate Body Report, *US – Softwood Lumber IV*, para. 64.

purpose of offsetting an injurious subsidy. The object and purpose of the *SCM Agreement* thus reveals that Members intended to allow for the use of countervailing duties to offset injurious subsidization under certain circumstances and subject to specific limitations.

574. We do not see that the object and purpose of the *SCM Agreement* provides clear indications as to the intentions of the drafters of the *SCM Agreement* in respect of double remedies in case of domestic subsidization. To the extent that the object and purpose of the *SCM Agreement* links the application of countervailing duties to their purpose—to offset injurious subsidization—this supports an interpretation of Article 19.3 that would render "inappropriate" the application of countervailing duties that, together with anti-dumping duties, exceed the full amount of the subsidy. We emphasize that we are not suggesting that the object and purpose of the *SCM Agreement* encompasses the imposition of disciplines on the use of anti-dumping duties.[1] Rather, we simply consider that the object and purpose of the *SCM Agreement* is not inconsistent with an approach that would accept that, in fixing the amount of countervailing duties that will be imposed, it is appropriate to take account of anti-dumping duties that are being levied on the same products and that offset the same subsidization.

575. The Panel rejected an argument by China based on the interpretation of Article 9.2 of the *Anti-Dumping Agreement* provided by the panel in *EC – Salmon (Norway)*.[2] Article 9.2 establishes that an anti-dumping duty "shall be collected in the appropriate amounts in each case", and is thus the provision in the *Anti-Dumping Agreement* that corresponds to Article 19.3 of the *SCM Agreement*. In *EC – Salmon (Norway)*, the panel found that the appropriate amount of an anti-dumping duty "must be an amount that results in offsetting or preventing dumping, when all other requirements for the imposition of anti-dumping duties have been fulfilled".[3] We consider that the panel's interpretation of Article 9.2 of the *Anti-Dumping Agreement* in *EC – Salmon (Norway)* is consistent with our interpretation of the phrase "in the appropriate amounts" in Article 19.3 of the *SCM Agreement*, as prohibiting the imposition of double remedies, and with the notion that the two agreements should be read together in a consistent and coherent manner. In fact, applying the reasoning of the panel in *EC – Salmon (Norway)*, an appropriate amount of

---

1 The Panel observed that China's arguments with respect to object and purpose implied that "it is the object and purpose of the SCM Agreement to impose disciplines not only with respect to the use of countervailing duties, but also of anti-dumping duties". The Panel expressed its view that "the object and purpose of Part V of the SCM Agreement is limited to imposition of disciplines with respect to the former". (Panel Report, para. 14.122)

2 Panel Report, para. 14.128.

3 Panel Report, *EC – Salmon (Norway)*, para. 7.705.

countervailing duty should be an amount that results in offsetting subsidization, with due regard being had to the concurrent application of anti-dumping duties on the same product that offset the same subsidization.

576. The Panel also considered as an "element of context" Article 15 of the Tokyo Round *Agreement on Interpretation and Application of Articles VI, XVI and XXIII of the General Agreement on Tariffs and Trade[1] (the "Tokyo Round Subsidies Code")*. According to the Panel, the fact that Article 15, which explicitly addressed the issue of the concurrent imposition of anti-dumping and countervailing duties on NME imports, was not carried forward in the *SCM Agreement* lent support to an interpretation of Articles 19.3 and 19.4 of the *SCM Agreement* as not addressing or encompassing the question of the permissibility of double remedies.[2]

577. Article 15 of the *Tokyo Round Subsidies Code*, entitled "Special situations", reads in relevant part:

1.In cases of alleged injury caused by imports from a country described in NOTES AND SUPPLEMENTARY PROVISIONS to the General Agreement (Annex **I**, Article **VI**, paragraph 1, point 2) the importing signatory may base its procedures and measures either

(a) on this Agreement, or, alternatively

(b) on the Agreement on Implementation of Article VI of the General Agreement on Tariffs and Trade.

578. Article 15 of the *Tokyo Round Subsidies Code* imposed upon an importing signatory a choice between the use of anti-dumping duties and the use of countervailing duties against imports from NMEs. This provision thus prohibited the concurrent application of the two types of duties, regardless of whether this in fact resulted in the imposition of double remedies.[3]

579. In our view, Article 15 of the *Tokyo Round Subsidies Code* cannot be considered as context within the meaning of Article 31 of the *Vienna Convention*. Article 31 does not refer to a predecessor agreement—that is, an agreement on the same matter that has ceased to exist and has been replaced by the agreement being interpreted—as context or as one of the elements to be taken into account together with the context. Rather, a provision in a

---

1 BISD 26S/56, entered into force in 1 January 1980.

2 Panel Report, para. 14.119.

3 As explained *supra*, paras. 541-544, "double remedies" does not refer simply to the fact that both anti-dumping and countervailing duties are imposed on the same product, but to circumstances in which the simultaneous application of anti-dumping and countervailing duties on the same imported products results, at least to some extent, in the offsetting of the same subsidization twice.

predecessor agreement may, at most, form part of the circumstances of the conclusion of a treaty under Article 32 of the *Vienna Convention* and thus be considered as supplementary means of interpretation.

580. In the present dispute, having reviewed Article 19.3 of the *SCM Agreement* and its relevant context[1], we do not consider it necessary to confirm the interpretation of Article 19.3 of the *SCM Agreement* by relying on supplementary means of interpretation, such as the circumstances of conclusion of the treaty. In any event, we are not persuaded that a provision that explicitly addressed the issue of the concurrent imposition of anti-dumping and countervailing duties in respect of imports from NMEs, clearly supports an interpretation of Articles 19.3 and 19.4 of the *SCM Agreement* "as not addressing or encompassing the question of the permissibility of double remedies".[2]

581. In particular, we are not persuaded that the existence in a predecessor agreement of a provision prohibiting the concurrent imposition of anti-dumping and countervailing duties to imports from NMEs allows an interpreter to conclude, *a contrario*, that, in the *SCM Agreement*, Members intended to allow double remedies. We have already cautioned, in respect of Article VI:5 of the GATT 1994, against mechanistic *a contrario* reasoning, and recalled that "omissions in different contexts may have different meanings, and omission, in and of itself, is not necessarily dispositive".[3] Article 15 of the *Tokyo Round Subsidies Code* does more than merely prohibit double remedies, in that it prohibits the concurrent application of anti-dumping and countervailing duties, regardless of whether they offset the same situation of subsidization. In the light of this, the absence of a provision like Article 15 of the *Tokyo Round Subsidies Code* in the *SCM Agreement* cannot be interpreted as indicating that Members intended to exclude from the scope of the *SCM Agreement* a different and narrower obligation, such as a prohibition on double remedies.

---

1 The Panel also considered China's Accession Protocol, which "contains no provision explicitly addressing the issue of double remedies even though it appears to allow for the use of countervailing duties while China remains an NME". For the Panel, the absence of any such provision also suggested that the drafters of Articles 19.3 and 19.4 of the *SCM Agreement* did not intend these provisions to address the issue of double remedies. (Panel Report, para. 14.121; see also para. 14.129) We do not agree with the Panel that the fact that China's Accession Protocol does not explicitly address the issue of double remedies suggests that Articles 19.3 and 19.4 of the *SCM Agreement* do not address double remedies. In our view, the fact that China's Accession Protocol does not exclude the application of countervailing duties to China while it remained an NME may equally be read as suggesting a shared understanding that China would be protected against the imposition of double remedies by the provisions of the *SCM Agreement*. On balance, however, we are not persuaded that the absence of a provision addressing double remedies in China's Accession Protocol suggests anything regarding the interpretation of Articles 19.3 and 19.4 of the *SCM Agreement*.

2 Panel Report, para. 14.119. See also para. 14.129.

3 Appellate Body Report, *Canada – Autos*, para. 138.

582. In sum, based on all of the above, we consider that the Panel erred in its interpretation of Article 19.3 of the *SCM Agreement* and failed to give meaning and effect to all the terms of that provision. Under Article 19.3 of the *SCM Agreement*, the appropriateness of the amount of countervailing duties cannot be determined without having regard to anti-dumping duties imposed on the same product to offset the same subsidization. The amount of a countervailing duty cannot be "appropriate" in situations where that duty represents the full amount of the subsidy and where anti-dumping duties, calculated at least to some extent on the basis of the same subsidization, are imposed concurrently to remove the same injury to the domestic industry. Dumping margins calculated based on an NME methodology are, for the reasons explained above, likely to include some component that is attributable to subsidization.

583. We, therefore, *reverse* the Panel's interpretation of Article 19.3 and, in particular, its findings that "the imposition of anti-dumping duties calculated under an NME methodology has no impact on whether the amount of the concurrent countervailing duty collected is 'appropriate' or not"[1], and that Article 19.3 of the *SCM Agreement* does not address the issue of double remedies.[2] We find instead that the imposition of double remedies, that is, the offsetting of the same subsidization twice by the concurrent imposition of anti-dumping duties calculated on the basis of an NME methodology and countervailing duties, is inconsistent with Article 19.3 of the *SCM Agreement*.

2. Article 19.4 of the *SCM Agreement* and Article VI:3 of the GATT 1994[3]

584. The Panel found that Article 19.4 of the *SCM Agreement* imposes a maximum limit on the amount of duties that may be levied, corresponding to the amount of subsidy that is found to exist[4], and that the use of an NME methodology in anti-dumping investigations does not have the effect of extinguishing the subsidy.[5] In the Panel's view, Article 19.4 is "oblivious

1 Panel Report, para. 14.128.

2 Panel Report, para. 14.129.

3 Article 19.4 of the *SCM Agreement* states:

No countervailing duty shall be levied on any imported product in excess of the amount of the subsidy found to exist, calculated in terms of subsidization per unit of the subsidized and exported product. (footnote omitted)

Article VI:3 of the GATT 1994 reads in relevant part:

No countervailing duty shall be levied on any product of the territory of any Member imported into the territory of another Member in excess of an amount equal to the estimated bounty or subsidy determined to have been granted, directly or indirectly, on the manufacture, production or export of such product in the country of origin or exportation, including any special subsidy to the transportation of a particular product.

4 Panel Report, para. 14.108.

5 Panel Report, para. 14.113.

to any potential concurrent imposition of anti-dumping duties", and, therefore, "the narrowly-crafted discipline contained in Article 19.4 of the *SCM Agreement* does not address situations of 'double remedies'."[1]

585. Accordingly, the Panel found that:

… China has failed to establish that the USDOC's use of its NME methodology in the anti-dumping determinations at issue, concurrently with its determination of subsidization and the imposition of countervailing duties on the same products in the four countervailing duty determinations at issue, was inconsistent with Article 19.4 of the SCM Agreement.[2]

586. For the same reasons, the Panel also found that:

… China has not established that the United States imposed duties in excess of the subsidy "determined to have been granted" in the investigations at issue inconsistently with Article VI:3 of the GATT 1994.[3]

587. China argues that the Panel erred in finding that Article 19.4 of the *SCM Agreement* does not address situations of double remedies and argues that, if a subsidy has been offset through the manner in which the importing Member calculates anti-dumping duties, the subsidy no longer "exists" within the meaning of Article 19.4, because it can no longer be attributed to the imported products as a cause of injury to domestic producers. China thus claims that the imposition of double remedies is inconsistent with Article 19.4 of the *SCM Agreement*, because it results in the imposition and levying of countervailing duties in excess of the subsidy "found to exist".[4] China makes similar arguments in respect of Article VI:3 of the GATT 1994.

588. The United States considers that Article 19.4 of the *SCM Agreement* is not concerned with the existence of subsidies, but with ensuring that any countervailing duties imposed do not exceed the subsidies attributable to the imported goods, in terms of subsidization per unit. The United States agrees with the Panel that, by its own terms, Article 19.4 only imposes disciplines with respect to *countervailing duties* (not anti-dumping duties), and is, thus, "oblivious to any potential concurrent imposition of anti-dumping duties".[5] We understand the United States to make the same arguments in respect of Article VI:3 of the GATT 1994.

589. In addressing China's claims under Article 19.3, we have explained that the

1 Panel Report, para. 14.112.

2 Panel Report, para. 14.123.

3 Panel Report, para. 14.136.

4 China's appellant's submission, paras. 499-509.

5 United States' appellee's submission, para. 396 (quoting Panel Report, para. 14.112).

provisions of the *Anti-Dumping Agreement* and the *SCM Agreement* should be interpreted together in a coherent and consistent manner, so as to avoid any possible circumvention of the rules governing, and ceilings on, anti-dumping and countervailing duties that are set forth in the respective provisions in the two agreements. We, therefore, disagree with the Panel's statement that "Article 19.4 of the SCM Agreement is oblivious to any potential concurrent imposition of anti-dumping duties."[1]

590. However, since we have already found that the imposition of double remedies is inconsistent with Article 19.3 of the *SCM Agreement*, we need not continue our analysis and address China's appeal with respect to the interpretation and application of Article 19.4 of the *SCM Agreement* and Article VI:3 of the GATT 1994. We consider, rather, that a ruling on the interpretation of Article 19.4 of the *SCM Agreement* or Article VI:3 of the GATT 1994 is unnecessary for purposes of resolving this dispute. The Panel's interpretation of these provisions is, in our estimation, moot and of no legal effect.

3. Conclusion

591. We have reversed the Panel's interpretation of Article 19.3 of the *SCM Agreement*. Because it was based on an erroneous interpretation of Article 19.3, we must also reverse the Panel's ultimate finding in paragraph 17.1(e)(ii)of the Panel Report that China did not establish that the United States acted inconsistently with its obligations under Articles 19.3[2], 10[3], or 32.1[4] of the *SCM Agreement*.

【思考题】

1. 为什么对同一进口产品征收的反补贴税和基于非市场经济计算方法得出的反倾销税会导致双重救济问题?

2. 出口补贴和国内补贴的区别及联系是什么?

Case2·拓展阅读

---

1 Panel Report, para. 14.112.

2 See also Panel Report, para. 14.130.

3 See also Panel Report, para. 14.138.

4 See also Panel Report, para. 14.139.

V

国际投资法

【内容摘要】

　　本章分为两节，精选两个 ICSID 投资仲裁案例。第一个案例是 Tokios Tokelės 公司诉乌克兰案（Tokios Tokelės v.Ukraine, ICSID Case No. ARB/02/18），该案仲裁庭对管辖权和实体问题分别做出了裁决，本节仅分析该案的管辖权问题。根据《华盛顿公约》第 25 条第 1 款的规定，ICSID 行使管辖权须符合三个条件：第一，争端性质适格，即争端系直接因投资而产生的法律争端；第二，争端当事方适格，即争端当事方分别是《华盛顿公约》缔约国和另一缔约国国民；第三，争端当事方书面同意将争端提交 ICSID 管辖。该案管辖权裁决书即围绕上述问题展开分析。第二个案例是谢业深诉秘鲁案（Tza Yap Shum v. The Republic of Peru ，ICSID Case No. ARB/07/6)，该案主要涉及征收以及征收的补偿标准问题。征收分为直接征收与间接征收，间接征收的认定一向是国际投资法领域的一个重要问题，此为本案争议的焦点之一。此外，征收的赔偿标准也是国际投资法领域的一个重要议题，这也是本案的另一个争议焦点。

Case1　Tokios Tokelės vs.Ukraine（ICSID Case No. ARB/02/18）

【案情说明】

一、案件事实

仲裁申请人 Tokios Tokelės 是一家根据立陶宛法律成立的企业，主要在立陶宛境内外从事广告、出版和印刷业务。1994 年，Tokios Tokelės 根据乌克兰法律成立了全资子公司 Taki spravy。Taki spravy 在乌克兰境内外从事广告、出版、印刷及相关业务。Tokios Tokelės 于 1994 年对 Taki spravy 进行了 17 万美元的初步投资，包括办公家具、印刷设备以及办公设施的建造和维修。从那时起，Tokios Tokelės 将 Taki spravy 的利润再投资于子公司，购买额外的印刷设备、计算机设备、银行股份和汽车。Tokios Tokelė 称在 1994—2002 年，它向在乌克兰的子公司共投资 650 多万美元。Tokios Tokelės 声称乌克兰政府当局对 Taki spravy 采取了一系列不合理的行动，违反了乌克兰和立陶宛之间的双边投资条约的义务，对其投资产生了不利影响。这些行动包括：（1）以执行国家税法为幌子进行了多次侵入性调查；（2）在国内法院提起无事实根据的诉讼，包括使 Taki spravy 签订的合同无效的诉讼；（3）对 Taki spravy 的资产进行扣押；（4）不合理地扣押 Taki spravy 的财务和其他文件；（5）诬告 Taki spravy 从事非法活动。Tokios Tokelės 称，政府当局采取这些行动是因为仲裁申请人 2002 年 1 月出版的一本书，该书正面描绘了乌克兰反对派领袖尤利娅·季莫申科。

Tokios Tokelės 反对被申请人即乌克兰政府当局的这种处理方式，并多次试图解决争端，包括会见地方税务官员，向税务和执法官员提出书面投诉，并向乌克兰总统发出申诉信函。但这些努力都没有成功，Tokios Tokelės 投诉的政府行动仍在继续。

Tokios Tokelės 及其全资子公司 Taki spravy 于 2002 年 8 月 14 日向国际投资争端解决中心（ICSID）提请仲裁，2003 年 7 月，被申请人乌克兰提出了管辖权异议。

二、裁决结果

ICSID 中心及其仲裁庭对该案具有管辖权。

【法律分析】

"ICSID"对国际投资案件具有管辖权应当满足三个条件，第一，争议一方为缔约国，另一方为另一缔约国国民。第二，争议是直接产生于投资的法律争议。第三，双方当事人同意将争端提交 ICSID 解决。具体到本案中则涉及四个问题：第一，Tokios Tokelės 是否是立陶宛公司；第二，申请人是否依乌克兰的法律法规进行了投资。第三，争端是否是因投资产生。第四，双方当事人是否同意将争端提交 ICSID 解决。

问题一：Tokios Tokelės 是否是立陶宛公司？

本案的申请人 Tokios Tokelės 是一家在立陶宛成立的公司，但是被申请人认为由于该公司 99% 的股权是具有乌克兰国籍的人拥有的，且乌克兰国民占其管理层的三分之二，所以申请人不是真正的立陶宛公司。被申请人称，如果 ICSID 仲裁庭具有本案管辖权，等于允许乌克兰国民对本国政府提起国际仲裁，这与 ICSID 公约的目的和宗旨不符，为避免这一结果，被申请人要求仲裁庭"刺破公司面纱"，即无视原告的注册国，并根据其实际控制人的国籍确定其国籍。

ICSID 公约第 25 条规定，只有当争议一方为缔约国，另一方为另一缔约国国民时，中心才具有管辖权。第 25 条（2）（b）进一步将"另一缔约国国民"界定为"包括具有作为争端一方的国家以外的某一缔约国国籍的任何法人"。ICSID 公约并没有给出确定法律实体国籍的方法，而将其留给缔约国自由决定。

仲裁庭强调尊重缔约方之间的条约对公司国籍的定义。《乌克兰—立陶宛双边投资条约》第 1 条（2）（b）规定："投资者系依据立陶宛的法律法规并在立陶宛领域内成立的任何机构。"申请人多次在立陶宛的维尔纽斯市登记注册并登记了具体的企业地址，是在立陶宛领土上建立的真正合法存在的实体。立陶宛政府对申请人的登记本身也表明，Tokios Tokelės 的建立符合该国的法律和条例。因此，根据《乌克兰—立陶宛双边投资条约》第 1 条（2）（b）的一般含义，申请人是立陶宛的投资者。仲裁庭认为尊重《乌克兰—立陶宛双边投资条约》中公司国籍的定义，既满足了当事方的期望，提高了争端解决程序的可预见性，并使投资者能够按条约合理安排其投资，以享受条约规定的法律保护。

仲裁庭认为虽然 ICSID 公约第 25 条第 2 款（b）项没有规定确定公司国籍的必要方法，但普遍接受的规则是，公司国籍是根据其所在地（siège social）或注册地确定的，在确定法人的国籍时，ICSID 仲裁庭一贯采用公司注册或所在地的标准，而不是控制权标准。因此，《乌克兰—立陶宛双边投资条约》中确立公司国籍的方法也不违背 ICSID 公约。

在做出上述结论后，仲裁庭进一步考虑了在国际法习惯承认的范围内，是否能超越缔约方之间条约的规定，用"刺破公司面纱"的衡平原则否认仲裁庭对本案的管辖权。在这方面，最重要的案件是巴塞罗那电车公司案（Barcelona Traction），在该案中，国际法院指出，刺破公司面纱的做法，作为国内法承认的一个例外，同样可以在国际法中发挥类似的作用。仲裁庭认为国内法中大量实践表明，刺破面纱是为了防止滥用法律人格特权，或为了防止逃避法律要求或义务。但是，在本案中，一方面被申请人未提出证据证明被申请人滥用立陶宛法律实体的地位，亦未提出为了保护第三人而必须刺破申请人的面纱从而拒绝 ICSID 管辖的主张，也没有证明申请人利用其公司国籍逃避法律要求或义务。另一方面仲裁庭也认为申请人的行为不构成滥用法律人格。申请人没有试图向被告隐瞒其国民身份，相反，根据立陶宛和乌克兰的法律，申请人作为立陶宛法律实体的地位已得到充分确立，而且为被告所熟知。Tokios Tokelės 是在乌克兰和立陶宛双边投资条约生效六年前成立的，被申请人也显然也并非为了根据双边投资条约对乌克兰在 ICSID 提起仲裁而创建。没有证据表明申请人将其国籍用于任何不当目的。

综上，根据《乌克兰—立陶宛双边投资条约》第 1（2）（b）条，申请人是立陶宛的"投资者"，因为它是"在立陶宛共和国境内根据其法律和法规设立的实体"。这种界定公司国籍的方法符合双边投资条约的现代实践，并符合 ICSID 公约第 25 条的客观要求。仲裁庭认为在《乌克兰—立陶宛双边投资条约》或 ICSID 公约中找不到任何依据，将缔约方对任何一方投资者的公司国籍的约定的定义搁置一边，而赞成根据控股股东的国籍确定公司国籍的标准。而且，仲裁庭也认为本案中并不存在需要刺破公司面纱的情形。基于此，仲裁庭认为 Tokios Tokelės 国籍国为立陶宛，其为适格的立陶宛投资者，从而也是《华盛顿公约》下的"另一缔约方之国民"。

问题二：申请人是否依乌克兰的法律法规进行了投资？

被申请人称，即使仲裁庭认定 Tokios Tokelės 是立陶宛的投资者，Tokios Tokelės 也没有按照条约的定义在乌克兰进行"投资"。更具体地说，Tokios Tokelės 没有证明其有足够的资本对其子公司 Taki spravy 进行初始投资，也没有证明资本来自乌克兰境外，对 Taki spravy 的投资因此不属于《乌克兰—立陶宛双边投资条约》和 ICSID 公约的范围，因为这两项条约的目的都是保护国际投资，即跨境投资。被申请人还称，即使判定 Tokios Tokelės 在乌克兰进行了投资，这些投资也不符合乌克兰法律，因此不包含在《乌克兰—立陶宛双边投资条约》的范围内。

ICSID 公约第 25 条规定，争端必须由"投资"引起，中心才有管辖权。但 ICSID 公约并未界定何为"投资"。成员方具有对投资进行定义的自由权，而这种自由权在本案中是通过双边投资条约来行使的。依《乌克兰—立陶宛双边投资条约》第 1 条第 1 款规定，"投资系根据东道国的法律，缔约一方的投资者在另一方境内投入的所有资产。"该条还进一步规定投资形式的变化不影响投资的性质。此外，该双边投资条约并不要求投资方用于投资的资本来自立陶宛，或并非来自乌克兰。

仲裁庭遵循一般的解释规则，即根据条约的目的和宗旨对条约中的"投资"进行解释，认为两国双边投资条约项下的"投资"在一般意义上被理解为"一缔约方的投资者花费资金或努力预期在另一缔约方领土内获得回报或利润的每一种资产"。换言之，申请人必须证明其在被申请人领土内进行了投资。申请人提供了大量证据，证明其从 1994 年投资 17 万美元开始，此后每年继续进行再投资，到 2002 年总投资超过 650 万美元。而且申请人还出示了 23 份"外国投资付款信息通知"的副本，显示申请人的投资是由乌克兰政府当局登记的。仲裁庭认为根据两国双边投资条约的规定，Taki spravy 企业和上述"信息通知"中所述财产都是申请人在乌克兰境内投资的资产。

被申请人乌克兰称，申请人在其名下注册的子公司并非乌克兰法律所承认的形式，且其所提供的法律文件也存在瑕疵，如缺乏必要之签署和公证。仲裁庭认为，这些不规范之处并不影响双边协定对投资的保护，因为条约关于投资应依据东道国法律的规定之目的，仅在于"防止双边协定被用来保护那些不应该受保护的投资，特别是可能非法的投资"。鉴于乌克兰已经将申请人的子公司登记为合法有效的企业，"基于细微错误而排除一项投资，不符合双边协定之目的和宗旨。"仲裁庭认为，被申请人注册了申请人的投资，就表明有争议之"投资"是根据乌克兰的国内法所进行的投资。

问题三：争端是否直接由投资引起?

根据 ICSID 公约第 25 条（1）中的规定，ICSID 对"直接由投资引起的"争端才有管辖权。为了满足直接性要求，争端和投资必须"合理地密切相关"。

被申请人据此辩称，本争议并非"直接由投资引起"，因为被指控的乌克兰政府当局的行为并非针对申请人拥有的有形资产，即其设施和设备。仲裁庭认为被申请人误解了第 25 条的管辖要求。要符合争端直接由投资引起的条件，被指控的政府行为不必是针对投资者的有形财产。如争端是由于投资本身或其投资的运作引起的，则符合直接性的要求，本案即属这种情形。

在本案中，每一项被指控的政府行为包括调查、扣押文件、对非法行为的公开指控，以及使合同无效和扣押资产的司法行动，都涉及申请人在乌克兰的子公司的业务。因此，仲裁庭认为争议是直接由申请人的投资引起。

问题四：双方当事人是否同意将争端提交 ICSID 解决?

根据《华盛顿公约》第 25 条第 1 款规定 ICSID 的争端当事方书面同意将争端提交"中心"管辖，是"中心"管辖的条件之一。本案中，《乌克兰—立陶宛双边投资条约》第 8 条第 2 款规定投资者有权将争端提交 ICSID 仲裁，此规定表明乌克兰同意将与投资者的争端提交仲裁，即该约定系乌克兰的书面同意，被申请人乌克兰未对此提出异议。

被申请人辩称，申请人的同意是不适当的，因为其同意书没有写明地址并直接寄给被申请人。此外，被申请人认为申请人未在启动 ICSID 程序之前给予同意，因此其同意亦是不及时的。最后，被申请人认为，申请人未按《乌克兰—立陶宛双边投资条约》第 8 条的规定，在六个月谈判期届满之后表示同意。

仲裁庭认为，公约没有规定书面同意必须采取的形式，更没有规定书面同意书必须寄给谁。此外，申请人无须在启动 ICSID 程序之前提交同意书，且《乌克兰—立陶宛双边投资条约》和 ICSID 公约均未要求申请人在必要的六个月谈判期结束后才表示同意。

【英文原文摘选】

IV. ANALYSIS OF RESPONDENT'S OBJECTIONS TO JURISDICTION

First Objection: Claimant Is Not a Genuine "Investor" of Lithuania

Arguments of the Respondent

The Respondent does not dispute that the Claimant is a legally established entity under the laws of Lithuania. The Respondent argues, however, that the Claimant is not a "genuine entity" of Lithuania first because it is owned and controlled predominantly by Ukrainian nationals. There is no dispute that nationals of Ukraine own ninety-nine percent of the outstanding shares of Tokios Tokelės and comprise two-thirds of its management.[1] The Respondent also argues, but the Claimant strongly contests, that Tokios Tokelės has no substantial business activities in Lithuania and maintains its *siège social*, or administrative headquarters, in Ukraine. The Respondent contends, therefore, that the Claimant is, in terms of economic substance, a Ukrainian investor in Lithuania, not a Lithuanian investor in Ukraine.

The Respondent argues that to find jurisdiction in this case would be tantamount to allowing Ukrainian nationals to pursue international arbitration against their own government, which the Respondent argues would be inconsistent with the object and purpose of the ICSID Convention.[2] To avoid this result, the Respondent asks the Tribunal to "pierce the corporate veil," that is, to disregard the Claimant's state of incorporation and determine its nationality according to the nationality of its predominant shareholders and managers, to what the Respondent contends is the Claimant's lack of substantial business activity in Lithuania, and to the alleged situs of its *siège social* in Ukraine.

In support of its request to "pierce the corporate veil," the Respondent makes three arguments, which we encapsulate as follows:

The context in which the ICSID Convention and the Ukraine-Lithuania BIT reference and define corporate nationality allows the Tribunal to disregard the Claimant's state of incorporation and determine its corporate nationality based on the nationality of its controlling shareholders, *i.e.*, to pierce the corporate veil;

---

1 Messrs. Sergiy Danylov and Oleksandr Danylov, who are nationals of Ukraine, own ninety-nine percent of the shares in Tokios Tokelės, and Ms. Ludmilla Zhyltsova, a national of Lithuania, owns the remaining one percent. *See* Request for Arbitration, at Annex 6, "Statute of the Closed Joint-Stock Company 'Tokios Tokelės'" at para. 3.6. Messrs. Danylov and Ms. Zhyltsova serve as managers of Tokios Tokelės. *See id.* at Annex 7.

2 "The Convention is designed to facilitate the settlement of investment disputes between States and nationals of other States. It is not meant for disputes between States and their own nationals." Christoph.

The Tribunal should pierce the corporate veil of the Claimant in this case because allowing an enterprise that is established in Lithuania but owned and controlled predominantly by Ukrainians to pursue ICSID arbitration against Ukraine is contrary to the object and purpose of the ICSID Convention and the Ukraine-Lithuania BIT, namely, to provide a forum for the settlement of *international* disputes; and

The jurisprudence of ICSID arbitration supports the use of a "control-test" rather than state of incorporation to define the nationality of juridical entities and it also supports piercing the corporate veil in certain circumstances that apply in the present case.

Nationality of Juridical Entities under Article 25 of the ICSID Convention

Article 25 of the Convention requires that, in order for the Centre to have jurisdiction, a dispute must be between "a Contracting State ... and *a national of another Contracting State...*"[1] Article 25(2)(b) defines "national of another Contracting State," to include "any juridical person which had the nationality of a Contracting State other than the State party to the dispute..." The Convention does not define the method for determining the nationality of juridical entities, leaving this task to the reasonable discretion of the Contracting Parties.[2]

Thus, we begin our analysis of this jurisdictional requirement by underscoring the deference this Tribunal owes to the definition of corporate nationality contained in the agreement between the Contracting Parties, in this case, the Ukraine-Lithuania BIT. As Mr. Broches explained, the purpose of Article 25(2)(b) is not to define corporate nationality but to: ... indicate the outer limits within which disputes may be submitted to conciliation or arbitration under the auspices of the Centre with the consent of the parties thereto. Therefore *the parties should be given the widest possible latitude to agree on the meaning of 'nationality' and any stipulation of nationality made in connection with a conciliation or arbitration clause which is based on a reasonable criterion.*"[3]

In the specific context of BITs, Professor Schreuer notes that the Contracting Parties enjoy broad discretion to define corporate nationality: "[d]efinitions of corporate nationality in national legislation or in treaties providing for ICSID's jurisdiction will be controlling for

---

1 H. Schreuer, THE ICSID CONVENTION: A COMMENTARY 290 (2001). Emphasis added.

2 *See* Aron Broches, "The Convention on the Settlement of Investment Disputes between States and Nationals of Other States," 136 RECUEIL DES COURS 331, 359-60 (1972-II).

3 ibid. at 361 (emphasis added); *see also* C.F. Amerasinghe, "Interpretation of Article 25(2)(B) of the ICSID Convention," in INTERNATIONAL ARBITRATION IN THE 21ST CENTURY: TOWARDS "JUDICIALIZATION"AND UNIFORMITY 223, 232 (R. Lillich and C. Brower eds. 1993).

the determination of whether the nationality requirements of Article 25(2)(b) have been met."[1] He adds, "[a]ny reasonable determination of the nationality of juridical persons contained in national legislation or in a treaty should be accepted by an ICSID commission or tribunal."[2]

Definition of "Investor" in Article 1(2) of the BIT

As have other tribunals, we interpret the ICSID Convention and the Treaty between the Contracting Parties according to the rules set forth in the Vienna Convention on the Law of Treaties, much of which reflects customary international law.[3] Article 31 of the Vienna Convention provides that "[a] treaty shall be interpreted in good faith in accordance with the ordinary meaning to be given to the terms of the treaty in their context and in light of its object and purpose."[4]

Article 1(2)(b) of the Ukraine-Lithuania BIT defines the term "investor," with respect to Lithuania, as "any *entity established* in the territory of the Republic of Lithuania in conformity with its laws and regulations."[5] The ordinary meaning of "entity" is "[a] thing that has a real existence."[6] The meaning of "establish" is to "[s]et up on a permanent or secure basis; bring into being, found (a … business)."[7] Thus, according to the ordinary meaning of the terms of the Treaty, the Claimant is an "investor" of Lithuania if it is a thing of real legal existence that was founded on a secure basis in the territory of Lithuania in conformity with its laws and regulations. The Treaty contains no additional requirements for an entity to qualify as an "investor" of Lithuania.

The Claimant was founded as a cooperative in 1989 and was registered by the municipal government of Vilnius, Lithuania on August 9 of that year.[8] In 1991, the founders of Tokios Tokelės agreed to reorganize the cooperative into a closed joint-stock company, which the municipal government of Vilnius, Lithuania registered on May 2, 1991.[9] According to the

---

1 Schreuer, at 286.

2 ibid.

3 *See, e.g., Mondev Int'l Ltd v. United States of America*, Award, Case No. ARB(AF)/99/2 (Oct. 11, 2002) 42 I.L.M. 85 (2003), at para. 43; *Emilio Agustín Maffezini v. Kingdom of Spain*, Decision on Jurisdiction, Case No. ARB/97/7 (Jan. 25, 2000), at para. 27; *Waste Management, Inc. v. United Mexican States*, Award, Case No. ARB (AF) /98/2 (June 2, 2000), 40 I.L.M. 56 (2001), at n. 2.

4 Vienna Convention on the Law of Treaties, art. 31(1) (May 22, 1969).

5 Emphasis added.

6 THE NEW SHORTER OXFORD ENGLISH DICTIONARY 830 (Thumb Index Edition 1993).

7 ibid. at 852.

8 Claimant's June 20, 2003 Submission of Documents, Vol. V, Annex 10.

9 ibid. at Annex 13.

Certificate of Enterprise, the address of Tokios Tokelės is Vilnius, vul. Seskines, 13-3. On August 11, 2000, the Ministry of the Economy of the Republic of Lithuania re-registered the Claimant as an enterprise and re-registered the Claimant's governing statute, both of which note the company's location as Sheshkines, 13-3 (or d. 13 kv. 3), Vilnius.[1] The Claimant, therefore, is a thing of real legal existence that was founded on a secure basis in the territory of Lithuania. The registration of Tokios Tokelės by the Lithuanian Government indicates that it was founded in conformity with the laws and regulations of that country. According to the ordinary meaning of Article 1(2)(b), therefore, the Claimant is an investor of Lithuania.

Article 1(2)(c) of the Ukraine-Lithuania BIT, which defines "investor" with respect to entities not established in Ukraine or Lithuania, provides relevant context for the interpretation of Article 1(2)(a) and (b). Article 1(2)(c) extends the scope of the Treaty to entities incorporated in third countries using other criteria to determine nationality—namely, the nationality of the individuals who control the enterprise and the *siège social* of the entity controlling the enterprise. The Respondent argues that the existence of these alternative methods of defining corporate nationality to *extend* the benefits of the BIT in Article 1(2)(c) should also allow these methods to be used to *deny* the benefits of the BIT under Article 1(2)(b). If the Contracting Parties had intended these alternative methods to apply to entities legally established in Ukraine or Lithuania, however, the parties would have included them in Article 1(2)(a) or (b) respectively as they did in Article 1(2)(c). However, the purpose of Article 1(2)(c) is only to extend the definition of "investor" to entities established under the law of a third State provided certain conditions are met. Under the well established presumption *expressio unius est exclusio alterius*, the state of incorporation, not the nationality of the controlling shareholders or *siège social*, thus defines "investors" of Lithuania under Article 1(2)(b) of the BIT.

The object and purpose of the Treaty likewise confirm that the control-test should not be used to restrict the scope of "investors" in Article 1(2)(b). The preamble expresses the Contracting Parties' intent to "intensify economic cooperation to the mutual benefit of both States" and "create and maintain favourable conditions for investment of investors of one State in the territory of the other State." The Tribunal in SGS v. *Philippines* interpreted nearly identical preambular language in the Philippines-Switzerland BIT as indicative of the treaty's broad scope of investment protection.[2] We concur in that interpretation and find that the object

---

1 Request for Arbitration, at Annexes 5-6.

2 *SGS Société Générale de Surveillance S.A. v. Republic of the Philippines*, Decision on Jurisdiction, Case No. ARB/02/6 (Jan. 29, 2004), at para. 116 ("The BIT is a treaty for the promotion and reciprocal protection of investments. According to the preamble it is intended 'to create and maintain favourable conditions for investments by investors of one Contracting Party in the territory of the other.' It is legitimate to resolve uncertainties in its interpretation so as to favour the protection of covered investments.") ("*SGS v. Philippines*").

and purpose of the Ukraine-Lithuania BIT is to provide broad protection of investors and their investments.

The object and purpose of the Treaty are also reflected in the Treaty text. Article 1, which sets forth the scope of the BIT, defines "investor" as "*any entity*" established in Lithuania or Ukraine as well as "*any entity*" established in third countries that is controlled by nationals of or by entities having their seat in Lithuania or Ukraine. Thus, the Respondent's request to *restrict* the scope of covered investors through a control-test would be inconsistent with the object and purpose of the Treaty, which is to provide broad protection of investors and their investments.

The Respondent also argues that jurisdiction should be denied because, in its view, the Claimant does not maintain "substantial business activity" in Lithuania. The Respondent correctly notes that a number of investment treaties allow a party to deny the benefits of the treaty to entities of the other party that are controlled by foreign nationals and that do not engage in substantial business activity in the territory of the other party.

For example, the Ukraine-United States BIT states, "[e]ach Party reserves the right to deny to any company the advantages of this treaty if *nationals of any third country* control such company and, in the case of a company of the other Party, that company has no substantial business activities in the territory of the other Party...."[1]

Similarly, the Energy Charter Treaty, to which both Ukraine and Lithuania are parties, allows each party to deny the benefits of the agreement to "a legal entity if *citizens or nationals of a third state* own or control such entity and if that entity has no substantial business activities in the Area of the Contracting Party in which it is organized."[2]

In addition, a number of investment treaties of other States enable the parties to deny the benefits of the treaty to entities of the other party that are controlled by nationals of the denying party and do not have substantial business activity in the other party. For example, the BIT between the United States and Argentina provides that "[e]ach Party reserves the right to deny to any company of the other Party the advantages of this Treaty if (a) nationals of any third country, *or nationals of such Party*, control such company and the company has no substantial business activities in the territory of the other Party...."[3]

These investment agreements confirm that state parties are capable of excluding from

---

1 Treaty between the United States of America and Ukraine Concerning the Encouragement and Reciprocal Protection of Investment, Mar. 4, 1994, at art. 1(2) (entered into force Nov. 16, 1996) (emphasis added).

2 The Energy Charter Treaty, Annex 1 to the Final Act of the European Energy Charter Conference, at art. 17(1), Dec. 16-17, 1994, Lisbon, Portugal, available at http://www.encharter.org/upload/1/TreatyBook-en.pdf (emphasis added).

3 Treaty between the United States of America and the Argentine Republic Concerning the Reciprocal Encouragement and Protection of Investment, Nov. 14, 1991, at art. 1(2).

the scope of the agreement entities of the other party that are controlled by nationals of third countries or by nationals of the host country. The Ukraine-Lithuania BIT, by contrast, includes no such "denial of benefits" provision with respect to entities controlled by third-country nationals or by nationals of the denying party. We regard the absence of such a provision as a deliberate choice of the Contracting Parties. In our view, it is not for tribunals to impose limits on the scope of BITs not found in the text, much less limits nowhere evident from the negotiating history. An international tribunal of defined jurisdiction should not reach out to exercise a jurisdiction beyond the borders of the definition. But equally an international tribunal should exercise, and indeed is bound to exercise, the measure of jurisdiction with which it is endowed.[1]

We note that the Claimant has provided the Tribunal with significant information regarding its activities in Lithuania, including financial statements, employment information, and a catalogue of materials produced during the period of 1991 to 1994.[2]

While these activities would appear to constitute "substantial business activity," we need not affirmatively decide that they do, as it is not relevant to our determination of jurisdiction.

Rather, under the terms of the Ukraine-Lithuania BIT, interpreted according to their ordinary meaning, in their context, and in light of the object and purpose of the Treaty, the only relevant consideration is whether the Claimant is established under the laws of Lithuania. We find that it is. Thus, the Claimant is an investor of Lithuania under Article 1(2)(b) of the BIT.

We reach this conclusion based on the consent of the Contracting Parties, as expressed in the Ukraine-Lithuania BIT. We emphasize here that Contracting Parties are free to define their consent to jurisdiction in terms that are broad or narrow; they may employ a control-test or reserve the right to deny treaty protection to claimants who otherwise would have recourse under the BIT. Once that consent is defined, however, tribunals should give effect to it, unless doing so would allow the Convention to be used for purposes for which it clearly was not intended.

This Tribunal, by respecting the definition of corporate nationality in the Ukraine-Lithuania BIT, fulfills the parties' expectations, increases the predictability of dispute

---

1 *See, e.g., Compañia de Aguas del Aconquija S.A. and Vivendi Universal (formerly Compagnie Générale des Eaux) v. Argentine Republic*, Decision on Annulment, Case No. ARB/97/3 (July 3, 2002). "In the Committee's view, the Tribunal, faced with such a claim and having validly held that it had jurisdiction, was obliged to consider and to decide it." *Id*. at para. 112. "[T]he Committee concludes that the Tribunal exceeded its powers in the sense of Article 52(1)(b), in that the Tribunal, having jurisdiction over the Tucumán claims, failed to decide those claims." *Id*. at para. 115.

2 Claimant's December 30, 2003 Submission of Documents, Annexes 1-11, Catalogues of Publications of Tokios Tokelės for 1991, 1992, 1993 and 1994.

settlement procedures, and enables investors to structure their investments to enjoy the legal protections afforded under the Treaty. We decline to look beyond (or through) the Claimant to its shareholders or other juridical entities that may have an interest in the claim. As the tribunal in *Amco Asia Corp. v. Indonesia* said in rejecting the respondent's request to attribute to the claimant the nationality of its controlling shareholder, the concept of nationality in the ICSID Convention is:

... a classical one, based on the law under which the juridical person has been incorporated, the place of incorporation and the place of the social seat. An exception is brought to this concept in respect of juridical persons having the nationality, thus defined, of the Contracting state party to the dispute, where said juridical persons are under foreign control. *But no exception to the classical concept is provided for when it comes to the nationality of the foreign controller, even supposing—which is not at all clearly stated in the Convention— that the fact that the controller is the national of one or another foreign State is to be taken into account*....[1]

Thus, the decision of this Tribunal with respect to the nationality of the Claimant is consistent with *Amco Asia* and other ICSID jurisprudence, as will be discussed further below.

Consistency of Article 1(2) of the BIT with the ICSID Convention

In our view, the definition of corporate nationality in the Ukraine-Lithuania BIT, on its face and as applied to the present case, is consistent with the Convention and supports our analysis under it. Although Article 25(2)(b) of the Convention does not set forth a required method for determining corporate nationality, the generally accepted (albeit implicit) rule is that the nationality of a corporation is determined on the basis of its *siège social* or place of incorporation.[2] Indeed, "ICSID tribunals have uniformly adopted the test of incorporation or seat rather than control when determining the nationality of a juridical person."[3] Moreover, "[t]he overwhelming weight of the authority... points towards the traditional criteria of

---

1 *Amco Asia Corp. and Others v. Republic of Indonesia*, Decision on Jurisdiction, Case No. ARB/81/1 (Sept. 25, 1983), 1 ICSID Reports 389, 396 (emphasis added) ("*Amco*").

2 Schreuer, at 278-79; *see also* G.R. Delaume, "ICSID Arbitration and the Courts," 77 AMER. J. INT'L LAW 784, 793-94 (1983); M. Hirsch, THE ARBITRATION MECHANISM OF T HE INTERNATIONAL CENTRE FOR THE SETTLEMENT OF INVESTMENT DISPUTES 85 (1993).

3 Schreuer, at 279-80 (citing *Kaiser Bauxite Company v. Jamaica*, Decision on Jurisdiction, Case No. ARB/74/3 (July 6, 1975), 1 ICSID Reports 296, 303 (1993); *SOABI v. Senegal*, Decision on Jurisdiction, Case No. ARB/82/1 (Aug. 1, 1984), 2 ICSID Reports 175, 180-81; *Amco*, at 396); *see also Autopista Concesionada de Venezuela, C.A. v. Bolivarian Republic of Venezuela*, Decision on Jurisdiction, Case No. ARB/00/5 (Sept. 27, 2001), 16 ICSID Review-FILJ 469 (2001), at para. 108 ("*Autopista*").

incorporation or seat for the determination of corporate nationality under Art. 25(2)(b)."[1] As Professor Schreuer notes, "[a] systematic interpretation of Article 25(2)(b) would militate against the use of the control test for a corporation's nationality."[2]

As discussed above, the Claimant is an "investor" of Lithuania under Article 1(2)(b) of the Ukraine-Lithuania BIT based on its state-of-incorporation. Although not required by the text of the Treaty, an assessment of the *siège social* of the Claimant leads to the same conclusion. Among the relevant evidence of *siège social*, the Claimant's registration certificate (issued by the Ministry of the Economy of Lithuania),[3] its statute of incorporation,[4] and each of the Claimant's "Information Notices of Payment of Foreign Investment" (registered by Ukrainian governmental authorities),[5] all record the Claimant's address as Vilnius, Lithuania. Contrary to the assertion of the Respondent, a nationality test of *siège social* leads to the same result as one based on state of incorporation.[6]

The second clause of Article 25(2)(b) provides that parties can, by agreement, depart from the general rule that a corporate entity has the nationality of its state of incorporation. It extends jurisdiction to "any juridical person which had the nationality of the Contracting State party to the dispute on [the date on which the parties consented to submit the dispute to arbitration] and which, *because of foreign control*, the parties have agreed should be treated as a national of another Contracting State…"[7] This exception to the general rule applies only in the context of an agreement between the parties. The Respondent asks the Tribunal to apply this exception in the present case, not to give effect to an agreement between the Contracting Parties, but, rather, to create an additional exception to the general state-of-incorporation or state-of-seat rule—in the absence of an agreement to that effect between the Parties.

We find no support for the Respondent's request in the text of the Convention. The second clause of Article 25(2)(b) limits the use of the control-test to the circumstances it describes, *i.e.*, when Contracting Parties agree to treat a national of the host State as a national of another Contracting Party because of foreign control. In the present case, the Claimant is not a national

---

1 Schreuer, at 281.

2 ibid. at 278.

3 Request for Arbitration, at Annex 5.

4 ibid.at Annex 6.

5 ibid. at Annex 13.

6 This is not a surprising result. *See* D.P. O'Connell, 2 INTERNATIONAL LAW 1041 (2d. ed. 1970) (stating, "[u]nder French law it is not possible for a corporation to have a *siège social* at a place other than that of incorporation …. The corporation laws of Continental countries provide that the charter of incorporation must designate this central office, and the inference is that it must be in the country of incorporation.").

7 Emphasis added.

of the host State nor have the parties agreed to treat the Claimant as a national of a State other than its state of incorporation.

The use of a control-test to define the nationality of a corporation to *restrict* the jurisdiction of the Centre would be inconsistent with the object and purpose of Article 25(2)(b). Indeed, as explained by Mr. Broches, the purpose of the control-test in the second portion of Article 25(2)(b) is to *expand* the jurisdiction of the Centre:

[t]here was a compelling reason for this last provision. It is quite usual for host States to require that foreign investors carry on their business within their territories through a company organized under the laws of the host country. If we admit, as the Convention does implicitly, that this makes the company technically a national of the host country, it becomes readily apparent that there is need for an exception to the general principle that that the Centre will not have jurisdiction over disputes between a Contracting State and its own nationals. *If no exception were made for foreign-owned but locally incorporated companies, a large and important sector of foreign investment would be outside the scope of the Convention.*[1]

ICSID tribunals likewise have interpreted the second clause of Article 25(2)(b) to expand, not restrict, jurisdiction. In *Wena Hotels Ltd. v. Egypt*, the respondent argued that Wena, though incorporated in the United Kingdom, should be treated as an Egyptian company because it was owned by an Egyptian national.[2] Egypt relied on Article 8.1 of the U.K.-Egypt BIT provision, which states:

[s]uch a company of one Contracting Party in which before such dispute arises a majority of shares are owned by nationals or companies of the other Contracting Party shall in accordance with Article 25(2)(b) of the Convention be treated for the purposes of the Convention as a company of the other Contracting Party.[3]

Egypt argued that this provision could be used to deny jurisdiction over disputes involving companies of the non-disputing Contracting Party that are owned by nationals or companies of the Contracting Party to the dispute. Wena, on the other hand, argued that this provision could be used only to extend jurisdiction over disputes involving companies of the Contracting Party to the dispute that are owned by nationals or companies of the non-disputing Contracting Party. Although the tribunal found that both interpretations of the BIT provision were plausible, it decided to adopt Wena's interpretation as the more consistent with Article 25(2)(b) of the Convention.

As the *Wena* tribunal stated, "[t]he literature rather convincingly demonstrates that Article

---

1 Broches, at 358-59 (emphasis added).

2 *Wena Hotels Ltd. v. Arab Republic of Egypt*, Summary Minutes of the Session of the Tribunal held in Paris on May 25, 1999, Case No. ARB/98/4, 41 I.L.M. 881, 886 (2002).

3 *Id.* at 887.

25(2)(b) of the ICSID Convention—and provisions like Article 8 of the United Kingdom's model bilateral investment treaty—are meant to expand ICSID jurisdiction."[1] The tribunal in *Autopista v. Venezuela* reached a similar result, concluding that the object and purpose of Article 25(2)(b) is not to limit jurisdiction, but to set its "outer limits."[2]

ICSID jurisprudence also confirms that the second clause of Article 25(2)(b) should not be used to determine the nationality of juridical entities in the absence of an agreement between the parties. In *CMS v. Argentina*, the tribunal states, "[t]he reference that Article 25(2)(b) makes to foreign control in terms of treating a company of the nationality of the Contracting State party as a national of another Contracting State *is precisely meant to facilitate agreement between the parties...*"[3] In the present case, there was no agreement between the Contracting Parties to treat the Claimant as anything other than a national of its state of incorporation, *i.e.*, Lithuania.

The second clause of Article 25(2)(b) does not mandatorily constrict ICSID jurisdiction for disputes arising in the inverse context from the one envisaged by this provision: a dispute between a Contracting Party and an entity of another Contracting Party that is controlled by nationals of the respondent Contracting Party.

In summary, the Claimant is an "investor" of Lithuania under Article 1(2)(b) of the BIT because it is an "entity established in the territory of the Republic of Lithuania in conformity with its laws and regulations." This method of defining corporate nationality is consistent with modern BIT practice and satisfies the objective requirements of Article of the Convention. We find no basis in the BIT or the Convention to set aside the Contracting Parties' agreed definition of corporate nationality with respect to investors of either party in favor of a test based on the nationality of the controlling shareholders. While some tribunals have taken a distinctive approach,[4] we do not believe that arbitrators should read in to BITs limitations not found in the

---

1 Wena Hotels Ltd. v. Arab Republic of Egypt, Summary Minutes of the Session of the Tribunal held in Paris on May 25, 1999, Case No. ARB/98/4, 41 I.L.M. 888 (2002).

2 *Autopista*, at para. 109 (quoting Broches).

3 *CMS Gas Transmission Company v. Republic of Argentina*, Decision on Jurisdiction, Case No. ARB/01/8 (July 17, 2003), 42 I.L.M. 788 (2003), at para. 51 (emphasis added) ("*CMS*").

4 *See, e.g., SGS Société Générale de Surveillance S.A. v. Islamic Republic of Pakistan*, Decision on Jurisdiction, Case No. ARB/01/13 (Aug. 6, 2003), 42 I.L.M. 1290 (2003). In this case, a Swiss company asserted claims against the Government of Pakistan for breach of contract and for breach of the BIT between the Swiss Confederation and Pakistan. Article 9 of that BIT provides for ICSID arbitration of "disputes with respect to investments...." *Id.* at para. 149. The provision does not in any manner restrict the scope of such disputes. Although the Tribunal recognized that BIT claims and contract claims "can both be described as 'disputes with respect to investment,'" it nonetheless decided—without support from the text or evidence of the parties' intent—to exclude contract claims from the scope of "disputes" that could be submitted to ICSID arbitration. *Id.* at paras. 161-62.

text nor evident from negotiating history sources.

Equitable Doctrine of "Veil Piercing"

Finally, we consider whether the equitable doctrine of "veil piercing," to the extent recognized in customary international law, should override the terms of the agreement between the Contracting Parties and cause the Tribunal to deny jurisdiction in this case.[1]

The seminal case, in this regard, is *Barcelona Traction*.[2] In that case, the International Court of Justice ("ICJ") stated, "the process of lifting the veil, being an exceptional one admitted by municipal law in respect of an institution of its own making, is equally admissible to play a similar role in international law."[3] In particular, the Court noted, "[t]he wealth of practice already accumulated on the subject in municipal law indicates that the veil is lifted, for instance, to *prevent the misuse of the privileges of legal personality*, as in certain cases of *fraud or malfeasance*, to *protect third persons* such as a creditor or purchaser, or to *prevent the evasion of legal requirements or of obligations*."[4]

The Respondent has not made a prima facie case, much less demonstrated, that the Claimant has engaged in any of the types of conduct described *in Barcelona Traction* that might support a piercing of the Claimant's corporate veil. The Respondent has not shown or even suggested that the Claimant has used its status as a juridical entity of Lithuania to perpetrate fraud or engage in malfeasance. The Respondent has made no claim that the Claimant's veil must be pierced and jurisdiction denied in order to protect third persons, nor has the Respondent shown that the Claimant used its corporate nationality to evade applicable legal requirements or obligations.

The ICJ did not attempt to define in *Barcelona Traction* the precise scope of conduct that might prompt a tribunal to pierce the corporate veil. We are satisfied, however, that none of the Claimant's conduct with respect to its status as an entity of Lithuania constitutes an abuse of legal personality. The Claimant made no attempt whatever to conceal its national identity from the Respondent. To the contrary, the Claimant's status as a juridical entity of Lithuania is well

---

1 Article 42(1) of the ICSID Convention states, "[t]he Tribunal shall decide a dispute in accordance with such rules of law as may be agreed by the parties. In the absence of such agreement, the Tribunal shall apply the law of the Contracting State party to the dispute (including its rules on the conflict of laws) *and such rules of international law as may be applicable*." Emphasis added.

2 For the sake of clarity, the Tribunal notes that *Barcelona Traction*, which held that incorporation is the only criterion for nationality in cases of diplomatic protection, is inapplicable with respect to agreements between the parties to treat companies of the host State as a national of the other Party under the second clause of Article 25(2)(b).

3 *See* Broches, at 360-361.

4 *Barcelona Traction, Light and Power Co., Ltd.* (*Belg. v. Spain*), 1970 I.C.J. 3 (Feb. 5), at para. 58 ("*Barcelona Traction*").

established under the laws of both Lithuania and Ukraine and well known by the Respondent. The Claimant manifestly did not create Tokios Tokelės for the purpose of gaining access to ICSID arbitration under the BIT against Ukraine, as the enterprise was founded six years before the BIT between Ukraine and Lithuania entered into force. Indeed, there is no evidence in the record that the Claimant used its formal legal nationality for any improper purpose.

Other Considerations Regarding Corporate Nationality

Although not necessary elements of our Decision, the section below addresses the relevant ICSID jurisprudence and the views of ICSID scholars raised by the parties that relate to the issue of defining corporate nationality.

a.*ICSID Jurisprudence*

The arbitral awards cited by the Respondent do not support a decision by this Tribunal to set aside the definition of nationality agreed to by the Contracting Parties. Among the awards cited, the Respondent quotes the following passage from *Banro American Resources Inc. v. Congo* in support of its request to pierce the corporate veil of the Claimant:

These few examples demonstrate that in general, ICSID tribunals do not accept the view that their competence is limited by formalities, and rather they rule on their competence based on a review of the circumstances surrounding the case, and, in particular, the actual relationship among the companies involved. This jurisprudence reveals the willingness of ICSID tribunals to refrain from making decisions on their competence based on formal appearances, and to base their decisions on a realistic assessment of the situation before them.[1]

The "few examples" to which the *Banro* Tribunal refers, however, are cases in which the Claimant, as the party that requested arbitration, was not the same entity as the party that consented to arbitration.[2] The *Banro* Tribunal suggests that, in these cases, the tribunals have been willing to consider the nationalities of the consenting party and the Claimant when making their determinations of jurisdiction.

In *Banro* itself, the Claimant's parent, Banro Resources (Canada), transferred shares in its Congolese investment to its subsidiary, Banro American (U.S.). The Tribunal stated that the Claimant, Banro American, could not avail itself of the consent expressed by its parent, Banro Resources, because Banro Resources, as a national of a non-Contracting Party, could not have validly consented to ICSID arbitration and, thus, could not transfer any valid consent

---

1 *Id.* at para. 56 (emphases added).

2 Respondent's Memorial, at 2.1.9 (citing *Banro American Resources, Inc. and Société Aurifère du Kivu du Maniema S.A.R.L. v. Democratic Republic of Congo*, Award, Case No. ARB/98/7 (Sept. 1, 2000), at para. 11 ("*Banro*")).

to its U.S. subsidiary.[1] Although the *Banro* Tribunal indicated that it "could have addressed the issue of *jus standi* of Banro American in a flexible manner,"[2] in the end, the Tribunal did not deny jurisdiction by piercing the Claimant's corporate veil. Instead, the *Banro* Tribunal denied jurisdiction to prevent Banro Resources from availing itself of diplomatic protection while its U.S. subsidiary pursued ICSID arbitration, which, if allowed, would contravene the object and purpose of Article 27 the Convention.[3]

Thus, the issue before the Tribunal in *Banro* and in the cases discussed briefly therein was not, as it is here, the proper method of defining the nationality of the claimant. In *Banro*, there was no dispute that the claimant was a national of the United States and Banro Resources was a national of Canada, both by virtue of their incorporation in those countries. The issue in *Banro* was whether the claimant of one nationality could benefit from the consent given by its parent company of another nationality. In the present case, it is undisputed that the Claimant made the request for arbitration and expressed consent to ICSID jurisdiction. Accordingly, the decision in *Banro* provides no justification for looking beyond the nationality of the Claimant, Tokios Tokelès, to other related parties or to its controlling shareholders.

The decision in *Autopista v. Venezuela* is similarly unhelpful to the Respondent. The Respondent's Memorial in the case before this Tribunal cites, in isolation, the following passage: "[a]s a general matter, the arbitral Tribunal accepts that economic criteria often better reflect reality than legal ones."[4] Although seemingly helpful, the text of the decision that follows the quoted passage directly undermines the Respondent's objection. In particular, the Tribunal states, "[h]owever, in the present case, such *arguments of an economic nature are irrelevant*. Indeed, exercising the discretion granted by the Convention, *the parties have specifically identified* majority shareholding *as the criterion to be applied. They have not chosen to subordinate their consent to ICSID arbitration to other criteria.*

As a result, the Tribunal must respect the parties' autonomy and may not discard the

---

1 *Banro*, at para. 10 ("This was the case, in particular, in two situations: when the request was made by a member company of a group of companies while the pertinent instrument expressed the consent of another company of this group; and when, following the transfer of shares, the request came from the transferee company while the consent had been given by the company making the transfer.").

2 *Id.* at para. 5.

3 *Id.* at para. 13.

4 *Id.* at paras. 13, 24. Article 27 states, "[n]o Contracting State shall give diplomatic protection, or bring an international claim, in respect of a dispute which one of its nationals and another Contracting State shall have consented to submit or shall have submitted to arbitration under this Convention, unless such other Contracting State shall have failed to abide by and comply with the award rendered in such dispute."Memorial, para. 2.1.9 (citing *Autopista*, para. 119).

criterion of direct shareholding, *unless it proves unreasonable.*"[1]

In the present case, as in *Autopista*, "arguments of an economic nature are irrelevant" where "the parties have specifically identified" the country of legal establishment "as the criterion to be applied" and "have not chosen to subordinate their consent to ICSID arbitration to any other criteria." This Tribunal, like the tribunal in *Autopista*, is obliged to respect the parties' agreement "unless it proves unreasonable."

Far from unreasonable, reference to the state of incorporation is the most common method of defining the nationality of business entities under modern BITs and traditional international law.[2]

The Respondent also cites *Loewen v. United States of America* to support its position.[3] In that case, the Canadian claimant declared bankruptcy during the arbitration proceedings and, immediately before going out of business, assigned its claim to a newly created Canadian corporation whose sole asset was the claim against the United States.[4]

The newly created corporation was wholly owned and controlled by the U.S. enterprise that emerged from the earlier bankruptcy proceeding. Although the claim remained at all times in the possession of a Canadian enterprise, the *Loewen* tribunal held that the assignment of the claim changed the nationality of the claimant from Canadian to U.S. origin. Accordingly, the tribunal denied jurisdiction because the claimant's nationality was not continuous from the date of the events giving rise to the claim through the date of the resolution of the claim, as the tribunal believed was required by customary international law.[5]

Although the *Loewen* tribunal denied that it pierced the claimant's corporate veil,[6] in reality, the tribunal did exactly that. Indeed, the tribunal could not have concluded that the nationality of the claimant had changed from Canadian to U.S. origin without piercing the claimant's corporate veil. Although one may debate whether veil piercing was justified in that case, the *Loewen* decision does not clarify the jurisprudence of veil piercing because the tribunal did not admit to, much less explain its reasons for, piercing the claimant's corporate veil.

As *Loewen* provides no additional guidance on the doctrine of veil piercing, we refer

---

1 *Autopista*, at paras. 119-120 (emphases added).

2 Schreuer, at 277.

3 Respondent's Reply, at 2.1.5.

4 *Loewen Group, Inc. and Raymond Loewen v. United States of America*, Award, Case No. ARB(AF)/98/3 (June 26, 2003), 42 I.L.M. 811 (2003), at paras. 220, 240.

5 *Id*. at para. 225.

6 *Id*. at para. 237.

instead to the jurisprudence of *Barcelona Traction*. As noted above, we are convinced that the equitable doctrine of veil piercing does not apply to the present case.

b.*Views of ICSID Scholars*

The Respondent also argues that some ICSID scholars encourage the application of the control-test to determine corporate nationality in the first clause of Article 25(2)(b) as well as the second, citing the views of Dr. Amerasinghe and Mr. Broches as discussed by Professor Schreuer. The Respondent, however, misinterprets the views of these scholars.

Dr. Amerasinghe does argue that Article 25 of the Convention allows tribunals to be "extremely flexible" in using various methods to determine the nationality of juridical entities, including the control-test.[7] He advocates this flexible approach, however, in the context of a challenge to jurisdiction where, unlike here, the parties to the dispute have not agreed on a particular method of determining the nationality of juridical entities. In addition, the Respondent fails to mention Dr. Amerasinghe's corollary rule of interpretation, that is, "every effort should be made to give the Centre jurisdiction by the application of the flexible approach."[8]

Likewise, Mr. Broches states that the text of Article 25(2)(b) "implicitly assumes that incorporation is a criterion of nationality."[9] He argues, however, that this provision does not preclude *an agreement between parties* to define juridical entities by methods other than state of incorporation, including ownership and control.[10] In other words, the Convention permits deviation from the general rule for defining the nationality of juridical entities, but only if there is an agreement between the Contracting Parties to do so. Here, there is no such agreement providing for deviation. On the contrary, the agreement under the Ukraine-Lithuania BIT confirms that the standard rule (incorporation) applies.

Traditional Approach under International Law

As with the Convention, the definition of corporate nationality in the Ukraine-Lithuania BIT is also consistent with the predominant approach in international law. As the International Court of Justice has explained, "[t]he traditional rule attributes the right of diplomatic protection of a corporate entity to the States under the laws of which it is incorporated and in whose territory it has its registered office. The two criteria have been confirmed by long

---

7 C.F. Amerasinghe, "The Jurisdiction of the International Centre for the Settlement of Investment Disputes," 19 INDIAN J. INT'L LAW 166, 214 (Apr.-June 1979).

8 *Id*. at 214-215.

9 Broches, at 360.

10 *Id*. at 360-361.

practice and by numerous international instruments."[1] According to *Oppenheim's International Law*, "[i]t is usual to attribute a corporation to the state under the laws of which it has been incorporated and to which it owes its legal existence; to this initial condition is often added the need for the corporation's head office, registered office, or its *siège social* to be in the same state."[2] Thus, the Ukraine-Lithuania BIT uses the same well established method for determining corporate nationality as does customary international law.

Conclusion of the Tribunal

The Tribunal concludes that the Claimant is an "investor" of Lithuania under Article 1(2)(b) of the BIT and a "national of another Contracting State," under Article 25 of the Convention.

Second Objection: The Claimant Did Not Make an "Investment" "in Accordance with the Laws and Regulations" of Ukraine

Argument of the Respondent: Claimant Has Not Shown that the Source of Capital Is Non-Ukrainian

The Respondent argues that, even if the Tribunal determines that the Claimant is an investor of Lithuania, the Claimant did not make an "investment" in Ukraine as defined by the Treaty. More specifically, the Respondent argues that the Claimant has not proved that it had sufficient capital to make the initial investment in its subsidiary, Taki spravy, nor that the capital otherwise originated outside Ukraine. According to the Respondent, the investment in Taki spravy therefore falls outside the scope of the Ukraine-Lithuania BIT and the ICSID Convention, as the purpose of both agreements is to protect international, *i.e.*, cross-border, investment. The Respondent also argues that, even if the Claimant is judged to have made investments in Ukraine, those investments were not made in accordance with Ukrainian law and thus are not covered by the Ukraine-Lithuania BIT.

"Investment" under Article 25 of Convention

Article 25 of the Convention requires that, in order for the Centre to have jurisdiction, a dispute must arise from "an investment." As with corporate nationality, the parties have broad discretion to decide the "kinds of investment they wish to bring to ICSID."[3] Indeed, "[p]recisely because the Convention does not define 'investment', it does not purport to

---

1 *Barcelona Traction*, at para. 70.

2 1 OPPENHEIM'S INTERNATIONAL LAW 859-60 (Sir Robert Jennings and Sir Arthur Watts eds., 9th ed. 1996) (footnotes omitted).

3 Schreuer, at 124.

define the requirements that an investment should meet to qualify for ICSID jurisdiction."[1] Parties have a "large measure of discretion to determine for themselves whether their transaction constitutes an investment for the purposes of the Convention."[2] Here, that discretion is exercised in the BIT.

Definition of "Investment" in Article 1(1) of the BIT

As mentioned above, Article 1(1) of the BIT defines "investment" as "every kind of asset invested by an investor of one Contracting Party in the territory of the other Contracting Party in accordance with the laws and regulations of the latter…." In addition, Article 1(1) provides that "[a]ny alteration of the form in which assets are invested shall not affect their character as an investment…." The Treaty contains no requirement that the capital used by the investor to make the investment originate in Lithuania, or, indeed, that such capital not have originated in Ukraine.

To phrase the Respondent's objection in the terms of the Treaty, it maintains that the assets of Taki spravy in the territory of Ukraine were not "invested by" the Claimant because the Claimant has not shown that it used non-Ukrainian capital to finance the investment. To assess the Respondent's objection, we follow the standard rule of interpretation: we apply to the terms of the Treaty their ordinary meaning, in their context, in light of the object and purpose of the Treaty. The ordinary meaning of "invest" is to "expend (money, effort) in something from which a return or profit is expected…"[3] The ordinary meaning of "by" is "indicating agency, means, [or] cause …"[4] Thus, an investment under the BIT is read in ordinary meaning as "every kind of asset" for which "an investor of one Contracting Party" caused money or effort to be expended and from which a return or profit is expected in the territory of the other Contracting Party. In other words, the Claimant must show that it caused an investment to be made in the territory of the Respondent.

The Claimant has provided substantial evidence of its investment in Ukraine, beginning with its initial investment of USD 170,000 in 1994, and continuing

---

1 *CMS*, at para. 51.

2 *See Fedax N.V. v. Republic of Venezuela*, Decision on Jurisdiction, Case No. ARB/96/3 (July 11, 1997), 37 I.L.M. 1378 (1998), at para. 22 (quoting Carolyn B. Lamm and Abby Cohen Smutny, "The Implementation of ICSID Arbitration Agreements," 11 ICSID Review-FILJ 64, 80 (1996)) ("*Fedax*").

3 THE NEW SHORTER OXFORD ENGLISH DICTIONARY, at 1410.

4 *Id.* at 310.

reinvestments[1] each year until 2002, for a total investment of more than USD 6.5 million.[2] Moreover, although the Treaty does not require the Contracting Parties to acknowledge the investments of entities of the other Contracting Party in order for such investments to fall within the scope of the Treaty, in this case, the Respondent has done so. In particular, the Claimant has produced copies of twenty-three "Informational Notice(s) of Payment of Foreign Investment," in which the Claimant's investments were registered by Ukrainian governmental authorities.[3]

The Respondent requests the Tribunal to infer, without textual foundation, that the Ukraine-Lithuania BIT requires the Claimant to demonstrate further that the capital used to make an investment in Ukraine originated from non-Ukrainian sources. In our view, however, neither the text of the definition of "investment," nor the context in which the term is defined, nor the object and purpose of the Treaty allow such an origin-of-capital requirement to be implied. The requirement is plainly absent from the text. In addition, the context in which the term "investment" is defined, namely, "*every* kind of asset invested by an investor," does not support the restriction advocated by the Respondent.[4] Finally, the origin-of-capital requirement is inconsistent with the object and purpose of the Treaty, which, as discussed above, is to provide broad protection to investors and their investments in the territory of either party. Accordingly, the Tribunal finds no basis on which to impose the restriction proposed by the Respondent on the scope of covered investments.

We conclude that, under the terms of the BIT, both the enterprise Taki spravy and the rights in the property described in the above-referred "Informational Notices," are assets invested by the Claimant in the territory of Ukraine. The investment would not have occurred but for the decision by the Claimant to establish an enterprise in Ukraine and to dedicate to this enterprise financial resources under the Claimant's control. In doing so, the Claimant caused the expenditure of money and effort from which it expected a return or profit in Ukraine.

Consistency of Article 1(1) of the BIT with the ICSID Convention

The Tribunal's finding under the BIT is also consistent with the ICSID Convention. The broad definition of "investment" in the Lithuania-Ukraine BIT is typical of the definition

---

1 The definition "investment" in Article 1(1), "every kind of asset invested by an investor" certainly includes reinvestments of the profits generated by the initial investments.

2 *See, e.g.*, Claimant's June 20, 2003 Submission of Documents, Vols. II-IV.

3 Request for Arbitration, at Annex 13.

4 Emphasis added.

used in most contemporary BITs.[1] Because the Convention leaves the definition of the term to the Contracting Parties, which in general have defined it broadly, there have been few cases in which the Respondent has challenged the underlying transaction as not being an "investment" under the Convention.[2] One such case was *Fedax N.V. v. Republic of Venezuela*. The treaty under which that dispute was arbitrated, the Netherlands-Venezuela BIT, defines "investment," like the Ukraine-Lithuania BIT, as "every kind of asset." In that case, the Respondent argued that the government-issued promissory notes held by the Claimant were not "investment(s)" because the Claimant had acquired the notes by way of endorsement from a Venezuelan company.[3] The Respondent argued that the Claimant had not made a "direct" investment in Venezuela, which the Respondent argued was required by the ICSID Convention.[4] In the following passage, the *Fedax* tribunal rejected the Respondent's argument and also underscored the broad definition of investment contemplated by the Convention:

[T]he text of Article 25(1) establishes that the "jurisdiction of the Centre shall extend to any legal dispute arising directly out of an investment." It is apparent that the term "directly" relates in this Article to the "dispute" and not the "investment." It follows that jurisdiction can exist even in respect of investments that are not direct, so long as the dispute arises directly from such transaction. This interpretation is also consistent with the broad reach that the term "investment" must be given in light of the negotiating history of the Convention.[5]

The Respondent in the present case also asks the Tribunal to narrow the scope of covered investments by adding a condition—in this case, an origin-of-capital requirement—not found in the instrument of consent or the Convention. The Respondent alleges that the Claimant has not proved that the capital used to invest in Ukraine originated from non-Ukrainian, sources, and, thus, the Claimant has not made a direct, or cross-border, investment. Even assuming, *arguendo*, that all of the capital used by the Claimant to invest in Ukraine had its ultimate origin in Ukraine, the resulting investment would not be outside the scope of the Convention. The Claimant made an investment for the purposes of the Convention when it decided to deploy capital under its control in the territory of Ukraine instead of investing it elsewhere. The origin of the capital is not relevant to the existence of an investment.

---

1 *See Fedax*, at para. 34 (citing Antonio Parra, "The Scope of New Investment Laws and International Instruments," in ECONOMIC DEVELOPMENT, FOREIGN INVESTMENT AND THE LAW 27, 35-36 (Robert Pritchard ed. 1996)); *see also* Rudolph Dolzer and Margaret Stevens, BILATERAL INVESTMENT TREATIES, 26-31 (1995).

2 *Fedax*, at para. 25.

3 *Id*. at para. 18.

4 *Id*. at para. 24.

5 *Id*. at para. 24.

That the ICSID Convention does not require an "investment" to be financed from capital of any particular origin was confirmed by the tribunal in *Tradex Hellas S.A. v. Republic of Albania*. In that case, the tribunal considered a definition of "foreign investment" under Albanian law that is substantially similar to the definition of "investment" in the Ukraine-Lithuania BIT: "every kind of investment in the territory of the Republic of Albania owned directly or indirectly by a foreign investor."[1] The tribunal found that the definition, "nowhere requires that the foreign investor has to finance the investment from his own resources ... the law provides for a broad interpretation of 'investment.'"[2] As in *Tradex*, the Claimant in the present case owns and controls the assets in Ukraine that have given rise to this dispute. The origin of the capital used to acquire these assets is not relevant to the question of jurisdiction under the Convention.

In our view, the ICSID Convention contains no inchoate requirement that the investment at issue in a dispute have an international character in which the origin of the capital is decisive. Although the Convention contemplates disputes of an international character, we believe that such character is defined by the terms of the Convention, and in turn, the terms of the BIT. Were we to accept the origin of capital as transcending the textual definition of the nationality of the Claimant and the scope of covered investment in the Ukraine-Lithuania BIT, we would override the explicit choice of the Contracting Parties as to how to define these terms. Ukraine, Lithuania and other Contracting Parties chose their methods of defining corporate nationality and the scope of covered investment in BITs with confidence that ICSID arbitrators would give effect to those definitions. That confidence is premised on the ICSID Convention itself, which leaves to the reasonable discretion of the parties the task of defining key terms. We should be loathe to undermine it.

Argument of the Respondent: Investment Not Made "in Accordance with Laws and Regulations" of Ukraine

According to the Respondent, even if the Claimant were found to have made investments, those investments were not made in accordance with Ukrainian law as required by Article 1(1) of the Ukraine-Lithuania BIT. For example, the Respondent argues that the full name under which the Claimant registered its subsidiary, "The Lithuanian subsidiary private enterprise The Publishing, Informational and Advertising Agency Taki Spravy,"[3] is improper because

---

1 *Tradex Hellas S.A. v. Republic of Albania*, Award, Case No. ARB/94/2 (Apr. 29, 1999) 14 ICSID Review-FILJ 161, at para. 105 (citing Albanian law).

2 *Id*. at para. 109.

3 Request for Arbitration, at Annex 8.

"subsidiary enterprise" but not "subsidiary *private* enterprise" is a recognized legal form under Ukrainian law.[1] The Respondent also alleges that it has identified errors in the documents provided by the Claimant related to asset procurement and transfer, including, in some cases, the absence of a necessary signature or notarization.[2] The Claimant disputes the Respondent's allegations.[3]

The requirement in Article 1(1) of the Ukraine-Lithuania BIT that investments be made in compliance with the laws and regulations of the host state is a common requirement in modern BITs.[4] The purpose of such provisions, as explained by the Tribunal in *Salini Costruttori S.p.A and Italstrade S.p.A v. Morocco*, is "to prevent the Bilateral Treaty from protecting investments that should not be protected, particularly because they would be illegal."[5]

Thus, the question before the Tribunal is whether the alleged violations establish that the assets invested by the Claimant were invested not "in accordance with the laws and regulations of" Ukraine. Under the Vienna Convention, the ordinary meaning of these terms "must emerge in the context of the treaty as a whole and in the light of its objects and purposes."[6] As discussed above, the object and purpose of the BIT is to provide broad protection for investors and their investments.

In the present case, the Respondent does not allege that the Claimant's investment and business activity—advertising, printing, and publishing—are illegal *per se*. In fact, as discussed above, governmental authorities of the Respondent registered the Claimant's subsidiary as a valid enterprise in 1994, and, over the next eight years, registered each of the Claimant's investments in Ukraine, as documented in twenty-three Informational Notices of Payment of Foreign Investment.[7] The Respondent now alleges that some of the documents underlying these registered investments contain defects of various types, some of which relate to matters of Ukrainian law. Even if we were able to confirm the Respondent's allegations, which would require a searching examination of minute details of administrative procedures in Ukrainian

---

1 Respondent's Memorial, at 2.2.2. Although the Certificate Regarding the State Registration of a Subject of Entrepreneurial Activity includes the phrase "The Lithuanian subsidiary private enterprise," as part of the name of the Claimant's subsidiary, the "organizational form" is recorded as "subsidiary enterprise." Request for Arbitration, at Annex 8.

2 Respondent's Reply, at Section 4.

3 Claimant's Rejoinder, at 48, 86-134.

4 Schreuer, at 130.

5 *Salini Costruttori S.p.A and Italstrade S.p.A v. Kingdom of Morocco*, Decision on Jurisdiction, Case No. ARB/00/4 (July 23, 2001), 42 I.L.M. 609 (2003), at para. 46.

6 Ian Brownlie, PRINCIPLES OF INTERNATIONAL LAW 634 (5th ed. 1998) (footnotes omitted).

7 Request for Arbitration, Annex 13.

law, to exclude an investment on the basis of such minor errors would be inconsistent with the object and purpose of the Treaty. In our view, the Respondent's registration of each of the Claimant's investments indicates that the "investment" in question was made in accordance with the laws and regulations of Ukraine.

Third Objection: The Dispute Does Not Arise from the Investment

In order for this Tribunal to have jurisdiction over a dispute, there must be an adequate nexus between the dispute and the Claimant's investment in the territory of the Contracting Party.

Article 25(1) of the ICSID Convention extends jurisdiction to any dispute "arising directly out of an investment." In order for the directness requirement to be satisfied, the dispute and investment must be "reasonably closely connected."[1] As Professor Schreuer notes, "[d]isputes arising from ancillary or peripheral aspects of the investment operation are likely to give rise to the objection that they do not arise directly from the investment ...."[2]

Article 8 of the Ukraine-Lithuania BIT, in turn, provides that an investor of one Contracting Party may submit to arbitration a dispute "*in connection with*" an investment in the territory of the other Contracting Party.[3] It may be held that the scope of arbitrable disputes under the Treaty is broader than that contemplated by Article 25(1) of the Convention which refers to any "dispute arising directly out of an investment."[4] Even if based only on the language of the Convention, however, the Respondent's contention is in any case bound to fail.

The Respondent argues that the present dispute does not "arise directly out of an investment" because the allegedly wrongful acts by Ukrainian governmental authorities (including unwarranted and unreasonable investigations of the Claimant's business, unfounded judicial actions to invalidate the Claimant's contracts, and false, public accusations of illegal conduct by the Claimant) were not directed against the physical assets owned by the Claimant, *i.e.*, its facilities and equipment.[5]

In this regard, the Respondent misapprehends the jurisdictional requirements of Article 25. For a dispute to arise directly out of an investment, the allegedly wrongful conduct of the government need not be directed against the physical property of the investor. The requirement of directness is met if the dispute arises from the investment itself or the operations of its

---

1 Schreuer, at 114.

2 *Ibid.*

3 Emphasis added.

4 Emphasis added.

5 Respondent's Memorial on Jurisdiction, at 12-16.

investment, as in the present case. The scope of this requirement was addressed by the first ICSID tribunal, *Holiday Inns S.A. v. Morocco*, which found jurisdiction over loan contracts that were separate but related to the investment agreement, emphasizing "the general unity of an investment operation."[1]

Thus, the Respondent's obligations with respect to "investment" relate not only to the physical property of Lithuanian investors but also to the business operations associated with that physical property. States' obligations with respect to "property" and "the use of property" are well established in international law. For example, the *Draft Convention on the International Responsibility of States for Injuries to Aliens*, defines a "taking of property" to include "not only an outright taking of property but also any such unreasonable interference with the use, enjoyment, or disposal of property as to justify an inference that the owner there of will not be able to use, enjoy or dispose of the property within a reasonable period of time after the inception of such interference."[2] Further, the Iran-U.S. Claims Tribunal found that "[a] deprivation or taking of property may occur under international law through interference by a state in the use of that property or with the enjoyment of its benefits."[3]

In the present case, each of the allegedly wrongful government actions—investigations, document seizures, public accusations of illegal conduct, and judicial actions to invalidate contracts and seize assets—involved the operations of the Claimant's subsidiary enterprise in Ukraine. Accordingly, we are satisfied that the present dispute arises directly from the Claimant's investment.

OBJECTIONS TO ADMISSIBILITY

First Objection: Claimant's Written Consent Was Improper and Untimely

Article 25(1) states, "jurisdiction of the Centre shall extend to any legal dispute... which the parties to the dispute consent in writing to submit to the Centre." The consent of the Ukraine is found in Article 8(2) of the Treaty, which provides that "the investor shall be entitled to submit the case to [arbitration] ..." It is well established that, "formulations [in a BIT] to the effect that a dispute 'shall be submitted' to the Centre'... leave no doubt as to the binding

---

1 Schreuer, at 116 (citing P. Lalive, "The First World Bank Arbitration (*Holiday Inns v. Morocco*)—Some Legal Problems," 1 ICSID Reports 645).

2 L. Sohn and R. Baxter, "Responsibility of States for Injuries to the Economic Interests of Aliens, AM J. INT'L L. 545, 553 (1961) (Article 10.3 of *Draft Convention on the International Responsibility of States for Injuries to Aliens*).

3 *Tippetts, Abbott, McCarthy, Stratton v. TAMS-AFFA*, Award No. 141-7-2, 6 Iran-U.S. C.T.R. 219, (June 22, 1984).

character of these clauses."[1] The Respondent does not contest that it has consented to ICSID arbitration.

The Respondent does argue, however, that the Claimant's consent was improper and untimely, and, thus, its claim should be inadmissible. As discussed above, the Claimant attached an unaddressed document entitled, "Letter of Consent to Arbitration," dated August 7, 2002, to its Request for Arbitration, which was received by ICSID on August 14, 2002.[2] The Claimant withdrew its request on October 17, 2002, and resubmitted it on November 22, 2002.

The Respondent argues that the Claimant's consent was improper because its Letter of Consent was not addressed and sent directly to the Respondent.[3] In addition, the Respondent argues that the consent was untimely because it was not given before the initiation of ICSID proceedings, which, according to the Respondent, is required by the Convention.[4] Finally, the Respondent argues that the Claimant's consent was untimely because it was expressed before the expiration of the six-month negotiating period required by Article 8 of the BIT.[5]

Each of the Respondent's arguments fails. First, the Convention does not stipulate the form that written consent must take, much less to whom it must be addressed and sent. As Dr. Amerasinghe explains, [t]he Convention requires *only* that the consent be in writing. Thus, it is not necessary that the consent of both parties be included in a single instrument. The consents may, indeed, be expressed in instruments of completely diverse character, and *not necessarily addressed to the other party* or made with particular reference to any dispute of arrangement with it.[6]

In fact, the Claimant need not have expressed its consent in a document separate from the RFA itself. As Professor Schreuer notes, "[i]t is established practice that an investor may accept an offer of consent contained in a BIT by instituting ICSID proceedings."[7] Thus, not only the

---

1 Schreuer, at 213.

2 Request for Arbitration, at Annex 1.

3 Respondent's Memorial on Jurisdiction, at 3.1.3.

4 *Id*. at 3.1.4

5 *Ibid*.

6 C.F. Amerasinghe, "The Jurisdiction of the International Centre for the Settlement of Investment Disputes," at 224 (emphases added).

7 Schreuer, at 218. As stated by the Tribunal in *SGS v. Philippines*, "the Claimant relies upon the consent to ICSID arbitration given by the Philippines in the BIT, combined with its own written consent contained in the Request for Arbitration. It is well established that the combination of these forms of consent can constitute 'consent in writing' within the meaning of Article 25(1), provided that the dispute falls within the scope of the BIT." *SGS v. Philippines*, at para. 31.

Claimant's letter but also the RFA itself satisfy the requirement to "consent in writing" to the jurisdiction of the Centre. As the Convention contemplates "no requirement that the consent either precede or follow the incidence of a particular dispute," neither does it require consent to precede or follow negotiations concerning a dispute.[1]

Further, the Claimant was not required to submit its consent prior to initiating ICSID proceedings. The Executive Directors' Report addresses the timing of parties' consent in paragraph 24: "[c]onsent of the parties must exist when the Centre is seized (Articles 28(3) and 36(3)) but the Convention does not otherwise specify the time at which consent should be given."[102] When an investor accepts a State's general offer of consent in a BIT, as in the present case, the timing of such an acceptance is proper as long as it occurs not later than the time at which the Claimant submits its request for arbitration.[103] There is no requirement that the Claimant's consent precede the request. Similarly, neither the BIT nor the Convention requires the Claimant to wait until after the requisite six-month negotiating period has ended before expressing its consent to ICSID jurisdiction. Article 8 of the BIT merely requires that there be a negotiating period of six months after a dispute arises before a claim may be submitted to arbitration. We are confident that this requirement has been fulfilled.

For the foregoing reasons, the Claimant's written consent satisfies the requirements of the ICSID Convention.

【思考题】

1. ICSID 行使管辖权需要满足哪些条件？

2. 确定法人国籍的标准主要有哪些？

3. 本案被申请人主张采取什么标准确定 Tokios Tokelès 的国籍？《乌克兰—立陶宛双边投资条约》约定以合种标准确定法人国籍？

Case1·拓展阅读

---

1 Amerasinghe, "The Jurisdiction of the International Centre for the Settlement of Investment Dispate Between States and Nationals of Other Sfates: British Yearbook of International Law, Nol.47.Issutl.1975.

Case2　Tza Yap Shum vs. The Republic of Peru（ICSID Case No. ARB/07/6）

【案情说明】：

一、案件事实

谢业深（Tza Yap Shum）是一名中国公民，他对秘鲁共和国提起仲裁，声称其违反了中国和秘鲁签订的双边投资条约，影响了他对 TSG del PerúS.a.C.（"TSG"）的投资。TSG 是一家秘鲁公司，主要为亚洲市场购买和出口鱼粉。谢业深投资 40 万美元，是持有 TSG90% 的间接股东。TSG 于 2002 年开始运营，2002—2004 年是秘鲁 12 个最大的鱼粉出口商之一，年销售额超过 2 000 万美元。TSG 的商业模式系与渔船签订采购鱼粉原材料的合同，同时对渔船提供融资。这些鱼粉原料由渔船直接运送到第三方加工厂，TSG 与第三方加工厂签约生产鱼粉，生产出来的鱼粉在准备出口之前一直存放在第三方工厂。TSG 从未直接处理任何产品，主要是起协调和提供资金融资的作用。尽管 TSG 没有从秘鲁银行获得融资，但它会利用秘鲁银行进行收付款等交易。

2004，秘鲁税务局（the Superintendencia Nacional de Administración Tributaria Tributaria, SUNAT"）开始对 TSG 进行审计，TSG 公司予以配合。该审计源于 TSG 在两年前向秘鲁税务当局申请销售税的部分退税，看起来是常规审计。审计期间，SUNAT 得出结论，TSG 的账簿没有充分反映鱼粉生产所用原材料的价值，因此，根据秘鲁税法，SUNAT 在分析中使用了"推定基数"，而不是基于 TSG 的账簿和记录。根据"推定基数"，SUNAT 得出结论，TSG 低报了销售额。于是 SUNAT 在 2005 年向 TSG 征收了大约 1 000 万秘鲁索尔（Peruvian solares）的税款和罚款。

审计后不久，SUNAT 还实施了临时措施，冻结 TSG 部分财产并指示所有秘鲁银行冻结与 TSG 交易的资金。秘鲁法律允许 SUNAT 在纳税人不合作（例如，未能披露重要信息）的情况下或因其他原因未能收到税款时采取临时措施。SUNAT 审计师为支持临时措施请求而编制的报告中表明请求采取临时措施是基于 TSG 的"非正常行为"。但是，该报告中唯一被引用的行为是 SUNAT 认定 TSG 的账簿未能准确反映公司的总销售额。随后，SUNAT 审计师提交了第二份报告，该报告中请求临时措施仍是基于 TSG 未能准确反映销售额，仅修改了审计师提出请求所依据的税法的具体条款。这两份报告都没有为审计师的结论提供具体的支持。此外，SUNAT 负责实施临时措施的执行司在实施临时措施之前没有要求审计师提供任何补充资料。

TSG 随后通过行政手段寻求救济，要求 SUNAT 取消临时措施，SUNAT 拒绝了 TSG 的这一申请，但减少了对欠税的计算。TSG 就 SUNAT 的决定向财政法庭（Fiscal

Tribunal）提起诉讼，财政法庭维持了临时措施，但进一步将补缴税金金额降低为约
3 100 000 秘鲁索尔。

SUNAT 采取临时措施后，TSG 无法利用秘鲁银行进行交易，销售额随后大幅下降，
最终，TSG 于 2005 年 3 月启动了债务重组程序，该程序起到暂停临时措施的效果以维
持经营。

随后 2006 年 9 月 29 日，谢业深作为申请人在 ICSID 针对秘鲁提起仲裁，声称
SUNAT 的审计决定及临时措施构成了对其投资的不合理间接征收，违反了中国与秘
鲁间于 1994 年签署的双边投资条约的规定，请求损害赔偿共计约 25 000 000 美元，
包括基于未来现金流而计算出的超过 57 000 000 索尔的损失和精神损害 15 000 000
索尔及其他。

二、裁决结果

2009 年 6 月 19 日，仲裁庭就其管辖权及权限（Jurisdiction and Competence）作出
裁决，裁定谢业深在 TSG 的投资利益构成中国和秘鲁双边投资下的"投资"，仲裁庭
对谢业深的征收赔偿请求享有管辖权。2011 年 7 月 7 日在对案件的最终裁决中，仲裁
庭认为 SUNAT 实施的临时措施构成随意攫取（arbitrary taking），是对谢业深投资的间接
征收，构成对中国和秘鲁间双边投资条约第四条的违反，应予赔偿损失。但是仲裁庭没
有采纳谢业深的损害赔偿计算方法，而是基于调整后 TSG 的账面价值计算损害赔偿，
裁定赔偿额为 US$786 306.24，并按美国国债利率计算利息。仲裁庭裁定仲裁费用由双
方平均分担。

【法律分析】

问题一：SUNAT 的审计是否构成对谢业深投资的间接征收？

征收问题向来是国际投资保护领域最具争议的问题之一，因为它不仅涉及投资者的
利益，还直接涉及国家主权问题，如何将间接征收行为与正常的国家管理行为相区别，
是认定是否构成间接征收的重点。 仲裁庭认为，SUNAT 对 TSG 进行审计是因为 TSG
在前几年要求退还大量销售税，因此，对 TSG 的审计是常规的审计。鉴于对国家的监
管和行政权力的尊重，SUNAT 在进行审计时的任何行为都不构成征收。

问题二：SUNAT 实施的临时措施是否构成对谢业深投资的间接征收？

仲裁庭认为 SUNAT 采取的临时措施构成间接征收，主要有两个原因。第一，
SUNAT 采取的临时措施严重干扰了 TSG 的运营。仲裁庭裁定，临时措施对所有受影响
的银行都具有法律约束力，阻止 TSG 继续与这些银行进行交易。鉴于 TSG 的商业模式
是利用秘鲁银行进行交易，临时措施对 TSG 的业务产生了严重和实质性的影响。仲裁
庭认为，根据 SUNAT 在审计期间获得的有关 TSG 如何融资和运营的信息，SUNAT 本

应知道临时措施是"对 TSG 运营能力的核心打击"。仲裁庭还注意到，由于采取了临时措施，TSG 的销售额从 2005—2006 年 8 000 万索尔剧减至 340 万索尔。第二，仲裁庭实施的临时措施具有任意性（arbitrary）。仲裁庭尊重和认同一国的税务主权及善意执法，国家不应为其行使主权和善意执法导致的损失承担赔偿责任，但需受限于国际公法及秘鲁法律、国际协定等要求的合理和非任意性原则 (the principle of reasonableness and non-arbitrariness)。本案中，法庭认为 SUNAT 未能遵守其内部指引及程序，这些内部指引和程序要求确定应对哪些具体资产采取临时措施；采取临时措施需合理基础及详尽的证据材料支撑；尽力避免干扰债务人的商业运营等。法庭还注意到，在采取临时措施之前，SUNAT 的执行部门也没有向审计师提出相关询问或要求提供补充资料。因此，法庭认定，SUNAT 的行为具有任意性质，给 TSG 造成了不合理的损失。

此外，虽然 TSG 采取了行政复议及司法救济手段，行政和司法机构并未充分分析 TSG 的诉求，而是不合理地支持了 SUNAT 的立场。因此，TSG 获得的仅是形式上而非实质上的法律救济。

基于上述原因，仲裁庭认定 SUNAT 的临时措施构成对谢业深投资的间接征收。

问题三：应当如何计算赔偿金额？

关于赔偿，仲裁庭指出，损害赔偿的标准是使仲裁申请人处于征收行为未发生时的状态所需的数额。双方一致认为，该金额应以 TSG 的价值为基础。然而，对于如何计算公司的价值，双方各执一词：谢业深要求以 TSG 的贴现现金流为基础计算损害赔偿金。秘鲁则辩称，公司调整后的账面价值才是适当的标准。法庭注意到，TSG 只运作了两年，其间现金流量为负。TSG 的杠杆率很高，在高风险渔业中运营，在 SUNAT 实施其临时措施时，它已经开始失去在渔业中的市场份额。有鉴于此，仲裁庭法庭未采纳谢业深计算损害赔偿的方法，而是采纳了被申请人的方法，即应根据 TSG 调整后的账面价值进行适当赔偿，并据此计算出赔偿为 786 306.24 美元。

但是，仲裁庭驳回了仲裁申请人要求精神损失赔偿的请求，认为 SUNAT 的行为不存在对投资者的身体的损害或损害的威胁，也并没有导致投资者身体或精神健康恶化或名誉受损，也不存在其他严重的不利后果。同时，仲裁庭也驳回了仲裁申请人 11% 的利息请求，认为该利率是 TSG 的融资利率，有风险因素，征收后不适用。最终裁定利息按美国十年国债的月平均利率计算。

问题四：仲裁费应如何承担？

仲裁庭注意到某些仲裁庭对费用裁决的不同看法，包括败诉方支付费用的原则和更为普遍接受的国际公法原则，即在仲裁期间各方都无恶劣行为的情形下，费用应由双方平等承担。仲裁庭认可双方当事人在仲裁期间的行为，裁定由双方均摊仲裁费用。

【英文原文摘选】[1]

I. THE FACTS

Tza Yap Shum ("Tza"), a Chinese national commenced this arbitration against the Republic of Peru ("Peru"), claiming violations of the BIT that affected his investment in TSG del Perú S.A.C. ("TSG"), a Peruvian company involved in the purchase and exportation of fishmeal, primarily for Asian markets. Tza is a 90% indirect shareholder of TSG, having made an investment of US$ 400,000. (para. 59-60, 74, 98) TSG commenced its operations in 2002 and between 2002 and 2004 was among the 12 largest exporters of fishmeal in Peru, with sales greater than US$ 20 million per year. TSG's business model consisted of contracting with, and financing, fishing vessels for the purchase of raw materials. Such raw material would be delivered directly by fishing vessels to third-party transforming plants, with which TSG contracted for the production of fishmeal. The produced fishmeal was warehoused at the third-party plants until ready for export. Thus, TSG never handled any products directly and served primarily as a coordinating and financing agent. TSG's comparative advantage in the industry consisted of access to financing from Tza's network of personal relationships with businesses and individuals. While TSG did not obtain financing from Peruvian banks, it used Peruvian banks to conduct its transactions, including the receipt of loans from abroad, the execution letters of credits from buyers abroad, and generally keeping track of its payments, costs, and accounts receivables.

In 2004, Peru's taxing authority, the Superintendencia Nacional de Administración Tributaria ("SUNAT"), commenced an audit of TSG, which was conducted with the company's cooperation. The audit appeared to be routine in nature and stemmed from TSG's requests in the prior two years of refunds of certain amounts paid in connection with sales taxes. During the audit, SUNAT concluded that TSG's books did not adequately reflect values for the raw material used in the production of fishmeal. SUNAT therefore, pursuant to the Peruvian tax code, utilized a "presumed basis" in its analysis rather than a basis based on TSG's books and records. Based upon the presumed basis, SUNAT concluded that TSG had underreported sales volumes. SUNAT, therefore, imposed back taxes and fines totaling approximately 10 million Peruvian solares ("S/.").

Shortly after the audit, SUNAT also imposed interim measures which had the effect of attaching certain limited assets of TSG and directing all Peruvian banks to retain any funds passing through them in connection with TSG's transactions. SUNAT is permitted under

---

1 由于该案裁决原文为西班牙文，此处的摘选系选自 ICSID 官网上提供的裁决的英文概略版，系由 Kenneth Juan Figueroa 所作。

Kenneth Juan Figueroa 先后毕业于耶鲁大学和哥伦比亚大学，在商事和投资仲裁领域有着丰富的经验。

Peruvian law to impose interim measures to ensure the payment of tax debts in "exceptional circumstances", 4 namely when the debtor has been uncooperative (by for example, failing to disclose material information) or when efforts to obtain payment of the tax debt would otherwise be unsuccessful. The report prepared by TSG's SUNAT auditor in support of the request for interim measures premised the request on TSG's "irregular behavior." The only behavior cited was SUNAT's determination that TSG's books had failed to accurately reflect the company's total sales volume. A second report was subsequently submitted by TSG's SUNAT auditor, which also premised the request on the failure to accurately reflect sales volumes and only modified the specific subsection of the Tax Code upon which the auditor based the request. Neither report provided specific support for the auditor's conclusions. Furthermore, SUNAT's executing division in charge of imposing interim measures (la División de Control de la Deuda y Cobranza) did not make any requests for additional information from the auditor before imposing the requested measures.

TSG challenged both SUNAT's audit determinations and its imposition of interim measures via administrative and judicial procedures available under Peruvian law. TSG commenced an administrative procedure requesting SUNAT to lift the interim measures on the basis that SUNAT had not adequately justified such measures. SUNAT rejected TSG's application, but reduced its calculation of back taxes. TSG also challenged SUNAT's decision before the Fiscal Tribunal, which affirmed the interim measures but further reduced the amount of back taxes to approximately S/. 3.1 million and ordered SUNAT to recalculate certain additional amounts.

The Claimant Tza, the 90% shareholder of TSG, thereafter commenced an ICSID arbitration claiming that SUNAT's audit determinations and interim measures constituted an unjustified indirect expropriation of its investment, in violation of the BIT. Tza sought over S/. 57 million based on the projected cash flow of TSG, in addition to S/. 15 million for moral damages, plus interest (at a rate of 11%) and fees and costs. Total damages demanded therefore approximated US$ 25 million.

On 19 June 2009, the Arbitral Tribunal issued a Decision on Jurisdiction and Competence in which it determined that Tza's interest in TSG constituted an investment for purposes of the BIT and that the Tribunal was competent to determine Claimant's expropriation claims. In its Final Award on the Merits, the Tribunal found that SUNAT's imposition of interim measures constituted an arbitrary taking and thus an indirect expropriation of Tza's investment. However, the Tribunal declined to adopt Tza's measure of damages, instead basing its calculation of compensation on the adjusted book value of TSG and awarding US$ 786,306.24, plus interest (at U.S. Treasury Bond rates). The Tribunal further ordered each party to split costs evenly.

II. Legal Issues Discussed in the Decision

(a) Whether SUNAT's audit constituted an indirect expropriation of Tza's investment.

The Tribunal found that the audit of TSG appeared to have been routine in light of TSG's request in prior years for large refunds on sales taxes. In light of the deference given to a State's regulatory and administrative powers, nothing in the conduct of SUNAT in conducting the audit constituted an expropriation. At the same time, the Tribunal also noted that TSG's challenges of SUNAT's determinations were not frivolous. (para. 95, 103, 113)

(b) Whether SUNAT's imposition of interim measures constituted an indirect expropriation of Tza's investment.

The Tribunal determined that the interim measures imposed by SUNAT were arbitrary in nature and constituted an expropriation for the following reasons: (i) The Interim measures significantly interfered with TSG's operations. The Tribunal found that the interim measures, which were legally binding on all affected banks, prevented TSG from continuing to transact with such banks. Given that TSG's business model used Peruvian banks to conduct its transactions, the interim measures presented a severe and substantial impact on TSG's business. The Tribunal found that, based on the information SUNAT obtained during its audit concerning how TSG was financed and operated, SUNAT should have known that interim measures were a "strike at the heart of the operative capacity of TSG." The Tribunal also noted that as a result of the interim measures, TSG's sales fell from an average of S/. 80 million for the 2005-2006 period to S/. 3.4 million for 2005-2006. Thus, the Tribunal distinguished the present case from the circumstances in LG&E Energy Corp. v. Republic of Argentina (ICSID Case No. ARB/01/ I), where it was held that the decrease in an investment's capacity and income generation, by itself, does not constitute expropriation. The Tribunal dismissed Peru's argument that the interim measures could no constitute an expropriation because they were ultimately suspended by TSG's restructuring proceedings. The Tribunal noted that SUNAT's interim measures were imposed for a period of one year and subsequently extended to be in effect for an additional two years. While the restructuring proceeding had the effect, under Peruvian law of suspending SUNAT's interim measures and allowing TSG to continue to operate through Peruvian banks, the Tribunal noted that the TSG could only resume normal operations once the restructuring proceedings concluded in June 2006. The Tribunal further noted that the restructuring proceedings were commenced at TSG's own initiative and were a reasonable and necessary response by TSG under the circumstances to mitigate its damages. The Tribunal determined that Peru could not rely on TSG's own efforts to justify or minimize the impact of SUNAT's actions.

(ii) SUNAT's imposition of interim measures was arbitrary. The Tribunal recognized the deference given to a State's regulatory and administrative powers and noted the general rule that a State is not liable for any losses resulting from the good faith application of general taxes and regulations. However, the Tribunal also noted that this deference is bound by the principle of reasonableness and non-arbitrariness reflected in public international law, as well as Peruvian law and treaty practice. Here, the Tribunal determined that SUNAT failed to comply with its own internal guidelines and procedures which required inter alia (i) a more precise identification of assets to be attached via interim measures, (ii) a reasoned basis for the "exceptional" remedy of interim measures accompanied by detailed evidentiary support, and (iii) efforts to avoid interfering with the debtor's business operations. The Tribunal also noted that SUNAT's executing division failed to make relevant inquiries or requests for additional information 7 from the auditor before imposing interim measures. As a result, the Tribunal found that SUNAT's actions were arbitrary in nature, resulting in unjustified losses on the part of TSG.

(iii) SUNAT's interim measures were ineffective. The Tribunal determined that while SUNAT's interim measures had a severe impact on the continued operations of TSG, they ultimately failed to be effective. The Tribunal noted that due in large part to the lack of precise identification of assets, such interim measures secured assets worth only US$ 172 out of the approximately US$ 4 million tax debt that resulted from the audit.

(iv) TSG did not have recourse to effective due process. The Tribunal recognized that TSG availed itself of administrative and judicial procedures to challenge the imposition of SUNAT's interim measures. However, the Tribunal held that such procedures did not amount to an adequate and effective legal recourse to SUNAT's decision. The administrative and judicial bodies that reviewed the interim measures failed to address and analyze sufficiently TSG's claims and, instead, adopted SUNAT's positions without a reasoned basis. The Tribunal found that TSG therefore had access only to formal, rather than substantive, legal recourse.

(v) TSG did not act in bad faith and did not fail to mitigate its damages. Finally, the Tribunal rejected respondent's arguments that Tza had conducted himself in bad faith because of the manner in which he organized his investment in TSG and TSG's failure to use funds reimbursed by SUNAT to pay his tax debt rather than TSG's business loans. The Tribunal noted that neither the structure of Tza's investment (and his delegation of authority to others) nor TSG's decision to pay off its business debts (and thereby mitigate its damages) evidenced bad faith. The Tribunal also rejected the argument that TSG failed to mitigate its damages by failing to request certain other 8 measures available to it under Peruvian law (e.g. requesting the executing division of SUNAT to substitute the interim measures or requesting waivers to make certain payments for the continued operation of TSG). The Tribunal found that it was doubtful that these additional measures would have been effective. It would therefore be unreasonable to expect TSG to exhaust these remedies. The Tribunal noted that TSG had mitigated its damages with the commencement of restructuring proceedings and that TSG's efforts to mitigate damages would be taken into account in the determination of damages.

(c) What is the appropriate compensation for expropriation?

With respect to compensation, the Tribunal noted that standard that the measure of damages is the amount needed to place the Claimant in the same position he would have been without the expropriatory act. Both parties were in agreement that this amount should be based upon the value of TSG. However, each party had different methods as to how to calculate the value of the company: Tza based his requested damages on the discounted cash flow of TSG, while Peru argued that the appropriate standard was the company's adjusted book value. The Tribunal rejected Tza's requested damages, which were based on the discounted cash flow of TSG. The Tribunal noted that TSG had been in operation for only two years during which its cash flow was negative. TSG was highly leveraged, operated in the high-risk fishing industry and had already begun to lose market share in the industry when SUNAT imposed its interim measures. In light of this, the Tribunal adopted Respondent's position that proper compensation should be based on TSG's adjusted book value, resulting in awarded compensation of US$786,306.24. The Tribunal rejected wholesale Claimant's request for moral damages. Relying on Lemire v. Ukrain (ICSID Case No. ARB/06/18), the Tribunal found that none of the conduct outlined in that case as justify moral damages (i.e. (i) physical harm or threat of harm to the investor, (ii) State action resulting in a deterioration of physical or mental health or 9 harm to reputation, and (iii) severe and substantial causes and effects of expropriation) existed here. Finally, the Tribunal also rejected Claimant's requested interest rate of 11%. This rate was based on the rates used by TSG for its financing, and thus incorporated a risk factor that the Tribunal determined was no longer applicable postexpropriation. Instead, the Tribunal adopted respondent's position that the appropriate interest rate should approximate the rate of return had the damages awarded been re-invested for a favorable return. The Tribunal therefore ruled that the interest rate on damages would be tied to the average monthly rate on 10-year U.S. treasury bonds. At the date of the Award, the interest awarded was US$227,201.30.

(d) Which party should bare the costs of arbitration?

The Tribunal observed the different perspectives of certain arbitral tribunals with respect to awards on costs, including the principle that the losing party pays (citing Methanex and EDF) and the more generally accepted public international law principle that costs should be borne equally by the parties, absent egregious conduct by one of the parties during the arbitration (citing Waste Management II). The Tribunal lauded the parties' conduct during the arbitration and concluded that it would not depart from the generally accepted practice of splitting costs equally between the parties.

III. Decision

SUNAT's imposition of interim measures constituted an indirect expropriation of Tza's investment. With respect to damages, the adjusted future cash flow of TSG was an inappropriate basis for compensation. Instead compensation was based upon the adjusted book value of TSG. Thus, Tza was awarded US$ 786,306.24 in compensation, plus interest (at U.S. Treasury Bond rates). No moral damages were awarded and costs were to be paid equally by each party.

【思考题】

1. 什么是间接征收?
2. 为什么仲裁庭认为 SUNAT 的审计不构成对谢业深投资的间接征收?
3. 仲裁庭裁定 SUNAT 的临时措施构成对谢业深投资的间接征收的主要理由是什么?

Case2·拓展阅读

VI

国际货币金融法

【内容摘要】

　　本章选取三个案例，案例一从劳动法的视角分析国际货币基金组织为实施其宗旨可以使用的工具，结合案例说明国际货币基金组织如何对各国产生影响；案例二探讨从 WTO 到 TPP 的金融服务监管范式转移，分析 TPP 有关金融服务监管的创新和变化；案例三分析雷曼公司跨国破产案，说明国际金融监管的复杂性。

Case1　The IMF's Approach to Labour Law in Practice

（Franz Christian Ebert, International financial institutions' approaches to labour law: The case of the International Monetary Fund, Adelle Blackett and Anne Trebilcock – 9781782549789, Downloaded from Elgar Online at 03/30/2017 08:11:34AM via University College London.）

【案情说明】

在国际组织中，国际金融组织引起的争议最多，尤其是国际货币基金组织（IMF）。虽然有人对国际货币组织的专业水平和高效表示赞赏，但是有些人则对其活动提出批评，认为基金组织的活动对各国主权进行了不当干涉，使全球贫困进一步恶化，沿用了殖民主义的模式。还有评论指出，由于基金组织存在偏好放松监管和市场自由化的趋势，导致其出台的政策方案对人权，尤其是社会经济权利带来负面影响。就劳动法而言，学者们对基金组织的政策方案展开了分析，指出其有时导致国内层面的劳动标准彻底解体。同时，基金组织与劳动法的关系似乎又存在复杂性。实际上，基金组织从一开始就明确表示支持国际劳工组织（ILO）的核心劳动标准，有时在自身开展的活动中提倡这些劳动标准和其他相关劳动标准。

基金组织通过开展运营活动，在实践中对劳动法采取了自己的方法，形成了自己的话语。利用各种工具实现其宗旨。结果，即便是不从基金组织获取资金援助的国家，也可能会在制定本国政策过程中受到基金组织的影响。基金组织的劳动话语就是明显的例证。基金组织的劳动话语存在自相矛盾之处，既提倡某种最低劳动标准，又主张国内劳动法"要灵活化"。重要的是，基金组织认为这两种方法都具有合理性，认为都有利于促进劳动者的利益。后者被认为旨在防止最恶劣的"劳动艰辛"，而前者则被视为是要促进创造就业，基金组织默示认为后者是劳动者的一项主要利益。实践中，虽然基金组织有时也提倡最低劳动标准，但是其作为放松监管者的角色要求减少干涉，通常对保护劳动者产生重大影响。结果，导致基金组织的劳动话语与其实践之间存在某些不一致。基金组织对劳动法的总体态度和上述不一致，至少可以依据基金组织工作人员对放松监管的偏好观念，在部分程度上得到解释。然而，基金组织的内部政治，尤其是来自主要股东的影响，与包括社会运动带来的外部压力一样，同样具有重要性，导致基金组织偏离自己政策方案的标准。最终，正是基金组织对这些外部压力的屈从，使其当前应对劳动法问题的方式存在可能的替代方案。

基金组织的劳动法话语存在含糊之处，使其政策方案与劳动者利益之间的矛盾得以化解。虽然这一方法有时使劳动法发生一些不大的有利变化，但其主要作用通常是广泛降低劳动标准。这种方法还导致话语与实践之间出现不一致，尤其是不断违反基金组织对国际劳工组织核心劳动标准的承诺。虽然基金组织对政治因素的屈从存在内部连贯性问题，但是也使其有机会对当前包括劳动法在内的政策进行变化。在基金组织活动相关政治和法律问责机制存在薄弱环节的情况下，这一点就显得更为重要。

【法律分析】

一、基金组织实现其宗旨可用的工具

基金组织的活动在历史上变动很大。虽然其早期活动的重点是工业化国家的收支平衡问题，但是基金组织随后将重心转移到发展中国家，其政策目标也不断从经济增长向减少贫困和创造就业发展。同时，其活动范围也迅速扩大，不仅涵盖"良好治理"问题，还涵盖更加广泛的经济和社会政策。

基金组织开展活动要采用各种不同的工具，最重要的是其资金援助贷款，这些贷款在期限、支付方式和准入要求上各不相同。而且，对"低收入国家"和"中—高收入国家"有不同的贷款要求。前者获得贷款享受特许条款，后者不享受特许条款，而适用市场化的利率。基金组织的资金援助项目在成员国提出请求后启动，随后基金组织工作人员对请求展开评估。接着，相关国家向基金组织提交一份"意向书"，必要时，意向书附带一份"有关经济和金融政策的备忘录"及其他技术文件。这些文件详细说明请求国作为获取资金援助前提条件而承诺履行的各项政策（即"前置条件"），前置条件有时涉及广泛的政策改革计划。实践中，这些文件在大多数情况下由基金组织工作人员起草。最后授予资金援助的决定，由基金组织执行董事会做出。贷款发放通常分不同档次进行，并要就确定的条件展开履约审查。发展中国家还要准备一份"消减贫困战略文件"，就其总体发展战略展开说明。

除资金援助之外，基金组织还影响成员国的政策。其主要手段是双边监督，尤其是基金组织第4条规定的磋商。磋商的主要目的，是通报基金组织执行董事会内部就汇率和宏观经济政策对国家层面的发展展开的讨论。然而，基金组织也使用这种磋商对成员国的公共政策提出建议。通常的磋商程序，涉及基金组织工作人员根据国家的任务起草报告，随后提交基金组织执行董事会讨论。工作人员报告不与直接的经济成果挂钩。然而，报告却会给相关国家施压，因为除其他主体外，该国的潜在投资者很可能会考虑这些报告。最后，基金组织还开展各种技术援助活动，尤其是要促进基金组织资金援助项目所要求的各项政策的实施。

二、基金组织的劳动法话语

基金组织的劳动法相关话语含有歧义。在基金组织最近的政策文件中，其基本立场是，各国应当"避免过度监管或极端无视劳动条件的'悬崖'"。建立在这种较为宽泛的表述基础之上，基金组织政策框架中的劳动法具有双面作用：首先，作为劳动市场灵活性的一种潜在障碍，阻碍经济增长和就业；其次，作为避免劳动者艰辛的一种工具。

（一）劳动法是经济增长和就业的障碍

这一点与基金组织应用于其劳动法相关政策的经济逻辑密切相关。劳动法需要两种灵活性。"微观灵活性"指劳动者能够跨公司、跨行业"进行重新分配"。"宏观灵活性"则涉及劳动成本和经济适应震荡的能力，主要受集体劳动合同和最低工资法的影响。因此，在授权集体谈判以设定最低基本工资标准的同时，基金组织赞同使用公司级的劳动合同安排。

就此而言，关键看基金组织如何使其政策方案合法化。有学者证明，基金组织和世界银行就各项人权采取的话语方式，对其经济政策提供支持。其做法是，将这些人权界定为市场而不是市场反作用的结果，使这些权利遵从市场逻辑。在劳动法领域，也明显存在类型的趋势。为了使其政策方案合法化，基金组织不仅提及宏观经济目标，还提及其所描述的劳动者利益。尤其是基金组织强调促进劳动者就业的重要性，而不是其雇用和工作条件。按照这一逻辑，劳动者在经济增长中获得利益，经济增长是创造工作机会的前提条件。因此，按照上述规定，放松劳动法监管也会释放利益。

基金组织认为，并不是要通过解聘保护法来保护"工作"，而是要通过失业救济来保护劳动者。这一话语的含义是，解聘保护法无法真正保护劳动者的利益。虽然基金组织实质上主张降低劳动标准避免解聘，而且事实上相关国家也不一定能够提供充足的失业救济，但是基金组织视失业救济是劳动者真正利益的保护者。同样，基金组织主张避免"双重就业保护"，即避免对临时工而不是固定劳动者给予较低就业保护。这里，基金组织将自身描绘成最弱势劳动者的保护者。同时，这一理念的主要目标似乎是彻底放松对就业保护立法的监管。

（二）劳动法是劳动者的一种最低保护工具

同时，基金组织工作人员要遵守指示，确保做出的政策能充分保护劳动者。这一点明显体现在基金组织对"包容性增长"目标的认同，既包括生产性就业，又包括机会的平等，在某种程度上，还包括结果的平等。明显的例子是基金组织对最低工资的立场，认为最低工资能够"降低收入的不平等"，成为避免剥削的底线。这里，劳动法被视为一种工具，可以减少经济制度的某些有害后果，其中包括基金组织宏观政策方案的后果。这就使基金组织的宏观经济政策具有一副"人文面孔"，既能化解认为基金组织的政策方案与劳动法不相容的争论，使基金组织较少受到指责，也能化解认为其对劳动者的利益漠不关心的争论。

然而，似乎较为明确的是，基金组织认为，劳动法提供的"充分保护"应限于最低标准，且主要关注"最弱势的劳动者"。因此，基金组织倾向于最低工资立法而不是集体劳动合同。而且，即便是对弱势劳动者的保护，基金组织似乎也是偏好社保领域的政策而不是劳动法工具。例如，就最低工资而言，基金组织并不赞同高标准，而是偏好通过将最低工资与社保领域结合在一起，进行二次分配。同样，基金组织的文件近来很少提及核心劳动标准，仅涉及工作场所男女平等问题。总体而言，各种情况表明，基金组织认为劳动法在保护劳动者免受社会艰苦方面仅发挥着有限作用。

【英文原文摘选】

4. THE IMF'S APPROACH TO LABOUR LAW IN PRACTICE

(a) The IMF as a Sporadic Promoter and Frequent Deregulator of Labour Law

The role of labour law-related aspects in the IMF's policy prescriptions has been subject to a considerable evolution. Since the late 1980s such conditions have become gradually more present in IMF conditionality. Similarly, in the IMF's surveillance independent of conditionality, labour law-related issues have become widespread.

Occasionally, the IMF has acted as a promoter of labour law. Especially during the late 1990s and early 2000s the IMF informally used its influence to bring about improvements of labour standards. An emblematic case is Indonesia which was at that time heavily struck by the Asian financial crisis. Here, the IMF political and economic leverage appears to have been instrumental for encouraging the ratification of five International Labour Organization (ILO) fundamental Conventions that the country had not yet ratified, starting with ILO Convention No. 87 on Freedom of Association and the Right to Organise. Furthermore, the IMF played an important role in obtaining the release of an imprisoned Indonesian trade union leader and reportedly reinforced the ILO's efforts to push for reform of the domestic laws on freedom of association and collective labour relations. Similarly, the IMF appears to have discussed matters relating to core labour standards with the Mexican Government on an informal basis during the negotiations of a financial arrangement in 1999. However, in recent years the prevalent area where the IMF has supported a strengthening of labour law has related to areas such as private sector minimum wage legislation. This has mainly concerned countries where the minimum wage had been very low in the first place.

Yet overall, the prevalent tendency of the IMF's activities has been a deregulatory one. According to Anner and Caraway, out of the Letters of Intent addressed to the IMF between 1998 and 2005, almost a third included commitments to render the labour market more "flexible." In other cases, deregulatory labour law reforms were not expressly made part of the programme's conditionality but were pushed through formal or informal political channels. The IMF's policy prescriptions have sometimes led to sweeping reforms of domestic labour law, significantly reducing the level of protection. An emblematic case is that of Argentina, which was subject to a severe structural adjustment programme set up by the IMF during the country's economic crisis starting in the late 1990s. This involved changes to individual labour law, e.g. an extension of the probation period, and collective labour law, including the introduction of the primacy of firm-level agreements over sectoral agreements.

Also, a number of recent IMF programmes concerning developing countries have included conditions related to labour law. For example, in the cases of Niger and the Kyrgyz Republic the conditions of the respective IMF programmes required the governments to undertake measures in order to increase 'labour market flexibility.' In Indonesia the IMF pushed the government to reduce labour law protection, including by reducing severance pay and facilitating the outsourcing of workers – only a few years after promoting the ILO's core labour standards in this country. Far-reaching labour law reforms have also recently been prescribed by the IMF together with the European Commission and the European Central Bank (the so-called 'Troika') to a number of EU member states. The most prominent example in this regard is Greece. Here, conditionality included significant restrictions of the temporal scope and effects of collective agreements, a freeze of automatic salary increases, and an imposed reduction of the minimum wage provided for by the national collective agreement. Similarly far-reaching were the reforms imposed by the programme regarding Portugal, including a reduction in statutory severance pay, a restriction on the possibility to increase the minimum wage, and several legislative measures to decentralize the collective bargaining system.

Finally, in some cases the IMF has promoted minor improvements of labour standards while demanding deregulatory labour law reforms on other fronts. This approach was, for instance, part of the IMF's adjustment programme for Mexico in the 1990s which involved a minimum wage increase while at the same time demanding the decentralization of collective labour relations. A more recent example is Djibouti, where the IMF supported deregulation of dismissal requirements but at the same time backed a moderate increase in the minimum wage in the public sector.

Importantly, the IMF does not systematically assess the effects of its policy prescriptions on workers. There is thus no systematic approach in place that could avoid 'hardship' for workers even though empirical research suggests that the IMF's structural adjustment programmes are correlated with a decline in workers' protection.

(b) Inconsistencies Between the IMF's Discourse on Labour Law and the Practice

(i) The link between the IMF's policy prescriptions and the objectives of growth and employment creation

In spite of the strong emphasis on the link between policy prescriptions providing for the deregulation of labour law and employment creation, in practice such a link cannot always be discerned. Indeed, in some cases the IMF has called for deregulating domestic labour law even though there was no evidence that this would foster the objective of employment creation. One example is the IMF's 2005 Article IV Report on South Africa. While the Report recommended deregulating the country's labour market to facilitate employment creation, its empirical part stated that 'other factors [than employment], not captured in this study, may also be playing an important role in keeping unemployment high in South Africa.' The use of labour law reform in terms of fostering employment creation was thus rather doubtful in this case. Similarly, the 2011 Article IV Report on Italy recommended a further deregulation of labour law even though that very Report had found in its empirical part that the earlier 'partial liberalization in the labor market may [actually] have undermined investment in human capital and innovation.' This made it seem unlikely that the proposed additional labour law reforms would lead to any positive results regarding growth and employment.

Conversely, it appears that the IMF has sometimes refrained from imposing its standard policy prescriptions even where this would have been clearly in line with its discourse. For example, in the late 1990s the IMF refrained from requiring South Korea to lower its statutory requirements regarding severance pay even though this was likely to hamper the adjustment programme envisioned by the IMF.

(ii) The IMF's compliance with its commitment to the ILO's core labour standards

The ambivalence within the IMF's activities relating to labour law is perhaps most striking when it comes to the core labour standards. Despite its commitment to these standards only one year after their adoption by the ILO, it appears that the IMF has repeatedly included conditions in its programmes that have driven the countries concerned into breaching these standards. This is particularly the case for workers' freedom of association and the right to collective bargaining. A well-publicised case in this regard has, again, been the case of Greece. Here, the ILO Committee on Freedom of Association found the labour law reforms imposed by the IMF and the other members of the 'Troika' to be in breach of the relevant principles in various respects.

Another illustrative case is that of Romania. In 2011, the Romanian Government had carried out a comprehensive labour law reform, which included lowering the restrictions on temporary employment and working time, extending probationary periods and decentralizing the collective bargaining system. IMF staff commented positively on these reforms, and it has been claimed that many – if not all – elements of the reform, had been asked for by the IMF. At the same time, the reform triggered doubts regarding its compatibility with ILO Convention No. 98. In 2011 and 2012, the ILO Committee of Experts identified several breaches in this regard and requested the government to remedy the situation. When the Romanian Government took action to bring the domestic labour law in line with the Convention, the IMF officially endorsed these steps. Yet, the unofficial position of the IMF appeared much less supportive of the ILO standards. A confidential note issued by the IMF and the European Commission contained propositions that were hardly compatible with ILO law. In particular, the note considered it 'critical to ensure compliance with the [IMF and EU financial assistance] programme' that elements relating to wages were excluded from collective bargaining at the national level. The note also recommended restricting the statutory protection against anti-union discrimination of 'elected and appointed [workers'] representatives […] to an appropriate number and timeframe.' These recommendations are in direct contradiction with ILO Conventions No. 87 and No. 98 and relevant principles as construed by the ILO's supervisory bodies. While an agreement ensuring the compatibility of the Romanian legislation with ILO standards was eventually reached, this case exemplifies the gap between the IMF's formal and factual commitment to the ILO's core labour standards.

5. THE ROLE OF IDEOLOGICAL BIAS, INTERNAL POLITICS AND EXTERNAL PRESSURE

This section looks at some of the factors determining the IMF's decision-making regarding labour law matters. A key issue in this regard concerns the sources used by the IMF as inputs regarding labour law. The IMF has repeatedly pointed to its lack of expertise in labour law issues and has declared its intention to fill this gap by drawing on the expertise of specialized international organizations, notably the World Bank and the ILO. Indeed, the IMF has engaged in some cooperation with the ILO, including by according the ILO observer status in the IMF Interim Committee in the 1990s and by carrying out pilot projects aiming to strengthen collaboration with the ILO at the country level.

Still, in the IMF's day-to-day work, ILO sources on labour standards have been used scarcely despite the fact that the ILO is generally considered the main international authority on labour law issues. Instead, just as at the level of discourse, World Bank resources have been the IMF's main reference point. This does not seem to be by accident given that the World Bank's approach regarding labour law is very similar to that of the IMF in terms of its deregulatory thrust. An illustrative case is the Doing Business Report's Index on 'Employing Workers', a World Bank flagship publication which used to rank national labour legislation according to the degree of 'flexibility' they provide to companies. The IMF has drawn on the Index's findings in its Article IV Reports and financial assistance programmes, usually reiterating its statements without any critical discussion. This is despite the fact that the Index had been heavily criticized for its methodological flaws, factual inaccuracies and doubtful theoretical assumptions with a strong anti-labour law bias. Although the World Bank stopped using the Index in 2009, the IMF has on some occasions continued to rely on it even after this date. This in combination with the IMF's refusal to engage with the relevant ILO documents illustrates the IMF staff's bias towards deregulation, going against both external evidence and its members' obligations under international law. This bias may, to some extent, also account for the aforesaid inconsistencies. One reason for this bias may lie in the dominance of conservative macroeconomic thinking within the IMF's staff whose members are recruited mainly from a narrow pool of Anglo-American economics faculties. As the IMF's internal evaluation body has highlighted, this has furthered 'groupthink' and other cognitive biases as a result of which policy issues are only examined under one paradigm whose basic assumptions are not questioned.

The IMF's policy decisions regarding labour law can, however, not be understood without considering certain additional factors. This concerns, first of all, factors relating to internal politics and in particular to the IMF's major shareholders. Research suggests that the interests of these shareholders, notably the United States, influence the level of intrusiveness of the conditions that are integrated into the IMF's programmes as well as the degree to which these conditions are actually enforced. While the influence of the major shareholders has often tended to reinforce the deregulatory thrust of the IMF's policy prescriptions, these dynamics have sometimes also worked in favour of labour standards. In particular, the main driver behind the IMF's interventions in favour of core labour standards at the end of the 1990s was the US Government, whose Executive Director repeatedly raised labour standards issues in the discussions within the Executive Board. Conversely, the fact that the US administration largely stopped putting labour issues on the IMF's agenda in the 2000s may explain, at least in part, why the IMF's efforts to promote the ILO's core labour standards have been reduced to close to zero in recent years.

Furthermore, while the IMF has tried to shield itself against external influences, it has reacted to and has been influenced by external actors, including social movements from the Global South. Research suggests that labour law-related conditionality is less prevalent where trade unions are politically influential than in countries where trade unions are weak. The IMF appears thus to be more sensitive to political pressure by domestic labour organizations than is often believed. Where opposition by labour and other organizations is sufficiently strong to put the programme's implementation in danger, some room for negotiations exists. In these cases, the IMF is likely to make concessions on the labour front in order to reduce the resistance to and ensure the success of the overall programme.

【思考题】

1. 国际货币基金组织为实现自己的宗旨有哪些可以使用的工具?
2. 国际货币基金组织的劳动法话语与其实践之间存在哪些不一致之处?

Case1·拓展阅读

Case2　Shifting Paradigm of WTO Financial Service Supervision

【案例说明】

金融服务在过去一段时间内被国际贸易谈判者和多边贸易体系视为二级主题，基本上被忽视。然而自 2008 年全球金融危机后，在国际经济法成为更加广泛讨论的领域以来，其重要性一直在稳步攀升。金融业最先通过 WTO《服务贸易总协定》及随附的《金融服务附件》进行国际监管，然而为了进一步开放并制定金融业标准和规则，仍然留有很多工作要做。TPP 文本有能力发挥重要作用，实现金融业市场准入自由化，并为金融业在全球层面的发展制定新的标准和准则。金融服务既是贸易问题也是投资问题，然而谈判者通常将这一问题纳入贸易"领地"，不承认其作为投资问题的重要地位。相反，TPP 的谈判者则遵守现代趋势，通过将其同时作为贸易与投资问题对待，增加了问题的连贯性，恰当地将金融服务市场设定为主要的投资场所。TPP 似乎已经成为国际经济法领域主要的新玩家，因此，通过强调金融服务可以按投资形式进行推广的理念有助于促进金融服务自由化。

通过分析可以得出以下几个结论。首先，TPP 有关金融服务的规定可以作为一种模式，未来用于双边和地区协议，最终用于多边论坛。《服务贸易总协定》的《金融服务附件》在金融服务自由化上迈出了最初的一大步，但是却存在许多局限性。尤其是《服务贸易总协定》实质上强调的是一般贸易自由化，虽然包含有一个简单的金融服务附件，但是停滞不前的多哈回合贸易谈判未能大幅度推进或增加现有贸易框架的内容。

相反，TPP 文本重申《服务贸易总协定》在市场准入上所做的努力，同时更倾力于打造系列金融服务自由化规则，其所坚持的理念是金融服务代表一种主要的跨境投资来源，故此也应当作为投资对待。这一投资导向的政策和策略，明显属于国际投资协定的范围。然而，这一议题在世界贸易组织中仅具有边缘性，属于《服务贸易总协定》中的第三种服务模式。此外，TPP 将金融服务单列一章，显示了金融服务业的重要性。纳入投资者—国家争端解决（ISDS）机制，使《TPP 协定》面临了许多挑战。不过，同传统的投资协定相比，在金融服务上对这种争端解决方法进行了大的变动，因为就金融服务采用了特定的系列规则，以化解国际投资界当前面临的各种合法性问题。其方法表现为这些规则要么采取对金融监管问题进行仲裁监督的方式，要么采取审慎例外条款的方式。

经审查可以发现，TPP 文本与《服务贸易总协定》不完整的金融服务标准存在差别，但是作为一种创新，其作用不应过分夸大。实际上，文本本身并不代表其最先偏离《服务贸易总协定》，在超越现有多边金融服务规则上，其只不过是遵循现代协定的趋势而已。因此，使这些现有规则显得越来越过时。《服务贸易总协定》签订之后起草的大量国际投资协定对金融服务做出了详细规定；除某些创新之外，TPP 的条款事实上与美国设定的现有标准非常一致。因此可以说，TPP 在许多方面凝结着美国《自由贸易协定》的做法，尤其是在金融服务投资上。美国达成的大多数安排，包括《北美自由贸易协定》，有特定的章节关于金融服务的规定，也有一章有关投资的规定，同 TPP 一样，都包含有一种特定的争端解决制度。这种审慎例外条款允许合作伙伴国政府采取审慎措施以维持金融稳定，且承认审慎性措施。而且，美国几乎所有国际投资协定在包含特定的适用于金融服务相关争议的国家—国家解决机制的同时，也允许将投资争议提交给投资者—国家争端解决机制 (ISDS)。

最后，虽然 TPP 中"金融服务"一章的规定似乎在若干事项上凝结着美国的做法，但《协定》本身有能力做出不同规定。与 WTO 无法跟上时代变化且无法设定新规则为新的贸易方向奠定基础不同，TPP 条文设立了新的系列规则，供十二个合作伙伴国家采纳，包括主要的市场主体和重要的全球经济体，而且可以在未来被不决定终止谈判的国家视为范本。目前，国际投资协定中的金融监管国家做法都存在碎片化和不一致之处。因此可以认为，TPP 这样的自由贸易协定越来越有价值，不仅可以在未来建立统一的金融服务自由化和监管模式，而且还在将来向外国投资者开放金融服务。就此而言，贸易与投资之间的界限将越来越模糊。

【案例分析】

众所周知，WTO 多哈回合贸易谈判近十五年来已经停滞不前，主要原因是具有决定性的农业经济问题，带着这一问题，所有人都希望 WTO 重现生机，进一步进行多边自由化。在这种情况下，与电子商务、竞争或投资等问题有关的贸易自由化及标准和规则制定，越来越采取双边和地区贸易协定的形式。

虽然大多数自由贸易协定最初是以双边方式或在区域市场范围内展开谈判的，但最近的趋势体现为在大的国家集团之间进行，即所谓的"元—区域"谈判。TPP 是已经签订的首份元—区域协定，有美国作为成员，该协定有能力发挥重要作用。

在某些方面，将金融服务作为综合自由贸易协定的组成部分展开谈判有其特定的意义。虽然 TPP 有关"金融服务"的第 11 章明显是涉及贸易与投资问题最重要的一章，但是有关"投资"的第 9 章和有关"服务贸易"的第 10 章也相当重要。

首先，TPP 有助于促进金融服务提供者进入外国市场，同《服务贸易总协定》确定的现行多边标准相比，TPP 做出了改进。其次，TPP 强调的理念是，金融服务越来越被视为是外国服务提供者和投资者发展的关键机会。因此，需要考察政策演化问题、向投资者和国家提供改进的争议解决机制的可能性以及包含各种重要的保障措施。最后，需要对 TPP 确定的"金融服务是投资场所"之标准与美国和非美国自由贸易协定等确定的标准进行对比。

【英文原文摘选】

TPP Promoting Financial Services as an Investment Playground: Crystalizing a Change in Approach from GATS?[1]

1 A More Comprehensive Framework for Financial Services

Market access for financial services was an important aspect of trade in services liberalization and a key element of TPP. The TPP Agreement, however, significantly differed from multilateral standard provided in the GATS' Annex on Financial Services, particularly in terms of the approach followed by the drafters.

To begin with, the GATS provides for general transparency and market access commitments as part of its general trade in services provisions. However, the issue of financial services has only been considered by means of the Agreement's Annex on Financial Services—which was designed and crafted too narrowly to allow for specific provisions on market access in relation to financial services—while the key negotiating objectives for financial services identified in the context of the 2005 Hong Kong Ministerial Conference have thus far been left unsolved. Likewise, GATS negotiations have not made the expected progress on discriminatory issues relating to quotas and the economic needs tests (which, as already mentioned, consist of placing duties upon the

---

1 Antoine P. Martin and Bryan Mercurio, TPP Promoting Financial Services as an Investment Playground: Crystalizing a Change in Approach from GATS? J. Chaisse et al. (eds.), Paradigm Shift in International Economic Law Rule-Making, Economics, Law, and Institutions in Asia Pacific, https://doi.org/10.1007/978-981-10-6731-0_13.

entry of new foreign products on a domestic market). Nor have the negotiations brought increased transparency in the legal and policymaking process through involving financial actors into the legislative procedures.

While the Annex clearly serves as an extension of the GATS to the financial services sector in that it provides for a specific framework which 'applies [the general GATS standards] to measures affecting the supply of financial services', it offers little detail as to how that specific framework shall operate. Instead, the Annex merely provides a general context through its large scope of application as well as definitions, guarantees that some exceptions can be allowed for 'prudential reasons... to ensure the integrity and stability of the financial system' and mandate that in disputes arising from such situations specific panels 'shall have the necessary expertise relevant to the specific financial service under dispute'. Apart from these, the Annex does not deliver substantial liberalization standards to the financial services industry with, as those provided through the general GATS instrument would typically apply.

The approach to financial services followed by the GATS drafters can be explained by the fact that financial services were never a negotiating priority in the Uruguay Round (which created the WTO and along with it the GATS). Given the complexity of the financial services sector, trade negotiators in the Uruguay Round were supported by officials from the various treasury departments who however had different views on the issues so that negotiations lingered for two years beyond the conclusion of the GATS and never played a big role in the multilateral trading system. Even the global financial crisis did not cause the Doha Round negotiators to prioritise, or even re-think, the issue. Instead, market access and subsidy issues involving agriculture remained at the centre of the multilateral negotiations under the WTO. As the difficulties with the Round continued to grow, easier small subsectors such as trade facilitation became the focus as any agreement, no matter how small, provided moral victories to the WTO and were viewed as possible impetuses to agreement on larger and more important issue. Alas, the Round has virtually died and with it the hopes of a comprehensive multilateral package for at least the short and medium term.

Often considered as a developed country issue by many in the developing world, the liberalization of the financial services sector was therefore addressed more comprehensively as part of FTA negotiations. There, the aim is clear—providing for market access opportunities while refining the prevailing standards. The TPP, in essence, is the latest and largest agreement to do so and, in contrast with the GATS, provides for more complete approach which grants specifically formulated market access opportunities to domestic financial services markets for foreign financial services providers.

Of course, similarities can be found from one agreement to the other. As in GATS, in particular, market access provisions in the TPP ensured that members could not place limitations on the number of foreign financial institutions willing to engage in local trade in financial services, could not impose quotas on the total value of financial service transactions or on the number of operations and outputs realized by foreign TPP entities, could not rely on the so-called economic needs test (ENT) which has traditionally imposed licensing procedures on foreign entities prior to the entry of a new foreign product on a domestic market and could not restrict the number of employees and the legal form of service suppliers. Moreover, and also as in GATS, the TPP text provided for regulatory transparency obligations which however have been specifically tailored for trade in financial services.

In contrast with the GATS and its Annex, however, the TPP's Chapter on Financial Services has been specifically drafted to make cross-border trade in financial services easy for all providers and provide these with specifically drafted and comprehensive rules on the matter. Relying on the core principle of National Treatment, the TPP text ensured that the parties allowed their counterparts' financial services suppliers access to domestic markets, and that their nationals—together with the persons located in their territories—were given the opportunity to purchase services originating from other TPP countries without being discriminated against. On the same grounds, the Agreement also promoted innovation in financial services as the parties committed to allow the introduction on domestic markets of new financial services and products that domestic suppliers would have been entitled to provide on domestic markets.

Furthermore, the TPP ensured that foreign financial actors could enjoy 'access to payment and clearing systems operated by public entities, and to official funding and refinancing facilities available in the normal course of ordinary business'. In addition, each party 'commit[ted] to promote regulatory transparency in financial services' and ensures that public participation amongst industry professionals is allowed for greater efficiency.

In terms of structural arrangements, last but not least, TPP would have also created a Committee on Financial Services with the mandate to supervise the implementation and further improvement of the Chapter provisions, consider issues regarding financial services that are referred to it by a Party and participate in the dispute settlement procedures as provided under the Investment Disputes in Financial Services provision (see below). The Agreement also provided parties with a 'consultation' mechanism to be used as a pre-dispute settlement tool in case interfering measures were to be identified.

All in all, therefore, the TPP provided a more comprehensive framework on the liberalization of financial services than that provided through the GATS Annex on Financial Services. There were, of course, some similarities in content as well as provisions which seemed to go further than under GATS. More significant, however, was perhaps the change in approach: while financial services under the GATS were merely considered a side topic relegated into an Annex, financial services have been considered by the TPP negotiators as an intrinsic part of the agreement which deserved a specific Chapter and thus would have benefited from tailor-drafted provisions aimed at building a dedicated liberalization framework.

2 Promoting Investment in Financial Services

Another significant feature of the TPP Chapter on Financial Services was the incorporation and reiteration of the various investment principles as applied in international investment law, and in line with the current standards and norms often incorporated into bilateral investment treaties (BITs) also referred to as International Investment Agreement (IIAs).

2.1 Policy Evolution

Various common standards of international investment law have been included into the TPP text, both as part of Chapter 9 on Investment and as part of Chapter 11 on Financial Services.

Chapter 9, on the one hand, would have provided the general investment framework under the TPP, including all of the core standards of protection enshrined under international investment law and systematically brought forward in BITs/IIAs: National Treatment (aimed at ensuring no discrimination between domestic and foreign investors), Most-Favoured-Nation (no discrimination between investors originating from different foreign countries), Minimum Standard of Treatment (including fair and equitable treatment (FET) and full protection and security under customary international law), not to forget expropriation and compensation permitting expropriation made for public purposes, in a non-discriminatory manner following a due process of law, and as long as prompt and adequate compensation is paid to the investor (as part of the established Hull formula); and the right of investors to repatriate profits. Chapter 11 on Financial Services, on the other hand, would have ensured that such investment standards and rules—i.e. National Treatment, MFN or Market Access—applied to measures adopted or maintained towards (a) financial institutions of another Party; (b) investors of another Party, and investments of those investors, in financial institutions in the Party's territory; and (c) cross-border trade in financial services.

The introduction of all of the common and core standards of investment law into the TPP was not unexpected given modern trends, but is worth noting because it points at a policy evolution which suggests that financial services are increasingly being developed and viewed as investments falling under the current foreign investment rules. Unsurprisingly, the standards included in the TPP are largely found in many other IIAs (and in the US Model BIT) but the TPP would have gone one step further in ensuring that principles such as the NT, MFN and the right of investors to repatriate profits were protected by placing them in both Chapters 9 and 11 of TPP.

Moreover, it is worth highlighting just how far provisions included in the TPP have advanced beyond the multilateral standard of the GATS. For example, the GATS' Annex on Financial Services and the related 'Understanding on Commitments in Financial Services' aim to facilitate the Commercial Presence of foreign service providers into the territory of any other Member (Mode 3) but do not provide for specific investment provisions and thus do not consider the possibility of treating financial services as a foreign investment. In addition, the TPP's investment standards would have been significantly more comprehensive than the standards included in GATS: MFN in the GATS has for instance being described as a 'general obligation' and NT as a 'specific commitment' but the GATS does not provide any provisions relating to a minimum standard of treatment, expropriation or compensation because it was never about setting investment rules but about facilitating trade in services. The protections for commercial presence (Mode 3), all in all, are therefore akin to investment protections but much shallower, less extensive, and lacking in direct enforcement to the benefit of the investor since only state to state dispute settlement methods provided under Article XXIII of the GATS would apply.

This means that although the TPP's provisions on investment were not revolutionary—since they largely repeated the US model and have been included in many recent IIAs—the agreement nonetheless would have constituted an advance on the multilateral standard in placing financial services as a self-standing playground for foreign investment whereas the GATS only considers financial services through an Annex which can be described as thin and lacking in detail. As mentioned previously, the Annex on Financial Services was finalised as a post-GATS political compromise which falls well short of TPP Chapter 11 in terms of both content and standards. Rather importantly, the mega-regional nature of the TPP, combined with the reality that for the largest economy and driver of the TPP, the US, there is for the most part little economic value in the agreement, suggests that the agreement is crystalizing US practice on the matter—that is, establishing financial services as a foreign investment and significantly departing from the multilateral rules on financial services, as an exercise in rulemaking and standard setting.

2.2 Evolutions on Dispute Settlement: Greater Investor Protection with Safeguards

As a reminder, dispute settlement in the WTO and therefore under the GATS Agreement and its Annex on Financial Services, is state-to-state, meaning that it is for governments to file and prosecute claims against the host government allegedly taking measures in contradiction with its obligations under the WTO covered agreements. In case of a dispute involving financial services, the parties would thus rely on an ad hoc panel of three individuals composed of financial services specialists from neutral countries but the affected companies would not be directly involved and would not stand to directly benefit in the form of say, monetary damages. The goal of dispute settlement, in such circumstances, is rather to ensure that Member States comply with their financial services obligations; that is, to return the equilibrium to the point where the expectations of the WTO "bargain" is restored between the Members. Dispute settlement in the WTO does not seek to punish offending Members or reward successful litigants. In most cases, compliance occurs through a modification or repeal of the offending measure(s) at issue. But as a general rule state to state disputes mechanisms would tend to make the decision to initiate a dispute a geopolitical decision, can be slow to deliver a decision and ultimately do not directly reimburse the private actor for damages.

As nearly all the IIAs negotiated by the US, the TPP was equipped with a much more comprehensive dispute settlement mechanism available to investors and borrowed in part from the specific investor-state dispute settlement (ISDS) provisions considered a key feature of bilateral agreements on investment promotion and protection. Such arbitral proceedings are aimed at insulating disputes involving foreign investors from the jurisdiction of host state courts, which may be influenced by domestic public interests and which will simply abide by domestic laws which in most cases tend to be at the heart of the relevant dispute. If successful, investors can receive monetary damages for the breach, but cannot force the respondent host state to amend or modify the law in question. Still, because such a direct remedy to investors is not available in the multilateral trade regime, the ISDS system has been rather well perceived by foreign investors which tend to see it as a reliable way to obtain justice without facing political pressure from home and host states alike.

The system of ISDS has produced legal standards over time which, for better or worse, are the result of a mix between more than three thousand IIAs containing different (though fairly coherent) standards, but the ISDS has been questioned on various grounds, particularly because of the ability of privately-appointed arbitral tribunals to bypass domestic courts or for a lack of predictability. The criticisms seem overblown and not entirely based on actual evidence or facts, but in any case in order to avoid criticism the TPP Chapter on Financial Services was more comprehensive than other investment treaties as it was based on a mix between an investor-state arbitral tribunal and a GATS-type of state-to-state specialist panel.

Two options were available here. On the one hand, disputes could be brought independently by an investor or by a state. In such situations, ISDS would have applied to disputes directly initiated by investors against a host state party — meaning that an investor of one party would have been able to directly challenge and claim damages against a government of another party while a state party willing to challenge a counterpart's measure relating to the regulation or supervision of financial institutions, markets or instruments would have relied on the state-to-state dispute resolution mechanisms provided for in Chapter 28. As a means to limit the negative consequences of investor-state disputes related to financial services— as this was for instance the case in the early years 2000 when Argentina faced multiple claims following its questioned management of an economic crisis—on the other hand, the TPP provided a quasi-safeguard giving partner countries a broader degree of sovereignty, regulatory freedom and control of the ISDS process. More specifically, if the respondent raised an 'exception' (as specified in Article 11.11) for prudential measures on prudential grounds, proceedings would be subject to a special procedure authorizing the respondent and the party of the claimant, through a Joint Committee of the financial regulatory authorities of the concerned TPP parties, to issue a binding joint interpretation on the matter —meaning 'any decision or award issued by the tribunal must be consistent with [the parties] determination'.

Moreover, where the parties could not reach agreement and make a determination within 120 days, the respondent or the Party of the claimant was entitled to request the establishment of a panel under the state-to-state dispute settlement mechanism contained in Chapter 28 to consider whether and to what extent the Article 11.11 (Exceptions) was a valid defence to the claim. The panel would then issue a final report to be transmitted to and binding on the disputing Parties and to the tribunal. Alternatively, if neither party requested a panel to make a determination and issue a final report, the ISDS claim could proceed without inference or interference.

This special procedure is important because it suggests that in presenting financial services as a focus point for foreign investment, the TPP was seeking equilibrium between the preservation of a forum for state-to-state debate and the practicality of arbitral litigation so as to balance applicable commitments and systemic stability.

Yet again, in providing such an improved dispute settlement possibility the TPP significantly differed from existing multilateral dispute settlement standards, but remained very much in line with the US FTA practice on the matter. In doing so, it solidified the trend of allowing businesses and investors the means to obtain reparation for breaches of a treaty which are detrimental to their investments in the financial services sector, but at the same time crafted a special provision for disputes involving measures taken in good faith and for prudential reasons whereby the decision to recognize (or otherwise) the legitimacy of the exceptional nature of the measures could be removed from ISDS arbitral proceedings and determined by a Joint Committee composed of representatives from each party to the dispute.

2.3 Additional Safeguards

In addition to the dispute settlement safeguard outlined above, the TPP provided an additional layer of protection to the public authorities in a number of different ways.

For instance, the TPP Agreement provided for an improved form of 'Denial of Benefits' provision which is worth mentioning because it departs from both the multilateral and US practice on the matter. Simply stated, Denial of Benefits clauses have traditionally been used in investment and trade agreements as a means to limit the granting of treaty benefits to non-party entities. Notably, however, the drafting and scope of application of such clauses differs. Under the GATS, for instance, benefits are denied on a very narrow manner, in relation to services supplied from/in the territory of a non-Member whilst US IIA practice denies treaty benefits 'to investors of a non-party if the host does not maintain diplomatic relations with the non-Party' or when the investor does not have a substantial business activity in the targeted country. In other words, benefits cannot be denied to service providers originating from a WTO Member under GATS, whereas in US IIAs benefits are denied to investing service providers located in the jurisdiction of the partner country but originating from non-party countries in which the US (or other host country) does not maintain diplomatic relations. The TPP Agreement departed from this standard, simply denying benefits to service providers owned or controlled by a person of a non-party or denying party, and on the basis of a lack of substantial activities in the territory. In doing so, TPP provided the parties with a means to significantly reduce forum shopping but would have left out the overt political motive behind the US practice.

Another safeguard was that of Article 11.11 of TPP, mentioned in the previous section. Article 11.11 provided the parties with the possibility to suspend market opening efforts for prudential reasons. More specifically, the provision stated that a party 'may prevent or limit transfers by a financial institution or cross-border financial service supplier […] through the equitable, non-discriminatory and good faith application of measures relating to maintenance of the safety, soundness, integrity, or financial responsibility of financial institutions or cross-border financial service suppliers'. This type of provision is very much in line with US IIA practice and, perhaps more importantly, confirms to the GATS standard. While GATS allows Members to adopt or maintain restrictions on trade in services notwithstanding existing commitments in case of 'serious balance-of-payments and external financial difficulties or threat', the Agreement's Annex on Trade in Financial Services allows taking measures for 'prudential reasons', i.e. the taking of measures similarly prevailing on existing multilateral commitments 'for the protection of investors, depositors, policy holders or persons to whom a fiduciary duty is owed by a financial service supplier, or to ensure the integrity and stability'. While there are critics of such provisions, who state that the prudential carve-outs in GATS and IIAs do not go far enough, the provision should allow for temporary measures taken in times of (or anticipated) crisis in order to maintain the integrity and stability of the financial system.

2.4 Financial Services in Non-US IIAs

At this point, it finally seems appropriate to consider the TPP's positioning of financial services as a form of foreign investment by comparing it to the various efforts conducted in non-U.S bilateral and regional arrangements lest the reader believe that it is only the US which provides for financial services in their bilateral and regional agreements. Of course, a comprehensive review is beyond the scope of this Chapter. Instead, we review the practice of a few select jurisdictions.

We start by reviewing another major player, the European Union (EU). The EU practice on financial services is not quite as consistent as that of the US. This can particularly be seen in the two most recent EU IIAs, that with Singapore and Canada. For example, while the EU–Singapore FTA comprises a general investment chapter and a general chapter on trade in services, financial services are merely considered as a sub-section of the latter thus making financial services a matter of trade rather than investment. In contrast, the EU—Canada FTA provides a more comprehensive approach to financial services. As with the TPP and most US agreements, the investment provisions do not directly apply to disputes relating to financial services but are regulated by Chapter 15's TPP-type dispute settlement provisions specifically adapted to financial services. As in the TPP, a Financial Services Committee may be called upon to produce a binding joint determination as to whether a disputed prudential measure is legitimate.

Elsewhere, ASEAN agreements are very much segmented and far less comprehensive, especially in regards to financial services. For example, while the extremely broad ASEAN Framework Agreement on Services does not mention financial services at all, the ASEAN Comprehensive Investment Agreement (ACIA) includes the classic investment protection standards together with the common exceptions aimed at preserving the Members' balance of payments, public order and the ability to enforce regulations while also providing for ISDS. The Agreement, however, provides no particular mechanisms for financial services and financial stability-related disputes, which are presumably simply handled in the same manner as any other investment claim. In a similar manner, both the ASEAN–China Investment Agreement and the ASEAN–China Agreement on Trade in Services merely mention financial services and incorporate para 2 of the GATS Annex on Financial Services as the applicable standard, meaning in practice the agreements provide no additional cover for financial services as investments and simply repeat the GATS's provision allowing for prudential exceptions. Taking another regional example, the Agreement establishing the ASEAN–Australia New Zealand Free Trade Area considers financial Services as an Annex to its Chapter 8 on Trade in Services but again does not expressly place the financial services sector as a particular playground for investors.

As a final example, we look at Australia's practice on the matter, which also is fairly inconsistent. For instance, Australia's FTAs with Chile or Korea suggest that Australian negotiators have made efforts to place financial services as an attractive sector in terms of investment since, as with the TPP approach, the agreements provide distinct chapters on financial services which reiterate the National Treatment, MFN and Market Access standards and provide specific dispute settlement mechanisms for investment disputes related to financial services. However, while one could assume that this reveals the evolution in Australian practice, in fact it does not. To illustrate, the recent China-Australia Free Trade Agreement (ChAFTA), which entered into force on 20 December 2015, merely places financial services as an opportunity for trade. Indeed, although the agreement contains a specific chapter on investment, it only considers financial services into an Annex to the Trade in Services Chapter without mentioning investment standards.

【思考题】

1. WTO 与 TPP 的金融服务监管范式有何不同？
2. WTO 与 TPP 的争端解决机制有何不同？

Case2·拓展阅读

| Case3   The Bankruptcy of Lehman Brothers Holdings, Inc. |

【案情说明】

雷曼是数百个法律实体组成的金融帝国，在许多国家设有分支机构和子公司，客户和资产分布于全球各地。其规模加上金融业务的复杂使得破产处理难上加难，该案的复杂性和索赔数额也远远超过历史上任何其他破产案件。由于关系到各国债权人的巨大利益，雷曼破产案引起了全世界范围内的一场激烈争斗。[1]

雷曼申请破产保护的文件显示，该公司总债务为 6 130 亿美元。其中，前 10 大无担保债权分别以债券、银行贷款（同业拆借）和信用证三种形式存在，金额超出 1 570 亿美元。花旗集团、纽约梅隆银行、日本青空银行和瑞穗金融集团位列雷曼最大的无担保债权人之列。花旗集团持有雷曼约 1 380 亿美元的债券资产，巴黎银行对雷曼的贷款敞口达 2.5 亿美元。摩根大通拥有 230 亿美元雷曼担保债权，是其最大的担保债权人。我国也有不少银行持有雷曼债券。雷曼申请破产保护的消息传出时，其债券价格应声大跌，多数雷曼相关债券价值几乎为零，雷曼次级债和优先股已被连降 15 档至 C 等级，低于"可投资"等级 11 档。债权人遭受巨大损失。

【法律分析】

一、破产保护并不意味着立即倒闭清算

根据美国《破产法》第 11 章的规定，雷曼作为破产保护申请人拥有 120 天的保护期。在此期间，为充分发挥公司管理层的效率、实现债务人财产的价值最大化，适用"占有中的债务人"制度。即，雷曼可以继续营业，现有的董事会和管理层将继续留任，在法院和股东的监督下运营业务，公司的股票和债券还可在证券市场上买卖，同时进行资产和债务结构重整，调整经营策略。所有重大经营决策无须取得多数债权人的同意，但是必须得到破产法庭的批准。但债权人有权反对出售公司的资产，而且实际上也经常反对出售负债公司的资产。一般而言，除非市场上存有出价更高之买家，法官将倾向接受雷曼兄弟处分资产之判断和决定。

二、债权人索债进入自动冻结程序

雷曼申请破产保护，其实是向债权人启动了自动冻结的程序。该程序是美国《破产法》中最强有力的规定之一，其目的是：给债务人一个喘息的空间，让债务人找出一条

---

1 参见周慧.雷曼破产案之法律分析 [J].银行家，2009（1）：114-117.

重整或清算的途径；同时，阻止债权人蜂拥至法院哄抢债务人所剩的财产。

根据美国《破产法》第 362（a）条规定，破产保护申请一经提起，即构成对下列行为的冻结：1. 之前对债务人实施的任何行政或司法程序；2. 任何催讨、征收或实现破产保护申请前产生的债权的行为；3. 根据法院之前作出的付款判决、针对债务人或债务人的特定财产实施的任何强制执行行为；4. 任何旨在占有或者控制债务人全部财产或者部分财产的行为；5. 任何对产生于破产保护申请前的债务追加创设、完成或执行担保权的行为；6. 债权人将其在破产保护申请前对债务人的负债与其债权进行抵销的行为。但是自动冻结并不禁止法庭内的有关程序和行为，也不排除法院针对特定的情况发布其他相关的禁令。自动冻结程序对一切主体均有约束力，包括自然人、各类企业和政府机构。其启动不以债权人的知晓为前提，无论债权人是否知道或者应当知道破产保护申请的提出，对债务人财产的个别执行均被认为可撤销或者当然无效，效力延续至破产程序终结之时。

如果债权人欲向雷曼索债，则必须申请破产法庭解除自动冻结程序。一般而言，达此目的的只能是有担保的债权人。如果债权人能够向法庭证明担保物的价值正在大幅度减损，且债务人并未采取措施保护债权人的担保权益，法庭可解除自动冻结程序，准许债权人重新占有担保物。而无担保债权人因为没有需要保护的担保财产利益，很少能够获得免于自动冻结的救济。

三、金融衍生品合约豁免条款增大案件不确定性

美国《破产法》第 9 章对于涉及金融衍生品交易的"金融合约"特别给予安全港保护，将破产约定条款无效、自动冻结程序等制度豁免适用于金融合约，也就是说，美国破产法对金融合约网开一面。在公司破产期内，这些金融衍生品之间行使冲抵、终止或加速到期等权利的协议仍然有效。美国金融合约安全港的主体范围非常广泛，在衍生产品领域涵盖了所有合约相对方。法律设计的主要考虑是，金融合约，尤其是金融衍生品合约几乎是大型机构投资者和中介机构的专属领地，高金额、高杠杆、高风险，同一主体往往是多份合约的相对方，牵一发而动全身。此时，如因某个当事方的破产导致金融衍生品合约无法顺利履行，将会导致合约相对方受到冲击，进而影响相对方之相对方，造成多米诺骨牌效应，危及金融衍生产品市场乃至整个金融市场的稳定和安全。

事实上，远期、信贷违约互换和回购协议这样的衍生品合约恰恰是这次金融风暴漩涡的中心，把衍生品排除在自动冻结程序之外，实际上提高了金融体系的系统性风险。由于衍生品合约不受自动冻结程序的约束，即使在其他合约被冻结的情况下，衍生品合约持有人也可以取消与交易方的合约并拿回抵押品，从而导致金融系统中其他方面的债权人无法获得清偿。雷曼是互换市场的主要玩家之一，它的崩溃让其所提供的信用保险在一夜之间化为乌有，还触发了针对该公司数十亿美元信贷违约互换的巨额清算。雷曼所涉及的衍生品合约条款极大地增加了破产案件的不确定因素。人们纷纷终止同雷曼之

间的衍生品合约，都想赶紧先拿回自己的那一份。这使得我国债权人追踪调查雷曼兄弟资产的过程更加坎坷，并需要在破产案外另行追讨有关债务。

四、法院的选择

理论上，对于债权人而言，重整要比破产清算的损失少一些。按照经验，如果公司进入破产清算程序，最终债权人拿回 10% 的投资就已经算万幸了。而重整环境下，结果会乐观一些，但债权人想要拿回 50% 以上投资的概率一般也不高。

对美国而言，雷曼的重整比清算更为有利，公司可以继续经营，雇员不至于大规模失业，债权人受偿状况也可能因债务的重整而得到改善，因而美国破产法院也更倾向于重整。实际上，美国就打着"更好地保护债权人利益"的《破产法》大旗，通过法院的批准，按照本国利益诉求对雷曼不断做出新的安排：2008 年 9 月 20 日，在美国纽约南区破产法院批准的收购中，巴克莱银行吞下雷曼有限的部分北美业务以外，还收购了雷曼加拿大、雷曼乌拉圭、雷曼 Sudamerica 公司，以及雷曼旗下针对高净资产个人客户的"私人投资管理"业务；9 月 21 日，日本野村证券买下雷曼在亚洲的业务；9 月 23 日，野村证券收购了雷曼的欧洲业务；10 月 16 日，美国法院批准了对 Neuberger Berman 在内的雷曼兄弟投资管理部门的破产拍卖竞标程序。

其实，雷曼公司破产案裹挟着政治考量。虽然美联储和美国政府均无权要求私人公司提交破产申请，但是美联储官员却必须遵守美联储和政府的指令，采取变相手段强迫雷曼公司董事会就范。实际上，美联储官员采取的行动，导致雷曼公司在 9 月 15 日无法获得充足的现金开展经营，最后不得不提交破产申请，进入破产程序。

【英文原文摘选】[1]

On September 15, 2008, the day Lehman Brothers Holdings Inc. (LBHI) filed for bankruptcy, its affiliates had over 930,000 derivative contracts outstanding. On October 3, 2008, Lehman Brothers Special Financing Inc. (LBSF), Lehman's primary swap affiliate, filed for bankruptcy as well. The fate of these contracts illustrates the challenges facing those who work with derivatives. According to litigation filings, by January 5, 2009, Lehman's counterparties had elected to terminate 900,000 of these contracts. The reasons they chose to do so, and the reasons other parties chose not to terminate, provide useful lessons.

Derivatives, in particular swaps, are of central importance to structured finance. Interest rate swaps, the primary focus of this article, are essential to the creation of credit products. An interest-rate swap can be used to match the obligations of a special-purpose vehicle (SPV) with its assets, converting fixed-rate payments into floating-rate payments, floating-rate payments

---

1 Henry A. Barkhausen, Some Lessons from Lehman Brothers, The Journal of Structured Finance (2010 Winter).

into fixed-rate payments, or floating-rate payments referencing one index into floating-rate payments referencing another index.

All of Lehman's contracts were governed by the 1992 Master Agreement promulgated by the International Swaps and Derivatives Association (ISDA). The 1992 Master Agreement is a standard agreement, intended to be used as a model by the derivatives industry. ISDA has also promulgated a schedule to the Master Agreement, through which parties to a derivative contract can customize their particular transaction.

The bankruptcy of one party to a derivative contract constitutes an event of default under Section 5(a)(vii) of the 1992 Master Agreement. The Schedule allows parties to specify either automatic or optional termination. Optional termination gives the non-defaulting party the *option* to declare termination after an event of default. Automatic termination means that an event of default automatically results in termination. Termination requires that the parties exchange payments to settle and close the transaction. The Schedule allows the parties two choices regarding termination: 1) they can choose between the Market Quotation and Loss methods for calculating the payment amount, and 2) they can choose between the First and Second Method of payment.

The Market Quotation method attempts to establish the market value of the derivative contract at the time of default, whereas the Loss method allows the non-defaulting party to estimate its "loss" as a result of the termination. The choice between the First and Second Method dictates the direction of payment. Under the Second Method, money can flow in either direction: if the non-defaulting party is in-the-money, then the defaulting party is obligated to pay the non-defaulting party. If the non-defaulting party is out-of-the-money, then the non-defaulting party is obligated to pay the defaulting party. Under the First Method, money can only flow from the defaulting party to the non-defaulting party: if the non-defaulting party is out-of-the-money, it need not pay the defaulting party.

Provisions in contracts which specify that the bankruptcy of one party will trigger a default or termination of the contract are normally prohibited under U.S. bankruptcy law. Section 365(e)(1) of the Bankruptcy Code, applying to "executory contracts," forbids contractual clauses specifying bankruptcy as a trigger for termination or modification of the contract. "Executory contract" is a bankruptcy term of art referring to contracts where performance is still due from both sides—a category that includes swaps. Section 560 provides that swaps are excepted from the prohibition in Section 365(e)(1). Section 560 specifically references the contract clauses prohibited by Section 365(e)(1), saying that such clauses *may* be used by a "swap participant" to cause the "liquidation, termination, or acceleration" of the swap agreement. Swap parties are allowed to have bankruptcy as a default trigger, even though other types of contracting parties are not.

According to litigation filings, most of Lehman's swaps used the Market Quotation and Second methods. That is, upon termination, the non-defaulting party determined the market price of its contract and 1) if the non-defaulting party's side was out-of-the-money, it made a payment, or 2) if its side was in-the-money, it presented a bill for the payment due to it. A survey of litigation filings also reveals that Lehman's swap contracts featured optional rather than automatic termination. This combination of choices skewed the incentives of Lehman's counterparties, and explains why most of them terminated in fairly short order.

If an executory contract has not been terminated, Section 365(d)(2) allows the debtor to either "assume" or "reject" it. Assumption entails the debtor reaffirming all the contract terms and agreeing to be bound by them post-bankruptcy. Rejection entails the opposite, with the debtor disallowing both the benefits and obligations of the contract. Under a Chapter 11 filing, the decision to reject or accept need not be made until a plan of reorganization is confirmed. This period of time can be quite lengthy. According to Lehman's "State of the Estate" presentation on November 18, 2009, its plan of reorganization is expected in the first quarter of 2010, representing one and a half years since Lehman's bankruptcy filing. What exactly is supposed to happen during this period before the plan is unclear under the Bankruptcy Code. It is unsettled whether non-defaulting parties to executory contracts are obliged to continue performing under those contracts, or whether they are entitled to withhold all or some performance. Previous case law seemed to suggest that such parties are obliged to continue performance. The First Circuit, deciding *In re Public Service Co. of New Hampshire*, 884 F.2d 11, 14 (1st Cir. 1989), held that during this period the "executory contract remains in effect and creditors are bound to honor it."

The potential obligation of Lehman's counterparties to continue their own performance created a double-edged incentive and explains why so many of them elected to terminate their contracts. If the counterparties did not terminate their derivatives contracts, they could be obligated to keep making payments to Lehman. If Lehman ended up owing the counterparties net payments under the swaps, the counterparties would have little chance of collecting the money. A counterparty owed swap payments is usually treated as an unsecured creditor under the Bankruptcy Code. As an unsecured creditor, it would probably be able to collect only a small fraction of the amount owing to it. However, if the counterparties ended up owing Lehman net payments on the swaps, then the bankruptcy trustee could sue them to collect the payments. The bankruptcy trustee would likely win, since the counterparties would be contractually obligated to make the payments. Accordingly, the incentives are all skewed in favor of termination. Not terminating the contract would have created the risk of having to make a net payment to Lehman even when there was no chance of receiving a net payment from Lehman.

This state of affairs was confirmed in the Metavante decision. In November 2007, Metavante, a financial-services technology company based in Milwaukee, entered an interest-rate swap with LBSF. Metavante agreed to make fixed-rate payments based on a notional value of $600 million, and LBSF agreed to make floating rate payments based on the same amount. These payments were to be netted against each other.

LBHI's bankruptcy filing on September 15, 2008 and LBSF's bankruptcy filing on October 3, 2008 both constituted events of default under Section 5(a)(vii) of the 1992 ISDA Master Agreement. Rather than sending a notice of default (triggering a termination of the contract) or continuing to send its net payments to LBSF, Metavante chose to do neither. It apparently hoped that 1) if its side of the derivative contract increased in value (interest rates rose), then it might be able to collect something from Lehman as an unsecured creditor (even if Lehman's estate was unable to pay the full amount owing to Metavante), or 2) if it ended up owing Lehman money on the swap (interest rates fell), Lehman's bankruptcy trustee would not be able to sue to collect because Lehman had defaulted under the contract.

Interest rates fell, and in May 2009 Lehman's trustee filed a motion in bankruptcy court to compel performance of Metavante's obligations. Metavante argued that it was not obligated to terminate the contract or continue to make payments. It pointed to Sections 2(a)(i) and 2(a)(iii) of the ISDA Master Agreement, which provide that the parties are obligated to make contract payments only if an event of default has not occurred. Commonly referred to as the "wait and see" provisions, these provisions allow parties to merely suspend payments after default, rather than fully terminate the contract. Metavante argued that it was not obligated to choose between continuing the contract and terminating, and was instead allowed to simply stop paying. Judge James M. Peck, the bankruptcy judge overseeing Lehman's bankruptcy, ruled in Lehman's favor, holding that the 1992 ISDA Master Agreement granted the non-defaulting party (Metavante) the option to either terminate the contract or continue it. He further held that Metavante's failure to act "promptly" meant that its "window to act" has passed, and Metavante no longer had the right to terminate the contract.

Judge Peck's Metavante decision leaves two open questions. First, there is little guidance as to how large the "window to act" is. How quickly must a non-defaulting party decide to exercise its right to terminate? Litigation filings reveal a fairly broad distribution of time used by counterparties before deciding to terminate their contracts. Most counterparties elected to terminate within three months of Lehman's filings, but a great many terminated more than three months later. This part of Judge Peck's ruling is less than satisfying. There is no provision, statutory or contractual, dealing with the loss of termination rights through waiver or any other means. The counterparties' delay is a reminder that these issues are complicated, and that time may be required before the counterparties can make informed decisions about whether to terminate. For Judge Peck to create an invisible line past which termination is prohibited injects uncertainty into bankruptcy proceedings.

Second, Judge Peck's decision creates confusion about the role of 2(a)(i) and 2(a)(iii), the ISDA provisions providing that parties are obligated to make payments only if a default has not occurred. What exactly these provisions permit non-defaulting parties to do, if anything, is not clear after Metavante. A 2003 Australian case, *Enron Australia v. TXU Electricity Ltd.*, dealt with the exact same issue and reached the opposite result. Enron Australia and TXU were party to several derivative contracts governed by the ISDA Master Agreement. At the time of Enron's bankruptcy, TXU was net out-of-the money on these contracts. Enron's bankruptcy, like Lehman's, constituted an event of default, and gave TXU the option to terminate the contract. TXU, like Metavante, choose not to terminate—as it would have faced a large termination payment to Enron's estate—and instead claimed that it had the *option*, not the obligation, to terminate. TXU, like Metavante, argued that 2(a)(iii) allowed it to withhold performance. The court agreed.

Neither Judge Peck's decision nor the Australian court's decision is optimally satisfying. As construed by the *TXU* court, 2(a)(iii) allows the non-defaulting party to suspend its performance indefinitely, effectively resulting in termination by other means. Despite TXU and Metavante's actions being essentially a form of termination, Judge Peck characterized them otherwise. Judge Peck held that Metavante's reliance on 2(a)(iii) was merely "withholding performance," and therefore prohibited by Section 365(e) of the Bankruptcy Code. The exception to 365(e), Section 560, which permits swap contracts to contain provisions providing that bankruptcy can lead to "liquidation, termination, or acceleration" of the contract, did not apply to Metavante's actions. For Judge Peck, "withholding performance" did not constitute termination, and therefore 2(a)(iii) did not fall within Section 560's safe harbor and is unenforceable within bankruptcy. The flaw in the *TXU* decision is that it seems to thwart the ISDA Master Agreement's designated termination provisions, instead allowing 2(a)(iii) to function as a termination provision. The flaw in Judge Peck's decision is that it declines to view Metavante's action as termination, even though that is what it seems to be. An alternate decision might have prohibited Metavante's action on contractual grounds, interpreting 2(a)(iii) as being true to its moniker as a "wait and see" provision. Under such an interpretation, 2(a)(iii) would permit a non-defaulting party to temporarily suspend payments before making a decision about termination, but it would not permit the non-defaulting party to wait indefinitely (what

Metavante wished to do and TXU actually did).

Presently, only a few thousand of Lehman's derivative contracts remain open out of the nearly one million open at the time of its bankruptcy filing. Most of the contracts still open are ones where Lehman's counterparties are far out-of-the-money, and the counterparties are trying to forestall making payments to Lehman. Some counterparties are choosing to continue to make their regular net payments rather than terminate the contract and be obligated to pay a lump-sum termination payment to Lehman's estate. Beaver Country Day School, a private secondary school outside Boston, is one such counterparty. Like Metavante, it agreed to make fixedrate payments to Lehman in exchange for floating-rate payments. As rates fell, it owed (and continues to owe) net payments to Lehman. Beaver has chosen to make those net payments rather than terminate the contract and be forced to pay its whole value.

Parties like Beaver have made a dangerous choice. Judge Peck ruled that Metavante had waived its rights to terminate because of the length of time that had elapsed since Lehman's default. The length of time since default for Lehman's contract with Beaver Country Day School has been no shorter, so, presumably, it and parties like it have also waived their right to terminate. Accordingly, they are obligated to keep making payments to Lehman's estate, though they cannot expect any of the benefit of the swap. That is, they can expect no future performance from Lehman.

Their best hope is that Lehman will choose to reject their contracts when Lehman formulates its plan of reorganization. Rejection would end the obligations of the counterparties to continue making net payments. Assumption, the alternative to rejection, would entail Lehman assigning the contract to another entity. Lehman itself could not assume the contract as it is in the process of dissolution. Assignment would actually be preferable to the current state of affairs for parties like Beaver Country Day School. Assumption and assignment of these contracts would result in the nondefaulting parties having more viable counterparties. At present, Beaver Country Day School is making payments on its swap contract without any reciprocal benefit—Beaver Country Day School is not actually getting any interest rate protection. But if the contracts are assumed and assigned, Beaver Country Day School would have a solvent counterparty. If interest rates rose, that new counterparty could be a credible provider of interest rate support.

In sum, Lehman's derivative contracts have seen three types of resolution. First, most counterparties opted to terminate their contracts shortly after Lehman's bankruptcy filing. They feared that keeping the contracts open was a lose-lose situation: if their side of the contract rose in value, they would be unable to collect; and if their side of the contract fell in value, Lehman's trustee could sue them. Second, some counterparties, like Metavante, chose neither to terminate nor to continue making payments. The subset of these parties that ended up owing money to Lehman has been pursued (successfully) by Lehman's trustee. Third, some counterparties, who have lost money on their contracts, are trying to avoid paying the full value of their obligation to Lehman. Parties like Beaver Country Day School have chosen to continue making regular net payments rather than be forced to make even larger termination payments.

【思考题】

1. 雷曼破产的主要原因是什么？
2. 雷曼公司破产案的复杂性体现在哪些方面？

Case3·拓展阅读

VII

国际税法

【内容摘要】

本章选取了国际税法中避免重复征税和反国际避税两个方面的经典案例。第一节为避免重复征税案例。避免重复征税是指国家间为了避免和消除向同一纳税人、在同一所得的基础上重复征税，根据平等互惠原则而签订的双边税收协定。各国征收所得税，都不同程度地基于所得来源地原则和纳税人居住地原则行使税收管辖权。如果纳税人居住地国与其取得所得的来源地国之间没有作出双方都能接受的协调安排，往往造成征税重叠，不仅会加重纳税人的负担，也不利于国际间的经济、技术和人才交流。因此，第二次世界大战后，随着国际间资金流动、劳务交流和贸易往来的发展，在国与国间签订避免双重税收协定，已日益受到重视。National Westminster Bank, PLC v. U.S., 512 F.3d 1347 (2008) 就是围绕英美之间的《避免双重征税条约》（Convention for the Avoidance of Double Taxation，以下简称《1975 年条约》）而产生的争议。该案例争议的焦点是 National Westminster Bank, US Branch（以下简称 Nat West）从其集团总部或其他分行借款而支付的资金利息是否可以在美国的税基中进行抵扣。美国联邦巡回上诉法院（United States Court of Appeals, Federal Circuit）通过对《1975 年条约》第 7（2）条进行解读，认为由常设国际金融企业（例如 NatWest 美国分公司）产生的利息支出可以在与该常设机构的日常活动有关的范围内进行抵扣。

第二节是打击通过转移定价进行国际避税的案例。转移定价是跨国公司内部的母公司与子公司之间、子公司与子公司之间提供产品、劳务或技术所采用的定价。转移定价是跨国公司经常使用的国际资金调度管理的手段，目的是使跨国公司避开一些东道国在资金调度上设置的政治和税收障碍并降低外汇交易成本。为了防止跨国公司不当利用转移定价的方式进行利润转移造成本国税收流失，各国政府相继对跨国贸易制定转移定价税制规则。通过规范和调整关联企业间的转移价格，以达到遏制和防止跨国公司利用关联交易进行避税、维护本国经济权益和市场公平竞争的目的。本节案例为欧盟委员会（EUROPEAN COMMISSION）发布的有关苹果公司避税的调查报告。该案中欧盟委员会认为爱尔兰政府对苹果公司的爱尔兰分公司给予有选择性的税收优惠，从而构成不正当的国家补贴，而该补贴有损欧盟共同市场的正当竞争，因而要求爱尔兰政府向苹果公司追缴相关的税款。

| Case1　Double Taxation Avoidance |

【案情说明】

案件事实

NatWest 是一家从事国际银行业务的英国公司。在 1981—1987 纳税年度，NatWest 通过六个常设分支机构（统称为"美国分行"）在美国进行批发银行业务。在纳税争议年度的美国联邦所得税申报表上，NatWest 要求扣除美国分行账簿上应计利息费用的扣除额。经审计，美国国税局（IRS）根据《财务条例》第 1.882-5 条规定的公式重新计算了利息费用扣除额。该公式不包括基于确定资产、负债和利息支出的考量而进行的分支机构间交易。该公式还根据固定比率或 NatWest 全球平均总负债与全球平均总资产之比估算美国分行持有的资本数量。根据美国国税局重新计算的利息费用扣除额，NatWest 的应税收入在所涉年份增加了约 1.55 亿美元。NatWest 得出结论，增加的收入将导致在美国产生至少 3 700 万美元的额外税收负担，而该笔税收无法在英国获得外国税收抵免。因此，NatWest 根据《1975 年条约》第 24 条，要求英国与美国进入主管当局程序，以解决双重征税问题。根据主管当局的程序，英国向 NatWest 提出了和解要约，NatWest 认为该要约未充分解决其双重征税问题。 NatWest 拒绝了和解要约，支付了额外的税款后，于 1995 年提起诉讼，声称 IRS（Inter Revenue Service）向 NatWest 之类的国际银行申请第 1.882-5 条的规定违反了《1975 年条约》的相关条款。美国初审法院与联邦上诉法院均支持了 NatWest 的主张，认定 IRS 的计算方法有违《1975 年条约》所规定的独立业原则。

【法律分析】

双方在初审法院和上诉法院均认可《 1975 年条约》要求美国分行像从 NatWest 分离出来的企业（即"独立企业原则"）一样被征税。 双方的争议在于适用独立企业原则的方式，包括①公司内部贷款（即美国分支机构和 NatWest 其他分支机构之间的分支机构贷款）的利息支出，以及②向美国分支机构分配资本。 上诉法院主要围绕上述问题进行了裁定。

一、常设机构原则

所谓常设机构原则，是指一国的税收居民企业取得的跨境营业所得（利润）只应在居民国一方被征收所得税，如果该企业通过设在来源地国的常设机构进行营业，则归属于该常设机构的利润可以在该来源地国一方被征收所得税。NatWest 在美国设立的 6 家分支机构被法院认定为常设机构，应就其获得的利润向美国纳税。

二、《1975 年条约》相关条款

《1975 年条约》第 7（2）条规定：除适用第 3 款的规定以外，缔约国一方企业通过设在缔约国另一方的常设机构在该缔约国另一方进行营业，应将该常设机构视同在相同或类似情况下从事相同或类似活动的独立分设企业，并同该常设机构所隶属的企业完全独立处理，该常设机构可能得到的利润在缔约国各方应归属于该常设机构。

在确定常设机构的利润时，应当允许扣除其进行营业发生的各项费用，包括行政和一般管理费用，不论其发生于常设机构所在国或者其他任何地方。

法院认为对于《1975 年条约》第 7 条的解释首先应采用广义解释，即根据条约的所适用的语言来解释相关条款，[1] 除非采用广义解释明显与缔约国的打算或预期相冲突。[2] 因而，在条约采用的措辞"不完全体现其目的"时，在解释相关条款时必须实现其基本目的。[3]

三、IRS 的纳税方式是否有违独立企业原则

针对 IRS 采用的应纳税款的计算方法，首先，上诉法院认为英国在《1975 年条约》于 1980 年正式生效前已在 1978 年认定其与独立企业原则相违而废除了该方法，说明作为缔约国之一的英国没有采用这种计算方法的打算。其次，对于 IRS 所采用的计算方法所依据的财税规则 (Treasury Regulation 1977) §1.861-8，上诉法院认为该条并没有明确规定在确定可扣除的利息支出时，不考虑分支机构间的交易。且常设机构与其他关联企业的交易在适用《1975 年条约》有相关规定时，其相对于属于国内法规则的 §1.861-8 具有优先适用的效力。

上诉法院进一步对《1975 年条约》第 7（2）条所采用的"相同或相似"进行解读。上诉法院认为第 7（2）条对独立企业原则进行界定时所采用的"相同或相似"的表述应理解为美国分行开展商业活动时所开展的业务活动和条件。也就是说，对美国分行征税时，应将其视为与美国分行从事的活动"相同或类似"的单独企业，也将其视为与美国分行从事活动的条件"相同或类似"下经营。很明显，为正确理解"相同或相似"条

---

1 Sumitomo Shoji America, Inc. v. Avagliano, 457 U.S. 176, 180, 102 S.Ct. 2374, 72 L.Ed.2d 765 (1982) [quoting Maximov v. United States, 373 U.S. 49, 54, 83 S.Ct. 1054, 10 L.Ed.2d 184 (1963)]; see also Xerox Corp. v. United States, 41 F.3d 647, 652 (Fed.Cir.1994) [citing United States v. Stuart, 489 U.S. 353, 365-66, 109 S.Ct. 1183, 103 L.Ed.2d 388 (1989)].

2 Xerox, 41 F.3d at 656 (citing Valentine v. United States, 299 U.S. 5, 11, 57 S.Ct. 100, 81 L.Ed. 5 (1936).

3 Great-West Life Assur. Co. v. United States, 230 Ct.Cl. 477, 678 F.2d 180, 183 (1982) [citing In re Ross, 140 U.S. 453, 475, 11 S.Ct. 897, 35 L.Ed. 581 (1891)]; accord Xerox, 41 F.3d at 652.

款，第 7（2）条中所使用的"完全独立"一词要求税务机关仔细审查涉及常设机构的企业内部交易，以确保准确地界定交易的性质并反映独立交易原则和价格。"相同或相似条件"的表达似乎支持 NatWest 的立场，即美国分行应按照其实际运作情况进行纳税，即使该分行的运营资金很少或没有免息资本。

在本案中，美国分行因其自有资本较低而需要在获得总部资金支持时支付相关利息。法院认为，《1975 年条约》的签署国期望由常设国际金融企业（例如 NatWest 美国分公司）产生的利息支出可以在与该常设机构的日常活动有关的范围内扣除。而 IRS 采用的估算利息公式拒绝抵扣该分支机构因其（实际）资本账户未达到美国国内法所规定的独立机构所需的"自我营运资金"而支付的利息是没有根据的。

【英文原文摘选】

512 F.3d 1347

United States Court of Appeals,

Federal Circuit.

NATIONAL WESTMINSTER BANK, PLC, Plaintiff–Appellee, v. UNITED STATES, Defendant–Appellant.

No. 2007–5028.

Jan. 15, 2008. Rehearing En Banc Denied April 21, 2008.

Synopsis

Background: United Kingdom corporation engaged in banking activity brought suit against United States for refund of income taxes paid by its United States branch on interbranch loan transactions, alleging that interest paid in such transactions should have been allowable as deduction. The United States Court of Federal Claims, James T. Turner, J., 44 Fed.Cl. 120, and Nancy B. Firestone, J., 58 Fed.Cl. 491 and 69 Fed.Cl. 128,granted summary judgment in part for taxpayer. United States appealed.

Holdings: The Court of Appeals, Gajarsa, Circuit Judge, held that:

deductions for interest expenses incurred on interbranch advances were authorized by Convention for Avoidance of Double Taxation;

government's unwavering, long-held position that contravened treaty's language and negotiation history, as well as contemporaneous expectations of United Kingdom, was entitled to minimal deference;

Convention did not allow for attribution of additional capital to branch;

trial court's denial of government's motion for reconsideration was not abuse of discretion;

government waived its argument before trial court that capital held by home office of United Kingdom bank should have been imputed to its United States branch for tax purposes; and corporate records of home office were not relevant to interest expense deduction for United States branch.

Affirmed.

GAJARSA, Circuit Judge.

This is a tax refund action brought by taxpayer National Westminster Bank PLC ("NatWest"), a United Kingdom corporation, for the tax years 1981–1987. The Government appeals from the judgment of the United States Court of Federal Claims ("trial court" or "court") that NatWest is entitled to a refund of $65,723,053 plus interest for the tax years at issue. Central to the trial court's judgment is the issue of whether the application of Treasury Regulation § 1.882–5 is consistent with the United States' obligations under Article 7 of the Convention for the Avoidance of Double Taxation and the Prevention of Fiscal Evasion with Respect to Taxes on Income and Capital Gains, U.S.-U.K., Dec. 31, 1975, 31 U.S.T. 5668 (the "1975 Treaty"). For the reasons stated below, we affirm.

BACKGROUND

The 1975 Treaty, which governs this dispute, was initially negotiated and signed by the United States and the United Kingdom in 1975.1 31 U.S.T. at 5668. As may be surmised from its title, the 1975 Treaty states that its purpose is "the avoidance of double taxation and the prevention of fiscal evasion with respect to taxes on income and capital gains." Id. at 5670. Of particular import to this case, Article 7 governs the taxing authority of the signatories with respect to the business profits of an enterprise operating in both countries. Id. at 5675-76.

NatWest is a United Kingdom corporation engaged in international banking activities. For the tax years 1981–1987, NatWest conducted wholesale banking operations in the United States through six permanently established branch locations (collectively "the U.S. Branch"). On its United States federal income tax returns for the years at issue, NatWest claimed deductions for accrued interest expenses as recorded on the books of the U.S. Branch. On audit, the Internal Revenue Service ("IRS") recomputed the interest expense deduction according to the formula set forth in Treasury Regulation § 1.882–5. The formula excludes consideration of interbranch transactions for the determination of assets, liabilities, and interest expenses. Treas. Reg. § 1.882–5(a)(5) (1981).2 The formula also imputes *1350 or estimates the amount of capital held by the U.S. Branch based on either a fixed ratio or the ratio of NatWest's average total worldwide liabilities to average total worldwide assets. Id. § 1.882–5(b)(2). Pursuant to the IRS's recalculation of the interest expense deduction, NatWest's taxable income was increased by approximately $155 million for the years at issue.

NatWest concluded that the increased income would result in an additional tax liability of at least $37 million in the United States for which a foreign tax credit would not be available in the United Kingdom. NatWest thus requested, under Article 24 of the 1975 Treaty, that the United Kingdom enter competent authority proceedings with the United States to resolve the double taxation issue. Pursuant to the competent authority proceedings, the United Kingdom presented NatWest with a settlement offer, which NatWest concluded did not sufficiently address its double taxation concerns. NatWest rejected the settlement offer, paid the additional taxes, and filed suit in 1995, claiming that the IRS's application of § 1.882–5 to an international bank such as NatWest violated the terms of the 1975 Treaty.

The 1975 Treaty

After the initial signing of the 1975 Treaty on December 31, 1975, certain provisions not at issue here were amended by three protocols signed between August 1976 and March 1979. 31 U.S.T. at 5668–69. The 1975 Treaty took effect on April 25, 1980. Id. at 5668. Article 7, entitled Business Profits, states as follows:

(1) The business profits of an enterprise of a Contracting State shall be taxable only in that State unless the enterprise carries on business in the other Contracting State through a permanent establishment situated therein. If the enterprise carries on business as aforesaid, the business profits of the enterprise may be taxed in that other State but only so much of them as is attributable to that permanent establishment.

(2) Subject to the provisions of paragraph (3), where an enterprise carries on business in the other Contracting State through a permanent establishment situated therein, there shall in each Contracting State be attributed to that permanent establishment the profits which it might be expected to make if it were a distinct and separate enterprise engaged in the same or similar activities under the same or similar conditions and dealing wholly independently with the enterprise of which it is a permanent establishment.

(3) In the determination of the profits of the permanent establishment, there shall be allowed as deductions those expenses which are incurred for the purposes of the permanent establishment, including a reasonable allocation of executive and general administrative expenses, research and development expenses, interest, and other expenses incurred for the purposes of the enterprise as a whole (or the part thereof which includes the permanent establishment), whether incurred in the State in which the permanent establishment is situated or elsewhere.

Id. at 5675–76 (emphasis added). Relating the terms of the 1975 Treaty to the present appeal, "a Contracting State" is the United Kingdom, "the other Contracting State" is the United States, "an enterprise" is NatWest, and "a permanent establishment" is the U.S. Branch. The emphasized portion of paragraph 2 sets forth the "separate enterprise principle" and frames the dispute in this case.

*1351 Treasury Regulation § 1.882-5

Treasury Regulation § 1.882-5 was proposed on February 27, 1980, adopted on December 30, 1980, and took effect on February 6, 1981. 46 Fed.Reg. 1681 (Jan. 7, 1981). As described by the Government, the regulation sets forth a formula for apportioning the interest expense of foreign corporations. The formula applies to all foreign corporations with permanent establishments in the United States and makes no exception for banks or other financial institutions.

At the outset, "[i]nter-branch loans, assets, liabilities, and interest expense amounts resulting from loan or credit transactions of any type between the separate offices or branches of the same foreign corporation are disregarded." § 1.882–5(a)(5). The deductible interest expense is then calculated according to a three-step formula. In step one, the permanent establishment's U.S.-connected assets—"total value of all assets of the corporation that generate, have generated, or could reasonably have been or be expected to generate income, gain, or loss effectively connected with the conduct of a trade or business in the United States"—are determined according to the books of the permanent establishment, exclusive of the intracorporate transactions disregarded under § 1.882–5(a)(5). § 1.882–5(b)(1). In step two, the permanent establishment's U.S.-connected liabilities are estimated either by multiplying the U.S.-connected assets by a capital ratio of 0.95 or by the ratio of the average total amount of corporate worldwide liabilities to the average total value of corporate worldwide assets. § 1.882–5(b)(2). In step three, the interest deduction is computed under either the "branch book/dollar pool method" or the "separate currency pools method." § 1.882–5(b)(3). The IRS used the branch book/dollar pool method to audit the U.S. Branch. Under this method, the permanent establishment is allowed an interest deduction on the larger of the U.S.-connected liabilities or the average total amount of liabilities, again exclusive of transactions disregarded under § 1.882–5(a)(5), shown on the books of the permanent establishment. § 1.882–5(b)(3)(i)(A), (B). The branch book/dollar pool method further specifies which interest rate(s) will be used to determine the total amount of the interest expense deduction. Id.

Proceedings in the Court of Federal Claims

The parties agree, both before the trial court and on appeal, that the 1975 Treaty requires that the U.S. Branch be taxed as if it were a separate enterprise from NatWest—the "separate enterprise principle." The parties differ with respect to the manner in which the separate enterprise principle treats (1) interest expenses on intracorporate loans (i.e., interbranch loans between the U.S. Branch and NatWest's other branches) and (2) the allocation of capital to the U.S. Branch. The trial court decided these issues in three separate summary judgment opinions and orders.

On cross-motions for partial summary judgment, the trial court concluded that the application of § 1.882–5 to a bank such as NatWest violated the terms of the 1975 Treaty. Nat'l Westminster Bank, PLC v. United States, 44 Fed.Cl. 120, 131 (1999) (Turner, J.) ("NatWest I "). During briefing, the United Kingdom submitted an amicus brief supporting the NatWest position and advocating the result arrived at by the trial court. See Br. Amicus Curiae of the U.K. 2–3 (hereinafter "U.K. Amicus Br."). Specifically, the court found that the § 1.882–5's exclusion of all interbranch transactions from the determination of the allowable interest expense violated the separate enterprise principle of the 1975 *1352 Treaty. NatWest I, 44 Fed.Cl. at 130. The court concluded that the separate enterprise principle required that the determination of the profits of the U.S. Branch be based on the books of account as the U.S. Branch would maintain them if it "were a distinct and separate enterprise dealing wholly independently with the remainder of the foreign corporation," without reference to the worldwide information of NatWest. Id. at 128. The books of account, however, "are subject to adjustment as may be necessary for imputation of adequate capital to the branch and to insure use of market rates in computing interest expense." Id. Subsequent to the issuance of the NatWest I opinion, Judge Turner retired and the case was transferred to Judge Firestone.

The parties then filed cross-motions for partial summary judgment regarding the manner in which the IRS should determine or estimate the amount of "adequate" capital held by the U.S. Branch. Nat'l Westminster Bank, PLC v. United States, 58 Fed.Cl. 491, 492 (2003) (Firestone, J.) ("NatWest II "). The Government argued that it was permitted to attribute capital to the U.S. Branch based on regulatory and marketplace capital requirements that applied to U.S. bank corporations—the "corporate yardstick." Id. at 495–96. NatWest argued that the 1975 Treaty did not permit the imputation of capital to the U.S. Branch based on capital requirements to which it was not subject. Id. at 496. The court ruled in NatWest's favor, concluding that the separate enterprise principle did not require or allow "the government to adjust the books and records of the branch to reflect 'hypothetical' infusions of capital based upon banking and market requirements that do not apply to the branch." Id. at 498. Rather, the court adopted NatWest's position that only capital actually allotted to the U.S. Branch is relevant to a determination of the U.S. Branch's tax liability and that the IRS may only allocate additional capital to the extent that the books of the U.S. Branch do not properly record allotted capital. Id. at 497–98.

After the decision in NatWest II, the U.S. moved to reopen discovery regarding the amount of capital that the books of NatWest's home office show as being allotted to the U.S.

branch. The government put forth a new theory that capital held by other branches should be imputed to the U.S. Branch, but the court found that the Government waived this theory by failing to present it during the briefing stage of NatWest II. Nat'l Westminster Bank, PLC v. United States, No. 95–758T (Fed.Cl. Jan. 18, 2005) (hereinafter "Order Denying Reconsideration ").

In the third summary judgment opinion, the trial court considered whether uncontroverted facts supported NatWest's assertion that, consistent with the holdings of NatWest I and NatWest II, the U.S. Branch was entitled to a refund of $65,808,076 plus interest. Nat'l Westminster Bank PLC v. United States, 69 Fed.Cl. 128, 131 (2005) ("NatWest III"). The court partially granted NatWest's motion for summary judgment and reached the following conclusions: (1) the books and records of the U.S. Branch were accurately maintained; (2) the six branch locations of the U.S. Branch constituted a single "permanent establishment" under the 1975 Treaty; (3) the U.S. Branch did not claim deductions based on interest expenses paid "on allotted capital or amounts to be treated as allotted capital"; (4) the U.S. Branch paid and received arm's-length interest rates on money market transactions; and (5) issues of material fact required a trial on whether the U.S. Branch paid and received arm's-length interest rates on clearing account transactions. Id. at 139–41, 144, 146–48. The parties then settled the remaining issue of interest rates on the clearing account transactions, and the *1353 court entered final judgment in NatWest's favor. The Government timely appealed to this court. We have jurisdiction pursuant to 28 U.S.C. § 1295(a)(3).

DISCUSSION

The Government presents three issues on appeal. First, the Government appeals the ruling of NatWest I and argues that the application of Treasury Regulation § 1.882–5 to NatWest is consistent with the expectations of the United States and the United Kingdom at the time the 1975 Treaty was negotiated, signed, and entered into force. Second, the Government appeals the ruling of NatWest II and submits that as an alternative to § 1.882–5, the proposed corporate yardstick method is a permissible means for imputing capital to the U.S. Branch. Last, the Government appeals the ruling of the Order Denying Reconsideration and requests that it be allowed to take discovery of NatWest's home office books to determine the capital actually allotted to the U.S. Branch. Should we uphold NatWest I, NatWest II, and the Order Denying Reconsideration, the Government does not appeal the trial court's ruling in NatWest III.

A grant of summary judgment by the Court of Federal Claims is reviewed de novo, drawing justifiable factual inferences in favor of the party opposing the judgment. SmithKline Beecham Corp. v. Apotex Corp., 403 F.3d 1331, 1337 (Fed.Cir.2005); Winstar Corp. v. United

States, 64 F.3d 1531, 1539 (Fed.Cir.1995) (en banc).

When construing a treaty, "[t]he clear import of treaty language controls unless 'application of the words of the treaty according to their obvious meaning effects a result inconsistent with the intent or expectations of its signatories.' " Sumitomo Shoji America, Inc. v. Avagliano, 457 U.S. 176, 180, 102 S.Ct. 2374, 72 L.Ed.2d 765 (1982) [quoting Maximov v. United States, 373 U.S. 49, 54, 83 S.Ct. 1054, 10 L.Ed.2d 184 (1963)]; see also Xerox Corp. v. United States, 41 F.3d 647, 652 (Fed.Cir.1994) [citing United States v. Stuart, 489 U.S. 353, 365–66, 109 S.Ct. 1183, 103 L.Ed.2d 388 (1989)]. Moreover, effect must be given to the intent of both signatories. Xerox, 41 F.3d at 656 [citing Valentine v. United States, 299 U.S. 5, 11, 57 S.Ct. 100, 81 L.Ed. 5 (1936)]. Thus, when the language of a treaty provision "only imperfectly manifests its purpose," we are required to give effect to its underlying purpose. Great–West Life Assur. Co. v. United States, 230 Ct.Cl. 477, 678 F.2d 180, 183 (1982) [citing In re Ross, 140 U.S. 453, 475, 11 S.Ct. 897, 35 L.Ed. 581 (1891)]; accord Xerox, 41 F.3d at 652 (" '[T]he ultimate question remains what was intended when the language actually employed ... was chosen, imperfect as that language may be.' " (second alteration in original) [quoting Great–West Life, 678 F.2d at 188)]. To this end, we must "examine not only the language, but the entire context of agreement." Great–West Life, 678 F.2d at 183.

The "entire context" of the 1975 Treaty is informed by, and is based on, the Office of Economic Cooperation and Development's ("OECD") 1963 Draft Double Taxation Convention on Income and Capital ("1963 Draft Convention"). See NatWest I, 44 Fed.Cl. at 125 n. 7; S. Exec. Rep. No. 95–18, at 15 (1978), as reprinted in 1980–1 C.B. 411, 427; Technical Explanation of the Convention between the Government of the United States of America and the Government of the United Kingdom of Great Britain and Northern Ireland for the Avoidance of Double Taxation and the Prevention of Fiscal Evasion with Respect to Taxes on Income and Capital Gains Signed at London, on December 31, 1975, as Amended by the Notes Exchanged at London on April 13, 1976, the Protocol Signed at London on August 26, 1976, and the Second Protocol signed at London on *1354 March 31, 1977, submitted to the Senate Foreign Relations Committee at hearings held on July 19–20, 1977, reprinted in 1980–1 C.B. 455, 473–74 (hereinafter "Technical Explanation"). As published, the model Articles of the 1963 Draft Convention issued as Annex I to a report of introductory and explanatory material. 1963 Draft Convention 5. Annex II consists of Commentaries on the Articles of the Draft Convention ("1963 Commentaries") that are "intended to be of great assistance in the application of the conventions and, in particular, in the settlement of eventual disputes." 1963 Draft Convention 18; see also NatWest I, 44 Fed.Cl. at 125. The Senate Report and the Technical Explanation both state specifically that Article 7 of the 1975

Treaty is based on or substantially similar to Article 7 of the 1963 Model Convention. See 1980–1 C.B. at 417, 461.

In NatWest I, the trial court concluded that the application of § 1.882–5 to the U.S. Branch of NatWest violated the separate enterprise principle of the 1975 Treaty. 44 Fed.Cl. at 131. Focusing on paragraphs 2 and 3 of Article 7, the trial court concluded that the plain language of the 1975 Treaty required that for a determination of the taxable income of the U.S. Branch, the U.S. Branch is to be regarded as an independent, separate entity dealing at arm's length with other units of NatWest as if they were wholly unrelated, except that the U.S. Branch may deduct, in addition to its "own" expenses, a reasonable allocation of home office expense. Words such as "distinct" and "separate" and the phrase "dealing wholly independently" (emphasis added) would appear to permit no other interpretation.

Id. at 124. The trial court also analyzed the 1963 Commentaries, which describe "'payments of interest made by different parts of a financial enterprise (e.g. a bank) to each other on advances, etc., (as distinct from capital allotted to them),' " as " 'narrowly related to the ordinary business of such enterprises.' " NatWest I, 44 Fed.Cl. at 127 (quoting 1963 Draft Convention 83–84, ¶ 15). Thus because § 1.882–5 expressly disregards payments of interest on these types of interbranch transactions, the court concluded that § 1.882–5 was inconsistent with the Treaty as applied to the U.S. Branch of NatWest.3 NatWest I, 44 Fed.Cl. at 130. The court further noted that if the U.S. Branch was a subsidiary of NatWest separately incorporated in the United States, the interest expense on transactions between the U.S. Branch and foreign NatWest branches would be subject to adjustment but would not be disregarded. Id. at 130 n. 11; see also Treas. Reg. § 1.482–2(a) (1984).

On appeal, the Government criticizes the trial court's conclusion in NatWest I on the following grounds: (1) the court ignored the 1975 Treaty's plain language; (2) the court misapplied the 1963 Commentaries that support the Government's position; (3) the court ignored the parties' shared expectations; and (4) the court did not accord proper deference to the "Treasury's consistent determination that the regulation is consistent with Article 7."

We agree with the trial court's analysis of the plain language of the 1975 Treaty. On a fundamental level, we do not read the separate enterprise language of Article 7, ¶ 2— requiring that the U.S. Branch's business profits be determined as "if it were a distinct and separate enterprise engaged *1355 in the same or similar activities under the same or similar conditions and dealing wholly independently with the enterprise of which it is a permanent establishment"—as permitting transactions between the permanent establishment and the enterprise to be disregarded. As did the trial court, we find the comparison to a separately incorporated U.S. subsidiary instructive. In that situation, intracorporate transactions recorded on the subsidiary's books are not disregarded, but are adjusted to reflect arm's length terms. See, e.g., Treas. Reg. § 1.482–2(a)(2) (1984) (defining "arm's length interest rate" as "the rate of interest which was charged, or would have been charged at the time the indebtedness arose, in independent transactions with or between unrelated parties under similar circumstances"). The plain language of the 1975 Treaty thus indicates that adjustment of the terms of intracorporate transactions is required and that the disregard of these transactions is prohibited.

To the extent that the Government submits that the "reasonable allocation" language of Article 7, ¶ 3 is relevant to whether § 1.882–5 is permissible under the 1975 Treaty, the Government misreads the treaty. With regard to allowable deductions for a determination of the profits of a permanent establishment, the 1963 Model Convention, which differs slightly from the 1975 Treaty, reads as follows:

In the determination of the profits of a permanent establishment, there shall be allowed as deductions expenses which are incurred for the purposes of the permanent establishment including executive and general administrative expenses so incurred, whether in the State in which the permanent establishment is situated or elsewhere.

1963 Draft Convention 46. The 1975 Treaty modifies this language by including a nonexclusive list of executive and general administrative expenses that are incurred on behalf of the enterprise as a whole (e.g., NatWest's worldwide enterprise including the U.S. Branch) and that may be partially allocated to the permanent establishment (e.g., NatWest's U.S. Branch).

In the determination of the profits of a permanent establishment, there shall be allowed as deductions those expenses which are incurred for the purposes of the permanent establishment, including a reasonable allocation of executive and general administrative expenses, research and development expenses, interest and other expenses incurred for the purposes of the enterprise as a whole (or the part thereof which includes the permanent establishment), whether incurred in the State in which the permanent establishment is situated or elsewhere.

31 U.S.T. at 5675–76 (emphasis added). Importantly, the "reasonable allocation" language refers to expenses, such as interest, that are "incurred for the purposes of the enterprise as a whole." Furthermore, a comparison of the Treaty to the 1963 Model Convention indicates that no reasonable allocation is necessary for expenses, such as interest, that are directly "incurred for the purposes of the permanent establishment."

As previously noted, the 1963 Draft Convention was published as part of a document that included the 1963 Commentaries, the purpose of which is " 'to illustrate or interpret the provisions' " and to " 'be of great assistance … in the settlement of eventual disputes.' "

NatWest I, 44 Fed.Cl. at 125 (quoting 1963 Draft Convention). Accordingly, the 1963 Draft Convention states that Article 7 "settles the question of the expenses which must be allowed as deductions in computing the profits of the permanent establishment." 1963 Draft Convention 12. Among these expenses that must be allowed are interbranch *1356 payments of interest "on advances, etc., (as distinct from capital allotted to [the permanent establishment])." 1963 Draft Convention 83–84, ¶ 15. This commentary indicates that § 1.882–5's disregard of interbranch transactions is inconsistent with the 1963 Draft Convention and the 1975 Treaty as modeled thereon.

On the separate enterprise principle specifically, the 1963 Commentary to Article 7, ¶ 2 states, "[T]he profits to be attributed to a permanent establishment are those which that permanent establishment would have made if, instead of dealing with its head office, it had been dealing with an entirely separate enterprise under conditions and at prices prevailing in the ordinary market." 1963 Draft Convention 82, ¶ 10. To determine these profits, "it is always necessary to start with the real facts of the situation as they appear from [t]he business records of the permanent establishment and to adjust as may be shown to be necessary the profit figures which those facts produce." Id. Exceptions to this rule, however, may exist where no separate accounts exist. Id. (allowing for formulaic allocation in the absence of separate accounts). The 1963 Commentary goes on to explain that adjustment to the accounts of the permanent establishment may be necessary in situations such as when the transactions between a permanent establishment and a head office do not reflect market pricing (i.e., market interest rates for financial enterprises). Id. at ¶ 11.

Consistent with the 1963 Commentary to Article 7, ¶ 2, the commentary to Article 7, ¶ 3 focuses on whether an expense is incurred by a permanent establishment, rather than whether the expense is paid to a foreign branch of the same worldwide enterprise. "[F]or the sake of removing doubts," the 1963 Commentary states that Article 7, ¶ 3 "specifically recognizes that in calculating the profits of a permanent establishment allowance is to be made for expenses, wherever incurred, that were incurred for the purposes of the permanent establishment." Id. at 83, ¶ 13. The commentary explicitly includes as a deductible expense "payments of interest made by different parts of a financial enterprise (e.g. a bank) to each other on advances, etc., (as distinct from capital allotted to them), in view of the fact that making and receiving advances is narrowly related to the ordinary business of such enterprises." Id. at 83–84, ¶ 15.

The Government argues that the use of formulaic allocations for taxing purposes by both parties during the period between the signing of the 1975 Treaty and its entry into force is evidence that the parties did not intend for the Treaty to prohibit the use of allocation formulas. The Government's position is undermined in two important respects. First, in 1978 the United

Kingdom abandoned its formula then in use after concluding that the formula was inconsistent with the separate enterprise principle. Second, the interest expense allocation formula used by the United States was significantly different than that prescribed by § 1.882–5.

The record demonstrates that during the negotiation period of the 1975 Treaty, the United Kingdom did employ a formulaic allocation when determining the interest expense deduction of a U.K. branch of a foreign (e.g., incorporated in the United States) bank. The Government's reliance on this use in furtherance of its appeal is misplaced. Referred to in the record as the "Price Waterhouse formula" ("PW formula"), the United Kingdom used the ratio of the bank's worldwide total free capital to total liabilities and compared the liabilities of the U.K. branch to the bank's total liabilities to allocate free capital to the U.K. branch for taxation purposes. NatWest II, 58 Fed.Cl. at 505–06. If the U.K. branch's allocated free capital was less *1357 than the net balance owed to the bank's head office, a formula was then used to calculate the interest rate on the remainder of the net balance (less an amount equal to allocated capital) that would be used to determine the amount of the deduction. Unlike § 1.882–5, the PW formula does not disregard transactions simply because they occurred between branches of the same worldwide enterprise. In addition, the United Kingdom abandoned use of the PW formula in 1978 after determining that the formulaic capital allocation violated the separate enterprise principle under the U.S.-U.K. treaty that was in effect before the 1975 Treaty entered into force in 1980. NatWest II, 58 Fed.Cl. at 505–06 (citing Counsel's Opinion (Dec. 7, 1978)). The separate enterprise language of that earlier treaty was nearly identical to the language of the 1975 Treaty,4 and the United Kingdom continued to maintain that the PW formula was equally violative of the supplanting language in the 1975 Treaty. See Inland Revenue, Banking Manual app. 9A, ¶ 3 (1994). This contemporaneous conduct of the United Kingdom supports the position taken in its amicus brief filed with the trial court—the United Kingdom has never interpreted the provisions of the 1975 Treaty as allowing a taxing authority to disregard interbranch transactions when computing the interest expense properly deductible by a permanent establishment. U.K. Amicus Br. 38–39; Letter from I.N. Hunter, Inland Revenue, to Donald E. Bergherm Jr., Assistant Commissioner (International), Internal Revenue Service (March 13, 1990) (Re: Request for Competent Authority Consideration Dated July 27, 1989).

Nor is the Government's position supported by its own conduct contemporaneous to the negotiations of the 1975 Treaty. The Government points to Revenue Ruling 78–423, 1978–2 C.B. 194 (concluding that the interest expense apportionment formulas of Treasury Regulation § 1.861–8 (1977) were permissible in view of the Business Profits article of the U.S.-Japan treaty, which was also based on 1963 OECD Model Convention), as supporting its argument that Treasury's consistent interpretation of § 1.882–5 is informative of the United States' intent as a signatory to the 1975 Treaty. This argument, however, overlooks the key difference between the allocation formula of § 1.861–8 and the formula of § 1.882–5—namely, that § 1.861–8 does not explicitly disregard interbranch transactions when determining the interest expense deductible by a permanent establishment. Treas. Reg. § 1.861–8(e)(2)(v), (vi) (1977) (apportioning appropriate amount of worldwide interest expense to permanent establishment). In addition, § 1.861–8 expressly stated that if treaty provisions apply to the determination of taxable income, the treaty takes precedence over the regulation.5 Treas. Reg. § 1.861–8(f)(1)(iv) (1977).

*1358 The Government submits that its unwavering, long-held position is to be accorded significant deference. The Government correctly notes that "[a]lthough not conclusive, the meaning attributed to treaty provisions by the Government agencies charged with their negotiation and enforcement is entitled to great weight." Sumitomo, 457 U.S. at 184–85, 102 S.Ct. 2374 (according great deference to agency's position where treaty's signatories, neither of which were parties to the lawsuit, agreed as to interpretation). Courts nevertheless "interpret treaties for themselves." Kolovrat v. Oregon, 366 U.S. 187, 194, 81 S.Ct. 922, 6 L.Ed.2d 218 (1961). Moreover, because we are to interpret treaties so as to give effect to the intent of both signatories, Xerox, 41 F.3d at 656, an agency's position merits less deference "where an agency and another country disagree on the meaning of a treaty," see Iceland Steamship Co., Eimskip v. U.S. Dep't of the Army, 201 F.3d 451, 458 (D.C.Cir.2000). Finally, this court, when considering different provisions of the 1975 Treaty, has declined to defer to Treasury's contemporaneous interpretation where it conflicted with the contemporaneous intent of the Senate. Xerox, 41 F.3d at 653–57 (rejecting agency's interpretation that was published during the ratification process and reasserted at trial).

The Government is correct to assert that it has unwaveringly interpreted § 1.882–5 as being consistent with the 1975 Treaty and other similar treaties based on the 1963 Draft Convention. See, e.g., Rev. Rul. 89–115, 1989–2 C.B. 130–31 (§ 1.882–5 consistent with 1975 Treaty); Rev. Rul. 85–7, 1985–1 C.B. 188 (§ 1.882–5 consistent with U.S.-Japan treaty). Indeed, in a report issued in 1984, the OECD itself acknowledged that the United States' interpretation of Article 7 of the 1963 Draft Convention 6 allowed for the application of § 1.882–5 to international financial institutions. Comments. on Fiscal Affairs, OECD, Transfer Pricing and Multinational Enterprises 59 (1984) (hereinafter "1984 OECD Report"). The 1984 OECD Report is, however, the earliest indication in the record of the Treasury's belief in the consistency between § 1.882–5 and the 1975 Treaty. Given the nine-year gap between the signing of the 1975 Treaty and the issuance of the 1984 OECD Report (and the four-year gap between the implementation of the 1975 Treaty and the issuance of the 1984

Report), the consistent position of the Treasury as of 1984 can hardly be read as dispositive of the issue of the intent of the United States and the United Kingdom in 1975 when the Treaty was signed—especially when considering that § 1.882–5 was not even proposed until February 27, 1980. Furthermore, to the extent that the 1984 OECD Report establishes that the United States had taken the position that § 1.882–5 is consistent with the 1975 Treaty, the report establishes that of the 24 OECD members (including the United Kingdom), the United States and Japan were the only two that interpreted the 1963 Draft Convention in this fashion. 1984 OECD Report 56–59. Thus, even if the United States' interpretation of the 1963 Draft Convention, and thereby the 1975 Treaty, can be established as of the publication date of the 1984 OECD Report, the United Kingdom's contrary interpretation is established as of the same date.

The record, therefore, contains no evidence prior to the 1984 OECD report that *1359 either party understood the separate enterprise principle as allowing a method of determining the interest expense of the U.S. Branch that disregards interbranch transactions. The predecessor to this court, however, did consider post-ratification conduct of the parties, "[i]n an appropriate case," to be relevant to the interpretation of a treaty's terms. Great–West Life, 678 F.2d at 189. In Great–West Life, the Court of Claims found that the government's proffered interpretation at trial was consistent with the legislative history of the treaty at issue, the "almost contemporaneous" subsequent legislative action, and the negotiation of later signed treaties. Id. at 188–89. It was this consistency that lent interpretive weight to the government's post-ratification conduct. Id. With respect to the 1975 Treaty, the United States' conduct after the adoption of § 1.882–5 is internally consistent as of the publication of the 1984 OECD Report, but the Government fails to adequately support its contention that this conduct is consistent with the expectations of the United States and the United Kingdom when the 1975 Treaty was signed. The record evidence of the United States' post-ratification conduct seems even less relevant in view of the signatories' contemporaneous acknowledgment that the Treaty is based on the 1963 Model Convention, the commentary to which explicitly authorizes deductions for interest expenses incurred on interbranch advances.

In sum, we find that the plain language of the 1975 Treaty—the separate enterprise principle—mandates that expenses incurred for the benefit of the U.S. Branch be deductible, including interest expenses paid to foreign branches of NatWest. Our reading of the plain language finds direct support in the 1963 Commentary and the contemporaneous understanding of the United Kingdom. Moreover, there is very little evidence that the contemporaneous understanding of the United States differed in any way from that of the United Kingdom. Lastly, the Government's current interpretation of the 1975 Treaty is entitled to minimal deference where it contravenes the treaty's language and negotiation history, as well as the contemporaneous expectations of the United Kingdom. For these reasons, we conclude that Treasury Regulation § 1.882–5 is inconsistent with the 1975 Treaty as applied to a permanent establishment of an international financial enterprise, e.g., the U.S. Branch of NatWest during the tax years at issue.

After rejecting the application of § 1.882–5 to the U.S. Branch in NatWest I, the court considered in NatWest II the method by which the books of the U.S. Branch should be adjusted for the "imputation of adequate capital to the branch and to insure use of market rates in computing interest expenses." NatWest I, 44 Fed.Cl. at 128; NatWest II, 58 Fed.Cl. at 494. The Government argued that the separate enterprise principle required the U.S. Branch to be taxed as if it were a separately incorporated institution and that the U.S. Branch should be deemed to hold an amount of interest-free capital equal to that required of similarly sized U.S. banks (6.996%, as compared to 5.668% for the largest U.S. banks)—the corporate yardstick. NatWest II, 58 Fed.Cl. at 495–96. Conversely, NatWest argued that the imputation of capital on any basis other than an as-necessary adjustment of the U.S. Branch's books to reflect actually allotted capital was improper under the 1975 Treaty. Id. at 496.

At issue is whether the separate enterprise principle was intended by the parties to require a permanent establishment to be taxed as a separately incorporated institution or to be taxed according to the reality of its situation and accounts as adjusted to reflect market pricing in its dealings with the home office. Id. at 497. *1360 The trial court adopted NatWest's position and concluded that " 'separate and distinct' does not mean the branch should be treated as if it were 'separately-incorporated,' but instead 'separate and distinct,' means separate and distinct from the rest of the bank of which it is a part." Id. The court thus held that capital may not be allocated under any formulaic approach, but rather, the capital held by a branch must be determined according to the books of the branch as may be adjusted to accurately characterize transactions and ensure the use of arm's length rates. Id. at 497–98. In support of its conclusion, the trial court noted that the capital determination method proffered by NatWest was consistent with the historic method used by the United Kingdom, as set forth in Inland Revenue, Banking Manual (1994). Id. at 506–07.

On appeal, the Government maintains that the separate enterprise principle allows the IRS to tax the U.S. Branch as if it were subject to the same regulatory and market capital requirements as a separately incorporated U.S. subsidiary. As before, our analysis begins with the language of the 1975 Treaty as informed by the 1963 Draft Convention and the expectations of the parties.

Turning again to the separate enterprise principle set forth in Article 7, ¶ 2, there shall in each Contracting State be attributed to that permanent establishment the profits which it might be expected to make if it were a distinct and separate enterprise engaged in the same or similar activities under the same or similar conditions and dealing wholly independently with the enterprise of which it is a permanent establishment.

31 U.S.T. at 5675. Under this language, the Government's position seems to focus on the "dealing wholly independently with" phrase as indicating that for tax purposes, the U.S. Branch should be taxed as if it possesses enough interest free capital to support its own operations, rather than rely on the capital of the worldwide NatWest enterprise. Conversely, the "same or similar conditions" language seems to support NatWest's position that the U.S. Branch should be taxed in a manner consistent with the actual conditions of its operation—a branch with operations that are funded with little or no interest free capital.

To the extent the parties' conflicting positions evidence ambiguity in the 1975 Treaty's language, we agree with the trial court that NatWest has espoused the better reading. The "same or similar" language of the separate enterprise principle refers to the activities and conditions in which the U.S. Branch conducted its business. That is, the U.S. Branch should be taxed as if it were a separate enterprise engaged in activities that are the "same or similar" to those activities in which the U.S. Branch engaged and as if it were operating in conditions that are the "same or similar" to the conditions in which the U.S. Branch conducted its activities. By way of contrast, the Government's reading of the separate enterprise principle requires that the "same or similar" language describe the activities of the hypothetical separate enterprise. That is, the U.S. Branch should be taxed as if it were engaged in activities that are the same or similar to those in which a separate enterprise would engage and as if it were operating in conditions that are the same or similar to those in which a separate enterprise would operate.

Under the proper reading of the "same or similar" clauses, it becomes clear that the "dealing wholly independently with" language requires taxing authorities to scrutinize intracorporate transactions involving a permanent establishment to ensure that the transactions are accurately *1361 characterized and reflect arm's length terms and pricing. Conversely, the Government's reliance on "dealing wholly independently with" is at odds with a proper reading of the "same or similar" clauses. To conclude that "wholly independently" requires that the U.S. Branch be taxed as if it were subject to regulatory and market capital requirements is to ignore the fact that the U.S. Branch does not operate under conditions in which it is subject to these requirements. In essence, the Government would read the "same or similar conditions" language out of the 1975 Treaty.

Our analysis of the 1975 Treaty's plain language is supported by the 1963 Draft Convention. The 1963 Commentary to Article 7, ¶ 2 states that the analysis of taxable business profits is to begin with the "trading accounts of the permanent establishment," but allows for a formulaic allocation of profits in circumstances where the permanent establishment does not maintain separate accounts from the home office. 1963 Draft Convention 82, ¶ 10. The commentary goes on to state:

It should perhaps be emphasized that the directive contained in paragraph 2 is no justification for tax administrations to construct hypothetical profit figures in vacuo; it is always necessary to start with the real facts of the situation as they appear from the business records of the permanent establishment and to adjust as may be shown to be necessary the profit figures which those facts produce.

Id. (emphasis added). In the instant case, the real facts of the situation are that the U.S. Branch is not required to maintain any minimal amount of capital. Therefore, because the corporate yardstick would essentially recharacterize loans that bear an interest expense as equity capital infusions based on regulatory and domestic market requirements that do not apply to the U.S. Branch, the corporate yardstick ignores the real facts of the U.S. Branch's situation and violates the 1975 Treaty as informed by the 1963 Draft Convention. As stated by the trial court in NatWest II, "The Commentary confirms that the purpose of any adjustment should be to reflect the real facts of the branch's transactions with the entity of which it is a part." 58 Fed.Cl. at 498.

The Government argues that because both parties used capital allocation formulae during the period of the 1975 Treaty's negotiation, the parties expected that the use of similar formulas, e.g., the corporate yardstick, would be permissible under the treaty. Specifically, the Government identifies the adoption of Treasury Regulation § 1.861–8 in 1977, see 49 Fed. Reg. 1195 (Jan. 6, 1977), and the United Kingdom's use of the PW Formula in support of its position. The record reveals, however, that the implementation or abandonment of these formulae provide little, if any, support for the Government's use of the corporate yardstick.

As discussed previously, § 1.861–8 used worldwide information of an international financial enterprise to allocate an interest expense to a permanent establishment doing business in the United States. Section 1.861–8, however, contained language expressly stating that applicable treaty provisions would take precedence over the regulation. Treas. Reg. § 1.861–8(f) (1)(iv) (1977). Thus, to the extent that § 1.861–8 conflicts with our reading of the 1975 Treaty and analysis of the signatories' expectations, the treaty governs.

More importantly, the analysis of the Queen's Counsel opinion when the United Kingdom abandoned the PW Formula in 1978 is particularly instructive. The opinion explicitly considered the appropriateness of treating a permanent establishment as "a company with independent *1362 shareholders," Counsel's Opinion 2 (Dec. 7, 1978), and speaks directly to the issue before us on appeal.

[I]n our view the Convention gives no authority to write into the branch accounts a level of capital which the branch does not have. To do this is to go against the scheme of Article III and the requirement of the paragraph (2) hypothesis that the United Kingdom branch is trading under "… the same or similar conditions…". This directs that the actual conditions under which the United Kingdom branch trades are taken into account. It is those conditions which dictate the expenses in question.

Accordingly the "notional interest formula", under which interest is disallowed to the extent that the (actual) capital account of the branch falls short of an amount (estimated by the Revenue) which would be required as "free working capital" by an independent banking enterprise is in our opinion unwarranted. The notional interest formula may very well result in the disallowance of actual expenditure which is attributable to the branch and that is something which Article III plainly does not authorise. Like the global apportionment referred to in paragraph 5 above the formula may offer a convenient method of avoiding the difficulties involved in the allocation of actual receipts and expenses, but in our opinion it is not sound in law.

Id. at 3 (alterations in original). This analysis of the separate enterprise principle (as similarly set forth in Article III of the previous U.S.-U.K. double taxation treaty, see supra note 4) led the United Kingdom to abandon the PW formula. U.K. Amicus Br. at 24–25. We are persuaded by the clarity of the Queen's Counsel's analysis that when the 1975 Treaty was negotiated, the parties did not understand the separate enterprise principle to allow for imputation of capital to the U.S. Branch according to estimates generated by the IRS's use of the corporate yardstick.

Having concluded that the corporate yardstick violates the 1975 Treaty as applied to the U.S. Branch, we uphold the trial court's decision in NatWest II. "[B]ranch profits must be based on the properly maintained books of the branch," subject to examination and adjustment where: "(1) an interest expense was deducted for advances to the branch that were not used in the ordinary course of its banking business; (2) an interest expense was deducted on amounts designated as capital on its books or on amounts that were in fact allotted to it for capital purposes, such as funding capital infrastructure; and (3) interest paid on inter-branch borrowing [that] was not at arms' length." NatWest II, 58 Fed.Cl. at 505.

Having upheld the trial court's decision in NatWest I and NatWest II, we turn now to the Government's appeal from the Order Denying Reconsideration. Following its ruling in NatWest II, the trial court issued a Scheduling Order that limited the scope of discovery regarding the "capital issue." Order Denying Recons. 1. In the Scheduling Order, the court stated that "the 'capital issue' does not include attributing capital to the U.S. branches from other National Westminster branches or its home office." Id. Thereafter, the Government filed Defendant's

Motion for Reconsideration of Court's July 16, 2004, Order, Limiting Scope of Capital Issue (hereinafter "Motion for Reconsideration"). The Government argued that United Kingdom banking regulations required NatWest to hold sufficient capital to support the operations of the U.S. Branch and that this capital should be attributed to the U.S. Branch for tax purposes. Mot. for Recons. 2. As evidence supporting its motion, the Government offered the expert *1363 report of Mr. Farrant and the decision of a Dutch court applying this capital allocation approach under a treaty similar to the 1975 Treaty. Id. at 1. The court denied the motion, concluding that the Government was seeking to introduce yet another capital allocation theory and thus waived this issue by failing to introduce it during briefing that gave rise NatWest II. Order Denying Recons. 3. Central to this conclusion was the court's finding that the Government did not dispute that it had for nine years been aware of NatWest's compliance with the United Kingdom banking regulations, yet had never sought to attribute capital held by foreign offices and branches to the U.S. Branch for tax purposes. Id. at 3.

We review the denial of a motion for reconsideration by the Court of Federal Claims for an abuse of discretion. Mass. Bay Transp. Auth. v. United States, 254 F.3d 1367, 1378 (Fed.Cir.2001). Likewise, the issue of waiver is also "within the discretion of the trial court, consistent with its broad duties in managing the conduct of cases pending before it." United States v. Ziegler Bolt & Parts Co., 111 F.3d 878, 882 (Fed.Cir.1997). An abuse of discretion occurs when a court misunderstands or misapplies the relevant law or makes a clearly erroneous finding of fact. PPG Indus., Inc. v. Celanese Polymer Specialties Co., 840 F.2d 1565, 1572 (Fed.Cir.1988).

The trial court's denial of the Motion for Reconsideration was not an abuse of discretion. The Government identifies no allegedly clearly erroneous finding of fact. In addition, having concluded that NatWest II was correctly decided, we find no misapplication of the relevant law. Discovery of NatWest's home office books was not necessary because the interest expense deduction for the U.S. Branch is to be determined according to the properly maintained books of the branch. We further find that the trial court did not abuse its discretion by finding that the Government had waived its argument that capital held by the NatWest home office should be imputed to the U.S. Branch for tax purposes.

CONCLUSION

We are persuaded that the signatories to the 1975 Treaty expected that the interest expenses incurred by a permanent establishment of an international financial enterprise, e.g., the U.S. Branch of NatWest, would be deductible to the extent the expenses were related to the permanent establishment's ordinary course of business. Accordingly, we conclude that Treasury Regulation § 1.882–5 and the corporate yardstick as applied to the U.S. Branch violate the 1975

Treaty. We further conclude that the Court of Federal Claims did not abuse its discretion by denying the Government's Motion for Reconsideration. The judgment of the Court of Federal Claims is therefore affirmed.

AFFIRMED

COSTS

No costs.

All Citations

512 F.3d 1347, 101 A.F.T.R.2d 2008-490, 2008-1 USTC P 50,140

Footnotes

1.The United States and the United Kingdom negotiated a new treaty that entered into force in 2003. Convention for the Avoidance of Double Taxation and the Prevention of Fiscal Evasion with Respect to Taxes on Income and on Capital Gains, U.S.-U.K., July 24, 2001, S. Treaty Doc. No. 107–19 (2002).

2.Section 1.882–5 remained unchanged for the tax years at issue but was amended in 1996. 61 Fed.Reg. 9329 (Mar. 8, 1996); 61 Fed.Reg. 15891 (Apr. 10, 1996). Section 1.882–5 was amended again in 2006 to comply with the renegotiation of the U.S.-U.K. treaty, as well as a renegotiated U.S.-Japan treaty. 71 Fed.Reg. 7448 (Aug. 17, 2006); 71 Fed.Reg. 56868 (Sept. 28, 2006).

3.The court also concluded that U.S.-connected liabilities under § 1.882–5 were impermissibly computed by reference to the worldwide assets and liabilities of NatWest rather than the operations of the U.S. Branch, NatWest I, 44 Fed.Cl. at 130, but the record demonstrates that the 0.95 capital ratio was used to calculate the U.S.-connected liabilities.

4.The business profits and separate enterprise language of the earlier treaty states, [T]here shall be attributed to such permanent establishment the industrial or commercial profits which it might be expected to derive if it were an independent enterprise engaged in the same or similar activities under the same or similar conditions and dealing at arm's length with the enterprise of which it is a permanent establishment.

Supplementary Protocol Amending the Convention of April 16, 1945, as modified by the supplementary protocols of June 6, 1946, May 25, 1954, and August 19, 1957, U.S.-U.K., March 17, 1966, 17 U.S.T. 1254.

5.The Government's reliance on Revenue Ruling 78–423 may also be mistaken in its assumption that the U.S.-Japan treaty considered therein is sufficiently similar to the U.S.-U.K. treaty at issue here. Rather than mandating deductions for "those expenses which are incurred for the purposes of the permanent establishment," 1975 Treaty, art. 7 ¶ 3, the U.S.-Japan treaty requires deduction for "expenses which are reasonably connected with [the] profits" of a permanent establishment, United States–Japan Income Tax Convention, Mar. 8, 1971, art. 8, ¶ 3, reprinted in 1978–1 CB 630, 634.

6.The OECD issued a new draft convention in 1977 that did not materially alter Article 7 of the 1963 Draft Convention. See NatWest II, 58 Fed.Cl. at 503, 504 n. 14.

【思考题】

1. 什么是避免重复收税？避免重复收税有什么积极作用？

2. 一个国家缔结或者参加的国际条约与其国内法之间产生冲突应如何解决？

3. 对于国际条约应如何进行解释？

Case1·拓展阅读

Case2　International Tax Avoidance （Transfer Pricing）

【案情说明】

一、苹果公司的避税模式

苹果公司通过设立两家爱尔兰子公司和一家荷兰子公司来达到避税的目的。首先，在爱尔兰投资设立了实际在爱尔兰运营的全资子公司——苹果销售国际公司（Apple Sales International，以下简称 ASI），由 ASI 在欧洲开展实际的经营活动，适用爱尔兰 12.5%企业税率，而 ASI 在美国按照其打钩规则视同为不存在。其次，在荷兰设立荷兰子公司。该荷兰公司在美国打钩选择非实体公司，按美国税法被视同不存在。最后，苹果美国母公司还在爱尔兰注册成立子公司苹果运营国际公司（Apple Operations International，以下简称 AOI），并在英属维尔京群岛（BVI）设立的鲍德温控股无限公司（Baldwin Holdings Unlimited）对其进行实际管理。因为爱尔兰政府为吸引国际企业，只要实际运营位于海外，原则上可以不用缴税，这家公司享有零税率优惠。

苹果美国母公司和 AOI，两公司签订成本分摊协议，共同研发无形资产，共同拥有无形资产，但是此前苹果美国母公司正在研发无形资产，因此，后加入研发的 AOI 公司需要"加入费"以进行合作研发，后期在此基础上买断欧洲地区的无形资产所有权，且交易定价符合美国转让定价要求。当一个苹果客户在 iTune 市场上购买一首歌或一个软件的时候，购买费就进入了 ASI 手中。其中的许可费（Royalty Payment）支付到荷兰子公司时，这笔许可费可以获得税收减免（Tax Reduction），从而使得这一部分许可费免征爱尔兰 12.5% 的企业所得税。荷兰子公司将该笔款以缴纳许可费的形式转给 AOI。根据爱尔兰税法，总部或者母公司在外国就认定为外国公司，且该爱尔兰运营公司把许可费收入汇到加勒比群岛总部时不需要向爱尔兰缴税。如此一来，购买费中的知识产权许可费就由 ASI 通过荷兰子公司流到 AOI，并最终流向 AOI 的总部避税天堂加勒比群岛。在整个收入转移过程中，苹果只需要缴纳荷兰低廉的交易税和部分爱尔兰低廉的所得税。根据苹果公司对外披露的财务报表，截至 9 月 30 日的 2012 财年，苹果公司在美国以外盈利所得税率仅为 1.9%。

二、案件过程

2013 年，欧盟成立了专项小组对成员国范围内的转移定价进行调查并于当年开启了对苹果公司的调查。2016 年 8 月欧盟出具了相关报告，认定爱尔兰对于苹果公司的税收优惠构成有违欧盟规定的不正当的国家补贴，要求爱尔兰向苹果公司追回 130 亿欧元的"非法国家援助"。

当前，爱尔兰政府已与苹果方面签订《托管账户框架行动协议》（Escrow Framework Deed）以执行欧盟委员会做出的向苹果追缴 130 亿欧元"非法国家援助"的最终裁定。但对于欧盟的上述裁定，苹果公司表示不服，向欧盟相关法院提起诉讼，其汇入托管账户的"非法国家援助"是欧盟委员会自行计算、确认的所得税加利息，这笔巨额资金的最终命运将取决于欧盟法院最早 2020 年才能做出的最终判决。有鉴于此，本节主要针对欧盟委员会的调查报告进行介绍。

【法律分析】

一、转移定价

转移定价（transfer pricing）是指跨国公司内部的母公司与子公司之间、子公司与子公司之间提供产品、劳务或技术所采用的定价。基于实现减少税收的目的，为这些交易设定的价格以及基于这些价格计算的所得金额有助于增加一个子公司的利润，并减少另一子公司的利润，从而确定两个实体的应税基础。因此，转移定价还涉及同一公司集团不同部分之间的利润分配，是跨国公司经常使用的国际资金调度管理的手段。因此，以这些转移价格来作为税基是不可靠的。为了避免转移定价减少税收，有必要确保应税收入的确定与私人经营者在类似情况下会申报的应税收入一致。欧盟委员会认为税务顾问提议并被爱尔兰税收局（Irish Revenue）在 2007 年的利润分配措施中所接受的方法实际上是转移定价 5 种常用方法中的交易净利润率法（the transactional net margin method, TNMM）。交易净利润率法，是指按照没有关联关系的交易各方进行相同或者类似业务往来取得的净利润水平确定利润的方法。

二、独立交易原则 Arm's length principle

独立交易原则是全球普遍适用，用以判定转让定价合理性的最基本的原则，即关联企业之间的内部交易应视为独立企业之间的交易，符合正常交易的原则。独立交易原则是约束关联企业间交易行为和税务当局调整转移定价行为的共同准则。为应对转移定价所带来的税基侵蚀，OECD 经合组织的《跨国企业和税务管理部门转移定价指南》2010 版 (*OECD Transfer Pricing Guidelines for Multinational Enterprises and Tax Administrations 2010*) 为"独立交易原则"的应用提供了指导，这是关于转移定价的国际共识，即出于税收目的对有关企业之间跨境交易的价格进行评估，独立交易原则要求关联企业之间的交易条件（价格、利润率等）与独立的交易双方在相似情形类似交易中应当采用的交易条件一致。独立交易原则为关联企业和独立企业提供了同等的税收待遇，尽量消除跨国公司利用转移定价达到减少税收负担的目的。但是在具体贯彻实施中，经常会遇到一些困难。独立交易原则的运用，主要是基于受控交易的条件与独立方"可比"交易的条件之间的比较。但是作为参照对象的可比非受控交易有时难以寻找。欧盟委员会一般适用 OECD 的上述指南确定跨国公司内部交易是否符合独立交易原则。[1]

三、不当国家补贴

（一）是否存在补贴

《欧盟运行条约》第 107（1）条规定：任何成员国以任何形式或通过国家资源提供的任何以偏爱某些企业或提供某些商品而扭曲或威胁扭曲竞争的援助，只要它影响成员国之间的贸易，均应与共同市场相抵触。因此，要使一项措施符合被认定为与共同市场相抵触，就必须满足以下累积条件：（ⅰ）该措施必须属国家所为，并通过国家资源提供资金；（ⅱ）它必须赋予其接受者利益；（ⅲ）优势必须是选择性的；（ⅳ）措施必须扭曲或威胁扭曲竞争，并有可能影响成员国之间的贸易。

本案中的主要问题是，这些税收优惠措施是否会给苹果公司带来选择性的优势，只要它能降低其在爱尔兰的应纳税额。如果可以证明存在选择优势，那么根据《欧盟条约》第 107 条第（1）款找到国家援助的其他两个条件就相对简单了。

（1）是否属于国家所为。有争议的税收措施是由爱尔兰政府机构——税收局提供的。在本案中，苹果使用这些税收措施来计算其在爱尔兰的企业所得税基础。爱尔兰税

1 Commission Decision 2003/755/EC of 17 February 2003, Belgian Coordination centres, OJ L 282, 30.10.2003, p. 55, recitals 89 to 95 and decision of 5 September 2002 in case C 47/01 German Coordination Centres, OJ 2003 L 177/17, para 27 and 28.

收局已接受这些计算，并在此基础上确定了应缴税款。

（2）是否有通过国家资源筹集资金的情况。有争议的税收措施导致苹果公司在爱尔兰的应纳税额降低，从而使爱尔兰政府失去了部分本可以获得的税收，这就导致了国家资源的损失。

（3）是否扭曲或威胁扭曲了欧盟共同市场的竞争。欧盟委员会认为苹果是一家活跃于全球的公司，在欧盟各个成员国开展业务，因此，任何有利于苹果的援助都会扭曲或威胁扭曲竞争，并有可能影响欧盟成员国之间的内部贸易。

（4）是否存在有选择的优势。欧盟委员会认为爱尔兰税务机构给予苹果公司的税收措施使得苹果公司所缴纳的税款低于类似的其他公司所缴纳的税款。

总之，在参照 OECD 的指南后，首先欧盟委员会认为爱尔兰税务局和苹果公司所达成 1991 年的税收措施中的应税税基及苹果各子公司间的利润分配是基于双方协商而没有通过参照可比交易加以证实且爱尔兰税务局也未按常规对此进行有关转移方面的调查并形成报告。其次，爱尔兰税务局对苹果公司 2007 年所采取的税收措施中虽采用了 TNMM 来确定转移定价，但欧盟委员会认为该方法将运营成本作为净利润的指标是不妥的。再次，欧盟委员会认为在苹果几个分公司间的利润分配规则有违独立交易原则，如 AOE 所分摊的 65% 的成本并无任何数据加以支撑。基于上述理由，欧盟委员会认为有争议的税收措施不符合独立交易原则。而通过这些税收措施，爱尔兰税收当局赋予了苹果有利的地位，且这些偏离了实际经济数据的税收措施事实上使苹果公司享受了较类似的其他公司更低的税负。因而，爱尔兰税务局的相关税收措施有违独立交易原则的范围，这些税收措施也应视为具有选择性。最后，欧盟委员会认为鉴于相关税收措施是在《欧盟运行条约》在爱尔兰生效后实施的，因此该措施构成了欧盟理事会（EC）659/1999 号条例第 1（c）条所指的新援助。

（二）补贴是否符合欧洲共同市场规则

如果符合 TFEU 第 107 条第 2 款和第 107 条第 3 款所列的例外情况，可以认为国家补贴措施与欧洲共同市场兼容。但是，爱尔兰所采取的相关税收措施并不符合例外情况的任何一条，该国也未就此进行抗辩。因此爱尔兰的相关税收措施而形成的国家补贴并不符合欧洲共同市场规则。

【英文原文摘选】

EUROPEAN COMMISSION

Brussels, 11.06.2014 C(2014) 3606 final

PUBLIC VERSION

Subject: State aid SA.38373 (2014/C) (ex 2014/NN) (ex 2014/CP) – Ireland Alleged aid to Apple Sir,

The Commission wishes to inform Ireland that, having examined the information supplied by your authorities on the measure referred to above, it has decided to initiate the procedure laid down in Article 108(2) of the Treaty on the Functioning of the European Union ("TFEU").

1. PROCEDURE

(1) By letter of 12 June 2013, the Commission requested Ireland to provide information on the practice of tax rulings in Ireland. In particular, the Commission requested information on any rulings granted in favour of Apple Operations International, Apple Sales International ("ASI") and Apple 2 Operations Europe ("AOE"). By letter dated 9 July 2013, Ireland submitted the requested information to the Commission.

(2) On 21 October 2013, the Commission requested additional information relating to Apple Inc., in particular, it requested information regarding all companies related to Apple which are tax resident in Ireland, all rulings in force and all elements essential to support the tax ruling as provided by the addressee of the tax ruling to the Irish tax authorities, the Office of the Revenue Commissioners ("Irish Revenue") and, in particular, the underlying tax advisor's report and, specifically, the rulings granted in 1991 and 2007. On 21 November 2013, the Irish authorities submitted the requested information, […][1].

(3) By letter of 24 January 2014, additional explanations regarding Apple Inc. were requested, in particular, on turnover figures. On 5 March 2014, the Irish authorities provided the requested information.

(4) By letter of 7 March 2014, the Commission informed the Irish authorities that it was investigating whether the tax rulings in favour of Apple constitute new aid and invited the Irish authorities to comment on the compatibility of such aid. Noting that the Commission had already requested, in its request of 21 October 2013, all essential elements underlying the tax rulings, the Commission invited Ireland to provide any additional information related to the transfer pricing arrangements on which the Irish tax authorities provided a positive opinion in the tax rulings of 1991 and 2007, […].

(5) On 25 March 2014, the Irish authorities replied to that request for information by submitting all the tax returns of Apple-related companies in Ireland since 2004. On 29 May 2014 the Irish authorities informed the Commission by letter that the turnover figures provided in their letter dated 5 March 2014 regarding Apple Operations Europe were not correct and provided corrected figures.

---

1 Parts of this text have been hidden so as not to divulge confidential information; those parts are enclosed in square brackets.

2. DESCRIPTION

2.1. Introduction to transfer pricing rulings

(6) This decision concerns tax rulings which validate transfer pricing arrangements, also known as advance pricing arrangements ("APAs"). APAs are arrangements that determine, in advance of intra-group transactions, an appropriate set of criteria (e.g. method, comparables and appropriate adjustments thereto, critical assumptions as to future events) for the determination of the transfer pricing for those transactions over a fixed period of time[1]. An APA is formally initiated by a taxpayer and requires negotiations between the taxpayer, one or more associated enterprises, and one or more tax administrations. APAs are intended to supplement the traditional administrative, judicial, and treaty mechanisms for resolving transfer pricing issues[2].

(7) Transfer pricing refers in this context to the prices charged for commercial transactions between various parts of the same corporate group, in particular prices set for goods sold or services provided by one subsidiary of a corporate group to another subsidiary of that same group. The prices set for those transactions and the resulting amounts calculated on the basis of those prices contribute to increase the profits of one subsidiary and decrease the profits of the other subsidiary for tax purposes, and therefore contribute to determine the taxable basis of both entities. Transfer pricing thus also concerns profit allocation between different parts of the same corporate group.

(8) Multinational corporations pay taxes in jurisdictions which have different tax rates. The after tax profit recorded at the corporate group level is the sum of the after-tax profits in each county in which it is subject to taxation. Therefore, rather than maximise the profit declared in each country, multinational corporations have a financial incentive when allocating profit to the different companies of the corporate group to allocate as much profit

---

1 APAs differ in some ways from more traditional private rulings that some tax administrations issue to taxpayers. An APA generally deals with factual issues, whereas more traditional private rulings tend to be limited to addressing questions of a legal nature based on facts presented by a taxpayer. The facts underlying a private ruling request may not be questioned by the tax administration, whereas in an APA the facts are likely to be thoroughly analysed and investigated. In addition, an APA usually covers several transactions, several types of transactions on a continuing basis, or all of a taxpayer's international transactions for a given period of time. In contrast, a private ruling request usually is binding only for a particular transaction. See, OECD Guidelines, paragraph 4.132.

2 OECD Guidelines, paragraph 4.123. Since APAs concern the remuneration for transactions that have not yet taken place, the reliability of any prediction used in an APA therefore depends both on the nature of the prediction and the critical assumptions on which that prediction is based. Those critical assumptions may include amongst others circumstances which may influence the remuneration for the transactions when they eventually take place.

as possible to low tax jurisdictions and as little profit as possible to high tax jurisdictions. This could, for example, be achieved by exaggerating the price of goods sold by a subsidiary established in a low tax jurisdiction to a subsidiary established in a high tax jurisdiction. In this manner, the higher taxed subsidiary would declare higher costs and therefore lower profits when compared to market conditions. This excess profit would be recorded in the lower tax jurisdiction and taxed at a lower rate than if the transaction had been priced at market conditions.

(9) Those transfer prices might therefore not be reliable for tax purposes and should not determine the taxable base for the corporate tax. If the (manipulated) price of the transaction between companies of the same corporate group were taken into account for the assessment of the taxable profits in each jurisdiction, it would entail an advantage for the firms which can artificially allocate profits between associate companies in different jurisdictions compared with other undertakings. So as to avoid this type of advantage, it is necessary to ensure that taxable income is determined in line with the taxable income a private operator would declare in a similar situation.

(10) The internationally agreed standard for setting such commercial conditions between companies of the same corporate group or a branch thereof and its mother company and thereby for the allocation of profit is the "arm's length principle" as set in Article 9 of the OECD Model Tax Convention, according to which commercial and financial relations between associated enterprises should not differ from relations which would be made between independent companies. More precisely, using alternative methods for determining taxable income to prevent certain undertakings from hiding undue advantages or donations with the sole purpose of avoiding taxation must normally be to achieve taxation comparable to that which could have been arrived at between independent operators on the basis of the traditional method, whereby the taxable profit is calculated on the basis of the difference between the enterprise's income and charges.

(11) The OECD Transfer Pricing Guidelines[1] (hereinafter the "OECD Guidelines") provides five such methods to approximate an arm's length pricing of transactions and profit allocation between companies of the same corporate group: (i) the comparable uncontrolled price method (hereinafter "CUP"); (ii) the cost plus method; (iii) the resale minus method; (iv) the transactional net margin method (hereinafter "TNMM") and (v) the transactional profit split method. The OECD Guidelines draw a distinction between traditional transaction methods (the first three methods) and transactional profit methods (the last two methods). Multinational corporations retain the freedom to apply methods not described in those guidelines to establish

---

1 Transfer Pricing Guidelines for Multinational Enterprises and Tax Administrations, OECD, 2010.

transfer prices provided those prices satisfy the arm's length principle.

(12) Traditional transaction methods are regarded as the most direct means of establishing whether conditions in the commercial and financial relations between associated enterprises are at arm's length[1]. All three traditional transaction methods approximate an arm's length pricing of a specific intragroup transaction, such as the price of a certain good sold or service provided to a related company. In particular, the CUP method consists in observing a comparable transaction between two independent companies and applying the same price for a comparable transaction between group companies. The cost plus method consist in approximating the income from goods sold or services provided to a group company. The resale minus method consists in approximating the costs of goods acquired from or services provided by a group company. Other elements which enter into the profit calculation (such as personal costs or interest expenses) are calculated based on the price effectively paid to an independent company or are approximated using one of the three direct methods.

(13) The transactional profit methods, by contrast, do not approximate the arm's length price of a specific transaction, but are based on comparisons of net profit indicators (such as profit margins, return on assets, operating income to sales, and possibly other measures of net profit) between independent and associated companies as a means to estimate the profits that one or each of the associated companies could have earned had they dealt solely with independent companies, and therefore the payment those companies would have demanded at arm's length to compensate them for using their resources in the intra-group transaction[2]. For this purpose, the TNMM relies on a net profit indicator which refers, in principle, to the ratio of profit weighted to an item of the profit and loss account or of the balance sheet, such as turnover, costs or equity. To this selected item, a margin is applied which is considered "arm's length" to approximate the amount of taxable profit. When the TNMM is used in combination with a net profit indicator based on costs, it is sometimes referred to as "cost plus" in exchanges between the taxpayer and the tax administration, but this should not be confused with the "cost plus method" described in the OECD Guidelines as described in the previous recital.

(14) The application of the arm's length principle is generally based on a comparison of the conditions in an intra-group transaction with the conditions in transactions between independent companies. For such comparisons to be useful, the economically relevant characteristics of the situations being compared must be sufficiently comparable. To be comparable means that none of the differences (if any) between the situations being compared could materiallyaffect the condition being examined in the methodology (e.g. price or margin),

---

1 OECD Guidelines, paragraph 2.3.

2 OECD Guidelines point 1.35.

or that reasonably accurate adjustments can be made to eliminate the effect of any such differences[1]. To establish the degree of actual comparability and then to make appropriate adjustments to establish arm's length conditions (or a range thereof), it is necessary to compare attributes of the transactions or companies that would affect conditions in arm's length transactions. The OECD Guidelines list as attributes or "comparability factors" that may be important when determining comparability: the characteristics of the property or services transferred; the functions performed by the parties, taking into account assets used and risks assumed (functional analysis); the contractual terms; the economic circumstances of the parties; and the business strategies pursued bythe parties.[2]

(15) The arm's length principle applies not only to transactions between separate companies within a group but also to "transactions" between a company and its permanent establishments, for example a branch. In fact, transfer pricing can also take place within one company if the company operates a branch or permanent establishment in a separate jurisdiction. In that case, the arm's length principle is applicable by analogy, as confirmed in the 2010 report on the attribution of profits to permanent establishments of the OECD[3].

2.2. The beneficiary: the Apple Group

2.2.1. The Apple Group

(16) The present decision concerns tax rulings on the attribution of profits to a branch granted by Ireland to the Apple Group, composed of Apple Inc. and companies controlled by Apple Inc. (hereinafter collectively referred to as "Apple"). Apple is headquartered in the United States of America ("US").

(17) Apple designs, manufactures and markets mobile communication and media devices, personal computers and portable digital music players. It sells different related software, services, peripherals, networking solutions and third-party digital content and applications. Apple sells its products worldwide through its retail stores, online stores and direct sales force, as well as through third-party cellular network carriers, wholesalers, retailers and value-added resellers. In addition, Apple sells a variety of third-party products compatible with Apple products, including application software and various accessories, through its online and retail stores.

(18) Apple sells to consumers, businesses and governments worldwide. Apple manages its business primarily on a geographic basis. The reporting geographic segments are Americas,

---

1 OECD Guidelines point 1.33.

2 OECD Guidelines point 1.36.

3 Report on the Attribution of Profits to Permanent Establishments, OECD, 2010.

Europe, Japan, Greater China, and Rest of Asia Pacific.

2.2.2. Apple's structure in Ireland

(19) Apple includes companies incorporated in Ireland as represented in the chart below (Apple Inc. is incorporated in the US, all other companies on the chart are incorporated in Ireland; of the companies incorporated in Ireland, Apple Operations International, ASI and AOE are not tax resident in Ireland).

(20) In 2013, Apple had worldwide net sales of USD 170,910 million and a net income of USD 37,037 million. In 2012 and 2011, net sales amounted to USD 156,508 million and USD 108,249 million respectively[1]. According to data provided by Apple to the Permanent Subcommittee on Investigations of the US Senate ("the Permanent Subcommittee"), ASI recorded pre-tax income for the years 2009-2011 as indicated in the table below[2].

(21) According to data provided by Apple to the Permanent Subcommittee, ASI's sales revenues for fiscal years 2009, 2010, 2011 and 2012, were USD 12.4 billion, USD 28.8 billion, USD 47.5 billion and USD 63.9 billion respectively[3]. This represents a 415% increase of sales revenues over the period 2009 to 2012.

(22) In their reply of 5 March 2014, the Irish authorities provided the following turnover figures for the Irish operations of AOE and ASI (as corrected by the submission by the Irish authorities dated 29 May 2014). These figures are calculated on the basis of the remuneration attributable to the Irish branch of the companies concerned as indicated in their tax returns.

(23) Based on those tax returns, the taxable income of the respective branches is reproduced in the table below[4]:

(24) The taxable income in the table above was taxed at 12.5%, except for limited components taxed at 25% mainly represented by interest payments received. Additionally to the taxable amounts calculated based on the percentages provided for in the ruling of 1997, the taxable basis is adjusted by a limited amount of tax reliefs. The effective tax payable amounts are represented in the table below:

---

1 Yearly figures at 28 September 2013. Apple's fiscal year is the 52 or 53-week period that ends on the last Saturday of September.

2 Apple does not report standalone accounting data for its subsidiary Apple Sales International, certain stand alone figures were reported in Exhibits of hearing of Offshore Profit Shifting and the U.S. Tax Code Part 2 (Apple Inc.) of the Permanent Subcommittee on Investigations of the US Senate, 21 May 2013.

3 Offshore profit shifting and the U.S. Tax Code-Part 2 (Apple Inc.), Hearing, Permanent Subcommittee on Investigations of the US Senate, 21 May 2013.

4 Tax reporting periods finish end September each year for 2010 and 2011 and for 2012 the figures provided do not cover September 2012 and onlyaccount for 11 months to end August 2012.

2.2.3. Apple Operations Europe (AOE)

(25) AOE, formerly Apple Computer Ltd., is a 100% subsidiary of Apple Operations International (an Irish-incorporated non-tax resident company with no branch in Ireland). AOE is an Irish incorporated non-tax resident company carrying on a trade through a branch in Ireland. The main activity of AOE's Irish branch is the manufacture of a specialised line of personal computers. The company's branch purchases materials from related companies and sells manufactured products to a related company according to specified requirements. AOE's Irish branch also provides shared services to Apple companies in Europe, the Middle East and Africa (EMEA) region, including payroll services, centralised purchasing and a customer call centre.

(26) AOE is party to a cost sharing agreement[1] whereby, together with other Apple Inc. subsidiaries, it shares R&D costs and risks of developing certain Apple products. Apple Inc. holds the legal title to all Apple IP, while AOE has IP rights under that cost sharing agreement. No rights in relation to the IP concerned are attributed to the Irish branch of AOE.

2.2.4. Apple Sales International (ASI)

(27) ASI, formerly Apple Computer International and originally Apple Computer Accessories Ltd., is a 100% subsidiary of AOE. ASI is an Irish-incorporated non-resident company that is carrying on a trade through a branch in Ireland. The main activities of the branch relate to:

§ procurement of Apple finished goods from third-party manufacturers (including a third-party manufacturer in China), [...], § onward sale of those products to Apple-affiliated companies and other customers, and § logistics operations involved in supplying Apple products from the thirdparty manufacturers to Apple-affiliated companies and other customers.

(28) All strategic decisions taken by ASI, including in relation to IP, are taken outside of Ireland. As with AOE, ASI is a party to the R&D cost sharing agreement with other Apple Inc. subsidiaries under which the total costs of the group's worldwide R&D are pooled. ASI's Irish branch has no authority to make decisions relating to Apple IP or the cost sharing agreement. No rights in relation to the Apple IP concerned are attributed to the Irish branch.

(29) According to the information provided by the Irish authorities, the territory of tax residency of AOE and ASI is not identified.

---

1 A cost sharing agreement is an agreement between companies of one group to share costs and benefits of developing intangible assets; it is a form of a cost contribution arrangement described in Chapter VIII of the OECD Guidelines.

2.3. The contested measure

2.3.1. Tax rulings in favour of AOE and ASI

(30) The present decision concerns rulings on profit allocation to branches granted by Irish Revenue in 1991 and 2007 in favour of AOE and ASI (referred to collectively as "the contested rulings" and separately as "the 1991 ruling" and "the 2007 ruling").

Apple Operations Europe (AOE)

(31) In 1991, a basis for determining Apple Computer Ltd.'s (subsequently AOE's) Irish branch net profit was proposed by Apple and agreed by Irish Revenue. According to that ruling, the net profit attributable to the AOE branch would be calculated as 65% of operating expenses up to an annual amount of USD [60-70] million and 20% of operating expenses in excess of USD [60-70] million. This was subject to the proviso that if the overall profit from the Irish operations was less than the figure resulting from this formula, that lower figure would be used for determining net profits. Operating expenses included in the formula were all operating expenses incurred by Apple Computer Ltd.'s Irish branch, including depreciation but excluding materials for resale and cost-share for intangibles charged from Apple-affiliated companies.

(32) In 2007, a revised approach for remunerating the Irish branch of AOE was agreed which was based on (a) a [10-20]% margin on branch operating costs, excluding costs not attributable to the Irish branch such as [...] and material costs, and (b) an IP return of [1-9]% of branch turnover in respect of the accumulated manufacturing process technology of the Irish branch.

Apple Sales International (ASI)

(33) In 1991, a basis for determining Apple Computer Accessories Ltd.'s (subsequently ASI) Irish branch net profit was proposed by Apple and agreed by Irish Revenue. According to that ruling, the net profit attributable to the ASI branch would be calculated as 12.5% of all branch operating costs, excluding material for resale.

(34) A modified basis for determining net profit was agreed for the ASI branch in 2007 with a [8-18]% margin on branch operating costs, excluding costs not attributable to the Irish branch, such as [...] and material costs.

2.3.2. Documents available to Irish Revenue when concluding the rulings

(35) The documents provided by Ireland as constituting all elements essential to support the 1991 ruling include [...] letters (dated [...] 1990, [...] 1990 and [...] 1991) and [...] faxes (dated [...] 1991 and [...] 1991) by [...] as tax advisor of Apple, one note of an interview dated

[…] 1990 and one note of a meeting dated […] 1991 by Irish Revenue, and a letter by Irish Revenue dated […] 1991 which confirms that the letters of [tax advisor] correctly reflect the agreement reached at the meeting of […] 1991. The agreement as described at recitals (31) and (33) is contained in the letter by[tax advisor] dated […] 1991.

(36) The following excerpt is taken from the note of the interview of […] 1990:

"[the tax advisor's employee representing Apple] mentioned by way of background information that Apple was now the largest employer in the Cork area with 1,000 direct employees and 500 persons engaged on a sub-contract basis. It was stated that the company is at present reviewing it's worldwide operations and wishes to establish a profit margin on it's Irish operations. [The tax advisor's employee representing Apple] produced the accounts prepared for the Irish branch for the accounting period ended […] 1989 which showed a net profit of $270 m on a turnover of $751 m. It was submitted that no quoted Irish company produced a similar net profit ratio. In [the [tax advisor's] employee representing Apple's view the profit is derived from three sources-technology, marketing and manufacturing. Only the manufacturing element relates to the Irish branch.

[The representative of Irish Revenue] pointed out that in the proposed scheme the level of fee charged would be critical. [The tax advisor's employee representing Apple] stated that the company would be prepared to accept a profit of $30-40 m assuming that Apple Computer Ltd. will make such a profit. (The computer industry is subject to cyclical variations). Assuming that Apple makes a profit of £100m it will be accepted that $30-40 m (or whatever figure is negotiated) will be attributable to the manufacturing activity. However if the company suffered a downturn and had profits of less than $30-40 m then all profits would be attribitable [sic] to the manufacturing activity. The proposal essentially is that all profits subject to a ceiling of $30-40 m will be attributable to the manufacturing activity.

[The representative of Irish Revenue] asked [the tax advisor's employee representing Apple] to state if was there any basis for the figure of $30-40 m and he confessed that there was no scientific basis for the figure. However the figure was of such magnitude that he hoped it would be seen to be a bona-fide proposal. As it was not possible to gauge the figure in isolation [the tax advisor's employee representing Apple] undertook to extract details of the actual costs attributable to the Irish branch."

(37) The following excerpt is taken from the note of the meeting dated […] 1991:

"in [the tax advisor's employee representing Apple's] view it was clear that the company was engaged in transfer pricing. The branch accounts for the accounting period ended […] 1989 showed a net profit of $269,000,000 on a turnover of $751,000,000. No company on the Irish stock exchange came close to achieving a similar result.

Revenue were not prepared to be conclusive as to whether the company was engaged in transfer pricing but were willing to discuss a profit figure for the Irish branch based on a percentage of the actual costs attributable to the Irish branch.

The proposal before the meeting was that the profit attributable to the Irish branch would be cost plus $[28-38]m and the capital allowances would not exceed $[8-18]m thereby leaving $[18-28]m chargeable to Irish tax. Based on the accounts for the accounting period ended [...] 1990 a profit of $[28-38]m represented 46% of the costs attributable to the Irish branch. It was pointed out that this figure greatly exceeded a figure of [10-20]% which is normally attributable to a cost center although it was readily conceded that a figure of [10-20]% was meaningless in relation to the computer industry. It was pointed out that a mark-up of 100% can be achieved in some industries and in particular the pharmaceutical industry. It was conceded however that the pharmaceutical and computer industries are not directly comparable. Following further discussions it was agreed that, subject to receiving a satisfactory outcome to the capital allowance question, to accept a mark-up of 65% of the costs attributable to the Irish branch. In addition it was agreed to accept a mark-up of 20% on costs in excess of $[60-70]m in order not to prohibit the expansion of the Irish operations[1].

(...) Arising from further discussions it was agreed that the capital allowances computations would be re-cast in Irish punts[2] and the normal rate of wear and tear[3] would be written for all years. In addition it was agreed that the company's claim would be restricted to a sum of $[1-10]m in excess of the sum charged for depreciation in the accounts. Based on the schedule of costs submitted for the period ended [...] 1990 this would ensure that the profits chargeable to Irish tax would be $[30-40]m.

(...) The format of the accounts to be submitted was then discussed. A proposal to submit a schedule of costs was not accepted. It was agreed that a full profit and loss account would be prepared and a royalty/head office charge would be taken for technology and marketing services provided by the group. In addition the full audited accounts of the company will be submitted.

(...) On a separate issue [the tax advisor's employee representing Apple] wished to agree a mark-up for a new company whose activities would be confined to sourcing raw material in the State. A mark-up of 10% was proposed and it was agreed following discussions to accept a mark-up of 12.5%".

(38) The letter by [tax advisor] dated [...] 1991 contains a capital allowances schedule

---

1 Emphasis added by the Commission.

2 Footnote added: punt refers to the Irish currency at the time of the ruling the Irish pound.

3 Footnote added: wear and tear refers to depreciation of material goods.

for Apple Computer Ltd. for the years 1985 to 1990. The fax dated [...] 1991 by [tax advisor] confirms the agreement by Apple to the following wording on the capital allowance which substitutes the wording on the capital allowance previously provided by [tax advisor] in the letter dated [...] 1991: "The capital allowance claimed will not exceed by USD [1-11]m of the depreciation charged in the accounts."

(39) The documents provided by Ireland as constituting all elements essential to support the 2007 ruling consists of a letter dated [...] 2007 by [...] as tax advisor of Apple. The letter contains the agreement as described at recitals (32) and (34). A second document provided by Ireland regarding the 2007 ruling is a letter dated [...] 2007 by Irish Revenue confirming agreement to the method of calculating the profits attributable to the Irish branches of AOE and ASI as explained in the letter by the [tax advisor's] employee representing Apple.

(40) Neither of the two documents provided regarding the 2007 ruling offer any explanation as to the figures "[10-20]%[of Irish located operating costs]/[19]% [of the annual turnover of AOE which is derived from products manufactured in Ireland]/[8-18]% [of operating costs of ASI]" agreed upon in that ruling, nor is there any indication as to how those figures are derived. The letter dated [...] 2007 contains a number of specifications as to how the agreed method will be applied. In particular, it is specified that "Irish located operating costs" of AOE, as well as operating costs of ASI for the avoidance of doubt, exclude [...], "above the line" costs such as material costs, customs, freight costs etc, once-off restructuring costs and capital costs.

(41) None of documents provided, in support of the contested rulings, contain either a transfer pricing report or any cost sharing agreement. According to exhibits of the hearing on Apple of the Permanent Subcommittee, AOE and ASI had a cost sharing agreement with Apple Inc.[1]. That agreement would have first been established in 1980. Under the current agreement, the Irish subsidiaries have the right to distribute Apple products in territories outside the Americas in exchange for contributing to jointly-financed R&D efforts in the US[2].

2.3.3. Information provided by the Irish authorities following the Commission's request

(42) As regards the agreements in the rulings in favour of AOE, the Irish authorities express the view in their letter of 25 March 2014 that AOE's Irish branch was essentially a contract manufacturer and provider of shared services for related Apple entities. The [10-

---

1 Exhibits of hearing of Offshore Profit Shifting and the U.S. Tax Code Part 2 (Apple Inc.) of the Permanent Subcommittee on Investigations of the US Senate, 21 May2013.

2 Testimony of Apple Inc. before the Permanent Subcommittee on Investigations US Senate, 21 May 2013.

20]% margin on the Irish-based costs of those low-risk functions, together with the [1-9]% of turnover return on manufacturing know-how developed by the Irish branch, delivered an aggregate attribution of profit to the Irish branch that would have been commensurate with the activities undertaken in Ireland.

(43) As regards the agreements in the rulings in favour of ASI, the Irish authorities express the view in their letter of 25 March 2014 that ASI's branch was considered to carry out routine, albeit important, functions in the procurement and onward sale and supply of goods for Apple. It would therefore have had no special valuable assets. Although the Irish branch arranged the procurement and onward sale and supply of goods (which did not pass though the Irish branch), the goods concerned derived their value largely from intangibles created in the US. There were also no indications that the Irish branch bore significant risks in relation to the activities of ASI.

(44) Furthermore, according to Irish authorities' letter of 25 March 2014, Irish Revenue was satisfied that the agreed margin on operating costs delivered a net profit commensurate with the value added by the Irish branch. On the basis of a branch-focused analysis of the operations undertaken in Ireland, it would have been clear that the main profit-generating functions and assets were not located in Ireland. All significant risks and all intellectual property would have been borne and economically owned elsewhere in the ASI enterprise or the Apple group and the profit attribution to the Irish branch would have represented full remuneration of its role in that process.

2.3.4. Information about the length of APAs in EU countries

(45) The 1991 ruling does not contain an expiry date and seems to have been in force until the 2007 ruling was issued. An overview of the length of validity of APAs concluded in a number of other Member States is provided in the table below[1]:

3. ASSESSMENT

3.1. Existence of aid

(46) According to Article 107(1) TFEU, any aid granted by a Member State or through State resources in any form whatsoever which distorts or threatens to distort competition by favouring certain undertakings or the provision of certain goods shall be incompatible with the common market, in so far as it affects trade between Member States.

---

1 International Transfer Pricing 2013/2014, PwC and Information on bi- or multilateral mutual agreement procedures under double taxation agreements for reaching Advance Price Agreements ("APA") aimed at granting binding advance approval of transfer prices agreed between international associated enterprises, 5 October 2006, German Federal Ministry of Finance.

(47) The qualification of a measure as aid within the meaning of Article 107(1) therefore requires the following cumulative conditions to be met: (i) the measure must be imputable to the State and financed through State resources; (ii) it must confer an advantage on its recipient; (iii) that advantage must be selective; and (iv) the measure must distort or threaten to distort competition and have the potential to affect trade between Member States.

(48) The main question in the present case is whether the rulings confer a selective advantage upon Apple in so far as it results in a lowering of its tax liability in Ireland. If the existence of a selective advantage can be shown, the presence of the other two conditions for a finding of State aid under Article 107(1) TFEU is relatively straightforward.

(49) As regards the imputability of the measure, the contested rulings were issued by Irish Revenue, which is part of the Irish State. In the present case, those rulings were used by Apple to calculate its corporate income tax basis in Ireland. Irish Revenue has accepted those calculations and, on that basis, set the tax due.

(50) As regards the measure's financing through State resources, provided it can be shown that the contested rulings resulted in a lowering of Apple's tax liabilityin Ireland, it can also be concluded that those rulings give rise to a loss of State resources. That is because any reduction of tax for Apple results in a loss of tax revenue that otherwise would have been available to Ireland[1].

(51) As regards the fourth condition for a finding of aid, Apple is a globally active firm, operating in various Member States, so that any aid in its favour distorts or threatens to distort competition and has the potential to affects intra-Union trade.

(52) Finally, as regards the presence of a selective advantage, it follows from the case-law that the notion of aid encompasses not only positive benefits, but also measures which in various forms mitigate the charges which are normally included in the budget of an undertaking[2]. At the same token, treating taxpayers on a discretionary basis may mean that the individual application of a general measure takes on the features of a selective measure, particularly, where the exercise of the discretionary power goes beyond the simple management of tax revenue by reference to objective criteria.[3]

(53) Accordingly, rulings should not have the effect of granting the undertakings concerned lower taxation than other undertakings in a similar legal and factual situation. Tax authorities, by accepting that multinational companies depart from market conditions in setting

---

1 Joined Cases C-106/09 P and C-107/09 P, Commission and Spain v Government of Gibraltar and United Kingdom [2011] ECR I-11113, paragraph 72.

2 Case C-143/99, Adria-Wien Pipeline, [2001]ECR,I-8365, paragraph 38.

3 Case C-241/94 France v Commission (Kimberly Clark Sopalin) [1996] ECR I-4551, paragraphs 23 and 24.

the commercial conditions of intra-group transactions through a discretionary practice of tax rulings, may renounce taxable revenues in their jurisdiction and thereby forego State resources, in particular when accepting commercial conditions which depart from conditions prevailing between prudent independent operators[1].

(54) In order to determine whether a method of assessment of the taxable income of an undertaking gives rise to an advantage, it is necessary to compare that method to the ordinary tax system, based on the difference between profits and losses of an undertaking carrying on its activities under normal market conditions. Thus, where a ruling concerns transfer pricing arrangements between related companies within a corporate group, that arrangement should not depart from the arrangement or remuneration that a prudent independent operator acting under normal market conditions would have accepted[2].

(55) In this context, market conditions can be arrived at through transfer pricing established at arm's length. The Court of Justice has confirmed that if the method of taxation for intra-group transfers does not comply with the arm's length principle[3], and leads to a taxable base inferior to the one which would result from a correct implementation of that principle, it provides a selective advantage to the company concerned.[4]

(56) The OECD Guidelines are a reference document recommending methods for approximating an arm's length pricing outcome and have been retained as appropriate guidance for this purpose in previous Commission decisions[5]. The different methods explained in the OECD Guidelines can result in a wide range of outcomes as regards the amount of the taxable

---

1 If, instead of issuing a ruling, the tax administration simply accepted a method of taxation based on prices which depart from conditions prevailing between prudent independent operators, there would also be State aid. The main problem is not the ruling as such, but the acceptance of a method of taxation which does not reflect market principles.

2 Commission Decision 2003/757/EC of 17 February 2003, Belgian Coordination centres, OJ L 282, 30.10.2003, p. 25, recital 95.

3 In particular, rulings allowing taxpayers to use improper transfer pricing methods for calculating taxable profits, e.g. the use of fixed margins for a cost-plus or resale-minus method for determining an appropriate transfer pricing may involve State aid- See Commission Decision 2003/438/EC of 16 October 2002 on State aid C 50/2001, Luxembourg Finance Companies, OJ L 153, 20.6.2003, p. 40, recitals 43 and 44; Commission Decision 2003/501/EC of 16 October 2002 on State aid C 49/2001, Luxembourg Coordination centres, OJ L 170, 9.7.2003, p. 20, recitals 46-47 and 50; Commission Decision 2003/755/EC of 17 February 2003, Belgian Coordination centres, OJ L 282, 30.10.2003, p. 25, recitals 89 to 95 and the related Joined Cases C- 182/03 and C-217/03 Belgium and Forum 187 v. Commission [2006] ECR I-5479, paragraphs 96 and 97; Commission Decision 2004/76/EC of 13 May 2003, French Headquarters and Logistic Centres, OJ L 23, 28.1.2004, p. 1, recitals 50 and 53.

4 See Joined Cases C- 182/03 and C-217/03 Belgium and Forum 187 v. Commission [2006] ECR I5479, paragraph 95.

5 Cf. Commission Decision 2003/755/EC of 17 February 2003, Belgian Coordination centres, OJ L 282, 30.10.2003, p. 55, recitals 89 to 95 and decision of 5 September 2002 in case C 47/01 German Coordination Centres, OJ 2003 L 177/17, para 27 and 28.

basis. Moreover, depending on the facts and circumstances of the taxpayer, not all methods approximate a market outcome in a correct way. When accepting a calculation method of the taxable basis proposed by the taxpayer, the tax authorities should compare that method to the prudent behavior of a hypothetical market operator, which would require a market conform remuneration of a subsidiary or a branch, which reflect normal conditions of competition. For example, a market operator would not accept that its revenues are based on a method which achieves the lowest possible outcome if the facts and circumstances of the case could justify the use of other, more appropriate methods.

(57) It is in the light of these general observations that the Commission will examine whether the contested rulings comply with the arm's length principle.

(58) The Commission notes, in the first place, that the taxable basis in the 1991 ruling was negotiated rather than substantiated by reference to comparable transactions. Moreover, according to the excerpt reproduced at recital (37), the authorities did not seem to have had the intention of establishing a profit allocation based on transfer pricing. Instead, according to that excerpt, Irish Revenue accepted the calculation of profit attributable to the branch of AOE on the basis of actual costs without this choice being reasoned in any way. The fact that the methods used to determine profit allocation to ASI and AOE result from a negotiation rather than a pricing methodology, reinforces the idea that the outcome of the agreed method is not arm's length and that a prudent independent market operator would not have accepted the remuneration allocated to the branches of ASI and AOE in the same situation, which serve as a basis for calculating the tax liability.

(59) Furthermore, Section V.C of the OECD Guidelines, although non-binding, lists the type of information that may be useful when determining transfer pricing for tax purposes in accordance with the arm's length principle[1]. Regarding the 1991 ruling, the Commission observes, in particular, that no transfer pricing report was included in the documents provided by the Irish authorities to support the calculation of taxable profits as confirmed in that ruling, which is a common manner by which a transfer pricing proposal is made to tax authorities.

(60) In the second place, the Commission recalls that the OECD Guidelines set certain requirements for the choice of the appropriate transfer pricing method to comply with the arm's length principle[2]. The method proposed by the tax advisor and accepted by Irish Revenue in the 2007 ruling for profit allocation is in effect the TNMM, with operating costs [...] as a net profit indicator. The choice of that particular net profit indicator is neither explained by the tax advisor nor by Irish Revenue, although that choice results in materially different outcomes

---

1 Paragraphs 5.16 to 5.27 of the OECD Guidelines, as well as paragraph 5.4 thereof.

2 See Chapter II , part I of the OECD Guidelines, in particular paragraph 2.8.

in the present case[1]. The 2007 ruling also fails to explain the choice of operating costs as net profit indicator rather than a larger cost basis, such as costs of goods sold. While costs can be an appropriate net profit indicator for routine functions or production process not requiring a specific valuable such as a unique intellectual property right, the 2007 ruling regarding the branch activities of AOE as described in recital (32) acknowledges the existence of a specific know-how in the branch which is remunerated at [1-9]% of branch turnover. The Commission therefore has doubts as to the appropriateness of the transfer pricing method chosen for the 2007 ruling.

(61) In the third place, the Commission notes several inconsistencies in the application of the transfer pricing method chosen when determining profit allocation to AOE and ASI that do not appear to comply with the arm's length principle.

(62) On the one hand, as regards the 1991 ruling, the Commission notes, first, that according to recital (37) the mark-up of 65% of the costs attributable to the AOE Irish branch appear to be reverse engineered so as to arrive at a taxable income of around USD [28-38] million, although according to recital (36) the figure of USD [28-38] million does not have any economic basis.

(63) Second, the margin on branch costs agreed in the 1991 ruling, as described at recital (31), is either 65% or 20% depending on whether the operating costs are below or above USD [60-70] million. According to the excerpt at recital (37), the reduction of the margin after a certain level above USD [60-70] million would have been motivated by employment considerations, which is not a reasoning based on the arm's length principle. In particular, the two margins of 20% and 65% are relatively far apart and, should the margin of 65% effectively constitute an arm's length pricing, the margin of 20% would be unlikely to fall within the same range of pricing, while applying the same degree of prudence.

(64) Third, on the amount of accepted capital allowances, which is restricted to USD [1-11] million in excess of the sum charged for depreciation in the accounts [see recital (38) above], this agreement is not motivated in economic terms nor substantiated by any

---

1 For example in 2011, the taxable profit of ASI represented only around [less than 0.2]% of the sales of ASI [see recitals (21) and (23)]. Therefore if a margin on sales indicator would have been retained as a net profit indicator, the resulting taxable profit would have been much higher, for any benchmark sales margin above [0.2]%. In detail, the turnover of the ASI subsidiary is taken as reference as no branch turnover seems to be reported [other than the turnover provided in recital (22) by the Irish tax authorities in 2014 and which are according to the submission calculated on the basis of the taxable basis and not according to accounting figures]. According to recital (21) the sales of ASI for 2011 amounted to USD 47.5 billion, which at the EUR/USD exchange rate 2011 average exchange rate of 1.3920, represents around EUR 34.1 billion. Comparing the 2011 taxable profit in Ireland of ASI of EUR [50,000,000 – 60,000,000] [see recital (23)] to this sales figure results in a margin on sales of around [less than 0.2]%.

methodology explained in the documents provided by Apple to Irish Revenue. According to the Taxes Consolidation Act 1997[1], a capital allowance can be claimed for plant and machinery expenditures if the plant and machinery are used for the purpose of a trade. However, the agreement on the amount, in particular on the level of the USD [1-11] million cap, does not seem justified by any actual plant or machinery expenditures, but was rather the result of negotiations, as described in recitals (36) and (37) above.

(65) Fourth, as regarding the duration of the 1991 ruling, this ruling was applied by Apple for fifteen years without revision. Even if the initial agreement was considered to correspond to an arm's length profit allocation, quod non, the open-ended duration of the 1991 ruling's validity calls into question the appropriateness of the method agreed between Irish Revenue and Apple to arrive to that allocation in the latter years of the ruling's application, given the possible changes to the economic environment and required remuneration levels. The Commission notes, in particular, that that duration is much longer than the length of APAs concluded by other Member States, as illustrated at recital (45) above.

(66) On the other hand, as regards the 2007 ruling, first, whereas according to the information reported in the note of the meeting of […] 1991 reproduced at recital (37) a mark-up of [10-20]% was considered "meaningless in relation to the computer industry", this mark-up was agreed in the 2007 ruling as a markup on the branch operating costs of AOE, while for ASI a lower mark-up of [818]% on operating costs was agreed. Although the required remuneration for the type of industry covered might have changed significantly between 1991 and 2007, there is an apparent contradiction between this statement and the subsequent agreement.

(67) Second, the profit allocation to the ASI Irish branch, agreed in the 2007 ruling, does not factor in the evolution of sales. In fact, according to recital (21) the sales income of ASI increased by 415% over the three years 2009-2012 to USD 63.9 billion[2]. For the same period, the operating costs as reflected by the taxable income (which represents around [8-18]%[3] of operating costs of the branch according to the ruling of 2007) increased by [10-20]% [see recital (23) above][4]. As a large part of the operating capacity of ASI as a whole seems to be located in Ireland, the discrepancy between the sales growth and the growth of the Irish operating capacity, cannot be explained.

---

1 Section 284 of chapter 2 of the Taxes Consolidation Act, 1997, http://www.irishstatutebook.ie/eli/1997/act/39/section/284/enacted/en/html

2 USD 63.9 billion in 2012 compared to USD 12.4 billion in 2009.

3 Because of the limited effect of interest income and of tax reliefs, the taxable income is not exactly equal to [8-18]% of operating costs, see recital (24).

4 EUR [40,000,000-50,000,000] in 2012 compared to EUR [30,000,000-40,000,000] in 2009.

(68) That discrepancy could point to an inconsistency in the allocation of turnover between ASI and its Irish branch. The income of ASI of USD 63.9 billion for 2012 and the respective amounts for previous years as indicated in recital (21) represent sales income, which is an active income and generates operating expenses. If the 415% increase in sales is only due to an increase in price and not an increase in volumes, it would not be inconsistent that the operating expense of the ASI branch only increase by [10-20]% over the same period. However if the sales volumes increased, the operating costs of either the Irish branch of ASI or the operating costs that ASI incurs outside of Ireland should have increased significantly as well. At this stage, the increase in sales cannot be related to a comparable increase in operating costs, which could point to an inconsistency in the profit allocation to the Irish activities.

(69) Based on the above, the Commission is of the opinion that the contested rulings do not comply with the arm's length principle. Accordingly, the Commission is of the opinion that through those rulings the Irish authorities confer an advantage on Apple. That advantage is obtained every year and on-going, when the annual tax liability is agreed upon by the tax authorities in view of that ruling.

(70) That advantage is also granted in a selective manner. While rulings that merely contain an interpretation of the relevant tax provisions without deviating from administrative practice do not give rise to a presumption of a selective advantage, rulings that deviate from that practice have the effect of lowering the tax burden of the undertakings concerned as compared to undertakings in a similar legal and factual situation. To the extent the Irish authorities have deviated from the arm's length principle as regards Apple, the contested rulings should also be considered selective.

(71) Given that the rulings were concluded after the entry into force of the Treaty in your country, the measure constitutes new aid within the meaning of Article 1(c) of Council Regulation (EC) No 659/1999. However, any potential recovery would be prescribed for aid granted before 12 June 2003, in accordance with Article 15 of that regulation.

3.2. Compatibility of aid

(72) As the measure appears to constitute State aid, it is necessary to examine whether that aid could be considered compatible with the internal market. State aid measures can be considered compatible with the internal market on the basis of the exceptions listed in Article 107(2) and 107(3) TFEU.

(73) At this stage, the Commission has no indication that the contested measure can be considered compatible with the internal market. The Irish authorities did not present any argument to indicate that any of the exceptions provided for in Article 107(2) and 107(3) TFEU apply in the present case.

(74) The exceptions provided for in Article 107(2) TFEU, which concern aid of a social character granted to individual consumers, aid to make good the damage caused by natural disasters or exceptional occurrences and aid granted to certain areas of the Federal Republic of Germany, do not seem to apply in this case.

(75) Nor does the exception provided for in Article 107(3)(a) TFEU seem to apply, which allows aid to promote the economic development of areas where the standard of living is abnormally low or where there is a serious unemployment, and for the regions referred to in Article 349 TFEU, in view of their structural, economic and social situation. Such areas are defined by the Irish regional aid map. This provision does not seem to applyin this case.

(76) As regards the exceptions laid in Article 107(3)(b) and (d) TFEU, the aid in question does not appear to be intended to promote the execution of an important project of common European interest nor to remedy to a serious disturbance in the economy of Ireland, nor is it intended to promote culture or heritage conservation.

(77) Finally, according to Article 107(3)(c) TFEU, aid granted in order to facilitate the development of certain economic activities or of certain economic areas could be considered compatible where it does not adversely affect trading conditions to an extent contrary to the common interest. The Commission has no elements at this stage to assess whether the tax advantages granted by the contested measure are related to specific investments eligible to receive aid under the State aid rules and guidelines, to job creation or to specific projects.

(78) At this stage, the Commission considers that the measure at issue appears to constitute a reduction of charges that should normally be borne by the entities concerned in the course of their business, and should therefore be considered as operating aid. According to the Commission practice, such aid cannot be considered compatible with the internal market in that it does not facilitate the development of certain activities or of certain economic areas, nor are the incentives in question limited in time, digressive or proportionate to what is necessary to remedy to a specific economic handicap of the areas concerned.

4. DECISION

In the light of the foregoing considerations, the Commission's preliminary view is that the tax ruling of 1990 (effectively agreed in 1991) and of 2007 in favour of the Apple group constitute State aid according to Article 107(1) TFEU. The Commission has doubts about the compatibility of such State aid with the internal market. The Commission has therefore decided to initiate the procedure laid down in Article 108(2) TFEU with respect to the measures in question.

The Commission requests Ireland to submit its comments and to provide all such information as may help to assess the aid/measure, within one month of the date of receipt of this letter. In particular:

• Provide the financial accounts of ASI and AOE for the period 2004-2013, in particular the P&L accounts. • In the case of ASI single out in the P&L the amount of passive income each year and specifying if such passive income comes from Ireland. • Provide the number of full time equivalent employees (hereinafter "FTE") of ASI and of AOE over the same period (each end of reporting period). Provide the FTE of the Irish branch of ASI and of AOE for the same period (each end of accounting period). • Provide the cost sharing agreement between Apple Inc., ASI and AOE in all its variations since 1989 until the last modification. • Describe in detail the type of intellectual property covered by the cost sharing agreement. The Commission requests your authorities to forward a copy of this letter to the potential recipient of the aid immediately.

The Commission wishes to remind Ireland that Article 108(3) of the Treaty on the Functioning of the European Union has suspensory effect, and would draw your attention to Article 14 of Council Regulation (EC) No 659/1999[1], which provides that all unlawful aid may be recovered from the recipient.

The Commission warns Ireland that it will inform interested parties by publishing this letter and a meaningful summary of it in the Official Journal of the European Union. It will also inform interested parties in the EFTA countries which are signatories to the EEA Agreement, by publication of a notice in the EEA Supplement to the Official Journal of the European Union and will inform the EFTA Surveillance Authority by sending a copy of this letter. All such interested parties will be invited to submit their comments within one month of the date of such publication.

【思考题】

1. 什么是转移定价？

2. 转移定价会产生什么危害？

3. 爱尔兰政府针对苹果公司所给予的税收优惠政策是否构成不正当的国家补贴？

Case2·拓展阅读

---

1 OJ L 83 of 27.3.1999, p. 1, last amended by Regulation 734/2013 of 22 July 2013 OJ L 204 of 31.7.2013, p.15.

VIII

国际经济贸易争端解决

【内容摘要】

　　本章分为三节，分别选取"DSM Dyneema v.s.Electromichaniku EPE"案、"韩国安城住房诉中国政府案"和"欧共体某些海关措施案"三个典型案例用来介绍和说明在国际货物贸易争端、国际投资争端和国际多边自由贸易体制内争端解决的不同特点。其中第一个案例主要涉及《联合国国际货物销售合同公约》（CISG）的适用问题，争议焦点包括 CISG 的适用问题，以及分批交货合同违约纠纷的解决。第二个案例涉及的核心问题包括 CISG 的初步异议程序适用和双边投资协定中最惠国待遇条款适用范围问题。第三个案例主要关注美国与欧共体之间关于欧共体境内海关措施的统一实施问题产生的贸易纠纷及其 WTO 框架内的解决，焦点在于 WTO 争端解决机构的职权管辖问题。

Case1 *DSM Dyneema* vs.*Electromichaniku EPE*（Greece 2009 Decision 4505/2009 of the Multi-Member Court of First Instance of Athens）

【案情说明】

一、案件事实

希腊警察通过国防部与希腊 SA 武器工业（Hellenic Weapon Industry of SA，以下简称 EBO SA）合作，就一批防弹背心进行国际采购。EBO SA 负责制造并向希腊警察提供这批防弹背心。在合同签订之前，EBO SA 向全球该类产品主要制造商发出了竞标邀请。其中，EBO SA 的一家附属公司，Electromichaniki Kimis EPE 的公司接到邀请后发出要约，表示愿意提供符合美国国家研究院 0101.03 保护标准的防弹背心，并承诺这批背心可以按照美国国家研究院方法在任何一家官方实验室进行测验。随后，在 Electromichaniki Kimis EPE 介绍下，EBO SA 向与 Electromichaniki Kimis EPE 有过合作关系的 DSM Dyneema 发出要约邀请，后者是一家抗冲击材料制造商。DSM Dyneema 随后参与了投标，并根据希腊国防部的要求提供了两种抗冲击材料供选择。其中一种 Dyneema UD-XSB31 为其最新研发的新型材料，但由于研发时间较短，无法提供实践数据。但 DSM Dyneema 保证该类产品完全符合技术手册的要求，并愿意自交付之日起提供 10 年质保。经评估后，EBO SA 和 Electromichaniki Kimis EPE 最终选定了 DSM Dyneema 的 Dyneema UD-XSB31 作为制造防弹背心的原材料。

2001 年 6 月 21 日，希腊国防部和 EBO SA 达成协议（no.16A/2001，以下简称 EBO 供货协议），协议中 EBO SA 承诺向希腊军方和希腊警察提供 10 020 件防护等级为ⅡA 的防弹背心和防护等级为Ⅲ的防弹板（bullet-proof slabs）。同时，EBO 供货协议约定，将由 EBO SA 全权负责对 DSM Dyneema 的质量检验。最终产品交付后，希腊国防部对其质量进行最终检验。基于 DSM Dyneema 的承诺，EBO SA 同样对最终产品提供 10 年质量担保。如发现任何质量瑕疵，希腊国防部有权在 20 天内就任何不符部分书面通知 EBO SA，要求修理或重做。合同特别约定，在担保期间内，如果货物瑕疵部分超过所收货物 10%，这种不符将被视为"系统性"的瑕疵，EBO SA 有义务免费对所有材料进行更换。

2001 年 7 月 4 日 DSM Dyneema 与 Electromichaniku EPE 签订销售合同，合同约定由前者向后者出售 155 000 延米 160 厘米宽、Dyneema UDX/SB31 型号的防弹材料，交

货地为雅典，总价款为 2 515 464.00 欧元，合同编号 No.46/2001，卖方在 2002 年 1—7 月按月分 7 个批次交付货物。买方采购和质检部门负责接收每一批货物并负责对材料进行初步检验。按照合同约定，卖方于 2001 年 7 月 15 日在银行担保下预付 40% 货款（100 618 560 欧元），余下货款在每收到一批货物后 30 天内分批支付。

合同同时约定，如卖方所交付材料不能完全符合合同要求，买方可以部分或全部拒收。当货物被部分或全部拒收后，卖方有义务在收到买方质量监督部门通知后 30 天内交付完全符合合同约定规格的货物，并由卖方自行承担由此产生的运输成本。卖方保证其所提供的材料不存在任何法律缺陷和任何其他明显或隐蔽瑕疵。

2001 年 6 月 12 日，买方向卖方预付 1 006 185.60 欧元（总货款 40%），卖方于 2002 年 1 月 11 日—7 月 19 日分 10 个批次交付了 125 129 延米材料，所交付货物均附有质量合格证书（quality compliance certificates），证书表明按照卖方采用的内部检验程序，材料符合可适用的制造规格；但也表示其提供的内部检验不影响买方对交付材料进行通常的检验。买方对前 6 个批次的材料按照合同约定支付了价款，但对于后 4 批次货物则并未付款，在卖方给出的 60 天宽限期届满后，买方仍未付款。

2002 年 9 月 25 日，双方就此展开交涉。交涉过程中，买方告知卖方其将在 2002 年 9 月底支付剩余价款；同时买方还首次告知卖方，希腊警察在 2002 年 9 月 20 日的测试中发现了问题。对此，卖方同意向买方提供全面协助，包括公开相关记录，并声明其会尽量消除相关问题。据介绍，希腊警察在前述测试中发现，背心正面拉链处接缝处测试中被洞穿。基于此，希腊警察认为 EBO SA 应该就故障原因进行分析，并将第 5 批货物退回。随后，买方拒绝支付剩余款项 438 771.58 欧元，同时通知卖方将拒收剩余的最后一批货物。卖方就此与买方数次交涉未果情况下，2002 年 7 月 19 日，卖方最后通知买方，如果后者在 14 天不能支付剩余款项，它将把未交付货物转售第三方。2002 年 10 月 8 日，买方传真通知卖方，称在希腊警方愿意支付相应款项情况下，它也将继续支付剩余款项。10 月 9 日，买方又通知卖方，称在完成故障原因分析之前将暂停剩余款项的支付。

2002 年 10 月 30 日，在买方代表在场情况下，希腊警方又进行了第二次测验，本次测验极为成功，并未出现第一次测验中的抗冲击能力不足的问题。对比两次测验之后，研究人员发现主要原因在于背心成品设计，以及第一次测试所选用的弹药类型。2002 年 12 月 6 日，卖方邀请第三方用同样材料设计了防弹背心并找到了解决办法。但买方对此不置可否，并未做出回应。2003 年 1 月 27 日，卖方再次催告买方收取剩余货物并支付剩余价款，但买方声称必须待其与希腊国防部商谈之后再做决定。2003 年 4 月 16 日，卖方再次催告支付剩余价款，并提出了设计方面的替代性解决方案，包括提供一种性能更好的改进型材料，但买方未做出回应。2003 年 10 月 27 日，买方与第三方供货商签订采购协议，同时买方通知卖方，基于 2002 年 9 月 20 日的测试，希腊警方已决定拒绝卖方所提供抗冲击材料，买方不再接受剩余批次货物，同时要求对已交付部分进行修理，买方同时要求减价 202 722 欧元以抵消修理和测试费用。至此，买方认为其最终应支付卖方价款为 34 464.45 欧元。2004 年 4 月 21 日，卖方否认了买方主张，要求买方支付剩余的 438 771.58 欧元价款并收取剩余货物。随后，在双方争端无法解决情况下，卖方向希腊雅典多员一审法院（Multi-Member Court of First Instance of Athens）提起诉讼。卖方诉讼请求包括：请求买方支付剩余价款 438 771.58 欧元，以及 5 000 000 欧元精神损害赔偿。

二、裁判结果

在将案件界定为国际货物贸易合同纠纷之后，法院通过适用《联合国国际货物销售合同公约》（CISG）和希腊相关国内法的规定对案件实体部分进行了判决。首先，卖方交付货物符合销售合同的要求。买方 2002 年 10 月 30 日进行的测验证明，最终产品的瑕疵源于产品设计方面，而非原材料。至于 2002 年 9 月 22 日进行的测验，法院认为该次测试并未按照合同约定进行符合国际标准的测验，因此出现的故障也无法证明卖方提供了有瑕疵的原材料。卖方也并非希腊军方与 EBO SA 之间合同的当事方，对于最终产品的质量它也不承担任何法律责任。法院进一步指出，对于买方对第 7、9、10 等三个批次货物主张宣告合同无效的抗辩，法院并未予以认可。对于剩余未交付货物，买方有义务接收货物并支付价款。最终法院判决买方赔偿卖方 729 627.80 欧元，包括前三个批次买方已经收货但尚未支付的货款，以及买方拒收的第 11 个批次货物货款。但对于卖方提出的精神损害赔偿，法院并未予以支持。

【法律分析】

本案属于一起典型的国际货物销售合同纠纷，重点涉及以下几个方面的问题：

（一）CISG 的适用

合同适用公约的条件规定在 CISG 第 1 条。包括直接适用和间接适用两种方式。直接适用的情况是指当营业地位于不同缔约国的当事人之间所订立的货物销售合同。间接适用，简单而言也就是指通过国际私法规则的指引适用某一缔约国的法律。本案卖方的主要营业地位于荷兰，而买方营业地在希腊。且希腊和荷兰均是 CISG 缔约国，因此符合直接适用条件。本案中，虽然双方合同约定适用希腊法律，但法院认为这种约定并不构成对 CISG 的默示排除。

（二）CISG 是否适用非财产性损失

本案中原告提出了精神损害赔偿。对此，法院认为 CISG 并未为该诉求提供相应的法律基础。理由在于，首先，CISG 并未涉及非财产性损失的规定。其次，基于 CISG 的损失可预见性理论，买方既不可能在主观上预见到此类损失的发生；客观上其在合同订立当时也没有义务预见到合同违约对当事方声誉的损害。

（三）分批交货合同部分不符的处理

法院通过适用 CISG 第 51 条等条款的规定，认为本案中前几个批次的货物已经为买方所收取并按照合同约定进行了验收，可认为卖方已交付与合同要求相符的货物，即便后几个批次交货不符，但因不构成系统性违约，因此买方应依据合同约定支付价款。法院进一步指出，根据 CISG 第 38 条 1 款的规定，买方必须在按情况实际可行的最短时间内检验货物或由他人检验货物。第 39 条 1 款规定，买方对货物不符合同，必须在发现或理应发现不符情形后一段合理时间内通知卖方，说明不符合同要求的情形，否则就丧失声称货物不符合同的权利。因此，法院认为，本案中的被告，也就是买方应在接收货物后，应在"实际可行的最短时间内"检验货物；并在发现或理应发现不符情形后的"合理时间内"通知卖方。但本案中买方并未履行上述义务，基于这一事实，法院裁定在这种情况下，应推定卖方交付货物与合同相符，买方要主张货物不符就必须承担相应的举证责任。此外，法院在参考意大利、德国等国家国内法院的判例，判定通知的合理时间为 1 个月。但法院并未就"实际可行的最短时间"进行解释和界定。

【英文案例裁决摘录】

Seller's Claim

On 28 July, the Seller （the "Claimant"） filed a claim （"Seller's Claim"） against the Buyer （the "Defendant"）.

1.Request to the Court

Based on this background, the Seller requests from the Court:

(1) to oblige the Buyer to pay to it the amount of €729,627.58, out of which the amount of €53,175.29, €239,537.09 and €146,059.20 with legal interest from the day following the date set for the settlement of the invoices referred to in the action, i.e., on 29 July 2002, 17 September 2002 and 17 September 2002 respectively, otherwise from the day following the date the extra-judicial written notice was sent, i.e., on 26 September 2002, otherwise from the day following the date the action was served upon it and until full payment, and the amount of €290,856.22 with legal interest from the day following the date the goods were loaded for shipment, i.e., on 31 July 2002, otherwise from the day following the date the extra-judicial notice was sent to it, i.e., on 26 September 2002, otherwise from the day following the date the action was served upon it and until full payment;

(2) to oblige the Buyer to pay the amount of €500,000.00 as compensation for moral damage it sustained;

(3) to order the publication of the purview of the judgment issued in two daily newspapers circulating throughout the whole Greek State;

(4) to declare the judgment provisionally enforceable; and

(5) to sentence the Buyer to pay its court expenses.

2. Ruling on Seller's Claim

"With this content and claims, the action under judgment, for the acceptance of the hearing for which, pursuant to the provision of Article 214A, para. 8 of the Code of Civil Procedure, the minutes dated 24 October 2005, jointly drawn up by the authorized attorneys-at-law Mr.D.Samoladas, I.Oikonomakis and D.Papaioannou of the litigants, is produced, from which it is concluded that the endeavor to extra-judicially settle the dispute failed, and it is subject, pursuant to the provisions of the above main thought, to the international jurisdiction of this Court, in accordance with the provisions of Articles 1§1, 2§1, 5§1, 23§1, 24, 60, 66§1, 68§1 and 76 of the (EC) Regulation 44/2001 of the European Council dated 22 December 2000, On International Jurisdiction and the Recognition and Enforcement of Judgments in Civil and Commercial Matters", which entered into effect on 1 March 2002, substituting the Brussels Convention, which (the regulation) supersedes and other provision of Greek law, in performance of Article 249 of the EC Treaty.

In particular:

(a) As regards the part of the action where the Seller seeks, on one hand, to be compensated by the Buyer for the total amount of €729,627.58, due to positive and negative loss it sustained from the refusal of the Buyer to settle the price of the goods delivered to it by the Seller and to accept the delivery of the last order, in accordance with the terms of their mutual contract no. 46/04 July 2001 and, on the other, the payment of the amount of €500,000.00 due to damage sustained to the international reputation of the Seller, because the Buyer declared the contract avoided and concluded a new contract with another supplier who is in direct competition with the Seller, the international jurisdiction of this Court is founded on a valid prorogation agreement which was concluded by the litigants [Article 23§1 of the (EC) Regulation 44/2001], setting out in clause 8.3 of the above sales contract executed, that for any dispute that may arise from the performance of the said contract, the Court of Athens would be competent. This agreement is valid, since both parties have their places of business in Member-States of the European Union (The Netherlands and Greece, respectively), they set out in writing that the competent courts would be the courts of a Member-State for the judgment of disputes concerning property which derive from a specific legal relation, i.e., the sales contract under judgment. In addition, the international jurisdiction of this Court is founded on the tacit prorogation [Article 24 of the (EC) Regulation 44/2001], since the Buyer appeared without contesting the international jurisdiction of this Court, and this Article applies, regardless of the contractual determination of the competent court by the litigants, in accordance to the provision of Article 23 of the above-mentioned regulation.

(b) As regards the part of the action where the Seller requests compensation for moral damages sustained due to a tort of the Buyer, consisting in slanderous talks against it, this Court has international jurisdiction, as being the court of the place where the fact that caused the moral damage of the Plaintiff （Seller） took place, according to the brief of the action (Article 5.3 of the (EC) Regulation 44/2001), otherwise of the place where the Defendant [Buyer] has its statutory place of business [Article 2§1, Article 60 of the (EC) Regulation 44/2001]. Furthermore, the action is accepted in substance and is brought before this Court in terms of jurisdiction (Articles 7, 9, 12, 13, 14.1 and 2, 19.1 and 42 of the Code of Civil Procedure) in order to be judged during the ordinary process and has been sufficiently defined, since it refers the founding facts (Articles 118 and 216 of the Code of Civil Procedure), except for the part where the Seller requests that the Buyer be obliged to pay to it the amount of €500,000.00 as compensation for moral damage Seller sustained from the slanderous talks against it, which is vague and cannot be judged by the Court, since it does not clearly exhibit the facts required in order to be legally founded. In addition, although the action is filed against a legal person, which does not commit a tort directly, but it is responsible for a tort committed by its bodies or persons drawing rights from it (employees, workers, etc.) in accordance with the provisions of Articles 71 and 922 of the Civil Code, which apply, pursuant to the provision of Article 26 of the Civil Code, as the law of the place where the tort (according to what is referred to in the action) of the Defendant Buyer was committed, no reference is made of the natural person (or natural persons) who committed the illegal action, by virtue of which the Seller's reputation was damaged, the special relationship of the said person with the Buyer, stating in particular that it acted as a body thereof or as a worker or employee or under any other capacity which connected it to the Buyer], as well as the cause of the said conduct (fraud or negligence) of the said person and if it acted within the limits of its duties or orders that it had taken from the Buyer. In addition, no reference is made in the action that the bodies or the persons drawing rights from the Buyer were aware or intentionally ignored the untruthfulness of the slanderous talks that the supported untrue talks causally exposed to great risk the credit of the Seller and that its property was causally damaged, since the above goods were exposed to risk. These deficiencies cannot be remedied with the pleadings, or with the reference to the context of another document, nor from the examination of evidence, since they contradict the provisions relating to the preliminary procedure of Article 111 of the Code of Civil Procedure, whose observance is *ex officio* examined by the Court. In this case, we are dealing with a "legal vagueness" of the action, since the substantial facts establishing its background are not referred therein. In this manner the Court cannot, on one hand, examine the brief of the action, and the Buyer cannot defend. Therefore, after the *ex officio* examination, the action, as to the above-mentioned part, must be rejected as being vague and unacceptable.

Furthermore, in accordance with the above referred thoughts, the action is legal, being founded on the provisions of Articles 1.1, 3, 4, 6, 7, 9, 25, 30, 31, 33, 35, 53, 57, 58, 59, 61, 62, 66, 67, 69, 74, 78, 99 and 100 of the Convention of the United Nations for the International Sale of Goods (CISG), Articles 340, 345, 346 of the Civil Code, 904§1 and 2 case (a), 907, 908 case (f) and 176 of the Code of Civil Procedure, except:

(a) the motion for the compensation of €500,000.00, due to the damage incurred to the international reputation of the Seller which was caused when the Buyer declared the contract avoided and concluded a new sales contract with a competitor of the Seller, since, even if the actual facts of the brief of the action are deemed true, they cannot establish the liability of the Buyer for monetary compensation of the Seller, since non-property damage is not compensated under the CISG, while based on the theory of foreseeability which applies to this contract, the invoked damage of the Seller to its professional reputation could not, based on the criteria referred to in the main thought, be foreseen by the Buyer (subjective foreseeability), neither was the Buyer obliged to have foreseen it (objective foreseeability) as a potential consequence of the contractual breach, throughout the contract.

(b) the subsequent motion thereof to order the publication of the purview of the judgment issued in two daily newspapers circulating throughout the Greek State, since no such provision is made in the CISG, neither within the context of the tort, for which the action was nevertheless rejected. Therefore, the part for which the action was deemed accepted and legal must be further examined as to the legal substance, given that the required court stamps with all legal surcharges in favor of the Jurists Fund (TN) and the Athens Lawyers Welfare Fund (TPDA) have been paid (see duplicate receipt No 6084100/20 November 2007 issued by the Tax Office of Athens and cash receipt voucher No 576051/20 November 2007 and 16.537/20 November 2007 of the Jurists Fund and Athens Lawyers Welfare Fund respectively).

The Buyer, *via* its written pleadings legally produced, reasonably opposes the action, raising allegations on its legal and substantial grounds, for the reasons illustrated in detail in the brief of its pleadings.

Furthermore, the Defendant-Seller claims that:

(1) The Buyer, during the period the risk was transferred, did not correspond to the terms of the sale contract dated 4 July 2001, since on 20 September 2002, during the ballistic tests of the bulletproof vest and the delivery, the committee responsible for ensuring the quality of the product, verified that the bulletproof vests were punctured and for this reason the action

must be rejected. This allegation of the Seller, in accordance with the above exhibited thoughts, constitutes an objection, which relies on the provisions of Articles 36(1), 38(1), 39, 60(b) and 67-69 of the CISG, since, based on the actual facts described in the brief of the pleadings, after the delivery of the bullet-proof type "DYNEEMA UDX/SB31" of the Seller, (the Buyer) did not proceed with the examination thereof within as short a period as is practicable in the circumstances, thus losing the right to notify the lack of conformity to the Seller, specifying the nature of the lack of conformity in detail, so as to reverse the burden of proof and causing the Seller to be obliged to prove that at the time the risk was transferred the above material corresponded to the sale contract under judgment.

(2) It has against the Buyer similar — as to their object — and due counterclaims concerning (a) expenses it incurred for repair and replacement of the Dyneema UD-SB31 material with aramidic material (Kevlar) in the bulletproof vests which amount to a total of €655,671.01 (103,750.77 + 314,758.62 + 43,247.36 + 193,914.26), (b) a total consideration of Euro 8,151.08 from the sale and delivery to it of 3,189 kg of pieces of the above material which resulted after the process (waste) and (c) a claim of the amount of € 7,680.87 which was assigned to it by "EBO S.A." in relation to its participation percentage in the cost of the ballistic tests conducted in November 2000 in the ballistic station of the University of Granfield in England, which, according to an inviolable term of the International tender for the procurement of antiballistic material, would be borne by the participating companies, pursuant to the events analytically referred to in the brief of the pleadings, which it suggests for set-off.

However, part of the claims of the Buyer against the Seller and in particular, the amount of €628,645.60 constitutes the content of the jointly judged action dated 21 December 2006 with brief deposit number 11867/2006, since there is identification of the background, motion and litigants between it and the objection for set-off raised (the reversal of the roles of the litigants has no legal importance), and thus the trial is pending, in accordance with the provision of Article 222§1 of the Code of Civil Procedure.

Consequently, whereas the objection for set-off raised by the Buyer via its pleadings dated 14 November 2007 has been raised at a later date than its action above, its hearing must, for the above-mentioned amount thereof which coincides with the amount of the said action, after being *ex officio* examined as a negative procedural condition of the trial (Court of Appeals of Athens [...] 7840/1995, Greek Justice [...] 1996.1123) be adjourned until the first trial is concluded, in accordance with Article 222§2 of the Code of Civil Procedure (Kerameas-Kondylis-Nikas, Interpretation of Code of Civil Procedure, Volume I, Article 222, notes 11 seq., page 485 seq., V. Vathrakokoilis, Interpretation of Code of Civil Procedure, Volume B,

Article 222, notes 6, 6a, 6b, 8, 14, 16, 38, 43, pp. 39-40, 42-43, 50, 52).

On the contrary, the claim of the Buyer for the amount of €43,247.36 which is suggested for set-off and which is not identified with the content and the extent of its above action, is legal, being founded on the provisions of Articles 440, 441 and 442 of the Civil Code, which apply to this case, in accordance with the content of the above main thought, following express choice of the litigants, by virtue of clause 8.4, to have the sales contract governed by the Greek Law, in accordance with the provision of Article 3§1, in conjunction with Article 10, par. d of the 1980 Rome Convention for applicable in contractual obligations, which was ratified by Greece with Law 1792/1988 and applies since 1 April 1991, the application of which is made in performance of the provision of CISG Article 7(2), since there is a gap therein as to the subject in question, which cannot be regulated based on a general principle thereof, and consequently there is an external gap.

(3) That the Seller participated in a four party legal relationship observing the terms and suggestions of the main parties, i.e., Ministry of Defense —"EBO S.A.", since it entered into the agreement as the sub-fabricator of the latter, adhering the terms of the international tender which it conducted for the procurement of ballistic material which would be used as raw material for the fabrication of bulletproof vests, as well as the terms of their mutual main contract No 016A/2001. That the selection of the Seller as the supplier of the material, was not a decision coinciding in its competency, but that of the two main parties. That when the defective conduct of the material of the Seller in the bulletproof vest was discovered, the main client (Greek Police) and "EBO S.A." demanded the replacement of the bulletproof vest type "DYNEEMA UDX/SB31" of the Seller with aramidic material, so as not to create any doubt as to the safety and not to endanger the human lives. That since the use of the above material of the Seller was objectively impossible, in order not to sustain any further damage it denied the latter the taking over of 29,871 meters of the said material. That the Seller, claiming the payment of Euro 290,856.22 for the non-delivered quantity of 29,871 meters of bulletproof material type "DYNEEMA UDX/SB31", it exercises its right in profound excess of the limits set by good faith, transactional customs and its social and financial purpose. This allegation, for the foundation of which on the provision of Article 281 of the Civil Code which applies hereto, efforts are made, in accordance with the above thoughts, constitutes an objection for abusive exercise of a right, but it is illegal and thus unacceptable, since the events described in the brief of the pleadings, based on which the conduct of the Seller will be judged, as the beneficiary, preceded the exercise of the right and the actual condition that has resulted, justifies the exercise thereof, since it does not profoundly exceed the limits set by the above provision, meaning that no impression of sound injustice is created as regards the benefit of the Seller-

beneficiary from the exercise of the right.

Buyer's Claim

On 21 December 2006, the Buyer (the "Claimant") filed a claim ("Buyer's Claim") against the Seller (the "Defendant").

1. Request to the Court

"Based on this background the (Buyer), invoking the provisions of the contract of sale, the legal provisions on pre-contractual liability, the legal provisions on tort, and in addition, the legal provisions on unjustified enrichment, requests from the Court, following the accepted limitation of its adjudicative motion to declaratory, with the pleadings and the oral statement of its authorized attorney-at-law, which was recorded in the Minutes [Article 223 section (b), 294, 295, section (b) and 297 of the Code of Civil Procedure]:

(1) that it be acknowledged that the Seller is obliged to pay to the Buyer the total amount of €628,245.60, of which the amount of Euro 193,914.26, €103,750.77 and €314,758.62 with legal interest thereupon, from the day following the date the action was served upon and until the full repayment, the amount of €8,151.08 with legal interest thereupon, from the day following the date the goods referred to in the background were taken over, by virtue of the invoice No. 76933/24 November 2004 of the carrier company, i.e., on 4 November 2004, otherwise from the day following the date the action was served upon and until the full repayment and the amount of €7,670.87 with legal interest from the date the Seller was notified in writing, i.e., on 22 February 2002, otherwise from the day following the date the action was served upon and until full repayment,

(2) that it be acknowledged that the Seller is obliged to pay to the Buyer the amount of €300,000.00 as compensation for moral damage the Buyer sustained, with legal interest thereupon, from the day following the date the action was served and until full repayment,

(3) that the publication of the purview of the judgment issued be ordered, in two daily newspapers circulating throughout the Greek State at the cost of the Seller,

(4) that the judgment be declared provisionally enforceable; and

(5) that the Seller be sentenced to pay its court expenses."

2. Ruling on Buyer's Claim

With this content and motions, the action under judgment is subject, for the acceptance of the hearing for which a statement of the authorized attorney-at-law of the Buyer Mr.G.Kakoulakis is produced, from which the failure of the endeavor for extrajudicial settlement of the dispute is concluded, pursuant to the content of the above main thought, to the international jurisdiction of this Court, pursuant to the provisions of Articles 1, 5, 23, 24, 66, 68 and 76 of the (EC) Regulation 44/2001 of the European Council, dated 22 December 2000 "On International Jurisdiction and the Recognition and Enforcement of Judgments in Civil and Commercial Matters" which entered into effect on 1 March 2002, substituting the Brussels Convention, which (the regulation) supersedes and other provision of Greek law, in performance of Article 249 of the EC Treaty. In particular:

(a) As regards the part of the action where the Buyer seeks the payment of compensation by the Seller, because the antiballistic material Dyneema SB31 that the Seller handed over to the Buyer did not conform, as regards the quality and nature, to the requirements of their mutual contract no. 46/04 July 2001, and thus the Buyer sustained positive and negative loss which amounted to a total of €612,423.65, the international jurisdiction of this Court is founded, on the one hand, on a valid prorogation agreement which was concluded by the litigants [Article 23.1 of the (EC) Regulation 44/2001] as mentioned above, setting out in clause 8.3 of the above sales contract executed, that for any dispute that may arise from the performance of the said contract, the Court of Athens would be competent and, on the other, on the tacit prorogation [Article 24 of the (EC) Regulation 44/2001], since the Seller appeared without contesting the international jurisdiction of this Court, and this Article does not apply, regardless of the contractual specification of the competent court by the litigants, in accordance to the provision of Article 23 of the above-mentioned regulation. Besides, from the review of the above clause, interpreted in accordance with Article 173 and 200 of the Civil Code, it is concluded that it was agreed that all disputes arising from their mutual sales contract would be subjected to the exclusive jurisdiction of this Court, without excluding the disputes based on tort and unjustified enrichment, i.e., those that are based on the sales contract, as well as those deriving from the performance of that contract, but which are based on the provisions on tort or unjustified enrichment. The above are concluded by the clear wording of the above clause, according to which all disputes deriving from the contractual relationship, as well as claims for unjustified enrichment are subject to the jurisdiction of this Court, since there is no distinction thereof, neither anything to the contrary can be concluded by the agreement between the parties.

(b) As to the part of the action where the Buyer claims compensation for €612,423.65, on the grounds of pre-contractual liability, this Court has the international jurisdiction in order to judge it, due to tacit prorogation [Article 24 of the (EC) Regulation 44/2001], since the Seller appeared without contesting the international jurisdiction and there is no case of exclusive international jurisdiction of another court, pursuant to Article 22 of the above regulation.

(c) As to the part of the action where the Buyer seeks the payment, on one hand, of the consideration of Euro 8,151.08 from the sale to the Seller of 3,189 kg, net weight, of pieces of material which remained after the process (waste), and on the other, the amount of Euro 7,679.87 which was assigned to it by "EBO S.A." against it, this Court has international jurisdiction to hear the dispute since it is located at the place where the Seller was required to perform the relevant obligations [Article 5 of the (EC) Regulation 44/2001].

Furthermore, this action is lawfully brought before this Court as to its *ratione materiae* and as to the location (Articles 7, 9, 12, 13, 14 and 2, 18 and 42 of the Code of Civil Procedure) in order to be heard during the ordinary procedure and it has been adequately defined, since it contains all necessary evidence in order to be raised by the Buyer against the Seller and clearly refers to the founding events which constitute its historical basis (Articles 118 and 216 of the Code of Civil Procedure). This is why the relevant allegation of the Seller about the vagueness of the action must be rejected as being groundless.

Besides, pursuant to the main body of the action, where the Buyer requests to be compensated by the Seller for the total amount of Euro 612,423.65, which is grounded on a pre-contractual liability of the latter, it must be accepted, given that it presents elements of foreign character, whereas although the Buyer has its place of business in Greece (Kymi, Euboea), the Seller has its place of business in the Netherlands, and the applicable provisions are the relevant provisions of the domestic Civil Code, as being the law not only tacitly chosen by the litigants from the invocation to the application of its provisions, but also since the *ex lege* obligation was connected more closely to Greek law, since the phase of negotiations began with the dispatch by the parent company of the Buyer "EBO S.A." which has its place of business in Greece, of a relevant proposition to, among others, the Seller, for the conclusion of a raw material sales contract (ballistic material) for the construction of bullet-proof vests.

According to the above-mentioned thoughts, the action, according to its basis which is founded on the sales contract, is legal, being founded on the provisions of Articles 1(1)(a), 3, 4, 6, 7, 9, 14, 15, 18, 23, 25, 30, 31, 33, 35, 36, 38, 39, 45, 53, 57, 58, 59, 61, 62, 66, 67, 74, 78, 99, 100 of the CISG, Articles 197, 198, 340, 345, 346, 455, 460 and 462 of the Greek Civil Code and Articles 70 and 176 of the Greek Code of Civil Procedure.

On the contrary, the following are not lawful and are rejected:

(a) The bases of the action founded on tort and unjustified enrichment, since these do not apply jointly with the provisions of the CISG, since in a different case, the risk for non-uniform application thereof of the CISG would emerge, and thus the Buyer would be entitled to claim damages only based on the provisions of the said Convention;

(b) The motion of the action by which the Buyer claims compensation for Euro 300,000.00 due to moral damage it sustained by the damage to its reputation caused by the

Seller, the disturbance of its commercial relationships with main and privileged customers, the Ministry of Defense and the Greek Police, and the harm of the prestige and credibility of its goods to them, since, even if the actual facts of the brief of the action are deemed true, they cannot establish the liability of the Seller for monetary compensation of the Buyer, since non-property damage is not remedied by the CISG. In addition, based on the theory of foreseeability which applies to this contract, the Seller could not, based on the criteria referred to in the main thought, foresee the damage claimed by the Buyer to its business reputation and credibility (subjective foreseeability), neither it was obliged to have foreseen it (objective foreseeability) as potential consequence of the contractual breach, throughout the contract;

(c) The subsequent motion of the action to order the publication of the purview of the judgment issued in two daily newspapers circulating throughout the Greek State, is denied since no such provision is made in the CISG, neither within the context of the pre-contractual liability or the provisions for the assignment;

(d) The subsequent motion of the action to have the issued judgment declared provisionally enforceable, after the limitation of its motion from adjudicative to declaratory, is also denied since a declaratory judgment, cannot, after being finally issued, be declared provisionally enforceable.

Therefore, the action in the part that was deemed accepted and legal must be further examined as to the legal substance, given that after its turn to declaratory, there is no obligation to pay, the court stamps with all legal surcharges in favor of the Jurists Fund (TN) and the Athens Lawyers Welfare Fund (TPDA).

The Seller, via its written pleadings legally produced, excepting the allegation of the vagueness of the action, reasonably opposes the Buyer's action, projecting allegations on its legal and substantial grounds, for the reasons illustrated in detail in the brief of its pleadings. Furthermore, the Seller claims that, since it delivered the shipments under judgment of the Material made from polyethylene type DYNEEMA SB31 for the fabrication of bullet-proof vests to the Buyer from January 2002 to July 2002, the Buyer, via the letter of its parent company "EBO S.A." No. 1471/9 October 2002 informed the Seller of the lack of conformity with the terms of the above contract, due to puncture of the material and the action under judgment was filed before this Court on 21 December 2006 and served upon the Seller at a latter date, thus rendering the Buyer's claims a subject of statutory limitation. This allegation is an objection and it is legal, being founded on the provisions of Articles 247, 277, 554 and 555 of the Civil Code (in conjunction with CISG Article 39), as applied before being replaced by Article 1. 1 of the Law 3043/2002 which entered into effect on 21 August 2002 (Article 14 of the said law) and which apply, since the sales contract under judgment was concluded prior to the effect of the said law, pursuant to the general principle of diachronic law, which is expressly established with the provisions of Article 2 of the Civil Code and Article 24 of the Introductory Act of the Civil Code, obligations under any cause, the producing events of which took place during the time of effect of a certain law which was later abolished or amended, are governed after the abolishment or amendment by the law in force at the time the said producing events took place.

Otherwise and in addition, even if it could be assumed that the claim of the Buyer was generated after the publication of the Law 3043/2002, since on 9 October 2002, by means of the letter of its parent company "EBO S.A." the Buyer informed the Seller of the lack of conformity to the terms of the above-mentioned contract, due to puncture of its material, and thus the statutory limitation which had not lapsed at the time was governed by the provisions of the above newer law, which is adopted by the diachronic law provision of Article 18 of the Introductory Law to the Civil Code, again the objection raised by the Seller for statutory limitation is legal, being founded on the above provisions, as in force following the replacement of Article 554 of the Civil Code with Article 1 of the Law 3043/2002, with which the statutory limitation for goods was prolonged from six months to two years.

In its defense and in order to rebut the objection for statutory limitation raised by the Seller, the Buyer alleges:

(a) That the Seller originally concluded the contract with its parent company "EBO S.A." fully accepting and entering into on 14 February 2000, without any reservations, the terms of the international tender for the procurement of the main antiballistic material, among which the minimum warranty for the goods was set to ten (10) years, thus guaranteeing the good status and conduct of its materials for ten years. That between "EBO S.A." as the awarding authority of the international tender, and the Seller, a contract was concluded in favor of a third party and namely it, within the context of which it promised the performance of the obligation and all other obligations deriving from it and as a result, since a ten-year warranty-period of liability of the Seller was set and the lack of conformity to the contract was established within the said deadline, i.e., on September 2002, its claim has not been subjected to statutory limitation. The Buyer's claim for the contractual prolongation of the period for statutory limitation of its claim is based on the provision of Article 556 of the Civil Code and constitutes a reasonable denial of the objection raised by the Seller for statutory limitation.

(b) That, by virtue of the contract no. 46/4 July 2001 it was agreed that the Seller, for the consideration of Euro 2,515,464, would deliver 155,000 meters of fabric Dyneema SB31, in successive partial deliveries which, by the nature of the contract itself, constituted supplies of a unified good. That due to the non-conformity on behalf of the Seller to the terms of the contract, the Buyer did not take over the last quantity of 29,871 meters of fabric Dyneema SB31 out of the order of 155,000 meters, and as a result, since the period for the statutory limitation of its claim did not commence, this claim is not subject to the said statutory limitation. This allegation of the Buyer, which is attempted to be founded on the provision of Article 555 of the Greek Civil Code and constitutes a justified denial of the objection for statutory limitation raised by the Seller, is rejected, since, according to the events referred to in the brief of the action, until the discovery of the problem in material of the Seller on September 2002, the Buyer had handed over to the Ministry of Defense approximately 6,900 bullet-proof vests, a fact which shows that the successive delivery installments were independent from each other and it was not the case of supply of a unified good, as the Seller claims with no legal grounds, and in any case the period for statutory limitation set out in the provision of Article 554 of the Civil Code, in accordance with the above main thought, commences not from the time the delivery of the goods sold by the Seller to the Buyer took place, but from the date, pursuant to the provision of CISG Article 39(1), the letter No. 1472/ […] of the parent company "EBO S.A." was notified to the Seller, i.e., on 9 October 2002. A different interpretational approach, consisting in the non-commencement of the statutory limitation when the goods have not been handed over, in case the buyer in a contract for partial installments declares the contract avoided as to a specific installment obligation due to the non-performance of the obligations of the seller which derive from the sales contract in accordance with the provisions of CISG Article 73(1), would result in a situation where the buyer's claims against the seller would be subject to prescription, which is unaccepted by all laws.

(c) That the Seller, being aware due to its extended experience and know-how at the time the risk was transferred to it, that the fabric Dyneem UDX/SB31 lost its antiballistic properties with respect to the type of vest which would be used, although it was obliged to notify the lack of the agreed quality, withheld it by means of fraud, in order to undertake the tender. That if it [the Buyer] had been aware that the material of the Seller had a different conduct and with respect to its intended use it could be deemed inappropriate, it would never have proceeded with the conclusion of the contract under judgment. This allegation of the Buyer is a counter-objection for statutory limitation and is legal, being founded on the provision of Article 557 of the Civil Code, whereas in this case the statutory limitation applies for a period of twenty (20) years. The above provisions of the domestic (Greek) Civil Code which regulate the statutory limitation of the buyer's claims against the seller, according to the content of the above-mentioned main thought, apply to this case, following the express choice of the litigants, by virtue of the clause 8.4, which provides that the sales contract under judgment will be governed by the Greek Law, pursuant to the provision of Article 3.1, in conjunction with Article 10 of the 1980 Rome Convention for applicable law in contractual obligations, which was ratified by Greece with Law 1792/1988 and applies since 1 April 1991, the application of which is made in performance of the provision of CISG Article 7(2), since there is gap therein as to the subject in question, which cannot be regulated based on a general principle thereof, and consequently there is an external gap, while Greece has not ratified the New York Convention for the statutory limitation in international sales of goods dated 14 January 1974.

Furthermore, the Seller, since it justifiably opposes the counter-objection raised by the Buyer under Article 557 of the Civil Code, since in its opinion, its liability as the manufacturer of the raw material, is exhausted in the specifications of the materials, which were successfully tested and confirmed not only prior to its selection as the supplier, but also during the new ballistic tests conducted on 30 October 2002 and 1 November 2002, argues that the Buyer did not try, by its own fault, to mitigate its damage, since it could achieve a higher safety limit for the bullet-proof vests via the addition of another polyurethane material weighting 24 g which could be supplied by it, worth Euro 0.33 per vest, which corresponded to the improvement of 6,900 vests and would amount to a total of Euro 2,777.00 instead of Euro 418,509.39 which it had to pay in order to repair the said vests. This allegation constitutes an objection and it is legal, being founded on the above referred to, in the main thought, provision of CISG Article 77.

Final conclusive part of the judgment

From the above actual events which were clearly proved, it is concluded that at the time the risk was transferred, the Seller delivered to the Buyer the agreed material Dyneema UDX/ SB31,160 mm wide in the quantity and kind that corresponded to the requirements of the sales contract dated 4 July 2001 under judgment, without any actual defects and equipped with the reasonably expected qualities which it presented, in the offer dated 14 February 2000 to Buyer's parent company "EBO S.A.", and which were confirmed during the ballistics tests conducted at Granfield University for the selection of the supplier of the above Buyer company, in which, after testing the conduct of the raw material and not its application to a specific vest design, it was selected as the most suitable one among other candidate materials (CISG Arts. 35 and 36) [D. Flambouras, "The International Sale" in Ch. Pamboukis (edit.), International Transactions Law, Athens, Law Library (to be published) par. 232].

In particular, the above shipments No.7, 9 and 10 of the material Dyneema UDX/ SB31 were dispatched by the Seller, accompanied by the relevant invoices and certificates of quality, they were taken over by the Buyer and successfully passed the quantitative and qualitative control tests conducted by the competent departments of purchasing and quality control thereof, without rejecting any quantity of material due to actual defect or deficiency of the reasonably expected qualities or because there was a qualitative deviation from the agreed upon specifications, since the material was indeed of fine quality and fulfilled in whole the specifications and its characteristics, for which the [Seller] as the raw material provider had guaranteed that it was free of any apparent or hidden defect, for a period of one (1) year which commenced from the delivery date, pursuant to Article 7.3 of sales contract no.46/2001.

The fine quality of the Dyneema UDX/SB31 material that the Seller delivered to the [Buyer] derives additionally from the ballistics tests conducted on 30 October 2002 in the ballistics station of "PYRKAL" within the context of which approximately eighty shots were taken in the same ballistic material and in particular in samples randomly selected from the batch 110097 Dyneema and mainly from the box No.DSM 2002203244, of which the vest was fabricated which, during the ballistic tests on 20 December 2002, was penetrated during the fifth shot, without any unusual conduct being exhibited by the material, so as to characterize it as suspicious for the failure. Based on these findings, the Failure Analysis dated 10 March 2003 reached the conclusion that, from the results of the ballistics tests, the failure of the bulletproof vest was not due to systematic failure of the antiballistic material Dyneema SB31 used.

Furthermore, as regards the penetration of the vest and the simulation specimen of the vest under examination which was performed during the ballistic tests with a submachine gun MP5 on 20 September 2002 and 1 November 2002, the following should be noted:

To begin with, the two ballistic tests were conducted in the ballistics station of "PYRKAL" which was not certified in accordance with the international standards; ammunition type 9 mmX19 Full Metal jacket Lot 304-IVI-879 was used, which was not the type provided for in Annex B of the main contract no. 016A/2001 between the Ministry of Defense and "EBO S.A."; while during the second test, high velocities v2 were measured (average 434 m/s) compared with the requirements of the specifications (426 m/s), while the five (5) shots were taken with an imaginable line on the simulation specimen of the type of vest under examination, instead of the triangular arrangement, with the keeping of specific distances of the points in which the material is hit, in accordance with the safety standard NIJ 010.03 and thus the results cannot be deemed safe and reliable.

However, based on the ballistic tests on the design simulation specimen, the above Failure Analysis concluded that this phenomenon was a strong indication of poor function of the antiballistic material Dyneema SB31 in this design. However, even if that was the case, the [Seller] did not bear any contractual liability for the conduct of the end product, i.e., the bulletproof vest. In particular, from the review of the context of contract no. 016/2001 between the Ministry of Defense and "EBO S.A." it is concluded with absolute clarity that the [Seller] was not a party therein and therefore it bore no liability whatsoever for the domestic manufacturing of the end product for the Ministry of Defense. The fact that, the Seller is mentioned in that contract as one of the sub-suppliers of "EBO S.A." (for the bulletproof cloth) with which the latter was going to conclude a procurement contract, in order to perform its further contractual obligations under the 16A/2001 contract with its counterparty, i.e., the Ministry of Defense, does not in any way alter the context of the sales contract no. 46/2001 concluded between the [Buyer] and the Seller.

Thus, upon execution on 4 July 2001 of the above contract, the Seller undertook the obligation to deliver to the Buyer 155,000 linear meters of raw material Dyneema UD-SB31, 160 cm wide. This contract makes no statement, in the form of reference or incorporation or annex, to the contact no. 016A/2001 between the Ministry of Defense and "EBO S.A" or to any of the annexes thereof, either in the call of the latter dated 14 January 2000 to the Seller for the submission of a financial offer, regarding ballistic material for the manufacture of a bulletproof vest, either in any other contractual text or document. On the contrary, pursuant to Article 9.2 of sales contract no. 46/2001, it was expressly agreed between the Buyer and the Seller that "this contract supersedes any other relevant text except in the case of apparent mistake which is mutually accepted by both parties". Consequently, since no reference was made to any other contract, text or document, except for sales contract no. 46/2001, only the terms and conditions referred therein would establish the contractual relationship between the Buyer and the Seller, excluding any contingency of application of any other contractual term. However, in this contract, while the Seller guaranteed the quality of the material Dyneema UD-SB31, no relevant clause was included, for the guaranteed proper design and manufacturing of the bulletproof vests, which one way or the other could not be performed by the Seller since, in its capacity as the supplier of antiballistic material, it was not in the position to undertake any liability for the storage conditions, the manner of cut and the manner of incorporation of its bulletproof material in the vest, from the occasional manufacture of bulletproof vests. Thus, although bulletproof vests fabricated with the material Dyneema UD are used by the police and the army in more than 50 countries of Europe, Asia and Northern and South America, proving in the most profound way that the antiballistic material of the Seller is suitable for the fabrication of bulletproof vests; nevertheless, the said company does not undertake, anywhere in the world, the liability for manufacturing omissions of defects of the bulletproof vests, whereas the fabrication thereof from other fabricators lies beyond the control of the Seller, which is exclusively limited to undertaking the liability only for any defects of the antiballistic material it supplies, which in this case, had an exceptional conduct in all ballistic tests performed. This is why the Seller in each shipment of the material Dyneema UD-SB31, issued a compliance certificate, which, after certifying that it met the fabrication specifications, made special reference that it was obliged to inspect the suitability of the said material for its actual application, as well as to conduct the regular audit of the material it took over.

In this manner, the exclusive responsibility for the necessary level of protection of the bulletproof vests ordered by the Greek Police, lay with "EBO S.A." since, by virtue of Article 9 of the contract no. 016A/2001 between "EBO S.A." and the Ministry of Defense, it had guaranteed the proper conduct of the materials supplied, and in a supervising manner, the Buyer, since in the contract no. 51/01/HMK/19 July 2001 it executed with "EBO S.A." which, it should be noted that it was executed at a later date than the contract 46/4 July 2001 executed with the [Seller], it had been specified that the above main contract no.016A/2001 constituted an annex and an integral executory part thereof, undertaking thus the obligation to observe the contractual obligations of "EBO S.A." to the Ministry of Defense. Indeed, by virtue of a relevant clause which was included in the contract no. 51/01/HMK/19 July 2001, "EBO S.A." or the Greek Police could request from the Buyer the replacement of a product, if any irregularity, defect or damage was discovered. For this reason, since the Seller was not a party to contract no. 016A/2001, it was not invited to attend the ballistic tests conducted by the Quality Control Team which was formed by virtue of the decision for the supervision of the performance of this contract, in any partial delivery of bulletproof vests from "EBO S.A." to the Ministry of Defense.

Most important, the above two penetrations could not be characterized as a systematic damage of the bullet-proof vests, since no penetration was noted, not only in the ballistic tests which were conducted in the ballistics station of "PYRKAL" on 4 September 2003, where shots were taken on material of the same batch as the one of the puncture dated 20 September 2002 and along the space created at the connection point of the two front parts of the vest, but also in ballistic tests that the Seller conducted in the shooting field and in the TNO Prins Maurits Laboratories in the Netherlands, with more than 300 shots and with much more powerful ammunition than the ones provided in the contract on a vest of the specific model it manufactured and in particular, along the space created at the connection point of the two front parts of the vest. In addition, prior to the event of 20 September 2002, 6,900 vests had been partially delivered to the Ministry of Defense, out of which, pursuant to clause 4.2 of Annex B of the contract no. 016A/2001, one sample from each of the ten (10) partial deliveries had been checked, and no puncture of the bulletproof vest was noted. Besides, in Article 9, par. 6 of the contract 16A/2001 between the Ministry of Defense and "EBO S.A.", the term "systematic damage" characterizes "the case where the same damage will occur in the same material within the period under warranty and at a percentage exceeding 10% of the delivered goods", which was not the case in this instance.

Following the above, since it was proved that, at the time the risk was transferred, the Seller fulfilled the requirements of sales contract no. 46/4 July 2001 under judgment, delivering to the Buyer the agreed upon Material Dyneema UDX/SB31, 160 wide in the quantity and kind that corresponded to the terms of this contract, without any actual defects and equipped with the reasonably expected qualities which it presented to the Buyer, the action dated 21 December 2006 with Brief Deposit Number 11867/2006 of the Buyer against the [Seller] [for Buyer's Claim, see paragraph 1.12.2 above], regarding its grounds which is founded in the sales contract and damages sustained by the Buyer due to the replacement of the material Dyneema UDX/SB31 with aramid fibers (Kevlar) are claimed, as well as the relevant objection which it raised and as it is based on the provisions of CISG Article 36(1), Article 39, Article 60(b) and Articles 67-69, must be rejected as being groundless in substance.

For the same reason, whereas the [Seller] is not responsible for monetary amounts that the Buyer spent for the replacement of the material Dyneema UD-SB31 with aramid material in the bulletproof vests, the objection to set-off that the latter raised, to the extent that it concerns the separate sum of €43,247.36 must be rejected as being groundless in substance.

Furthermore, the Court, based on the above actual events which were proven, cannot be led to the judgment that a pre-contractual liability of the Seller is established in the sense that during the phase of negotiations with "EBO S.A." and the Buyer the Seller intentionally violated the principles of good faith and transactions morals, i.e., its main two obligations which were mostly enforced by the said principles, those of transparency and protection of the counterparty. However, it is a true fact that Mr. Johan Kunst, in his facsimile sent on 3 March 2003 to the Buyer seems to acknowledge that the combination of the material Dyneema SB31 with a specific design of some antiballistic vests could create some issues. Nevertheless, in no case could it be deemed that the Seller, during the process and participation in the international tender and also during the execution of sales contract no. 46/2001 between itself and the [Buyer], intentionally omitted to notify of, even though it was aware of, due to its extended experience and know-how in the industry, the differentiations in the conduct of the material of Dyneema UD-SB31 as regards the design of the bulletproof vest and under which conditions and circumstances was that suitable, i.e., it could not sustain puncture, in order to mislead the Buyer as to the suitability of the material and thus persuade it to execute the relevant contract, since such an action presupposes that there was indeed an improper function of the above antiballistic material in this specific design of the bulletproof vest that the [Buyer] manufactured, which in this case, was not proved.

From the fact and only that the material Dyneema UD-SB31 is produced each year in thousands of tons or millions of meters and it is used as raw material throughout the world for the manufacturing of bulletproof vests, in many applications, from various specialized manufacturers, its completeness is presumed, at first, for any type of bulletproof vest. The Seller not only did not violate the principles of good faith and transaction morals, as the [Buyer] alleges without legal grounds, but fully respecting and observing the obligations of transparency and protection of "EBO S.A." and the [Buyer] during the phase of negotiations, it clearly notified them, in Annex 4 of its offer dated 14 February 2000 for the order of the Ministry of Defense to "EBO S.A." that the material Dyneema UD-SB31 was a new product in the market not existing for a long period of time, and thus it had no data of actual experience, a fact that alone could lead to rejection, otherwise to endangering the selection of the offered antiballistic material of the Seller.

Besides, from the review of the above facsimile sent by Mr. Johan Kunst, it is clearly concluded that he, with the pretext of the ballistic tests which were conducted in the ballistics station of "PYRKAL" on 30 October and 1 November 2002, focused on the problem of the combination of the specific design of bulletproof vests and special ammunition used, which differ from those included in the specifications issue of the Seller, pointing out that there was no connection between the quality of the material and the performance of the bulletproof vests. However, in any case, even if we could assume that the above antiballistic material of the Seller responds differently regarding its design and the type of bulletproof vest, again, the obligation of transparency and protection of "EBO S.A." and the Buyer was not extended to this point, since the latter two companies ought to and could be informed of this fact by conducting their own thorough research, given that both companies, according to their statutory object, had a similar extended experience and know-how, the [Buyer] had additionally commercially co-operated with the Seller during 1994, when it had purchased from the latter the unidirectional (UD) Dyneema, thus being aware of the exact specifications of the said material. Based on these thoughts, the action dated 21 December 2006 with Brief Deposit Number 11867/2006 of the Buyer against the [Seller], as regards its legal grounds which is founded in a pre-contractual liability and damages that the Buyer sustained due to execution of the sales contract no. 46/2001 under judgment are claimed, must be rejected as being groundless in substance.

From the counter-contractual contract breaching conduct of the Buyer, the Seller sustained a positive loss which amounts to a total of €438,771.58, and consists of the sum of the invoices no. 13196/30 May 2002, 13439/19 July 2002 and 13440/19 July 2002 which concern orders for 5,641 m., 24,600 m. and 24,600 m. of the material Dyneema UDX/SB31 that it delivered to the buyer, with respective prices of €53,175.29, €239,537.09 and €146,059.20, which Buyer owes with legal interest thereupon, from the day following the date agreed for their settlement (due payment date), i.e., on 29 July 2002 and 17 September 2002, respectively.

Besides, the declaration of the contract avoidance by the Buyer, in relation to the 11th loading of the above sold quantity of 29,871 m. after the deduction of 40% of the advance payment, i.e., €290,856.22 was wrong, since the Seller fully complied with the requirements of the sales contract no. 46/2001 under judgment, and the actual reason, in accordance with the facsimile dated 11 February 2003, which the Buyer sent to the [Seller] was that it did not actually need them, thus [the avoidance declaration] not releasing both parties from their contractual obligations and the value of the material sold which was duly manufactured and offered by it was due for payment to the Seller, without the said order being executed due to fault of the above Buyer company. Therefore, the Seller also sustained negative loss that amounted to €290,856.22 which corresponds to 60% of the total agreed price, which the Buyer owes along with legal interest from the day following the date it was extra-judicially notified by the Seller, i.e., 26 September 2002. Consequently, the total positive and negative loss that the [Seller] sustained amounts to €729,627.80 (€438,771.58 + 290,856.22).

Furthermore, it was proved that the Buyer being aware of the relevant clause incorporated in the offer of the [Seller] dated 14 February 2000 to "EBO S.A." under which it accepted to purchase the items of the material Dyneema UDX/SB31 that would be left over the process (waste) for 5 German Marks per kg, dispatched to the Seller, issuing the invoice — weigh note No. C01/HMK/19 October 2004, via the transport company "SUPERTRANS — INTERNATIONAL FORWARDING & LOGISTICS ORGANIZATION" as shown in the invoice of the latter No. 0000076933/24 November 2004, out of the total quantity of approximately 125.000 meters delivered, a quantity of gross weight 4,522 kg and net weight 3,189 kg which was the net product after the process, which was shipped to sixteen customers and its total value amounted to €8,151.08, calculated for €2.56/kg which corresponded to the five (5) German Marks/kg and which the Seller has not yet settled.

However, despite the above offer of the latter to the Buyer, no such clause was incorporated in the sales contract no. 46/2001 under judgment that they executed. Thus, given that in Article 9.2 of the said contract it was specified that it supersedes any other relevant document, it is clearly evident that the Seller had no contractual obligation to take over the quantity of the antiballistic material which would be left over from the process, paying the respective amount and, for this reason, it does not owe the amount of €8,151.08 to the Buyer, which corresponded to the above quantity delivered to it, which, it should be noted, questions, claiming that it weighed 2,280 kg, as it can clearly be concluded from the letter of Mr.Josse

Kunst to it, dated 4 November 2004.

Furthermore, the terms of the International Tender Notice for the procurement of antiballistic material with Protocol No. 403/DM/ct/P255/24 January 2002, included, among other things, clause No. 4.4, on the one hand, which provided that the persons participating in the tender, would bear the cost of the evaluation tests that would be realized for the selection of the supplier, and, on the other hand, clause 4.6, which prohibited the non-acceptance of the terms or the raising of claims by the participants. These clauses were accepted by the [Seller] since it filed its offer dated 14 February 2000 and participated in the ballistic tests realized on behalf of "EBO S.A." in November 2000 in the ballistic station of the Granfield University in England. Next the said center issued and dispatched to "EBO S.A." the invoice no.c 20299/20 November 200 requesting to be paid the amount of €10,927.50 for the ballistic tests, and indeed "EBO S.A." paid the said amount with a bank order in the Bank of Attica S.A. on 15 March 2001, as evidenced by the receipt voucher — remittance no. 1803/16 March 2001 of the Bank of Attica to the said University. Thereafter, "EBO S.A." allocated the costs of ballistic tests to each participating company and the amount that corresponded to the Seller for 78 shots, was €4,680, notifying it at first on 5 February 2001 with its document under protocol number 31/210 and once again on 18 October 2001, with its relevant letter, in order for the Seller to immediately pay the above-mentioned participation cost. The Seller, as it is clearly concluded by the letter of Mr. Kyriakos Sachanides dated 24 October 2001, accepted its debt. Due to assumption by the Buyer of the project for the manufacturing of bulletproof vests, "EBO S.A." assigned to it the above claim, notifying the Seller of this assignment on 22 February 2002, by means of its document under protocol number 312/AK/AG/Im, dispatching to it at the same time a copy of the results of the ballistic tests and a copy of the invoice that the Granfield University issued, inviting it to credit the amount of €4,580.00 which corresponded to €7,670.87 with the issuance of the relevant credit note on account of the Buyer, so as to set it off with the existing debit balance. However, the Seller did not pay the above amount, which, after the alteration of the adjudicating claim of the action judged, it owes along with legal interest thereupon, from the date following the service of the action dated 21 December 2006, with Brief Deposit Number 11867/2006 of the Buyer against it.

Following the above actual events which were proved and in accordance with the above-illustrated thoughts:

(1) The action of the Seller dated 28 July 2005 with Brief Deposit Number 7147/2005 against the Buyer must be partially accepted as being grounded in substance and the Defendant Buyer must be forced to pay to the Plaintiff Seller the total amount of €729,627.80, out of which:

(a) the amount of €53,175.29 along with legal interest thereupon from the day following

29 July 2002;

(b) the amount of €239.537.09 along with legal interest thereupon from the day following 17 September 2002;

(c) the amount of €146,059.20 along with legal interest thereupon from the day following 17 September 2002; and

(d) the amount of €290,856.22 along with legal interest thereupon from the day following 26 September 2002.

As regards the motion requesting that the judgment be declared provisionally executory, given that it was not concluded that the Buyer enjoins the benefits of the State, the Court judges that there are no material grounds to enforce the provisional execution of the judgment or that delay in the execution of the judgment may cause substantial damages to the Seller. This is why the relevant motion must be rejected as being groundless in substance. The Court expenses for this action must be allocated based on the outcome (win and loss) of each of the opponents (Article 178 and 191, par.2 of the Code of Civil Procedure) as specifically set out in the purview.

(2) The action dated 21 December 2006 with Brief Deposit Number 11867/2006 of the Buyer against the Seller, must be partially accepted as being grounded in substance and it must be acknowledged that the Defendant Seller is obliged to pay to the Plaintiff Buyer the amount of €7,670.87 along with legal interest thereupon, from the date following the date of service of the action.

Finally, the court expenses for this action, must be allocated based on the outcome (win and loss) of each of the opponents (Articles 178 and 191, par. 2 of the Code of Civil Procedure) as specifically set out in the purview.

For These Reasons

The Court

— Judges the action dated 28 July 2005, with Brief Deposit Number 7147/2005, the action dated 21 December 2006 with Brief Deposit Number 11867/2006, the garnishment dated 3 December 2007 with Brief Deposit Number 11608/2007 of the procedural guarantor and the additional intervention dated 25 February 2008 with Brief Deposit Number 2017/2008, with both opponents present.

— Rejects whatever was judged in the rationale as being rejected.

— Obliges the Defendant Buyer to pay to the Plaintiff Seller the total amount of €729,627.80, out of which:

(a) the amount of €53,175.29 along with legal interest thereupon from the day following 29 July 2002;

(b) the amount of €239.537.09 along with legal interest thereupon from the day following

17 September 2002;

(c) the amount of €146,059.20 along with legal interest thereupon from the day following 17 September 2002; and

(d) the amount of €290,856.22 along with legal interest thereupon from the day following 26 September 2002.

— Suspends the trial of the set-off objection, to the part thereof that refers to the rationale of this judgment, until the issue of a final judgment for the action dated 21 December 2006 with Brief Deposit Number 11867/2006 of the [Buyer] against the Seller.

— Imposes against the Defendant Buyer a part of the court expenses of the Plaintiff Seller, which it sets at the amount of €25,000.00.

— Accepts in part the action dated 21 December 2006 with Brief Deposit Number 11867/2006.

— Acknowledges that the Defendant Seller is obliged to pay to the Plaintiff [Buyer] the amount of €7,670.87 along with legal interest thereupon, from the date following the date of service of the action.

— Imposes against the Defendant Seller a part of the court expenses of the Plaintiff [Buyer], which it sets to the amount of €270.00.

— Rejects the additional intervention dated 25 February 2008 with Brief Deposit Number 2017/2008.

— Imposes against the party additionally intervening, the court expenses of the opponent against whose the additional intervention is made, which it sets at the amount of €500.00.

The Court Reporter

(Signature)

Konstantinos Protonotarios

【思考题】

1. 本案原告的所有诉讼请求是否均能依据 CISG 得以解决，为什么？

2. 按照 CISG 的规定，分批交货合同中部分批次发生违约时应如何处理？

Case1·拓展阅读

| Case2　Ansung Housing CO., LTD. vs. People's Republic of China（ICSID Case No. ARB/14/25）　|

【案情说明】

一、案件事实

2006 年 12 月 12 日，韩国安城住房株式会社（Ansung Housing Co., Ltd.，简称安城住房）与中华人民共和国江苏省射阳港口产业园区管委会（后文简称管委会）签订一份有关高尔夫球场建设投资协议。协议约定由安城住房在射阳建设高尔夫球场及豪华公寓、会所等附属设施，并由其享有相应经营权益；同时，管委会约定不在相关地区为其他企业颁发高尔夫球场许可。项目按约定分两期进行。项目动工后不久，射阳管委会提出，按照中国房地产管理政策，其无法再按照原定价格提供第一期工程所需的 300 亩土地，转而要求安城住房按照中国政策要求就此公开竞买。一期工程竣工后，管委会并未及时提供二期用地。此外，在安城住房高尔夫项目建设期间内，管委会并未阻止其他中国建设公司在未经许可情况下在同一地区建设高尔夫球场。在垄断该地区内高尔夫球场经营未果导致无法盈利情况下，2011 年 9 月，安城住房在亏损 1 380 万美元的情况下迫不得已以 120 万美元低价转让了高尔夫球场所有权。2014 年 10 月 7 日，安城住房依据韩国与中国签订的《双边投资保护协定》，以中国政府为被申请人，将案件提交 ICSID 请求仲裁。同年 11 月 4 日，ICSID 立案［Ansung Housing Co., Ltd. v. People's Republic of China（ICSID Case No. ARB/14/25）］，并依据《华盛顿公约》第 37 条（2）款（b）项成立仲裁庭。

2016 年 9 月 15 日，仲裁庭开庭审理。中方根据《仲裁规则》第 41 条（5）款的规定，依据中韩投资保护协定第 9 条 7 款有关 3 年仲裁时效的规定，主张本案已经超出仲裁时效，因此安城住房的仲裁请求"显然不具有法律依据"。此外，双边投资保护协定的最惠国待遇条款也不适用于仲裁时效，基于此，请求仲裁庭驳回仲裁请求。但安城住房认为，直到 2011 年 12 月它才知悉其损失，而且仲裁时效的截止日期应该是提交仲裁意向通知的日期或提交仲裁申请书的日期，因此其仲裁请求并未过仲裁时效。安城住房进一步提出，即便超出了中韩双边投资保护协定规定的仲裁时效，按照最惠国待遇原则，其也有权援引其他条约中的较长时效规定。

二、裁判结果

通过对《仲裁规则》第 41 条（5）款"明显缺乏法律依据"中"明显"一词的解释，肯定了超出仲裁时效构成"明显缺乏法律依据"的事项，进而对安城住房是否超出

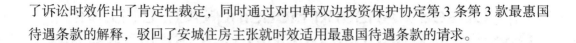

了诉讼时效作出了肯定性裁定，同时通过对中韩双边投资保护协定第 3 条第 3 款最惠国待遇条款的解释，驳回了安城住房主张就时效适用最惠国待遇条款的请求。

【法律分析】

本案主要涉及三个方面的问题：第一，《仲裁规则》第 41 条（5）款中"明显缺乏法律依据"的标准是什么，超出仲裁时效是否构成"明显缺乏法律依据"事由？第二，安城住房仲裁请求是否超出了仲裁时效？第三，最惠国待遇条款是否适用于时效？

（一）安城住房仲裁请求是否"明显缺乏法律依据"

按照《仲裁规则》第 41 条初始异议程序的规定。该款规定如下："除非双方另有约定，在仲裁庭组成后 30 天内，在仲裁庭首次开庭之前，可以基于对方请求"明显缺乏法律依据"而提出异议。该当事方应尽可能准确地详细说明异议理由。在给对方当事人就此异议提出表达意见后，仲裁庭应在首次开庭时或开庭后及时通知当事方对于异议的决定。……"中方正是依据该款规定提出了初始异议。

中方认为，按照 ICSID 在"环球石油公司诉约旦案"（"Trans-Global Petroleum v. Jordan"）案中对初始异议中有关"明显"（manifestly）的解释称，所谓"明显"，系要求被申请人"清晰、明显、轻松且快速地提出反对意见"。同时在判断初步异议问题时，仲裁庭应假设仲裁请求中事实部分的主张为真实的，除非所提供的事实显然不可信、轻率、无理、不准确或基于恶意而提供。因此，中方主张，《仲裁规则》第 41 条（5）款实质是要回答这样一个问题，即"假定所主张事实为真，诉求是不是一个法律问题。"换言之，第 41 条（5）款设置之目的在于允许仲裁庭撤销明显缺乏法律价值的仲裁请求。同时，针对安城住房以 ICSID 秘书处仲裁请求登记行为作为其请求具有法律依据的证明的主张，中方反驳认为，第 41 条（5）款的目的就是对秘书处筛选权力（screening powers）的一种补充，登记行为本身并不构成对初步异议问题的预判。中方进一步指出，与简易注册程序仅考虑申请人的单方面主张不同，初步异议程序是对相关法律原则的一种全面和对抗式的探究。此外，中方还特别引用了《仲裁规则》修订过程中立法工作组中一名成员的观点证明，时效问题完全可以在第 41 条（5）款中加以解决。安城住房则认为，如果仲裁庭认为仲裁请求中的事实部分并非明显轻率或荒谬，且非经深入调查无法做出判断时，就应当在事实问题上支持安城住房，驳回初步异议。仲裁庭最终认可了安城住房所述的事实。

（二）安城住房仲裁请求是否超出了仲裁时效

中方主张仲裁时效的起算日是指安城住房首次知道或应当知道其投资项目受损之日，即 2011 年 10 月之前，终止日应为案件向 ICSID 登记之日即 2014 年 11 月 4 日。据此，根据中韩投资协定，已过 3 年诉讼时效。安城住房认为中国政府在土地提供方面持续不作为，因此安城住房只有在投资目的完全落空时方可确定其损害，因此时效起算日应为 2011 年 12 月 17 日，因此尚未超出 3 年仲裁时效。仲裁庭在综合考察相关细节后认为，按照中韩投资协定第 9 条（7）款规定，双方已经明确约定仲裁时效起算日为首次知悉损失之日起算，因此按照文义解释，仲裁时效起算日应为 2011 年 10 月之前。

（三）最惠国待遇条款是否适用于时效

安城住房认为时效问题属于实体性权利范围，而且即便属于程序性权利，按照 ICSID 先例，最惠国待遇条款同样可以适用。考虑到中国与其他国家之间签订的投资协定中多数未规定仲裁时效，因此安城住房可以通过适用最惠国待遇条款援引中国与他国签订的投资协定中的规定，适用较 3 年更长的仲裁时效。对此，中方认为仲裁时效属于程序性事项，而中韩投资协定第 3 条（3）款已经明确限定了最惠国待遇条款仅适用于东道国领土范围内投资和商业行为，因此本案中最惠国待遇条款不能扩张适用于仲裁时效。仲裁庭最终肯定了中方主张。

【英文案例裁决摘录】

I.The Parties' Respondent's Position

(1) respondent's Position

Respondent recites that ICSID Arbitration Rule 41(5) provides for early dismissal of claims that are "manifestly without legal merit," and the Tribunal must render an award under ICSID Arbitration Rule 41(6) if it finds either that the dispute is not within the Centre's jurisdiction or that the claims are "manifestly without legal merit."[1] Respondent relies on the Rule 41(5) analysis of the ICSID tribunal in Trans-Global Petroleum v. Jordan ("Trans-Global"), which subsequent tribunals have cited with approval:

[T]he ordinary meaning of the word "manifestly" requires the respondent to establish its objection clearly and obviously, with relative ease and despatch. The standard is thus set high. Given the nature of investment disputes generally, the Tribunal nonetheless recognizes that this exercise may not always be simple…. The exercise may thus be complicated; but it should never be difficult.[2]

Respondent, again citing to Trans-Global, posits that a Rule 41(5) decision would "assume the truth of the factual allegations in the request for arbitration unless a given factual obligation was manifestly 'incredible, frivolous, vexatious or inaccurate or made in bad faith.'"[3] China asserts that Ansung erroneously suggests that a claim can survive a Rule 41(5) challenge "if

---

1 R. 41(5) Obj., para. 7. See also R. 41(5) Obj., para. 11 (noting "…subsequent tribunals have repeatedly confirmed, any legal defect in the claim may be the subject of a Rule 41(5) application, whether concerning the tribunal's jurisdiction or the merits.").

2 R. 41(5) Obj., para. 10〔citing RLA-009, Trans-Global Petroleum, Inc. v. Hashemite Kingdom of Jordan, ICSID Case No. ARB/07/25, para. 88 (Decision on the Respondent's Objection Under Rule 41(5), May 12, 2008) ("Trans- Global")〕.

3 R. 41(5) Obj., para. 12 (citing Trans-Global, para. 105).

a tribunal is of the opinion that…the facts in the claim are not patently frivolous or absurd."[1] According to Respondent, the question under Rule 41(5) instead is "whether, assuming the truth of the credible allegations made, the claim fails as a matter of law."

When considering Rule 41(5) applications, Respondent explains that "tribunals weigh the right granted to the respondent 'to have a patently unmeritorious claim disposed of before unnecessary trouble and expense is incurred in defending it' against the general requirements of due process."[2]

With respect to Claimant's reliance on the Secretary-General's registration of the Request, Respondent notes that ICSID Arbitration Rule 41(5) was proposed to complement the Secretary-General's screening powers, so registration does not prejudge the Rule 41(5) question presented to the Tribunal.[3] Unlike the short registration process, which considers only the claimant's ex parte submissions, the Rule 41(5) procedure has a "full, adversary exploration of the relevant legal principles."[4] Respondent further notes that an article written by a member of the working group that prepared the Rule 41 amendments recognized that temporal objections were appropriate for resolution under Rule 41(5).[5]

(2) Claim's Position

Claimant, like Respondent, relies on the Trans-Global decision to interpret the scope of ICSID Arbitration Rule 41(5), but contends that the Trans-Global tribunal "held that the provision applied only to clear and obvious cases of 'patently unmeritorious claims.'" Ansung concurs with China's reliance on that tribunal's elucidation of the meaning of the adjective "manifestly," by requiring the respondent to establish its objection "clearly and obviously, with relative ease and despatch."[6] Claimant concludes that, to meet the necessary element of "manifestly," "Respondent must pass a demanding and rigorous test by demonstrating that its objection has such clarity, certainty, and obviousness."[7]

Claimant further argues that, "for the purpose of the 41(5) Objection, if a tribunal is of the opinion that (i) the facts in the claim are not patently frivolous or absurd, and (ii) the tribunal

---

1 R. Obs., para. 18 (citing Cl. First Obs., para. 13).

2 R. 41(5) Obj., para. 13 [citing RLA-012, Global Trading Resource Corp. and Globex International, Inc. v. Ukraine, ICSID Case No. ARB/09/11, para. 34 (Award, December 1, 2010) ("Global Trading")].

3 R. Obs., para. 19.

4 Ibid.

5 Ibid. [referencing RLA-007, A. Antonietti, The 2006 Amendments to the ICSID Rules and Regulations and the Additional Facility Rules, 21(2) ICSID Rev. 427, 439 (2006)].

6 Ibid.

7 Cl. First Obs., para. 8.

would not be able to decide the questions presented to it without an in-depth scrutiny of factual allegations, then it must resolve such a factual question in favour of the claimant and reject the 41(5) Objection."[1]

Claimant asserts that the factual background set out in its Notice of Intent and Request for Arbitration meets the temporal requirement of Article 9(7) of the China-Korea BIT at a *prima facie* level.[2] Furthermore, according to Ansung, a Rule 41(5) objection is not appropriate for contesting the existence of temporal jurisdiction, as further factual disclosure is required for a proper assessment of this objection.[3]

Claimant also asserts that "[g]iven that the ICSID Secretary-General registered Ansung's Request for Arbitration, this shows that from the Secretary-General's perspective, Ansung's claim is not 'manifestly outside the jurisdiction [of the Centre].'"[4]

(3) Tribunal's Analysis

The test for a preliminary objection under ICSID Arbitration Rule 41(5) is whether "a claim is manifestly without legal merit." The Tribunal agrees with the Parties that the test of "manifestly" is well articulated by the Trans-Global tribunal, and so will require Respondent to establish its objection "clearly and obviously, with relative ease and despatch."

In deciding the objection, the Tribunal accepts the facts as pleaded by Ansung. The Tribunal need not decide China's argument that it must ignore facts that are "incredible, frivolous, vexatious or inaccurate or made in bad faith," as it does not find that the facts pleaded by Ansung fall into these categories.

With regard to the import of the Secretary-General's registration of Ansung's Request for Arbitration, the Tribunal agrees with China that registration does not and cannot prejudge an application under ICSID Arbitration Rule 41(5). Registration follows the Secretary-General's early screening process, at which point she bases her registration decision only "on the basis of the information contained in the request."[5] If registration were to vouch for the manifest legal merit of a request for arbitration, Rule 41(5) would never lead to early resolution and would serve no purpose.

Where a respondent's Rule 41(5) objection is concerned with a limitation period, as China's is, a tribunal's decision on such an objection constitutes a decision as contemplated by Rule 41(6) regarding a lack of jurisdiction of the Centre and of its own competence as well as

---

1 Cl. First Obs., para. 13.

2 Cl. Second Obs., para. 3.

3 Ibid.

4 Cl. First Obs., para. 69.

5 ICSID Convention, Art. 36(3).

regarding manifest lack of legal merit due to a lack of temporal jurisdiction. As set out below, this is the situation here.

II.ARTICLE 9(7) OF THE CHINA-KOREA BIT — LIMITATION PERIOD

To recall, Article 9(7) of the China-Korea BIT provides:

[A]n investor may not make a claim pursuant to paragraph 3 of this Article if more than three years have elapsed from the date on which the investor first acquired, or should have first acquired, knowledge that the investor had incurred loss or damage.

Classically, the start date for such a temporal limitation period is known as the *dies a quo* and the end date as the *dies ad quem*.

1. Respondent's Position

(1) *Dies a Quo*

Turning first to the *dies a quo* for the prescription period in the Treaty, Respondent emphasizes that Article 9(7) is precise in setting the *dies a quo* as "the date on which the investor first acquired, or should have first acquired, knowledge that the investor had incurred loss or damage."[1] Relying on prior decisions by NAFTA tribunals interpreting the substantially similar time limitation language in the NAFTA, China argues that the Treaty Article 9(7) language addresses "knowledge of the fact that there has been a loss, not knowledge of the quantum lost." Moreover, Respondent asserts, "a claimant may not rely only on loss from the last of a series of similar and related State actions alleged to constitute a breach."[2]

Accepting the facts set out in Claimant's Request for Arbitration, Respondent asserts that Ansung "necessarily knew of the fact that it had incurred loss or damage on some date prior to the disposal of its investment in October 2011," the date on which Ansung sold its entire investment in Sheyang-Xian "in order to avoid further losses."[3] According to Respondent, the Tribunal need not decide an exact date because the first date of losses (being earlier losses) necessarily was prior to October 2011.[4]

In Respondent's Observations, China underscores that Ansung has attempted to change its story in its First Observations by concentrating on "a continuing omission" by the local government in late 2011, as opposed to allegations in the Request for Arbitration that the Committee began affirmatively breaching the Investment Agreement by withholding land in

1 R. 41(5) Obj., para. 1 [citing C-001, China-Korea BIT, Art. 9(7)].

2 R. 41(5) Obj., para. 25 [citing RLA-008, Grand River Enterprises Six Nations, Ltd., et al. v. United States of America, NAFTA/UNCITRAL, para. 81 (Decision on Jurisdiction, July 20, 2006) ("Grand River")].

3 R. 41(5) Obj., para. 2 [citing RFA, paras. 12 and 60 (emphasis added by Respondent)]. See also R. 41(5) Obj., paras. 27-30.

4 R. 41(5) Obj., para. 31.

2007, and engaged in "outright repudiation" in 2008 by forcing Ansung to pay a higher price for use of the 300 mu.[1] Respondent also asserts that, in Claimant's First Observations, Ansung modified, without explanation, its story that it disposed of its investment in October 2011 by alleging that it began negotiations with an unnamed Chinese individual at an unspecified time and finally agreed to transfer its shares at the agreed price only on December 17, 2011.[2]

China contests Ansung's belated reliance on December 17, 2011 as the *dies a quo*. According to Respondent, although this may have been the date Ansung fully liquidated and realized its losses, it is not the date on which "Ansung first knew or should have known that its project incurred a loss."[3] Citing to prior decisions including Mondev International Ltd. v. United States, China contends that Claimant's assertions fail as a matter of law because the three-year period commences when a claimant knows "of the fact that some loss has occurred, not upon its full realization".[4]

Respondent challenges Claimant's "continuing omission" argument, first, for lack of support in Ansung's own allegations and the applicable jurisprudence.[5] The alleged breaches based on local government conduct between 2007 and 2010, for example the demand for an increased price for the 300 mu, were not ones with continuing character pursuant to the rules on State responsibility, as each breach was "complete even if it has continuing ongoing effects…." Respondent contends that Claimant cannot convert these breaches into continuing breaches simply by alleging that it tried and failed to resolve the situation.

Second, China dismisses Ansung's "continuing omission" justification that, as the Committee did not explicitly repudiate its prior assurances to provide the additional 1,500 mu, Ansung's original plan for a 27-hole golf course remained viable up to the date, in mid-December 2011, that Ansung sold its phase one 18-hole golf course and clubhouse. In addition to being incoherent, Respondent considers this justification to be a legal characterization of Ansung's factual allegations that fails as a matter of law. If viewed as an allegation of fact, however, China urges the Tribunal to disregard it as not credible.

From a legal perspective, Respondent asserts that tribunals have consistently rejected similar theories of "continuing breach" through a "continuing omission" for purposes of

---

1 R. Obs., paras. 9-12.

2 R. Obs., para. 14.

3 R. Obs., para. 3.

4 R. Obs., para. 35 [finding support in RLA-006, Mondev International Ltd. v. United States of America, ICSID Case No. ARB(AF)/99/2, para. 87 (Award, October 11, 2002); RLA-040, Spence International Investments, LLC, Berkowitz, et al. v. Republic of Costa Rica, ICSID Case No. UNCT/13/2, para. 213 (Interim Award, October 25, 2016) ("Spence")].

5 R. Obs., paras. 4, 38 et seq.

calculating a limitations period. For example, as in Corona v. Dominican Republic, Claimant relies in this case on the local government's absence of action for its "continuing omission" theory; however, as in Corona v. Dominican Republic, "that silence did not 'produc[e] any separate effects on [the] investment other than those that were already produced by the initial decision[s]' and acts."

Moreover, even if considered "continuing acts," China emphasizes that Ansung's final transfer of shares on December 17, 2011 "would not change the fact that Ansung first knew or should have known of the fact of loss from the breaches prior to 4 November 2011" or before October 2011.

Respondent also criticizes Claimant's reliance on Pac Rim v. El Salvador, because that case "did not even address application of a limitation period." Nor can Ansung rely on UPS v. Canada, as that case addressed a textually different limitation clause that required knowledge of both breach and loss, and the tribunal's approach has been "severely criticized and not followed by later tribunals." Most recently, in Spence v. Costa Rica, the tribunal found:

While it may be that a continuing course of conduct constitutes a continuing breach, the Tribunal considers that such conduct cannot without more renew the limitation period as this would effectively denude the delimitation clause of its essential purpose, namely, to draw a line under the prosecution of historic claims. Such an approach would also encourage attempts at the endless parsing up of a claim into ever finer sub-components of breach over time in an attempt to come within the limitation period. This does not comport with the policy choice of the parties to the treaty.

Finally, Respondent argues that Claimant's interpretation of Treaty Article 9(7) would render that Article without effect. If a State's inaction could itself renew a time limitation period, or if final disposal of an investment were required for the limitation period to begin, the investor would fully control when the period would start, thereby "rendering it illusory" and undermining the legal stability served by limitation periods.[1]

(2) *Dies ad Quem*

Turning to the *dies ad quem* for the three-year limitation period, Respondent argues that the end date must be November 4, 2014, the date on which ICSID registered Claimant's Request for Arbitration."[2] This means that, on China's case, the *dies a quo* had to have been after November 4, 2011.

In support of its position, China recites that Article 9(7) of the China-Korea BIT refers

---

1 R. Obs., para. 54.

2 R. 41(5) Obj., paras. 3, 45 [citing Institution Rule 6(2)].

to "the date on which the investor...make[s] a claim pursuant to paragraph 3 of this Article,"[1] and paragraph 3 of Article 9 in turn addresses how the dispute shall be submitted to arbitration. Therefore, according to China, the *dies ad quem* "is when an investor makes a claim in the sense of submitting the dispute to arbitration."[2]

In specific, China asserts that ICSID Institution Rule 6(2) precisely establishes when a dispute is submitted and the proceeding begins: "[a] proceeding under the Convention shall be deemed to have been instituted on the date of registration of the request." When an investor chooses ICSID arbitration, Institution Rule 6(2) "determines when an 'investor...make[s] a claim pursuant to paragraph 3 of this Article 9,'" because "in the ICSID system there is no arbitration unless and until the Secretary-General registers the request."[3] Applying Article 31 of the VCLT to interpret the plain terms of Treaty Article 9(3) and (7), China submits that an "investor does not make an ICSID claim or submit a dispute to ICSID arbitration until that claim is registered by the Secretary-General."

Respondent contests Claimant's position that the date of the original Notice of Intent constitutes "making a claim" within the meaning of Article 9(7) of the China-Korea BIT. China insists that the provision is clear that "a claim is made only when the dispute is submitted under the arbitration rules specified in Article 9(3)." China disagrees that the China-Korea BIT text can support Ansung's efforts to draw a distinction between the "claim" reference in Article 9(7) and "the dispute" reference under Article 9(3), as Article 9(5) treats those terms as synonyms. Nor does China find any linguistic or textual support for Claimant's contention that there is a distinction between "making" and "submitting" a claim in either the English, Korean or Chinese versions. Citing Apotex Inc. v. United States as an example, Respondent reiterates that prior tribunals interpreting "substantially identical" provisions "have held that 'making a claim' refers to the definitive activation of an arbitration procedure," which a notice of intent could not meet.[4]

China also challenges Ansung's argument that ICSID claimants would be inconvenienced if the plain terms of Article 9(7) were strictly applied, as prior tribunals have confirmed that a limitation clause is "a legitimate legal mechanism to limit the proliferation of historic claims" and "generations of NAFTA claimants have succeeded without difficulty in navigating" such

---

1 R. 41(5) Obj., para. 32 (citing C-001, China-Korea BIT, Art. 9(7) (emphasis added by Respondent).

2 R. 41(5) Obj., para. 32 [citing C-001, China-Korea BIT, Art. 9(3)].

3 R. 41(5) Obj., para. 3 [citing Institution Rule 6(2)]. See also R. 41(5) Obj., para. 33.

4 R. Obs., paras. 2, 26 [citing RLA-032, Apotex Inc. v. Government of the United States of America, NAFTA/UNCITRAL, para. 301 (Award on Jurisdiction and Admissibility, June 14, 2013) ("Apotex")].

provisions.[1]

Finally, Respondent asserts that Claimant errs in suggesting that China's position is that the Request's transmission establishes the *dies ad quem*, and it reiterates its position that under Article 9(7) of the Treaty a claim is made in an ICSID arbitration when the proceedings are instituted, on the date of registration.

(3) Conclusion

In sum, Respondent submits that Claimant "instituted this ICSID arbitration more than three years after the date on which it acquired knowledge that it had incurred loss or damage." Based on Ansung's own pleadings, it first learned that it incurred loss or damage related to its Sheyang-Xian golf course project at some point before October 2011. This is more than three years before November 4, 2014, when ICSID registered Ansung's case. Consequently, "[u]nder the plain terms of Article 9(7)…[Ansung's] claim is barred by the text of the consent it relies upon to invoke the jurisdiction of this Tribunal," and "[t]he lack of legal merit of its claims is manifest."

2. Claimant's Position

(1) *Dies a Quo*

To determine the proper start date for its claim, Ansung emphasizes that the China-Korea BIT provides a cause of action in Article 9(1) for loss or damage arising from the breach of the Treaty obligations,100 and "the loss or damage set out in Article 9(7) is also understood to relate to those arising from the Respondent's multiple breaches of the China-Korea BIT."101 According to Ansung, it could ascertain its loss or damage under Article 9(7) "only after its expectation and plan for the 27-hole golf course was completely frustrated, owing primarily to the government's continued inaction in providing the additional land for the second phase of the Project."

Ansung alleges that it "obtained information assisting it in recognizing possible losses only around December 17, 2011…when the circumstances leading to the losses became unavoidable, thereby driving Ansung to sell the business to the Chinese purchaser."[2] Therefore, the *dies a quo* for purposes of Treaty Article 9(7) must be December 17, 2011, as the date when Claimant "first acquired or should have first acquired knowledge" of loss or damage.[3] This position, says Claimant, is consistent with the tribunal's view in Pope & Talbot, Inc. v. Canada that "actual damage, rather than predicted future damage" is required to trigger a prescription

---

1 R. Obs., para. 28 (citing Spence, para. 208).

2 Cl. First Obs., para. 31.

3 Cl. First Obs., para. 32.

period.[1]

Claimant contests Respondent's argument that it knew that it had incurred loss triggering the limitation period by reason of local government action before October 2011. Ansung's loss instead was a consequence of government inaction concerning the second allotment of 1,500 mu of land, which inaction could not lead to a claimable loss while Ansung continued to try to resolve the situation with the government.[2] Relying on Pac Rim v. El Salvador and UPS v. Canada, Claimant notes that continuing host State omissions have been held to be treaty breaches, and such continuing omissions push the temporal boundaries of the relevant limitation period.[3]

In its Second Observations, Claimant asserts that "the key question to be examined pursuant to Article 9(7) of the China-Korea BIT is when Ansung actually or constructively acquired knowledge of the incurred losses resulting from the frustration of its legitimate expectation." The answer alleged is that "[b]efore Ansung transferred its shares in December 2011, Ansung could not know that its legitimate expectation [to develop a 27-hole golf course and condominiums] was frustrated and, therefrom, it incurred losses." Claimant contests Respondent's position that the local government's failure to allot the second phase land must be characterized (for prescription purposes) as a discrete breach that occurred before December 2011. According to Ansung, the government "failed to provide the second phase land for more than a year without any express repudiation and with even further assurance to give the land," which "actually or constructively matured into a breach only in mid-December 2011."[4]

Similarly, Claimant maintains that even if the Tribunal should find that that the government's separate acts between 2007 and 2010 were severable breaches falling before the three-year limitation period, the Tribunal would still have jurisdiction. This is because such earlier breaches could not affect Ansung's claims based on the local government's separate ongoing breach of its commitment to provide the second phase land. Alternatively, and relying on UPS v. Canada, Ansung argues that the local government's continuing omission concerning the second phase land effectively renewed the three-year period and "may render the first damage incurred from the renewed omission to fall within the prescription period of the China-Korea BIT."[5] Claimant challenges Respondent's efforts to undermine the UPS case and thereby

---

1 Cl. First Obs., para. 31 [citing CLA-003, Pope & Talbot, Inc. v. Government of Canada, UNCITRAL, para. 12 (Award, February 24, 2000)].

2 Cl. First Obs., para. 35.

3 Cl. First Obs., paras. 36-37.

4 Cl. First Obs., para. 33.

5 Cl. Second Obs., paras. 15-17, 20, 23 (emphasis in original).

avoid the application of the continuing breach principle. Claimant also distinguishes the Corona case, where the host State took an affirmative measure and thereafter remained silent in the face of the claimant's request that it reconsider the measure; in the present case, the government never acted and instead simply withheld the second parcel of land, making it a "continuing breach" of its promise.[1]

(2) *Dies ad Quem*

According to Claimant, although Article 9(7) of the China-Korea BIT explicitly precludes an investor from making a claim if the three-year time period has expired, the Treaty does not define the meaning of the phrase "make a claim."[2] Claimant posits that "a claim is made when the notice of intent is submitted."

In support of its position, Ansung highlights Article 9(5) of the Treaty, which addresses how an investment dispute may be settled. Article 9(5) requires that a claimant investor provide a written notice of intent to the respondent State at least 90 days before its claim can be "submitted" to arbitration. As its Notice of Intent and Request for Arbitration are substantially similar and as, according to Ansung, a notice of intent clarifies the nature of the dispute and the investor's intention to resolve it, it is unreasonable to calculate the limitation period from the date of the Request for Arbitration and reduce the period by 90 days. Moreover, Article 9(3) of the Treaty permits the respondent State to require the investor to go through the domestic administrative review procedure for four months before submission to international arbitration, which could reduce the limitation by a further four months. Given that, according to Ansung, the submission of a dispute to arbitration is only "a formalistic process, whereas making the claim is the more substantive step…the prescription period applies to the substantive step, i.e. submitting the notice of intent." Finally, Ansung suggests that "a dispute is 'a disagreement on a point of law or fact, a conflict of legal views or of interest'" and that the notice of intent and the subsequent acts can help crystalize a "dispute," which until that point remains a "claim," in order to support its view that "the prescription period applies only to the notice of intent."

In its Second Observations, Claimant reiterates its position that the end date must be the date of its Notice of Intent, and adds that, in the alternative, this could be the date of the filing of the Request for Arbitration. Claimant alleges that Respondent "fails to identify any relevant authorities demonstrating that a registration date becomes the date when a claim was first made," and, by contrast, "there are supporting legal authorities that treat the date of Notice of

---

1 Cl. Second Obs., paras. 18-19.

2 Cl. First Obs., para. 40.

Intent or the filing date of the Request for Arbitration as the date for making a claim."[1]

Claimant reasserts that the China-Korea BIT distinguishes between a "claim" and a "dispute."[2] For a claim to crystallize into a dispute, the investor must first give the Respondent a "notice of intent" which will become a dispute when the respondent State refuses the claim. Ansung argues that it first "made a claim" seeking relief for its losses, for purposes of Article 9(3) of the Treaty, through its Notice of Intent to China on May 19, 2014. Ansung rejects China's argument that the terms "investment dispute" and "claim" are used synonymously and suggests that "while every dispute includes a claim, every claim does not mature into a dispute."[3] Claimant opposes Respondent's assertion that there is no distinction between "making" and "submitting" a claim, and disagrees with the use of the Apotex and Feldman decisions on grounds that these decisions do not interpret the phrase "make a claim" objectively, but rather in the context of NAFTA provisions. Ansung notes that the NAFTA uses "claims" consistently and does not refer to "disputes," so the NAFTA jurisprudence does not provide a useful comparison. Ansung further argues that the teleological approach put forward by Respondent "constitutes a failure to apply the rules of treaty interpretation in international law and reduces the protections" granted by the Treaty.

In the alternative, and citing Vannessa Ventures v. Venezuela, Claimant contends that the latest possible cut-off date is October 7, 2014 when it filed its Request for Arbitration. Although the Secretary-General has the power under Article 36(3) of the ICSID Convention to screen requests for arbitration before registration, Ansung argues it would be "absurd to suggest that the cut-off date within the meaning of the China-Korea BIT will change depending on the time taken by the ICSID Secretary-General to register the Request for Arbitration," especially as the Secretary-General's screening power "does not prejudice the tribunal's power to examine its own competence."

(3) Conclusion

In sum, Claimant submits that, taking the facts it alleges as true, it meets the three-year limitation period in Article 9(7) of the China-Korea BIT. Ansung "came to know, or should have come to know, of its loss or damage around December 17, 2011" and it made a claim with its Notice of Intent on May 19, 2014, approximately two-and-a-half years later. Alternatively, Claimant submits that it made a claim with the filing of its Request for Arbitration on October 7, 2014, which also meets the three-year limitation period in Article 9(7) of the China-Korea BIT. Consequently, Ansung's claim cannot be considered manifestly meritless on grounds that

---

1 Cl. Second Obs., para. 4(2).

2 Cl. Second Obs., para. 29.

3 ibid.

it is time-barred.

3. Tribunal's Analysis

As the time limitation question before the Tribunal is one of treaty interpretation, the text of Article 9(7) of the China-Korea BIT bears repeating:

Notwithstanding the provisions of paragraph 3 of this Article, an investor may not make a claim pursuant to paragraph 3 of this Article if more than 3 years have elapsed from the date on which the investor first acquired, or should have first acquired, the knowledge that the investor had incurred loss or damage.

It also bears repeating that, under ICSID Arbitration Rule 41(5), China must establish that Ansung's claim is "manifestly without legal merit" on the basis of the facts as pleaded by Ansung.

(1) *Dies a Quo*

Turning first to the start date for the three-year limitation period in Article 9(7), the record is clear that Claimant repeatedly pleaded facts setting the date at which it "first acquired...the knowledge...that [it] had incurred loss or damage" to be before October 2011. As set out in the Factual Background section above, which is based on the facts as pleaded by Claimant:

(a) Most important, in the Request for Arbitration (paragraph 12), Ansung pleaded that it "was forced to dispose of its entire investment in Sheyang Xian in October 2011 in order to avoid further losses. Specifically, Ansung was forced to sell its shareholdings in the Subsidiaries to a Chinese purchaser at a price significantly lower than the amount that Ansung had invested toward the project" (emphasis added). This indicates Ansung had knowledge that it had incurred loss or damage before October 2011.

(b) In the Request for Arbitration (paragraph 55), Ansung pleaded that its subsidiary Mirage "was unable to meet the repayment date of June 2011 for the [loan] arranged by the Committee" (emphasis added), and "Ansung was unable to produce sufficient returns from its investments in the [joint venture] and Mirage as to justify their continued existence." It was also in June 2011 that Ansung employees suffered harassment from Committee officials and the local government refused to provide police protection. This indicates Ansung had knowledge of loss or damage incurred by June 2011.

(c) In the Request for Arbitration (paragraph 60), Ansung pleaded that "in October 2011, Ansung had no alternative but to dispose of its entire assets of the golf business, including its shareholding in the Subsidiaries, to a Chinese purchaser at a price significantly lower than the amount that Ansung had invested toward the project, causing serious financial losses and damage to Ansung" (emphasis added). This indicates Ansung had knowledge of incurred loss or damage by October 2011.

(d) Ansung pleaded several other facts indicating knowledge of incurred damage, at least to the prospects of its golf course project, well before October 2011. As early as 2007, it observed the development of a competing golf course at Sheyang Island Park, which went into operation in 2009.135 In 2007 and 2008, Ansung was compelled to pay a higher price for the additional 300 mu of land for phase one than originally agreed, following what Ansung described as "the Committee's outright repudiation" of the Investment Agreement (emphasis added).

After these multiple and clear pleadings, the Tribunal cannot accept Ansung's attempts to characterize these pre-October 2011 dates in its Observations and at the Rule 41(5) Hearing as mere background information.

Nor can the Tribunal accept Ansung's main argument that it incurred loss or damage for Article 9(7) purposes "only after its expectation and plan for the 27-hole golf course was completely frustrated, owing primarily to the government's continued inaction in providing the additional land for the second phase of the Project" (emphasis added), and when it sold its shares in the joint venture on December 17, 2011.

Ansung ignores the plain meaning of the words "first" and "loss or damage" in Article 9(7). The limitation period begins with an investor's first knowledge of the fact that it has incurred loss or damage, not with the date on which it gains knowledge of the quantum of that loss or damage. Ansung's actual sale of its shares on December 17, 2011 marked the date on which it could finalize or liquidate its damage, not the first date on which it had to know it was incurring damage.

As aptly stated by the ICSID tribunal in the Interim Award in Spence v. Costa Rica, "the limitation clause does not require full or precise knowledge of the loss or damage.... such knowledge is triggered by the first appreciation that loss or damage will be (or has been) incurred. It neither requires nor permits a claimant to wait and see the full extent of the loss or damage that will or may result."

The Tribunal acknowledges Claimant's legal argument that a continuing omission by a host State, such as alleged here, is recognized as a breach, for example in Pac Rim v. El Salvador, and that damages for such a continuing breach may be measured from different times after the first incident of that omission. As noted by the UPS tribunal, a "continuing course of conduct might generate losses of a different dimension at different times."

However, even assuming a continuing omission breach attributable to China, which the Tribunal must assume, and even assuming Ansung might wish to claim damages from a date later than the first knowledge of China's continuing omission — for example, from November 2, 2011, when Ansung tentatively agreed to transfer its shares or even December 17, 2011, when Ansung's commercial patience ran out — that could not change the date on which Ansung first knew it had incurred damage. And it is that first date that starts the three-year limitation period in Article 9(7). To allow Claimant to adjust that date of first knowledge by selecting the date from which it wants to claim damages for continuing breach would be, to borrow from the Spence decision, to allow an "endless parsing up of a claim into ever finer sub-components of breach over time in an attempt to come within the limitation period."

To conclude, based on the facts as pleaded by Claimant, Ansung "first acquired, or should have first acquired, the knowledge that [it] had incurred loss or damage" in connection with its ill-fated golf course project in Sheyang-Xian for purposes of Article 9(7) of the Treaty on a date before October 2011. The record does not provide an exact date, but it is reasonable to assume a date close to October, in late summer or early autumn 2011.

(2) *Dies ad Quem*

Turning to the *dies ad quem* for the applicable three-year limitation period, the Tribunal finds that, on the basis of the plain language in Article 9(7) of the China-Korea BIT, the end date is the date on which an investor deposits its request for arbitration with ICSID.

The interpretive steps are not difficult. Article 9(7) instructs that an investor "may not make a claim pursuant to paragraph 3 of this Article" more than three years after the *dies a quo*. Paragraph 3 of Article 9, in turn, instructs that "the dispute shall be submitted, at the option of the investor, to [as relevant here] ICSID." In coming to this conclusion, the Tribunal finds itself in agreement with the Decision on Jurisdiction in Vannessa Ventures v. Venezuela, where the ICSID tribunal had to determine when a dispute was submitted and found that the "relevant document regarding the interruption of the statute of limitation is therefore the Request for Arbitration."

In the Tribunal's view, this combination of paragraphs 3 and 7 of Article 9 of the China-Korea BIT excludes the two alternative end dates championed by the Parties in their primary cases.

First, Claimant correctly points out that Article 9(5) of the Treaty requires an investor to take the preliminary step of giving the Contracting Party a written notice of intent. However, as a matter of plain text, the Article 9(5) notice of intent is not "submitted...to ICSID," as required by Article 9(3).

Second, for similar reasons, the date on which ICSID registers the request for arbitration is, by definition, subsequent to the date the dispute is "submitted...to ICSID." Moreover, the

Tribunal agrees with Claimant that it would be unreasonable to subscribe to the Contracting Parties the intention that the end date of the Article 9(7) limitation period would be dependent upon the uncertain date of registration of a request for arbitration, which may depend upon a number of extraneous factors (no matter how efficient ICSID's registration process has become).

In light of the Tribunal's interpretation, it is not necessary to address the Parties' arguments concerning interpretation of the potentially different meaning of the words "dispute" and "claim" in the ICSID Arbitration Rules.

Claimant deposited the Request for Arbitration with ICSID electronically on October 7, 2014 and physically on October 8, 2014. Either date is more than three years after late summer or early autumn 2011, or the beginning of October 2011.

Consequently, Ansung submitted its dispute to ICSID and made its claim for purposes of Article 9(3) and (7) of the Treaty after more than three years had elapsed from the date on which Ansung first acquired knowledge of loss or damage. The claim is time-barred and, as such, is manifestly without legal merit.

III. ARTICLE 3 OF THE CHINA-KOREA BIT — MFN TREATMENT

To recall, Article 3 of the China-Korea BIT provides:

Each Contracting Party shall in its territory accord to investors of the other Contracting Party and to their investments and activities associated with such investments by the investors of the other Contracting Party treatment no less favourable than that accorded in like circumstances to the investors and investments and associated activities by the investors of any third State (hereinafter referred to as "most-favoured-nation treatment") with respect to investments and business activities [defined in paragraph 1 as "the expansion, operation, management, maintenance, use, enjoyment, and sale or other disposal of investments"], including the admission of investment.

....

Treatment accorded to investors of one Contracting Party within the territory of the other Contracting Party with respect to access to the courts of justice and administrative tribunals and authorities both in pursuit and in defence of their rights shall not be less favourable than that accorded to investors of the latter Contracting Party or to investors of any third State.

(1) Claimant's Position

Should the Tribunal find that Ansung made its claim after the three-year limitation period, Claimant argues in the alternative, in its First and Second Observations, that the MFN Clause in

Article 3(3) of the China-Korea BIT operates to save the claim from being time-barred.[1]

First, after noting that MFN clauses operate to allow investors to import substantive rights from other treaties, Ansung argues that the principle of extinctive prescription is considered a substantive (rather than a procedural) right both in international law and in many civil law countries, including Korea and China. Claimant then relies on a twopage table of 81 Chinese BITs to contend that most Chinese BITs do not have any prescription period.144 Because the three-year limitation period in Article 9(7) of the China-Korea BIT "is less favorable to foreign investors than those investors protected by BITs which do not contain such a prescription period," Ansung claims the protection of other Chinese treaties lacking prescription periods.

Second, even if the three-year period in Article 9(7) is considered to be procedural rather than substantive, Ansung contends that "[m]any tribunals and commentators are of the view that MFN clauses should be interpreted broadly" and be extended to the important procedural protection of arbitration provisions. In its First Observations, Ansung refers to a "stream of jurisprudence"147 supporting its MFN argument, to be developed at a later stage of the proceedings, which allegedly shows that China's Rule 41(5) Objection does not meet the requisite legal threshold.148 In its Second Observations, Ansung reiterates that such jurisprudence "will insulate" its claims from China's jurisdictional defense, by supporting its use of Chinese treaties without limitations periods.

Third, contesting China's treaty interpretation position, Ansung argues that the terms"treatment" and "investment activities" in Article 3(3) of the Treaty should be broadly interpreted to include dispute settlement procedures, because investor-State arbitration is critical to protect investment activities.150 Moreover, Claimant submits that the geographical limitation "within the territory" found in the MFN Clause of the Treaty does not prevent application of the MFN Clause to the dispute settlement clause.151 Ansung puts forward case law to support its arguments.152 Ansung refers to Siemens v. Argentina, where the tribunal interpreted the phrase "activities related to investment," included in an MFN clause, to be sufficiently wide to include settlement of disputes. Such an interpretation allowed the claimant in Siemens to access another treaty that did not condition international arbitration on waiting 18 months after initiation of the domestic judicial process.153 Furthermore, Ansung relies on AWG v. Argentina, where the tribunal interpreted an MFN clause similar to Article 3(3) of the China-Korea BIT — covering an investor's "management, maintenance, use, enjoyment or disposal of their investments" — to apply to dispute settlement and allow the claimant to avoid having to submit its dispute first to local courts.

---

1 Cl. First Obs., paras. 56 et seq.

Ansung contests China's contextual argument that Article 3(5) of the Treaty, which provides MFN treatment with respect to "access to courts of justice and administrative tribunals and authorities", demonstrates that Article 3(3) is unrelated to dispute settlement. Ansung argues that Article 3(5) on its face "comprehensively covers all kinds of domestic judicial or administrative proceedings" and therefore not international dispute settlement. Ansung further suggests that China's argument regarding references to its treaty practice fails, because, among other things, the treaties submitted by China are later than the China-Korea BIT, which "makes the Respondent's analysis…less convincing", and also refers to general treaty practice on MFN clauses.[1]

In its Second Observations, Ansung emphasizes the importance of the alleged substantive nature of the prescription period, as tribunals are more likely to import substantive standards than procedural protections from third party treaties through the MFN clause.

(2) Respondent's Position

In its Observations responding to Claimant's First Observations, Respondent contests Ansung's reliance on the MFN Clause in Article 3(3) of the China-Korea BIT to save its claim from being dismissed as time-barred under Article 9(7). China emphasizes that Article 3(3) does not apply either in general to investor-State dispute settlement provisions or in particular to China's temporal condition to consent to arbitration in Article 9(7).

First, China argues that Ansung's invocation of the MFN Clause in Article 3(3) fails as a matter of treaty interpretation. The text of Article 3(3) limits MFN treatment to the host State's territory and covers only "investment and business activities," which phrase is defined in Article 3(1) to cover "the expansion, operation, management, maintenance, use, enjoyment, and sale or other disposal of investments" — and does not include dispute settlement. The Treaty context confirms that Article 3(3) does not cover dispute settlement. This is because Article 3(5) separately provides for MFN treatment for dispute resolution by access to courts and administrative tribunals, demonstrating that the Contracting States do not consider Article 3(3) to apply to dispute settlement.

Respondent asserts that the Contracting States' treaty practice further confirms that Article 3(3) does not apply to dispute settlement. The 2012 trilateral agreement on investment between China, Korea and Japan similarly limits MFN treatment to "investment activities" encompassing "management, conduct, operation, maintenance, use, enjoyment and sale or other disposition of investments," and the States expressly state their understanding that this MFN treatment does not extend to dispute settlement. The 2015 comprehensive free trade agreement between China and Korea is to similar effect.

---

1 Cl. Second Obs., paras 62-69.

Second, Respondent argues that Claimant erred in equating Article 9(7) of the Treaty with the principle of extinctive prescription under international law. Article 9(7) explicitly conditions a Contracting State's consent to arbitration under Article 9(3) "on the submission of a claim within a precisely delimited and unqualified time period," which, under the plain Treaty terms, is "both an integral part of the investor-State dispute-resolution mechanism and a condition to China's consent to arbitration." In comparison, extinctive (or equitable) prescription arises under customary international law and "represents a form of the common-law notion of laches," requiring an assessment of State negligence without a fixed time period. Article 9(7), says China, is "akin to a statute of limitation that fixes an unyielding, specific time limitation for bringing a claim and specifies the beginning and end date for the calculation."

Third, China contends that Ansung errs in categorizing either equitable prescription or Article 9(7) as a substantive obligation. While in customary international law prescription is a question of admissibility rather than merits, "Article 9(7) is explicitly framed as a condition to consent to arbitration and therefore presents a question of jurisdiction."

Finally, Respondent emphasizes that Claimant has failed to specify a treaty with more favorable treatment as a matter of time limitation, and so has failed to demonstrate more favorable treatment than Article 9(7) of the China-Korea BIT.

IV. Tribunal's Analysis

Ansung's alternative defense to China's Rule 41(5) Objection is that, because China has entered into other bilateral investment treaties with third States that do not prescribe a temporal limitation for an investor initiating an arbitration claim against the host State, Ansung is entitled to invoke the MFN Clause in Article 3(3) of the China-Korea BIT to disregard the three-year limitation period in Article 9(7) of the Treaty.

The Tribunal accepts that the ambit of an MFN clause is dependent on its wording. Article 3(3) of the China-Korea BIT relevantly provides:

Each Contracting Party shall in its territory accord to investors of the other Contracting Party and to their investments and activities associated with such investments by the investor of the other Contracting Party treatment no less favorable than that accorded in like circumstances to the investors and investments and associated activities by the investors of any third State (hereinafter referred to as "most-favoured-nation treatment") with respect to investments and business activities [defined in paragraph 1 as "the expansion, operation, management, maintenance, use, enjoyment, and sale or other disposal of investments"], including the admission of investments.

A plain reading of this Article does not extend to MFN treatment for a State's consent to arbitrate with investors and, in particular, not to the temporal limitation period for investor-State arbitration in Article 9(7) of the China-Korea BIT. The Tribunal considers that Article 9(7) pertains to the Contracting State's consent to arbitration, and so it is irrelevant whether under municipal law prescription is a matter of substance or procedure. The import of Article 9(7) of the China-Korea BIT is a matter of international law, as correctly pointed out by Respondent and as is reflected in the International Law Commission's Articles on State Responsibility.

The Tribunal's conclusion in relation to the MFN Clause in Article 3(3) of the China-Korea BIT also becomes clear by reference to Article 3(5) of the Treaty. This Article offers specific MFN protection in relation to an investor's "access to courts of justice and administrative tribunals and authorities." In marked contrast to those domestic avenues, such express reference to international dispute resolution is conspicuously absent in the MFN Clause in Article 3(3).

As the Tribunal finds that the wording of the MFN Clause in Article 3(3) of the Treaty is clear, it is not necessary to give further consideration to additional arguments or previous arbitral decisions on the interpretation of other MFN clauses or treaty practice. The plain reading of Article 3(3) and its interpretation leave no doubt that China has established its Rule 41(5) Objection with regard to the MFN Clause "clearly and obviously, with relative ease and despatch," contrary to Claimant's allegation.

For these reasons the Tribunal does not consider that Article 3(3) of the China-Korea BIT assists Claimant in preventing its claim from being manifestly time-barred under Article 9(7) of the Treaty.

To conclude, the Tribunal has carefully considered Respondent's Rule 41(5) Objection, the Observations from both Parties, and the presentations from counsel at the Rule 41(5) Hearing. The breadth and depth of the Parties' submissions has enabled the Tribunal to provide its oral ruling after deliberating at the end of the First Session and Rule 41(5) Hearing. In specific, to borrow language from the Trans-Global tribunal, the Tribunal was able to determine that China established its Rule 41(5) Objection "clearly and obviously, with relative ease and despatch" and its determination proved not to be "difficult."

Accepting the facts as pleaded by Claimant to be true, the Tribunal finds Ansung's claim to be time-barred under Article 9(7) of the China-Korea BIT and not protected by operation of the MFN Clause in Article 3(3) of the Treaty. The Tribunal finds the claim hence to be manifestly without legal merit under ICSID Arbitration Rule 41(5).

In light of the reasoning above, Respondent's alternative request that the Tribunal hear the question of the application of Article 9(7) of the China-Korea BIT as a preliminary question pursuant to ICSID Arbitration Rule 41(4) is moot.

V.COSTS

Article 61(2) of the ICSID Convention provides:

In the case of arbitration proceedings the Tribunal shall, except as the parties otherwise agree, assess the expenses incurred by the parties in connection with the proceedings, and shall decide how and by whom those expenses, the fees and expenses of the members of the Tribunal and the charges for the use of the facilities of the Centre shall be paid. Such decision shall form part of the award.

This provision gives the Tribunal discretion to allocate all costs of the arbitration, including attorney's fees and other costs, between the Parties as it deems appropriate.

(1) Claimant's Position

In its Statement of Costs of January 17, 2017, Claimant seeks the following costs: (i) costs of ICSID arbitration, including the lodging fee, amounting to US$ 175,000; (ii) wire transfer fee for the lodging fee, amounting to KRW 54,340; and (iii) professional fees and disbursements of Bae, Kim & Lee LLC, amounting to KRW 433,772,145.169.

In support of its costs request, Claimant asserts that, "although there is no set principle for allocation of costs in ICSID arbitrations, the Tribunal in one well-cited award Romak v. Uzbekistan was compelled to conclude after reviewing prior jurisprudence that there is a 'general practice in investment treaty arbitration disfavoring the shifting of arbitration costs against the losing party' and that 'a general trend has developed that arbitration costs should be equally apportioned between the Parties, irrespective of the outcome of the dispute.'"

Claimant asks the Tribunal to follow this "general trend" and exercise its discretion under Article 61(2) of the ICSID Convention to order each Party to bear its own costs and divide the ICSID costs (including the fees and expenses of the Tribunal) equally. Ansung offers three reasons for this allocation, in the circumstances of this case: first, Ansung, which is a small investor, has suffered substantial loss as a consequence of China's actions, and "pursued the instant claim in good faith and on sound substantive ground;" second, Ansung presented its case "in the most procedurally efficient and economical manner;" and, third, the Rule 41(5) Objection issues were novel issues of law.171 As to the third reason, Claimant emphasizes that "the Tribunal was called on to rule on the novel legal questions of (i) whether MFN applies to limitations provisions in a BIT, and (ii) how to interpret 'knowledge that the investor had incurred loss or damage' under Article 9(7) of the BIT."

In Claimant's Response, Ansung reiterates the novelty of these legal arguments and emphasizes that "the applicability of a MFN clause to limitation periods has never been tested by an investment treaty tribunal previously."

Ansung rejects China's argument that the upholding of a Rule 41(5) objection automatically requires an ICSID tribunal to award all costs to the respondent. In support, Ansung cites Global Trading Resource v. Ukraine, in which the tribunal "gave much weight to the parties' conduct in apportioning costs and did not give any consideration to the review threshold under Rule 41(5)."

Claimant also challenges the level of Respondent's legal costs, which are almost double Ansung's costs. This disparity is unreasonable, Ansung contends, because China filed only two briefs totaling 47 pages, participated in a one-day hearing, and did not have to prepare a comprehensive submission equivalent to Claimant's Request for Arbitration. Ansung objects to Respondent's "attempts [at] justifying its excessive costs by arguing that it needed to prepare a defense to Ansung's allegedly shifting arguments and conflicting factual assertions." Ansung points out that China did not raise this "shifting arguments" contention until November 2016, while most of its legal costs were incurred before September 2016 and one-third of the sums claimed by the Zhong Lun law firm had been paid by July 2015.

Finally, Ansung requests the Tribunal to disregard China's "unsolicited" and "fresh" request for post-Award interest. Ansung alleges that this request falls outside the scope of the Statements of Costs and outside the Tribunal's instructions allowing Respondent to file observations on Claimant's Statement of Costs, which did not address interest.

(2) Respondent's Position

In its Statement of Costs of January 17, 2017, Respondent seeks the following costs: (i) costs of ICSID arbitration, amounting to US$ 149,985.00; (ii) disbursements relating to Chinese Government representatives' attendance at the Rule 41(5) Hearing in Singapore, amounting to US$ 6,471; (iii) Dentons' invoiced legal fees and disbursements, amounting to EUR 356,590.80; and (iv) Zhong Lun's invoiced total legal fees, amounting to CNY 3,330,900.33 with fees capped at CNY 1,850,000.00 (including disbursements of CNY 200,000).

In Respondent's Observations on Costs, China contests Ansung's depiction of the general approach to allocation of costs being "pay-your-own-way," citing the words of the ICSID tribunal in Arif v. Moldova that "a 'more modern strand is for the costs to be awarded on the basis of the relative success of the parties in the arbitration.'" Ansung argues that the "costs follow the event" principle is "particularly adapted to cases where the losing party's arguments are rejected for fundamental lack of merit" and "particularly suited to the context of a successful Rule 41(5) objection." China relies on the RSM v. Grenada award, in which the tribunal "had no difficulty applying the 'costs follow the event' principle and ordered the unsuccessful claimant to bear the entirety of the arbitration costs in a case where the claims were rejected for manifest lack of legal merit following a successful Rule 41(5) objection."

Respondent objects to Claimant's arguments in favor of cost-sharing. First, even if Ansung is a small investor and made a good faith mistake in assessing its case, there is no basis for the Tribunal to presume that Ansung's substantive claims would have proven meritorious. Second, Claimant "cannot claim being efficient" by bringing a claim that was dismissed for a manifest lack of legal merit. Third, the issues presented were not novel, as "[n]umerous investor-State tribunals have rejected claimants' claims on the basis of similar temporal objections to the application of a treaty" and China's objections were based "on the clear wording of Article 9(7) of the China-Korea BIT which the Tribunal had no difficulty applying in this case."

Finally, China emphasizes that its costs were "reasonable and proportionate to the total amount of work that was needed to prepare a defense against Ansung's shifting arguments and conflicting factual assertions." Further, Respondent achieved an early dismissal of the case "through an expedited procedure introduced specifically to address frivolous claims filed against the ICSID Contracting States."

(3) Tribunal's Analysis

The Tribunal's decision in favor of Respondent's Rule 41(5) Objection constitutes a decision as contemplated by Arbitration Rule 41(6) regarding a lack of jurisdiction of the Centre and of its own competence as well as regarding manifest lack of legal merit due to a lack of temporal jurisdiction.

The Tribunal need not venture into the discussion about whether there is a general trend in ICSID practice favoring the "costs follow the event" approach or "pay-your-own-way" approach to allocation of costs. The Tribunal is satisfied that, under the circumstances in this case, Respondent is entitled to its reasonable costs. The Tribunal's determination that Ansung's claim manifestly lacks legal merit as time-barred necessarily means that the claim should not have been brought, and China should not bear the reasonable costs for successfully defending the claim at the Rule 41(5) stage.

Even accepting the novelty of Ansung's arguments concerning the applicability of MFN treatment to limitations provisions in BITs in general and the proper interpretation of Article 9(7) of the China-Korea BIT ("knowledge that the investor had incurred loss or damage"), novelty is not necessarily a test of even prima facie validity.

Even further accepting that Ansung is a small investor in an unfortunate position, proceeding in good faith against China, these points are irrelevant to the allocation of costs following acceptance of the Rule 41(5) Objection. Nor is efficiency in an Arbitration Rule 41(5) objection procedure necessarily a factor relevant to costs allocation, as an Arbitration Rule 41(5) objection procedure is by definition designed to promote efficiency.

This is not to say that costs could and should never be apportioned between the parties following a successful Rule 41(5) objection. In this regard, the Tribunal notes Claimant's reliance on Global Trading Resource v. Ukraine, in which the tribunal granted Ukraine's Rule 41(5) objection but chose not to allocate costs between the parties. However, as pointed out by Claimant itself, the Award dates to 2010, and the tribunal opined that "given the newness of the Rule 41(5) procedure and given the reasonable nature of the arguments concisely presented to it by both parties, the appropriate outcome is for the costs of the procedure to lie where they fall." In comparison, the Rule 41(5) procedure is no longer new and the Tribunal has found in this case that Claimant's limitations arguments were not reasonable.

This leaves the question of the reasonableness of the amount of costs claimed by Respondent. Having considered the circumstances and the entire record carefully, the Tribunal determines to apportion only 75 percent of Respondent's costs to Claimant. This is not because China claimed substantially higher costs than Ansung claimed, as percentage comparisons ignore issues such as market rates and individual fee arrangements. Rather, the Tribunal considers that the legal costs sought by China, even noting the fee cap for the Zhong Lun law firm, are disproportionate to the extent of the Rule 41(5) Objection submissions and one-day hearing.

Turning to post-Award interest, Ansung is incorrect in suggesting that China made a "fresh" request for post-Award interest in its Observations on Claimant's Submissions on Costs. The record reflects that China requested post-Award interest, at a commercially reasonable rate to be set by the Tribunal, in its Rule 41(5) Objection, in its Observations and in its Statement of Costs. The Tribunal determines to award post-Award interest, on the terms set out below.

To conclude, the Tribunal decides to assess all of the direct costs of the proceeding and 75 percent of Respondent's legal fees and expenses against Claimant.

The direct costs of the proceeding include: (i) the fees and expenses of each Member of the Tribunal; (ii) payments made by ICSID for other direct expenses, such as those related to the conduct of hearings (e.g., court reporting, Maxwell Chambers' charges, courier services, and estimated charges related to the dispatch of this Award); and (iii) ICSID's administrative fees.

These costs amount to (in US$):

Arbitrators' fees and expenses:

Professor Lucy Reed	US$ 29,987.20
Dr. Michael Pryles	US$ 29,444.84
Professor Albert Jan van den Berg	US$ 33,589.05

Other direct expenses (estimated)	US$ 14,500.00
ICSID's administrative fees	US$ 32,000.00
Total	US$ 139,521.09

The above costs have been paid out of the advances made to ICSID by the Parties in equal parts. Once the case account balance is final, the ICSID Secretariat will provide the Parties with a detailed financial statement, and the remaining balance will be reimbursed to the Parties in proportion to the advances they made.

Accordingly, the Tribunal orders Claimant to pay Respondent US$ 69,760.55 for the expended portion of Respondent's advances to ICSID and US$ 4,853.25 plus EUR 267,443.10 plus CNY 1,387,500 to cover 75 percent of Respondent's legal fees and expenses, plus interest at the rate of three-month LIBOR plus two percent, compounded quarterly, such interest to run from the 90th day after the date of dispatch of this Award on any unpaid portion of the amounts due under this Award until the date of payment.

VI.DECISION

For the reasons set forth above, the Tribunal decides as follows:

(1) Dismisses with prejudice all claims made by Claimant, Ansung Housing Co., Ltd., in its Request for Arbitration, pursuant to ICSID Arbitration Rule 41(5).

(2) Awards Respondent, the People's Republic of China, its share of the direct costs of the proceeding in the amount of US$ 69,760.55, plus 75 percent of its legal fees and expenses in the amount of US$ 4,853.25 plus EUR 267,443.10 plus CNY 1,387,500, plus interest at the rate of three-month LIBOR plus two percent, compounded quarterly, such interest to run from the 90th day after the date of dispatch of this Award on any unpaid portion of the amounts due under this Award until the date of payment.

Appellate Body Report, EC-Selected Customs Matters, WT/DS315/AB/R, 2006-11-13.

【思考题】

1. 本案中，为什么中韩双边投资协定中的最惠国待遇条款不能适用于仲裁时效？
2. ICSID 仲裁规则的初始异议程序在何种情况下启动？

Case2·拓展阅读

Case3　European Communities–Selected Customs matters（DS315）

【案情说明】

一、案件事实

2004 年 9 月 21 日，美国认为欧共体 (EC) 有关海关分类和估价，以及限制或禁止某些进口的措施、欧洲理事会第 2913/92 号规定中的 "共同体关税守则"、第 2454/93 号规定中有关 "共同体关税守则" 实施规定、欧洲理事会颁布的 "共同海关关税" 以及其他相关措施分别违反了 GATT1994 第 10 条 3 款（a）项和（b）项的义务，因此请求依据《关于争端解决规则与程序的谅解》（DSU）与 EC 就此进行磋商，磋商无果后，美国于 2005 年 1 月 13 日向 WTO 申请成立专家组以解决相关争议。

在专家组审理过程中，美欧除了对有关实体问题存在争议外，专家组职权范围的确定也是本案在程序方面的核心争议。按照 DSU 第 7 条 1 款的规定，除非当事方另有不同约定，则专家小组应按照 WTO 相关协定的有关规定，审查当事方提交到 DSB 的有关事项，对其进行调查并作出裁定。因此，专家组的职权范围，是由申诉方提交给 DSB 的有关设立专家组的申请书所确定。在本案中，美国作为申诉方请求 DSB 设立了专家小组。但对于专家小组审理美国根据 GATT1994 第 10 条 3 款（a）项所提诉求的具体职权范围，争端当事方和专家小组以及上诉机构均存在不同意见。

专家组认为，确定争议的具体措施，应结合申诉方的指控进行，即按照被指控方违反的具体 WTO 义务来界定。WTO 专家小组或上诉机构的主要任务在于确定被诉措施是否与其 WTO 下具体义务相一致。既然本案中起诉方美国所指控的事项为 EC 海关措施违反了 GATT1994 第 10 条 3 款（a）项的有关规定。即 EC 海关没有以统一、公正和合理的方式执行第 10 条 1 款所述之法律、条例、决定和裁定。那么 WTO 专家组的工作便是就此进行裁定，指明所涉及的法律、条例、决定或裁定及其适用的领域。在本案中也就是要裁定《EC 海关税则》及其实施条例、《EC 共同海关税则及商品分类编码制度》、《EC 统一关税表》以及相关措施在申请书所列举的海关执行方式是否符合上述 "统一、公正与合理" 的要求。

EC 认为，既然美国诉求为请求 WTO 专家组裁定 EC 海关法律的实施方式，故 WTO 专家组裁判范围应限定为裁定 EC 被诉海关法在实施或执行方面是否存在违反 GATT1994 第 10 条 3 款相关义务，而不是对海关法律法规本身的合法性进行裁判。而且，从美国起诉书中可以明显看出，美国的诉求是请求裁定 EC 海关措施的实施方式（the manner）是否合法，而非措施本身。美国起诉书中虽然列举了 EC 相关海关法律法规，但这种列举也旨在表明其所质疑的执行措施的法律依据，并不意味着所列举的法律法规本身的合法性属于本次诉讼的争议事项范畴。但美国认为，既然根据 DSU 第 6.2 条的规定，DSB 的职责在于明确"所争议事项"（the measures at issue），因此，所争议事项当然包括构成 EC 海关法的法律法规、决定和裁定。

二、裁判结果

2006 年 6 月 16 日，专家小组提交了报告。报告根据美国就 EC 在海关税则分类、海关估价和海关程序三个方面的指控进行了调查并得出结论：

在海关税则分类上，EC 在个人电脑网卡、滴灌产品税则分类未违反 GATT1994 第 10 条 3（3）项的规定，但有关遮光布内衬税则决策的行政程序，以及装有数字视频接口的液晶显示监测器的税则分类违反了 GATT 第 10 条 3（3）项的规定，但美国的其他三项诉求因举证不能未获支持。

在海关估价的海关管理方面，专家组裁定 EC《实施规定》第 147 条（1）款的规定未能在成员国以统一形式实施，构成对 GATT1994 第 10 条 3（a）的违反。但另一项类似指控，因美国举证不能未获支持。

在海关行政管理程序方面，专家组裁定 EC 基于《EC 海关编码》第 78 条（2）款实施措施，以及各成员国海关处罚法的实施均没有违反 GATT1994 第 10 条 3（a）款。同时，关于《EC 海关编码》第 502（3）、第 552 条的规定是否违反 GATT1994 第 10 条 3（a）款规定，因美国举证不能而未获支持。同时专家组裁定，EC 在对管理活动提供及时审查方面没有违反 GATT1994 第 10 条 3（b）项之规定。

2006 年 8 月 14 日和 28 日，美国和 EC 分别就专家组报告中部分裁定内容提出上诉，同年 11 月 13 日，WTO 上诉机构做出上诉裁定，就专家组职权范围、GATT1994 第 10 条 3（a）项适用，以及第 10 条 3（b）项解释等部分问题肯定了专家组裁定。

【法律分析】

本案在程序和实体上均存在争议，程序上主要涉及专家组职权问题，实体层面则主要涉及 GATT1994 第 10 条 3 款相关规定的适用和解释问题。

（一）WTO 专家组的职权范围

根据 WTO/DSU 第 7 条第 1 款的规定，除非争端当事方另有约定，专家组将按照争端各方援引的 WTO 协定的相关规定，审查各方所提交给争端解决机构的事项，提出调查结果。换言之，专家组的职权范围（terms of reference）主要根据申诉方的争端解决申请书来确定。本案中，鉴于双方并未就专家组职权范围另做其他约定，因此，专家组法定职权范围将主要根据美国争端解决申请书（WT/DS315/8）来确定。然而，就美国根据 GATT1994 第 10 条 3（a）项所提出诉求，专家组的具体职权范围各方却存在争议，概括而言，争议主要集中在以下几个方面：

1. 争议解决范围界定

在本案中，美欧双方对于专家组争议解决范围存在争议。美国认为，其质疑的对象是 EC 海关法执行方式。但是方式本身不构成措施，因此，美国在争端解决申请书当中提到的争议措施（measures at issue）系指构成 EC 海关法的相关法律、法规、决定和裁定。但 EC 认为，争议解决范围应是美国申请书中所指控的 EC 的具体措施，而非措施据以实行的法律法规。对此，专家组认为，在本案中，根据美国的指控，EC 若干海关措施违反了 GATT 第 10 条 3（a）项的规定，按照 GATT 的要求，每一缔约方应以统一、公正和合理的方式管理有关海关归类、海关估价、关税税率、国内税费、有关产品进出口相关的转账、销售、分销、运输、保险、仓储检验、展览、加工、混合等方面的法律、法规、判决和裁定。对此，专家组首先解释了"争议措施"（measures at issue）。专家组认为，按照《争端解决程序谅解》第 6.2 条，设立专家组的请求应以书面形式提出。请求应确认争议措施并提供一份足以说明申诉请求的法律基础概要。简言之，DSU 第 6.2 条包含两个基本要求：（1）确认所争议的具体措施；（2）简要提出申诉请求的法律依据。在强调了"争议措施"界定的重要性之后，专家组特别引述了上诉机构的观点："原则上，任何 WTO 成员的作为或不作为均可构成争端解决程序中理解的措施。在通常的案件中，无论是国家还是其行政部门的作为或不作为都可以称之为措施。"因此，专家组认为，所谓措施不仅指具体情形下的特定行动，同时也包括那些具有一般性和可能适用的规则或规范制定。换言之，专家组认为，WTO 成员方的规则和规范本身也能构成所谓的措施。专家组还进一步从 GATT 和 WTO 的目的角度出发论证了上诉解释的合理性，它谈到，WTO 和 GATT 的目的不仅在于保护现有的贸易，同时还希望能够为未来的贸易活动提供一个安全和可预测的环境。因此，如果将措施仅仅局限于具体的贸易措施而忽略对那些具有一般适用性的规则的审查将与这一目标相冲突。最终专家组将本案争议的具体措施界定为"EC 海关当局对《EC 海关守则》及其实施条例、《EC 海关税则及商品分类编码制度》、《EC 统一关税表》及相关制度等在申诉请求中被列举的海关管理措施。"

对此，上诉机构认为专家组在对具体争议措施界定方面存在两个问题。第一，专家小组不应依据申诉请求中提及的 WTO 义务来界定具体争议措施。事实上，界定具体争议的范围，应从《争端解决程序谅解》第 6.2 条的规定进行，凡任何可归因于 WTO 成员方的作为或不作为均可称为争端解决程序的"措施"。第二，专家组职权范围的确定和执行问题是两个相互独立的问题，不应该将其混为一谈。以执行手段来界定专家小组职权范围不仅不符合逻辑，还会造成不必要的混乱，因为执行手段允许存在一定的灵活性，只要其行为符合 WTO/GATT 的相关要求即可。上诉机构进一步指出，专家组在解读美国申诉请求时存在错误解读。实际上，美国在申诉请求第一段就已经明确声明了其质疑的对象，即其所列有关 EC 的法律、条例、决定或裁决的整体执行情况。这一声明已经足够让当事方和第三方知晓申诉措施。至于第三段的内容实际上只是对第一段申诉内容的补充说明而已。

2. 美国诉求的范围与性质

在一般性解决了争议范围之后，具体到本案中，在美国诉求的具体范围与性质的认定上，专家组将美国诉求限定为申请书第三段所列明的欧共体具体管理措施，而没有对 EC 海关管理的总体设计问题提出质疑。对此，美国不予认可，在上诉中，美国指出，专家组错误的将争议措施限定为申请书中所列举的具体措施，而没有将申诉书中的请求作为一个整体加以考虑。美国指出，其申请书第三段的内容实际上只具有说明的意义，其目的在于支持美国对 EC 海关法律法规整体执行上不符合 GATT1994 第 10 条 3（a）项规定予以补充说明，其本身并不构成一项单独的诉求，或指向被诉的具体措施。实际上，美国的诉求是要求专家组审查 EC 是否提供了相应的机制或手段来确保欧共体海关法律制度在成员国的统一实施。美国据此认为，专家组对美方申请书中诉讼请求存有误解，不仅混淆了主张，同时也混淆了主张的论据。美国这一主张得到了上诉机构的支持，其同样认为，上诉机构应将申请书视为一个整体看待，在美国请求专家组将 EC 海关整体执行情况予以审查的意图已经表露于其申请书中的情况下，专家组应对此予以审查。

3. 专家组职权管辖的时效范围

另一个与专家组职权范围密切相关的一个争议点在于，专家组对于专家组成立之前或之后的被诉行政行为是否有审查权。专家组认为其不仅有权审查在其成立时有效的措施，对于成立前后 EC 采取的措施，只要这些措施为美国申请书所涵盖，专家组便有权加以审查。对此，EC 表达了不同意见。EC 认为，在职权范围的时效范围的确定上，专家组采取了一种过于宽泛的解释方式。EC 认为，原则上，专家组仅应考虑那些在其成立时存在的措施。因此，专家组宣称其对在此之前和之后的措施均有权审查的说法，EC 表示反对。同时，对于专家组关于管理方式属于没有明确起始和结束点的看法，EC 也拒绝予以认同。EC 认为，专家组这种宽泛认定方式将导致尴尬的后果：对于那些过去发生的，也已经不再有任何影响的违规行为，如果没有结束点的话，将被认为仍在持续；而那些尚未发生的活动，则因没有起始点将被视为已经发生。专家组将 GATT1994 第 10 条 3（a）项中的"管理"视为一种"没有任何时间边界的现象"违反了 DSU 第 6.2 条的正当程序权，因为要求被告为过去的管理活动是否违法的作出准备是"过度困难的"，而将未来可能出现的管理行为纳入审查范畴则让案件的诉讼标的变成一个"移动的目标"。专家组的这种做法也会让遵守变得不可能。因为如果管理不存在起止点的话，任何被诉方将不可能证实它已经修改了它的管理方式以遵守 GATT1994 第 10 条 3（a）项的规定。综上，EC 认为专家组关于他职权的时效范围认定违反了 DSU 第 7.36 和 7.37 两条的规定。美国对此表示反对，美国认为，EC 的上述说法混淆了既有的海关法管理和专家组成立以前的海关管理活动，以及在专家组审理过程中作为 EC 未统一实施管理的证据呈示的内容。在美国看来，EC 误读了专家组对作为"持续过程的管理"

和"管理的具体事例"之间的区别。对于上述争议，上诉机构裁定专家组虽有权将 EC 有关执行行为作为证据，但是专家组的确未能将措施与证据两者区分开来，前者有时效限制，但后者不具有。

（二）EC 海关措施是否违反 GATT1994 第 10 条 3（a）项

由于专家组认为其无权对 EC 海关管理体系的整体设计与结构进行审查，所以其在报告中只对美国申请书第三段所列举的一些管理行为进行了审理。对于前述专家组的审查结果，上诉机构主要针对以下几个方面的内容作出了裁定。

1. 成员国执行 EC 海关法的处罚条款和审计程序

专家组界定的"执行"是指 EC 海关法律法规的适用，而不是法律本身，但美国认为专家组对"执行"一词的解释存在错误。对此上诉机构援引了此前"EC 香蕉案"和"EC 家禽案"中上诉机构的解释后支持了 EC 的支持。上诉机构认为，按照 GATT1994 第 10 条 3（a）项的规定，其主要调整对象是成员方"贸易法规的公布和执行"，因此，有必要将被执行的法律文件与落实这些文件的文件或执行的法律文件区分开来。换言之，申诉方无权对被执行文件的实质内容提出申诉，但对于落实这些文件的政策性文件导致了对有关海关法律法规执行的不统一、不公正或不合理的执行，申诉方可以提出申诉，但申诉方应负举证责任。

对于 EC 成员国之间处罚条款和审计程序的不同是否违反 GATT1994 第 10 条 3（a）项，专家组做出了否定回答，对此美国提出了上诉。但上诉机构最终仍支持了 EC 主张，但对裁定理由进行了修改。专家组做出上述结论的理由是法律本身不构成执行行为，对此上诉机构表达了不同看法，上诉机构认为，EC 成员国法律本身的不同不足以证明违反了统一执行 EC 海关法律的要求，但起诉方必须证明处罚条款的适用导致了 EC 海关法的非统一适用，但美国对此并未提出足够证据。

2. 海关统一管理要求是否适用于执行程序

上诉中，EC 提出专家组要求将 GATT1994 第 10 条 3（a）项解释为要求 EC 成员国采取统一的执行程序是错误的。但从专家的实际解读来看，专家组的裁定并未做出这样的认可，而只是提请注意执行和执行程序有关，不过并不认为执行程序的差异会导致对 GATT 第 10 条 3（a）项的违反。最终，上诉机构认为 EC 在这一点上存在误读。但上诉机构也并未因此肯定美国的上诉主张，同样，上诉机构认为美国在这一点并未完成举证责任。

3. 遮光布衬里的关税分类

在有关遮光布衬里的海关分类上，专家组认为 EC 违反了 GATT1994 第 10 条 3（a）款规定。理由在于，德国海关参照了一项仅适用于德国的解释参考标准，而未参考其他成员国海关当局的做法。但上诉机构推翻了专家组这一结论，认为执行包括执行程序，但并不要求执行程序也采用统一的形式。要认定一项执行程序导致了不统一的执行，仅

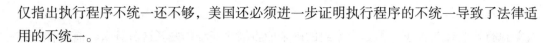

仅指出执行程序不统一还不够，美国还必须进一步证明执行程序的不统一导致了法律适用的不统一。

4. 附数字视频互动功能的液晶显示器的关税分类

专家组裁定欧共体在附数字视频互动功能的液晶显示器的关税分类方面违反了GATT1994第10条3（a）款，理由是，按照EC的关税税则分类，此类商品既可以被归类到计算机显示器，也可能被归类为录像显示器。按照《EC共同海关税则》，前者的进口关税为零，但后者进口关税为14%。在EC成员内部，荷兰将其归类为录像显示器，而其他成员国则将其归类为计算机显示器，因此违反了统一执行海关法律的要求。上诉中，EC提出了三项抗辩理由：第一，专家组据以作出裁定的证据属于专家组成立之后的EC的执行行为；第二，专家组未能根据DSU第11条的要求对事实作出客观评价；第三，专家组未考虑《EC第2171/2005号规则草案》以及EC中期审查阶段提交的167、168和169号证据。对此上诉机构均予以驳回。上诉机构重申了专家组成立之前或之后的事实均可视为证据的观点；对于EC认为专家组未能对事实进行客观评估的观点，上诉机构认为专家组是在分析了大量不同证据基础上做出的，因此并未违反对事实进行客观评估的义务。最后，上诉机构指出，专家组事实上有对《EC第2171/2005号规则草案》进行过讨论，虽然并未如EC所期待的那样进行讨论，但专家组作为事实裁判者，对此有自由裁量权。至于EC中期审查阶段提交的证据，依据"EC沙丁鱼案"确立的先例，上诉机构认为中期阶段不适于出示新的证据。

5. 连续销售条款的执行

《〈EC海关守则〉实施条例》第147条第1款规定了所谓的连续销售条款，按照该条规定，EC将以进口商品进入EC的最后销售环节以外的销售环节作为海关估价基础的条件。对此，美国指控EC部分成员国在执行该条款时附加了事先同意的要求，而部分成员国则没有，由此造成了执行上的不统一。在专家组审理阶段，因EC举证不利，专家组最终裁定EC违反了GATT1994第10条3（a）款。对此EC上诉中提出，在本案中，美国并未能提供充分的证据，在此情形下，专家组就将举证责任转移给EC是不当的。上诉机构最终认可了EC的上述主张，肯定了在美国未能提供充分证据情况下应承担举证不力的后果，而不是将举证责任转嫁给EC。

（三）关于GATT1994第10条3（b）款

按照GATT1994第10条3（b）款的规定，每一缔约方应维持或尽快设立司法、仲裁或行政庭或行政程序，目的在于迅速审查和纠正与海关事项有关的行政行为。此类法庭或程序……的决定应由此类机构执行，并应适用于此类机构的做法……。美国认为，EC各成员国设立的旨在对海关当局的行政行为进行审查和纠正的司法、仲裁或行政机构决定仅在本国境内有效，但不能约束其他成员国的海关部门，因此有违GATT1994第10条3（b）款。专家组认为，虽然该款规定并未直接就这一问题给出答案，但通常情况下，大多数法律体系中初审法院和机构的实体管辖权和地域管辖权是有限的，要求他们的司法机关等约束成员方境内所有行政机构是不合理的。美国认为专家组在这一认定上存在错误。美国提出的理由是，该款在"机构"一词上使用了复数形式，并且未作出任何限定，因此指的不是一个或几个机构，而应该是全体机构。对此上诉机构首先肯定了GATT1994第10条3（b）款是有关初审的，在此基础上，上诉机构结合了文义解释、上下文解释和条约目的解释等方法对这一问题进行解释得出结论认为，该款规定并不能解释为要求成员国司法或仲裁机构的裁判必须约束成员方境内全体行政机构。因此，在这一问题上，上诉机构维持了专家组的结论。

【英文案例裁决摘录】

下文摘录的是上诉机构报告部分内容。

I. The Panel's Terms of Reference

Claims of Error by the United States — Appellant

The United States requests the Appellate Body to reverse the findings of the Panel concerning its terms of reference. According to the United States, the Panel erred in three respects: first, in finding that, under Article 6.2 of the DSU, the measure at issue must be the "manner of administration"[1] when a claim is made under Article X3(a) of the GATT 1994; secondly, in finding that the specific measure at issue in this dispute was confined to the six areas of customs administration identified in the third paragraph of the request for the establishment of a panel by the United States (the "panel request");[2] and finally, in concluding that, due to the wording and content of the panel request, the United States was precluded from challenging the European Communities' system of customs administration "as a whole".

(1) The "Measures at Issue" for Purposes of a Claim under Article X3(a) of the GATT 1994

According to the United States, the Panel erroneously found that, when a violation of Article X3(a) of the GATT 1994 is alleged, the measure to be identified in the panel request must be a "manner of administration". For the United States, in making this finding, the Panel relied primarily on what it described as "an inter-linkage between the reference to the term 'measure' in Article 19.1 of the DSU and to the term 'measures at issue' in Article 6.2 of the DSU."[3] The Panel also reasoned that, under Article 19.1 of the DSU, a Member breaching Article X3(a) of the GATT 1994 would be required "to alter the manner in which the relevant

---

1 WT/DS315/R 16 June 2006, Panel Report, para. 7.20.

2 Request for the Establishment of a Panel by the United States, WT/DS315/8 (attached as Annex III to this Report).

3 United States' appellant's submission, para. 45 (referring to Panel Report, para. 7.14).

laws, regulations, decisions and/or rulings are being administered in order to abide by that recommendation."[1]

The United States contends that this reasoning of the Panel is flawed because a "manner of administration" is not a "measure" but, rather, a description of how a measure operates. The United States adds that this approach blurs the distinction between measures and claims. By finding the "manner of administration" to be the measure at issue, the Panel confused the measure at issue in an Article X:3(a) dispute with the obligation under that provision. The United States also argues that the Panel's reasoning leads to illogical consequences for complaints under other WTO provisions as well, because, under such an approach, the measure at issue is not "distinguishable" from the legal basis of the complaint for purposes of Article 6.2 of the DSU Regarding the "inter-linkage" between Articles 6.2 and 19.1 of the DSU identified by the Panel, the United States points out that the mere fact that a breach of Article X3(a) may be removed by changing a law's administration cannot be a basis for concluding that the law is not the measure at issue. The United States argues that, although Article 19.1 of the DSU contemplates a recommendation that a Member bring a measure into conformity with a covered agreement, it is silent as to how this is to be done.

(2) Confinement of the Measures at Issue to Certain Areas of Customs Administration

The United States contends that the Panel erred in confining the specific measures at issue to the areas of customs administration indicated in the panel request, because the Panel failed to construe the panel request "as a whole". The United States also argues that the Panel confused arguments, on the one hand, with measures and claims, on the other hand. For the United States, had the Panel construed the panel request "as a whole", it could not have avoided the conclusion that, first, the specific measures at issue were the Community Customs Code, the Implementing Regulation, the Common Customs Tariff, the TARIC, and, for each of these measures, all amendments, "implementing measures, and other related measures"; and, secondly, that the legal basis of the complaint was the administration of those measures in a manner inconsistent with Article X3(a) of the GATT 1994. The United States emphasizes that the list of areas of customs administration provided in the panel request was only illustrative, aimed to give an indication of the argument underlying the United States' claim, and did not constitute the claim itself or the specific measures at issue. According to the United States, the Panel read individual phrases in the panel request in isolation, focusing on "particular text … taken out of its context". The United States maintains that the Panel's characterization of the illustrative list as a specification of the measures at issue "ignored the introduction to the

---

1 Ibid., para. 46 (referring to Panel Report para. 7.21).

list, which stated that 'lack of uniform, impartial and reasonable administration of the above-identified measures is manifest in differences among member States in a number of areas, including, but not limited to, the following.'"

The United States also points out that the Panel gave no consideration to the fact that the request included a claim that the absence of mechanisms or institutions to secure uniform administration in the European Communities' system of customs administration "as a whole" results in a breach of Article X3(a).[1] For the United States, the Panel missed the fundamental point that "nowhere in the system as a whole … are there mechanisms or institutions which achieve the uniformity in administration which Article X3(a) requires".[2] With respect to the analogy made by the Panel to the EC — Computer Equipment dispute, the United States considers that the Panel erred because, in EC — Computer Equipment, the scope of the measures at issue depended on the identity of the products subject to the measures; also, the claim put forward in that case was not "systemic" and did not relate to the system "as a whole".[3]

The United States considers that the Panel's approach led to a confusion of claims and measures, on the one hand, with arguments, on the other hand. The United States does not believe it was required to list the areas in which the manner of administration of the specific measure at issue was inconsistent with Article X3(a); however, in the view of the United States, such a list made the panel request more transparent, in that it anticipated certain arguments the United States would make in its submissions and statements to substantiate its claims. For the United States, rather than understanding the discussion in the panel request as intended, the Panel mischaracterized it as "an elaboration of what it understood to be the measure at issue".[4]

(3) Challenging the European Communities' System of Customs Administration "As a Whole"

The United States contends that the Panel erred by construing the panel request to exclude a claim that the European Communities' system of customs administration "as a whole" results in nonuniform administration of European Communities customs law in breach of Article X3(a) of the GATT 1994. For the United States, the Panel erred in considering that, in order to challenge the European Communities' system of customs administration "as a whole", the United States would have had to list separately "each and every area of customs administration". This aspect of the Panel's reasoning, the United States argues, would make

---

1 United States' appellant's submission, para. 61.

2 Ibid.

3 Ibid., para. 62.

4 Ibid., para. 66.

it "virtually impossible" to challenge a responding Member's system "as a whole" or overall. The United States maintains that the panel request made it clear that its claim related to the European Communities' system of customs administration "as a whole", because it identified the measures that constitute the main instruments of European Communities customs legislation and addressed the manner of administration of these instruments collectively.[1] For the United States, the heart of the problem is that "the European Communities administers its customs law through separate, independent customs authorities and does not provide any institution or mechanism to reconcile divergences automatically and as a matter of right when they occur.[2] The United States underlines that, throughout the panel request, the measures at issue were discussed collectively, and that this "is precisely what one would expect in a panel request challenging a system of customs administration as a whole."[3]

According to the United States, the Panel's interpretation of the panel request rested on its view that the word "manner", as used in the panel request, was not related to "the design and structure of something", and the Panel assumed that a challenge to the design and structure of the European Communities' system of customs administration must refer to "actions taken and/or procedures and institutions existing at the European Communities level". For the United States, these aspects of the Panel's reasoning are problematic; given that the very essence of the Article X3(a) obligation is the "manner" of administration of certain types of measures, it would be "illogical to assume that [the] use of the word 'manner' in a claim involving Article X3(a) of the GATT 1994 necessarily suggests that the claim does not relate to a Member's system of customs administration as a whole." Furthermore, the United States is of the view that, because "the defining characteristic of the design and structure of the European Communities' system of customs administration … is the absence of procedures and institutions" at the European Communities level, a challenge to the design and structure of this system must necessarily address administration undertaken by member State customs authorities.

The United States considers that it clearly articulated a challenge to the European Communities' system of customs administration in the panel request. The United States submits that the absence of an explicit reference to the terms "as such" or "*per se*" in the panel request does not preclude a claim with respect to the European Communities' system of customs administration "as a whole". What is important, the United States argues, is that the responding party be aware of the claim against it so that its ability to defend

---

1 United States' appellant's submission, para. 69.

2 Ibid. para.72.

3 Ibid. para.74.

itself is not prejudiced. For the United States, it is clear from statements by the European Communities at meetings of the DSB, and from the European Communities' submissions and statements during the Panel proceedings, that the European Communities was aware that the United States had made a claim with respect to the European Communities' system of customs administration "as a whole". For the United States, the "consistent articulation" by the United States throughout the Panel proceedings of a claim concerning the European Communities' system of customs administration "as a whole" is "a strong indication that the European Communities did not suffer any prejudice on account of any lack of clarity in the panel request".[1]

II.Arguments of the European Communities — Appellee

The European Communities submits that the Panel did not err in finding that the measure at issue was only the "manner of administration" of European Communities customs law in the specific areas identified by the United States in the panel request. Furthermore, the European Communities agrees with the Panel's conclusion that its terms of reference did not include a claim against the European Communities' system of customs administration "as a whole", or "as such".

(1) The "Measures at Issue" for Purposes of a Claim under Article X3(a) of the GATT 1994

The European Communities agrees with the Panel that the measure at issue with respect to the United States' claim under Article X3(a) of the GATT 1994 is the "manner of administration" of European Communities customs law.[2] The European Communities considers that, by referring to the "manner of administration", the Panel did not blur the distinction between the measure at issue and the claims under Article X3(a). The Panel used the term "manner of administration" to distinguish "administration" (the measure at issue in this dispute) from the laws and regulations of general application under Article X:1 of the GATT 1994, which are the subject of administration. According to the European Communities, the Panel used the term "manner of administration" synonymously with "administration". The European Communities is of the view that this "minor ambiguity" is not enough to reverse the Panel's finding that when a violation of Article X3(a) is claimed, the panel request must identify a "manner of administration".[3]

The European Communities contends that the United States is trying to confuse the

---

1 United States' appellant's submission, para. 77.

2 European Communities' appellee's submission, para. 97.

3 Ibid., para. 92.

laws to be administered with their administration. In this respect, the European Communities observes that, in EC — Bananas III, the Appellate Body distinguished, in the context of Article X3(a), between the administration of the laws and the laws to be administered.106 According to the European Communities, the panel request refers to the manner of administration, "clearly distinguishes the administration from the laws which are being administered", and, thus, "identifies the 'administration', rather than those laws, as the measure at issue in the dispute."

(2) Confinement of the Measures at Issue to Certain Areas of Customs Administration

For the European Communities, the Panel was fully justified in concluding that the measure at issue was only the administration of customs law in the areas identified in the third paragraph of the panel request. The European Communities reiterates that, in this case, the measure at issue is not the set of legal instruments listed in the first paragraph of the panel request but, rather, their administration. The European Communities submits that the United States is trying to engage in a selective reading of the panel request by asking the Appellate Body to ignore the third paragraph of the panel request. Furthermore, given the "vast body of law" referred to by the United States in the first paragraph of the panel request, it would not have been possible for the European Communities to prepare adequately its defence purely on the basis of a challenge against the administration of European Communities customs law "as a whole" without specifying the relevant provisions or sectors. In the view of the European Communities, "an identification of the specific issue or provision with respect to which a claim of non-uniform administration is made was ... necessary ... to protect [its] due process rights".[1]

The European Communities contends that the Panel correctly referred to the general principle set out in EC — Computer Equipment that "what is necessary for identification of the 'specific measures at issue' depends on the circumstance of the case." [2]In the circumstances of the present case, given the vast body of law to which the United States referred, the Panel was justified in requiring specification of areas of customs administration.

Regarding the terms "including but not limited to" contained in the third paragraph of the panel request, the European Communities relies on the Appellate Body Report in India — Patents (US) in asserting that "these words cannot have the effect of including, contrary to the requirements of Article 6.2 [of the] DSU, the administration of the entire body of [European Communities] customs law into the Panel's terms of reference." The European Communities

---

1 European Communities' appellee's submission, para. 94.

2 Ibid., para. 105.

adds that the United States' interpretation of this phrase would reduce the third paragraph of the panel request to inutility and would "prejudice the defendant's due process rights by leaving the actual subject matter of the case unclear."[1]

(3) Challenging the European Communities' System of Customs Administration "As a Whole"

According to the European Communities, the Appellate Body should uphold the Panel's findings that the United States' claims regarding the European Communities' system "as a whole" and "as such" are outside its terms of reference. The European Communities considers the "as a whole" claim to be outside the Panel's terms of reference because the measure at issue is "only the European Communities' manner of administration in the areas of customs law specifically identified in the Panel request". The European Communities also maintains that "it is thus incorrect to suggest that the European Communities' system of customs administration could be assessed 'as a whole', independently of the specific needs and requirements of the sector or area in question, and the tools and mechanisms existing in such area."

The European Communities argues that the panel request did not indicate that the United States intended to challenge the European Communities' system of customs administration "as such". For the European Communities, the panel request identified as the measure at issue the "manner of administration", and these terms are "diametrically opposed to those which one could have expected to be used in the case of a challenge against a measure 'as such'."[2] Regarding the United States' argument that the measures at issue were the instruments listed in the first paragraph of the panel request, and that they constitute the main instruments of the European Communities customs legislation, the European Communities reiterates its view that the measures at issue are not these instruments but, rather, their administration in the areas listed in the third paragraph of the panel request. The European Communities adds that its system of customs administration is broader than the instruments listed in the first paragraph of the panel request, because it includes other instruments such as the EC Treaty itself and more specific instruments existing in the field of customs cooperation, or budgetary and financial control.[3]

With respect to the United States' reliance on a number of statements made by the parties during or outside the Panel proceedings, the European Communities recalls that "the compliance of a panel request with Article 6.2 of the DSU must be assessed primarily on the face of the panel request". The European Communities reiterates that at no point did it

---

1 Ibid.

2 European Communities' appellee's submission, para. 129.

3 Ibid. para.128.

recognize or acknowledge that its system of customs administration "as such" was the measure at issue in this dispute.

(4) Temporal Limitations of the Panel's Terms of Reference

The European Communities contends that the Panel took an excessively wide approach to the temporal reach of its terms of reference. For the European Communities, a panel may, in principle, consider only measures that are in existence at the time of its establishment and, therefore, the Panel erred in considering that it had "a general competence to also consider measures which 'predate' or 'post-date' its establishment." The European Communities refers to past Appellate Body and panel reports in support of its arguments. The European Communities argues that, furthermore, the manner of administration "cannot be regarded as a 'continuum' without a clear start or end point", contrary to what the Panel suggests. According to the European Communities, the Panel's approach would produce absurd results: it would imply that "violations which occurred far in the past and which no longer have any current effect could be claimed to be continuing because 'administration has no end point'"; similarly, "violations which had not yet occurred at the time the Panel was established might be regarded as indicative of violations pre-dating the Panel's establishment because administration 'has no starting point'."[1]

The European Communities considers that, on the basis of the panel request, it was entitled to assume that the complainant's case related to measures in existence at the time of the Panel's establishment. The European Communities contends that, by defining "administration" under Article X3(a) of the GATT 1994 as a "phenomenon without any boundaries in time", the Panel violated the due process rights of the defendant protected by Article 6.2 of the DSU, because the preparation of the defense for past instances of administration is "unduly difficult", and including future instances of administration in the measure at issue would make the subject matter of the case a "moving target".[2]

The European Communities also argues that the Panel's reasoning would render establishing compliance almost impossible. If administration has no clear start or end point, it would be difficult for a WTO Member found to be in violation of Article X3(a) to establish that it has altered its manner of administration so that compliance with Article X3(a) is achieved. The European Communities contends that "the Panel's approach to the temporal limitations to its terms of reference is incompatible with Article[s] 7.1 and 6.2 of the DSU" and requests the Appellate Body to reverse the Panel's findings on the temporal limitations of its terms of reference.

---

1 Ibid. para.65.

2 European Communities' other appellant's submission, para. 66.

The United States is of the view that the Panel did not err in its approach to the temporal scope of its terms of reference. The United States observes that the legal instruments it identified as the measures at issue in the panel request were in existence on the date when the Panel was established. For the United States, the European Communities' argument "confuses administration of European Communities customs law in existence when the Panel was established with individual acts of administration that occurred prior to establishment and with evidence that came to light during the panel proceeding that confirm the existence of non-uniform administration at the time of panel establishment." For the United States, the Panel correctly explained that "it would take account of individual instances of administration pre-dating and post-dating panel establishment not to determine whether each established a WTO-inconsistency in its own right, but as a means of elucidating the manner of administration that may be in existence at the time of panel establishment." The United States considers that the Panel referred to individual acts of administration that pre-dated its establishment "not as potential breaches of Article X3(a) of the GATT 1994 in and of themselves, but as evidence of the manner of administration of the relevant provisions of [European Communities] customs law."[1]

The United States is also of the view that the European Communities misreads the logical distinction the Panel made between administration as an ongoing phenomenon and individual instances of administration.227 For the United States, although the European Communities has referred to the general principle that a panel may consider only measures in existence at the time of panel establishment, it made "no distinction between acts of administration themselves being considered as potential breaches of Article X3(a) and acts of administration being considered as evidence of an ongoing course of administration that potentially is a breach of Article X3(a)." The United States points out that nothing in the text of Article X3(a) or its context suggests that a breach of Article X3(a) "is demonstrated only when individual acts of administration in existence on the date a panel is established diverge." According to the United States, the European Communities' view is that administration is not a continuum, and that only individual acts of administration in existence at the time of panel establishment can be challenged as breaching Article X3(a). If this understanding were correct, the United States argues, the obligation of uniform administration under Article X3(a) would be rendered "ineffective" and would not meet the minimum standards of predictability for traders set out in Article X3(a).

Regarding the European Communities' argument concerning events that post-dated the Panel's establishment, the United States maintains that, contrary to the European Communities'

1 European Communities' other appellant's submission, para. 82; Panel Report, paras. 7.102-7.113 and 7.119.

assertions, the Panel's references to evidence post-dating its establishment do not show the Panel overstepping its terms of reference. According to the United States, "they show the Panel properly took account of evidence relevant to understanding the manner of administration of European Communities customs law existing at the time of panel establishment."[1]

III. Verdict of the Appellate Body

With respect to the Panel's terms of reference, the United States' appeal can be divided into three issues. The first issue raised is whether the Panel erred in finding that, "when a violation of Article X3(a) of the GATT 1994 is being claimed, the relevant request for establishment of a panel must identify the manner of administration that is allegedly non-uniform, partial and/or unreasonable." [2](infra, Section IV.A) The second issue is whether the Panel erred in finding that the specific measure at issue in this dispute is "the manner of administration ... of the Community Customs Code, the Implementing Regulation, the Common Customs Tariff, the TARIC and related measures" and, furthermore, that it was confined to the six areas of customs administration specifically identified in the third paragraph of the request for the establishment of a panel by the United States (the "panel request") .[3] (infra, Section IV.B) While these two issues relate to the identification of the specific measure at issue, the third issue raised by the United States relates to the Panel's construction of the nature and scope of the claim set out in the panel request. With respect to this third issue, the United States contends that the Panel erred in finding that, due to the wording and content of the panel request, the United States was precluded from challenging the European Communities' system of customs administration "as a whole" or "as such". (infra, Section IV.C)

In its other appeal, the European Communities contends that the Panel erred in its interpretation of the temporal scope and limitations of its terms of reference in respect of "steps and acts of administration that pre-date or post-date the establishment of a panel". [4](infra, Section IV.D)

1.Interpretation of the Term "Measures at Issue" under Article 6.2 of the DSU

The first issue is whether the Panel erred in finding that the "measure at issue" for purposes of a claim under Article X3(a) of the GATT 1994 must be the "manner of administration" that is allegedly non-uniform, partial, and/or unreasonable. The Panel was of

---

1 United States' appellee's submission, para. 51.

2 Panel Report, para. 7.20.

3 ibid, para. 7.33.

4 Panel Report, para. 7.37.

the view that the term "measures at issue" in Article 6.2 of the DSU should be interpreted in the light of the specific WTO obligation that is allegedly being violated by that measure in a particular dispute. The Panel considered that this approach is necessary because the "measure at issue" identified in the panel request will be the subject of a recommendation, pursuant to Article 19.1 of the DSU, if that measure is found to be in violation of a WTO obligation.

Based on this general proposition, the Panel turned to the interpretation of the nature of a "measure at issue" with respect to the obligation contained in Article X3(a) of the GATT 1994. The Panel considered that the essence of the obligation under this Article is to "administer [the legal instruments of the kind described in Article X1] in a uniform, impartial and reasonable manner". For the Panel, "this essential aspect of the obligation contained in Article X3(a) of the GATT 1994 implies that when a violation of Article X3(a) of the GATT 1994 is being claimed, the … request for establishment of a panel must identify the manner of administration that is allegedly non-uniform, partial and/or unreasonable." The Panel further reasoned that, if a WTO Member were found to be in violation of Article X3(a), this would mean that the manner in which the legal instruments are being administered by that Member is not uniform, impartial, or reasonable. In order to comply with a recommendation made under Article 19.1 of the DSU to bring the measure at issue into conformity with Article X3(a) of the GATT 1994, "the Member would need to alter the manner in which the relevant laws, regulations, decisions and/or rulings are being administered". 314 Thus, for the Panel, the specific WTO obligation alleged to be violated and the means of compliance with a recommendation made under Article 19.1 of the DSU should govern the identification of the specific measure at issue under Article 6.2 of the DSU. The Panel therefore found that, for purposes of a claim under Article X3(a), the "measure at issue" to be identified in the panel request under Article 6.2 of the DSU must be the "manner of administration" of the legal instruments of the kind described in Article X:1 of the GATT 1994.[1]

On appeal, the United States challenges this interpretation of the Panel. For the United States, "manner of administration" is not a "measure"; rather, it is, "[a]s the Panel uses the term, … a description of how a measure operates so as to breach an Agreement provision." The United States emphasizes that the Panel's reasoning blurs the distinction between "measures" and "claims". [2]The United States also finds fault with the Panel's recourse to Article 19.1 of the DSU in identifying the measure at issue. The United States point out that, "because DSU Article 19.1 requires that the breaching 'measure' be brought into

---

1 Panel Report, para. 7.17.

2 United States' appellant's submission, para. 47.

conformity", it does not follow that "the measure in the case of Article X:3(a) must be the 'manner of administration' of 'laws, regulations, judicial decisions or administrative rulings,' rather than the laws, regulations, judicial decisions, or administrative rulings themselves." For the United States, "[t]he mere fact that a breach of Article X:3(a) may be removed by changing a law's administration is not a basis for concluding that the law is not the measure at issue."[1] The United States also argues that the Panel's reasoning leads to illogical consequences for complaints not only under Article X:3(a) of the GATT 1994 but under other WTO provisions as well, because, under this approach, the measure at issue will not be "distinguishable" from the legal basis of the complaint, namely, the claim under Article 6.2 of the DSU.

The European Communities agrees with the Panel that the measure at issue with respect to the United States' claim under Article X:3(a) in this dispute is the "manner of administration" of European Communities customs law. The European Communities argues that, by referring to the "manner of administration", the Panel did not blur the distinction between the measure at issue and the claim under Article X:3(a). According to the European Communities, the Panel used the term "manner of administration" to distinguish "administration"—which is the measure at issue under Article X:3(a)—from the laws, regulations, judicial decisions, and administrative rulings of general application under Article X:1 of the GATT 1994, which are the subject of administration. The European Communities is of the view that the Panel used the term "manner of administration" synonymously with "administration", and submits that this "minor ambiguity" is not enough to reverse the Panel's finding that, when a violation of Article X:3(a) is claimed, the panel request must identify the "manner of administration". The European Communities contends that the United States is trying to confuse the laws to be administered with their administration. The European Communities points out that the panel request itself refers specifically to the manner of administration, "clearly distinguishes the administration from the laws which are being administered", and, thus, "identifies the 'administration', rather than [the] laws, as the measure at issue in the dispute".[2]

We are thus called upon to determine whether the Panel erred in finding that, when a violation of Article X:3(a) of the GATT 1994 is being claimed, the "measure at issue" must necessarily be the "manner of administration" of the legal instruments of the kind described in Article X:1, and that such legal instruments cannot themselves be identified as the "measures at issue".

---

1 United States' appellant's submission, para. 47.

2 European Communities' appellee's submission, para. 96.

We begin our analysis with the text of Article 6.2 of the DSU, which provides:

The request for the establishment of a panel shall be made in writing. It shall indicate whether consultations were held, identify the specific measures at issue and provide a brief summary of the legal basis of the complaint sufficient to present the problem clearly. In case the applicant requests the establishment of a panel with other than standard terms of reference, the written request shall include the proposed text of special terms of reference.

Article 6.2 sets forth the requirements applicable to a request for the establishment of a panel. As the Appellate Body stated in US — Carbon Steel, there are two distinct requirements, namely:

… identification of the specific measures at issue, and the provision of a brief summary of the legal basis of the complaint (or the claims).[1]

These two requirements relate to different aspects of the complainant's challenge to measures taken by another Member. The "specific measure" to be identified in a panel request is the object of the challenge, namely, the measure that is alleged to be causing the violation of an obligation contained in a covered agreement. In other words, the measure at issue is what is being challenged by the complaining Member. In contrast, the legal basis of the complaint, namely, the "claim" pertains to the specific provision of the covered agreement that contains the obligation alleged to be violated. A brief summary of the legal basis of the complaint required by Article 6.2 of the DSU aims to explain succinctly how or why the measure at issue is considered by the complaining Member to be violating the WTO obligation in question. This brief summary must be sufficient to present the problem clearly. Taken together, these different aspects of a panel request serve not only to define the scope of a dispute, but also to meet the due process requirements.

Pursuant to Article 7.1 of the DSU, a panel's terms of reference are governed by the request for the establishment of a panel. In other words, the panel request identifies the measures and the claims that a panel will have the authority to examine and on which it will have the authority to make findings. The question of whether a measure falls within a panel's terms of reference is a threshold issue, distinct from the question of whether the measure is consistent or not with the legal provision(s) of the covered agreement(s) to which the panel request refers. Therefore, questions pertaining to the identification of the "measures at issue" and the "claims" relating to alleged violation of WTO obligations, set out in a panel request, should be analyzed separately.

At the heart of the Panel's reasoning stands the proposition that the term "measure at issue" in Article 6.2 of the DSU should be interpreted in the light of the specific WTO

---

1 Appellate Body Report, US — Carbon Steel, para. 125.

obligation that is raised in a particular claim. This reasoning appears to us to be flawed. The Panel's proposition would introduce uncertainty because the identification of the measure would vary depending on the substance of the legal provision invoked by a complainant and the interpretation that a panel might give to that provision. As we noted above, Article 6.2 of the DSU sets out "two distinct requirements" applicable to requests for the establishment of a panel: "identification of the specific measures at issue, and the provision of a brief summary of the legal basis of the complaint (or the claims)" sufficient to present the problem clearly.[1] These two requirements are conceptually different and they should not be confused. In finding that the term "measures at issue" in Article 6.2 should be interpreted in the light of the specific WTO obligation that is alleged to be violated, the Panel blurred the distinction between measures and claims.

In our view, a complainant is entitled to include in its panel request an allegation of inconsistency with a covered agreement of any measure that may be submitted to WTO dispute settlement. In US — Corrosion-Resistant Steel Sunset Review, the Appellate Body provided guidance on the types of measures that may be the subject of dispute settlement. Relying on, inter alia, Article 3.3 of the DSU, which refers to "situations in which a Member considers that any benefits accruing to it directly or indirectly under the covered agreements are being impaired by measures taken by another Member", the Appellate Body stated that "in principle, any act or omission attributable to a WTO Member can be a measure of that Member for purposes of dispute settlement proceedings."[2] As long as the specificity requirements of Article 6.2 are met, we see no reason why a Member should be precluded from setting out in a panel request "any act or omission" attributable to another Member as the measure at issue.

The Panel considered that, when a violation of Article X:3(a) of the GATT 1994 is claimed, the measure at issue must necessarily be a "manner of administration" because, if such a violation is found, the WTO Member concerned would need to alter the manner of administration in order to comply with a recommendation made pursuant to Article 19.1 of the DSU. In our view, this reasoning of the Panel is flawed because it conflates the threshold question of whether a measure falls within a panel's terms of reference with the question of the means of implementation in the event that a violation is found. Through the recommendation under Article 19.1, the Member found to have violated a provision of a covered agreement is required to take corrective action to remove the violation. The recommendation envisaged in Article 19.1 concerns the stage of implementation and not

---

1 Appellate Body Report, US — Carbon Steel, para. 125.

2 Appellate Body Report, US — Corrosion-Resistant Steel Sunset Review, para. 81.

the question of whether a measure falls within a panel's terms of reference. Moreover, the Member concerned has a degree of discretion with respect to the nature and type of action that it undertakes in order to achieve compliance. Therefore, we have difficulty in understanding how the means of compliance with a recommendation under Article 19.1 of the DSU should govern the identification of the specific measure at issue in a panel request. We agree, in this respect, with the United States that "the mere fact that a breach of Article X:3(a) may be removed by changing a law's administration is not a basis for concluding that the law is not the measure at issue."

In US — Upland Cotton, the Appellate Body emphasized that the nature of a recommendation a panel may make under Article 19.1 of the DSU with respect to a measure "is not … dispositive of the preliminary question of whether a panel can address claims in respect of that measure".[1] In that case, the Appellate Body had to address the issue of whether an expired measure can be a "measure at issue" within the meaning of Article 6.2 of the DSU. The Appellate Body rejected the United States' argument that, because an expired measure is not susceptible to a recommendation under Article 19.1 of the DSU, it cannot be a "measure at issue" under Article 6.2. For the Appellate Body, the question of whether a panel can address claims in respect of an expired measure is to be distinguished from the question of whether that measure is susceptible to a recommendation under Article 19.1. Although the issue addressed by the Appellate Body in US — Upland Cotton is not identical to that raised by the United States' appeal in this case, the Appellate Body's reasoning in US — Upland Cotton supports our position that Article 19.1 of the DSU does not place restrictions on the type of measure that can be identified in a panel request under Article 6.2 of the DSU.

Interpreting the term "measure at issue" in Article 6.2 of the DSU in the light of the substance of the specific WTO obligation that is allegedly being violated[2] would generate uncertainty and complexity in WTO dispute settlement proceedings. When drafting a request for the establishment of a panel, the complainant would have to foresee the possible restrictions that the substance of the legal provisions might impose on the type of measure that could be challenged. The identification of the measures at issue in the panel request might prove to be even more complex where the challenge concerns a plurality of provisions of the covered agreements. Moreover, the existence, nature, and scope of possible restrictions would depend on the panel's interpretation of the substance of those legal provisions. The respondent might also be placed in an uncertain situation in presenting its defence because it would have to guess what the panel would identify as the measure at issue on the basis

---

1 Appellate Body Report, US — Upland Cotton, para. 272.

2 Panel Report, para. 7.17.

of the panel's interpretation of the substance of the alleged violation. This could lead to unnecessary litigation on a panel's terms of reference, as the responding party may choose to contend at a preliminary stage that, in the light of the substance of the legal provision on which a specific claim is based, the measure identified in the panel request does not fall within the panel's terms of reference.

In the light of these considerations, we reverse the Panel's finding, in paragraph 7.20 of the Panel Report, that the "measure at issue" for purposes of a claim under Article X:3(a) of the GATT 1994 must necessarily be "the manner of administration that is allegedly non-uniform, partial and/or unreasonable."

2. Confinement of the Measures at Issue to Areas of Customs Administration

We next address the issue of whether the Panel erred in finding that the specific measure at issue in this dispute was "the manner of administration ... of the Community Customs Code, the Implementing Regulation, the Common Customs Tariff, the TARIC and related measures", and furthermore, that it was confined to the areas of customs administration identified in the third paragraph of the panel request.

In the first paragraph of the panel request, the United States stated that it "considers that the manner in which the European Communities ... administers its laws, regulations, decisions and rulings of the kind described in Article X:1 of the ... GATT 1994 ... is not uniform, impartial and reasonable, and therefore is inconsistent with Article X:3(a) of the GATT 1994."[1] Also, in the third paragraph of the panel request, the United States asserted that the lack of uniform, impartial, and reasonable administration of measures relating to customs matters is manifest in differences among member States of the European Communities in a number of areas. The United States went on to state that these areas include, but are not limited to:

(1) classification and valuation of goods;

(2) procedures for the classification and valuation of goods, including the provision of binding classification and valuation information to importers;

(3) procedures for the entry and release of goods, including different certificate of origin requirements, different criteria among member States for the physical inspection of goods, different licensing requirements for importation of food products, and different procedures for processing express delivery shipments;

(4) procedures for auditing entry statements after goods are released into the stream of commerce in the European Communities;

(5) penalties and procedures regarding the imposition of penalties for violation of customs

---

1 Request for the Establishment of a Panel by the United States (attached as Annex III to this Report).

rules; and

(6) record-keeping requirements.

The Panel was of the view that "[t]he terms of the United States' request for establishment of a panel indicate that it challenges the manner of administration of certain aspects of [European Communities] customs law."[1] According to the Panel, "[t]he request clarifies that the administration challenged by the United States is that undertaken by the 'national customs authorities of [European Communities] member States'", and that "the specific forms of administration by national customs authorities challenged by the United States under Article X:3(a) of the GATT 1994 include, inter alia, laws, regulations, handbooks, manuals and administrative practices."

The Panel stated that "the requirements in Article 6.2 of the DSU, including the obligation to specifically identify the 'measure at issue', serve the important due process objective of notifying the parties and third parties to a dispute of the nature of the complainant's case". The Panel noted that the United States had challenged measures that "cumulatively contain, literally, thousands of different provisions [that] relate to a vast array of different customs areas, and may entail administration in a multitude of diverse ways." In the light of this, the Panel considered that, "in the context of this dispute, the specificity requirement in Article 6.2 of the DSU additionally requires the identification of the customs areas in the context of which the obligation contained in Article X:3(a) of the GATT 1994 is alleged by the United States to be violated", because "without such additional specificity regarding the customs areas at issue, the European Communities would not have been accorded its due process right to be informed of the nature of the United States' claim under Article X:3(a) of the GATT 1994."[2]

Also, the Panel drew an analogy with the Appellate Body Report in *EC – Computer Equipment*, where the Appellate Body noted that, even though "Article 6.2 does *not* explicitly require that the products to which the 'specific measures' at issue apply be identified … with respect to certain WTO obligations, in order to identify 'the specific measures at issue', it may … be necessary to identify the products subject to the measures in dispute". According to the Panel, because, in the context of the present case, the "measure at issue" is the manner of administration of instruments relating to customs matters, the "identification of the areas of customs administration at issue is necessary to *specifically* identify the 'measures at issue' in the same way as suggested by the Appellate Body in *EC – Computer Equipment*" with respect to the products subject to the measure at issue in that case.[3]

---

1 Panel Report, para. 7.25.

2 id, para. 7.30.

3 id, para. 7.31.

The Panel noted:

1. the United States' Claims regarding Article X:3(a) of the GATT 1994

(a) The Panel's Interpretation of the Term "Administer" in Article X:3(a) of the GATT 1994

The United States submits that the Panel erred in its interpretation and application of the term "administer" in Article X:3(a) of the GATT 1994, and its consequent treatment of differences in penalty provisions and audit procedures among the member States of the European Communities. The Panel itself noted that the existence of substantive differences in penalty provisions and audit procedures among member States is not disputed between the parties. In the United States' view, these divergences in laws among the member States, in and of themselves, lead to non-uniform administration of European Communities customs law in breach of Article X:3(a). The United States asserts that the arguments it made with respect to the Panel's approach to divergences in penalty laws apply equally with respect to the Panel's approach to audit procedures.

The United States agrees with the Panel that measures are administered when they are "put into practical effect". The United States contends that penalty and audit regimes put the measures subject to those regimes into practical effect because they encourage compliance with, and deter breaches of, those measures. The United States submits that the different penalty regimes put European Communities customs law into effect differently among the member States and that this amounts to a failure by the European Communities to administer its customs law in a uniform manner.

Further, the United States refers to the Panel's finding that "the substantive content of penalty laws of the member States used to enforce [European Communities] customs law cannot be viewed as acts of administration". [1] The United States contends that a breach of Article X:3(a) can be substantiated not only by particular "acts of administration", but also by the laws themselves. According to the United States, if divergences between individual acts of administration (for example, individual impositions of penalties for identical breaches of European Communities customs law) constitute non-uniform administration, then, a fortiori, divergences in the penalty provisions that govern the individual acts of administration carried out by different customs authorities must also constitute non-uniform administration.

The United States alleges that the Panel's findings in the present case are inconsistent with the findings regarding Article X:3(a) of the GATT 1994 made by the panel in Argentina – Hides

---

1 Panel Report, para. 7.444 (quoted in United States' appellant's submission, para. 113).

and Leather. In the view of the United States, the Panel should have recognized the distinction that the panel in Argentina – Hides and Leather recognized between measures of general application whose manner of administration is at issue under Article X:3(a), and measures of general application that put the measures at issue into practical effect.

Furthermore, the United States submits that the Panel's reasoning concerning penalty laws is contradicted by other parts of the Panel Report. In the United States' view, the Panel recognized that a measure of general application may be put into practical effect through an instrument that happens also to be a measure of general application, and that it is appropriate to consider the substance of that instrument to determine how the measure at issue is being administered. In this respect, the United States mentions two aspects of the Panel Report: first, with respect to the tariff classification of blackout drapery lining, the Panel referred to the fact that one customs authority (in Germany) relied on an interpretative aid not relied on by customs authorities of other member States; and secondly, with respect to LCD monitors with DVI, the Panel referred to the substance of a Tariff Notice issued by the United Kingdom customs authority and a decree issued by the Dutch customs authority as showing a lack of uniform administration of the European Communities classification rules at issue. The United States submits that the Panel itself considered the substance of a measure of general application concerning blackout drapery lining and LCD monitors with DVI to determine how the Common Customs Tariff was being administered. In the United States' view, the same rationale should have been applied to the administration of penalty provisions.

With respect to the Panel's finding concerning differences in audit procedures among the member States of the European Communities, the United States submits that the Panel erred in limiting the scope of the claim to the non-uniform administration of Article 78(2) of the Community Customs Code. The United States submits further that, even if the Panel had been correct in limiting its examination to Article 78(2) of the Community Customs Code, the Panel's reasoning was based on an incorrect interpretation of the term "administer" in Article X:3(a) of the GATT 1994. The United States contends that the error in the Panel's analysis is essentially the same as the error in its analysis of penalty provisions. Therefore, the United States considers the arguments it presented in the context of penalty provisions equally valid in the context of audit proceedings.

In the event that the Appellate Body reverses the Panel's findings regarding penalty provisions and audit procedures, the United States requests the Appellate Body to complete the Panel's analysis and to find that divergences in penalty provisions and audit procedures in the European Communities amount to non-uniform administration of European Communities customs law in breach of Article X:3(a).

(b) Completing the Analysis with respect to the "As a Whole" Challenge of the United States under Article X:3(a) of the GATT 1994

In the event the Appellate Body reverses the Panel's finding that its terms of reference regarding the United States' claim under Article X:3(a) of the GATT 1994 do not include a challenge to the European Communities' system of customs administration "as a whole", or an "as such" challenge with respect to the design and structure of this system, the United States requests the Appellate Body to complete the analysis and find that the design and structure of the European Communities' system of customs administration "as a whole" is inconsistent with Article X:3(a). The United States submits that, in this dispute, "a reversal of the Panel's findings without a completion of the analysis would fail 'to secure a positive solution to the dispute'".[1]

The United States submits that the analysis can be completed on the basis of undisputed facts and the Panel's findings of fact regarding the European Communities' system of customs administration. The United States recalls that "the crux of the United States' claim ... was that the existence of a system of customs administration in which separate, independent authorities exercise judgment in interpreting and applying European Communities customs law, without any procedures or institutions to ensure against divergences or to reconcile them promptly and as a matter of right when they occur necessarily constitutes a lack of uniform administration, in breach of Article X:3(a). The United States points to statements made by the Panel with respect to various mechanisms and institutions in the European Communities that, according to the European Communities, are supposed to ensure against divergences or to reconcile divergences when they occur. The United States mentions as particular examples, the Customs Code Committee, Article 10 of the Treaty Establishing the European Communities (the "EC Treaty"), and the system of preliminary reference of questions of European Communities customs law to the Court of Justice of the European Communities (the "ECJ").[2] The United States also refers to the Panel's statement that the European Communities' system of customs administration "as a whole" is "complicated and, at times, opaque and confusing". According to the United States, by these various statements, the Panel rejected the European Communities' argument that the institutions and procedures to which the European Communities referred ensure the uniform administration of European Communities customs law. Thus, for the United States, in the light of the Panel's statements regarding "the institutions and mechanisms the European Communities held out as securing uniform administration of European Communities customs law, completion of the Panel's analysis should be straightforward" and should lead to the

---

1 United States' appellant's submission, para. 159.

2 id, paras. 103, 104, and 105.

conclusion that "the European Communities' system of customs administration as a whole is inconsistent with the European Communities' obligation of uniform administration under Article X:3(a) of the GATT 1994."

2. the European Communities' Claims regarding Article X:3(a) of the GATT 1994

(a) The Panel's Interpretation of the Term "Administer" in Article X:3(a) of the GATT 1994

The European Communities submits that the Panel was correct to distinguish between the laws to be administered and the administration of those laws, and disagrees with the United States that laws themselves can constitute administration. According to the European Communities, the administration of a law or a regulation of general application, by definition, implies its application in concrete cases.

The European Communities argues that the Panel did not err in finding that substantive differences in the penalty laws of the member States of the European Communities, in and of themselves, do not constitute a violation of Article X:3(a) of the GATT 1994.

According to the European Communities, the United States did not demonstrate that differences in the penalty laws of the member States lead to non-conformity in the administration of European Communities customs law. The European Communities explains that, although administrative or penalty provisions applicable to violations of customs law are set out in the individual laws of the member States, the member States do not have complete freedom in the determination of the appropriate level of penalties. Rather, in accordance with the binding principles of European Communities customs law, sanctions for the violation of customs law that member States provide must be effective, proportionate, and dissuasive. In the European Communities' view, these principles ensure uniform application of customs law throughout the European Communities.

The European Communities emphasizes that the objective of ensuring uniform application of European Communities customs law does not require full harmonization of penalty provisions among the member States, and that differences in penalties do not necessarily lead to a lack of uniformity in the application of the provisions. The European Communities submits that, if sanctions are dissuasive and effective, then it must be assumed that the related substantive provisions will be respected, regardless of differences in the level of sanctions applicable. The European Communities contends that the United States has not provided any evidence concerning the actual nature and level of sanctions imposed by the laws of member States for specific violations of customs provisions. Therefore, in the European Communities' view, the United States has not established that differences in penalty laws result in differences in the administration of European Communities customs law.

With respect to the administration of audit procedures, the European Communities submits that the Panel was correct to find no violation of Article X:3(a). The European Communities disagrees with the United States that the same arguments it submitted when challenging the Panel's findings with respect to penalty laws apply with equal force to the Panel's findings with respect to audit procedures. In the European Communities' view, these claims are substantially different, because audit procedures are not primarily set out in member States' laws. The European Communities asserts that uniform practice in this respect is ensured by the Community Customs Audit Guide.

The European Communities notes the discretionary character of Article 78(2) of the Community Customs Code but argues that, nevertheless, the mere exercise of discretion in one way or another does not constitute non-uniform administration.132 The European Communities submits that "the [United States] has not provided any evidence to substantiate its allegation that there are significant differences in the audit procedures followed by the … member States", and "has also not been able to demonstrate what impact, if any, such differences would have on the uniform administration of European Communities customs law."

Regarding the United States' request that the Appellate Body complete the analysis under Article X:3(a) with respect to penalty provisions and audit procedures, the European Communities maintains that the Panel did not make the necessary findings of fact and that there are no undisputed facts on the record that would enable the Appellate Body to complete the analysis.

(b) Completing the Analysis with respect to the "As a Whole" Challenge of the United States under Article X:3(a) of the GATT 1994

In the event that the Appellate Body reverses the Panel's findings regarding its terms of reference, the European Communities submits that the Appellate Body is not in a position to complete the legal analysis and should decline to find that the European Communities' system of customs administration "as a whole" and "as such" is inconsistent with Article X:3(a) of the GATT 1994.

The European Communities disagrees with the United States that there are enough factual findings made by the Panel, or enough undisputed facts on record, that would enable the Appellate Body to find that the European Communities' system of customs administration "as such" and "as a whole" is inconsistent with Article X:3(a). According to the European Communities, the Panel's statements to which the United States refers are isolated remarks in the Panel Report where the Panel commented on individual aspects of the European Communities' system of customs administration. These statements, the

European Communities argues, would not allow the Appellate Body to assess whether the European Communities' system of customs administration "as a whole" and "as such" is in conformity with Article X:3(a) of the GATT 1994, given that they do not contain findings of fact in this regard, and were not intended by the Panel to constitute such findings. The European Communities notes that these statements are contained in a section where the Panel set out its understanding of the European Communities' system of customs administration as "context" for the evaluation of the United States' claims regarding individual instances of application.

Furthermore, the European Communities emphasizes that the Panel observed, inter alia, that "the United States did not demonstrate that the design and structure of the European Communities' system of customs administration, including components thereof, necessarily result in a violation of Article X:3(a) of the GATT 1994". Thus, in the European Communities' view, the Panel explicitly confirmed that the United States did "not even come close" to establishing that the European Communities' system of customs administration "as such" and "as a whole" entails a violation of Article X:3(a) of the GATT 1994.

Finally, the European Communities submits that the United States' claim regarding the European Communities' system of customs administration "as a whole" is a claim that has not been explored by the Panel, and the Panel has therefore not made any legal findings and interpretations on this claim that the Appellate Body could reverse. For the European Communities, a claim of violation of the obligation of uniform administration directed against individual instances of application is fundamentally different from a claim directed against a system of customs administration "as such" and "as a whole". Adjudging the claim regarding the European Communities' system of customs administration "as such" and "as a whole" would, therefore, violate the due process rights of the participants, and of the European Communities in particular. Appellate Body proceedings have to take place within a narrow time-frame, and are focused on issues of law and legal interpretations. For the European Communities, such proceedings are manifestly not suited for investigating a claim against a system of customs administration "as a whole" and "as such".

3. the United States' the Panel's Interpretation of Article X:3(b) of the GATT 1994

The United States submits that the Panel erred in finding that the tribunals and procedures for review of customs administrative actions in the European Communities are consistent with Article X:3(b) of the GATT 1994, despite the fact that their decisions do not govern the practice of all the agencies entrusted with administrative enforcement throughout the territory of the

European Communities.

The United States notes that review tribunals or procedures of the European Communities consist of the courts of various member States. Each court issues decisions that govern the practice of only the agency in the respective member State. The United States claims that, in reaching its conclusion concerning interpretation and application of Article X:3(b), the Panel made a number of interpretive errors. In the United States' view, the Panel misconstrued the ordinary meaning of the terms "the agencies" and "such agencies"; confused the concepts of "implement" and "govern the practice of "; and failed to take into account the context provided by Article X:3(a) of the GATT 1994. The United States submits that the Panel effectively disregarded the ordinary meaning of those terms when it stated that "it is difficult to know what significance should be attached, if any, to the reference to agencies in the plural." The United States submits that the ordinary meaning of the plural form encompasses "the agencies"—without limitation—as opposed to only one such agency or just "some of" or a subset of "the agencies". The United States argues that the use of the plural form contemplates multiple agencies and, given the absence of any basis in the text for distinguishing among multiple agencies, it must contemplate all the agencies entrusted with administrative enforcement.

Furthermore, in the United States' view, Article X:3(b) must be read in the light of the obligation of uniform administration in Article X:3(a) of the GATT 1994. According to the United States, the review of decisions that are inconsistent with "established principles of law or the actual facts" contemplated by Article X:3(b) also embodies the principle of uniform administration. The United States submits that procedures leading to decisions that have effect only in particular regions of a WTO Member's territory are therefore inconsistent with Article X:3(b). In addition, the United States alleges that the Panel did not give meaning to the two distinct requirements of "govern the practice" and "implement" in Article X:3(b). In the United States' view, the Panel assumed incorrectly that, if a decision can be implemented by a single agency, then the decision need govern the practice of only that agency, even though, pursuant to Article X:3(b), it must be effectuated by "such agencies" entrusted with administrative enforcement. The United States submits that Article X:3(b) does not contemplate such a geographical limitation of the "govern the practice" requirement.

With respect to the Panel's assessment of what is "reasonable" in the light of "most legal systems", the United States submits that the Panel ignored the feature that distinguishes the system of the European Communities from most legal systems, namely, that most legal systems have only one central agency entrusted with enforcement of customs law. The United States points out that this is not the case in the European Communities because its legal system combines review tribunals with geographically limited jurisdiction with customs authorities whose practice is limited to particular geographical regions. In the United States' view, this results in a geographically fragmented administration of the customs law in the European Communities.

4. the European Communities' The Panel's Interpretation of Article X:3(b) of the GATT 1994

The European Communities argues that the Panel was correct in finding that the European Communities has not violated Article X:3(b) of the GATT 1994, because this provision does not require that the review of administrative action relating to customs matters must have effect throughout the territory of the European Communities.

As a general matter, the European Communities notes that all disputes concerning European Communities law that are not subject to the jurisdiction of the ECJ and the Court of First Instance of the European Communities (the "CFI") fall within the competence of the national courts of the member States. The European Communities explains that national courts have a dual function: when deciding a dispute governed by national law, they form part of the national legal order; when deciding a case governed by European Communities law, they belong, from the functional point of view, to the European Communities' legal order.

The European Communities points out that, in the case of actions brought before a national court that relate to the interpretation of an issue of European Communities law, the national court may request the ECJ to interpret a question of European Communities law (referred to as "references for a preliminary ruling"). Member State courts, against whose decisions there is no judicial remedy under national law, are required to refer issues of interpretation of European Communities law to the ECJ. Since European Communities customs law is implemented through the customs authorities of the member States, an appeal for judicial review is lodged before the court of the member State whose customs authorities have issued the decision. According to the European Communities, the main objective of the preliminary reference procedure is to guarantee the proper and uniform interpretation and application of European Communities law throughout all the member States, while avoiding the establishment of a long and expensive appellate system before the ECJ. The European Communities notes that a preliminary ruling by the ECJ is binding on the national court hearing the case in which the ruling is given, and that it has effect also on persons who are not parties to the case referred. The European Communities points out that, in exceptional cases, a right of appeal against member State customs decisions may also be available directly to the CFI.

The European Communities submits that the Panel gave the correct meaning to the terms "the agencies entrusted with administration enforcement" and "such agencies" in Article X:3(b) of the GATT 1994. In the European Communities' view, the Panel correctly explained that the use of the plural when referring to "agencies" in Article X:3(b) could flow from the fact that the review "tribunals and procedures" required under the same provision are also referred to in the plural. The European Communities disagrees with the United States' argument that the use of the singular in the proviso indicates that only one entity within a WTO Member should be permitted "to pursue" the review. In the European Communities' view, the proviso covers the "central administration of any of those agencies existing in the WTO [M]ember".

In response to the United States' argument that the Panel failed to give meaning to the distinct requirements in Article X:3(b) that review decisions must be "implemented by" and "govern the practice of" such agencies 154, the European Communities submits that the differences between the terms "to implement" and "govern the practice of" are irrelevant for interpreting the term "the agencies". Furthermore, the European Communities notes that the absence of an express reference to Article X:3(a) in Article X:3(b) of the GATT 1994 contrasts with the explicit reference by Article X:3(c) to Article X:3(b) of the GATT 1994. The European Communities agrees with the Panel that this absence precludes an inference that the obligation to ensure review of administrative action under Article X:3(b) could be read as simultaneously requiring uniform administration in accordance with Article X:3(a) of the GATT 1994, because "such an interpretation would amount to merging different requirements that are currently contained in separate subparagraphs of Article X of the GATT 1994." The European Communities argues that this interpretation is also supported by the negotiating history of Article X. The European Communities concurs with the Panel that it would not be reasonable to infer that "first instance independent review tribunals and bodies, whose jurisdiction in most legal systems is normally limited in substantive and geographical terms, should have the authority to bind all agencies entrusted with administrative enforcement throughout the territory of a Member".

Finally, the European Communities submits that the United States' interpretation would lead to a major conflict between the Marrakesh Agreement Establishing the World Trade Organization (the "WTO Agreement") and the EC Treaty, because the creation of a central European Communities customs court of first instance would require a profound constitutional amendment of the EC Treaty that would require ratification by its 25 member States. The European Communities recalls that, when the WTO Agreement was negotiated and concluded, the United States never raised any concern about the European Communities' system of judicial review, which had already existed for almost 40 years.

【思考题】

1.WTO 争端解决机构职权管辖范围如何确定？

2. 设立专家组之前和之后的行政措施和行政行为是否属于专家组的职权范围？

Case3 · 拓展阅读